Dedication

To my family – on all sides of 'the
Pond':
especially the two Franks,
my father and brother

New Introductory
Reader in
Sociology

Nelson

Thomas Nelson and Sons Ltd
Nelson House   Mayfield Road
Walton-on-Thames   Surrey
KT12 5PL   UK

51 York Place
Edinburgh
EH1 3JD   UK

Thomas Nelson (Hong Kong) Ltd
Toppan Building 10/F
22A Westlands Road
Quarry Bay   Hong Kong

Distributed in Australia by
Thomas Nelson Australia
480 La Trobe Street
Melbourne   Victoria 3000
and in Sydney, Brisbane, Adelaide and Perth

© Mike O'Donnell 1987
First published by Harrap Limited 1983
(under ISBN 0–245–53935–2)

Third impression published by Thomas Nelson and Sons Ltd 1985

Second Edition published 1988
ISBN 0–17–4481403
NPN: 987654321

Phototypeset by Input Typesetting Ltd, London SW19 8DR
Printed and bound in Great Britain by
Butler & Tanner Ltd, Frome and London

Contents

CONTENTS

vi

CONTENTS

SECTION 8

SECTION 9

SECTION 10

CONTENTS

CONTENTS

SECTION 19

Preface

The main reason for a second edition of this Reader is to provide a fuller coverage of the staple topics of sociology. Stratification, poverty, politics, gender, family and education are now given much fuller coverage. I have also extended most other sections to a greater or lesser extent. A second reason for this edition is to improve the book as a learning instrument. Questions have been provided at the end of every reading, except in Section 1. The new readings are generally shorter and most of the longer ones carried over from the first edition have been trimmed. The remaining longer readings have been clearly split into 'digestible' portions. The format of shorter extracts with questions enables the readings to be used as stimulus material. The questions are primarily intended to test understanding, interpretation and evaluation of the specific reading but some range more widely or invite a greater degree of personal judgement than is usually required in response to the shorter passages typically used in 'A' level examinations. It would be spurious to claim that these questions are objective means of assessment. In particular, the suggested mark allocation, while reflecting the different skills involved in parts of questions, should be taken as approximate. The questions could serve as much as a focus for discussion on note-taking as titles for essays. The new formating of the readings in this edition reflects in the broadest way my work in helping to construct the new (1987) 'AS' level sociology syllabus and on the revision of the current 'A' level (AEB). However, the prime purpose of the Reader is not to provide stimulus material but to give access to original sources to students generally fed on a heavy textbook diet.

The balance of the readings remains as originally conceived. It is a mix of the classics, some authoritative contemporary pieces, and is peppered with contributions included for their current relevance. I hope it will be obvious which is which! As in the first edition, the sociological perspectives are fully represented throughout. However, I have retreated still further from the *perspective format* which has never seemed to me an adequate basis on which to present the discipline.

Mike O'Donnell
September 1987

Notes

1. Where extracts have been taken from American publications, the spelling and punctuation have been left unchanged.
2. Where it seems useful, original cross-references have been left within readings.

Acknowledgements

For the second time, Caroline Riddel has given me essential help in completing a book. I thank her without reservation. Gina Garrett's comments on draft material have been as informed and useful as ever. My colleagues, Jim Pey and Murray Morrison, have both made helpful suggestions, several of which I have adopted. I am grateful to my students for being patient, but by no means passive, guinea-pigs for the testing of much of the following material. It was not possible to give formal thanks to Pat Mayes for the help she gave me in preparing for publication the companion to this volume, 'A New Introduction to Sociology'. I would like to thank her now. Finally, if writing is notoriously a lonely enterprise, it is also, in a sense, a selfish one. For those who may have missed me, I promise not to keep myself to myself quite so much in the future.

Finally, Helen Huckle of Harrap started me on one book and has seen me through to the end of another. I would like to thank her for her help and support and for allowing me a loose rein.

Note to the Second Editon

There is a price to be paid for the isolated time spent in writing any book and not only by the author. My warmest thanks to those whose patience and kindness I have allowed myself to put upon. These include Jillian Brown, Pat Mayes, Marie Taylor, Hal Westergaard and Brian Dutton. At Nelson, Elizabeth Johnston, Christine Considine, Graham Taylor and, in the final stages, Philippa Whitbread, all helped me to turn my wodges of typescript and photocopies into a book. As always, the final product must be put down to me.

The Nature of Sociology: Theoretical Perspectives and Concepts

Readings 1–5

This section on the nature of sociology begins with a short extract from the American sociologist, Charles Wright Mills (1916–62). There follow readings from Karl Marx, Max Weber, Emile Durkheim and Herbert Blumer. I draw upon Mills first, not because he is a greater sociologist than the others, but because he sought to synthesise the work of other leading sociologists and to explain the nature of sociology to a wider public. The brief reading from Mills is an attempt to present the theoretical framework of the discipline in the broadest possible way. Further, at the conclusion of the passage, Mills makes perhaps his most celebrated observation – that sociology can help people relate 'public issues' to 'private troubles' (e.g., relating business investment or government policy to being personally unemployed). This seems to me still the most important contribution of the subject, and Mills develops the point in his *The Sociological Imagination* (Oxford University Press, 1959. See especially pp. 3–11).

An equal admirer of both Marx and Weber, Mills was also well aware of the contribution to social science of American thinkers like George Mead. Marx, Weber and Durkheim had an unparalleled understanding of social structure and of how individual behaviour is formed and limited by social context. Mead examined and explained in more detail than they the way individual thought and action affect society as well as being influenced by it. Although Marx, Weber and, to some extent, Durkheim also explored the issue of individual consciousness, the piece from Herbert Blumer which summarises the essence of Mead's analysis seems to me to be a better presentation of the matter, partly because he was able to avail himself of advances in psychological knowledge not available to them.

Note: Questions on theory are given at the end of Section 19.

1   C. Wright Mills: The Classic (Sociological) Tradition

The following extract from C. Wright Mills merits close reading. He does not attempt a precise definition of sociology but indicates the scope and concerns of the subject. He suggests that it is the type of questions sociologists ask that characterise the discipline. In his words: 'These questions are generally of wide scope: they concern total societies, their transformations, and the varieties of men and women that inhabit them'. This is, indeed, a broad brief but, as Mills indicates, there is a need for a discipline concerned with overviewing the nature of social structure and change and of the relationship of individuals and groups to society. Such a discipline must inevitably call upon more specific subject areas, such as economics and political science, but it uses them within a wider framework of analysis encompassing the whole of society. The frameworks of analysis (or 'models', as Mills calls them) developed by different sociologists do vary. As the following readings will show, Marx and Weber differed on a number of significant points in their models or, to use the current preferred term, 'perspectives', on society. It is crucially important to notice, however, that Mills considered that these models or perspectives should be revised and refined with reference to the empirical (practical) research that they help to guide. Finally, Mills does not deny the usefulness of limited, small-scale research, but what he clearly insists on is that such work needs to be interpreted in the full social context. The readings from Marx, Weber, Durkheim and Blumer that follow are intended to give a general idea of their models of society but they do not, of course, cover every major theory and concept employed by these writers in developing and applying their models.

Reading 1 From C. Wright Mills, *Images of Man* (George Braziller, Inc., 1960), pp. 1–4.

The study of man contains a greater variety of intellectual styles than any other area of cultural endeavor. How different social scientists go about their work, and what they aim to accomplish by it, often do not seem to have any real common denominator. Some consider themselves to be working in close parallel with chemists and physicists; others believe they share the aims, if not the methods, of novelists and even of poets. These of course are the extreme limits of 'social science' practice and proclamation. Between these extremes there are many ways of thinking, many conceptions and methods, ideas and just plain notions. Let us admit the case of our critics from the humanities and from the experimental sciences: social science as a whole is both intellectually and morally confused. And what is called sociology is very much in the middle of this confusion.

It will not quite do to excuse this condition by saying that the social sciences are after all very young. In the first place, they are not so very young, or rather they are young only if one restricts – rather arbitrarily, I believe – 'social science' to some one or another more recent phase of work. In the second place, to say that they are young implies, or even assumes, that such studies may be understood to be going through some sort of biographical cycle, like an individual, to be growing in a more or less straight line towards maturity. But of course, the question is: if they were 'mature,' what then would they be? No one has answered this question in a way that is altogether convincing to those who are working in the social sciences.

There is an amusing little game played nowadays – especially in England – by literary people, a few physical scientists, and by historians. It consists of criticising what they take to be sociology as a pretentious discipline having no firm conceptions and agreed-upon propositions. Behind this criticism there is the standard or the model of the physical sciences. The practitioners of sociology, they are saying, only ape these in an often ridiculous way, and accordingly: there is nothing much to sociology.

Such criticism is quite well taken – and quite irrelevant. It is true that many sociologists are ridiculous in their attempts to ape what they take to be physical science. But the point of irrelevance in this

3

criticism is the standard chosen. The standards that ought to be used by critics of current social study and reflection are those that have slowly accumulated in the classic tradition. I know the idea is hard to grasp for those not acquainted with this tradition – and especially in the face of the current pretensions of many social scientists – but it is the only way in which criticism might be useful to the working student of man and society.

The classic tradition is difficult to characterise in a brief and coherent way. Like any intellectual tradition, it can be grasped only by exposure to the variety of books that compose it. Any brief statement defining the tradition can only be a single interpretation – in fact, a distinguishing mark of the 'classic' is probably that it is subject to a variety of interpretations! For what it may be worth, my own interpretation rests mainly upon the kinds of questions that its practitioners ask and the manner in which they go about answering them.

Most of the ideas of the classic sociologists are not of the sort that can readily be shaped for precise testing. They are interpretive ideas, orienting us to various ways of looking at social realities. They are attempts to state the general historical trend, the main drift, of modern society, or, to use Dr. Ruth Glass's phrase, the 'state and the fate' of societies in our time. They are attempts to make sense of what is happening in the world and to gauge what may be going to happen in the near future.

The classic sociologists are not inhibited by what are now the boundary lines of academic disciplines or specialties. In their work what are now called political science, social psychology, economics, anthropology and sociology are all used – and integrated so as to form a master view of the structure of society in all its realms, the mechanics of history in all their ramifications, and the roles of individuals in a great variety of their psychological nuances.

But the important thing about the classic sociologists is that even when they have turned out to be quite wrong and inadequate – as for example Spencer was in his notion of the trend from military to industrial society – even then, by their work and by the way in which they did it they reveal much about the nature of society, and their ideas remain directly relevant to our work today.

But how, it may be asked, can these men be so often wrong and yet remain so great? The answer lies, I think, in a single characteristic of their work: their 'great ideas' consist of what might be called 'models,' in contrast to specific theories or detailed hypotheses. In these working models are contained statements of (1) the elements to which attention must be paid if we are to understand some particular feature of society or a society as a whole, and (2) the range of possible relations among these elements. The elements are not left merely to interact in some vague way. Rightly or wrongly, they are constructed in close and specific interconnection with one another, and causal weights are assigned to each. These imputed connections and weights of course are specific theories.

In short, the classic sociologists construct models of society and use them to develop a number of theories. What is important is the fact that neither the correctness nor the inaccuracy of any of these specific theories necessarily confirms or upsets the usefulness or the adequacy of the models. The models can be used for the construction of many theories. They can be used for correcting errors in theories made with their aid. And they are readily open: they can themselves be modified in ways to make them more useful as analytic tools and empirically closer to the run of fact.

It is these models that are great – not only as contributions to the history of social reflection and inquiry, but also as influences on subsequent sociological thinking. They, I believe, are what is alive in the classic tradition of sociology. And I think, too, that they are the reason why so persistently there have been, under quite varied circumstances, so many 'revivals' of the thinkers presented in these pages; in short, why their works are 'classic.'

The classic tradition, then, may not be defined by any one specific method, certainly not by the acceptance of any one theory of society, history, or human nature. Once that is acknowledged, a usable definition is simple enough – although its application in selecting a book of illustrative readings is by no means automatic. The classic tradition is most readily defined by the character of the questions that have guided and do now guide those who are part of it. These questions are generally of wide scope: they concern total societies, their transformations, and the varieties of individual men and women that inhabit them. The answers given by classic sociologists provide conceptions about society, about history and about biography, and in their work these three are usually linked closely together. The structure of society and the mechanics of history are seen within the same perspective, and within this perspective changes in human nature are also defined.

But it is not only the scope and the interrelations of their questions and the fact that they are 'soaked in history' that define the classical workmen. It is also the fact that their intellectual problems are relevant to the public issues of their times, and to the private troubles of individual men and women. More than that – they have helped to define more clearly the issues and the troubles and the intimate relations between the two. People have read Spencer and Marx and Weber and Michels not only to become informed. They have read in a search for orientation and out of their reading they have gotten orientation.

2 Karl Marx and Friedrich Engels: Class Conflict

Marx's analysis of social structure and change is, perhaps, the major example of the kind of sociological model or perspective referred to by Mills. At the core of the Marxist model of society is the theory of class conflict. It is a theory of social structure and of social and historical change. For Marx, society is made up of classes, and it is the conflict of classes that brings about change. The two major examples of class conflict cited in the extract are those between the bourgeoisie and the landed aristocracy – resulting in the bourgeois period – and between the bourgeoisie and the proletariat or working class which Marx anticipated would result first in the dictatorship of the proletariat and then in a classless society. The key to understanding the ebb and flow of class conflict is the changing relationship of classes to the means of production (land in the feudal period, industrial machinery in the bourgeois). The bourgeoisie gradually gained control over production in the late feudal/early modern period and, as the final section of the extract shows, Marx thought the proletariat would eventually take over control of the means of production from the bourgeoisie.

Marx's theory of class conflict undoubtedly illuminates historical and contemporary change and has had world-wide influence. In some countries Marxism (or, rather, local varieties of it) is a matter of faith. As sociologists, however, we cannot approach Marxism in this way but must examine it critically as we would any other sociological model. Sociological models help us to understand society but they cannot predict the future.

KARL MARX AND FRIEDRICH ENGELS

As sociologists, then, we cannot agree with Marx that 'the victory of the proletariat is . . . inevitable' although we are entitled to believe this or hope for it as individuals or as members of a particular political party. In making this statement Marx was claiming too much predictive power for his model, but this criticism does not deny its immense usefulness when employed as a dispassionate tool of sociological analysis. Like all sociological tools (or models and theories) it is open to further development and improvement.

Reading 2 From Karl Marx and Friedrich Engels, *The Communist Manifesto* (Penguin, 1981), pp. 79–93.

Bourgeois and proletarians

The history of all hitherto existing society is the history of class struggles.

Freeman and slave, patrician and plebeian, lord and serf, guild-master and journeyman, in a word, oppressor and oppressed stood in constant opposition to one another, carried on an uninterrupted, now hidden, now open fight that each time ended, either in a revolutionary reconstitution of society at large, or in the common ruin of the contending classes.

In the earlier epochs of history, we find almost everywhere a complicated arrangement of society into various orders, a manifold gradation of social rank. In ancient Rome we have patricians, knights, plebeians, slaves; in the Middle Ages, feudal lords, vassals, guild-masters, journeymen, apprentices, serfs; in almost all of these classes, again, subordinate gradations.

The modern bourgeois society that has sprouted from the ruins of feudal society has not done away with class antagonisms. It has but established new classes, new conditions of oppression, new forms of struggle in place of the old ones.

Our epoch, the epoch of the bourgeoisie, possesses, however, this distinctive feature. It has simplified the class antagonisms. Society as a whole is more and more splitting up into two great hostile camps, into two great classes directly facing each other – bourgeoisie and proletariat.

From the serfs of the Middle Ages sprang the chartered burghers of the earliest towns. From these burgesses the first elements of the bourgeoisie were developed.

The discovery of America, the rounding of the Cape, opened up fresh ground for the rising bourgeoisie. The East-Indian and Chinese markets, the colonisation of America, trade with the colonies, the increase in the means of exchange and in commodities generally, gave to commerce, to navigation, to industry, an impulse never before known, and thereby, to the revolutionary element in the tottering feudal society, a rapid development.

The feudal system of industry, in which industrial production was monopolised by closed guilds, now no longer sufficed for the growing wants of the new markets. The manufacturing system took its place. The guild-masters were pushed aside by the manufacturing middle class; division of labour between the different corporate guilds vanished in the face of division of labour in each single workshop.

Meantime the markets kept ever growing, the demand ever rising. Even manufacture no longer sufficed. Thereupon, steam and machinery revolutionised industrial production. The place of manufacture was taken by the giant, modern industry, the place of the industrial middle class by industrial millionaires, the leaders of whole industrial armies, the modern bourgeois.

Modern industry has established the world market, for which the discovery of America paved the way. This market has given an immense development to commerce, to navigation, to communication by land. This development has, in its turn, reacted on the extension of industry; and in proportion as industry, commerce, navigation, railways extended, in the same proportion the bourgeoisie developed, increased its capital, and pushed into the background every class handed down from the Middle Ages.

We see, therefore, how the modern bourgeoisie is itself the product of a long course of development, of a series of revolutions in the modes of production and of exchange.

Each step in the development of the bourgeoisie was accompanied by a corresponding political advance of that class. An oppressed class under the sway of the feudal nobility, an armed and self-governing association in the mediæval commune; here independent urban republic (as in Italy and Germany), there taxable 'third estate' of the monarchy (as in France); afterwards, in the period of manufacture proper, serving either the semi-feudal or the absolute monarchy as a counterpoise against the nobility, and, in fact, cornerstone of the great monarchies in general – the bourgeoisie has at last, since the establishment of modern industry and of the world market, conquered for itself, in the modern representative state, exclusive political sway. The executive of the modern state is but a committee for managing the common affairs of the whole bourgeoisie . . .

The bourgeoisie, during its rule of scarce one hundred years, has created more massive and more colossal productive forces than have all preceding generations together. Subjection of nature's forces to man, machinery, application of chemistry to industry and agriculture, steam navigation, railways, electric telegraphs, clearing of whole continents for cultivation, canalisation of rivers, whole populations conjured out of the ground – what earlier century had even a presentiment that such productive forces slumbered in the lap of social labour?

We see then: the means of production and of exchange, on whose foundation the bourgeoisie built itself up, were generated in feudal society. At a certain stage in the development of these means of production and of exchange, the conditions under which feudal society produced and exchanged, the feudal organisation of agriculture and manufacturing industry, in one word, the feudal relations of property became no longer compatible with the already developed productive forces; they became so many fetters. They had to be burst asunder; they were burst asunder.

Into their place stepped free competition, accompanied by a social and political constitution adapted to it, and by the economic and political sway of the bourgeois class.

A similar movement is going on before our own eyes. Modern bourgeois society with its relations of production, of exchange and of property, a society that has conjured up such gigantic means of production and of exchange, is like the sorcerer who is no longer able to control the powers of the nether world whom he has called up by his spells. For many a decade past the history of industry and commerce is but the history of the revolt of modern productive forces against modern conditions of production, against the property relations that are the conditions for the existence of the bourgeoisie and of its rule. It is enough to mention the commercial crises that by their periodical return put the existence of the entire bourgeois society on its trial, each time more threateningly. In these crises a great part not only of the existing products, but also of the previously created productive forces, are periodically destroyed. In these crises there breaks out an epidemic that, in all earlier epochs, would have seemed an absurdity – the epidemic of over-production. Society suddenly finds itself put back into a state of momentary barbarism; it appears as if a famine, a universal war of devastation had cut off the supply of every means of subsistence; industry and commerce seem to be destroyed. And why? Because there is too much civilisation, too much means of subsistence, too much industry, too much commerce. The productive forces at the disposal of society no longer tend to further the development of the conditions of bourgeois property; on the contrary, they have become too powerful for these conditions, by which they are fettered, and so soon as they overcome these fetters, they bring disorder into the whole of bourgeois society, endanger the existence of bourgeois property. The conditions of bourgeois society are too narrow to comprise the wealth created by them. And how does the bourgeoisie get over these crises? On the one hand, by enforced destruction of a mass of productive forces; on the other, by the conquest of new markets, and by the more thorough exploitation of the old ones. That is to say, by paving the way for more extensive and more destructive crises, and by diminishing the means whereby crises are prevented.

The weapons with which the bourgeoisie felled feudalism to the ground are now turned against the bourgeoisie itself.

But not only has the bourgeoisie forged the weapons that bring death to itself; it has also called into existence the men who are to wield those weapons – the modern working class – the proletarians.

In proportion as the bourgeoisie, *i.e.*, capital, is developed, in the same proportion is the proletariat, the modern working class, developed – a class of labourers, who live only so long as they find work, and who find work only so long as their labour increases capital. These labourers, who must sell themselves piecemeal, are a commodity, like every other article of commerce, and are consequently exposed to all the vicissitudes of competition, to all the fluctuations of the market . . .

The proletariat goes through various stages of development. With its birth begins its struggle with the bourgeoisie. At first the contest is carried on by individual labourers, then by the work people of a factory, then by the operatives of one trade, in one locality, against the individual bourgeois who directly exploits them. They direct their attacks not against the bourgeois conditions of production, but against the instruments of production themselves; they destroy imported wares that compete with their labour, they smash to pieces machinery, they set factories ablaze, they seek to restore by force the vanished status of the workman of the Middle Ages.

At this stage the labourers still form an incoherent mass scattered over the whole country, and broken up by their mutual competition. If anywhere they unite to form more compact bodies, this is not yet the consequence of their own active union, but of the union of the bourgeoisie, which class, in order to attain its own political ends, is compelled to set the whole proletariat in motion, and is moreover yet, for a time, able to do so. At this stage, therefore, the proletarians do not fight their enemies, but the enemies of their enemies, the remnants of absolute monarchy, the landowners, the non-industrial bourgeois, the petty bourgeoisie. Thus the whole historical movement is concentrated in the hands of the bourgeoisie, every victory so obtained is a victory for the bourgeoisie.

But with the development of industry the proletariat not only increases in number; it becomes concentrated in greater masses, its strength grows, and it feels that strength more. The various interests and conditions of life within the ranks of the proletariat are more and more equalised, in proportion as machinery obliterates all distinctions of labour, and nearly everywhere reduces wages to the same low level. The growing competition among the bourgeois, and the resulting commercial crises, make the wages of the workers ever more fluctuating. The unceasing improvement of machinery, ever more rapidly developing, makes their livelihood more and more precarious; the collisions between individual workmen and individual bourgeois take more and more the character of collisions between two classes. Thereupon the workers begin to form combinations (trade unions) against the bourgeois; they club together in order to keep up the rate of wages; they found permanent associations in order to make provisions beforehand for these occasional revolts. Here and there the contest breaks out into riots.

Now and then the workers are victorious, but only for a time. The real fruit of their battles lies, not in the immediate result, but in the ever expanding union of the workers. This union is helped on by the improved means of communication that are created by modern industry, and that place the workers of different localities in contact with one another. It was just this contact that was needed to centralise the numerous local struggles, all of the same character,

11

into one national struggle between classes. But every class struggle is a political struggle. And that union, to attain which the burghers of the Middle Ages, with their miserable highways, required centuries, the modern proletarians, thanks to railways, achieve in a few years.

This organisation of the proletarians into a class, and consequently into a political party, is continually being upset again by the competition between the workers themselves. But it ever rises up again, stronger, firmer, mightier. It compels legislative recognition of particular interests of the workers, by taking advantage of the divisions among the bourgeoisie itself . . .

Of all the classes that stand face to face with the bourgeoisie today, the proletariat alone is a really revolutionary class. The other classes decay and finally disappear in the face of modern industry; the proletariat is its special and essential product. The lower middle class, the small manufacturer, the shopkeeper, the artisan, the peasant, all these fight against the bourgeoisie, to save from extinction their existence as fractions of the middle class. They are therefore not revolutionary, but conservative. Nay more, they are reactionary, for they try to roll back the wheel of history. If by chance they are revolutionary, they are so only in view of their impending transfer into the proletariat; they thus defend not their present, but their future interests; they desert their own standpoint to place themselves at that of the proletariat.

The 'dangerous class,' the social scum, that passively rotting mass thrown off by the lowest layers of old society, may, here and there, be swept into the movement by a proletarian revolution; its conditions of life, however, prepare it far more for the part of a bribed tool of reactionary intrigue.

In the conditions of the proletariat, those of old society at large are already virtually swamped. The proletarian is without property; his relation to his wife and children has no longer anything in common with the bourgeois family relations: modern industrial labour, modern subjection to capital, the same in England as in France, in America as in Germany, has stripped him of every trace of national character. Law, morality, religion, are to him so many bourgeois prejudices, behind which lurk in ambush just as many bourgeois interests.

All the preceding classes that got the upper hand, sought to fortify their already acquired status by subjecting society at large to their conditions of appropriation. The proletarians cannot become masters of the productive forces of society, except by abolishing their own previous mode of appropriation, and thereby also every other previous mode of appropriation. They have nothing of their own to secure and to fortify: their mission is to destroy all previous securities for, and insurances of, individual property.

All previous historical movements were movements of minorities, or in the interest of minorities. The proletarian movement is the self-conscious, independent movement of the immense majority, in the interest of the immense majority. The proletariat, the lowest stratum of our present society, cannot stir, cannot raise itself up, without the whole superincumbent strata of official society being sprung into the air.

Though not in substance, yet in form, the struggle of the proletariat with the bourgeoisie is at first a national struggle. The proletariat of each country must, of course, first of all settle matters with its own bourgeoisie.

In depicting the most general phases of the development of the proletariat, we traced the more or less veiled civil war, raging within existing society, up to the point where that war breaks out into open revolution, and where the violent overthrow of the bourgeoisie lays the foundation for the sway of the proletariat.

3 Max Weber: Social Order and Power (Class, Status, Party)

Although Weber recognised the major importance of class in analysing social stratification (the division of society into different groups), he considered that Marx put too exclusive an emphasis upon it. He argued that two other major forms of social division or stratification occur: party (or political divisions) and status (divisions based on different grades of honour or prestige). Unlike Marx, he did not consider that these two additional forms of stratification are necessarily subordinate to, or dependent upon, class. The example he gives in the passage of the 'typical American boss' is intended to show that 'economically conditioned power' or, more succinctly, high economic class, does not guarantee high status nor, though he does not make the point here, great political power. Weber referred to economic position as economic class and status position as social class; as the previous example shows the two need not be closely related, although in practice they usually are.

Weber's analysis of class-situation in terms of market-situation (which includes the ability to offer services as well as the ownership of property) results in a much more highly differentiated concept of class structure than that of Marx. Yet, as is made clear in the section 'communal action flowing from class interest', Weber does not attribute the same range of characteristics to class as does Marx. He makes a crucial and perhaps insufficiently appreciated distinction between class and community. Communities are groups that experience a feeling of belonging and, in Weber's view, members of economic classes do not always share such feelings. He suggests that Marx too readily thought that they did (although, in fairness to Marx, his concept of false-consciousness shows that he was aware that they sometimes did not). For Weber, therefore classes are not necessarily nor naturally communities although they may sometimes act as such.

Weber argues that status groups rather than classes are 'normally communities'. He suggests that equality of esteem and similarity of life-style can generate a sense of mutual identity, even when economic inequalities exist. He goes on to explain the usually exclusive nature of status groups. It is worth re-emphasising that, unlike Marx, he believed that status stratification could exist independently of, and sometimes be more important than, class stratification. The concept of status is central in Weber's thought and is covered here substantially. The quite complex treatment of status, caste, ethnicity and race may be considered again when race is studied.

The brevity of the final section on parties should not undermine its significance. By applying the term 'societalisation' to parties, Weber means that, however they are made up (i.e., whether of classes or status groups or both), they seek power in order to affect society.

The 'talented author' to whom Weber refers is Karl Marx.

Reading 3 From Max Weber as edited by C. Wright Mills, *From Max Weber* (Routledge and Kegan Paul, 1970), pp. 180–5, 186–91, 194–5.

Economically determined power and the social order

Law exists when there is a probability that an order will be upheld by a specific staff of men who will use physical or psychical compulsion with the intention of obtaining conformity with the order, or of inflicting sanctions for infringement of it.* The structure of every legal order directly influences the distribution of power, economic or otherwise, within its respective community. This is true of all legal orders and not only that of the state. In general, we understand by 'power' the chance of a man or of a number of men to realise their own will in a communal action even against the resistance of others who are participating in the action.

'Economically conditioned' power is not, of course, identical with 'power' as such. On the contrary, the emergence of economic power may be the consequence of power existing on other grounds. Man does not strive for power only in order to enrich himself economically. Power, including economic power, may be valued 'for its own sake.' Very frequently the striving for power is also conditioned by the social 'honor' it entails. Not all power, however, entails social honor: the typical American Boss, as well as the typical big speculator, deliberately relinquishes social honor. Quite generally, 'mere economic' power, and especially 'naked' money power, is by no means a recognised basis of social honor. Nor is power the only basis of social honor. Indeed, social honor, or prestige, may even be the basis of political or economic power, and very frequently has been. Power, as well as honor, may be guaranteed by the legal order, but, at least normally, it is not their primary source. The legal order is rather an additional factor that enhances the chance to hold power or honor; but it cannot always secure them.

The way in which social honor is distributed in a community between typical groups participating in this distribution we may call the 'social order.' The social order and the economic order are, of

* *Wirtschaft und Gesellschaft*, part III, chap. 4, pp. 631–40. The first sentence in paragraph one and the several definitions which are in brackets do not appear in the original text. They have been taken from other contexts of *Wirtschaft und Gesellschaft*.

course, similarly related to the 'legal order.' However, the social and the economic order are not identical. The economic order is for us merely the way in which economic goods and services are distributed and used. The social order is of course conditioned by the economic order to a high degree, and in its turn reacts upon it.

Now: 'classes,' 'status groups,' and 'parties' are phenomena of the distribution of power within a community.

Determination of class-situation by market-situation

In our terminology, 'classes' are not communities; they merely represent possible, frequent, bases for communal action. We may speak of a 'class' when (1) a number of people have in common a specific causal component of their life chances, in so far as (2) this component is represented exclusively by economic interests in the possession of goods and opportunities for income, and (3) is represented under the conditions of the commodity or labor markets. (These points refer to 'class situation,' which we may express more briefly as the typical chance for a supply of goods, external living conditions, and personal life experiences, in so far as this chance is determined by the amount and kind of power, or lack of such, to dispose of goods or skills for the sake of income in a given economic order. The term 'class' refers to any group of people that is found in the same class situation.)

It is the most elemental economic fact that the way in which the disposition over material property is distributed among a plurality of people, meeting competitively in the market for the purpose of exchange, in itself creates specific life chances. According to the law of marginal utility this mode of distribution excludes the non-owners from competing for highly valued goods; it favors the owners and, in fact, gives to them a monopoly to acquire such goods. Other things being equal, this mode of distribution monopolises the opportunities for profitable deals for all those who, provided with goods, do not necessarily have to exchange them. It increases, at least generally, their power in price wars with those who, being property-less, have nothing to offer but their services in native form or goods in a form constituted through their own labor, and who above all are compelled to get rid of these products in order barely to subsist. This mode of distribution gives to the propertied a monopoly on the possibility of transferring property from the sphere of use as a 'fortune,' to the sphere of 'capital goods'; that is, it gives them the entrepreneurial function and all chances to share directly or indirectly in returns on capital. All this holds true within the area in which pure market conditions prevail. 'Property' and 'lack of property' are, therefore, the basic categories of all class situations. It does not matter whether these two categories become effective in price wars or in competitive struggles.

Within these categories, however, class situations are further differentiated: on the one hand, according to the kind of property that is usable for returns; and, on the other hand, according to the kind of services that can be offered in the market. Ownership of domestic buildings; productive establishments; warehouses; stores; agriculturally usable land, large and small holdings – quantitative differences with possibly qualitative consequences; ownership of mines; cattle; men (slaves); disposition over mobile instruments of production, or capital goods of all sorts, especially money or objects that can be exchanged for money easily and at any time; disposition over products of one's own labor or of others' labor differing according to their various distances from consumability; disposition over transferable monopolies of any kind – all these distinctions differentiate the class situations of the propertied just as does the 'meaning' which they can and do give to the utilisation of property, especially to property which has money equivalence. Accordingly, the propertied, for instance, may belong to the class of rentiers or to the class of entrepreneurs.

Those who have no property but who offer services are differentiated just as much according to their kinds of services as according to the way in which they make use of these services, in a continuous or discontinuous relation to a recipient. But always this is the generic connotation of the concept of class: that the kind of chance in the *market* is the decisive moment which presents a common condition for the individual's fate. 'Class situation' is, in this sense, ultimately 'market situation.' The effect of naked possession *per se*, which among cattle breeders gives the non-owning slave or serf into the power of the cattle owner, is only a forerunner of real 'class' formation. However, in the cattle loan and in the naked severity of the law of debts in such communities, for the first time mere 'possession' as such emerges as decisive for the fate of the individual. This is very much in contrast to the agricultural communities based on labor. The creditor-debtor relation becomes the basis of 'class situations' only in those cities where a 'credit market,' however primitive, with rates of interest increasing according to the extent of dearth and a factual monopolisation of credits, is developed by a plutocracy. Therewith 'class struggles' begin.

Those men whose fate is not determined by the chance of using goods or services for themselves on the market, e.g. slaves, are not, however, a 'class' in the technical sense of the term. They are, rather, a 'status group.'

Communal action flowing from class interest

According to our terminology, the factor that creates 'class' is unambiguously economic interest, and indeed, only those interests involved in the existence of the 'market.' Nevertheless, the concept of 'class-interest' is an ambiguous one: even as an empirical concept it is ambiguous as soon as one understands by it something other than the factual direction of interests following with a certain probability from the class situation for a certain 'average' of those people subjected to the class situation. The class situation and other circumstances remaining the same, the direction in which the individual worker, for instance, is likely to pursue his interests may vary widely, according to whether he is constitutionally qualified for the task at hand to a high, to an average, or to a low degree. In the same way, the direction of interests may vary according to whether or not a *communal* action of a larger or smaller portion of those commonly affected by the 'class situation,' or even an association among them, e.g. a 'trade union,' has grown out of the class situation from which the individual may or may not expect promising results. (Communal action refers to that action which is oriented to the feeling of the actors that they belong together. Societal action, on the other hand, is oriented to a rationally motivated adjustment of interests.) The rise of societal or even of communal action from a common class situation is by no means a universal phenomenon . . .

In any case, a class does not in itself constitute a community. To treat 'class' conceptually as having the same value as 'community' leads to distortion. That men in the same class situation regularly react in mass actions to such tangible situations as economic ones in the direction of those interests that are most adequate to their average number is an important and after all simple fact for the understanding of historical events. Above all, this fact must not lead to that kind of pseudo-scientific operation with the concepts of 'class' and 'class interests' so frequently found these days, and which has found its most classic expression in the statement of a talented author, that the individual may be in error concerning his interests but that the 'class' is 'infallible' about its interests . . .

Status honor

In contrast to classes, *status groups* are normally communities. They are, however, often of an amorphous kind. In contrast to the purely economically determined 'class situation' we wish to designate as 'status situation' every typical component of the life fate of men that is determined by a specific, positive or negative, social estimation of *honor*. This honor may be connected with any quality shared by a plurality, and, of course, it can be knit to a class situation: class distinctions are linked in the most varied ways with status distinctions. Property as such is not always recognised as a status qualification, but in the long run it is, and with extraordinary regularity. In the subsistence economy of the organised neighborhood, very often the richest man is simply the chieftain. However, this often means only an honorific preference. For example, in the so-called pure modern 'democracy,' that is, one devoid of any expressly ordered status privileges for individuals, it may be that only the families coming under approximately the same tax class dance with one another. This example is reported of certain smaller Swiss cities. But status honor need not necessarily be linked with a 'class situation.' On the contrary, it normally stands in sharp opposition to the pretensions of sheer property.

Both propertied and propertyless people can belong to the same status group, and frequently they do with very tangible consequences. This 'equality' of social esteem may, however, in the long run become quite precarious. The 'equality' of status among the American 'gentlemen,' for instance, is expressed by the fact that outside the subordination determined by the different functions of 'business,' it would be considered strictly repugnant – wherever the old tradition still prevails – if even the richest 'chief,' while playing billiards or cards in his club in the evening, would not treat his 'clerk' as in every sense fully his equal in birthright. It would be repugnant if the American 'chief' would bestow upon his 'clerk' the condescending 'benevolence' making a distinction of 'position,' which the German chief can never dissever from his attitude. This is one of the most important reasons why in America the German 'clubby-ness' has never been able to attain the attraction that the American clubs have.

Guarantees of status stratification

In content, status honor is normally expressed by the fact that above all else a specific *style of life* can be expected from all those who wish to belong to the circle. Linked with this expectation are restrictions on 'social' intercourse (that is, intercourse which is not subservient to economic or any other of business's 'functional' purposes). These restrictions may confine normal marriages to within the status circle and may lead to complete endogamous closure. As soon as there is not a mere individual and socially irrelevant imitation of another style of life, but an agreed-upon communal action of this closing character, the 'status' development is under way.

In its characteristic form, stratification by 'status groups' on the basis of conventional styles of life evolves at the present time in the United States out of the traditional democracy. For example, only the resident of a certain street ('the street') is considered as belonging to 'society,' is qualified for social intercourse, and is visited and invited. Above all, this differentiation evolves in such a way as to make for strict submission to the fashion that is dominant at a given time in society . . .

'Ethnic' segregation and 'caste'

Where the consequences have been realised to their full extent, the status group evolves into a closed 'caste.' Status distinctions are then guaranteed not merely by conventions and laws, but also by *rituals*. This occurs in such a way that every physical contact with a member of any caste that is considered to be 'lower' by the members of a 'higher' caste is considered as making for a ritualistic impurity and to be a stigma which must be expiated by a religious act. Individual castes develop quite distinct cults and gods.

In general, however, the status structure reaches such extreme consequences only where there are underlying differences which are held to be 'ethnic.' The 'caste' is, indeed, the normal form in which ethnic communities usually live side by side in a 'societalised' manner. These ethnic communities believe in blood relationship and exclude exogamous marriage and social intercourse. Such a caste situation is part of the phenomenon of 'pariah' peoples and is found all over the world. These people form communities, acquire specific occupational traditions of handicrafts or of other arts, and cultivate a belief in their ethnic community. They live in a 'diaspora' strictly segregated from all personal intercourse, except that of an unavoidable sort, and their situation is legally precarious. Yet, by virtue of their economic indispensability, they are tolerated, indeed, frequently privileged, and they live in interspersed political communities. The Jews are the most impressive historical example.

A 'status' segregation grown into a 'caste' differs in its structure from a mere 'ethnic' segregation: the caste structure transforms the horizontal and unconnected coexistences of ethnically segregated groups into a vertical social system of super– and subordination. Correctly formulated: a comprehensive societalisation integrates the ethnically divided communities into specific political and communal action. In their consequences they differ precisely in this way: ethnic coexistences condition a mutual repulsion and disdain but allow each ethnic community to consider its own honor as the highest one; the caste structure brings about a social subordination and an acknowledgment of 'more honor' in favor of the privileged caste and status groups. This is due to the fact that in the caste structure ethnic distinctions as such have become 'functional' distinctions within the political societalisation (warriors, priests, artisans that are politically important for war and for building, and so on). But even pariah people who are most despised are usually apt to continue cultivating in some manner that which is equally peculiar to ethnic and to status communities: the belief in their own specific 'honor.' This is the case with the Jews.

Only with the negatively privileged status groups does the 'sense of dignity' take a specific deviation. A sense of dignity is the precipitation in individuals of social honor and of conventional demands which a positively privileged status group raises for the deportment of its members. The sense of dignity that characterises positively privileged status groups is naturally related to their 'being' which does not transcend itself, that is, it is to their 'beauty and excellence' ($\varkappa\alpha\lambda o$-$\varkappa\alpha\gamma\alpha\theta\iota\alpha$). Their kingdom is 'of this world.' They live for the present and by exploiting their great past. The sense of dignity of the negatively privileged strata naturally refers to a future lying beyond the present, whether it is of this life or of another. In other words, it must be nurtured by the belief in a providential 'mission' and by a belief in a specific honor before God. The 'chosen people's' dignity is nurtured by a belief either that in the beyond 'the last will be the first,' or that in this life a Messiah will appear to bring forth into the light of the world which has cast them out the hidden honor of the pariah people. This simple state of affairs, and not the 'resentment' which is so strongly emphasised in Nietzsche's much admired construction in the *Genealogy of Morals*, is the source of the religiosity cultivated by pariah status groups. In passing, we may note that resentment may be accurately applied only to a limited extent; for one of Nietzsche's main examples, Buddhism, it is not at all applicable.

Incidentally, the development of status groups from ethnic segregations is by no means the normal phenomenon. On the contrary, since objective 'racial differences' are by no means basic to every subjective sentiment of an ethnic community, the ultimately racial foundation of status structure is rightly and absolutely a question of the concrete individual case. Very frequently a status group is instrumental in the production of a thoroughbred anthropological type. Certainly a status group is to a high degree effective in producing extreme types, for they select personally qualified individuals (e.g. the Knighthood selects those who are fit for warfare, physically and psychically). But selection is far from being the only, or the predominant, way in which status groups are formed: political membership or class situation has at all times been at least as frequently decisive. And today the class situation is by far the predominant factor, for of course the possibility of a style of life expected for members of a status group is usually conditioned economically.

Status privileges

For all practical purposes, stratification by status goes hand in hand with a monopolisation of ideal and material goods or opportunities, in a manner we have come to know as typical. Besides the specific status honor, which always rests upon distance and exclusiveness, we find all sorts of material monopolies. Such honorific preferences may consist of the privilege of wearing special costumes, of eating special dishes taboo to others, of carrying arms – which is most obvious in its consequences – the right to pursue certain non-professional dilettante artistic practices, e.g. to play certain musical instruments. Of course, material monopolies provide the most effective motives for the exclusiveness of a status group; although, in themselves, they are rarely sufficient, almost always they come into play to some extent. Within a status circle there is the question of intermarriage: the interest of the families in the monopolisation of potential bridegrooms is at least of equal importance and is parallel to the interest in the monopolisation of daughters. The daughters of the circle must be provided for. With an increased enclosure of the status group, the conventional preferential opportunities for special employment grow into a legal monopoly of special offices for the members. Certain goods become objects for monopolisation by status groups. In the typical fashion these include 'entailed estates' and frequently also the possessions of serfs or bondsmen and, finally, special trades. This monopolisation occurs positively when the status group is exclusively entitled to own and to manage them; and negatively when, in order to maintain its specific way of life, the status group must *not* own and manage them.

The decisive role of a 'style of life' in status 'honor' means that status groups are the specific bearers of all 'conventions.' In whatever way it may be manifest, all 'stylisation' of life either originates in status groups or is at least conserved by them. Even if the principles of status conventions differ greatly, they reveal certain typical traits, especially among those strata which are most privileged. Quite generally, among privileged status groups there is a status disqualification that operates against the performance of common physical labor. This disqualification is now 'setting in' in America against the old tradition of esteem for labor. Very frequently every rational economic pursuit, and especially 'entrepreneurial activity,' is looked upon as a disqualification of status. Artistic and literary activity is also considered as degrading work as soon as it is exploited for income, or at least when it is connected with hard physical exertion. An example is the sculptor working like a mason in his dusty smock as over against the painter in his salon-like 'studio' and those forms of musical practice that are acceptable to the status group. . . .

Parties

Whereas the genuine place of 'classes' is within the economic order, the place of 'status groups' is within the social order, that is, within the sphere of the distribution of 'honor.' From within these spheres, classes and status groups influence one another and they influence the legal order and are in turn influenced by it. But 'parties' live in a house of 'power.'

Their action is oriented toward the acquisition of social 'power,' that is to say, toward influencing a communal action no matter what its content may be. In principle, parties may exist in a social 'club' as well as in a 'state.' As over against the actions of classes and status groups, for which this is not necessarily the case, the communal actions of 'parties' always mean a societalisation. For party actions are always directed toward a goal which is striven for in a planned manner. This goal may be a 'cause' (the party may aim at realising a program for ideal or material purposes), or the goal may be 'personal' (sinecures, power, and from these, honor for the leader and the followers of the party). Usually the party action aims at all these simultaneously. Parties are, therefore, only possible within communities that are societalised, that is, which have some rational order and a staff of persons available who are ready to enforce it. For parties aim precisely at influencing this staff, and if possible, to recruit it from party followers.

In any individual case, parties may represent interests determined through 'class situation' or 'status situation,' and they may recruit their following respectively from one or the other. But they need be neither purely 'class' nor purely 'status' parties. In most cases they are partly class parties and partly status parties, but sometimes they are neither. They may represent ephemeral or enduring structures. Their means of attaining power may be quite varied, ranging from naked violence of any sort to canvassing for votes with coarse or subtle means: money, social influence, the force of speech, suggestion, clumsy hoax, and so on to the rougher or more artful tactics of obstruction in parliamentary bodies.

4 Emile Durkheim: Society, Social Facts and the Individual

Marx, Weber and Durkheim were all committed to the view that individual behaviour can be explained largely in terms of the influence of society on the individual. In C. Wright Mills' terms, the burden of their work is structural, although in the case of Weber this emphasis is balanced by his repeated insistence that sociology should focus upon understanding the meanings individuals themselves attribute to their actions. By contrast, Durkheim did not dilute his structural bias with any such concern. His exclusive study was how 'social facts', as he called them, exercise a 'controlling' and 'coercive' power over the individual. Social facts are all the ideas, values, norms and sentiments that 'exist' in society and which form the way the individual comes to think, believe and feel. Thus, newspapers, the church and the family may be the vehicles through which these social facts which constrain the individual are conveyed. Durkheim himself gives the educational system as an example of an institution that transmits values, attitudes and norms, i.e. social facts, which structure and constrain individual behaviour. Elsewhere, he describes the socialising influence of the educational system as 'almost impossible to resist'. This piece by Durkheim should be contrasted with the reading from Herbert Blumer which makes the contrary emphasis. In my view, Blumer's analysis needs to be accepted as a necessary corrective to Durkheim's excessive and deterministic emphasis on social facts. Stripped of its excess, however, Durkheim's position can be regarded as complementary rather than antagonistic to Blumer's.

Although this extract is about Durkheim's methodology, it implies a clear perspective on social structure. It is the positivistic perspective that sociology is concerned with the effect of social structure (social facts and their inter-relations) on people. In Durkheim's view, the interpretation of individual motive and meaning lay outside the scope of sociology.

Reading 4 From Emile Durkheim, *The Rules of Sociological Method* (The Free Press, 1964), pp. 1–4.

Before inquiring into the method suited to the study of social facts, it is important to know what facts are commonly called 'social.' This information is all the more necessary since the designation 'social' is used with little precision. It is currently employed for practically all phenomena generally diffused within society, however small their social interest. But on that basis, there are, as it were, no human events that may not be called social. Each individual drinks, sleeps, eats, reasons; and it is to society's interest that these functions be exercised in an orderly manner. If, then, all these facts are counted as 'social' facts, sociology would have no subject matter exclusively its own, and its domain would be confused with that of biology and psychology.

But in reality there is in every society a certain group of phenomena which may be differentiated from those studied by the other natural sciences. When I fulfil my obligations as brother, husband, or citizen, when I execute my contracts, I perform duties which are defined, externally to myself and my acts, in law and in custom. Even if they conform to my own sentiments and I feel their reality subjectively, such reality is still objective, for I did not create them; I merely inherited them through my education. How many times it happens, moreover, that we are ignorant of the details of the obligations incumbent upon us, and that in order to acquaint ourselves with them we must consult the law and its authorised interpreters! Similarly, the church-member finds the beliefs and practices of his religious life ready-made at birth; their existence prior to his own implies their existence outside of himself. The system of signs I use to express my thought, the system of currency I employ to pay my debts, the instruments of credit I utilise in my commercial relations, the practices followed in my profession, etc., function independently of my own use of them. And these state-ments can be repeated for each member of society. Here, then, are ways of acting, thinking, and feeling that present the noteworthy property of existing outside the individual consciousness.

These types of conduct or thought are not only external to the individual but are, moreover, endowed with coercive power, by virtue of which they impose themselves upon him, independent of his individual will. Of course, when I fully consent and conform to them, this constraint is felt only slightly, if at all, and is therefore unnecessary. But it is, nonetheless, an intrinsic characteristic of these facts, the proof thereof being that it asserts itself as soon as I attempt to resist it. If I attempt to violate the law, it reacts against me so as to prevent my act before its accomplishment, or to nullify my violation by restoring the damage, if it is accomplished and reparable, or to make me expiate it if it cannot be compensated for otherwise.

In the case of purely moral maxims; the public conscience exercises a check on every act which offends it by means of the surveillance it exercises over the conduct of citizens, and the appropriate penalties at its disposal. In many cases the constraint is less violent, but nevertheless it always exists. If I do not submit to the conventions of society, if in my dress I do not conform to the customs observed in my country and in my class, the ridicule I provoke, the social isolation in which I am kept, produce, although in an attenuated form, the same effects as a punishment in the strict sense of the word. The constraint is nonetheless efficacious for being indirect. I am not obliged to speak French with my fellow-countrymen nor to use the legal currency, but I cannot possibly do otherwise. If I tried to escape this necessity, my attempt would fail miserably. As an industrialist, I am free to apply the technical methods of former centuries; but by doing so, I should invite certain ruin. Even when I free myself from these rules and violate them successfully, I am always compelled to struggle with them. When finally overcome, they make their constraining power sufficiently felt by the resistance they offer. The enterprises of all innovators, including successful ones, come up against resistance of this kind.

Here, then, is a category of facts with very distinctive characteristics: it consists of ways of acting, thinking, and feeling, external to the individual, and endowed with a power of coercion, by reason of which they control him. These ways of thinking could not be confused with biological phenomena, since they consist of representations and of actions; nor with psychological phenomena, which exist only in the individual consciousness and through it. They constitute, thus, a new variety of phenomena; and it is to them exclusively that the term 'social' ought to be applied. And this term fits them quite well, for it is clear that, since their source is not in the individual, their substratum can be no other than society, either the political society as a whole or some one of the partial groups it includes, such as religious denominations, political, literary, and occupational associations, etc. On the other hand, this term 'social' applies to them exclusively, for it has a distinct meaning only if it designates exclusively the phenomena which are not included in any of the categories of facts that have already been established and classified. These ways of thinking and acting therefore constitute the proper domain of sociology. It is true that, when we define them with this word 'constraint,' we risk shocking the zealous partisans of absolute individualism. For those who profess the complete autonomy of the individual, man's dignity is diminished whenever he is made to feel that he is not completely self-determinant. It is generally accepted today, however, that most of our ideas and our tendencies are not developed by ourselves but come to us from without. How can they become a part of us except by imposing themselves upon us? This is the whole meaning of our definition. And it is generally accepted, moreover, that social constraint is not necessarily incompatible with the individual personality.

5 Herbert Blumer on George Mead: Symbolic Interaction, Self and Society

The following reading from Herbert Blumer is an attempt to present faithfully and clearly some of the basic concepts of George Mead, generally regarded as the founding father of symbolic interactionism. I present this reading here because it is an absolutely unambiguous statement of the importance of individual understanding, choice, and creativity in the social process. As Blumer says: 'The key feature in Mead's analysis is that the human being has a self.' This self is conscious of itself and of others and, mainly through language, is capable of meaningful communication with others – i.e. is capable of symbolic interaction (words being symbols).

Blumer's emphasis, through Mead, on the self's ability to plan or 'construct' action should be balanced against the tendency of the structural perspectives of Marx, Weber and Durkheim to stress the opposite – the influence of society upon the individual. It is true that one can find in Weber a considerable emphasis on the potential variety of individual motivation and action and in Marx a recurrent humanistic concern, but it is mainly through the symbolic interactionist perspective that this crucial awareness of individuality has been expressed in modern sociology. Not that symbolic interactionists fail to take account of the undoubted effect of society on the individual, but they make quite plain that this does not occur to the extent that it obliterates individuality.

Reading 5 From Herbert Blumer, 'Symbolic Interaction,' in Arnold M. Rose *ed.*, *Human Behavior and Social Process* (Houghton-Mifflin, 1962), pp. 179–84.

A view of human society as symbolic interaction has been followed more than it has been formulated. Partial, usually fragmentary, statements of it are to be found in the writings of a number of eminent scholars, some inside the field of sociology and some outside. Among the former we may note such scholars as Charles Horton Cooley, W. I. Thomas, Robert E. Park, E. W. Burgess, Florian Znaniecki, Ellsworth Faris, and James Mickel Williams. Among those outside the discipline we may note William James, John Dewey, and George Herbert Mead. None of these scholars, in my judgment, has presented a systematic statement of the nature of human group life from the standpoint of symbolic interaction. Mead stands out among all of them in laying bare the fundamental premises of the approach, yet he did little to develop its methodological implications for sociological study. Students who seek to depict the position of symbolic interaction may easily give different pictures of it. What I have to present should be regarded as my personal version. My aim is to present the basic premises of the point of view and to develop their methodological consequences for the study of human group life.

The term 'symbolic interaction' refers, of course, to the peculiar and distinctive character of interaction as it takes place between human beings. The peculiarity consists in the fact that human beings interpret or 'define' each other's actions instead of merely reacting to each other's actions. Their 'response' is not made directly to the actions of one another but instead is based on the meaning which they attach to such actions. Thus, human interaction is mediated by the use of symbols, by interpretation, or by ascertaining the meaning of one another's actions. This mediation is equivalent to inserting a process of interpretation between stimulus and response in the case of human behaviour.

The simple recognition that human beings interpret each other's actions as the means of acting toward one another has permeated the thought and writings of many scholars of human conduct and of human group life. Yet few of them have endeavored to analyse what such interpretation implies about the nature of the human being or about the nature of human association. They are usually content with a mere recognition that 'interpretation' should be caught by the student, or with a simple realisation that symbols, such as cultural norms or values, must be introduced into their analyses. Only G. H. Mead, in my judgment, has sought to think through what the act of interpretation implies for an understanding of the human being, human action, and human association. The essentials of his analysis are so penetrating and profound and so important for an understanding of human group life that I wish to spell them out, even though briefly.

The key feature in Mead's analysis is that the human being has a self. This idea should not be cast aside as esoteric or glossed over as something that is obvious and hence not worthy of attention. In declaring that the human being has a self, Mead had in mind chiefly that the human being can be the object of his own actions. He can act toward himself as he might act toward others. Each of us is familiar with actions of this sort in which the human being gets angry with himself, rebuffs himself, takes pride in himself, argues with himself, tries to bolster his own courage, tells himself that he should 'do this' or not 'do that,' sets goals for himself, makes compromises with himself, and plans what he is going to do. That the human being acts toward himself in these and countless other ways is a matter of easy empirical observation. To recognise that the human being can act toward himself is no mystical conjuration.

Mead regards this ability of the human being to act toward himself as the central mechanism with which the human being faces and deals with his world. This mechanism enables the human being to make indication to himself of things in his surroundings and thus to guide his actions by what he notes. Anything of which a human being is conscious is something which he is indicating to himself – the ticking of a clock, a knock at the door, the appearance of a friend, the remark made by a companion, a recognition that he has a task to perform, or the realisation that he has a cold. Conversely, anything of which he is not conscious is, *ipso facto*, something which he is not indicating to himself. The conscious life of the human being, from the time that he awakens until he falls asleep, is a continual flow of self-indications – notations of the things with which he deals and takes into account. We are given, then, a picture of the human being as an organism which confronts its world with a mechanism of making indications to itself. This is the mechanism that is involved in interpreting the actions of others. To interpret the actions of another is to point out to oneself that the action has this or that meaning or character.

Now, according to Mead, the significance of making indications to oneself is of paramount importance. The importance lies along two lines. First, to indicate something is to extricate it from its setting, to hold it apart, to give it a meaning or, in Mead's language, to make it into an object. An object – that is to say, anything that an individual indicates to himself – is different from a stimulus; instead of having an intrinsic character which acts on the individual and which can be identified apart from the individual, its character or meaning is conferred on it by the individual. The object is a product of the individual's disposition to act instead of being an antecedent stimulus which evokes the act. Instead of the individual being surrounded by an environment of pre-existing objects which play upon him and call forth his behavior, the proper picture is that he constructs his objects on the basis of his on-going activity. In any of his countless acts – whether minor, like dressing himself, or major, like organising himself for a professional career – the individual is designating different objects to himself, giving them meaning, judging their suitability to his action, and making decisions on the basis of the judgment. This is what is meant by interpretation or acting on the basis of symbols.

The second important implication of the fact that the human being makes indications to himself is that his action is constructed or built up instead of being a mere release. Whatever the action in which he is engaged, the human individual proceeds by pointing out to himself the divergent things which have to be taken into account in the course of his action. He has to note what he wants to do and how he is to do it; he has to point out to himself the various conditions which may be instrumental to his action and those which may obstruct his action; he has to take account of the demands, the expectations, the prohibitions, and the threats as they may arise in the situation in which he is acting. His action is built up step by step through a process of such self-indication. The human individual pieces together and guides his action by taking account of different things and interpreting their significance for his prospective action. There is no instance of conscious action of which this is not true.

The process of constructing action through making indications to oneself cannot be swallowed up in any of the conventional psychological categories. This process is distinct from and different from what is spoken of as the 'ego' – just as it is different from any other conception which conceives of the self in terms of composition or organisation. Self-indication is a moving communicative process in which the individual notes things, assesses them, gives them a meaning, and decides to act on the basis of the meaning. The human being stands over against the world, or against 'alters,' with such a process and not with a mere ego. Further, the process of self-indication cannot be subsumed under the forces, whether from the outside or inside, which are presumed to play upon the individual to produce his behavior. Environmental pressures, external stimuli, organic drives, wishes, attitudes, feelings, ideas, and their like do not cover or explain the process of self-indication. The process of self-indication stands over against them in that the individual points out to himself and interprets the appearance or expression of such things, noting a given social demand that is made on him, recognising a command, observing that he is hungry, realising that he wishes to buy something, aware that he has a given feeling, conscious that he dislikes eating with someone he despises, or aware that he is thinking of doing some given thing. By virtue of indicating such things to himself, he places himself over against them and is able to act back against them, accepting them, rejecting them, or transforming them in accordance with how he defines or interprets them. His behaviour, accordingly, is not a result of such things as environmental pressures, stimuli, motives, attitudes, and ideas but arises instead from how he interprets and handles these things in the action which he is constructing. The process of self-indication by means of which human action is formed cannot be accounted for by factors which precede the act. The process of self-indication exists in its own right and must be accepted and studied as such. It is through this process that the human being constructs his conscious action.

Now Mead recognises that the formation of action by the individual through a process of self-indication always takes place in a social context. Since this matter is so vital to an understanding of symbolic interaction it needs to be explained carefully. Fundamentally, group action takes the form of a fitting together of individual lines of action. Each individual aligns his action to the action of others by ascertaining what they are doing or what they intend to do – that is, by getting the meaning of their acts. For Mead, this is done by the individual 'taking the role' of others – either the role of a specific person or the role of a group (Mead's 'generalised other'). In taking such roles the individual seeks to ascertain the intention or direction of the acts of others. He forms and aligns his own action on the basis of such interpretation of the acts of others. This is the fundamental way in which group action takes place in human society.

The foregoing are the essential features, as I see them, in Mead's analysis of the bases of symbolic interaction. They presuppose the following: that human society is made up of individuals who have selves (that is, make indications to themselves); that individual action is a construction and not a release, being built up by the individual through noting and interpreting features of the situations in which he acts; that group or collective action consists of the aligning of individual actions, brought about by the individuals' interpreting or taking into account each other's actions. Since my purpose is to present and not to defend the position of symbolic interaction I shall not endeavor in this essay to advance support for the three premises which I have just indicated. I wish merely to say that the three premises can be easily verified empirically. I know of no instance of human group action to which the three premises do not apply. The reader is challenged to find or think of a single instance which they do not fit.

Sociological Methods

Readings 6–12

The following selection of six extracts covers the range of socio-logical research methods from the fairly large social survey to the most qualitatively sensitive of methods, participant obser-vation. Large-scale social surveys are designed to produce infor-mation or data about a substantial group of people. Usually only a sample of the total group or population of interest to the researcher is possible. As Willmott and Young make clear, it is essential that the sample be representative of the total popu-lation of interest, otherwise the generalisations based on the survey will be unreliable. The discovery of facts and, particularly, of the relationships (e.g. causal or correlational) between facts is very much in the positivist tradition of Comte and Durkheim. However, none of the following readings, including the one from Willmott and Young, is exclusively, or even predominantly, posi-tivist in method.

Although the extracts are arranged roughly in positivist-inter-pretist spectrum, it is significant that none of the authors appears to consider herself or himself to be exclusively committed to one or other type of method. They all either use, or suggest that they would use if necessary, both quantitative and qualitative methods. So, for many modern sociologists, the choice of a particular method depends on its appropriateness to a particular research project and not on any rigid commitment to either a positivist or an interpretist approach.

6 Michael Young and Peter Willmott: A Sample Survey, Inter-views and Analysis of Results

It is quite possible that even students coming fresh to sociology will have heard of Willmott and Young's famous work, *Family and Kinship in East London* (1957). Certainly, it is a classic of British sociology. It would be easy to choose a more recent example of a fairly large social survey (933 people in the main sample), but it would be difficult to find a clearer presentation of the basic procedures of sampling, interviewing and analysis of results than that given in the methodological appendix of this work. This remains true despite recent criticisms of the supposed romanticism of this and other studies of working class communities carried out in the 1960s.

Willmott and Young's findings cannot be fairly summarised in a sentence or two but, basically, they tell the story of how relationships, based on extended families and kin living close together in the East End's Bethnal Green, disappear when nuclear families move out to new housing estates such as Green-leigh. To this writer, part of the appeal of this study is the easy way in which the authors combine several methods of social research to complementary effect. They give due weight and respect to various sampling and statistical techniques whilst recognising that more humanly sensitive methods are necessary to understand the quality of feelings and relationships.

To understand the following passage, it must be realised that it is only a part of Willmott and Young's methodological appendix. Elsewhere they describe how they selected their four samples (numbers bracketed): the General Bethnal Green Sample (933 men and women from electoral registers); the Bethnal Green Marriage Sample (45 couples); the Greenleigh Marriage Sample (47 couples); and the Grammar School Sample (24 females). The first part of the passage refers mainly to the Marriage Sample interviews. These were intensive interviews of up to three hours, to provide data for comparing family life in the two areas. The General Bethnal Green survey was conducted mainly by questionnaire and brief follow-up interviews to provide general data. The part of the extract titled 'Analysing the Results' concerns the total survey. It is not necessary to be familiar with the statistical terms used by the authors to understand their essential points.

Reading 6 From Michael Young and Peter Willmott, *Family and Kinship in East London* (Penguin, 1969) pp. 207–11.

How the marriage sample interviews were carried out

We used a schedule of questions, but the interviews were much more informal and less standardised than those in the general survey. Answers had to be obtained to all the set questions listed (though not necessarily in the same order), but this did not exhaust the interview. Each couple being in some way different from every other, we endeavoured to find out as much as we could about the peculiarities of each couple's experiences and family relationships, using the set questions as leads and following up anything of interest which emerged in the answers to them as the basis for yet further questions. After each interview we wrote up, from our notes, a full interview report, including where possible people's verbatim remarks.

The marriage samples being of couples, the interviewing gave rise to some difficulties. We would have preferred to see husband and wife separately, but we found it in practice impossible to do this. What we were able to do was call in the daytime and, if the wife was at home and willing to be interviewed, interview her then, calling back to see her husband, usually in her presence also, one evening. We actually saw 21 out of 45 wives separately in this way in Bethnal Green, and 24 out of 47 at Greenleigh. Such an approach requires flexibility in conducting the interview. Some questions were specifically addressed to the wife or to the husband, while others we felt could be answered by either or both. In fact, since two refused, only 43 husbands were interviewed in Bethnal Green; we considered however that we had full enough information from both the wives to justify including the couples in our analysis.

In the main the people interviewed had no prior notice that we were coming. In the general survey, the interviewers called on those whose names and addresses were in their lists and, after explaining the purpose of the survey and assuring them that their anonymity would be preserved, asked if they would agree to help. If they said no, that was the end of the matter; if they said yes, they were either interviewed on the spot or a later appointment was made. We did the same thing ourselves when approaching the people in the Greenleigh sample for the first time. With the Bethnal Green marriage sample we reminded people of the earlier visit and asked if they would be prepared to cooperate further, just as we did when we called back on the Greenleigh sample. The approach to the members of the grammar school sample usually had to be less personal. Since many of the girls now lived at a distance from Bethnal Green, and since in any case our first task was to find them, our initial contact with most of them – and with some of the parents also – was by letter.

Analysing the results

The interviews completed, our next job was to order the information collected in them and make what sense we could of it. As will now be clear, the material was of two kinds. There was straightforward factual information in a form capable of statistical analysis, principally from the general sample but to some extent from the others as well, and there were, from the various series of 'intensive' interviews, detailed individual accounts.

Let us explain first how we set about the statistical analysis, which was carried out with the help of Philip Barbour. The general survey yielded a battery of information about nearly a thousand people. Since it would have been beyond our capacities to deal with all this material accurately and speedily by hand, the analysis was undertaken mechanically. Information about each person in the general sample was transferred from the interview schedule to a punched card, and the various tables required were produced with the help of a machine called a 'Counter-Sorter'. Briefly the procedure was to sort the cards according to one piece of information, say people's sex or age, counting them at the same time, and then once more to sort each of the selected groups according to another piece of information, say where people's parents lived, again counting those in the different categories – parents living in the same house, the same street, elsewhere in Bethnal Green, and so on. For separate analysis, we punched a further set of cards giving information about all the married children of the people in the sample, and another set of all their brothers and sisters. We have seldom cited tables from these additional groups in the book, but they were extremely useful in providing additional tables to compare with those about the informants themselves. For instance, from married people in the sample with parents alive we had information about parent-child relationships; and we had an independent set of information, through a different generation of people in the sample, about the relationships of all their married children with them. Comparisons of this kind, where the results from both sets of cards tallied, gave us more confidence in the findings.

Since the numbers in the other samples were so much smaller, the statistical analysis of them could be done better by hand. For each couple interviewed in the marriage samples and for each of the ex-grammar-school girls, we prepared a card setting out the standardised information, so that we had altogether three sets of these cards, each of which could be manually sorted, grouped, and counted to produce the required tables.

As well as carrying out the analysis, we did what we could to check on the 'representativeness' of our samples and to test the reliability of the findings. One indication of the reliability of the general sample could be provided by comparing its members, in respect of their age, sex, marital state, and so on, with the proportions shown in the 1951 Census for Bethnal Green as a whole. Four years had of course elapsed between the Census and our general survey, but we thought it unlikely that there had been any major changes in matters like these, and when the various comparisons showed only minor differences between the proportions in the sample and those in the Census, this suggested to us that the sample was, in the main, probably a fairly 'representative' one.

There were also a number of recognised statistical techniques that could help in interpreting the various analyses we carried out. For one thing, with the appropriate formula, we could calculate the margin of error likely to apply to any particular finding, and could thus judge the validity of generalising from it to the 'population' concerned. This kind of calculation showed, for instance, that since 8 per cent of the people in our general sample were Jewish, the proportion of Jews among the adult population of Bethnal Green as a whole (in 1955, when the survey was done) was likely to be between 2 per cent and 14 per cent. Or to take another example, as 55 per cent of the married women in the general sample with mothers alive had seen them in the previous day, between 47 per cent and 63 per cent of those in the borough population would probably have done the same. Another thing open to us was to apply the appropriate 'tests of statistical significance' to any difference that appeared in the analysis (the difference, for instance, between the proximity of married men and married women to their parents) and see whether the difference observed was likely to arise in the sample by chance alone. In deciding whether any particular finding should be regarded as valid, we also considered whether it seemed to be consistent with other, related findings (the preponderance of the mother-daughter tie, for example, stood out quite clearly from the many analyses with different samples we undertook on these subjects). And if any table suggested a specially important correlation, we went on to do a series of further tables (or employed 'multi-variate analysis', to use the technical term) to try to see if the differences that had appeared were explained by other incidental differences, hitherto concealed from us, in the various groups under examination.

But the statistical material, essential though it was, had its obvious limitations. We had set out from the beginning with the deliberate intention to combine statistical analysis with the kind of detailed description and individual illustration that could come only from fairly free and lengthy interviews and from personal observation, because we thought that this would give a more rounded – and more accurate – account than either method alone. In interpreting the survey findings, we could draw upon the detailed interview reports from the marriage samples, and also the notes and impressions from our observation in the two districts. As we have explained in the Introduction, one of us lived with his family in Bethnal Green during the period of the survey; and this provided local contacts which opened the way to additional material on family and community patterns in the borough (the detailed account of one woman's half-hour shopping trip, on pp. 106–7, is an example). We both also tried to supplement this with as much personal observation and participation as possible in Bethnal Green and in Greenleigh as well.

We thus had a range of information of different kinds – figures, detailed interview reports, personal accounts and impressions – and in writing the book we drew on all these sources. We moved from the tables to the descriptive material for illustration and explanation of what had been statistically established, or perhaps for a refined interpretation which would take us back to the figures once more for further analysis. Or we sometimes began with an impression from the interviews, or an idea suggested by something we had observed, and turned to the various sources of statistical information in a search for some way to test or explore it. Through this process of exploration, moving to and fro between the different types of information and discussing together the meaning of the often complex evidence, the final report of this survey came to be fashioned. This method inevitably has its dangers. We have tried, in what we have written, to respect the appropriate statistical procedures and to avoid bias or tendentiousness. But the extent to which the final account is a personal interpretation, shaped and coloured by our own interests and sympathies, predispositions and unconscious prejudices, should be borne in mind by the reader.

Question

1. *(a)* *What problems could arise from the 'more informal and less standardised' interviews with the marriage samples?*

(10 marks)

(b) *What are the 'obvious limitations' of statistical material? You may use examples from other statistical data besides those given here.*

(15 marks)

7 Ann Oakley: A Small-scale Social Survey (Sample Selection and Measurement Techniques)

The following extract is from Appendix 1 of Ann Oakley's *The Sociology of Housework*. The survey is an attempt to find out what women feel about housework, particularly their levels of satisfaction or dissatisfaction with it. The sample of 40 is stratified into a middle-and a working-class group. Crucially, Oakley distinguishes between 'feelings' and 'orientation' towards housework. Orientation describes the general attitude of women towards the 'traditionally female' role of housework, and feeling describes their response to the housework they actually have to do. Whilst Oakley found that most of the respondents were positively oriented to housework 'in theory' (this being especially true of working class women), the majority found that, in practice, it was monotonous, fragmentary, and had to be done at an excessive pace. Oakley's major finding was that feelings of 'dissatisfaction with housework' predominate.

The extract brings into focus two general aspects of methodology. First, is the selection of the sample itself. Its size is small and the issue of representativeness is therefore raised. Second, the research combines quantitative and qualitative aspects. Indeed, it can be said that Oakley is essentially trying to quantify, or at least give a precise assessment of specific qualitative experiences, i.e. satisfaction or dissatisfaction with housework. In order to convey something of the problems associated with 'measuring' qualitative phenomena, I have included part of Oakley's section on measurement techniques. Here I present in full only her comments on 'rating' satisfaction with housework and exclude those on satisfaction with marriage and child-rearing.

Reading 7 From Ann Oakley, *The Sociology of Housework* (Martin Robertson, 1974), pp. 198–201.

This appendix contains more detailed information about methodological aspects of the housework study than is given in the text. It covers two areas: (1) methods of selecting the forty housewives interviewed; and (2) procedures used to assess 'satisfaction' and other areas of women's responses. These assessments play a key part in the analysis of the research findings.

1 Sample selection

For the purposes of developing an interview schedule, ten pilot interviews were carried out some weeks before the main survey interviewing (which took place between January and March 1971). The ten respondents for the pilot interviews (five 'working class', five 'middle class' on the basis of husband's occupation) were chosen simply by knocking on doors in two areas: one working class, one middle class.

The main sample of forty women was selected from the practice lists of two general practitioners in London – one in a predominantly working-class, one in a predominantly middle-class, area. The names of potential respondents were selected from the practice lists on an alphabetical basis. Two names were selected for each letter of the alphabet – the first two names occurring of married female patients born between 1940 and 1950, with at least one child under five. These criteria were used in order to obtain a relative homogeneous sample of young housewife-mothers. Seventy-one names were yielded by this method. Each doctor was then asked whether any physical or mental illness in his view justified the exclusion of patients from the research sample. They were also asked to indicate the ethnic group of the patients chosen, and West Indian, West African and Indian patients were then withdrawn from the sample list; those remaining were all either Irish-born or British-born women. Again, the purpose of controlling ethnic group was to increase the homogeneity of the sample.

After excluding individuals on the basis of ethnic group, the sample size was reduced to sixty-five. The procedure then used was to call at the address given on the medical card, using the doctor's name as an introduction, stating the aim of the research ('to find out what housewives think about housework') and inviting co-operation. Names were taken in alphabetical order, one from each letter in both class lists until a total of forty interviews had been obtained. The sample of forty was equally divided into working-class and middle-class groups, using the main criterion of husband's occupation. A fairly high proportion of patients in the working-class area had moved since the address on the medical card had been given; in most cases the new address was not available, but when it was, and when it was within the same local area, the potential respondent was followed up.

In sixteen cases out of the total forty, the woman agreed to be interviewed straight away. In the remaining cases an appointment was made for some future time. In no case in which a woman was contacted was there any refusal to co-operate, although in two cases the appointment offered was so far ahead (due to a sick husband and a holiday respectively) that it seemed better to substitute another respondent. Table 1 gives a summary of data relating to sample size and reasons for failure to interview. In each of the seven 'failed to contact' cases the address was visited five times, over a period of a few days and at different times of the day.

Table 1 Size of sample drawn and reasons for failures to interview

	Number
Sample drawn	65
Moved, unable to trace	16
Failed to contact	7
Contacted, not interviewed	
(i) refused	0
(ii) offered appointment too far ahead	2
Sample interviewed	40

The interviews were completed in one session using a tape

recorder, and lasted between one and a quarter and three and a half hours, with an average of about two hours.

2 Measurement techniques

A number of ratings of satisfaction and other aspects of the housewife's work situation were based on the interview responses. Levels of satisfaction with housework, child-care, marriage, employment work and life generally were assessed separately from each other. In addition as assessment was made of each woman's level of identification with the housewife role, and of the degree to which she specified standards and routines for housework activity. The marital relationship was rated as 'segregated' or 'joint' on the two areas of decision-making and leisure activities, and, lastly, an assessment was made of the husband's level of participation (as reported by his wife) in housework and child-care tasks.

One possible procedure in making ratings of this kind is to ask respondents themselves to make the assessments – for example, to place themselves on a 'scale' of satisfaction ('highly satisfied', 'satisfied', 'unsatisfied' and so forth). Although this approach has the merit of requiring no interpretation on the part of the researcher, it also has the disadvantage that different respondents may use different yardsticks in making their assessments, and the researcher has no way of judging these. A strategy similar to self-report is the use of 'standardised' questions to obtain ratings of satisfaction or some other attitudinal/behavioural dimension. Undermining the utility of both self-report and standardised question-answer procedures is the problem of 'conventionalisation' – the tendency of people to choose the socially desirable response – which results in a reporting distortion of the phenomenon under study. Thus, for example, people tend to say they are satisfied with marriage when asked a direct question about marital satisfaction, since this response has a higher social acceptability than one stating dissatisfaction. Because of the drawbacks associated with these methods, the ratings for the research were all undertaken by the interviewer-researcher.

Satisfaction ratings

In view of the tendency of people to respond positively when asked for a direct report of their satisfaction, the question 'Are you satisfied/dissatisfied with work/marriage/child-care?' was not asked in the present survey. Instead a number of questions were asked to elicit responses on which assessments of satisfaction/dissatisfaction could be made.

(1) For *satisfaction with housework*, the particular questions were:

(i) 'Do you like housework?' This is clearly a focused question, but it was employed for two reasons: first, because the more neutral question 'What do you feel about housework?' was greeted with some confusion in the pilot interviews. For working-class house-wives it appeared to lack intelligibility, and middle-class women tended to answer it by making general statements about their domestic role-orientation (e.g. 'I don't mind being a housewife really'). The second reason for using this question was that it proved immensely useful as a 'way in' to the whole area of housework attitudes; its simplicity enabled some rapport to be established between interviewer and respondent.

(ii) A second approach was to ask about attitudes to particular work tasks. Thus, questions were asked about six basic household activities: cleaning, shopping, cooking, washing up, washing and ironing.

(iii) A third group of questions related to the experiences of monotony, fragmentation, excessive pace, social isolation and 'captivity' in housework. These questions formed part of the attempt to understand the housewife's experience of housework, but they were also asked to achieve some degree of comparability with other studies.

(iv) Two last questions, asked in the final section of the interview, invited the housewife to compare her present work satisfaction with alternatives experienced by her in other roles, or alternatives which she might conceive of as potentially open to her. (Where these more general questions provoked responses which gave information about other areas of satisfaction – employment work, for instance – responses were taken into account in the assessment of other areas of satisfaction.)

Question

1. (a) *What was the possible value of the pilot survey to the researcher?*
(5 marks)
(b) *Comment on the sample (e.g. its size and degree of homogeneity) in terms of the problem of representativeness and of generalisation.*
(8 marks)

(c) Comment on the techniques used by Ann Oakley to assess satisfaction. What problems do sociologists face in measuring experiences like satisfaction?

(12 marks)

8   Paul Corrigan: A Qualitative Approach: A Variety of Methods

The following extract is from the first chapter of Paul Corrigan's *Schooling the Smash Street Kids.* Corrigan's research is a committed attempt to understand the 'kids" experience of school in their own terms – and only then to relate this experience to the structural realities of the wider world. His assumption is that the way the kids think and act will at least make sense to them if not, often, to others (such as teachers and the police). He does them the credit of trying to find out how *they* 'see things'. To do this, he uses a variety of sociological methods, including questionnaires, interviews, general observation and just chatting with the lads. Amusingly, he explains that the most intimate method of observation – participant – was not open to him. His height (six foot four) precluded it!

The major conclusion that Corrigan draws from the qualitative side of his research is that the kids feel themselves to be relatively powerless. They *have* to go to school. They *have* to do a job. The necessity and compulsion is there, even though school and work might be boring. Much of their activity can be understood as an attempt to enliven otherwise dull proceedings. Indeed, that is how they explain it themselves. Observing all this, Corrigan is provoked to ask why they should be in so powerless a position. He does not explain this in terms of their personal failure, but in terms of the needs of the capitalist system and of the functioning of the educational system within it. To do this, he uses the historical method. He illustrates, perhaps rather than proves, that historically the governmental, business, and educational establishments have required that the state educational system should control and teach conformity to working-class children. According to him, the educational system was developed largely for that purpose from the second half of the nineteenth century.

In blending successfully micro and macro sociological

45

analysis, Corrigan shows that different sociological methods can be used in a complementary way. Methodological variety can be a strength of the discipline rather than a sign of fragmentation.

Reading 8 From Paul Corrigan, *Schooling the Smash Street Kids* (Macmillan, 1979), pp. 14–17.

The questionnaire

In asking the boys to answer a questionnaire I realised that I was doing something far from original. Yet there were sets of background information about the boys' experiences which could only really be gained by this method. I needed some information before I could use the more sensitive techniques of structured interview, observation and just plain chatting. So I administered a questionnaire myself to groups of boys in both schools.

I gave the questionnaires to 48 boys from Municipal School and 45 from Cunningham. I asked the headmasters to provide me with boys who were most probably leaving that year. (Since the school-leaving age had not at the time been raised, this meant that they were all nearly 15.) In answer to all the other more specific questions from the headmasters I simply answered that I wanted a 'cross-section'. Both said that the boys that they selected represented their year quite well; both warned me that there were several terrors and horrors in the group; both said that there were some 'good lads' in it.

I gave the questionnaires to the boys, preceded by a patter which I hoped would allay some of their fears. There were a variety of techniques used in the questionnaire, but in the pilot survey and throughout I realised the tremendous difficulty of collecting information from people whose thoughts are not expressed in the same way as the researcher's. Many of the boys found difficulty in writing at all, and a few of them just didn't write anything or answer any questions. All the time I stressed that I did not mind if they didn't write sentences and that one word would do in sentence completion. Overall the questionnaire tried to get round this as much as possible by providing a spread of different methods of articulation: Importantly, too, I gave out the questionnaires to *groups* of boys, giving them much more confidence since they were filling them in with their mates.

The interview

I interviewed all the boys in Municipal School that I had given the questionnaire to. It is important to stress why I didn't interview any of the boys from Cunningham School as it says a lot about the way in which sociological research *actually happens* (rather than the way in which sociologists write about their research). The headmaster of Cunningham School was not too pleased at the thought of me going to his school two or three times a week with my tape recorder and could well have stopped me interviewing half-way through. Therefore, since the interviews were to be supplemented by general observations about the way in which the school worked, I thought it might be better to concentrate on getting to know the social relationships involved with one school. At the same time, in analysing the two schools' answers to my questions, I discovered no significant difference between the responses of the two sets of boys. This was surprising, since from the outside the schools appeared so different, but in another way it was not surprising at all, since the whole message that the research ends up saying is that school is school for these boys, and it is the structure of perceived compulsion that makes it such an oppressive experience.

Other methods

Apart from the questionnaires and interviews there were other ways of obtaining information which were used throughout my research. It is these that are generally forgotten when sociologists write up their research. Most importantly as far as the understanding of these schools is concerned, I spent a lot of time just in the school, looking, trying to understand the way in which structures worked. This provided me with insights which made a lot of the interpretation of the other data possible. It directed my reading in certain directions. I also spent some time just chatting to boys at lunchtimes; in these situations the research process is seen as a two-way process. They were making sense of my world as much as I was making sense of theirs. They asked about drugs, student demonstrations, politics, sex, pop music, football, south of Teesside, and all the other things which are so very odd to them. Towards the end of the research they could have written a fairly good report on what it is like for a working-class postgraduate to live in a fairly bourgeois town (Durham) but do research in a working-class area of a city. But of course these boys at the end of the research go down the pits or into the Navy. THEY don't get to write the books.

Getting to know these boys in this way allowed me some greater understanding of their school experiences. It also directed my research and my methods in a different way. It forced me to look at the education system of this country historically in order to try and find out why these boys had to go to school. Thus one of the methods of investigation became the use of the historical method.

Conclusion

What this chapter has tried to do is show the similarity between the sociological methods that I used to try to make sense of a problem I was interested in, and the ways in which ordinary people make sense of their world. It may appear a mess and imprecise; yet I believe that it represents much more fully the real way in which an analysis of a situation makes sense of the world for people. Whether sociology is a science, a craft or a philosophy, it is nothing if it fails to discuss the experienced problems of ordinary people; and it is nothing if it fails to do this in a way which people can understand.

Therefore in the following five chapters I have arranged my research around five questions which I consider of social importance. At the beginning of each chapter I have outlined one sort of answer to the question – the answer with which I entered my research. Then I use large chunks of the kids' words about their worlds to try and supply another answer to the question. The distance between these two answers does, I think, measure the distance between sociology and the experienced world. Thirdly, I try to follow some of the leads that the boys' words had given me in terms of other areas of research. Fourthly, I provide a very different sort of answer to the question that the chapter is based upon. The result may appear less structured than most sociological research, yet it will provide the reader with a view of what it is like to do research, and what it is like to learn and change one's opinions and ideas whilst doing it. I think the research answers some questions and asks a lot of others; overall it shows the vital importance of actually getting down to trying to understand the real world and not taking the obvious answers as the right ones.

You can't solve a problem? Well get down and investigate the present facts and the past history! When you have investigated a problem, you will know how to solve it. Only a blockhead cudgels his brains on his own or together with a group to 'find a solution' or 'evolve an idea' without making an investigation. It must be stressed that this cannot possibly lead to any effective solution or to any good ideas.

Questions

1. (a) Evaluate the 'method' by which the author 'chose' his 'cross-section of pupils' from the two schools.

(5 marks)

(b) What do you think the advantages and disadvantages of administering the questionnaires to groups of boys rather than individuals might be?

(5 marks)

2. (a) Why does the author consider that it did not matter very much that he only interviewed the boys from Municipal School and not from Cunningham? Do you agree?

(5 marks)

(b) Comment briefly on the absence of girls from the sample.

(5 marks)

3. The author has adopted less formal 'sociological methods' (in addition to questionnaires and interviews), to try 'to make sense of' the boys' world that are much the same as the ways they themselves use to try to understand their 'world'. Comment on this claim.

(10 marks)

9 Ken Pryce: Participant Observation

The following extract is from the methodological appendix of Ken Pryce's *Endless Pressure*, a book which is fast becoming a classic of participant observation. The study is an attempt to apply or put into operation Weber's concept of *life-style* to describe the way of life of members of the West Indian community in Bristol.

Even more than most participant observational studies, this is 'an insider's view', (Pryce's phrase) because the author himself is a West Indian. Yet, at the start of his research, Pryce was unfamiliar both with Bristol as a whole and the St Paul's area in particular which was the focus of much of his research. The following extract finds him attempting to gain a foothold on life in the St Paul's district. Especially worth noting is his self-conscious sense of difficulty at being both a participant and a researcher (observer). His remark that many 'insights and hypotheses . . . were developed in the actual process of investigation' is reminiscent of a comment by William Foote Whyte, author of a participant observational study of a Chicago gang, that: 'As I sat and listened, I learned the answers to questions that I would not even have had the sense to ask if I had been getting my information solely on an interviewing basis.'

There is much similarity, then, between the participant observer and the 'true story' teller. The difference lies in the researcher's ability to use a variety of helpful concepts (life-style itself is one of them) and methods. Nevertheless, I am not sure that there is any real difference between, say, George Orwell's *Down and Out in Paris and London* and Pryce's own 'tale' of West Indian life in St Paul's.

Not surprisingly, Pryce finds a variety of different life-styles among Bristol's West Indian community. He uses an interesting range of terms to describe various groups, some of which appear here. 'Hustlers' are mainly unemployed, younger West Indians who make, or 'hustle' a living, sometimes resorting to drug-pushing or pimping. 'Main-liners' are those West Indians who aspire to success in the 'white' dominated world. 'In-betweeners' are those who retain a foot in both black sub-culture and the white mainstream. 'Saints' refers to religiously orientated members of the West Indian community.

Reading 9 From Ken Pryce, *Endless Pressure* (Penguin, 1979), pp. 279–82.

The main method adopted for the research on which this study is based was participant observation. Participant observation, because it deposits one inside the culture of the group studied and forces on one the role of involved actor and participant, affords the academic researcher a unique opportunity of getting the right leads and following through situations whereby he can replace superficial impressions with more accurate insights. By combining his 'outsider' perception with an insider's view of the way of life under consideration, the researcher can thus get behind the statistical shapes and patterns and explore at first hand the wide variety of adaptive responses he encounters, studying them from the value position of the people themselves, in their own terms and on their own ground. All the time he does this through prolonged, intensive direct exposure to actual life-conditions over a relatively long period of time. Not only can the findings of this intensive approach supplement and add significance to data gathered by more quantitative techniques, they can generate fruitful hypotheses which quantitative research can later refine and test.

The St Paul's area in Bristol – problems of orientation

When I started my research in Bristol, not only the coloured community, but the entire city of Bristol was totally unfamiliar to me. Getting to know the St Paul's area was especially difficult, because initially I was living outside it in trendy middle-class Clifton, the university area.

My entrance into St Paul's and environs was gained concurrently at three separate points. The first point of entry was through Shanty Town – the domain of the hustler and the teeny-bopper. My introduction to Shanty Town took place on my first night in Bristol while I was prowling around on my own in the city centre. As I was boarding a No. 11 bus going into the St Paul's district, a very friendly and garrulous Jamaican – a man in his early thirties – saw me and asked me if I was new in Bristol. He had heard me ask the conductor if the bus would take me to the section of the city where black people lived. Without revealing my true identity as a researcher, I told him I was a Jamaican like himself and that I was a student, but that I was new in Bristol and was interested in finding the Panorama Club (which already I had heard so much about from my new acquaintances in Clifton). My concealment of my role as a researcher was not intended to deceive, but merely to sustain the rapport which I was developing with the stranger. The man asked me my name. I told him, and he said his name was Segie. It turned out Segie was an ex-hustler who wanted to keep as far away from St Paul's as possible, because, to use his own words, he didn't want to get 'mixed up'. Segie said he was lucky always to meet West Indians on their first day in Bristol and told me of similar instances of meeting newcomers to Bristol in pubs and in the streets. I paid my first visit to the Panorama Club that night with Segie, though he said he hated going there. After the club I accompanied him to Grosvenor Road, where he bought 'johnny cakes' in the Sea-Island Café and hung around until he was able to find a friend from whom he could buy a 'smoke'. Segie hated the hustling scene, but he still visited the café regularly to buy 'drugs'. After that he took me to his flat in Montpelier, where we ate and drank together, and of course, smoked. Segie, who was a painter and decorator by trade, was out of work at the time. However, he worked when he felt like it, and this was usually in summer. Segie said he had just stopped working and would not work again until next summer; his woman would support him through the winter. She was away at the time as she had just got a job on a passenger ship as a stewardess. When we parted that night we agreed to meet again.

My second introduction to West Indians in Bristol was through a law-abiding West Indian working man. I was given his name by my head of department, who told me it would help my acquaintance with the West Indian community if I could meet this man, who could then arrange further contacts for me. The man turned out to be a mainliner and our first meeting took place at a commemoration service in honour of the then recently deceased Norman Washington Manley, ex-Prime Minister of Jamaica. At this service, which was held at an Anglican church in St Paul's, I met several other main-liners, including Prescott and Harry Saunders, who was then well in with that crowd, but who later rejected the mainline orientation to become an in-betweener. All the individuals I later came to regard as the principal West Indian mainliners were there. My main contact introduced me to the others and I found I was warmly welcomed and instantly accepted as one of them, despite the fact that we were meeting for the first time. In this group it was not necessary to be guarded about my true identity as a researcher. That very same night I received more than one invitation from people in the group to have dinner with them. I was also introduced to several English people, mostly women in the teaching profession who helped to make up the social circle of mainliners.

My third contact with the West Indian community was through saints and their churches, and it took place at around the same time as I was beginning to multiply my friendships with West Indians in other sections of the West Indian community. The three completely different ways in which I was gaining entrance to the field situation were helpful in that they exposed me almost simultaneously to three sections of the black community which were socially dissimilar both in their style and quality of life. They afforded me a kind of panoramic view of the West Indian scene.

Having gained entry into the St Paul's area, the second major problem was to work out a focus for the research. This was a difficulty inasmuch as I did not enter the field with any preconceived idea of what I would find. I only knew that I wanted to study life-styles and that I would go about it in a way that would make full use of my identity as a West Indian. I had no worked-out theory or hypothesis I was going to develop, no blueprint for action apart from my undergraduate training in sociology, and my only knowledge of life-style was limited to a single reading of Ulf Hannerz's book, *Soulside*. I didn't even know then that my method of investigation would be purely observation and participation. Participant observation became more and more necessary the more qualitative the investigation became. My first hunch came only after weeks in the field, when it was agreed with one of my thesis advisors that I would start my research with an investigation into West Indian church people as a clearly identifiable group in the black community. Even then the situation was pretty vague as I still did not know exactly what I would study when I got into the church. The findings on the church, as well as all the other insights and hypotheses that later were to form the substance of the thesis, were developed in the actual process of investigation.

Questions

1. (a) *The author tends to stress the appropriateness of participant observation to his topic of research but what problems might he also encounter using this method (some of which he hints at himself)?*

    (10 marks)

    (b) *Contrast the author's description of how his research developed with more traditional positivist models of scientific and social scientific research.*

    (15 marks)

2. *How, if at all, does the above kind of participant observational study differ from simply giving an account of one's experiences?*

    (10 marks)

METHOD

10 John H. Goldthorpe: The Personal Document

The following reading is from John H. Goldthorpe *et al.*, *Social Mobility and Class Structure in Modern Britain*. The book is based on data produced by the Oxford Survey on Social Mobility of 1972. This passage describes the research problems that arose as a result of the authors' attempt to produce qualitative data on 'the experience of social mobility' in order to balance the predominantly quantitative nature of the rest of their data.

Arguably, the personal document produces the most qualitative of all data. Personal recollection or life-history is not, of course, a source of data proper to sociology. Social and cultural historians use it more. Most usefully, Goldthorpe offers some remarks about the value of this form of data against some other forms of qualitative data, and against quantitative data. He discusses issues of validity and representativeness, and briefly touches on how it is possible to use subjective data to illuminate wider, collective issues. To do this, the data must meet the criteria of 'rational intelligibility' or, in everyday language, it must make sense. The student is invited to explore some of these issues by answering the questions at the end of the passage.

The extract below is from the 1974 follow-up study to the main survey.

Reading 10 From John H. Goldthorpe, *Social Mobility and Class Structure in Modern Britain* (Clarendon Press, 1980), pp. 217–22.

In designing our 1974 follow-up study, the importance of investigating in some way the subjective experience of mobility, or immobility, of those men who were respondents to our national inquiry was readily apparent to us. In critiques of mobility research, as undertaken by standard survey procedures, the question has several times been raised of how far the mobility or immobility that is observed by the investigator in terms of movement between occupational or class groupings of his own devising in fact corresponds with his respondents' actual awareness of having been mobile or immobile. And indeed evidence has been produced to suggest that the degree of this correspondence may in some instances be sufficiently low to call into question the validity of such research, at least where its central concern is with the implications of mobility for social action and social structure. For, clearly, the study of any aspect of the consequences or concomitants of mobility must become more problematic than ever if some wide divergence prevails between the investigator's and actors' ideas of what should count as mobility. Moreover, even if the investigator is prepared, on theoretical grounds, to give privilege to his own categories over those of actors, the extent and nature of the discrepancy that exists between the two sets of constructs must in itself remain an obvious matter for further inquiry.

Problems of method

While recognising, then, the need to give some place in our analyses to our respondents' own awareness and understanding of their mobility, we were, however, faced in this respect with a major problem of data collection. In basing our follow-up study on a number of relatively small subsamples, drawn from respondents to our 1972 investigation, our aim was to obtain more detailed information – complementary to that collected in 1972 – from a few hundred respondents that it was feasible to collect and process from a sample of over 10,000. But one unavoidable consequence of subsampling was that the men selected for re-interview could be located in any of the 417 primary sampling units of the 1972 inquiry, and were thus far more widely scattered geographically, throughout England and Wales, than would be usual in a survey inquiry on the scale that was planned. This meant therefore that it was not economically or administratively possible for us to deploy our own fieldwork team for the follow-up study, and that we had rather to draw on the services of an established social-research agency with a nationally organised field force. So far as the collection of essentially factual information was concerned, this proved to be in no way a disadvantage: the interviewers employed by the agency with whom we collaborated had a high level of skill and experience in taking respondents through structured, though often very complex and detailed, series of questions. But, on the other hand, since our interviewers did not for the most part have any specifically sociological training, limitations were clearly imposed on the extent to which we could make use of a less structured approach. In particular, what would have been our preferred method for investigating respondents' subjective mobility experience, that is, the use of open-ended questions followed up by 'informed' probing, was effectively precluded by the character of our field force, and we were therefore obliged to search for an alternative, second-best possibility.

Perhaps the most obvious resort was to develop, in this respect also, the kind of structured interview items that our field force would have been capable of administering. However, on due consideration, we decided against this option because of the doubts that we felt about the degree of validity of the data that would be thus generated. From various pieces of pilot work that we had undertaken, it was clear that we could expect to find quite wide diversity in the meanings which mobility had for our respondents, and in the ways in which they conceived its various contexts and correlates. In turn, then, it seemed to us scarcely possible to devise any one conceptual schema that could serve as the basis for structured questioning *and* in terms of which the views of our respondents could be represented, without the risk of serious distortion. We could, to be sure, have formulated, from the standpoint of our own theoretical interests, a series of 'closed' questions relating to mobility awareness etc., and could have expected, in the main, to have received answers to them. But these answers would have constituted data of very dubious utility to us in our attempt to investigate, precisely, the degree to which, in regard to mobility, our categories and those of our respondents might be discrepant.

Since therefore it appeared that neither structured nor unstructured questioning could be satisfactorily taken up as a means of obtaining the kind of material we sought, the implication was that this material would have to be collected in some way other than through the interview itself. In these circumstances, the method that came most readily to mind – as indeed the classic alternative to the interview (or questionnaire) in the history of social research – was that of the 'personal document', and specifically in the form of the individual 'life-history'. Moreover, this method was one which could be regarded as being especially apt to our purpose of eliciting our respondents' own understanding of their mobility. Angell, for example, has defined a personal document as 'one which reveals a participant's view of experiences in which he has been involved', and has represented the essential aim in collecting such documents as being 'to obtain detailed evidence as to how social situations appear to the actors in them and what meanings various factors have for the participants'. Likewise, Becker explicitly contrasts 'data formulated in the abstract categories of [sociologists'] own theories', which is characteristic of survey research, with the kind of material obtained from life histories which is expressed 'in the categories that seemed most relevant to the people . . . studied'. The distinctive feature of the life-history approach, Becker argues, is in 'assigning major importance to the interpretations people place on their experience', and its distinctive value is in 'giving us insight into the subjective side of much-studied institutional processes'.

We decided thus to try as far as possible to link the collection of life-histories, focused on our respondents' mobility experience, to our basic survey approach, and proceeded in fact in the following manner. Each respondent to our follow-up inquiry was asked at the end of his interview if he would be willing to help us further in our research by writing for us what we referred to as a set of 'life-history notes'. The respondent was provided with a leaflet explaining in more detail what we had in mind and including a list of questions which we would particularly like him to cover. The first two paragraphs of the leaflet and the list of questions are reproduced below. Assurances were given that any material supplied would remain confidential to members of the research team and would not be used in our research reports in any way that would permit an individual to be identified. Those respondents who agreed to write notes were provided with a stamped addressed envelope in which to forward them to us, and were also told how to contact members of the research team in the case of any queries.

Extracts from the life-history notes leaflet

You have already supplied us with a good deal of basic information about your education, work, family, etc. What we are now asking you to do is to tell us something about how, looking back, you view the course of your life – its patterns, its turning points, its light and shade.

Below we have a list of questions. If you would write a paragraph or so in answer to each of these, this should give us the kind of notes that we want. On the other hand, you may wish to arrange what you write in your own way, taking these questions simply as a guide to the points which chiefly interest us. (Remember in any case that you need not go over again the basic facts that you have already given us) . . .

Questions we would like to cover in your life history of notes

1. What are the biggest differences between the job and way of life of your father (or the head of your family) when you were about 14, and your job and life now? What do you think are the reasons for these differences?

2. What pattern has your working life mainly followed from the time of your first full-time job up to now? A steady advance to better and better jobs? A series of disappointments? Repeated ups and downs? A series of jobs that were just different from each other, rather than being better or worse? Or some other pattern?

3. Do you think there have been any important turning points or major crises in your working life? If so, what were they?

4. How important has luck been in your working life, compared with other things (such as family background, the way you were brought up, or your own character and abilities)? Do you feel that the same applies to most other people, or has your case been unusual? Can you give examples of how luck, or whatever it was, worked in your case?

5. How important has your work been to you in your life as a whole? Have other things had to take second place to it? Or have you taken the jobs you have because they gave you a chance to do other things? Have you ever turned down a good job because it would have meant giving up something that mattered more?

6. What have been your main goals during your working life? To work at something that interests you for its own sake? To earn more? To provide for the future? To be able to live in a particular way, or in a particular place? Or something else?

7. How far, and in what ways, do you see yourself as 'successful' in your job or in other aspects of your life? And in what ways, if any, as a 'failure'? Do you think success in your work matters more, or less, than success in other things?

8. Have you found that success in your working life has had generally good effects on your life outside work, or has success had its costs? Has any failure you may have had in your work

had a bad effect on life outside work, or have other things made up for it? For example, how has success or failure affected your family, or the kinds of friends you have made?

As can be seen, the questions that we wished respondents to consider were posed in everyday language, in an entirely open-ended form and, we hoped, in such a way as to give a respondent every encouragement to 'tell his own story'. To judge at least from the sets of notes that we received, the questions were in general found meaningful and indeed stimulating. Few men answered them in a merely perfunctory fashion, and in the large majority of cases the notes that were written ran from 500 to 1,500 words in length. A number of men wrote what amounted to autobiographical sketches, several thousand words long. Moreover, from the extracts from these notes that will subsequently be cited, it will be apparent that there were often displayed a remarkable sharpness of both observation and expression, and that new perspectives on virtually all aspects of mobility were opened up.

However, the chief problem that we anticipated with the procedure we followed, and which did in fact arise, was that of persuading respondents actually to produce notes. Only a small minority refused at the outset to undertake the task; but despite two, or in some cases three, reminders, a majority even of those who had agreed in principle to write notes still failed to do so. In the end, usable notes were secured from 274 men, representing 38 per cent of the 652 respondents to our 1974 study or 27 per cent of the total number of 926 men who were selected for re-interview from our 1972 respondents. Differences in the proportions supplying life history notes among our groupings of intergenerationally stable and mobile respondents are shown in the following Table.

What we succeeded in obtaining was thus a body of material which, while substantial in itself and apparently highly illuminating of the mobility experience of those who had supplied it, related none the less to the experience of only a minority of the men in our subsamples, and which had in consequence to be viewed with, to say the least, extreme caution so far as its representativeness was concerned. In turn, then, it was this deficiency in our data which largely conditioned the decisions that we made regarding their analysis and use. For example, there seemed little point in taking

METHOD

Returns of life-history notes by mobility pattern

Mobility pattern	Number returning usable notes	Percentage of all re-interviewed (1974)	Percentage of all selected for re-interview
Stable in Class I	33	44	32
Stable in Classes III-V	35	34	26
Stable in Classes VI and VII	53	34	23
Directly mobile to Class I	33	33	-(a)
Indirectly mobile to Class I	68	45	-(a)
All upwardly mobile to Class I	101	40	33
Downwardly mobile from Class I	25	37	27
All	247	38	27

Note: (a) The distinction between direct and indirect mobility did not apply in the selection of men for re-interview in 1974.

our life-history material as being, so to speak, a direct substitute for the kind of material that we might have obtained from interviews, and subjecting it to systematic quantitative treatment as, for example, through techniques of content analysis. In other words, it did not seem appropriate, given that our material derived from only a relatively small proportion of our respondents, to try to extract from it attitudes and beliefs to be taken as the attributes of specific individuals, which could then be related to other of their attributes such as, say, features of their mobility experience as expressed through the categories of our earlier analyses. It was, rather, evident to us that, from a quantitative standpoint, our life-history data would have to be used in a much cruder and more limited way. The only objective which in fact appeared feasible was to identify, for each of our groupings of stable and mobile respondents, those themes and their main variations within the life-history notes supplied by its members which could, even with our very imperfect data, be reasonably regarded as salient ones; or, where the degree of diversity was such that no dominant theme could be discerned, to give as full an idea as our data would allow of the range of this diversity.

At the same time, though, it appeared to us also important to try to exploit our life-history material in a qualitative as well as a quantitative fashion; and, specifically, to use this material as a basis not only for describing our respondents' experience of mobility from their own point of view but further for making this experience 'understandable'. The personal document has been widely regarded as a means whereby individuals differently located in the social structure can communicate with each other: in Becker's words, 'it tells us what it means to be a kind of person we have never met face to face'. But, for such communication to be effective, some basis of understanding – some way of 'bridging the gap' between the subjectivity of the writer of the document and that of the members of his audience – is obviously required. The key assumption that we would make in this respect is the following: that the medium through which this bridging must ultimately be achieved, in so far as it can be achieved at all, is that of rational intelligibility. In other words, we would argue that to the extent that one claims to understand the beliefs and attitudes or the actions or, more generally, the responses to events and circumstances of other persons, one is in effect claiming that, within the given situation, they are intelligible to one in rational terms: once the facts of the situation, as one may establish them, are taken into account, it is apparent to one how, at least from the observed actors' own standpoint, their beliefs, attitudes, actions, etc. are related to their situation and to each other in a rational manner.

Thus in what follows we shall try as far as possible to bring out, for each of our groupings of respondents, the 'subjective logic' of the life-history notes that they presented by considering, on the one hand, the rationally intelligible (rather perhaps than the quantitatively important empirical) relationships that prevail between their dominant themes and certain factual aspects of the mobility, and also of the present social situation, of the men in question; and, on the other hand, the internal coherence that exists among these dominant themes and some at least of their variants. We shall, that is to say, attempt to interpret the collectively significant content of the life-history accounts of our several groupings of respondents in such a way that our conception of the understandability of these accounts is made explicit. At the same time, though, we hope that the amount of purely descriptive material provided, together with the data of our previous chapters, will be sufficient to give the reader some basis for forming his own view of the appropriateness of these interpretations. Finally, in this respect we may note that the implications of the incompleteness of our collection of life-history notes will be rather less serious for our interpretive efforts than in regard to quantitative analysis. If the data from which we shall work are in fact unrepresentative, the effect of this will not be in itself to invalidate the interpretations that are offered; rather, it would at most imply that some aspects of our respondents' mobility experience, because inadequately represented in our data, might be left uninterpreted.

Questions

1. (a) *What does validity mean? Why might the structured interview not have produced valid data in this case?*

(5 marks)

(b) *Why do the authors express 'extreme caution' about the representativeness of their data?*

(5 marks)

(c) *Why is it sometimes less necessary and important for the researcher to interpret in detail qualitative than quantitative data?*

(5 marks)

2. *With reference to the reading, discuss Howard Becker's contrast between 'data formulated in abstract categories of [sociologists'] own theories' and material expressed 'in the categories that seemed most relevant to the people . . . studied'.*

(15 marks)

11 Frank Coffield, Carol Borrill, and Sarah Marshall: People–oriented Research

The title of this introduction is mine rather than that of the authors of the following reading. It seems to me that in researching their group of young working class people, they were consistently guided by an awareness and respect for the needs and opinions of the young people themselves. This attitude constantly appears throughout the following extract. Thus, they invite their subjects to choose their own 'pseudonyms'; they decide not to use data which, though useful, might be considered too personal; and, most telling of all perhaps, they estimate the size of their 'sample' as 'around fifty' on the basis, not of precise contact figures, but because they 'established good relationships for two-and-a-half years with around fifty'. What is apparent here is a link between ethics, choice of methods and findings. Initially, I planned to title my introduction to this reading – 'Ordinary Research: Ordinary People'. This was perhaps an inept attempt to indicate that Coffield and his co-researchers adjusted their research in response to a variety of everyday problems, including, of course, those of their research subjects. This theme is explored and illustrated in some detail in H. Newby and C. Bell *eds., Doing Sociological Research* (Macmillan, 1981). This title was also intended to suggest that their research was aimed at the problems of 'ordinary' young people rather than delinquents or the spectacularly stylish.

Despite the extremely flexible and qualitative nature of the research, it is, of course, finally filtered through the researchers' own theoretical framework. Another reading from this book is given in the section on Poverty and Inequality (Reading 32).

Reading 11 From Frank Coffield, Carol Borrill and Sarah Marshall, *Growing Up At the Margins: Young Adults in the North East* (Open University Press, 1986), pp. 1–6.

Between January 1982 and August 1984 we carried out two-and-a-half years' fieldwork in a study of 'around fifty' working-class young women and men in the north east of England. They were aged between sixteen and twenty-eight when we first met them.

The project was jointly funded by the SSRC (now the ESRC) and Durham University and was part of the SSRC's research initiative into 'Young People in Society'. The main aims of the initiative were to study older adolescents and young adults; to encourage research that tried to relate individuals to their social surroundings, to concentrate on young people growing up in society rather than to focus on problems such as delinquency; and to encourage approaches based on talking to young people in their homes, in pubs and night clubs and in and out of jobs.

In aims and approach, our project sought to embrace all these points. Our sample covered a wider than usual age range, reflecting the lack of chronological age barriers outside institutional settings such as school or administrative categories such as 'sixteen to nineteen-year-olds'. We also included women and men in equal numbers because too frequently in the past the focus has been on one or other sex. The early concentration on studying boys and young men from Thrasher (1927) and Whyte (1955) to Parker (1974) and Willis (1977) has been partially corrected by more recent studies of young women by McRobbie and Garber (1975), Davies (1979), Griffin (1985) and Breakwell (1984). The book considers *both* young women and men and how they interact, which is after all one of the main activities of the age group.

Our methods were also very different from the standard approach of the mass media and of professional conferences on adolescence, both of which tend to sensationalise the scabrous deeds of a few rampant or exotic adolescents. Too often, discussions of young people are confined to a catalogue of 'teenage problems' such as glue sniffing, schoolgirl pregnancies, vandalism, aggro and delinquency. In contrast, our fieldwork constantly underlined the essential normality and conformity of most young adults. Our aim, then, is to present a rounded account of their lives which puts issues such as crime or drunkenness into perspective.

We also accept that discussing such issues as unemployment and social security rates with sixteen to twenty-eight-year-olds involves us in taking a political stand. We attempted to reflect this political stance in our research by combining theory and method, and by inviting the young adults to join us in an examination of the main issue in their lives. For example, we encouraged them wherever possible to decide on the main questions and areas to be discussed rather than always supplying them ourselves. We negotiated our accounts of their lives with the young people and for the most part we met with confirmation and approval. We are inclined, however, to challenge the notion of Rom Harré (1980) that relatively inarticulate, unreflective and inexperienced young people can be 'the prime sources of *theories* about their actions and thoughts' (our emphasis). It would be disingenuous of us not to admit that the selection from the wealth of data we collected, the organisation of the material, and the final conclusions are all our work, although heavily influenced by discussions with young adults.

In trying always to recognise the distribution of power between ourselves and our sample, we constantly restated our promise of confidentiality. Asking them to choose their own pseudonyms for this book resulted in further insights into some of their characters.

Kirsty and Clara chose their names because they preferred them to their own, Asia named herself after a little three-year-old girl down her road and Shuk decided on hers because she liked her friend Shuk at work. Joe (Tetley) and Scotch were influenced in their choice by their favourite beer, and Jimi named himself after Jimi Hendrix, while Max and Ricky were indicating their favourite film stars from action-packed 'macho' movies. Troy later denied that he had chosen his name: 'I must have been drinking at the time'. He had been, but he was pleased to learn that he had changed from his first choice of Sinbad!

We also decided to omit a large amount of the richest (traceable) data, on the principle that those who are researched own the facts of their own lives and have the right to decide what should and should not be published. The paramount concern in our type of research is to protect those who have participated from unwelcome attention. Many of the young women and men said they did not mind whether they were identifiable or not, and some even wanted their photographs to be included. For us, the ethics of our relationship demanded that anonymity rule the day, even at the cost of some of the best illustrative material.

We have tried to produce a text in clear, simple English, devoid of the jargon of the social sciences which is becoming impenetrable even to students of the subject. We want to speak directly to as many young adults as possible as well as to students of the social sciences and to those professionals in the civil service, politics, education and the social services who take daily decisions affecting young people. This book has not been written for the academic specialist.

Three points of style in particular illustrate three major themes in the book: age, gender and region. First, the notion of age: young people in British society are neither fish nor fowl nor good red herring. There is not even an appropriate term to describe this section of the population. 'Kids' is patronising, 'teenagers' is similarly dismissive, 'adolescents' is unattractive and never used by the people so described, according to Simmons and Wade (1984), 'children' is insulting (although used by many professionals), 'youth' rhymes with 'uncouth', and even 'young adults' appears grudging in its recognition of status. 'Young people' is less objectionable, but bland. In the absence of any other terms, we have decided to use the latter two, and just as often we refer simply to either 'the women and the men', in an attempt to accord sixteen to twenty-year-olds some status or to the 'lasses and lads', which was the phrase employed by the young people themselves. The lack of an acceptable phrase typifies the anomalous position of young people in western societies.

Second, throughout the text we have regularly put women first, both in terms of style (the women and the men, Kirsty and Phil) and in order of our considerations of the two sexes. This came from Carol and Sarah's awareness that, in team discussions, all three of us unthinkingly discussed the males in our sample first, and only afterwards would we turn to consider the females. We therefore made the conscious decision to consider the women first and we believe this has made them more visible both in our thinking and in these pages (see Marshall and Borrill, 1984).

Our third stylistic and political point concerns the representation of the Geordie dialect. Our first preference was to include as much dialect as possible to provide splashes of local colour, but we have been persuaded that this approach might be seen by North Easterners as patronising. They disagree among themselves about who is entitled to be called a Geordie and whether it is desirable to speak Geordie. In the event, we have compromised, by including some dialect words, which are listed in a glossary, but generally keeping phonetic spelling to a minimum. Our reasons are the same as those given by Jack Common (1954, p. 149), whose autobiography about growing up in the North East faced the same problem:

> Most of the characters are of course people who speak in dialect . . . Readers may wonder why they are not treated to the traditional outbreaks of funny spelling and if in their absence they are expected to regard all dialogue as being conducted in Standard English. They are not. Funny spelling is avoided . . . just because it won't work in this case . . . Try to spell the north eastern dialect and the result is something nobody can understand for more than a line or two . . . The short way out is to print all plain.

We worked with young adults from three different areas in the North East to which we gave the pseudonyms Shipton, Milton and Hillsborough. Shipton and Hillsborough were urban town and city respectively and Milton was a large rural area incorporating a number of small towns and villages.

We met these groups after a series of initial visits to various parts of the North East and interviews with officials from agencies including Education departments, the Careers Service, the police and the Manpower Services Commission (MSC) to give us some notion of the official version of local provision for young people.

In Shipton, we met the group in January 1982 through the local Technical College. They were all participating in the MSC's Youth Opportunities Programme (YOP). We attended a 'Life and Social Skills' course and a residential weekend away with twenty-four YOP 'trainees' of both sexes.

The second group we contacted at the same time through the Milton Training Workshop where we carried out interviews and group discussions with six young women and six young men during the first six month period.

Over these early months, we concentrated on building up good relationships with our sample. Once the young people (at this stage eighteen women and eighteen men) had finished their government schemes, we kept in touch with them at informal monthly meetings in pubs, cafes or in their homes, seeing them in small groups or on a one-to-one basis. We then concentrated on getting to know our sample well and building up an easy atmosphere of mutual trust, disclosure and respect.

In September 1982, work began in the third area, Hillsborough, where contact was made with a 'natural group' of eight men aged sixteen to twenty-eight. They all lived on the same estate, Marlow Dene, and were all unemployed. With the help of a local youth project, we had regular weekly meetings with the lads and a series of evening meetings with a small group of women from a nearby estate. After ten months, contact was also established with the wives and girlfriends of the men.

As fieldwork started later with the Hillsborough group, contact was deliberately more intensive: we spent whole days with the lads plus several residential periods organised through the youth project. As it was an informal group, however, the circumstances of their everyday lives (for example, commitments to partners and family ties) affected the attendance of individual members. This drifting in and out highlighted the constantly changing patterns of young adults' lives.

Intensive fieldwork in all three areas ended in August 1983. Over the following year, however, we maintained regular contact by letter, telephone and with occasional meetings in order to keep up with any changes in their lives. We also held special feedback sessions to give the women and men the opportunity to comment on our ideas and emerging conclusions. We met them for a final time in August 1984.

Although unstructured interviewing and observation of individuals, couples and groups were our principle methods of gaining information, we also devised some basic questionnaires and asked young people to complete diaries for us. We deliberately employed a mixture of methods in order to check and recheck the validity of our data.

When discussing the size of our sample, we have always referred to 'around fifty' young women and men. Perhaps an explanation of the word 'around' would help as much as anything to convey the qualitative nature of our work. Unlike most research projects, we are unable to give a simple answer to the question: what is the size of your sample? Some young people, for instance, faithfully turned up to meet us for over a year and then, for a variety of reasons such as searching for work in London, or going steady with their lass or lad or moving home, they stopped seeing us. Others slowly became members of our project because they were the partners or close friends of our original contacts. Again, our sample size varied depending on whether we stress the depth or the regularity of contact established with us. For instance, we met Clara infrequently, but gained as much information about her life and the life of her street in ten minutes as we did from, say, Winnie after hours of monthly meetings. The type of information we received also varied: we learnt more, for instance, about relationships with partners from the women than from the men. The sample number changed, therefore, from week to week throughout the life of the project. In all, we met far more than fifty young people but we are claiming to have established good relationships for two-and-a-half years with around fifty. What matters, however, in a study such as ours is not the seductive certainty produced by percentages or statistical tables but the quality of the understanding reached and of the explanations offered. Surveys of large numbers of young people by means of questionnaires have their place and importance, but the very technique prevents much being discovered about the nature of young adults' personal relations or how they develop tactics or strategies to cope with unemployment, for instance.

The size of our sample was not the only variable that changed constantly over time. Some moved away from the parental home to set up on their own. Only fourteen women and men were kept on after their government training schemes ended and were in full-time employment for the period of the study. All the others moved on and off schemes and in and out of jobs, particularly when they were still eligible for youth training placements in the early stages of our fieldwork. We were in fact monitoring a moving picture with constant scene changes rather than a still; and those behind the camera changed their angle and their view as much as those in front of it.

Question
1. (a) *What evidence is there that the research team was concerned with the well-being of their subjects?*

(5 marks)

(b) *Illustrate how the research team tried to obtain data which closely expressed the young people's views and feelings.*

(5 marks)

(c) *What does this reading suggest to you about the role of ethics in sociological research?*

(5 marks)

Activity
1. *Write your own question (to the value of 25 marks) on this or another reading in this section.*
2. *Exchange questions with another member of your group.*
3. *Make sure you understand precisely what the question you have been given means.*
4. *Answer the question you have been given.*

12 Valerie Yule: Observing Adult-Child Interaction – An Example of a Piece of Research Anyone Could Do

As one of my students remarked on reading this piece of research by Valerie Yule – 'I could do that'. So could we all. I have included this reading in the methods section because it describes such a simple and repeatable piece of research, although its content is interesting enough and highly relevant under Section 9.

As Valerie Yule says, 'It is research that costs nothing: you only need to take a clipboard on streets and buses, and watch how adults behave with children.'

In fact, there is a little more to the research than that. Although Yule appears not to have formulated a specific hypothesis, she had a clear area of enquiry in mind – the quality of adult-child interaction. She observed 85 adult-child pairs for three minutes each, and matched each pair with a pair of adults. It is not clear whether she took notes only *during* the periods of observation or whether she also added notes from recollection (not quite so reliable a technique). However, her data are clearly based on very close observation as her list of negative interactions makes clear. In interpreting her findings, Yule draws on what is apparently a wide knowledge of child-rearing in other cultures and of psychology. She concludes that while most parents may not abuse their children, many are 'tough' and insensitive to them. The implication seems to be that, in this climate, child abuse might easily flourish. Abuse is not so much a deviant aberration as the extreme end of so-called 'normal' behaviour. Her comments are informed by a lively humanitarian concern – as her final sentence vividly illustrates.

Reading 12 Valerie Yule, 'Why are parents so tough on children', in *New Society*, 27 September 1986, pp. 444–6.

The little boy was about 18 months old and sat in the front seat of the bus. The enormous pom-pom on his woolly hat was bouncing with the movement of the bus, and he clutched at it and sang, 'Jinger bow, jinger bow'. Everyone was smiling until his mother reached over and smacked him hard. 'Stop that and behave yourself.'

The two year old girl slid off her seat on to the next one, to look out of the window, chattering to herself. Her young mother grabbed her by the back of the collar, swung her back and planted her down with a cuff. 'Stop fooling around, you little horror. I'll wring your neck next.' An elderly man said, 'Leave her be, she's only small.' 'I'm not going to have her behaving like an animal,' said Mum.

A child in a pusher was crying at a bleak, windy bus stop. A bystander offered her a coloured autumn leaf to divert her. The child took it with curiosity, but the parent threw it away. 'She's only interested in food.'

None of these young mothers would feature in a social worker's enquiries about child abuse. However, while most homes operate in private (fortunately for adults' civil liberties), parental behaviour in public can be observed at any time. It is research that costs nothing: you only need to take a clipboard on streets and buses, and watch how adults behave with children. Patterns of parental behaviour in public may well link up with grimmer statistics of destructive child abuse. The cruelty of the pathological abusers may increase or decrease in line with the behaviour towards children by the 'normal' parents around them.

I carried out my own study in the streets, shops and buses of a provincial city. I watched a series of adult-child pairs for three minutes each, all of them matched with another pair of people for comparison. There were 85 of each set of pairs. I watched them on sunny afternoons, in places that were not crowded and not at peak hours, so that people were not busy hurrying, or dodging in the traffic.

The pairs that did not include a small child might be male/female, all-female or all-male. They ranged from teenage to elderly. But whoever they were, within my three-minute observation period, four-fifths had some speech together, or at least a glance or a smile. All their behaviour towards each other was courteous. In fact, it is only when they are drunk or together in large groups that adults or teenagers are likely to abuse each other in the streets.

By contrast, only a quarter of the child-adult pairs had any communication within two minutes of watching, and under half within three minutes. For two-fifths of my sample what took place was negative. This is what happened:

☐ Seven adults crossed roads telling their children to look out or hurry up, but none of them looked at the children they were speaking to. Five yanked the child by arm or hand.

☐ Six children cried in pushers. Three were smacked, two given sweets round the side of the pusher without a glance at them, and one was ignored.

☐ Four children in shops were told to behave themselves in varying degrees of severity, and one was then pacified with sweets.

METHOD

☐ Four children on buses were scolded or smacked for misbehaviour, following complete inattention.

☐ Four children at bus stops were told to behave or keep still, and one was cuffed.

☐ Four children tried to talk to adults who paid no attention.

☐ Three children tried to talk to adults and were rejected.

☐ Three children had their clothes adjusted on buses without one word spoken.

☐ Two children were pulled out of pushers without any prior warning.

☐ Two men talked to their small children as they walked along the street.

☐ One child in a bus cried and was ignored.

☐ One mother talked to her child about going home, without looking at it.

☐ One grandmother talked to a seven year old about buying mother a birthday present.

☐ One mother in a bus pointed out to a three year old child all the sights through the window, with a lively discussion together.

☐ One (Asian) mother in the bus watched her baby's face as she cuddled it.

☐ Eight adult couples chatted while one pushed a pusher containing a wakeful but passive toddler.

For the rest, the adults took no notice of the children they were with, even in some pairs that I watched for up to ten minutes. The most typical adult-child couple consisted of a young woman staring ahead with a sombre face, as if tuned in to some dumb misery of her own (which must surely affect the child) while the child walked, sat, lay or was carried, with a blank expression on its face.

This picture of widespread adult rudeness to children is unlikely to be local. It fits in with too many current stereotypes in the media for one to dismiss it too easily. There is a contrast with previous stereotypes – from, say, the 1920s to the 1950s – about what adults think and feel about children, and how to behave to them. These are now often dismissed as 'sentimental.' The current stereotype of behaviour is not merely that of the deprived and disadvantaged still perpetuating their deprivation and disadvantage in the way they treat their young. It is popular at the trendy end, too. The humour of *Punch* or Posy Simmonds shows well-educated middle class parents who are hairtrigger-irritable and impatient, offensively rude to their young, and quite incredibly helpless to cope with even the slightest manifestation of children's ignorance or curiosity. Parents often act exactly as if *they* were the children, and children should be excessively tactful towards *them*.

A recent series of cartoons by Heath in the *Guardian* shows parents perceiving their child as a gigantic monster. I privately draw my parallel cartoon of the real situation. The child, accurately, sees the parents as gigantic and untrustable owners, who behave in a distracted and unnecessary fashion.

Previous stereotypes were of adults calm in the midst of chaos, if not actually delighting in objectively less than delightful offspring. Even 30 years ago, the average parent was shown as having some sense of perspective and knowledge of parenting skills when a toddler, for example, blew bubbles into its food (a recent martyrdom which drew expletives from Posy Simmonds's Mr and Mrs Weber). Stereotypes are not *only* cliches: they are models people may follow.

Clinical psychologists in the Western world are constantly faced by parents who are 'driven up the wall' by normal childish behaviour, which they make worse through ignorance of how to respond. What has happened to make parents now feel so incompetent, martyred and irritable? Why can't they enjoy their children?

Observing the pleasure that adults in other cultures still have in children, and enjoying their company myself, I conclude that rude parental behaviour in public is part of a total social problem. But none of the factors involved is, I think, irreversible.

The martyrdom of young mothers comes partly from feelings of low social status – even among those teenagers who become pregnant in order to obtain status. How does a young mother with toddlers, parcels and pusher feel as she struggles unaided on to a bus, without a courteous hand or smile from anyone? Where is the media coverage of the delightful sides of child-rearing? The world of adult television is practically childless.

The martyrdom comes also through incompetence. You hate doing what you know you are doing badly. The main contributory cause here may be 'ageism' – a segregation which shares with racism and sexism that underlying fear of difference from oneself. Mother-with-toddler groups proliferate, to share 'problems', but young parents have little social communication with older parents who may have 'solutions.' They have been almost brainwashed to keep clear of Nana.

METHOD

Freud's greatest mistake was to misinterpret the great physical enjoyment felt in the loving cuddling of children. Notions of pleasurable contact with children have become genitalised. The deviation called 'paedophilia' now gets more publicity than the basic human instinct to enjoy fondling small children.

In the not so distant past, it was seen as an amusing sign of the ignorance and inexperience of new parents that they feared that their baby was too fragile to handle with confidence; they pushed the prams over the kerb with infinite care and judgment. Today's climate turns ignorance another way. Adults think children are tougher than they are, or ought to be toughened.

One research study that I think needs to be urgently done is whether babies suffer any permanent damage when they are rattled severely over uneven pavements from the age of three weeks or less, in the modern springless light strollers. On some streets these may be the infant's equivalent of working a pneumatic drill. This is the first human generation in history to be subject to such early rattling. We have not begun to think about possible long-term effects. May rattled children grow up with more jangled and irritable nervous systems, and fewer powers of concentration, than children used to smoother movement?

I have heard a young parent say proudly – and his baby was six weeks old – 'We know other parents who smack their babies to keep them quiet. We think that is terrible. All you need to do is shake them.'

Some people are involved in arguments about when an embryo becomes human. This is an urgent question today, but it has a strange quality about it when young parents ask you in all seriousness, 'When does a child become human?'

Question

1. (a) Briefly summarise Valerie Yule's findings on adult-child interactions. How reliable a basis for generalisation about adult-child communication do you consider them to be?

(10 marks)

(b) Critically consider the link Valerie Yule makes between her findings on 'patterns of parental behaviour in public' and 'grimmer statistics of destructive child abuse'.

(15 marks)

(You may find it helpful to study Reading 45 before answering part (b) of this question).

Activity

1. *Select an area of social life you would like to observe and could practically do so.*
2. *Decide on the number of observations you wish to make (10 to 20 is likely to be a practical limit).*
3. *Select your methodology and plan your research.*
4. *Carry out your research and report back.*

(*Note*: If you decide to do research as a group, the size of your sample could be bigger – although this will require more co-ordination when you process your data).

SECTION 3

Socialisation and the Family

Readings 13–17

In the selection of readings on the family, I have focused on the related issues of family functions, stability and problems, particularly in relation to the modern family. This has meant that historical and comparative issues are only incidentally dealt with. However, these perspectives on the family receive some coverage in the Gender and Age sections which also deal with changing family roles (see, especially, Readings 33 and 45).

The first reading on the family is by Ronald Fletcher. Whilst acknowledging a variety of stresses on the family, his main emphasis is on its vitality, adaptability, and comparative stability. In the 1960s it was critics such as anthropologist, Edmund Leach, and radical psychiatrist, R. D. Laing, who presented the 'darker side' of family life only barely acknowledged by Fletcher. They argued that the small, closed nuclear family easily led to pressured and sometimes destructive relationships. Leach drew on his knowledge of anthropology to illustrate that child-rearing can be successfully accomplished by several kin, thus saving the time and energy of the natural mother. Laing's work in family therapy suggested to him that the intense relationships of the nuclear family so valued in Western culture often contain elements of domination and aggression which can lead to great conflict and unhappiness. What was needed in Britain was more empirical work to substantiate and develop these theoretical postulations. In fact, what has been produced is a growing body of work on wife battering and child abuse. The former is more a product of women's studies than any conscious attempt to explore Laing's analyses. The reading from Jan Pahl on wife battering soberly and shockingly records its extent and explains it mainly in the context of patriarchal domination. Reading 45 (and especially the latter part), by Neil Postman, deals in part with child abuse.

The smallest conceivable family unit is the one parent family. In the mid-nineteen eighties, one in eight families were of this type – reflecting mainly the increase in the divorce rate but also the rise in the percentage of children born to unmarried women (about seventeen per cent). In the reading on one parent families by Ellis Cashmore, I have selected a piece which shows just how hard life can be for a single parent rather than one that attempts to assess the arguments for and against this type of family.

The reading by Robert Chester provides more contemporary statistical support and analysis for much the same position as that taken by Ronald Fletcher. Statistics are invariably open to more than one interpretation and some cited by Chester could be interpreted as evidence of nuclear family fragmentation – at least, at the margins.

The reading from Mary Maynard's *Houseworkers and their Work* focuses on family roles, particularly that of houseworker. She cites convincing evidence that, contrary to some commentators, women still do most of the housework, and that, contrary to popular misconception, it is hard work.

Because the family is often the first sociological topic studied, I have tried to keep the readings in this section simple. The readings in the gender section tend to be more theoretical and most of them are relevant to the family (see, especially, Readings 33 and 34).

13 Ronald Fletcher: The Continuing Functions of the Family

This extract is a robust statement that the family both fulfils its 'essential' functions and also contributes to the needs of its members through its links with the wider network of institutions of the modern state (e.g. health, social welfare). In Fletcher's view the family is busier than ever, both fulfilling its essential functions as well as expanding its commitment to most non-essential ones.

Following R. M. MacIver, Fletcher denotes the following as the essential and non-essential functions of the family. It will help to present these in tabular form as the paragraph in which Fletcher deals with them is rather dense.

FAMILY

Essential Functions
1. Stable satisfaction of sex need
2. Production and rearing of children
3. Provision of a home

Non-essential Functions
1. Government
2. Economic
3. Education
4. Health
5. Religious
6. Recreation

Fletcher strongly disagrees with MacIver's view that the family has been 'stripped of' its non-essential functions by the modern state. The bulk of the extract establishes links between the family and state which, in Fletcher's view, add up to increased work and responsibility for both. On balance, the non-essential functions of the family take up more, not less, time and effort.

The brief section on policy given here is particularly interesting. Fletcher argues that the range and extent of the functions of the modern family mean that it requires more, not less, state help. He appears to envisage a 'forward looking' partnership between the family and the state. This contrasts with some of the more recent sociological and political comment which favours less state 'interference' (and help) for the family (see Ferdinand Mount, *The Subversive Family: An Alternative History of Love and Marriage* (Counterpoint, 1982). The policy section, and the couple of pages preceding it, should be interesting to re-read in the light of the comments in Reading 14 on the family as a 'private' or 'social' institution.

Fletcher first made the analysis in this reading in the early nineteen sixties. The text shows its age in Fletcher's rather bland treatment of the position of women and in his somewhat unproblematic view that the family is still essentially stable. However, the key issue about the family remains, what does it do and how well does it do it? Fletcher sets up this debate very well from a committed functionalist and pro-family point of view.

Reading 13 From Ronald Fletcher, *The Family and Marriage in Britain* (Penguin, 1973), pp. 204–25 – edited.

The functions of the family

The first conclusion which the foregoing analysis seems to warrant is that it is quite untrue to say that the family in contemporary Britain has been 'stripped of its functions' and has, as a consequence, become of diminished importance as a social institution. On the contrary, the modern family fulfils *more* functions, and in a far more detailed and sophisticated manner, than did the family before or during the nineteenth-century development of industrialisation.

When sociologists speak of the 'functions' of an institution they have two things chiefly in mind: the human needs and purposes (whether intended or not) which the institution exists to satisfy, and the 'functional interconnections' which the institution has with the wider network of institutions in society – the ways in which it is interdependent in its operation with the other institutions in the whole social system. In both senses of the word 'function' our conclusion holds good. The family is now concerned with a more detailed and refined satisfaction of needs than hitherto, and it is also more intimately and responsibly bound up with the wider and more complicated network of social institutions in the modern state than it was prior to industrialisation.

This conclusion can be demonstrated by taking the functions enumerated by MacIver and considering each of them in turn.

If we take, first of all, the 'essential' functions of the family – the satisfaction of the sexual needs of the married couple, the careful upbringing of children, and the provision of a satisfactory home for its members – it is perfectly clear that the modern family – entailing the equal status of wife and husband and their mutual consideration in marriage; the high status of children; and the improved standards of income, housing, household equipment – aims at, and achieves, a far more satisfactory and refined provision for these needs than did either the pre-industrial family or the family of early industrial Britain, in which women were inferior and subjected, women and children were frequently exploited within or outside the family, and conditions in the home were so deplorably inadequate.

What is not commonly stressed, however, in stating this qualitative improvement in the 'essential' functions of the family is that the demands upon the members of the family for the satisfactory performance of them have become increasingly heavy. Professor Titmuss has made this point admirably. In *Essays on the Welfare State*, he writes:

> That the children of the large working-class families of fifty years ago helped to bring each other up must have been true; no single-handed mother of seven could have hoped to give to each child the standard of care, the quantity of time, the diffusion and concentration of thought, that most children receive today. In this context, it is difficult to understand what is meant by those who generalise about the 'lost' functions of parents in the rearing of children.

And in his contribution to the conference on *The Family:*

> Society is in process of making parenthood a highly self-conscious, self-regarding affair. In so doing, it is adding heavily to the sense of personal responsibility among parents. Their tasks are much harder and involve more risks of failure when children have to be brought up as individual successes in a supposedly mobile, individualistic society rather than in a traditional and repetitious society. Bringing up children becomes less a matter of rule-of-thumb custom and tradition; more a matter of acquired knowledge, of expert advice. More decisions have to be made because there is so much more to be decided; and as the margin of felt responsibility extends so does the scope for anxiety about one's children.

As the expected standards of fulfilment of the 'essential' functions of the family have improved, therefore, so have the demands for responsibility on the part of members of the family increased . . .

There is little doubt, then, that the 'essential' functions of the family, centred upon sexual relationships, parenthood, and home-making, are fulfilled far more satisfactorily in the modern family than they were in the family of the distant or the recent past. It is more interesting, however, to consider the so-called 'non-essential' functions of the family, which, the generalisation states, have been increasingly fulfilled outside the family by the specialised agencies of the modern state.

Government

If we begin with MacIver's function of 'government' in the family, and take this to mean the family's government of its own affairs and the activities of its members, it would seem that the modern family is just as much concerned with this function as was the family in Britain before industrialisation. But if we interpret this function more widely it can be seen that a great and important change has taken place. In the modern family, both husband and wife are recognised citizens of the state. Both have a voice and a vote in deciding upon the acceptance or rejection of those policies of the state which affect the conditions of the family. The adult members of the modern family are now, in a democratic community, largely responsible for determining those provisions of public health, public education, economic security, which, taken together, determine the conditions and the destinies of the family. In the pre-industrial family, husband and wife had no such voice. The members of the modern family are now, therefore, drawn far more closely into the tasks of government than ever before. They enjoy far greater degrees of responsibility for government, and, correspondingly, far greater demands are made upon their capacities for responsibility.

This function has considerably increased in effectiveness and in importance in the modern family.

Economic functions

Secondly, let us consider the 'economic functions' of the family, and the generalisation that the modern family is no longer an 'economic unit'. Certainly the modern family is not a productive unit as was the case with labouring-class families in agriculture and domestic industry; but to leap to the conclusion that the modern family is in *no* important sense an economic unit is unwarranted . . .

The family remains an important economic unit from the viewpoint of the patterning of consumption, or, as the economist would put it, of the 'consumer's outlay'. This expenditure of family income – whether this is contributed by one or more members, and whether it is to any great extent 'pooled' or not – is still patterned not solely on 'individual preferences' but also on the needs of the family as a whole and the preferences of the family as a group. Advertisers are clearly aware of this, and sometimes play upon it to a rather nauseating extent, as may be seen by watching television advertisements for some foodstuffs, soap powders, holiday arrangements, and the like. Furthermore, although the degree and extent of this throughout the country cannot be said to be known, it is probable that there is still, to some extent, a 'pooling' of proportions of family incomes for the upkeep of the family as a whole, and for the improvement of the home. Indeed, if one is to judge from the present concentration upon schemes of furnishing, schemes of interior decoration, 'do-it-yourself' techniques with appropriate tool-kits, and from the extent to which families devote themselves to improving their 'homes and gardens' along these lines, the present-day concern for the improvement of the family's household must be held to be very considerable indeed . . .

Education

Thirdly, let us consider the 'educative' functions of the family.

In the more limited sense of providing the basis for the 'socialisation' of the child during its earliest years of complete dependence, the modern family is just as much an educative unit as was the pre-industrial family, with the difference that in these earlier times children did not possess the status they now have and were introduced, in their upbringing, to harsh and impoverished conditions in which they were often exploited, whereas the child now enjoys a high status and is increasingly treated as an end in himself. With increased public regulation and public aid, and possibly with an increased sensitivity to new psychological knowledge and opinion, the upbringing of the child is undertaken in a far more considerate and careful, perhaps even fastidious, manner. . . .

Here again, therefore, it is clear that the provision of public eduction by 'specialised agencies' has not by any means 'stripped' the family of its educative functions; it has in fact increased the nature and the extent of these functions. The family is drawn more intimately into the network of educational institutions than ever before, and has to meet new demands and new responsibilities in this sphere.

Health

Precisely the same considerations apply to the functions of the family in caring for the health of its members in the context of the provisions of public health services.

It can hardly be maintained in any serious sense that the family in pre-industrial Britain provided for the health of its members, beyond doing its best (by employing a bizarre equipment of semi-magic and old wives' tales) to prevent and endure the sufferings of ill-health and early death. Now, however, from the very conception of the child onwards, provisions for the maintenance and further-ance of both bodily and mental health are made. There are family allowances for the child, pre-natal and post-natal provisions for mother and child; medical, dental, and other services are easily and cheaply available for all members of the population, together with economic benefits during periods of ill-health, and an extended hospital service. These services and benefits are certainly provided by 'specialised agencies' going beyond the family; but, here again, they have not been simply 'given by the state'. These public provisions are the outcome of political policies which stemmed from the desires of parents and which had to meet with their support and approval, and they continue to be financially maintained by the public at large. The effective provision of them has not, by any means, stripped the family of the function of caring for the health of its members . . .

Religious functions

Not so much can be said about the 'religious' functions of the family.

In what sense the pre-industrial family could be said to perform 'religious' functions is, to my mind, very far from being clear. Increasingly, the view seems to be emerging that the working classes were never extensively represented in, concerned about, or catered for by the religious denominations during the eighteenth and nine-teenth centuries . . .

However, there is no doubt that religious beliefs and sanctions have been considerably challenged during the past hundred years or so. All one can do here is to state a personal view. It seems to me:

(a) that, whatever the constellations of beliefs and practices held by parents (Roman Catholic, Jewish, agnostic, or whatever they may be), it is still in the context of the family that these beliefs and practices are first encountered by the child, so that the family continues to be extremely influential in this respect, and

(b) that the general growth of a more liberal attitude in these matters – i.e., that children should come to their views on such important questions by way of their own careful deliberation, and not by means of dogmatic family indoctrination – is all to the good . . ..

Recreation

Similarly with regard to recreation, it is dubious to what extent we can say that the recreative activities of people in pre-industrial Britain, such as they were, were provided by the family itself. Recreative activities, even in pre-industrial Britain, seem to have involved groups going beyond the family. The picture of the large, contented family practising its manifold recreations in the cosy fire-lit homestead is itself something of a caricature. Indeed, it would be interesting if someone would tell us precisely what *were* the recreations carried on by the pre-industrial family within the home and how much leisure time people were able to devote to them.

Certainly, however, the provision of public entertainment has increased and now exists extensively outside the home. Cricket matches, football matches, tennis matches, boxing matches, athletics matches, pubs, clubs, cinemas, concerts of music, exhibitions of paintings and sculpture, horse-racing meetings, 'stock-car' destructions, angling societies (the list would obviously take up several pages) have all proliferated, and have all taken people outside the home. But how these developments can be said to have disturbed recreation in the family, or to have stripped the family of its recreative functions, is not easy to see . . .

Indeed, we must bear in mind the considerable increase in leisure time available to the majority of families. Leisure time has made possible the proliferation of recreative activities. These family recreations have not superseded something already existing in earlier days, they have been *added* to the experience of most families. Michael Young and Peter Willmott give a pointed illustration of this:

The reduction of working hours after 1918, and again after 1945, has made a difference to every family. The spread of the five-day week has created the 'week-end', a new term and a new experience for the working man. With it has come the sight of young fathers wheeling prams up Bethnal Green Road

on a Saturday morning, taking their little daughters for a row
on the lake or playing with their sons on the putting green . . .

This is not a picture of family life disrupted by individual
recreation; the 'week-end' seems rather to have provided the opportunity for an extension of family recreation. The same picture is
given in the previously mentioned talk by Mark Abrams. 'Once,'
he says, 'the working-class husband sought to escape from the
crowded shabbiness of his home to the warmth and conviviality of
"pubs" or the club rooms of voluntary associations . . . But now,
as far as shabbiness and smartness are concerned, the boot is on the
other foot; so the new man stays at home . . .' Moreover, quite apart
from the enjoyment of 'common fire-side relaxations', including
television, 'it is primarily in the home that the worker now has his
greatest opportunities for exercising and enjoying his
craftsmanship'.

I conclude, then, that the idea that the family in Britain has been
'stripped of its functions' during the process of industrialisation is
false. Both in the sense of being concerned with a more detailed
and refined satisfaction of the needs of its members, and in the
sense of being more intricately and responsibly bound up with the
wider institutions of society, the functions of the family have
increased in detail and in importance. As the provisions of wider
agencies have been increased, the functions of the family have not
been diminished, but have themselves been correspondingly
extended. These wider provisions are *additional* to the conditions of
the family in pre-industrial Britain; they have not superseded functions which the family at that time fulfilled within itself; and they
have positively added to the expectations which society has of the
family. These more detailed and extended functions have been, as
we have seen, the outcome of substantial moral improvements. To
say, then, that the family has 'declined in importance as a social
institution' and that it has suffered a 'moral decline' is quite false.
The family has simply *changed* in such ways as to become adjusted
to the demands of a highly complex industrial and urban society,
and in such ways as substantially to reform the miserable conditions
of the pre-industrial and early industrial family alike. The wider
public provisions which have been made have not denuded the
family of its importance. On the contrary, they have been the manifestation of a *continually increasing recognition of its importance*. They

have been effected in order to aid the family in fulfilling functions whose importance has been gradually acknowledged.

This conclusion is stated in rather a different way by Professor Titmuss, who claims that the family of today must be considered *more* of a social institution than hitherto:

> No longer is the family taken for granted as it was, like progress, in Victorian England. Again, like economic progress, it was in those Victorian days essentially a private affair; a closed area for the cultivation or neglect of private affections and private ambitions; a parking place for the exploration of patriarchal authority. Private ambitions are now matters of public interest, not least to the Commissioners of Inland Revenue, while, in discovering the family, we have simultaneously discovered that the quality of its internal life is also a matter of public concern. In this sense, *the family of today is a social institution.* The health and stability of the community is now seen to rest on the health and stability of its families; the social health of the individual personality is now judged to depend in great measure upon the quality of parent-child relationships. These are accepted generalities today; fifty years ago they were not.

Attitudes towards social policy

This first conclusion has important implications for the attitudes we should adopt when considering social policies with regard to marriage and the family. If our assumption is that the family has declined as a social institution, morally or otherwise, then we shall tend to adopt a backward-looking approach to social policy, indeed a reactionary approach. And there seems to be, at the present time, an all too powerful tendency to adopt a backward-looking point of view which is both false and dangerous. There are many who appear to believe that, in attempted reforms, we have gone 'too far, too fast', and that in our efforts to create a Welfare State we have given rise to irresponsibility and moral decay.

If, however, our conclusion is that, as an outcome of many social improvements, we are, as a society, expecting of the family that it should possess a knowledge of, and should utilise responsibly, the wider network of agencies and provisions of which it is a central element, and also that the family should perform many functions of a more fastidious standard of excellence, then our attitude will be one of helping to clarify this situation for the members of society, of helping them to see clearly and act effectively in relation to these extended responsibilities. Similarly, if we decide that the stresses and strains experienced in family relationships are not the outcome of moral decay, but the unforeseen consequences of improved social policies, we shall adopt the forward-looking view of seeking to reconsider and renew our study of the nature of these problems, to understand those apparent entailments of previous policies which we had not fully anticipated, and to formulate further and effective policies to deal with them. We shall recognise that great improvements have been made, that we need to consolidate them, and then make efforts to move beyond them – to resolve the new problems which have arisen. But it is wise always to bear in mind that social reforms never solve human problems once for all; they only solve particular problems to some degree, and are always likely to bring into being new problems which were not foreseen. When these new problems arise, we should not think of going back upon the reforms which have been made, but should realistically appraise them in a reliable historical perspective and then deal with them in such a way as to improve the conditions and relationships of human life still further.

The conclusion of our analysis is, clearly, that this latter, forward-looking attitude to social policy is the only one which can be justified. As part of this attitude to policy, however, it should also be recognised that many problems stemming from the apparent inadequacies and shortcomings of some families are not only due to the fact that reforms have been effected, but are a direct consequence of the fact that even the reforms we have mentioned *have not yet gone far enough*. Thus, any child neglect resulting from the increased employment of women is in some measure due to the fact that the provisions for child care envisaged in earlier acts – for example, the provision of nursery schools envisaged in the 1944 Education Act – have not in fact been implemented. The provision of any kind of nursery service has thus tended to be regarded as a provision for the unfortunate, rather than a normal and desirable service for the ordinary family.

Question
1. (a) Briefly summarise Fletcher's description of the functions of the modern family.

(10 marks)
(b) To what extent does Fletcher's description correspond to the 'functioning' of a family with which you are familiar?

(15 marks)

14 Jan Pahl: Is Wife Battering a Form of Male Control over Women?

Private Violence and Public Policy, edited by Jan Pahl, contains an account of her own survey of 42 battered wives and of other research contributions on the issue. The following is an extract from her introduction to the book which overviews research in the area. This topic is relatively new to sociology, yet it is so important that it merits a lengthy extract. In fact, the author divides her analysis into three parts which are quite open to separate consideration.

The first part does the basic job of defining and describing the violence of husbands against wives and of documenting its extent. The extent of the violence is assessed in terms of official statistics, the proliferation of women's refuges in Britain in recent years, and on the basis of a limited number of studies.

The second part of the extract attempts to offer a framework of explanation for violence against wives. Jan Pahl gives two types of explanation, individual and social–structural, of which she finds the latter more generally applicable. The following phrase from the extract sums up the structural explanation of violence between husbands and wives 'as the extension of the domination and control of husbands over wives'. Pahl cites comparative and historical evidence to show just how widespread and persistent this form of violence is.

The third section considers the vital fact that wife battering occurs within what Western societies consider the 'private' sphere of life – the family. The police and other public agencies have tended to consider such violence as outside the full measure of their social control. Many battered women and their husbands have taken the same attitude. This has made preventing the violence and dealing with its perpetrators much more difficult.

Current research is also establishing a high level of violence and, additionally, sexual abuse of children within families. 'Patriarchal' violence against wives and children is thus becoming apparent as a major problem of family life. In the nineteen sixties and early seventies, R.D. Laing and Edmund Leach wrote of the oppression, restriction and abuse that they saw as the 'darker side' to nuclear family life. Current research gives some specific support to their generalisations.

Reading 14 From Jan Pahl *ed.*, *Private Violence and Public Policy: The Needs of Battered Women and the Responses of the Public Services* (Routledge and Kegan Paul, 1985), pp. 4–15.

What do we mean by violence against wives?

It is important to recognise that violence can take many forms and that it includes both *physical* and *mental* assault. The evidence from many studies is that the violence experienced by wives is both prolonged and severe. In my own study 62 per cent of the women had been subjected to violence for three or more years, and the injuries which they had suffered ranged from cuts and bruises, through broken bones and damaged eyesight, to a ruptured spleen, stab wounds and a fractured skull. The findings of this small study are confirmed by the results of a much larger study undertaken at the same time in all the refuges of England and Wales by Binney, Harkell and Nixon. This larger study found that 73 per cent of women in refuges had put up with violence for three or more years. Thirty per cent of the women who were interviewed in this study had suffered life-threatening attacks or had been hospitalised for serious injuries such as having bones broken. The rest of the sample had experienced assaults which included being kicked, pushed into fires or through glass, being thrown against walls or down stairs, being punched and having their hair pulled out. Sixty-eight per cent said that mental cruelty was one of the reasons why they left home (Binney, Harkell and Nixon, 1981). Dobash and Dobash found that the women they interviewed in Scottish refuges had experienced a variety of different forms of violence. This violence ranged from a single slap, usually experienced early in the marriage, to an attack involving kicking, punching and choking: on occasions the men would use belts, bottles or weapons. The most typical attack involved punches to the face and/or body, and kicks (Dobash and Dobash, 1980, p.106). One definition of the problem is that 'a battered wife is a wife or cohabitee who has suffered persistent or serious physical assault at the hands of her partner' (Marsden, 1978): however, to this definition must be added the comment of many women, that 'the mental battering was worse than the physical battering'.

There is some dispute about whether we should use the words 'battered women' or 'battered wives'. The former term is a reminder that women can be battered by their co-habitees and ex-husbands as well as by their spouse. The latter term is a reminder that, whatever the legal status of the couple, the violence takes place in a marriage-like situation. That is to say that the couple have children in common, that they share a home or have shared a home, and that the woman is likely to be financially dependent on the man.

What is more significant is that we use the term 'battered wives' rather than 'violent husbands'. It is rather as though the problem of international terrorists hijacking aeroplanes was described as 'the problem of hostages'! The effect of this renaming of the problem is to shift attention from the instigators of the violence to its victims, and the shift tends to make it easy to blame the victim for the problem and to encourage a search for solutions among the victims rather than among the violent partners. This misnaming is probably no accident. A great many people hold to the view that battered women are somehow responsible for what has happened to them, and this view is expressed in such statements as 'the woman must have done something to deserve it' or 'women must enjoy it really, otherwise surely they would leave'. The tragedy is that battered women themselves share the popularly held assumption that they are to blame for what is happening: they continue to blame themselves and to feel guilty about the violence, and this is one reason why they do not leave but continue to endure the violence.

The evidence from my own study is that, of the women who remarried between the two interviews, not one was being abused in her new relationship. On the other hand, every refuge has stories about individual men, each one of whom, when one woman has finally obtained a divorce from him on the grounds of cruelty, marries again and starts to batter yet another woman. *It is the men who are violence-prone and not the women.* When we are considering short-term help for battered women, in the form of legislative changes, better services or more refuges, then it makes sense to talk of the problem of battered women. But when we consider more long-term fundamental solutions we should remember that the problem is more accurately described as *the problem of violent husbands*.

What proportion of all violence takes the form of violence against wives? There are considerable difficulties in answering this question since so much violence, both inside and outside the home, goes unrecorded. The best sources of evidence are police records, but even these pose problems, especially in the case of private crimes such as wife assault and rape, where the victims are often reluctant to report the crime because of feelings of guilt, shame and loyalty. There is considerable 'shrinkage': crimes may occur but may not be reported to the police: they may be reported but not recorded. And then, of course, more 'shrinkage' occurs between the crime being recorded and the case coming to court.

Table 1 Offences involving violence reported to selected police departments in Edinburgh and Glasgow in 1974

Offence	Total number of offences	Percentage of offences
Violent: Family		
Wife assault	776	24.14
Alleged wife assault	32	1.00
Husband assault	13	0.40
Child assault	110	3.42
Parent assault	70	2.18
Sibling assualt	50	1.56
	(1051)	(32.70)
Violent: Non-family		
Male against male	1196	37.20
Male against female	292	9.08
Male against police	452	14.06
Female against female	142	4.42
Female against male	53	1.65
Female against police	29	0.90
	(2164)	(67.31)
Total	3215	100.00

Source: Dobash and Dobash (1980)

However, there does seem to be agreement between a number of different sources which suggest that assault of wives by their husbands is by far the most common form of family violence. Important evidence comes from the study of Dobash and Dobash, who analysed the police records of Edinburgh and Glasgow. Their findings are presented in Table 1. This table shows that the most common form of violence is that which takes place between unrelated males, which makes up 37 per cent of all recorded violent incidents. The second most common form of violence is wife assault, which makes up 25 per cent of all recorded violent crime. By comparison, the other forms of violence between family members, such as assault on husbands, on children, elderly parents and siblings, are relatively insignificant. When one thinks of the attention which is directed towards street violence, concern with assault on wives seems long overdue. What we are discussing in this book represents one-quarter of all violent crime. (See also McClintock, 1963: Chester and Streather, 1972).

We must remember, however, the differential rates of both the reporting and the recording of crimes of violence. It is unlikely that assault on a policeman will go unrecorded, and so we can consider the recorded total of these offences as a reasonably accurate reflection of the occurrence of assaults. On the other hand, assaults on wives and on children are very much less likely to end up as entries in police records and so the recorded totals must be seen as under estimates of the true extent of these problems. After careful and detailed interviews with large numbers of abused wives, the Dobashes concluded that only about 2 per cent of all such assaults are ever reported to the police (Dobash and Dobash, 1980, p.164).

One important measure of the extent of wife abuse is the dramatic proliferation of refuges in Britain over the past few years. From the setting up of the first refuge for battered women in Chiswick in 1971, the number has grown so that by 1981 there were about 200 refuges scattered across the country. The majority of these refuges are affiliated to the Women's Aid Federations of England, Scotland, Wales and Northern Ireland. They provide safe accommodation for women and their children, advice of whatever sort the woman requires and support for as long as she needs it. The fact that most refuges are usually extremely overcrowded suggests that the women who go to them represent the desperate tip of a very large iceberg. The Women's Aid Federation calculate that in any one year about 12,000 women and 21,000 children will use refuge accommodation, and that at any one time about 1,000 women and 1,700 children will be living in refuges (Women's Aid Federation, 1980a). However, provision of refuges is still very far from the level recommended by the Select Committee on Violence in Marriage which proposed that 'One family place per 10,000 of the population should be the initial target' (Select Committee Report, 1975, xxvi).

Another question concerns the extent of violence in family life and within marriage. A difficulty here is that so little is known about the extent of violence in ordinary families. Most of our knowledge about wife abuse comes from the accounts of wives who have gone to refuges, or from studies of divorcing couples. In both instances it seems likely that a greater proportion of middle-class, as opposed to working-class violence, goes unreported.

The only large study to have investigated violence in the general population was carried out in the United States by Straus, Gelles and Steinmetz. The first paragraph reads:

> Drive down any street in America. More than one household in six has been the scene of a spouse striking his or her partner last year. Three American households in five (which have children living at home) have reverberated with the sounds of parents hitting their children. Where there is more than one child in the home, three in five are the scenes of violence between siblings. Overall, every other house in America is the scene of family violence at least once a year (Straus, Gelles and Steinmetz, 1980).

This study showed that, while in any one year violence occurs in 16 per cent of American marriages, if the entire marriage period is considered, violence has occurred in 28 per cent of American marriages. Though wives are violent as well as husbands, the damage inflicted by husbands is more dangerous, causes more harm, and is more frequently inflicted.

In Britain, Hanmer's study of community violence to women showed that 59 per cent of the women interviewed had experienced violent or threatening attacks during the previous year, 21 per cent of these at home (Hanmer, 1983). What about violence within marriage? Drawing together such evidence as there is, Marsden suggested that serious violence takes place in up to 5 per cent of British marriages and less serious violence in about another 1 per cent (Marsden, 1978). These percentages are, however, extremely tentative and perhaps the most realistic answer to our question was given by the Select Committee Report:

> Despite our efforts, we are unable to give any estimates of what the likely numbers are: several witnesses talked to us in terms of the tip of an iceberg and this seems to us to be correct. Most witnesses agreed, and this is almost certainly correct, that all strata of society are involved, although the better off are perhaps less likely to seek outside help. (Select Committee, 1975)

2 Why does violence occur?

Broadly speaking, there are two approaches to causal analysis of this problem. The first approach locates the problem within the individuals concerned and seeks to explain the violence in terms of deviant or pathological personalities. The work of Faulk, for example, which was concerned with men who had been convicted of wife abuse, showed that a majority of them could be classified as being mentally ill in one way or another (Faulk, 1974). However, other studies have not so far confirmed this finding, which was, of course, carried out with an unusual group in that all the men had actually been convicted of assault. Several researchers have found a link between violence and excessive consumption of alcohol. In my own study 52 per cent of the women said that their husbands often drank to excess, and this is similar to the proportions recorded by Gelles (1974) and Gayford (1975). However, it has been suggested that drunkenness should be seen not as a 'cause' of violence but as a condition which co-exists with it. Thus men who wish to carry out a violent act may become intoxicated in order to have the courage to perform the act. After violence has occurred both the man and his wife may excuse his behaviour on the grounds that since he had been drunk he could not be held responsible for what had happened.

Violent personalities are also seen as being a consequence of childhood experiences. The study carried out by Straus, Gelles and Steinmetz showed that people who grew up in violent homes were more likely to use violence than those who had not. Thus one in ten of husbands who grew up in violent families were wife beaters in the sense of serious assault, and this is over three times the rate for husbands who did not grow up in such homes. However, the researchers point out that it would be a mistake to put too great a burden on what is learned in the family. To see this one needs only to look at the violence rates for children of non-violent parents. These rates show that a considerable amount of violence is perpetrated by people whose parents were not violent to them and not violent to each other. The family may be a training ground for violence, but for a fuller explanation we have to look to the wider society (Straus, Gelles and Steinmetz, 1980). There is now a considerable number of studies which put forward a variety of causal explanations of wife abuse. For more extended discussion of these see especially Freeman (1979), Hanmer (1978) and Martin (1978). In general it can be said that causal analyses of the problem are divided between the individual and the social-structural approach.

The second approach locates the problem in a broader social-structural context and focuses, not narrowly upon the individual, but upon the whole social situation within which the violence takes place. Here explanation is in terms of social context rather than in terms of individuals, and here new light can be thrown upon the behaviour of individuals. For example, this explanation would look beyond the link between drunkenness and battering to consider the way in which some cultures see both phenomena as symptoms of masculinity and male dominance. The social-structural explanation would, similarly, look beyond the fact that a drunken man committed an assault, to recognise that if he assaults a policeman he is likely to be prosecuted, while if he assaults his wife it is likely to be labelled a 'domestic dispute' for which police intervention is kept to a minimum. And this explanation would see the fact that some women return again and again to their violent husbands, not as a result of some sort of sado-masochism, but as a consequence of the inadequate help given to battered women and the hardships experienced by women who are trying to bring up children by themselves.

The legitimisation of violence by the wider society is an important part of this broader structural approach. This legitimisation is woven into a culture at every level, from the level of popular saying to the level of legislation. An important part of this legitimisation is the denial that wife abuse takes place, or the assertion that its occurrence is rare and is confined to unusual or deviant couples. In recent years, however, evidence has accumulated to confirm that violence against wives occurs in many very different societies, and at all social levels. It would be incorrect to see violence as confined to Britain and to the working class within Britain. Throughout this book reference is made to British and American studies. However, it is important to note the existence of studies of wife abuse in Germany (Hagemann-White, 1981), Israel (Saunders, 1982), the Mediterranean (Loizos, 1978), Amazonia (Chagnon, 1968) and Mexico (Roldan, 1982), and the existence of refuges or shelters for battered women in Britain, the United States, Holland, West Germany, Switzerland, Belgium, Canada, France, Australia, New Zealand and Israel (Dobash and Dobash, 1980). Schlegel rated forty-five societies and showed that three-quarters of them permitted husbands to be aggressive towards their wives (Schlegel, 1972).

Just as wife abuse takes place in the majority of societies, so it has been condoned throughout most of history. Historically the tradition of accepting wife assault is longer than the tradition of deploring it. Until the nineteenth century British law gave to husbands the right to beat their wives for what was called 'lawful correction', and it was only excessive beating that was frowned upon. The law reflected and upheld a hierarchical and patriarchal family structure. This tradition was summarised by Blackstone in the late eighteenth century as follows:

> The husband also might give his wife moderate correction. For as he is to answer for her misbehaviour the law thought it reasonable to entrust him with this power of restraining her, by domestic chastisement in the same moderation that a man is allowed to correct his servant or children. (Blackstone, 1966, vol. 1. 432) . . .

Any explanation of wife assault needs to be located in the broader social context, and in particular in the context of the structural and ideological forces which shape the relationships between men and women both within marriage and in the wider society. Straus summed up the conclusions of the recent large-scale survey of violence in American families by saying, 'the causes of wife-beating are to be found in the very structure of American society and its family system' (Straus, 1978, 41: see also Breines and Gordon, 1983).

A very careful and detailed British study of wife beating was that carried out by Dobash and Dobash in Scotland. In that study the assaults which the women had endured were investigated not as isolated incidents, but as part of the whole relationship between the couple, as it had developed from courtship to marriage to child bearing and rearing. The Dobashes concluded:

> We propose that the correct interpretation of violence between husbands and wives conceptualises such violence as the extension of the domination and control of husbands over wives. This control is historically and socially constructed. The beginning of an adequate analysis of violence between husbands and wives is the consideration of the history of the family, of the status of women therein, and of violence directed against them. This analysis will substantiate our claim that violence in the family should be understood primarily as coercive control. (Dobash and Dobash, 1980, 15)

Clearly it is important, not simply to describe the violence inflicted by one individual on another, but to extend the analysis to take into account the social and economic context within which the violence takes place. The literature on wife abuse has pointed to a number of different aspects of marriage and family life as being conducive to the occurrence of violence. One aspect which has not so far received much attention, however, is the fact that the violence takes place in the privacy of the family home and within what is defined as the most private of all relationships. It is to this aspect of the problem that we now turn.

3 Public and private

The dichotomy between public and private must be of concern to those who seek to understand the roots of violence against wives and to those who want to help the victims of violence in the home. In a culture which, both explicitly and implicitly, assumes fundamental linkages between such concepts as 'woman', 'wife', 'family', 'home', and 'private', it is no accident that violence against a woman, perpetuated by her husband within their family home, is somehow seen as a different sort of crime from violence against a stranger in a public place. We can see these linkages exemplified in many different statements which have been made on the subject, most especially in the justifications for non-intervention given both by violent husbands, and also by people who might well have intervened had the violence occurred between strangers in a public place. The following example comes from the Select Committee Report on *Violence in Marriage*. The first is an extract from the evidence presented by the Association of Chief Police Officers:

> It is important to keep 'wife battering' in its correct perspective and realise that this loose term is applied to incidents ranging from a very minor domestic fracas where no Police action is really justified, to the more serious incidents of assaults occasioning grievous bodily harm and unlawful woundings. Whilst such problems take up considerable Police time during say, 12 months, in the majority of cases the role of the Police is a negative one. We are, after all, dealing with persons 'bound in marriage', and it is important for a host of reasons, to maintain the unity of the spouses. (Select Committee Report, 1975, 366)

This statement suggests that the intervention of the state is less appropriate when the individuals concerned are linked by family ties as opposed to being strangers, and when the incident takes place in a private rather than a public place. To question this is not to advocate that there should be a policeman in every bedroom nor is it to argue for the abolition of privacy or of domestic life. However, for our topic it is important to consider more carefully the ways in which the public-private boundary is defined: more specifically, it is important to consider *whose privacy* is being respected or violated in particular circumstances. We shall argue that the notion of privacy is not an absolute value, that some people's privacy appears to be more inviolate than other people's privacy, and that by looking at how 'the private' is defined and maintained we can understand a great deal about the nature of power relations in a particular society.

Question
1. *(a) Indicate the extent and seriousness of the problem of violent husbands.*

(8 marks)

(b) Do you regard wife battering as an aspect of male dominance and control? Explain your view.

(8 marks)

(c) Does the evidence of male violence within the family suggest that the state ought to intervene more in this 'private' area?

(9 marks)

(Question sections (a), (b) and (c) refer to extract sections 1, 2 and 3 respectively).

15 Ellis Cashmore: The One Parent Family 'Alternative'

Currently, about one family in eight in Britain is headed by a single parent. Broadly, the literature on one parent families presents two images. Catherine Itzin, *Splitting Up: Single Parent Liberation* (Virago, 1980), and Jean Renvoize, *Going Solo: Single Mothers By Choice* (Routledge and Kegan Paul, 1985), present a positive picture. For their mothers, single parenthood can be an alternative to an oppressive or dependent relationship. Significantly, however, most of Renvoize's sample of over 30 mothers or mothers-to-be are middle class, as most voluntarily single parents seem to be. However, in actuality the majority of single parents are working class and their experience is much less of a 'liberation'. Ellis Cashmore's sample of over 250 lone parents, mainly women, were introduced to him by various social service departments and voluntary organisations. True, for a few of them single parenthood represented a desperate bid for a kind of freedom but, for most, it proved a hard choice, if choice at all, leading to poverty and loneliness.

There follow two extracts from Cashmore's book. The first is part of a case study of Sarah Rand whose experience of poverty and personal stress is typical of many of the lone parents interviewed by Cashmore. The second extract focuses on what policies should be adopted to improve the situation of one parent families. One way or another, what the suggestions amount to is more money for single parents. Only then, will the potential for liberation in parenthood be realisable for the majority of single parents.

The second part of the reading refers to the *Finer Report* (1974). Had it been accepted, the report would have ensured a minimum income above Supplementary Benefit for the great majority (90 per cent) of one parent families but at the price of a means test.

Reading 15 From E.E. Cashmore, *The World of One Parent Families: Having To* (Counterpoint, 1985), pp. 201–3, and 278–82.

The phrase 'My life is in pieces', uttered by Sarah Rand, encapsulates. the situation of the women in this chapter, and their views contrast quite starkly with those of Joy White and the others who found single parenthood a positive force in their lives. For Sarah, being a lone parent means problems, of which the central one is bad housing. Sarah, 32 and a mother of one, sees her own particular problems as stemming from her accommodation – a tenth-floor flat in a highrise tower block.

'People muck about with the lifts for a start and the engineers who are meant to repair them don't do anything about it. They just let the residents cope, which is a bit awkward when you've got kids to cart up and down ten flights or more. Then, if there's a lift working, you get on and the stench is unbelievable 'cause somebody's urinated in it. If you have to use the stairs, somebody's always done it there as well. All over the walls, there's graffiti: "NF" or "Blacks out", and all these sort of slogans. You've got a drying-room. It's like a brick room and it's got a drain in the middle and it's got a grid so you can dry clothes in there. In some flats, you haven't got balconies. You've got nowhere at all to dry nappies and a person on Social Security can't afford disposable ones; they're a luxury even to somebody at work.

The baby never has any fresh air for the simple reason that it's hard to get outdoors. If the mother goes to work, then she's able to put the baby in a daycare centre and then she won't experience half the things that a mother on Social Security will. She's better off in that she'll only see the block of a night. But, then again, if somebody's playing their music and she's gotta get up for work and got the baby to look after and get it to the daycare nursery, then she'll be shattered 'cause you can't sleep with all the noise.'

Sarah didn't have her first child until she was 30. She suffers from systemic lupus erythematosus (SLE), which resulted in her losing three children by her ex-husband. This was a factor contributing to her eventual divorce at 29. She then met a man and, to her surprise, conceived. Her son is now 2 and she lives in a tenth floor, one-bedroomed flat, from which she moves only when necessary. 'With a 2–year old child, it's a big deal every time I want to set foot outside. I've got to think about dressing him and getting the pram up and down ten flights. So I tend to stay in a lot.'

Her single carpet is threadbare and her furniture obviously well-used. The place seems to reflect Sarah physically: worn, tired and ready to break apart. Her thinning hair is arranged to cover a bald patch caused by the SLE but aggravated by her constant, nervous scratching. She blew up from 9 stone to 11½ during her initial treatment, but has now been reduced to a fragile 8 stone.

'I couldn't say I've ever been a healthy person, but I've never suffered as badly as I have since Danny came along and I got put in here. I was up here a year and four months without seeing anybody except my mum and a health visitor once a week. It's ever so lonely and that's the one thing I hate: loneliness. When I get with people, I talk non-stop: it's a terrible reaction to having too much talk pent up.

I'm still lonely now: I go down and see my friend on the fifth floor who's got a little girl; she is on her own, but she has got a boyfriend now. I go down and see her, but Danny doesn't get on with her little girl: they fight and, really, it is more like hard work going down to see her because you have to keep breaking them up all the time. You can't relax. It doesn't really break up the monotony and the boredom. My life has so much variety that I could live it blindfolded.

I suffer with my nerves; well, I had a depression a few months ago now and it was pretty bad. I don't know what hit me but it was just like being hit by a bloody hammer one day. I just couldn't see a light. I thought everything was crowding in on me. So I used to sit in here and I used to go deeper and deeper and there was no one to outlet my feelings to. I used to think I'm going to scream. The baby went through a bad patch at that time as well; he was getting on my nerves and wouldn't do as he was told, running riot. And I couldn't go down to see Vera because the kids were fighting. Everything came at once so I went down the doctor's for help. I suppose I chose the wrong doctor. I was in such a state that I was crying from here to the doctor's surgery and everybody in the surgery was going, "What's the matter, love?", and the baby was lying on the floor and he was kicking me. I was going, "Oh God, I can't cope." I was pulling my hair out. I thought, "Try and control yourself." So I went and splashed some water on my face. The doctor's reaction was terrible. He just said, "We deal with the physical side of the body only here, not the mental side; go home, pull yourself together and grow up."

Well, a few days after that, I had a letter and it says, "You are being asked to call on a Welfare Dayworker to see about your little boy being taken away from you for a few days." I can imagine the doctor's words: "She's come down to my surgery and she's told me she can't cope with her little boy any longer." And I was thinking "No, they are not going to take my baby away," and I panicked. I was just pulling myself together too.

Anyway, I didn't go down. A worker came to assess him on his birthday and I told her about my feeling depressed and she said, "Come and see me." I said, "Well, I wasn't going to come and see you because of this letter." So she said, "Well I'm glad you pulled yourself together now, but we are always there." I said, "Well, I know that, but when you want help, you don't actually go for it; you are so deep, you don't want to bother with it."

I've been forced to like the estate. I don't like being stuck up this high, I hate the flat, I detest it. I desperately want a garden, but I suppose every parent wants one. I want a place that I can feel is a home and this place has never been home to me . . .'

Liberated but caught

Some feminists have argued plausibly that the poverty of one parent families is not due to their family status at all and that past recommendations have failed to recognise the fact that, as Fran Bennett puts it, 'many of these disadvantages arise simply because the vast majority of single parents are women' (1983, p.192). Bennett's view is that debates about whether parents are better off out of work (the unemployment trap) or whether they will lose net income with taxable wage rises are conducted in sex-neutral terms, but relate in the main only to married male workers with financially dependent families. Sara Delamont expresses the view of modern society: 'While the man who is not engaged in paid work is either ill or deviant or a victim of harsh economic circumstances, the reverse is true for women' (1980, p. 100). Delamont argues that, even in the 1980s, the working career woman is just as much a deviant as a non-working man. Women are regarded as only subsidiary earners and therefore dependent on men.

One of the objections to the Finer scheme, apart from the obvious degradation implied by the means test, was that it involved a cohabitation rule. For example, a woman's benefits would be stopped should she be found to be cohabiting with a man, in which case their combined incomes would count as the means. The women's movement has charged that this cohabitation rule 'implies that a heterosexual relationship must and should involve financial dependence (or maintenance in return for sexual and other services)' (Bennett, 1983, p. 200). Of course, it doesn't necessarily follow that a man living with a woman is materially supporting her. In the present study, a subgroup of twenty-two mothers living in what were described as 'transitory relationships' (cohabiting for three months or less) was interviewed: in only ten cases did the male cohabitee contribute half or more of the family's total financial input. Even allowing for a degree of inaccuracy in estimates, the conclusion seems to be that women cohabiting do not necessarily draw material support from their men. In some circumstances, the idea that the man would lend active support was laughable: as Sandra Melville, a mother of two boys, commented, 'As far as he's concerned, my kids are my own and it's my job and their father's to keep them. The most he gives 'em is some chocolate or sweets. He don't want the responsibility.'

There have been all manner of suggested revisions to the current benefit system to improve the material conditions of one parent families. Those accepting the Finer recommendations (which were not accepted by the government) in a broad sense argue that, as Jonathan Gathorne-Hardy and others have put it, 'Divorce is the modern death, and it should be treated like that' (1983, p. 202). Like widows, all lone parents should automatically and by right receive a moderate means-tested sum of money, which should not be appreciably affected by whether the parent works or not. The sum should be non-contributory. As Gathorne-Hardy argues, 'society insures against the consequences of death, of old-age, of ill-health, of car accidents and other inevitabilities. It should insure against divorce' (1983, p. 203).

A more radical view is that women should receive an income as a right in order to rid themselves of their traditional economic dependence on men. At one extreme was the call of the Women's

Liberation Movement at their 1977 Conference for a version of Finer's Guaranteed Minimum Income for every individual person regardless of sex or whether they were in or out of work. It was an extraordinary and unrealistic demand and one that encouraged scepticism. On the one hand, it could encourage employers to hold down wages, knowing that workers would be subsidised by the state. On the other hand, it would have been far too expensive to operate.

Even the less extreme view that all women, regardless of status, should be granted a sum is, as Bennett puts it, 'threatening to a conservative or a traditionalist view of the family which stresses the natural, wholesome goodness of the nuclear family in its idealised, rigid form' (1983, p. 200). True, divorce has been made administratively easier; but the custodial parent will be hard-pressed to avoid some sort of material deprivation, especially if she is a woman. To alleviate that situation would be to encourage more divorces. And, to many, that isn't a desirable prospect. If life was made easier for divorcees with children, for unmarried parents wanting to break up or for parents simply wishing to remain solo, then the supposition is that the institution of marriage, so vital to the religious, educational and economic system of society, would show cracks. As Townsend argues, official recognition of the needs of one parent families has been inhibited by 'fears that any such support or recognition might tend to perpetuate and increase the numbers of such families and so erode the institution of marriage' (1979, p. 772).

Still, as I stated at the outset, the one parent population will continue to grow as more parents opt to go it alone, as more divorces split parents and as more ephemeral *de facto* relationships become the norm. There is also likely to be an upsurge in the number of one parent fathers following the recommendations of the Matrimonial Causes Procedure Committee. Of course, the ambitions of many lone parents (32 per cent) extend only to remarriage and, of the remainder, many others will unexpectedly find partners and re-enter a nuclear unit. Yet the phenomenon of one parent families will not pass away as the individuals concerned go back to the 'mainstream' of family life. The spread of feminist consciousness alone will guarantee that many mothers adopt the one parent approach to rearing children.

Sheer numbers will ensure that the questions raised throughout this book will be sustained. Questions like: is the presence of both mother and father a prerequisite for a child's satisfactory development; are one parent families a viable, legitimate (albeit alternative) family form in modern society; is one parenthood significant enough to require special welfare considerations? The interface of groups prompting these questions and an incomprehending wider society with a different morality will produce many problems.

As I've stressed, many see in the maligned group the potential for a new, invigorating freedom, particularly for women. My conclusions are more guarded: although I also see the emancipatory dimension of parents breaking free of the constraints of marriage and raising children in a foxhole situation, I'm forced to recognise the new problems lone parents are forced to face: low incomes, high rates of poverty, fewer employment opportunities, restricted access to choice accommodation, limited nursing and childcare facilities. I'm not suggesting that they need another partner; I'm suggesting that they need another partner's income. It is this material fact that instils in me sufficient caution to say that one parenthood seems destined to remain only a potentially liberating force – for the majority anyway. The economic gap between one and two parent families is one that will have to be closed if lone parents are to realise some of the ambitions that have been set for them or to which they personally aspire.

I hope I have shown that, for most lone parents, society generates a subtle – and, sometimes, not-so-subtle – barrage of discrimination. If one parenthood is to be a liberation, then society must respond at all levels, from the institutional to the personal. In this book, I have attempted to inform that response by offering a series of insights into both the costs and benefits of being a lone parent. My conclusions must be that the one parent unit is a functional and adequate environment for the personal growth and general development of both parent and children. It presents a vigorous and, to many, perplexing challenge to existing social arrangements. But my enthusiasm is tempered by the view that society's established order is, in many ways, not rising to the challenge and will be reluctant to introduce any reforms designed to alleviate the poverty in which many lone parents live. Writers like myself will acknowledge the prevalence of one parent families and applaud their defiance; policymakers are unlikely to do so.

Like a butterfly emerging from a chrysalis only to find itself caught in a collector's net, the lone parent has broken free from the creaking conventions of the nuclear family, only to become the captive of another less tangible setup.

Question
1. (a) Describe and account for the problems experienced by Sarah Rand.

(10 marks)

(b) Critically review the policy suggestions in respect to one parent families presented in the reading.

(15 marks)

16 Robert Chester: The Nuclear Family is Normal

The preceding two readings may have left the impression that family life is often rough and even violent and that, as a result, the family is vulnerable to instability and break-up. Robert Chester's article does not directly address the quality of family life but is a robust statement saying that, in statistical terms, the nuclear family is normal. The great majority are born into one and establish one of their own.

The crucial statistics on which Chester bases his case are that, at any one time, about 80 per cent of people live in households headed by married couples, of which three-quarters contain children (83 per cent of all children). In most of those families both partners work. Chester uses the term 'neo-conventional family' to describe this family unit. Without much difficulty, he also establishes that, notwithstanding minor counter trends, marriage is overwhelmingly the norm in Britain.

Having established his norm, Chester then marches relentlessly through the statistics and picks off apparent deviations as relatively marginal. On current trends, one in three marriages may be heading for divorce, but this also means that two-thirds survive until the death of a partner. In any case, most divorcees remarry. Whilst showing sensitivity to the problems of single parent families and step-families, Chester again puts them in statistical perspective.

Clearly, Chester feels that the case for the predominance of the 'neo-conventional' family needs to be argued and he selects his evidence accordingly. A balanced picture of changes in the lifestyles of individuals, couples and families does require other trends and interpretations to be considered. Several other articles in this book examine in some detail the stresses and conflict only touched on by Chester. However, stress is not the only factor to consider. The trend to smaller families and smaller households (about 50 per cent contain only one or two people!) is equally noteworthy. Many more adults are spending large periods of their lives in the immediate absence of children – a social trend worthy of much more analysis.

Reading 16 From Robert Chester, 'The Rise of the Neo-Conventional Family' in *New Society*, 9 May 1985, pp.185–8.

Most adults still marry and have children. Most children are reared by their natural parents. Most people live in a household headed by a married couple. Most marriages continue until parted by death. No great change seems currently in prospect.

As headlines, such facts are the demographic equivalents of small earthquakes in Chile with nobody killed. They seem a far cry from current preoccupations about the family. Attention has focused on the rise in divorce, cohabitation and one-parent families, and the fall in marriage and birth rates.

Social alarmists fear the death of the family. This same thing is welcomed by radical voices which assert the need for alternatives. The casual belief is fostered that only a diminishing minority now lives in the traditional 'nuclear' family of two parents with their children. The facts give no justification for these beliefs.

Of course, some changes have occurred in marriage and family patterns. Their importance cannot be ignored. But they must be seen in the context of major continuities in family life. Let us begin by looking at families and households. What is really going on here?

Much play is made of the supposed pluralism and diversity of contemporary family forms. The first column of the table shows that only 40 per cent of households consist of married couples living with children. Figures like this lead to the claim that it is wrong to describe the typical family as a unit of parents plus children, and that this cannot be used as a basis for policy-making, either. It is further said that a stricter stereotype – breadwinning husband plus housewife – applies to only 15 per cent of households and, more restrictively still, that men with two dependent children and a non-employed wife constitute only 5 per cent of all workers. Statements of this kind have a formal truth. But they are severely misleading if they are looked at in isolation.

Households and people in households: 1981

type of household	% of households	% of people
one person	22	8
married couple	26	20
married couple with dependent children	32	49
married couple with independent children	8	10
lone parent with dependent children	4	5
other	9	8

source: modified from 'Social Trends, 13', figures for Great Britain

The second column of the table shows that you get a very different picture if you consider people rather than the units they live in. In fact, six out of ten people (59 per cent) are currently in parents-plus-children households. A further 20 per cent of people are married couples who mostly have had, or will have, children. The 8 per cent living alone are mostly the elderly widowed, or else younger people who are likely to marry. At any one time, about 80 per cent of people live in households headed by a married couple. Three-quarters of these families contain children, who represent 83 per cent of all children.

The point is that snapshots of *household types* are misleading about *families*, and they ignore the life cycle. Even with universal marriage and parenthood, and no divorce or early death, there would always be many non-nuclear-family households, because the parents-plus-children unit is a developmental phase. But it is one which is normal and is still experienced by the great majority.

Nor does the fact that only 15 per cent of households consist of breadwinner husband plus housewife, undercut the social importance of nuclear families. This means insisting that the definition must include a fully-dependent housewife, which makes it rather an Aunt Sally argument. One significant family change is in the proportion of wives with jobs: up from 22 per cent in 1951, through 38 per cent in 1966, to 58 per cent now. Employed wives are thus now statistically normal in Britain. But employed married mothers are still (just) a minority at 49 per cent. Only 14 per cent of all married mothers have full-time jobs, and most of these have older children.

The pattern is of married women withdrawing from the labour force to become mothers, and some of them taking (mostly part-time) work as their children mature. This is important for family life, but it is scarcely a drastic re-ordering of the conventional model. The new pattern seems established and accommodating enough to be dubbed the 'neo-conventional family.' Certainly, it does not mean that the nuclear family has been abandoned as the normal experience.

Myths about marriage

Another area of myth relates to marriage. What is happening here? Is there really a flight from marriage, as is sometimes claimed?

Marriage rates among the under–30s have recently declined in most Western countries. The trend began in Sweden and Denmark in the middle 1960s, spread to Britain, America and West Germany in the early 1970s, and to France somewhat later. This contrasts with the 1950s, when British marriage rates were rising, particularly at ages under 25. The proportion of first marriages involving a teenage bride grew from 17 per cent in 1951 to 29 per cent in 1961. Teenage marriage rates continued to increase during the 1960s, while rates at other ages remained stable. But since then, marriage rates have fallen at all ages under 30. This is especially true of the under–25s, and outstandingly true of teenagers, where the rate has more than halved. In 1983, one in five spinsters marrying was a teenager, as against one in three in 1971. Whereas one in eleven of teenage women got married in 1971, only one in 24 did so a decade later. But, again, the figures must be put in context. They do not prove a flight from marriage.

Demographers know that the marriage rates each year can fluctuate widely, without necessarily reflecting change in the proportion of people who will eventually marry. The major influence on fluctuations is the timing of marriage. How rapidly marriage rates fall when age at marriage changes is shown by the history of people born in 1931 and 1936. They had very strong differences in marriage rates at younger ages, but almost no difference in the proportions married by the age of 30. It *may* be that the current younger generations will show some shortfall in marriage, compared with the past. But the difference is likely to be small. Mainly we seem to be witnessing a delay in the timing of marriage, rather than a fall-off in getting married at all.

It is sometimes held that reduced marriage rates indicate a growing preference for what demographers call 'consensual unions' over marriage. The evidence certainly suggests a considerable increase in cohabitation during the 1970s. Of women marrying for the first time in 1979, about 19 per cent said they had lived with their husband beforehand. This contrasts with 2 per cent for marriages between 1961 and 1965, and 7 per cent in 1970–73. By definition, however, this was cohabitation as a temporary transitional phase, not a permanent alternative to marriage. Among women who remarry, the reported incidence of living together beforehand is much higher (over 60 per cent). This suggests cohabitation as an interim measure where partners may not yet be free to marry.

How many people go in for living together as a permanent alternative to marriage? To pin this down, the first step is to distinguish single women from the divorced/separated. Of the divorced or separated, about 19 per cent of those aged between 18 and 49 reported themselves as currently cohabiting in 1980– 81. This contrasted with 9 per cent of single women, 6 per cent of widows, and 3 per cent of all women in the age group. Divorced and separated women, in fact, accounted for 44 per cent of all cohabiting women.

The General Household Survey also suggests an important distinction among single cohabiting women. Almost half of these began by telling the interviewer they were married, but later said they were not; the remainder acknowledged from the start that they were living together. This seems to indicate a real difference. The supposedly 'married' women had, on average, cohabited for twice as long as those who simply said they were 'living together'; and about half the 'married' women had children, while the others were mainly childless.

In practice, only about 2 per cent of single women aged between 18 and 49 are living and bearing children in 'consensual unions' which may be permanent. This is less than seven in a thousand of all women in their age-group.

Again, this scarcely seems a flight from traditional paths. It firmly associates Britain with one of the two cohabitation patterns now apparent in Western Europe. Scandinavian marriage rates fell earlier, faster and farther than elsewhere. The fall in legitimate births was matched by a rise in births to consensual unions (a third of all births in Sweden). This is not the pattern in France, West Germany or Britain, where the decision to have a child is usually accompanied by marriage. The Scandinavian pattern could possibly evolve here, but there is no sign of this on current evidence.

Where marriage takes place is it imminently threatened with breakdown? Western countries have mostly had similar divorce trends since 1945. There was a postwar spate, a decline to a plateau through the 1950s, a strongly rising trend from around 1960, and a recent high plateau. An associated trend is a widespread move from 'matrimonial offence' (like adultery or cruelty) to 'marriage breakdown' as the basis of divorce. The British divorce rise in the 1970s is often attributed to our 1971 reform of the grounds for divorce.

Yet this reform probably mattered less than some suppose. Divorce had already been going up by 9 or 10 per cent a year from 1960. The annual number of petitions in England and Wales rose from 26,000 in 1959 to around 170,000 now. Current projections suggest that one in three of recent marriages may end in divorce. These figures are large, though they also mean that marriages are still preponderantly ended by death. A historical perspective is helpful. During much of this century, low death and divorce rates accustomed this country to great stability of marriage. But in the 19th century, marital disruption through death and divorce combined was closely parallel to now. Proportionately more children were affected.

Observers often note an association between teenage marriage and divorce. Teenagers who marry have twice the divorce risk of people who marry aged 20 to 24. On current rates, over half the teenage marriages will end in divorce. But the effects of youthful marriage as such are hard to disentangle. Pregnant brides also have a high divorce risk, and premarital pregnancy often precipitates teenage marriage. There is evidence to suggest that precocious childbearing may be more divorce-disposing than marriage age in itself. Social class complicates the issue. Unskilled manual workers have particularly high divorce rates, and teenage marriage is especially associated with lower occupational groups.

So a constellation of age, reproductive and economic factors offers a poor prognosis for marriage. But the specific effect of age is

111

uncertain. Presumably, however, the decline in teenage marriages will ultimately cut the numbers who divorce.

Good data on social class and divorce have only recently been available. The pattern is not what it used to be thought. The annual divorce rate for husbands in social class V (unskilled workers) is four times that for class I (professional occupations), at 30 and 7 per 1,000 respectively. But the rates for the intervening classes (containing the great majority of couples) do not form a progression between these extremes. For classes II, III and IV (lower middle class, skilled workers, and the semi-skilled), the rates fluctuate around 15 per 1,000. There is no inverse relationship between class and divorce. The differences between the small extreme social groups must reflect their own particular circumstances.

About one in three of divorcees are childless, and one in ten only have independent children. There is a persistent belief that childlessness is positively associated with divorce. But recent work suggests that enhanced divorce risk is associated with *both* childlessness *and* above-average childbearing. The lowest divorce risk lies with the well-spaced, two-child family. Divorce hits about 160,000 children a year. More and more of them are under five (22 per cent in 1976, but 29 per cent in 1983), because divorce is being obtained earlier in marriage. Recent projections anticipate that almost one child in five will undergo parental divorce before they reach the age of 16.

For children the most immediate consequence of divorce is life in a one-parent family, the numbers of which rose from 570,000 in 1971 to about 900,000 in 1981, mainly via divorce and separation. About one in eight of all families with dependent children are now headed by lone parents, predominantly mothers (87 per cent), and about 1.5 million children are involved. There is much evidence that, in current social circumstances, the one-parent family is a vulnerable context for living. The exposure of so many children to vulnerability causes great anxiety. But a proper concern for their well-being need not obscure the fact that four-fifths of children will continue to grow up living with both their natural parents.

The remarrying kind

The family remains very popular, even among the divorced. The commonest consequence of divorce for both sexes is still remarriage, rather than cohabitation or celibacy. One study found that 56 per cent of men, and 48 per cent of women, remarried within 4½ years of divorce, and mostly within the first year. Unsurprisingly, younger divorcees are more given to remarriage than older ones. Less predictably, the presence of children seems to change neither the incidence or the speed of remarriage, at least if there are fewer than three of them.

Remarriage rates declined for both sexes during the 1970s. But this does not mean that divorcees are less likely to remarry. The numbers of divorcees have been rising very quickly. Given the necessary interval between divorce and remarriage, the rates were almost bound to fall. Evidence suggests that, in the longer run, 65 or 70 per cent of divorcees remarry. A third of all marriages now are remarriages for at least one partner (36 per cent in 1983, as against 14 per cent in 1961).

More remarriage has meant more redivorcing. The divorce risk for a divorced groom is 1½ times that for a same-age bachelor. For a divorced bride, it is twice that for a comparable spinster. In 1983 one divorce in five was a second or subsequent divorce for one or both partners. The number of divorces to couples both in a first marriage has actually diminished by more than 5 per cent since 1980. But the overall plateau is sustained by the increase in redivorce.

If there are children, remarriage creates step-families, which mostly means they shift from being in a one-parent family to living with natural mother plus stepfather. This was the current situation for 4 per cent of all children in 1979, though of course the cumulative proportion who experience this will be higher. Stepfamilies outwardly resemble the conventional family, but they have dynamics which are certainly different and possibly more problematical. A National Stepfamily Association was founded recently to provide support.

Altogether it is clear that there have been many changes in family behaviour in Britain: later marriage, greater susceptibility to divorce, a greater tendency for wives to work, and cohabitation as a temporary and childless phase in relationships between couples. But there is a very strong framework of continuity. The family based on a married couple living with their children, and committed to a permanent relationship, is still the norm. On the evidence, most people will continue not only to spend most of their lives in a family environment, but also to place a high value on it.

To say this is not to ignore the diversity of styles among families of conventional form, or the problematical aspects of family life. Still less is it to discount the existence of other domestic forms (like the single-parent family), which may not yet be sufficiently acknowledged and regarded. It is important, nevertheless, to remember that these are minorities, which for various reasons excite attention disproportionate to their number.

Discontinuities in the family get more notice than continuities partly because they often involve stress or other grounds for social concern. Traditionalists point to them as signifying the decline of the family. Feminists and other objectors to the conventional family have an obvious interest in derogating it. Some people in the poverty lobby emphasise family pluralism in order to get better treatment for non-conventional households. Lobbies for various minority forms of family life seek to legitimise what is often still regarded as deviant.

But to win support for policies which help those who need it, it should not be necessary to obscure the factual prevalence of conventional family arrangements; nor is it necessary to try to demote the nuclear family. If policy-making goes that way (as may be happening at the margin), then it will go against the grain of majority family behaviour.

Question

1.   (a) Summarise Chester's data and comments on:
        (i) The size of households
        (ii) The popularity (or otherwise) of marriage
        (iii) The growth in the number of single parent families.
        (About a paragraph each).

(12 marks)

(b) In what ways do you agree and disagree with Chester's picture of the 'neo-conventional family'?

(13 marks)

17 Mary Maynard: The 'Myth' of the Symmetrical Family (and Aspects of the Houseworker Role)

This reading is about contemporary housework and the house-worker role. It provides the necessary descriptive starting point without which a more theoretical attempt to understand the relationship of housework to society would not be possible. What is given here, then, is a description of the sexual division of labour, some estimates of who does most of the housework (mainly women), and an overview of research on what the experience of housework is like.

The reading is divided into the following five sections:

1. *The sexual division of labour* – in which the concept is defined and the view is refuted that the symmetrical family form (i.e. equality of roles) is becoming dominant.

2. *Time–budget studies* – this section surveys studies of the amount of time the two sexes spend on housework. Even women employed outside the home tend to do proportionately much more housework than their husbands.

3. *Changes in the nature of housework* – in which it is argued that supposedly 'labour saving' household technology tends to increase the standards and goals of housewives rather than save them time. The function of housewives as consumers in capitalist society is also dealt with.

4. *The experience of housewives* – this section overviews who does housework (mainly women) and what they feel about it. Roughly summarised, five points are made. Research suggests that housewives

   (a) feel unappreciated, and bored with the more repetitive aspects of housework

   (b) establish their own (often obsessively high) standards

   (c) like the sense of autonomy, of 'being one's own boss'

   (d) find their children satisfying but frustrating

   (e) tend to be dissatisfied with being full-time housewives and mothers (largely because of the loneliness and isolation they experience).

5. *The problems of contemporary research* – *(The need for theoretical explanation)*—Maynard observes that the concept of the sexual division of labour is descriptive as is the material used to illustrate it in the reading. More theoretical explanations of the houseworker role are given in Section 7.

Reading 17 From Mary Maynard 'Contemporary Housework and the Houseworker Role' in Graeme Salaman *ed.*, *Work, Culture and Society*, (Open University Press, 1985), pp. 137–44.

1 The sexual division of labour

A review of the historical material indicates the complexity of the changes in domestic labour which accompanied industrialisation. But although different authors emphasise differing aspects of these changes, there is agreement that household tasks were largely female tasks and that there continued to be a distinction between those duties and responsibilities performed by women and those carried out by men. At its most simple this is described as the sexual division of labour. This is the demarcation between male and female roles and the separation of the sexes into gender specific areas of work, family commitment and psychological identity. Women are regarded, and see themselves, as responsible for home and domestic life. Even when they are engaged in paid employment (also highly sex-segregated), their primary responsibility is for the family and its members. Men, on the other hand, are primarily breadwinners and are expected to have less involvement with their families. This division between the sexes is legitimated on the grounds that it is natural, necessary and a biological inevitability. It is taken for granted that the social world is, and should be, organised in this way.

Although the sexual division of labour was clearly a feature of nineteenth-century life and remains a central dimension in the organisation of contemporary society, some sociologists have claimed that, particularly within the home, a strict segregation of duties and obligations is breaking down. It is argued that the family structure in Western society is evolving in such a way that women's and men's roles are becoming more 'symmetrical'. More women are working outside the home in addition to performing their traditional family roles, and men are increasing their investment in the family, while maintaining their work commitments. This symmetrical family form is regarded as the dominant mode of family organisation for the future. It implies a movement towards a balance between the involvement of husband and wife in the two spheres of domestic and paid work (Young and Willmott, 1975).

Such a view has some resonance with the current picture of family life depicted by the mass media. This picture is based on an interpretation of two particular socio-economic trends. Firstly, it is said that, since the number of women doing paid work has increased substantially, some sharing of household tasks is now the norm. Secondly, the growth in household technology is presumed to have removed the drudgery from female domestic work, saved a substantial amount of time in its performance and rendered most tasks so simple that they can be undertaken by any household member (Bose, 1982). Such an account also appears to set the conditions for a symmetrical family form and the gradual breakdown of a domestic division of labour based on sex.

But despite the predominance of this view, a vast amount of empirical evidence suggests otherwise. This evidence is of two kinds: American time-budget surveys, and sociological surveys and studies of housework and the housewife which are mainly British in origin.

2 Time-budget studies

In recent years a number of time-budget studies have measured time spent on housework and other activities such as paid work and leisure. Such research generally involves either asking respondents to record their activities for specified time intervals over a number of days, or having them keep diaries registering the number and nature of tasks performed and the amount of time spent on each. The findings are remarkably consistent.

One study, for example, completed in the late sixties, shows that women who have no employment outside the home work an average of fifty-seven hours per week on such activities as preparing and clearing up after meals, washing, cleaning and tidying the house, taking care of children and other family members and shopping (Walker and Woods, 1976). More recent research shows women spending similar amounts of time on domestic tasks, to the extent that if it was paid employment it would certainly be regarded as full-time work (Berk and Berk, 1979).

For women employed outside the home, it appears that the more waged work they do, the fewer hours they spend on housework but the longer their overall working week. It has been reported that women who are in paid employment for more than thirty hours per week work a total of seventy-six hours in all, including an average of thirty-three hours spent on housework (Walker and Woods,

1976). Yet those husbands whose wives have the longest work weeks, have the shortest work weeks themselves. It appears that the husbands of wives in waged work do not spend any more time on housework than those with full-time housewives. This apparent lack of responsiveness by husbands to women's waged work is corroborated by other research, including a 1976 study of 3,500 couples in the United States. Wives employed outside the home worked substantially more hours every day than either their husbands or full-time housewives. They also spent about double their weekday time for housework doing domestic chores on their days off, whereas husbands, and even full-time housewives, had the weekend for increased leisure (reported in Hartmann, 1981).

This burden increases substantially when there are very young children, or many children, in the family. In either case the wife's work week expands to meet the needs of the family. Research shows that in families with a child under one year old, the typical full-time houseworker spends nearly seventy hours a week in housework (Walker and Woods, 1976); nearly thirty hours of this is spent in child care. The typical father spends five hours a week on this task, but reduces his time spent on other work around the house, such as home repairs, decorating and cleaning the outside of windows, so that his total domestic commitment does not increase. When the wife is employed outside the home for fifteen or more hours a week, the average husband spends two hours more per week on child care, increasing his overall household labour to twenty hours. His wife spends over fifty hours on housework, indicating that the amount of time spent on housework by the employed woman increases substantially with the presence of young children.

In addition, researchers do not appear to regard the housework or childcare activities of husbands as particularly significant (Berk and Berk, 1979). They point out that men are more likely to be occupied in this way after dinner. At this time child care typically consists of playing with and talking to children, which is not particularly burdensome. Moreover, while husbands are occupied in this way, their wives are tied up with the less than exciting after dinner chores. When men are involved with other domestic tasks it is frequently because their wives have to leave for employment after dinner and so are not themselves available to perform them.

Thus the activities of husbands are a form of back-up, or reserve labour, for a series of tasks which remain primarily the women's responsibility. Most married women still spend a considerable part of every day performing the necessary and most time-consuming work in the household. It is also noteworthy that the work week of domestic labourers is longer than that of the average person in the labour-force. Thus it is clearly demonstrated that although waged women do less housework than their unwaged counterparts, this has little effect on the allocation of particular tasks within the home. Domestic labour is still very rigidly differentiated along sex lines and this division appears to be constant across localities, regions and nations (Gershuny, 1982; Robinson, 1977; Szalai, 1972). Time-budget data indicate that there has been no significant change in the sexual division of labour within the household.

3 Changes in the nature of housework

One significant finding suggests that during the last century there has been an alteration in the content, although not in the amount, of housework performed (Bose, 1982; Cowan, 1976; Vanek, 1974). Although technological changes were slower in reaching the home than the workplace, they did begin to enter the more affluent homes towards the end of the nineteenth century. However, major techno-logical developments did not affect the households of most of the population until the early decades of the present century. The significance of these developments cannot be underestimated. As Rothschild says, 'Gas and electricity for cooking, heating, and lighting; indoor plumbing; and the washing machine dramatically reduced filthy and back-breaking labor for the housewife' (Roths-child, 1983). Labour-saving devices such as refrigerators, vacuum cleaners, freezers and convenience foods have also made activities such as cooking and cleaning easier. This has led one commentator to suggest that technological changes in the home have been on a par with, and as important as, those of the Industrial Revolution (Cowan, 1976).

Thus fifty or sixty years ago a large proportion of a housewife's time would have been spent in heavy routine and repetitive jobs such as fetching, hand-laundry and cleaning. Today, time is more likely to be spent on managerial activities, particularly child care and planning shopping expeditions. The continuing emphasis on the physical, moral and emotional stability of childhood as a significant component of mothering has obviously influenced the amount of time women spend on child-rearing. But despite the increased availability of household technology, the purchase of appliances and gadgets does not necessarily alleviate woman's domestic role (Bose, 1982; Cowan, 1976). Rather, it is suggested that the more technology present in a household, the more time is spent in its acquisition, use and maintenance. For example, food mixers encourage the preparation of more ambitious meals, and washing machines, together with higher standards of cleanliness, mean that more washing is carried out more often. Indeed, Parkinson's Law seems to operate, keeping women's housework at a constant level despite improvements in household technology. The situation appears to have changed very little over the last fifty years, since the amount of time devoted by full-time housewives to housework has remained remarkably stable during this time (Vanek, 1974). Moreover, household technology has been developed on an individual, familial basis, thus increasing the privatised nature of the domestic work which women perform. Despite the many developments made in this area, housework remains decentralised and is performed in isolated, relatively inefficient units. For all these reasons it has been argued that instead of challenging the sexual division of labour within the home, modern technology has tended to support, and even reinforce, the traditional allocation of domestic roles (Rothschild, 1983; Thrall, 1982).

Additionally, the increase in the number and range of goods available for purchase, together with the focus of advertisers on the mother and housewife as the major consumer, have made the home the centre of consumption. Women are the major consumers in our society. They are responsible for most of the expenditure on food, clothing and footwear and for the purchase of most household and chemists' goods. They are also largely responsible for the actual decision to buy most goods in the consumer durable section (Scott, 1976). Moreover, shopping and consuming should not be regarded as synonymous. Whereas the former refers to the physical process of buying goods, the latter involves a whole set of social and psychological factors surrounding the ultimate decision to purchase a particular item. The act of buying can be performed fairly quickly; the process of consuming can be a very complex and drawn-out business (Scott, 1976).

4 The experience of housewives

Sociological studies and surveys of housework corroborate the findings from time-budget studies. This research has been conducted mainly via interviews aimed at eliciting the nature of the work involved, strategies of coping and the meaning that housework has for the houseworker. Despite its differing orientation, the evidence concerning the sexual division of labour within the home continues to be overwhelming.

Oakley's much quoted research (1974) indicates that only 15 per cent of husbands in her sample assisted with housework and 25 per cent with child care. Her work reveals that husbands performing such tasks were still regarded as household aids, while the woman remained responsible for ensuring that tasks were completed, and for the daily management of housework and child care. A similar study found that the husbands of both waged and unwaged wives helped around the house on a spasmodic rather than a regular basis and were more likely to be involved in jobs outside than inside the house (Hunt, 1980). Moreover, this research corroborates the time-budget findings that husbands do slightly more in the home when wives are employed, but less than when both of the couple are employed but childless. The waged wife still does a double shift and has to revert to being a full-time houseworker at the weekend, when she catches up on her chores. Even the professional wife of the dual career family retains her domestic responsibilities. A number of studies report that husband's child care is still regarded, not as a part of the role of being a father, but as a favour to the wife (Gavron, 1968; Ginsberg, 1976; Hunt, 1980; Oakley, 1974). The man's involvement with children is again revealed as recreational rather than physical, involving playing and talking with children, thereby freeing the mother to perform domestic work.

The sociological evidence suggests that only a very small minority of men participate in domestic work on anything like an equal basis. This finding holds regardless of whether wives work outside the home or whether they are full-time houseworkers.

The qualitative material concerning the experience of being a housewife reveals that a series of contradictions and conflicts are involved. Firstly, the ideology surrounding domestic labour defines it as non-work and many wives report that their husbands think they 'get off lightly' with little to do all day (Hunt, 1980; Oakley,

1974). The conditions under which housework is performed, however, often resemble factory-like and assembly-line organisation. This is particularly so in the morning, when the housewife's major job is organising those of the family who have to leave the house to do so on time. Other aspects of domestic work also resemble the conditions of other forms of work. For example, housewives comment on the monotony of the activities and their repetitive nature, since many jobs have to be done daily and seem never-ending (Hunt, 1980; Oakley, 1974). Additionally, housework is experienced not as a single activity but as a collection of hetero-geneous acts, which are often contradictory and demand a variety of skills and actions.

Secondly, in order to cope with a job where there are no set specifications and standards, and where it is difficult to judge how much work is adequate, housewives devise their own standards and routines (Oakley, 1974). In the absence of formal rules for procedure and obvious rewards, such as wages, the satisfactory fulfilment of one's own standards and routines can bring its own psychic recompense. This process of self-rewarding is significant in a job which, because of its nature, draws attention from other household members only when tasks have not been properly completed. However, bringing coherence and self-reward to work in this way can lead to the loss of autonomy and constraint on creativity. For some women the imposition of rigid job specifications can lead to an obsession with tidiness and cleanliness, 'the houseproud wife', and to guilt and anxiety if housework is not performed to the self-defined standards.

Thirdly, one of the aspects of their work particularly liked by housewives is the sense of autonomy and of 'being one's own boss' which it conveys. Moreover, the women in Oakley's sample chose cooking and shopping as their most favoured activities. This seems to be because cookery has an element of creativity attached to it and, of course, is closely associated with woman's self-image as nurturer and carer. Shopping, on the other hand, is a public activity, involving social contact and freedom from the more menial house-hold tasks. Paradoxically, however, the more women set themselves schedules and routines for housework, the less autonomy they have and the less time is available for the pleasurable domestic duties. A conflict emerges between spending time on tasks which are enjoyed and working through the schedule of less agreeable jobs.

Fourthly, a similar contradiction is associated with children. Women overwhelmingly report child care as one of the most satisfying aspects of housewifery (Gavron, 1968; Oakley, 1974). However, children continually impinge upon and interrupt the household routine, extending the length of time spent in basic tasks and eroding those periods set aside for particular involvement with them. In addition, there is a conflict between the object of housework as a means of controlling dirt and tidiness, and the present 'progressive' notion of childhood, which emphasises the importance of freedom in the early years (Davidoff, 1976). The new tolerance of disruptive behaviour is particularly incompatible with the ideal image of good household management. Often the competition between children and housework presents an obstacle to job satisfaction for the housewife (Oakley, 1974).

Fifthly, a sizeable majority of housewives openly express dissatisfaction with their work, particularly with housework, and menial chores. Nearly 70 per cent of the housewives in one study (Oakley, 1974) and nearly two-thirds in another (Ginsberg, 1976) were dissatisfied with being full-time housewives and mothers. Clearly not every woman perceives contradictions and ambivalence in her houseworker role and not every housewife is dissatisfied. But mothers continually refer to the fact that they are staying at home because of the children, whilst recognising that this contributes significantly to their loneliness and isolation (Gavron, 1968; Ginsberg, 1976; Oakley, 1974). Women can derive considerable satisfaction and enjoyment from their children, yet still find the day to day work of child care highly frustrating. This is yet another aspect of the guilt and frustration which researchers have identified as part of the housewife role. More poignantly, it appears that those women with pre-school children are more likely to feel isolated and lonely, and to be dependent on drugs. Evidence indicates that feelings of conflict and low self-worth are related to the high consumption of psychotropic drugs (such as tranquillizers, sedatives and anti-depressants) among women with pre-school children (Ginsberg, 1976). There is also evidence that work outside the home can protect women against psychiatric disorder (Bose, 1982; Gavron, 1968; Ginsberg, 1976). But this leads to a final contradiction since the majority of females are channelled into paid work which is often limited by a sense of what would be compatible with their domestic responsibilities. A principle of 'occupational compatibility' is in operation: the job opportunities which are open or closed to women, and the beliefs held about women as paid workers are coloured by real and imaginary ideas about the limited availability and competence of women because of their domestic work. The woman who wishes to escape from the houseworker role will inevitably find that all social relations are organised around the assumption that women are responsible for housework and child care (Berk, 1980).

5 The problems and contemporary research

The time-budget and sociological evidence describes a situation where the typical houseworker is female and where a rigid sexual division of domestic labour ensures that women retain responsibility for the completion of household tasks and child care. However, although providing a comprehensive picture of contemporary house-work, this picture is rather unsatisfactory because of its essentially descriptive nature. The houseworker appears in an isolated domain of her own, cut off from the wider context of the world outside. Moreover, the use of the dichotomic concept 'sexual division of labour' as a focus for analysis underplays the possible inequalities in a relationship and makes it difficult to address questions of power and dominance. Put simply, to organise our understanding of house-work in terms of the sexual division of labour is merely to redescribe empirical regularities without attempting to explain them. The 'sexual division of labour' is a descriptive, not a theoretical, concept. It helps to organise our empirical material but does no more. To move beyond mere description it is necessary to ask questions of a more general, contextual and theoretical nature. This can be demonstrated by looking at some recent socio-economic approaches to housework.

Question.
1. *Do you consider that 'symmetrical' conjugal (husband-wife) roles are typical of the contemporary family?*

(25 marks)

SECTION 4

Education

Readings 18–22

There are two main themes running through this section. The first is the relationship between education and the economy and the second is the educational disadvantage experienced by certain social groups. Both themes appear to a greater or lesser extent in all the readings.

The first reading by A. G. Watts is on the relationship between educational institutions and employment. Watts' perspective is not narrowly economic but is steeped in the findings of recent educational sociology. In his first section on occupational selection, he undermines the myth of 'credentialism' by reference to the work of Berg, and Bourdieu and Passeron among others. His second section refers to the work of Bowles and Gintis, Ashton and Field, and Paul Willis and suggests that class socialisation, in and outside schools, deeply distorts the goal of open competition between individuals for educational and career success. In discussing orientation and preparation for work within schools, Watts draws on his own considerable knowledge. He concludes that, far from being the channel to better jobs, many vocational courses lead to low status and rewards. On the question of orienting students to the world of work, he observes that some teachers fear they may be being pushed by government towards indoctrination. This is a point on which he might have elaborated. A related aspect is the issue of social control. Some critics have argued that a major motive behind recent initiatives in vocational training, particularly the Youth Training Scheme (YTS), is to serve as an alternative to unemployment 'to keep the kids off the streets'. In this interpretation the role of the teacher becomes that of 'soft cop' and students are potential dupes of a system of training for largely non-existent jobs. Of course, this is not a static situation – both the availability of jobs and the quality of education and training could improve.

The extract from Stephen Ball's *Beachside Comprehensive*

examines the role of teachers in educational success and failure. Like other researchers before him, Ball finds that teachers academically differentiate pupils partly on the basis of social class and that this contributes to the formation of pro – and anti-school sub-cultures. The reading from Paul Willis' *Learning to Labour* explores the continuity between anti (or counter) school culture as lived by working class 'lads' and the shop floor culture of their 'dads'. Reading this passage it is hard to deny Willis' argument that the values and behaviour the lads learn, in and out of school, is a preparation for their future work. This puts the role of school and teacher in context – they are reproducing agents of existing cultural patterns and groups rather than initiators of new cultural forms and possibilities. Individuals may break from the grip of childhood socialisation as a result of school experience, but the educational system cannot itself change society.

However, society does change and, even in the few years since Willis wrote, the demand for the labour of the traditional working class has greatly diminished. It remains to be seen how their energy will be channelled and culture transformed in the conditions of the late twentieth century. What seems apparent is that the educational system is hardly likely to function largely to reproduce a culture which is well on the wane.

The extract from Dale Spender's *Invisible Women* continues the theme of cultural reproduction. In this instance, it is how the ideology and practice of patriarchy is reproduced in schools that is discussed. This reading is one of several in the book which challenge males to look closely at the fine detail of patriarchal domination.

A. H. Halsey reasserts a cautious and qualified liberal optimism in the face of what may be regarded as the radical pessimism of some of the preceding readings. Although his major target is Pierre Bourdieu, his arguments can also be read as a reply to Paul Willis. Halsey contends that the educational system can certainly help to equalise class inequalities, including cultural inequalities. This is not an easy optimism, however, as he considers that the bulk of the job still has to be done.

18 A. G. Watts: Education and Employment

The usefulness of this extract is that it condenses much familiar and crucial material into a simple and coherent framework. Watts describes four functional links or 'bonds' between education and employment:
1. Selection
2. Socialisation
3. Orientation
4. Preparation

Selection refers to the process of sorting out and categorising pupils according to given occupational levels. As Watts indicates, and as later readings in this section show, class and gender as well as ability play a part in this process. The socialising function of the school is not confined to socialisation for work – it also includes personal, moral, political and social aspects. However, socialisation for work is a key area and merits the attention Watts gives it. He briefly describes how pupils come to *identify* with and accept their role in certain occupational areas. The third and fourth bonds are very particular to the education/employment connection. Orientation refers to the way in which the general awareness of students about work and its importance is raised. This includes careers education and learning about work in a wide sense, e.g. about industry or wealth creation. Preparation for work involves acquiring specific job and vocational skills. As Watts points out preparation is not always as useful as it seems at first sight.

A feature of Watts' account is that it combines functional analysis (the 'bonds' can be regarded as functions) with radical perspective. Many Marxists would find it quite acceptable.

Reading 18 From A. G. Watts, 'Education and Employment: The Traditional Bonds' in Roger Dale *ed.*, *Education, Training and Employment: Towards a New Vocationalism* (Pergamon, 1985), pp. 13–20.

In broad terms, four functions which educational institutions can play in relation to employment can be distinguished: those of selection, socialisation, orientation, and preparation. Each will now be briefly examined in turn.

EDUCATION

1 Selection

Over the past century or so, there has been a steady movement from the ascription of status by birth to the achievement of status through education. As a result, the educational process has ceased to be concerned simply with the transmission of skills and values: increasingly it has taken on the functions of allocating and selecting as well as training individuals for their adult roles (Banks, 1976, p. 5). Particular educational qualifications are now necessary prerequisites for entry to many occupations, and are used in selection by many employers. The case for credentialism of this kind is partly based on a utilitarian principle of *efficiency*, recognising the importance of developing the society's talents to the full and deploying them to maximum effect, so that the most able people can find their way into the most important and demanding jobs. In part, too, it is concerned with *equity*, making it possible for the social status of individuals to be determined by their talents and their efforts rather than by the accidents of birth.

It is important to recognise that in practice credentialism seems to satisfy neither of these principles very satisfactorily. In terms of efficiency, the relationship between educational qualifications and degree of success in an occupation is often very low (for American evidence on this, see Hoyt, 1965; Collins, 1979. pp. 19– 20). This may be partly because professional associations, in the search for reduced supply and increased status, are constantly upgrading the educational qualifications required for entry (Dore, 1976, pp. 24–28; Watts, 1973b); the same process is used by employers seeking convenient ways of restricting the number of job applicants to a manageable size. As Berg (1970) has shown in the United States, this process of meritocratic inflation can proceed to a point where, far from adding to workers' productivity and satisfaction, it reduces them because the workers are over-qualified and their skills are not being utilised. Moreover, many of the attributes which are most important in determining occupational success – social skills, for example – are not measured by educational qualifications. Such qualifications are thus often used as criteria for occupational entry not because they are relevant but because they are administratively convenient and publicly defensible.

Their defensibility is largely due to the appearance they give of being socially equitable. But here, too, there is room for scepticism.

Bourdieu and Passeron (1977) argue that schools trade in exclusive forms of 'cultural capital' based on the symbols, language forms, structure and meanings of bourgeois culture, and that students with access to such cultural capital – primarily through their families – do well in school because educational achievement is measured in terms of the skills and the knowledge which the cultural capital provides. Certainly it is the case that upper-middle-class children born in the period 1930–49 were three times as likely as lower-middle-class children to reach a university, and nearly 12 times as likely as lower-working-class children to do so (Halsey, 1975, p. 14). Admittedly these differentials were lower than for children born during the period 1910–29, suggesting some reduction of social class inequalities of access to educational opportunities. Westergaard and Resler (1975, pp. 324–6), however, have suggested that this moderate widening of education as an avenue of ability has been counteracted by a concomitant contraction of other channels of mobility – notably independent entrepreneurial activity and mid-career promotion up the rungs of bureaucratic hierarchies – resulting from, among other things, increased attention to educational quali-fications in schools and colleges. As a result, they argue, creden-tialism and the expansion of educational provision are likely to have had little or no net impact on social mobility. Even if one does not argue such an extreme case, it is clear that credentialism does not remove inequalities, and that even if it diminishes them to some extent, it adds apparent legitimacy to those that remain.

Moreover, the extent of the use made of educational qualifications should not be exaggerated. As Maguire and Ashton (1981) demon-strate, employers do not in practice place such emphasis on educational qualifications as schools often imagine they do. At the higher levels of the occupational hierarchy, qualifications are often necessary but not sufficient: employers use them as a convenient pre-selection device when deciding which applicants to consider more closely, but thereafter pay little attention to them. At the lower occupational levels, qualifications are frequently used simply as crude measures not of cognitive abilities but of such normative qualities as perseverance and capacity for hard work, or are ignored altogether.

Nonetheless, the process of credentialism has had a powerful effect on education. It has increased the demand for education; it has also affected its nature. In surveys conducted in Ireland, Raven

(1977) found that the goals to which primacy was attached by pupils, ex-pupils, parents, teachers and employers – for example, the fostering of personal qualities and capabilities like initiative, self-confidence, and the ability to deal with others – received scant attention in schools and, as a result, were poorly attained. Teachers and pupils worked not towards the goals which they believed to be the most important from an educational point of view, but towards goals that could be assessed in a manner acceptable for the award of educational qualifications. The result was to restrict what went on in schools to activities that were narrowly utilitarian and instrumental in scope. The available evidence indicates that much the same is true in Britain.

This process contains many ironic contradictions. Intrinsic educational values are subordinated to the extrinsic need to provide tickets to employment. Yet the content of these 'tickets' has very little direct vocational relevance, and its indirect relevance is much more pertinent to white-collar than to other occupations. The content is controlled not by employers but, ultimately, by the universities. For at each stage of the educational system, the content of the curriculum tends to be determined by the needs not of those who will 'drop out' at that stage, but of those who will go on to the next; and at the apex of this structure stand the universities, which in addition exert a powerful influence on school examination boards. Their control 'protects' the school curriculum from vocational influence, in line with the heritage of Williams' 'old humanists'. The status of subjects tends to be measured by the extent to which they have moved away from utilitarian or pedagogic traditions and have become 'academic' (Goodson, 1983).

The result is an extension to almost all school pupils of an academic curriculum very like that previously offered only to the few in the grammar schools. This curriculum is experienced by many young people as irrelevant to their immediate and future interests. The notion that the traditional liberal curriculum has some particular intrinsic virtue which work-oriented subjects do not, as a medium through which spiritual, intellectual and aesthetic powers can be developed, is itself open to question (Peterson, 1975, p. 95). But even if it were true, the chances of achieving these ends with pupils suspicious of such a curriculum are greatly diminished by the examination system, which means that these pupils see the curriculum chiefly as a means of labelling them as failures through an opaque process based on restricted academic criteria. They are aware that the applicability of these criteria outside the educational world is highly disputable, particularly in the non-professional and non-clerical jobs for which many of them are destined. Moreover, although the whole process is justified to them by the supposed need to perform a sorting and preselection function for employers, this service in reality is not as widely used by employers as is commonly supposed; and because of their limited vantage point, pupils tend to underestimate even the extent to which it is used (see Gray *et al.*, 1983, pp. 136–41).

Thus although the examination system provides an effective motivational spur for some, it is counter-productive for others, and can indeed alienate them permanently from formal learning. It also more generally develops an instrumental attitude to learning and work in which intrinsic motives such as actual enjoyment of working hard are rejected and regarded as socially unacceptable (Turner, 1983). Indeed, Flude and Parrott (1979, pp. 67– 68) consider that 'it is the attitudes and values engendered by public examinations, and the image of education which this adolescent, academic steeple-chase provokes in parents, teachers and pupils, which represent the main barrier to the development of recurrent education'.

2 Socialisation

The second function which educational institutions can play in relation to employment is that of influencing students' attitudes to the world of work, and to their own function within it, through the formal and informal organisation of educational institutions and the social relations within them. In the United States, Bowles and Gintis (1976) have argued that in many key respects the structure and social relations of education accurately reflect and reproduce the structure and social relations of the work-place. Both are organised hierarchically; in both, alienated workers are motivated by extrinsic rewards (examination marks in school, pay at work); and in both, work tasks are fragmented. This 'close correspondence between the social relationships which govern personal interaction in the work place and the social relationships of the educational system' (*ibid.*, p. 12) means that schools nurture, within young people of different types, attitudes and behaviour consonant with their likely future levels of participation in the labour force. Those destined for managerial and professional occupations are presented during their educational careers with situations in which they are asked to be autonomous, independent and creative; those destined for the shop-floor are subjected to custodial regimes which stress obedience to rules, passivity and conformity.

In the British context, Ashton and Field (1976) have described how the identities of pupils destined for different occupational levels are established or reinforced by the identities created within their schools. Thus those destined for 'extended careers' – characterised by long training and the continuing prospect of advancement – come to see themselves as possessing superior abilities, to see the successful performance of their allotted school tasks in the light of the long-term rewards associated with the entry into a 'good career', and to understand the importance both of personal advancement and of loyalty to the organisation. The importance of 'getting on' and of 'making something of themselves' is also transmitted to those destined for 'short-term careers' – in skilled manual trades, technical occupations, and some forms of clerical and secretarial work – which again are characterised by formal training but which offer little chance of advancement beyond a certain level. Here, though, the organisational structure of the school, including streaming and more informal channelling mechanisms, restricts their access to the certification required for entry to extended careers.

Finally, those destined for 'careerless occupations' – which require little training and offer no prospects of promotion and little or no intrinsic job satisfaction – receive derogatory messages which, as we have seen, teach them to see themselves as 'failures'. Their realisation that academic subjects have no rewards to offer them persuades them instead to seek some alternative sources of reward or satisfaction in the here and now – for example, through persistent rule-breaking and 'messing about'. Not only are these young people committed to semi-skilled and unskilled work by their educational experience, but their self-image of being academically inferior, their concern with obtaining extrinsic rewards as immediately as they can, and their desire to leave school as soon as possible, all mean that jobs of this kind have certain attractions. As Willis (1977) points out, this means that the very forms of resistance used within a school counter-culture by alienated groups of working-class boys lead them to make a largely willing entry into unskilled forms of labour, in which they are subsequently trapped – a powerful, even poignant, form of 'self-induction'. They even presage the forms of resistance – skiving etc. – which will enable them to cope with the monotony of such jobs.

Such analyses can evidently be applied too rigidly, to a point where they become mechanistic and deterministic. Clearly there are many respects in which schools do not reproduce the values and social relations of the workplace. Indeed, some influential commentators in recent years have argued that schools do not mirror the world of work well enough, but instead encourage patterns of dependency and immaturity which inhibit the process of transition to adulthood and to employment (Bazalgette, 1978a; Scharff, 1976). Clearly, too, the divisions between the groups distinguished by Ashton and Field are not as rigidly marked as the description above might suggest. The movement from a 'sponsored' to a 'contest' system – however incomplete it may have been – means that the forces of socialisation have been weakened somewhat, because the point of differentiation has been postponed, and its rigidity relaxed to some extent. Teachers have become more resistant to the notion that they should be performing a 'sorting' function, and adapting pupils to accept low-level jobs which make little use of their potential. Such resistance has indeed proceeded to a point where numbers of employers have grown concerned about the discrepancies between the expectations and attitudes that school-leavers have been encouraged to develop and the demands that will realistically be made of them (for a useful analysis of these and other differences of view between teachers and employers, see Bridges, 1981). Nonetheless, the changes that have taken place in opening up opportunities within educational institutions are often more apparent than real: for example, secondary school pupils continue to be sifted by teachers in terms of their perceived aptitudes, despite the rhetoric of pupils making their own subject 'choices' (Woods, 1979, especially chapter 2). The process of socialisation into employment remains a strong feature of the educational system – all the stronger because it is often implicit rather than explicit, and hidden even to the teachers who promote it.

3 Orientation

The third function is concerned with deliberate curricular interventions designed to help students to understand the world of employment, and to prepare for the choices and transitions they will have to make on entering it. To some extent it can be seen as an attempt to reinforce the process of socialisation where it is not proving sufficiently effective. Alternatively, it can also be seen as being designed to make the process more visible and therefore open to questions and deliberation – to make it a learning process rather than merely a conditioning process.

This orientation function has two distinguishable facets. One is *careers education*, which is concerned with helping students to prepare for their individual career choices and transitions. From its traditionally peripheral position within education, based on narrow concepts of information-giving and individual interviewing, careers guidance in the early 1970s increasingly came to be incorporated into the curriculum itself (Schools Council, 1972; DES, 1973; Watts, 1973a). Many schools and other educational institutions now have curricular programmes focused around four broad aims: 'opportunity awareness', covering awareness of the range of alternatives open in and around the world of work, the demands they make, and the rewards and satisfactions they offer; 'self awareness', covering awareness of the distinct abilities, interest, values, etc., that define the kind of person one is and/or wishes to become; 'decision learning', covering development of decision-making skills; and 'transition learning', covering development of skills to cope with the transition to work and subsequent career transitions (Law and Watts, 1977). Some schools establish careers education as a separate 'subject'; some integrate it into a broader programme of social and personal education; and some seek to 'infuse' it across the traditional areas of the curriculum. A survey conducted in 1975–8 by Her Majesty's Inspectorate (DES, 1979a, p. 230) found that half of secondary schools had a programme of this kind in the fourth and fifth years for all their pupils, and a further 12–15 per cent a programme for some of their pupils. Careers-education programmes have also been introduced in higher education (Watts, 1977b) and for adults (Watts, 1980). The notion that careers-education programmes can help people to participate actively in the decisions that determine their lives has been questioned by Roberts (1977, 1981), who argues that in reality people's lives are largely determined by the opportunity structure, and that many people have to accept what they can get. This has been disputed by other writers (e.g. Daws, 1977, 1981; Law, 1981a, 1981b), who have argued that there remains sufficient scope for such programmes to have an impact.

The second facet of the orientation function is *learning about work*, as part of social and political education within (in particular) schools. The central concept here is that all school pupils – regardless of when and where they are to work themselves, and as part of the preparation for their role not of *worker* but of *citizen* – should be taught to understand the place of work in society. Various approaches have been developed, including curriculum courses on 'industry' and related topics, and infusion of such topics into traditional subjects across the curriculum. There has also been emphasis on experiential methods, including work experience, work simulation, and the use of 'adults other than teachers' (including employers and trade unionists) in the classroom (see Jamieson and Lightfoot, 1982; Watts, 1983a).

A particular concern behind many such programmes has been the notion that young people should understand the process of wealth generation in general and the role of manufacturing industry in particular. Discussion of such matters is in principle welcomed not only by the political right but also by the left, so long as it is possible to regard the *status quo* as open to challenge and question (see e.g. Edgley, 1977). In practice, however, the boundaries set by government statements and the like tend to be narrow, and to avoid any suggestions that the matters under discussion are disputable or politically controversial. Some teachers thus fear that if they engage in such issues, they will be compelled to engage in a form of indoctrination. Accordingly, they sometimes prefer to evade the issues altogether (Beck, 1981, p. 89). Significantly, the most effective project in this area – the Schools Council Industry Project – has disarmed such suspicions by having the support of the Trades Union Congress as well as the Confederation of British Industry, and has adopted a low-profile approach in which emphasis has been placed not on centrally-produced policy statements and curriculum materials, but on encouraging local curriculum development which is experience-based and in which the teachers' role is shared to a much greater extent than is usual with employers, unionists and other members of the community (see Jamieson and Lightfoot, 1982).

4 Preparation

The fourth and final function is that of promoting the acquisition of specific skills and knowledge which students will be able to apply in a direct way after entering employment. As we have seen, this function was strongly evident in the practice of education up to the Industrial Revolution, if only in relation to certain occupations. Subsequently it has diminished in prominence, certainly within schools and universities. The general view has come to be that such preparation should properly be left to employers and to other post-school institutions like colleges of further education and polytechnics. It is argued, for example, that introducing significant vocational training into schools would require resources, equipment and expertise which schools rarely possess. It would also run the danger of limiting pupils' occupational horizons prematurely, and – unless great care was taken – it might develop knowledge and skills which would be inappropriate to, or would rapidly become outdated in, a changing labour market. Further, it is pointed out that many of the skills that are most important at work are generic skills like numeracy and literacy; if schools concentrate on these, then they are providing a form of preparation but without closing options unnecessarily.

On the other hand, it is recognised that what the Brunton Report in Scotland felicitously termed the 'vocational impulse' (SED, 1963, p. 24) can be a powerful incentive to learning. Also, unless steps are taken to introduce a wider range of vocational skills into the school curriculum, the effects of schooling may be to establish a bias in favour of the white-collar occupations to which, as was suggested earlier, the academic forms of learning used in schools tend to be most relevant. The result may be to raise aspirations which cannot be met, and to develop attitudes that impede occupational flexibility.

On the whole, however, the tendency until recently has been to limit the extent to which schools have been involved in vocational preparation. The vocational courses set up in many secondary-modern schools in the 1950s to yield the motivational advantages of the 'vocational impulse' largely disappeared with comprehensive reorganisation, and teachers became resistant to them, for reasons already mentioned. Even employers tended on the whole to bear out the findings of the Carr Committee (National Joint Advisory

Council, 1958, p. 23) that 'the overwhelming majority of industries are of the opinion that education given at school before the minimum school-leaving age is reached should be general rather than vocational in character' and should not engage in offering 'some sort of vocational instruction which industry itself is much better qualified to give'. Trade unions, too, consistently opposed vocational education in school, on the grounds that it would operate to the disadvantage of working-class children, who would be bound to be pressurised into forms of work which were more appropriate to their social station than to their innate aptitudes and abilities (Jamieson and Lightfoot, 1982, p. 39). Certainly the evidence from such programmes in the United States indicates that, narrowly defined, they are almost invariably limited to low-attaining students and lower-level occupations, that they restrict access to higher-status and better-paid jobs, and that they accordingly acquire a stigma which limits and in time discredits their appeal (Grubb and Lazerson, 1981). In short, the irony of vocational-preparation programmes is that they tend to deprive their students of access to what in terms of status and income must be regarded as the *real* vocational prizes.

Questions

1. *The extract refers to Bowles and Gintis' argument that there is a 'close correspondence between . . . social relations . . . in the work place and the social relations of the educational system'. With reference to the extract critically present and illustrate this argument.*

(10 marks)

2. *Discuss the advantages and disadvantages of vocational education.*

(15 marks)

3. *'Ability is not the major factor determining occupational status.' Discuss.*

(25 marks)

(This question requires familiarity with additional material – for instance, see sections on education and social class in standard textbooks).

19 Stephen Ball: Pro- and Anti-School Sub-cultures

Stephen Ball's *Beachside Comprehensive* is one of the most recent in an influential series of participant observational studies of the effects of streaming on pupil sub-cultural formation and academic performance. The first of these was David Hargreaves' *Social Relations in a Secondary School* (1967). Hargreaves' work showed how, in the case of Lumley Secondary Modern School, streaming and teacher labelling greatly contributed to the formation of pro- and anti-school sub-cultures. Colin Lacey's study of Hightown Grammar School illustrated the same processes of *differentiation* and *polarisation* there. Both noted that polarisation into separate and antagonistic sub-cultures increased as the boys (both schools were male single sex) proceeded through the schools.

A student of Lacey, Stephen Ball's study generously reflects his tutor's work. A notable difference, however, is that Ball chose a mixed sex school in which to carry out his study. In selecting a comprehensive school Ball completes the trilogy of secondary modern, grammar and comprehensive. Again, streaming or, more precisely, 'banding' of pupils fosters pro- and anti-school sub-cultures. Ball finds that social class plays a significant part in how teachers differentiate pupils. The on-going process of teacher labelling contributed to the hardening of the sub-cultures with band one attracting most of the positive stereotyping, and band two most of the negative. After the first term, little movement between bands occurred and even movement between forms within bands took place mainly on 'social rather than academic grounds'.

In this extract, Ball described sub-cultural formation in the fourth and fifth years. His data suggest a more complex typology of pupil sub-cultural formation than Hargreaves' or Lacey's:

	Pro-school		Anti-school	
1. Supportive	2. Manipulative		1. Passive	2. Rejecting

Still more recent work suggests that, in addition to supportive (pro-school) and rejecting (anti-school) pupils, there are perhaps a majority who are just 'ordinary kids'. Perhaps the groups Ball describes as 'manipulative' and 'passive' could be re-categorised in this way. This line of analysis is developed in Bob Coles' article on recent work on youth (Reading 48).

Reading 19 From Stephen Ball, *Beachside Comprehensive: A Case-Study of Secondary Schooling* (Cambridge University Press, 1981), pp. 116–21.

The fourth and fifth years

Looking back over the first three years of secondary schooling at Beachside, represented in the experience of the two case-study forms, a clear picture emerges of two polarised pupil sub-cultures. In general terms, there is a band 1 pro-school sub-culture which is dominated by values which are positively oriented to the school and to the teachers, and a band 2 and 3 anti-school sub-culture which is dominated by values which are negatively oriented to the school and to the teachers. This, then, is a model essentially similar to those identified by Hargreaves (1967: 162) and Lacey (1970). But it is important to mention that, as Hargreaves notes, 'to posit the existence of such sub-culture is to propose a model or "ideal type" of the school's cultural structure'.

In fact, this general model must be qualified to take into account both the extent of cultural polarisation within forms in each band as well as between bands, and the number of pupils who do not adhere clearly to either set of values, who have been described as ambivalent. As I have attempted to show in the previous chapter, this polarisation and differentiation of sub-cultures is a *process*. It is clear that the bifurcated structure becomes more rigid and more complex over time and also becomes more correlated with academic achievement, but these sub-cultural groups are clearly identifiable at least as early as the second year at Beachside.

However, in this process of evolution in the social life and related cultural affiliations of the pupils, the period during the third year is particularly important as a time of considerable social development for almost all pupils. In particular, it is a time of transition from a clearly home-centred and school-based social life to one that is to a much greater extent independent of both. The impact of this social development on the *school lives* of the pupils is not, however, the same for all. The peer-group cultures to which children belong may, as Bronfenbrenner (1971) suggests, be 'deviant' for all, but in this context they only appeared to become *alternative* cultures for some. Many of the pro-school pupils who were clearly identified by their teachers as 'good pupils' also participated in the trends and tastes of the pop media culture and played in neighbourhood street gangs.

However, it was those pupils who were identified as anti-school by their teachers who increasingly tended to adapt or revert to these systems of commitment as *alternatives* to the culture of the school, their 'anti-schoolness' becoming less school-based and less a manifestation of negative polarity – that is to say, those pupils were no longer dependent upon a reversal of school norms and values as a source of alternative status and opposition. The difference between these anti-school pupils and the pro-school pupils lies in the 'use' made of their environmental cultures within the school, and the degree of insulation between them and the school culture – that is, the extent to which they were 'brought into' the formal school contexts where they would normally have been defined by teachers as irrelevant. In moving on to examine the social organisation of pupils in the fourth and fifth years at Beachside, it is apparent that for some anti-school pupils their involvement in a social life independent of the world of school becomes crucially important in the way in which they order, interpret and handle their experience of schooling.

Out of school, many of these adolescents had jobs, went to pubs and to dances, and were able to make their own decisions or to participate in the decision-making of the social group. They participated in or aspired to much of an 'adult working-class culture'. However, the values of physical prowess, self-determinance and collective behaviour to which they adhered clashed fundamentally with the value-system of the school – academic prowess, long-term goals, subordination, and individual effort in competition with others. That is not to suggest that the pupils who aspired to adult working-class culture did not also *have* long-term goals. The real difference between them and the pro-school pupils lay in their rejection of the school as a means of achieving these goals. Indeed, this would not be irrational, given the lack of success they had thus far experienced at school and the improbability of their achieving future success in school, at least in any way that would objectively change their immediate prospects of employment. These pupils had rejected the long-term goals *of the school*

Some part at least of these pupils' alternative views of themselves, outside their ascribed role as pupil (alternatives which are available to all), derives from the new status attributed to teenagers by the commercial system in recognition of their economic independence and greater social freedom. This contributes to the creation of a conception of self for the pupil which is very different from the child-based conception of the pupil of earlier generations. The school is stressing conformity, uniformity, and the acceptance of the role of compliant pupil (passed down through the paternalistic system: 'teacher knows best'), while outside the normative influence of the teacher-centred school culture, the pressures on the pupils stress an individual freedom of choice and social sophistication that is incompatible with this traditional pupil role. For the pupils who belong to anti-school groups their greater economic and social autonomy outside school takes them out of the cultural world of schooling, and, to use Coleman's (1961) term, they are 'released' into the delinquescent working-class culture of the 'corner boy'. However, the constraints of finishing a compulsory school career maintain these pupils on the periphery of this life-world, especially in that they lack some of the fundamental role-relationships of such a culture, most particularly work-relationships. What appears to be happening here is a complicated set of interactions and accommodations between the media-relayed teenage leisure culture, the dominant adult culture, and the subordinate situated working-class culture.

Conventionally, the sociologists of education have tended to take over the teachers' view of the disruptive anti-school pupil and, with a few recent exceptions, have failed to take into account the pupils' own systems of relevance. Ian Birksted (1976: 74), an anthropologist, provides one of the few views of education from the other side, from the pupils' point of view:

Adolescents whom I did participant observation with inside and outside of school during their fourth and fifth year at a comprehensive, did not see school as an organisational principle of their lives. They evaluated the usefulness to them of exams in terms of their occupation plans for the future. This evaluation governed their perception of the usefulness of school and their performance at school. Thus school achievement and performance can be seen as strategies decided upon by pupils in terms of their perception of ends and means. A group of boys who were seen as hostile by the teachers and who would be classified by sociologists as one of the under-achieving cliques 'that the school most needs to teach', can only be thus labelled by ignoring the logic and meaning of their decisions, strategies and tactics. What school-staff call failure, and colluding educational sociologists call under-achievement, is an externally imposed one-dimensional judgement applied across the board, which does not take into account the reality of each adolescent's plans and personal and socio-cultural meanings.

As in Birksted's study, the anti-school pupils at Beachside who were normally viewed as failures by their teachers, can alternatively be seen as rationally weighing up the value of school in terms of returns to their immediate goals and life plans, accepting those parts of the experience of schooling that they saw as valuable and rejecting the rest. It is only logically reasonable to label these pupils *en bloc* as school failures, if one views them as striving after rewards that the school has to offer. Anti-school pupils at Beachside, by the time they entered their fourth and fifth years, had ceased to be participants in any real sense in the socio-cultural world of schooling. It was apparent that they had come to see school as an alien institution, whose teachers denied them status-rewards, and that access to environmental or latent cultures provided status-alternatives and forms of satisfaction not available to them within the competitive and achievement-oriented school culture. One implication of this must be that the expressive culture of the school, as well as its organisation, is a major factor contributing to the generation of extreme forms of antipathy for, and disaffection from, school. In the fourth and fifth years all the pupils exercise a greater degree of social autonomy and are more involved in adolescent social activities than in the first three years at school. Most of them are beginning to participate as equals in certain areas of adult social life. As I have suggested, their status outside school is changing. For some, this involves a further separation from the culture of the school and the values of their teachers. However, those pupils who continue to accept these values also change status within the school; the greater social maturity attributed to them by the staff often brings them into a closer involvement with the 'world of school'. This usually means greater participation in extra-curricular activities and more informal contacts with the staff. At Beachside this meant participation in drama productions and music, as well as 'social community' activities, fêtes, collecting money for charities, school holidays and trips, school parties and dances, etc. Thus, although the standards set by their adolescent peer-group and the cultures of adolescence become more important for pro-school pupils, so do the standards set by the school and the expectations held by their teachers. In the eyes of the anti-school pupils, the pro-school pupil is low in status and social maturity. In the eyes of their teachers the pro-school pupils are high in status and social maturity, and it is the anti-school pupils who are viewed as immature and socially naïve. The pro-school pupils are often those who are destined for the sixth form, and their school-based social life in the fourth and fifth years can be seen to be an anticipatory socialisation. Once in the sixth form, relationships between pupils and staff become even more informal.

Both Lacey (1970) and Hargreaves (1967) suggest that the latter years of compulsory schooling are likely to witness an increase in the complexity of pupil sub-cultures, especially with regard to the impact of external adolescent, working-class and pop media cultures. But both continue to regard the pro- and anti-sub-cultures that they describe as existing in these latter years as in themselves unitary groups. While both qualify their model of pupil relationships to the extent that some pupils cannot be neatly classified into either sub-cultural extreme, neither suggests that these opposing sub-cultures may themselves become sub-divided and that informal groupings may become differentiated and polarised *within* these aggregate classifications of pro- and anti-school. However, it seems too simplistic to view the outcome of the countervailing pressures of school life and social life in terms of the continuation of merely a bifurcated pro- and anti-school system of polarised sub-cultures. Rather, these pressures or peer groups v. teacher and academic pursuits v. leisure pursuits give rise to a further proliferation of adaptation-strategies *within* the pro- and anti-school divisions. I shall attempt to describe a fourfold classification of such strategies below, but it may be that even this model does not do justice to the pupils' social world. Certainly, for instance, it would be possible to introduce pop media and pop-cult phenomena as further complicating and cross-cutting factors – for example, rock-and-roll, punk-rock, soul, etc.

But even excluding these factors there is a further breakdown of attitudes and friendship allegiance within the pro- and anti-school cultures at Beachside which reflect different kinds of commitments to and rejections of the normative order of the school. These different kinds of commitment and rejection may be classified as follows, in terms of their approximation to the components of the typology of pupils' informal social systems suggested by Lambert *et al.* (1973).

Pro-school

1. Supportive of the formal system. These pupils share normatively in a conception of school as 'education'. This would be similar to Etzioni's 'moral involvement' (1961:66).
2. Manipulative of the formal system. These pupils use features of the formal social system to their own ends. They have a utilitarian view of school and are concerned mainly with a concrete return on the investment of their time and energy, in terms of getting 'exam passes' and 'qualifications'. This would be similar to Etzioni's 'calculative involvement' (1961:66). These pupils' attachment to the school is weak compared with that of the previous group. As indicated by Etzioni, calculative involvement designates an orientation of low intensity, which can be engendered in either positive or negative attitudes towards those in power.

Anti-school

1. Passive. These pupils ignore aspects of the formal structure of schooling, as well as the teachers' authority in particular areas. They maintain a considerable degree of insularity between their private world and the demands of their teachers without resorting to active intransigence.
2. Rejecting. These pupils reject the goals and the authority of the school. This line of adaptation is represented, for instance, by the anti-school pupils in 3TA. It would be similar to Etzioni's 'alienative involvement' (1961:65).

These 'lines of adaptation', and there may be others, may be used to describe the attitudes and behaviour of individual pupils or of particular social groups or friendship groups. Once again, however, it should be said that not every individual can be neatly fitted into one or other of the categories. There are some pupils who display patterns of behaviour appropriate to more than one category. But this must be expected, for, as Lacey (1970) points out, extreme deviance in either a pro- or an anti-school direction leads to unpopularity. Without the reinforcement of a strong peer-group most pupils were *flexible* in both attitude and behaviour. In general terms, however, few pupils at this stage in their school careers see their commitment to school totally in terms of a normative identification with the school culture. Many more tend to view school calculatively, as a provider of negotiable qualifications, and some reject both the values of the school culture and its products.

The changes in values that take place within the pupils' social worlds are concomitant with the changes in the social organisation of friendship discussed in the previous chapter. But the changes in pupils' attitudes and behaviour over this time cannot be explained entirely in terms of greater participation in life-worlds outside school. Factors related to the pupils' continuing experience of school are still of major importance. One of these factors, the processes of option choice and allocation which take place at the end of the third year, is examined in the following chapter. This allocation of pupils to different options is of crucial importance in the comprehensive school, for it is the point of formal structural differentiation in the school careers of comprehensive pupils. It is, as we shall see, as fundamental to their future life-chances as was the 11 plus examination in the tripartite system.

Question

1. (a) *In what circumstances do peer groups provide an* alternative *culture to that of the school?*

(5 marks)

(b) *Describe the alternative basis of cultural values and goals with which anti-school peer groups tend to identify.*

(5 marks)

(Refer also to Reading 20.)

20 Paul Willis: Counter-school Sub-culture and Shop-floor Sub-culture

The general culture of a society is the way of life to which most of its members more or less conform. Whereas functionalists stress the necessity of conformity to cultural norms (normative conformity) so that society can function in an orderly manner, Marxists emphasise that unquestioning conformity favours the wealthy and powerful at the expense of the poor and exploited. Within most cultures, at least most modern cultures, there are groups which live in ways that are sufficiently distinctive from the mainstream to be termed sub-cultures. Class sub-cultures are one example, youth sub-cultures another. Of course, these sub-cultures are never entirely or even substantially cut-off from the dominant culture and, indeed, in the case of upper- and upper-middle-class sub-culture they will tend to be little different from it.

In this extract from *Learning to Labour* Paul Willis writes about working-class sub-culture or, more precisely, working-class-male sub-culture. He is concerned mainly with the workplace but constantly draws parallels between the workplace and the school in terms of the cultural values expressed in each. His method of research is that of ethnography i.e., precise and detailed (participant) observation. Willis finds the following to be characteristic of working-class cultural values and life-style: a cult of masculinity (including more than a smattering of sexism); an ability to gain an immediate control over either the work or, in the case of the 'lads', the school situation; a rough but often witty humour – both verbal (kidding) and physical (the practical joke); a belief that practicalities – the ability to solve 'real' problems – matter more than mere theory. Willis comments that on the last point they are only partially correct because the ability to theorise is a major means of gaining access to the middle class and so to greater power and resources. Realistically, however, most of the 'lads' and their 'dads' know that the middle class does not have room for them and, further, many may still feel class solidarity (identity and loyalty) even in a period when the size of Britain's traditional proletariat is decreasing.

Although some of the vocabulary Willis uses is quite technical, the themes of his presentation are clear.

Reading 20 From Paul Willis, *Learning to Labour. How Working Class Kids Get Working Class Jobs* (Saxon House, 1977), pp. 52–59.

The main emphasis so far has been upon the apparently creative and self-made forms of opposition and cultural style in the school. It is now time to contextualise the counter-school culture. Its points of contact with the wider working class culture are not accidental, nor its style quite independent, nor its cultural skills unique or special. Though the achievements of counter-school culture are specific, they must be set against the larger pattern of working class culture in order for us to understand their true nature and significance. This section is based on fieldwork carried out in the factories where 'the lads' get jobs after leaving school, and on interviews with their parents at home.

In particular, counter-school culture has many profound similarities with the culture its members are mostly destined for – shopfloor culture. Though one must always take account of regional and occupational variations, the central thing about the working class culture of the shopfloor is that, despite harsh conditions and external direction, people do look for meaning and impose frameworks. They exercise their abilities and seek enjoyment in activity, even where most controlled by others. Paradoxically, they thread through the dead experience of work a living culture which is far from a simple reflex of defeat. This is the same fundamental taking hold of an alienating situation that one finds in counter-school culture and its attempt to weave a tapestry of interest and diversion through the dry institutional text. These cultures are not simply layers of padding between human beings and unpleasantness. They are appropriations in their own right, exercises of skill, motions, activities applied towards particular ends.

The credentials for entry into shopfloor culture proper, as into the counter-school culture, are far from being merely one of the defeated. They are credentials of skill, dexterity and confidence and, above all, a kind of presence which adds to, more than it subtracts from, a living social force. A force which is *on the move*, not supported, structured and organised by a formal named institution, to which one may apply by written application.

The masculinity and toughness of counter-school culture reflects one of the central locating themes of shopfloor culture – a form of masculine chauvinism. The pin-ups with their enormous soft breasts plastered over hard, oily machinery are examples of a direct sexism but the shopfloor is suffused with masculinity in more generalised and symbolic ways too. Here is a foundryman, Joey's father, talking at home about his work. In an articulate way, but perhaps all the more convincingly for that, he attests to that elemental, in our

culture essentially masculine, self-esteem of doing a hard job well –
and being known for it:

> I work in a foundry . . . you know, drop forging . . . do you
> know anything about it . . . no . . . well you have the factory
> down in Bethnal St with the noise . . . you can hear it in the
> street . . . I work there on the big hammer . . . it's a six tonner.
> I've worked there twenty-four years now. It's bloody noisy,
> but I've got used to it now . . . and it's hot . . . I don't get
> bored . . . there's always new lines coming and you have to
> work out the best way of doing it . . . You have to keep
> going . . . and it's heavy work, the managers couldn't do it,
> there's not many strong enough to keep lifting the metal . . .
> I earn eighty, ninety pounds a week, and that's not bad, is
> it? . . . It ain't easy like . . . you can definitely say that I earn
> every penny of it . . . you have to keep it up you know. And
> the managing director, I'd say 'hello' to him you know, and
> the progress manager . . . they'll come around and I'll go . . .
> 'Aright' [thumbs up] . . . and they know you, you know . . .
> a group standing there watching you . . . working . . . I like
> that . . . there's something there . . . watching you like . . .
> working . . . like that . . . you have to keep going to get
> enough out.

The distinctive complex of chauvinism, toughness and machismo
on the shopfloor is not anachronistic, neither is it bound to die
away as the pattern of industrial work changes. Rough, unpleasant,
demanding jobs which such attitudes seem most to be associated
with still exist in considerable numbers. A whole range of jobs from
building work to furnace work to deep sea fishing still involve
a primitive confrontation with exacting physical tasks. The basic
attitudes and values most associated with such jobs are anyway still
widely current in the general working class culture, and particularly
in the culture of the shopfloor. The ubiquity and strength of such
attitudes is vastly out of proportion to the number of people actually
involved in heavy work. Even in so-called light industries, or in
highly mechanised factories where the awkwardness of the physical
task has long since been reduced, the metaphoric figures of strength,
masculinity and reputation still move beneath the more varied and
visible forms of workplace culture. Despite the increasing numbers

of women employed, the most fundamental ethos of the factory is still profoundly masculine.

Another main theme of shopfloor culture – at least as I observed and recorded it in the manufacturing industries of the Midlands – is the massive attempt to gain informal control of the work process. Limitation of output or 'systematic soldiering' and 'gold bricking' have been observed from the particular perspective of management from Taylor onwards, but there is evidence now of a much more concerted – though still informal – attempt to gain control. It sometimes happens now that the men themselves to all intents and purposes actually control at least manning and the speed of production. Again this is effectively mirrored for us by working class kids' attempts, with the aid of the resources of their culture, to take control of classes, substitute their own unofficial timetables, and control their own routines and life spaces. Of course the limit to this similarity is that where 'the lads' can escape entirely, 'work' is done in the factory – at least to the extent of the production of the cost of subsistence of the worker – and a certain level of activity is seen as necessary and justified. Here is the father of one of 'the lads', a factory hand on a track producing car engines, talking at home:

Actually the foreman, the gaffer, don't run the place, the men run the place. See, I mean you get one of the chaps says, 'Alright, You'm on so and so today'. You can't argue with him. The gaffer don't give you the job, they swop each other about, tek it in turns. Ah, but I mean the job's done. If the gaffer had gi'd you the job you would . . . They tried to do it one morning, gi'd a chap a job you know, but he'd been on it, you know, I think he'd been on all week, and they just downed tools (. . .) There's four hard jobs on the track and there's dozens that's . . . you know, a child of five could do it, quite honestly, but everybody has their turn. That's organised by the men.

Shopfloor culture also rests on the same fundamental organisational unit as counter-school culture. The informal group locates and makes possible all its other elements. It is the zone where strategies for wresting control of symbolic and real space from official authority are generated and disseminated. It is the massive presence of this informal organisation which most decisively marks off shopfloor culture from middle class cultures of work.

Amongst the workers it is also the basis for extensive bartering, arranging 'foreigners' and 'fiddling'. These are expanded forms of the same thing which take place in school amongst 'the lads'. The informal group on the shopfloor also shows the same attitude to conformists and informers as do 'the lads'. 'Winning' things is as widespread on the shopfloor as theft is amongst the lads, and is similarly endorsed by implicit informal criteria. Ostracism is the punishment for not maintaining the integrity of the world in which this is possible against the persistent intrusions of the formal. Here is the father of another of 'the lads' on factory life:

> A foreman is like, you know what I mean, they're trying to get on, they're trying to get up. They'd cut everybody's throat to get there. You get people like this in the factory. Course these people cop it in the neck off the workers, they do all the tricks under the sun. You know what I mean, they don't like to see anyone crawlin' (. . .) Course instead of taking one pair of glasses [from the stores] Jim had two, you see, and a couple of masks and about six pairs o'gloves. Course this Martin was watching and actually two days after we found out that he'd told the foreman see. Had 'im, Jim, in the office about it, the foreman did, and, (. . .) well I mean, his life hasn't been worth living has it? Eh, nobody speaks to him, they won't give him a light, nobody'll give him a light for his fag or nothin' . . . Well, he won't do it again, he won't do it again. I mean he puts his kettle on, on the stove of a morning, so they knock it off, don't they, you know, tek all his water out, put sand in, all this kind of thing (. . .) if he cum to the gaffer, 'Somebody's knocked me water over', or, er, 'They put sand in me cup' and all this business. 'Who is it then?'. 'I don't know who it is'. He'll never find out who it is.

The distinctive form of language and highly developed intimidatory humour of the shopfloor is also very reminiscent of counter-school culture. Many verbal exchanges on the shopfloor are not serious or about work activities. They are jokes, or 'pisstakes', or 'kiddings' or 'windups'. There is real skill in being able to use this language with fluency: to identify the points on which you are being 'kidded' and to have appropriate responses ready in order to avoid further baiting.

This badinage is necessarily difficult to record on tape or represent, but the highly distinctive ambience it gives to shopfloor exchanges is widely recognised by those involved, and to some extent recreated in their accounts of it. This is another foundry worker, father of one of the Hammertown 'lads', talking at home about the atmosphere on his shopfloor:

> Oh there's all sorts, millions of them [jokes]. 'Want to hear what he said about you', and he never said a thing, you know. Course you know the language, at work like. 'What you been saying about me?' 'I said nothing.' 'Oh you're a bloody liar', and all this.

Associated with this concrete and expressive verbal humour is a well-developed physical humour: essentially the practical joke. These jokes are vigorous, sharp, sometimes cruel, and often hinged around prime tenets of the culture such as disruption of production or subversion of the boss's authority and status. Here is the man who works in a car engine factory:

> They play jokes on you, blokes knocking the clamps off the boxes, they put paste on the bottom of his hammer you know, soft little thing, puts his hammer down, picks it up, gets a handful of paste, you know, all this. So he comes up and gets a syringe and throws it in the big bucket of paste, and it's about that deep, and it goes right to the bottom, you have to put your hand in and get it out . . . This is a filthy trick, but they do it (. . .) They asked, the gaffers asked X to make the tea. Well it's fifteen years he's been there and they say 'go and make the tea'. He goes up the toilet, he wets in the tea pot, then makes the tea. I mean, you know, this is the truth this is you know. He says, you know, 'I'll piss in it if I mek it, if they've asked me to mek it' (. . .) so he goes up, wees in the pot, then he puts the tea bag, then he puts the hot water in (. . .) Y was bad the next morning, one of the gaffers, 'My stomach isn't half upset this morning'. He told them after and they called him for everything, 'You ain't makin' our tea no more'. He says, 'I know I ain't not now'.

It is also interesting that, as in the counter-school culture, many of the jokes circle around the concept of authority itself and around its informal complement, 'grassing'. The same man:

> He [Johnny] says, 'Get a couple of bread pudding Tony [a new worker] we'll have them with our tea this afternoon see. The woman gi'd him some in a bag, he says, 'Now put them in your pocket, you won't have to pay for them when you go past, you know, the till' (. . .) Tony put 'em in his pocket didn't he and walked past with his dinner (. . .) When we came back out the canteen Johnny was telling everybody that he'd [i.e. Tony] pinched two pieces of bread pudding (. . .)he told Fred, one of the foremen see, 'cos Fred knows, I mean . . . Johnny says, 'I've got to tell you Fred', he says, 'Tony pinched two pieces of bread pudding', I mean serious, the way they look you know (. . .) he called Johnny for everything, young Tony did, Fred said, 'I want to see you in my office in twenty minutes', straight-faced you know, serious. Oh I mean Johnny, he nearly cried (. . .) We said, 'It's serious like, you're in trouble, you'll get the sack', you know and all this (. . .) they never laugh. He says, 'What do you think's gonna happen?'. 'Well what can happen, you'll probably get your cards' (. . .) 'Oh what am I gonna do, bleeding Smith up there, he's really done me, I'll do him'. I say, 'Blimey, Tony', I says, 'It ain't right, if other people can't get away with it, why should you 'a' to get away with it'. 'Ooh'. Anyway Fred knocked the window, and he says, 'Tell Tony I want him'. He says, 'You've got the sack now Tony', you know. 'Hope I haven't', he says, 'I dunno what I'm gonna do' (. . .) After they cum out, laughing, I said, 'What did he say to you Tony'. He says, 'He asked me if I pinched two pieces of bread pudding', so I couldn't deny it, I said I had. He says, 'All I want to know is why you didn't bring me two pieces an' all.'

The rejection of school work by 'the lads' and the omnipresent feeling that they know better is also paralleled by a massive feeling on the shopfloor, and in the working class generally, that practice is more important than theory. As a big handwritten sign, borrowed from the back of a matchbox and put up by one of the workers, announces on one shopfloor: 'An ounce of keenness is worth a whole library of certificates'. The shopfloor abounds with apocryphal stories about the idiocy of purely theoretical knowledge. Practical ability always comes first and is a *condition* of other kinds of knowledge. Whereas in middle class culture knowledge and qualifications are seen as a way of shifting upwards the whole mode of practical alternatives open to an individual, in working class eyes theory is riveted to particular productive practices. If it cannot earn its keep there, it is to be rejected. This is Spanksy's father talking at home. The fable form underlines the centrality and routinisation of this cultural view of 'theory'.

> In Toll End Road there's a garage, and I used to work part-time there and . . . there's an elderly fellow there, been a mechanic all his life, and he must have been seventy years of age then. He was an old Hammertown professional, been a professional boxer once, an elderly chap and he was a practical man, he was practical, right? . . . and he told me this (. . .) I was talking to him, was talking about something like this, he says (. . .) 'This chap was all theory and he sends away for books about everything', and he says, 'Do you know', he says, 'he sent away for a book once and it came in a wooden box, and it's still in that box 'cos he can't open it'. Now that in't true, is it? But the point is true. That in't true, that didn't happen, but his point is right. He can't get at that box 'cos he don't know how to open the box! Now what's the good of that?

This can be seen as a clear and usually unremarked class function of knowledge. The working class view would be the rational one were it not located in class society, i.e. that theory is only useful insofar as it really does help to do things, to accomplish practical tasks and change nature. Theory is asked to be in a close dialectic with the material world. For the middle class, more aware of its position in a class society, however, theory is seen partly in its social guise of qualifications as the power to move up the social scale. In this sense theory is well worth having even if it is never applied to nature. It serves its purpose as the *means* to decide precisely which bit of nature one wants to apply it to, or even to choose not to apply it at all. Paradoxically, the working class distrust and rejection of theory comes partly from a kind of recognition, even in the moment that it oppresses, of the hollowness of theory in its social guise.

EDUCATION

Question
1. (a) How do 'the lads' prepare themselves for 'working class' jobs?
(15 marks)
(b) To what extent do schools reinforce 'the lads'' behaviour and expectations?

(10 marks)

Note: You will need to refer to Reading 19 and other sources to answer part (b).

21 Dale Spender: Classroom Interaction and Gender

Until the nineteen eighties, most studies of classroom inter-action focused on teacher stereotyping of pupils on the basis of class. Work by Hargreaves, Lacey and Ball and by Nell Keddie established a tendency among many teachers to favour pupils who reflected their own, middle class values and norms and negatively to label those who did not. Could a similar process be occurring in relation to gender? In the following extract, Dale Spender refers to a range of material which suggests that this is so.

Cultural reproduction – whether of class or gender – is largely an unconscious process. Spender suggests that teachers are probably unaware of the way in which they may reinforce male dominance and female docility. However, she cites data which suggests that sometimes students *do* notice the greater atten-tion boys often get and further supports her case using evidence provided by videos. Teacher and pupil awareness of the problem of gender stereotyping in the classroom is by no means a guarantee that it will be solved. Girls who assert themselves are likely to be labelled 'unladylike', boys who receive less attention as a teacher attempts less gender biased teaching strategies may 'make trouble' or even feel victimised themselves. In a section not included here, Spender goes on to discuss the various attention seeking devices of some male pupils, certain of which border on intimidation. Pointedly, Spender suggests that whatever the solution to patriarchy in the classroom, it does not lie in females aping male behaviour.

154

DALE SPENDER

Reading 21 From Dale Spender, *Invisible Women: The Schooling Scandal*
(Writers and Readers Cooperative, 1982), pp. 54–60.

Historically, men have excluded women. They have proved that
women are inferior and wrong and therefore do not deserve the
same consideration and opportunities as men. Historically men have
interrupted and silenced women and have catered for the interests
of men. But anyone who assumed that this was only history would
be being misled, for this same process continues today in most of
the classrooms of this country, where, in mixed-sex classes, males
are the authority figures, males do the talking, and lessons are
designed to cater for male interests because, as most teachers
acknowledge, if males do not get what they want, they are likely to
make trouble. At this moment, female students are being dismissed
in class in exactly the same way as their foremothers have been
dismissed, and the experience of women is no more likely to be the
substance of the curriculum in a mixed-sex school than the experience of women has been the substance of our social knowledge.

It is not difficult to establish who gets the teachers' attention in
class, and numerous studies report that boys get most of it in mixed-
sex classrooms (see Sears and Feldman, 1976, for an overview of
this, and Birgit Brock-Utne, n.d.). But while it has been known for
a long time that boys get so much more attention from teachers
than do girls, not surprisingly, few attempts have been made to
explain this phenomenon or to speculate on its significance: in a
society where men are perceived as more important such statistics
can simply serve to confirm what we already know about male
'supremacy' and are therefore taken for granted rather than made
the subject of further enquiry.

Teachers themselves are very often unaware of the way they
allocate their time and it is not uncommon to ask teachers whether
they give more attention to one sex than the other, and to have
them vehemently protest that they do *not* and that they treat both
sexes equally. But when their next lesson is taped it is often found
that over two-thirds of their time was spent with the boys who
comprised less than half of the class. Most teachers do not
consciously want to discriminate against girls, they say they do want
to treat the sexes fairly, but our society and education is so structured that 'equality' and 'fairness' mean that males get more attention (see Spender, 1981, a).

If the teachers do not know that they give more attention to boys, and more *positive* attention that enhances the image of boys, the students *do* know. In her recent study in Cambridge, Michelle Stanworth (1981) asked the students who it was who received the attention in class and what sort of attention they received and the students indicated that it was overwhelmingly boys who received the attention and who were given the knowledge that they were important and liked.

In classroom discussion, said the students, boys predominated: for every four boys who participated, there was only one girl. When teachers asked questions they asked two boys to every one girl, and when teachers provided praise and encouragement three boys received it to every one girl. And in these classes there were more girls than boys.

The students themselves provided the data that the boys asked twice as many questions as the girls and made twice as many demands of the teachers' time. And both the boys and the girls stated that teachers are more concerned about boys, they consider boys more conscientious and capable, they get on better with the boys, they enjoy teaching the boys more and are twice as likely to consider boys the model pupils (Stanworth, 1981).

Despite what teachers may think or say they are doing, from the perspective of female and male students there is consensus that boys are considered more important, more authoritative, more deserving and worthy of attention, and this knowledge possessed by the students adds to the confidence of the boys (who go on to say more and demand more attention) and undermines the confidence of the girls (who react by saying less and by attracting less attention). These are the lessons learnt in the classroom from kindergarten to college.

Teachers who teach the lesson that boys are more important than girls are not debased and cruel individuals who are deliberately trying to create or reproduce a sexist society: on the contrary many can be consciously trying to combat sexism. When I and many others have actively tried to change our patterns of behaviour in the classroom, when we have tried to change the proportion of time spent with the girls, the curriculum materials we use, the topics we set for discussion, we have often been spectacularly unsuccessful and for numerous reasons (see also Elizabeth Sarah, *Interaction in the Classroom*).

One reason is that sexism is so pervasive and embedded in our ways of looking at the world that we are sometimes unaware of the extent to which it controls our actions so that even when we feel that we are being just and fair, or even showing 'favouritism' to the girls, empirical evidence can indicate otherwise. Because we take it so much for granted that boys are more important and deserve more of our time and attention, giving the girls 35% of our time can feel as if we are being unfair to the boys.

While it is 'normal' to devote most of our efforts to boys, then even giving slightly more than one third of our attention to the girls seems to be a significant intervention and feels like making an effort to achieve equality.

I have taped many lessons that I and other teachers of mixed-sex classes have taught and there have been numerous occasions when the explicit aim has been to spend an equal amount of time with both sexes. At the end of the lesson I have felt that I managed to achieve that goal – sometimes I have even thought I have gone too far and have spent *more* time with the girls than the boys. But the tapes have proved otherwise. Out of ten taped lessons (in secondary school and college) the maximum time I spent interacting with girls was 42% and on average 38%, and the minimum time with boys 58%. It is nothing short of a substantial shock to appreciate the discrepancy between what I *thought* I was doing and what I actually *was* doing.

Other teachers have also been reasonably confident that they have achieved their aim of allocating their time equally between the sexes only to find when the tapes have been analysed, that spending approximately 38% of their time with girls feels like *compensating* the girls, feels like artificially constructed equality.

'I was so conscious of trying to spend more time with the girls that I really thought I had overdone it' one teacher said in amazement when she listened to the evidence of the tape and worked out that in her interaction with the students only 36% of her time had been spent with girls. 'But I thought I spent more time with the girls' said another who found that she had given them 34% of her attention, 'and', she added 'the boys thought so too. They were complaining about me talking to the girls all the time.'

It should not be surprising that the students should share a similar notion of fairness with their teachers, for we are all members of the same society which accords more significance to males. In the classrooms where teachers were trying to allocate their time equally, their efforts did not go unnoticed by the students, and despite the fact that the teachers were unsuccessful, and were able to spend only slightly more than one third of their time with the girls, many of the boys protested that slightly more than one third was unfair, and that they were missing out on their *rightful* share of teacher attention.

'She always asks the girls all the questions' said one boy in a classroom where 34% of the teacher's time had been allocated to girls. 'She doesn't like boys and just listens to the girls' said another boy where boys had interacted with the teacher for 63% of the time; and these are among some of the more 'polite' protests. From this it would seem that in a sexist society boys assume that two thirds of the teacher's attention constitutes a fair deal and if this ratio is altered so that they receive less than two thirds of the teachers' attention they feel they are being discriminated against.

Many exercised pressure on their teachers in the classroom but some even went further and either complained, or threatened to complain, to those in authority, about the preferential treatment girls were receiving when allocated more than one third of the teachers' time. And this is another reason that teachers are unable to give an equal allocation of time to the sexes – many of the boys are against it, they make trouble and they get results.

Every teacher must try to gain the interest and co-operation of the class. There is only one teacher and many students, and if there is to be 'order' as it is generally understood, then teachers are usually in the position of trying to utilise the interest and goodwill of those whom they are required to teach. In today's classrooms, the point of view of students is often taken into account – in some areas – far more than is generally acknowledged and it makes common sense to many teachers to enlist the co-operation of their students.

But many males will co-operate only when it is their interests that are taken into account. This means that teachers are not always free to introduce either the forms of discussion or materials they would like. Rather than catering for the class as a whole, in mixed-sex classrooms they may find that they are being manipulated by a group of boys who will engage in uncooperative and disruptive behaviour if they do not get material they find interesting.

This raises the question of what is interesting in general in our society. It has already been established that knowledge about women is not valued – is not considered interesting or significant except by a few funny feminists – and therefore, even if knowledge about women were readily available it would not serve the purpose of claiming the attention of the respect of some boys. On the contrary, introducing knowledge about women (and trying to spend more time in interaction with female students) is more likely to result in a riot than in reasoning.

What is considered inherently interesting is knowledge about men. Because men control the records, and the value system, it is generally believed that it is men who have done all the exciting things: it is men who have made history, made discoveries, made inventions and performed feats of skill and courage – according to men. These are the important activities and only men have engaged in them, so we are led to believe. And so it is that the activities of men become the curriculum.

Making male knowledge the substance of the curriculum is a multifaceted process. A part is played by those who determine what the values of society will be, a part is played by the policy makers and a part is played by the researchers who produce knowledge about men; but a part is also played by male students in mixed-sex classrooms who insist that their interests be catered for – often exclusively. Many teachers can document what happens in a mixed-sex classroom where boys are not the focus of attention – there is trouble!

If boys do not get what they want then many of them are likely to be uncooperative and in a sexist society their lack of co-operation is often expressed in sexist ways. In a society where males are expected to be aggressive, to be authoritative, forceful and masterful, then in many respects boys are only doing what is expected of them if they act in an aggressive manner when registering their protests. Many teachers and students see it as quite legitimate for boys to make trouble, to prevent others from participating, to impose their values on others who may not share them, if they do not get what they want.

'The boys get upset if we try to talk about girls' things' said one female student, 'I suppose it's only right really.' When I asked her whether the girls got upset about having to do only boys' things she said, 'It's not the same. We don't mind doing their things. Sometimes we get upset but we don't say much.' When girls are required to do 'boys' things' they don't make as much noise, they don't mount the same disruptive protests. Girls do not impose their values on the boys, nor do they manipulate the teachers in this way.

Because teaching is so closely allied with classroom control in our society (an arrangement which might be altered if women were to have a say) teachers simply cannot afford to have a classroom of unruly boys who are not interested in the lesson and who are bent on causing trouble. The boys get the results – the lessons are directed towards them!

When Katherine Clarricoates (1978) interviewed primary teachers they provided clear evidence that they geared their classes to the interests of boys (despite the fact that they also claimed they treated the sexes equally) because that was the only way the class could be controlled.

'Boys are more difficult to control' said one teacher. 'Yes' said another 'they're ever so lively and boisterous.'
'It's important to keep their attention . . . otherwise they play you up something awful.'

'The boys are more difficult to settle down to their work . . . they don't seem to have the same self discipline as the girls do, so it's important to direct the subject at them.'

'I'd tend to try and make the topic as interesting as possible so that the boys won't lose their concentration and start fidgeting . . .'

'It's a bit harder to keep the boys' attention during a lesson . . . at least that's what I've found so I gear the subject to them more than I do the girls who are good at paying attention in class'. (Clarricoates, 1978; pp. 356–357).

This is part of the significance of teacher attention being directed to boys. This is why *teachers give them more attention and offer them more praise and encouragement, and why boys talk more, make more demands, question and challenge more.* This is the process *whereby the* male *experience becomes the* classroom *experience, whereby education duplicates the patterns of the wider society.*

For girls who are expected to be dependent and docile, any objections they may have to being inculcated in the male experience can take a different form. Their failure to co-operate can lead to withdrawal, to either 'getting on with the work' and not expecting it to be meaningful or interesting, or to quietly opting out in the corner. Either way, such behaviour of the girls is not likely to be seen as evidence that teachers cannot control their classes, for in most classrooms it is the noise level which is used as the criterion for teacher efficiency, and inside and outside education it is the male who makes the more noise.

The students know that girls are expected to be quiet and docile (and this has numerous consequences) and when Angele Parker (1973) questioned students, both sexes stated that asking questions, challenging the authority of teachers, demanding reasons and explanations – in short behaving in an active way in the classroom – was a masculine activity. And both sexes know that girls who do not conform to these expectations are likely to be punished.

Over and over again my own research has exposed the double standard which operates in the classroom. When boys ask questions, protest, or challenge the teacher (or other students) they are often met with respect and rewards; when girls engage in exactly the same behaviour they are often met with punishment and rebuke. For boys who demand attention and explanations there is *not even a term in the language* to label their undesirable behaviour, but there is for girls – they are unladylike! It is expected that boys should stand up for themselves, that they should assert themselves, and even if and when this may be inconvenient for a teacher, it is behaviour from boys that is still likely to be viewed positively. After all, boys will be boys!

It is not expected that girls should act in an independent manner, and if they do, their behaviour is frequently seen as inappropriate, is viewed negatively, and in many cases is classified as 'a problem'.

Teachers can continue to treat their students in this sexually differentiated way and at the same time report their behaviour as fair and just, precisely because in our society males are perceived as more important. It feels fair and just to pay more attention to males, to accord more significance to their behaviour and more legitimacy to their demands. In a society where it is normal for males to receive preferential treatment, it is also normal to provide such preferential treatment in school.

EDUCATION

Question

*1. (a) What evidence is given in the extract that male pupils tend to
receive more of the teacher's attention than female pupils?*
(5 marks)
*(b) The following quotation is from the extract: 'In a society where
it is normal for males to receive preferential treatment, it is also
normal to provide such preferential treatment in school'. Explain
and comment on this statement.*
(20 marks)

**22 A. H. Halsey et al.: Theories of Cultural Capital (Bourdieu)
and the Liberal Idea of Equality of Opportunity**

The following extract from the concluding chapter of *Origins
and Destinations* falls into two distinct parts. First, Halsey offers
an empirically grounded refutation of theories that the
educational system serves merely to reproduce existing cultural
advantage (or 'capital' in Bourdieu's terms). Second, he presents
three definitions of equality of opportunity and examines how
far any of them have been achieved in the British educational
system between the 1930s and 1960s.

There is no doubt that in attacking theories of cultural reproduction, Halsey's main target is French Marxist sociologist,
Pierre Bourdieu. The latter argues that the educational system
and the qualifications it bestows help to legitimate (justify) and
reproduce a class society. Halsey concludes that as far as Britain
is concerned although cultural capital influences selection for
secondary school, afterwards it is of 'minimal' importance. He
argues that the material aspects of class are much more significant in explaining inequality of educational achievement. Finally,
in the first section, he calculates the wastage of talent caused
by class disadvantage.

In the second part of this extract in which Halsey discusses
equality of educational opportunity, he continues the theme of
class disadvantage in education. His crucial third definition of
equality of educational opportunity is that there should be equal
access to superior forms of education for children of similar
intelligence, regardless of class *in fact* as well as in law. He
concludes that such is not the case. In referring to secondary

education he writes pessimistically that: 'This picture of unequal access to the superior secondary schools has remained depressingly constant over time'.

The educational disadvantage of the working class is cumulative in that proportionately more working- than middle-class children leave full-time education at each 'exit-point' (for example, post 'O' level/CSE or post 'A' level). However, for those that do survive, the effects of material or secondary class inequality become less, the longer they remain in the educational system. Nevertheless, as Halsey is aware, this is scant comfort, given that the survivors are relatively so few.

One or two of Halsey's terms need explaining. The 'service class' is the professional, managerial, technical and administrative middle class. HMC is short for Head Masters' Conference – HMC public schools tend to be more elite ones. A few statistical terms such as 'logistic curve' occur in the extract. These references can be ignored without detracting significantly from the sense of the passage.

Reading 22 From A. H. Halsey *et al.*, *Origins and Destinations: Family, Class, and Education in Modern Britain* (Clarendon Press, 1980), pp. 198–205.

Our fundamental theoretical concern has been with the question of whether education can change the class character of childhood. A strong strand in liberal traditions of political and social thought is that it can. We began this book with a recognition of the cautious optimism of political arithmeticians on this issue.

But against the optimism of the liberal educational reformers has to be set the pessimism of the Left and the Right. On the Left writers such as Bourdieu have argued that the educational system serves merely to reproduce the distribution of cultural capital. Those who can receive what the school has to give are those who already are endowed with the requisite cultural attributes – with the appropriate cultural capital. A parallel argument comes from the Right. Bantock argues that many working-class children are 'for cultural reasons likely to be inhibited from gaining the best of what is offered them even if they were to be offered "Chances" in these terms; and this because they have already been formed by historical socio-cultur forces which make the segment of "high" culture for them meaningless.' Their political differences do not prevent them from arriving at the same hypothesis: the culture of the working class (as opposed to their measured IQ or material circumstances) will inhibit them from taking advantage of what the school has to offer.

To test this hypothesis we looked first at the proportion of 'first-generation' grammar- and technical-school boys. In our sample as a whole, the great majority of those who attended selective secondary schools came from homes where both parents had been to non-selective schools. Eighty per cent of boys at the technical schools and two-thirds of those at the grammar schools came from homes with no tradition of formal academic schooling. Even at the apex of the educational system, 88 per cent of the boys at university came from families in which neither parent was a graduate, and 41 per cent from homes in which neither parent had been to selective schools. The state system of education, therefore, gave 'superior' education to vast numbers of boys from 'uneducated' homes. It is the dissemination rather than the reproduction of cultural capital that is more apparent here. And even within the private sector there has been a large minority of boys from these less educated backgrounds. Only the independent HMC schools could really be said to maintain a 'cycle of privilege' in which cultural capital is reproduced among those from educated homes.

In other words, the educational system has undoubtedly offered chances of securing cultural capital to large numbers of boys to whom the ethos of the grammar and technical schools was new. But did 'historical socio-cultural forces' mean that these chances were largely spurious, that there was *formal* but not *effective* opportunity for these first-generation grammar-school boys? The answer is an unequivocal No. As we have noted, two-thirds of our respondents at grammar school were 'first generation', and two-thirds of these went on to secure some kind of academic credential. Moreover, their chances of success were very little different from those of second-generation grammar-school boys. The kind of education which the parents had received was of little value as a predictor of success or failure in the grammar schools.

It might be objected that our use of the variable 'parental education' does scant justice to the notion of cultural capital, but another method yields the same result. We used path analysis in Chapter 9 to explore the determinants of educational attainment, incorporating two measures of family background which we labelled 'material circumstances' and 'family climate' respectively. Our estimates of the effects of material circumstances are based on multiple correlations between the various dependent variables and a group of five measured independent variables: father's class, domestic amenities, owner occupation, council-house tenancy, and number of siblings. In contrast, 'family climate' is a hypothetical variable representing all those sources of similarity between certain measured specified characteristics of brothers that have not been captured by the material circumstances variable. It could represent parental interest and encouragement, linguistic competence, genetic endowment, or indeed income, in so far as these factors are not picked up by the variables in the 'material circumstances' group. 'Family climate' is thus a rag-bag, but it is a capacious rag-bag which is likely to provide ample room for the variables which Bourdieu and Bantock have in mind, in so far as these are distinct and separable from social class: and if they are not separable from social class, their arguments reduce to triviality. It will give us then an estimate of the *maximum* effect which the parents' cultural capital is likely to have on the respondents' cultural capital.

The results are clear. Cultural capital influences selection for secondary school but thereafter its importance is minimal. The effect of 'family climate' on the respondent's school-leaving age or examination success is wholly indirect, being mediated by type of secondary school and, to a lesser extent, by IQ. Among boys who attended the *same* type of secondary school 'family climate' does not discriminate between the academic successes and failures. IQ is slightly better as a discriminator, and 'material circumstances' better still, although we should note that none of these variables, not even 'material circumstances', is a particularly powerful discriminator among boys within a given type of school.

At all events, it would seem to be class, not culture or IQ, which is the more important source of, for example, early leaving from grammar school. Our evidence holds no comfort for those who would believe that class differences in educational attainment reflect a fair distribution of opportunities to those with the intellectual ability or cultural capacity to profit therefrom.

We can go further still. Our evidence suggests that 'the pool of ability' – the number of children with the capacity to obtain O-Levels, A-Levels, or university degrees – was larger than is usu?l' supposed. We have tested a theory of the demand for edµ' which assumes that the numbers staying on to take O-Levels and A-Levels would continue to grow until all those believed by themselves and their teachers to have the ability to qualify in fact do so. The theory predicts that the demand for education will follow a logistic curve, a curve shaped like an elongated S, and that the demand will be saturated when the 'pool of ability' is exhausted. Though the dangers of extrapolation must again be emphasised, logistic curves derived from this theory explain 99 per cent of the variance and predict that eventually 80,000 boys each year would stay at school until the age of 17 and 55,000 to the age of 18. In comparison, however, official figures show that by the end of our period the actual numbers staying on were of the order of 73,000 and 48,000 respectively. Wastage of talent therefore continues and was massive over most of the period with which we have been concerned. Given that by the 1970s the number of boys obtaining at least one A-Level was actually somewhat larger than the number staying on until eighteen, we may reasonably conclude, assuming current conceptions of educability, that *at least* 7,000 boys each year could have obtained A-Level passes but were not in fact remaining at school long enough to do so. Further back in time, of course, the wastage was much greater. In the early 'sixties it was running at an annual rate of around 30,000, and in the early 'fifties it would have been well over 40,000.

These figures bring out clearly the enormous strides that have been made since the Second World War in the provision of sixth-form education, but this past progress cannot be a source of current complacency. We have shown that the chances of becoming an undergraduate have declined for boys with A-levels. Two-thirds of them went on to university in the 'fifties, but only half of them did so in the 'sixties. The expansion of the universities failed to keep pace with the expansion of the sixth forms – a reminder of one of the recurrent features of the British educational system – inequity between generations caused by educational inflexibility. Able children unfortunate enough to have been born in years of baby boom were at a serious disadvantage in the competition for university places compared with their siblings born a few years earlier or later.

At university level, then, there is a double wastage. There are the children who could have obtained A-Levels, but failed to stay at school long enough. And there are the children who obtained A-Levels but failed to find a university place because of the unresponsiveness of our system to changes in the demand for education. Our evidence also shows that much of this was a wastage of working-class talent. We found in Chapter 8 that the service class demand for sixth-form education had already reached saturation level by the end of our period. Thirty-eight per cent of the service class were already staying on until the age of 18 in our predicted saturation level. Assuming that these were the cleverest 38 per cent of the service class, then boys with measured IQ at least as low as 113 were staying on until 18 and obtaining A-Levels. Our IQ assumptions entail that 14 per cent of working-class boys had measured IQ scores above 113, but only 6 per cent in fact stayed on until 18. It follows that the proportion of working-class boys reaching A-Level, and *pari passu* securing places at university, could comfortably be doubled without any necessary lowering of standards. At the time that our youngest cohort was of university age, the working class was obtaining less than half the number of places which, by service-class standards, it was entitled to.

Equality of opportunity

So far then, our retrospective view is that the optimists rather than the pessimists deserve support. The optimism in question has been essentially liberal. But the main legacy of the liberal tradition is, of course, a combined intention and prediction that modernising the education system would mean realising the principle of equality of opportunity. This educational policy, it might reasonably be demanded, should be evaluated in the terms of the liberal tradition in which it was formed. However, equality of opportunity is a phrase with many different meanings. A minimal definition of it can be described as formal equality of opportunity with the implication that no legal barrier exists to prevent a child from entering any form of education in the way that Jews were once kept out of Oxford and Cambridge, or black Africans are excluded from white South African universities. In this minimal sense formal equality of opportunity existed in the British schools throughout our period. The real debate, at least in the years before 1944, turned on strengthening the definition to take account of inequalities of circumstances, and especially financial ones. It was these, whether in the form of school fees or earnings foregone where boys stayed on beyond the statutory leaving age, that were in dispute: and the 1944 Act brought the final elimination of fee paying in state selective secondary schools. If, therefore, we define equality of opportunity in a second way to include the elimination of financial barriers then the reduction of these through the expansion of free places before 1944 and their total abolition after 1944 was clear progress towards equality of opportunity. At the same time, however, the existence of the private sector at both primary and secondary level, and the absence of maintenance grants for secondary-school children beyond the statutory school-leaving age, prevented full realisation of this stronger definition of the ideal aimed at through liberal reform.

It is also important and relevant to this second definition of equality of opportunity to notice the financial implications of a developing non-financial selective system. As we have seen, the 1944 Act continued the growth of selective secondary schooling and, particularly in the 1960s, there was expansion of higher education on a selective basis. The costs of the different forms of education have been such that success in the selective process did not diminish but, if anything, widened the distance between those who got most and those who got least out of the public purse towards the cost of their schooling.

Given, then, that the selective stakes became, if anything, higher it is all the more crucial to note the actual distribution between social classes of educational costs, educational experience and examination results. In consequence, the third definition of equality of opportunity on which we have concentrated is one which compares the relative chances of access to schools and qualifications which were, *substantively* as distinct from *formally*, open to the children of different social classes. In effect, taking the word 'equality' to have its normal meaning in common speech, the definition now shifts from equality of opportunity to equality of outcome.

This third meaning of equality of opportunity in the sense of equality of access to superior forms of education yields a much less comforting picture. At the secondary-school stage access has been more unequal at the higher levels of the academic hierarchy as we have defined it. Class differentials are most extreme in the case of the independent HMC schools; a boy from the service class had nearly forty times the chance of his working-class peer of entering one of these schools. In the case of the Direct Grant schools his chance was twelve times as good, and in that of the grammar schools it was three times as good. Only in the technical schools has there been equality of class chances, and even this apparently more equitable distribution of opportunity has had much more to do with their lower standing in the academic pecking order than with the fairness of their methods of selection; relatively few boys from the service class went to the technical schools simply because so many had already gone to notionally superior secondary schools.

In general, then, class chances of access vary according to position in the academic hierarchy. The only clear exception is that of the minor independent schools. We have ranked these below the grammar schools (a position confirmed by their O-Level and A-Level records), but the service-class boy had nearly eighteen times the chance of the working-class boy of securing a place at one. Another possible exception is that of the major independent schools. We placed these at the head of the academic hierarchy. Though on most criteria of academic achievement they are virtually indistinguishable from the Direct Grant schools, they are socially far more exclusive. The private schools represent a bastion of class privilege compared with the relatively egalitarian state sector. The hybrid Direct Grant schools, before they were abolished, uncomfortably straddled the divide.

Class differentials in access are necessarily reflected in school differences of class composition. Only the technical schools contained anything resembling a representative cross-section of the population, while the HMC schools remained socially the most exclusive. About 90 per cent of those at the private schools came from the service and intermediate classes. In contrast, over one-third of boys in the state grammar schools came from the working class. Admittedly, the grammar schools may have served more to assimilate these working-class boys into middle-class life and culture than to break down class boundaries, but the social experience they offered must undoubtedly have been significantly different from that of the private sector. Tawney's judgement accordingly retains its force:

A special system of schools, reserved for children whose parents have larger bank accounts than their neighbours, exists in no other country on the same scale as in England. It is at once an educational monstrosity and a grave national misfortune. It is educationally vicious, since to mix with companions from homes of different types is an important part of the education

169

of the young. It is socially disastrous for it does more than any other single cause, except capitalism itself, to perpetuate the division of the nation into classes of which one is almost unintelligible to the other.

This picture of unequal access to the superior secondary schools has remained depressingly constant over time. For the selective secondary schools as a group, chances of access rose at all levels of the class structure in the middle of our period, leading to some slight narrowing of class differentials, but they then fell back again to levels very like those of a generation earlier. Thus the likelihood of a working-class boy receiving a selective education in the mid 'fifties and 'sixties was very little different from that of his parents' generation thirty years earlier.

If we disaggregate selective schooling into its component types of school, however, we find a more complex pattern. Chances of private schooling traced the inverted U that was followed by selective schools as a whole. Twenty-six per cent of the service class attended some form of private secondary school – HMC, non-HMC, and Direct Grant – in our earliest cohort. This percentage crept up to 27 and then to 29 in the succeeding two cohorts, only to fall back to 25 among the most recent cohort. The working-class percentage followed a parallel but lower path, starting at 0.5, rising to 2.3, and falling back to 1.1

With the grammar and technical schools, on the other hand, an inverted J rather than an inverted U provides a better picture of the path. Grammar-school chances steadily improved for all three social classes among the first three cohorts, followed by small and uneven retrogression in the final cohort. As a result, class differentials narrowed appreciably; in the first cohort the service-class boy's chance was over four times that of his working-class contemporary, but in the final cohort it was little more than twice as high. But what was given to the grammar schools was taken away from the technical schools. Here the inverted J is turned the other way round. Small increases at the beginning of our period were followed by a long and steady decline, and what the working class gained through the expansion of the grammar schools, they largely lost through the decline of the technical schools. Over the period as a whole 100 working-class families sent an extra eight boys to grammar schools, but eight fewer to technical schools.

So much, then, for patterns of entry to the secondary schools. But what of exit? The short answer is that class differentials widen at each rung up the educational ladder. The boy from the working class was much more likely than his service-class contemporary to drop out of school as soon as the minimum leaving age was reached, was less likely to continue his school career into the sixth form, and less likely to enter a university or some other form of education after school. As we have shown, there was persistent class difference in survival rates, and inequalities thus increased. A service-class boy in our sample was four times as likely as his working-class peer to be found at school at the age of 16, eight times as likely at the age of 17, ten times as likely at the age of 18, and eleven times as likely to enter a university.

On the other hand, despite the continuing class differences, survival rates also show a tendency to converge. The secondary effects of stratification, as Boudon termed them, although reasserting themselves on each higher rung of the educational ladder, do so with less and less vigour. For the school population as a whole, the biggest difference is at the minimum school-leaving age; over three-quarters of our working-class respondents dropped out at this stage whereas about three-quarters of those from the service class stayed on. But at the gate of the university the gap narrowed appreciably. Of those who had survived long enough in the educational system to secure at least one A-Level or Higher School Certificate, 63 per cent from the service class went on to university, while the working-class percentage was not so greatly lower at 53 per cent. *For those who survive*, inequalities of opportunity are much reduced, although not entirely eliminated. They are, however, a small and select band. Less than one in forty of our working-class respondents acquired Higher School Certificate or an A-Level pass compared with one in four from the service class. The convergence of the survival rates, therefore, occurs too late in the school career to be relevant to more than a tiny handful of working-class children. Inequalities of opportunity have already done their damage at earlier stages of the school career.

However, patterns of exit from the secondary schools offer a slightly more encouraging trend than patterns of entry. Sustained expansion replaces the inverted U. The picture is at its most encouraging if we focus on the percentage staying on until 16 or later. In the earliest cohort a boy from the service class had nearly six times the chance of his working-class contemporary of being found in school at the age of 16: in the final cohort his chance was less than three times as high. But even this optimism must be tempered by the finding that while the *rate of increase* was greater for the working class, their *absolute* gains were less. Thus for every 100 working-class boys there were an extra twenty-two staying on until 16 or later by the end of our period; but for every 100 service-class boys there were an extra twenty-six staying on. In this sense, then, the difference between the classes had actually widened until, in 1974, the raising of the school-leaving age brought statutory equalisation.

The proportion of 18 year olds staying on at school again shows steady expansion with larger absolute gains going to the service class. An extra twenty-two service-class boys for every 100 stayed on till 18, but for the working class the increment was a meagre three per 100. In consequence, relative chances as well as the absolute differences widened.

In summary, school inequalities of opportunity have been remarkably stable over the forty years which our study covers. Throughout, the service class has had roughly three times the chance of the working class of getting some kind of selective secondary schooling. Only at 16 has there been any significant reduction in relative class chances, but even here the absolute gains have been greater for the service class. If the 'hereditary curse upon English education is its organisation upon lines of social class', that would seem to be as true in the 1960s as it was in 1931 when Tawney wrote.

Questions
1. *In Halsey's view, what disadvantages working class children most — cultural or material 'deficit'?*

(5 marks)

2. *(a) Define equality of opportunity.*

(5 marks)

(b) To what extent is there equality of educational opportunity in Britain?

(20 marks)

SECTION 5

Social Class

Readings 23–29

An understanding of social class must still begin with the primary analysis of Marx and Weber and for this the student is referred back to Readings 2 and 3. Where next to go for theoretical enlightenment is less obvious. I have chosen to begin this section with a pair of readings, one of which sharply departs from Marxist class analysis whilst the other discusses Marxist ruling class theory sympathetically, if critically.

Probably the two dominant theories of social structure and change in the post-war period are modernisation theory (or the theory of industrial society) and Marxism (in a number of varieties). There is a relationship between modernisation theory and Functionalism, but the parcelling up of the teaching of sociology into separate 'perspectives' has served to obscure some of the major points of agreement and disagreement between these two approaches. There is no need to offer an 'idiot-guide' to Marxism here, but some readers may not be familiar with the theory of industrial society. The following is a summary of its main points drawn from an analysis by Anthony Giddens (*Sociology: A Brief but Critical Introduction*, Macmillan, 1982):

1. The transition from 'traditional societies' to 'modern societies' is the way in which change in the contemporary world is conceptualised.
2. The transition from traditional to industrial society is a progressive historical movement, particularly in the increase in equality of opportunity.
3. Class conflict in advanced industrial society is increasingly abating.
4. The rise of liberal democracy is seen as a compatible, if not essential, element accompanying the transition from tradition to modernity.
5. All industrial societies, including Communist, tend to

173

develop important similarities (especially in organisation and stratification). This is known as 'convergence theory'.

6. The traditional industrial society model is applied to analysing the 'underdeveloped' world which is seen as needing 'development'. This is usually termed 'modernisation theory'. (See Section 8, especially Readings 35 and 39).

In the case of the first two readings, the student has to judge whether Dahrendorf or Scott's account is more correct. Has class conflict declined with the onset of 'industrial society', as Dahrendorf maintains, or is it still the fundamental structural reality of 'capitalist society'? as John Scott suggests.

The third reading is included for its simplicity (despite some jargon) and contemporary relevance. The authors, John Rentoul and Andrew Lumsden, crudely divide mid-eighties Britain into three groups – the very rich, the mass of comfortably and getting better off, and the poor (mostly becoming relatively worse off). This analysis is presented with no theoretical justification but it provides a useful perspective on contemporary class divisions and inequality. Most of the detail of the article describes the wealth and life-style of the rich and the leading role of the royal family among them.

To attempt a clear exposition of what Anthony Giddens refers to as 'the problem of the "new middle" class' is to risk burial in a theoretical quagmire. The 'problem' is whether the 'new' or 'non-capitalist' middle class is more correctly categorised as middle or working class, or neither. Giddens differentiates the 'new middle class' from the working class but also finds important differences within the 'new middle class' itself. For instance, he sharply differentiates between higher professionals and the less well-paid and lower status white collar employees ranging from nurses to laboratory assistants.

In Reading 27 Mike Saks discusses neo-Weberian and Marxist analyses of the class position and social contribution of professionals. Saks touches on issues such as whether professionals mainly serve themselves or 'the community' and the relationship of professionals to capital and government.

Twenty years ago (1966), David Lockwood categorised the working class into deferential traditionalist, proletarian tradition-

RALF DAHRENDORF

alist and privatised workers. Marxists would deny that the divisions between these groups were (or are) as deep as Lockwood suggested but few would debate the importance of his insight and observations. Lockwood focused on a key 'figure' in post-war social and political development – the privatised, instrumental worker. The cultural preferences and political behaviour of privatised workers are emerging as central to the kind of society Britain is becoming.

One reading on the working class is, of course, quite insufficient. The following section on Inequality and Poverty (Section 6) continues with issues related to the working class, and Section 10 is also largely concerned with this topic. Similarly, the stratification of women requires more analysis than the single reading given here. Section 7 rights the balance.

23 Ralf Dahrendorf: The Decomposition of Capital and the Decomposition of Labour – Industrial rather than Capitalist Society?

The rather long-winded title of this section is intended to convey that Dahrendorf has extremely important, if controversial, things to say about the nature of capitalist *and* industrial society. I stress capitalist *and* industrial society because Dahrendorf distinguishes clearly between the two. He argues that the division of 'modern' societies into two conflicting classes characteristic of, for instance, nineteenth-century capitalist Britain is no longer the case. Here, he argues that, far from forming unified classes, both the capitalist class and the working class have 'decomposed'. In a passage not given here, he also contends that the 'middle class' is, in fact, divided into a variety of separate interest groups. He concludes, therefore, that the bourgeois-proletariat conflict at the core of capitalist society no longer dominates what he now calls industrial society (i.e. industrial but *not* capitalist). He even doubts whether industrial conflict, which he considers to occur more between management and labour than between capital and labour, is truly class conflict in the old sense. It is immediately economic, not broadly social and political in nature; it is certainly not, as Marx thought, the

175

crux of a fundamental conflict which would form the basis of revolution.

Whatever one thinks of this analysis – and it has been opposed powerfully by Marxists and others – it is compelling and massively influential. What it means for the analysis of social change is worth considering.

Reading 23 From Ralf Dahrendorf, *Class and Class Conflict in Industrial Society* (Routledge and Kegan Paul, 1959), pp. 41–3, 48–51.

Ownership and control, or the decomposition of capital

Marx was right in seeking the root of social change in capitalist society in the sphere of industrial production, but the direction these changes took turned out to be directly contrary to Marx's expectations. With respect to capital, he had, in his later years, at least a vision of what was going to happen, as his brief and somewhat puzzled analysis of joint-stock companies shows. Joint-stock companies were legally recognised in Germany, England, France, and the United States in the second half of the nineteenth century. Laws often indicate the conclusion of social developments, and indeed early forms of joint-stock companies can be traced back at least to the commercial companies and trade societies of the seventeenth century. But it was in the nineteenth and early twentieth centuries that this type of enterprise first gained wide recognition and expanded into all branches of economic activity. Today, more than two-thirds of all companies in advanced industrial societies are joint-stock companies, and their property exceeds four-fifths of the total property in economic enterprises. The enterprise owned and run by an individual, or even a family, has long ceased to be the dominant pattern of economic organisation. Moreover, the stock of companies is dispersed fairly widely. Three per cent of the adult population of the Federal Republic of Germany, and approximately 8 per cent of that of the United States, own one or more shares of joint-stock companies. Probably the proportion in other countries is somewhere between these extremes. For purposes of the present analysis, we may add to joint-stock companies the co-operative enterprises and those owned by the state, which command an ever-increasing proportion of the national wealth in contemporary societies. All these together, and their growth in the last decade, leave little doubt about the significance of this change.

It is not surprising that sociologists should have shared, from an early date, the interest of lawyers and economists in these new and rapidly expanding types of organisation. There is, moreover, on the whole an astonishing degree of consensus among sociologists on the implications of joint-stock companies for the structure of industrial enterprises, and for the wider structure of society. If one wants to distinguish between points of view, one might contrast a rather more radical with a somewhat conservative interpretation of this phenomenon. Marx was, in this sense, the founder of the radical school; surprisingly enough, however, most of his later adherents took the more conservative view.

According to the radical view, joint-stock companies involve a complete break with earlier capitalist traditions. By separating what has come to be called ownership and control, they give rise to a new group of managers who are utterly different from their capitalist predecessors. Thus for Marx, the joint-stock company involves a complete alienation of capital 'from the real producers, and its opposition as alien property to all individuals really participating in production, from the manager down to the last day-laborer'. In other words, by separating ownership and control, the joint-stock company reduces the distance between manager and worker while at the same time removing the owners altogether from the sphere of production and thereby isolating their function as exploiters of others. It is merely a step from this kind of analysis to the thesis that, as Renner has it, the 'capitalists without function' yield to the 'functionaries without capital,' and that this new ruling group of industry bears little resemblance to the old 'full capitalists'. Burnham, Geiger, Sering, and others followed Marx (and Renner) in this radical interpretation of the social effects of joint-stock companies.

The conservative view, on the other hand, holds that the consequences of the apparent separation of ownership and control have been vastly overrated. It is argued that in fact owners and controllers, i.e., stockholders and managers, are a fairly homogeneous group. There are often direct connections between them, and where this is not the case, their outlook is sufficiently similar to justify insisting on the old assumption of a homogeneous class of capitalists opposed to an equally homogeneous class of laborers . . .

Skill and stratification, or the decomposition of labor

While Marx had at least a premonition of things to come with respect to capital, he remained unaware of developments affecting the unity of homogeneity of labor. Yet in this respect, too, the sphere of production which loomed so large in Marx's analyses became the starting point of changes that clearly refute his predictions. The working class of today, far from being a homogeneous group of equally unskilled and impoverished people, is in fact a stratum differentiated by numerous subtle and not-so-subtle distinctions. Here, too, history has dissolved one position, or role, and has substituted for it a plurality of roles that are endowed with diverging and often conflicting expectations.

In trying to derive his prediction of the growing homogeneity of labor from the assumption that the technical development of industry would tend to abolish all differences of skill and qualification, Marx was a genuine child of his century. Only the earliest political economists had believed that the division of labor in manufacturing would make for an 'increase of dexterity in every particular workman' (Adam Smith) by allowing him to refine the 'skill acquired by frequent repetition of the same process' (Babbage). Already in the following generation, social scientists were quite unanimous in believing that the processes of industrial production 'effect a substitution of labor comparatively unskilled, for that which is more skilled' (Ure), and that the division of labor had reached a phase 'in which we have seen the skill of the worker decrease at the rate at which industry becomes more perfect' (Proudhon). Marx was only too glad to adopt this view which tallied so well with his general theories of class structure: 'The interests and life situations of the proletariat are more and more equalised, since the machinery increasingly obliterates the differences of labor and depresses the wage almost everywhere to an equally low level'. 'The hierarchy of specialised workmen that characterises manufacture is replaced, in the automatic factory, by a tendency to equalise and reduce to one and the same level every kind of work that has to be done'.

Indeed, so far as we can tell from available evidence, there was, up to the end of the nineteenth century, a tendency for most industrial workers to become unskilled, i.e., to be reduced to the same low level of skill. But since then, two new patterns have emerged which are closely related on the one hand to technical innovations in production, and on the other hand to a new philosophy of industrial organisation as symbolised by the works of F. W. Taylor and H. Fayol. First, there emerged, around the turn of the century, a new category of workers which today is usually described as semiskilled. As early as 1905, Max Weber referred to the growing importance of 'the semiskilled workers trained directly on the job'. By the 1930's, the theory had become almost commonplace that 'there is a tendency for all manual laborers to become semiskilled machine minders, and for highly skilled as well as unskilled workers to become relatively less important' (Carr-Saunders and Jones). The semiskilled differ from the unskilled not so much in the technical qualifications required from them for their work, as in certain less easily defined extrafunctional skills which relate to their capacity to accept responsibility, to adapt to difficult conditions, and to perform a job intelligently. These extrafunctional skills are acquired not by formal training (although many semiskilled workers receive this also), but by experience on the job; yet these 'skills of responsibility' constitute a clear line of demarcation between those who have them and the unskilled who lack both training and experience. Apart from the semiskilled, there appeared, more recently, a new and ever-growing demand for highly skilled workers of the engineer type in industry. Carr-Saunders and Jones, in their statement above, still expected the simultaneous reduction of unskilled as well as skilled labor. Today we know – as Friedmann, Geiger, Moore, and others have pointed out – that the second half of this expectation has not come true. Increasingly complex machines require increasingly qualified designers, builders, maintenance and repair men, and even minders, so that Drucker extrapolates only slightly when he says: 'Within the working class a new shift from unskilled to skilled labor has begun – reversing the trend of the last fifty years. The unskilled worker is actually an engineering imperfection, as unskilled work, at least in theory, can always be done better, faster and cheaper by machines'.

Because of changing classifications, it is a little difficult to document this development statistically. As for the unskilled, a slight decrease in their proportion can be shown for England where, in 1951, they amounted to 12.5 per cent of the occupied male population, as against 16.5 per cent in 1931. In the United States, an even sharper decrease has been noted, from 36 per cent of the labor force in 1910 to just over 28 per cent in 1930 and, further, to less than 20 per cent in 1950. But statistics are here neither very reliable nor even indispensable evidence. Analysis of industrial conditions suggests quite clearly that within the labor force of advanced industry we have to distinguish at least three skill groups: a growing stratum of highly skilled workmen who increasingly merge with both engineers and white-collar employees, a relatively stable stratum of semiskilled workers with a high degree of diffuse as well as specific industrial experience, and a dwindling stratum of totally unskilled laborers who are characteristically either newcomers to industry (beginners, former agricultural laborers, immigrants) or semi-unemployables. It appears, furthermore, that these three groups differ not only in their level of skill, but also in other attributes and determinants of social status. The semiskilled almost invariably earn a higher wage than the unskilled, whereas the skilled are often salaried and thereby participate in white-collar status. The hierarchy of skill corresponds exactly to the hierarchy of responsibility and delegated authority within the working class. From numerous studies it would seem beyond doubt that it also correlates with the hierarchy of prestige, at the top of which we find the skilled man whose prolonged training, salary, and security convey special status, and at the bottom of which stands the unskilled man who is, according to a recent German investigation into workers' opinions, merely 'working' without having an 'occupation' proper (Kluth). Here as elsewhere Marx was evidently mistaken. 'Everywhere, the working class differentiates itself more and more, on the one hand into occupational groups, on the other hand into three large categories with different, if not contradictory, interests; the skilled craftsmen, the unskilled laborers, and the semiskilled specialist workers' (Philip).

In trying to assess the consequences of this development, it is well to remember that, for Marx, the increasing uniformity of the working class was an indispensable condition of that intensification of the class struggle which was to lead, eventually, to its climax in a revolution. The underlying argument of what for Marx became a prediction appears quite plausible. For there to be a revolution, the conflicts within a society have to become extremely intense. For conflicts to be intense, one would indeed expect its participants to be highly unified and homogeneous groups. But neither capital nor labor have developed along these lines. Capital has dissolved into at least two, in many ways distinct, elements, and so has labor. The proletarian, the impoverished slave of industry who is indistinguishable from his peers in terms of his work, his skill, his wage, and his prestige, has left the scene. What is more, it appears that by now he has been followed by his less deprived, but equally alienated successor, the worker. In modern industry, 'the worker' has become precisely the kind of abstraction which Marx quite justly resented so much. In his place, we find a plurality of status and skill groups whose interests often diverge. Demands of the skilled for security may injure the semiskilled; wage claims of the semiskilled may raise objections by the skilled; and any interest on the part of the unskilled is bound to set their more highly skilled fellow workmen worrying about differentials.

Again, as in the case of capital, it does not follow from the decomposition of labor that there is no bond left that unites most workers – at least for specific goals; nor does it follow that industrial conflict has lost its edge. But here, too, a change of the issues and, above all, of the patterns of conflict is indicated. As with the capitalist class, it has become doubtful whether speaking of the working class still makes much sense. Probably Marx would have agreed that class 'is a force that unites into groups people who differ from one another, by over-riding the differences between them' (Marshall), but he certainly did not expect the differences to be so great, and the uniting force so precarious as it has turned out to be in the case both of capital and of labor.

Question
1. (a) *What evidence and arguments does Dahrendorf give for the decomposition of capital?*

(10 marks)

(b) *What evidence and arguments does Dahrendorf give for the decomposition of labour?*

(10 marks)

(c) *Briefly, how convincing do his arguments appear from the vantage point of the late nineteen eighties?*

(5 marks)

24 John Scott: Britain: Ruling Class, Political Elite or Power Bloc?

The first response of the reader to this extract may be that it is in the wrong section – that it ought to be included under 'politics'. In fact, class and power are deeply connected as this extract illustrates. The issue discussed in this reading is whether the economically very wealthy are also politically a ruling class.

Very usefully, Scott begins by summarising both Marxist ruling class theory and various forms of elite theory. He then attempts to establish whether there is a British upper class and, having done so, whether it is also a ruling class. In giving evidence for the existence of an upper class, he presents substantial economic but limited cultural data. In establishing that a wealthy and unified upper class exists, Scott refutes the managerial position of Dahrendorf.

But is the upper class also a ruling class? Scott concludes that it is not – largely because 'there is not a perfect association between membership in the upper class and membership in the political elite'. However, he makes the important argument that the upper class is very well placed to achieve political dominance provided that it allies itself with other social groups. These alliances constitute a 'power bloc' – a term Scott finds more accurate in the British political context than either 'ruling class' or 'elite'.

Reading 24 From John Scott, 'Does Britain Still Have a Ruling Class?' in *Social Studies Review*, Vol 2, No 1, September 1986, pp. 2–7.

The Marxist position

The classic formulation of the concept of a ruling class comes, of course, from Karl Marx. The orthodox Marxist position has maintained that the division of society into opposed social classes involves a fusion of economic and political power in the hands of the bourgeoisie and the exploitation and oppression of the proletariat. Bourgeoisie and proletariat – the capitalist and the working classes – are mutually antagonistic social groupings, and the working class can improve its situation only by building up its own power base outside the formal structures of society. Collective organisation, class consciousness and political leadership are the bases of working-class power and will ensure the revolutionary overthrow of the capitalist class and the wholesale transformation of society.

The bourgeoisie, for its part, has a dual power base. It is the economically dominant class, having powers of ownership and control over the means of production; and it is the politically dominant class, monopolising the levers of power within the state. The modern state, whether liberal or authoritarian, is not a neutral instrument of administration, but a tool of class dominance. In the conflict between bourgeoisie and proletariat the state becomes the 'executive committee' of the bourgeoisie, acting at the behest and in the interest of the capitalist class as a whole. The position of the bourgeoisie as a ruling class is reinforced further by its dominance in the cultural sphere, which ensures that the prevailing ideas are mere ideological expressions of its interests and function to legitimate and obscure its power (Marx and Engels 1848).

The Italian and German theoretical traditions

The mainstream of research within the social sciences, however, has rejected this straightforward equation of economic and political power. Researchers have drawn heavily on the Italian and German theoretical traditions which have emphasised the analytical independence of the two sources of power and which introduced the concept of 'elite' to understand the collective organisation of political power.

The Italian writers Mosca and Pareto were key figures in the 'neo-Machiavellian' tradition of political analysis, which stressed the importance of political sovereignty as the essential bulwark against social dislocation. The late achievement of independence and political unification in Italy highlighted this question in a practical way, and led political theorists to attempt to theorise the mechanisms of power in a sovereign state. Mosca and Pareto argued for the inevitability of minority rule, the former using the phrase 'ruling class' to refer to any politically dominant minority. Pareto sought to distance himself from the Marxist phraseology completely, and referred instead to the existence of elites. The active, organised minority in any society constitutes the elite and is able to rule over the disorganised majority which constitutes the 'mass'. The opposition of elite and mass, and the continual 'circulation of elites', is the social dynamic of political behaviour.

In Germany also historians and philosophers were concerned to theorise and legitimate the power of a centralised nation state, reflecting once more the late achievement of political unification in Germany. Weber was closely involved, both intellectually and politically, in these debates, and his analyses of party and bureaucracy in the modern state were allied with a concern to counter the Marxist conflation of political and economic power. The phenomena of class, status and party, Weber argued, were analytically distinct, their interrelationships in particular historical settings being a matter for empirical determination. Weber's stress on the autonomy of party politics is furthered in the work of his student Robert Michels, who became an influential figure in Italian thought after his move to that country. Michels formulated the famous 'iron law of oligarchy', which holds that any politically organised group will find itself headed by a small minority: the need for effective action buttresses the power of the leadership, which thereby becomes detached from the mass of its supporters.

The ideas behind the 'elitist' tradition

What are the core ideas of this 'elitist' tradition of social thought? Pareto originally attempted to base his idea of the elite on natural inequalities. The 'Pareto curve' – still widely used in economics – was an attempt to measure mathematically the distribution of innate skills and abilities, and Pareto argued that such phenomena as the distribution of income and wealth would follow a similar curve. Those who were found at the top end of each distribution could be regarded as the 'elites' of their respective areas, and there would be a close association between each of the hierarchies. Political power, Pareto felt, should be found in the hands of that segment of the overall elite – the governing elite – which actually undertakes an important part in the activity of government. Pareto recognised, however, that the actual governing elite in a society may not be drawn exclusively from those at the top of the hierarchies of ability and advantage, and he was led to formulate a more general model of political rulership which had a more adequate sociological basis.

Elite dominance for Pareto was rooted in organisational ability and the factors which later writers have termed 'the three C's' – consciousness, cohesion and conspiracy – and power was vested in whoever could achieve these conditions. Pareto argued that the inevitability of elite rule was founded in the requirement for organisational ability which lay at the heart of the state. Elite rule is a constant fact of history despite the replacement of one elite by another in the succession of historical periods. Pareto recognised two types of political leaders, which he termed 'lions' and 'foxes'. Lions excel in force and coercion, and Pareto claimed that they embody a deep-rooted instinct or sentiment for stability and order. Foxes, on the other hand, embody sentiments of imagination and creativity and excel in cunning and manipulation. The skills of both lions and foxes enter into political rule, though the balance between them will vary from one situation to another. Any particular elite, therefore, will have a predominance of one or the other type of leader. But whatever their origin and particular skills, elites are liable to see their power weakening in the course of their rule. As they succumb to the privileges of office, elites become less effective and so more liable to infiltration by 'foxes' or overthrow by 'lions'. In this way, Pareto argued for the continued 'circulation of elites'.

Ruling class or political elite?

Many of the details of this model of the political process have been rejected, or simply forgotten, by later researchers, but the critique of democracy to which it led has remained a powerful influence. Pareto and Michels agreed that democracy was little more than a sham. In a liberal democracy all the large parliamentary parties formed parts of the political elite, and the most that resulted from an election was a shift in the composition of the elite. The elite itself persisted as a force separate from the masses to whom it was nominally responsible. Mosca was more favourably disposed towards democracy than was Pareto, the teacher and follower of Mussolini, and he felt that the degree of popular influence possible in a democratic regime was an important advance over other forms of elite rule. It is perhaps in this view that the origins of the modern 'elitist theory of democracy' are to be found.

This theory of democracy prevailed amongst American writers of the 'pluralist' school, who argued that democratic politics involves the competition for dominance among a plurality of competing elites – organised labour, business groups, political parties, voluntary associations, pressure groups, and so on. According to this view, the modern democratic state is simply the neutral arena within which these elite groups compete, and the mechanisms of popular election and lobbying ensure that no one elite is able to dominate the exercise of political power. This political pluralism is seen as incompatible with the concept of a ruling class, not least because it is assumed that the class structure no longer corresponds to the classic Marxian picture – if indeed it ever did. Pluralists hold that modern societies are continuous stratification hierarchies, in which each status level merges imperceptibly into its neighbours. Furthermore, each stratum is able to form a plurality of interest groups and so is able to enter into the democratic competition to determine the composition of the elite.

This view of the stratification system and its associated theory of democracy has been rejected by a number of important researchers, for whom the concept of 'elite' nevertheless remains a leading idea. Mills (1956) and Domhoff (1967) argue that there remains a fundamental class division between the wealthy and propertied owners and controllers of large-scale businesses, on the one hand, and the middle and working classes on the other. The propertied class, furthermore, follows a privileged and exclusive pattern of schooling, has a high level of intermarriage, and is virtually closed to recruitment from outsiders. This class is able to dominate politics, so forming a power elite; and Mills argues that the terminology of 'economic class' and 'power elite' is preferable to the Marxist conflation of the two in the concept of the ruling class. The power elite brings together the economic leadership and the political and military leadership, though all members of the power elite share a common class origin and social background.

The key issues to have emerged in the debate over the ruling class, therefore, concern (a) whether or not a propertied upper class still exists, and (b) whether politics is dominated by such a class. In order to answer the question 'Does Britain still have a ruling class?' the evidence on each of these areas must be reviewed.

The development of the upper class in Britain

Although there is widespread agreement that Britain did once have a sharply defined upper class, many researchers have argued that the twentieth century has seen its demise. This upper class was formed in the late nineteenth and early twentieth century from the landed, commercial and manufacturing classes of earlier periods, but it was unable to sustain its position in the face of the economic trends of the twentieth century. I intend to argue against this view, and so will initially outline the development of the propertied classes in Britain.

Early capitalist development in Britain led to the formation of two distinct classes of landowners in the sixteenth century, the landed magnates and the landed gentry. The magnates were the dominant force in land-ownership, owning large estates which frequently spread over two or more counties. Their orientation towards their land was predominantly as *rentiers*, as capitalist land-owners living on the rental income from their land. The farmers who rented this land from them and the independent gentry of small landowners were dependent on and subordinate to the magnates, but by the eighteenth century the division between magnates and gentry had become far less sharp and the two groups comprised segments within a unified class of landed rentiers.

For much of the nineteenth century the 'upper class' was virtually coterminous with the 'landed class'. But economic dominance was not exclusively a feature of land ownership. The capitalist development which transformed 'feudal' landholders into landed rentiers was initiated and implemented by commercial capitalist interests centred on market trading and international finance. The merchant 'bourgeoisie', which had crystallised as a distinct and important class by the fifteenth and sixteenth centuries, controlled the import and export trade, and ensured that domestic production became increasingly oriented to the market system. By the eighteenth century, this class of merchants and financiers held a strong position in the commercial centres of London, Bristol, Glasgow and Liverpool, and showed a high degree of internal specialisation.

In London especially, merchants were divided into East and West India merchants and into specialisation by commodity – spice, tea, cloth, bullion, and so on – and there were, in addition, specialist bankers who dealt with landowners and provincial merchants. Some of the provincial merchants were involved in the provision of finance to the industrial undertakings which produced the goods in which they traded, but the owners of the numerous manufacturing enterprises spawned in the industrial revolution depended mainly on the capital provided by their own families. Thus, nineteenth century Britain had three relatively distinct upper classes – landed, commercial and manufacturing – each of which was sharply divided from the classes below them. But this objective economic division was not reflected directly in popular images of class. Landed antipathy to trade and industry, and the obviously superior wealth of some of the largest landowners, led the manufacturing and commercial classes to perceive themselves, and to be perceived by others, as 'middle class'. These wealthy and powerful 'middle classes', however, were clearly demarcated by wealth and lifestyle from the lower middle class of shopkeepers, artisans, and clerks, and their generally privileged position makes it realistic to regard them, economically speaking, as 'upper class'.

This was reflected in the slow fusion of land, commerce, and manufacturing which took place in the later part of the nineteenth century. As the scale of manufacturing industry increased, leading to demands for capital which could not normally be met by the manufacturers themselves, so links between the London financiers and the manufacturers were established and strengthened. At the same time, the depression in agricultural rentals in the last third of the century reduced the incomes of many landowners and forced them to raise mortgages through their bankers or to sell parts of their estates. This closer integration of land and commerce was furthered by the increased involvement of many landowners in mining, railways, and urban development, and a number were recruited as directors of the large joint stock companies formed at the turn of the century. By the early years of the twentieth century it was possible to speak of a unified upper class with its roots in the increasingly intertwined areas of land, commerce and manufacturing.

The managerialist position

It has been widely accepted, even amongst those responsible for shaping the Labour Party's views on equality, that this 'business class' lost its power during the 1940s and 1950s. Partly as a result of the policies of the postwar Labour Government and partly because of internal changes in business, their control over the levers of economic power had crumbled. Most importantly, it was claimed that there had been a transfer of power from owners to managers, from the upper class to the new middle classes. As a result, the wealthy families lost their function in the system of production and faced a continuous and effective attack upon their wealth. The upper classes had become simply irrelevant.

In a previous article (Scott 1986) I argued that this managerialist position could not be sustained. The managerialist case rests upon inadequate evidence and faulty theory. In advanced capitalist societies there has been a move away from personal and family ownership of business to more impersonal structures of ownership. The transfer of shares from private individuals to financial intermediaries – pension funds, insurance companies and banks – has led to a 'depersonalisation' of property.

In Britain this has involved the emergence of 'control through a constellation of interests' in many of the largest business enterprises. The large financial intermediaries comprise a dominant bloc of shareholders, but their interests are too diverse to allow them to pursue a common policy. The directors and managers cannot ignore their interests – as the managerialists assume – but neither are they the mere tools of the financial intermediaries. The board of directors is, therefore, the focus of corporate control. It is the arena in which shareholders, lenders, and executives come together to exercise control over the strategy to be pursued by the enterprise. A key question in considering the survival of a capitalist upper class in Britain, therefore, is the source of recruitment to company boards. Are those who actually shape the policies of the business world drawn from the world of the propertyless 'new middle class' or from surviving wealthy families? And if they come from wealthy families, what is the connection between their personal wealth and the impersonal structure of corporate property?

An economically privileged upper class

Although the majority of directors are salaried employees, this does not mean that they are *merely* salaried employees. Research has shown that there are two sources of privilege and power which buttress their position and serve to differentiate them from the mass of salaried 'middle-class' managers. First, they are participants in the exercise of control and, as such, are able to determine their own conditions of employment. While they do not always have personal ownership of the company for which they work, or even a substantial percentage holding in its capital, the mechanisms through which they are recruited and dismissed and through which their pay and fringe benefits are determined are different from those regulating other forms of work.

Second, the majority of directors are indeed substantial shareholders and, therefore, have an additional source of income. While their percentage holding in any particular company may be very small, the monetary value of shares held is considerable and directors tend to hold shares in a wide range of companies. Top corporate 'management' and the large personal shareholders are one and the same group. The shareholdings of directors give them an interest in the success of the business system as a whole: their general financial interests are identical to those of the financial intermediaries, and their shareholdings are often managed on a day-to-day basis by bank investment departments. There is, therefore, a fusion of interest between directors and the structure of depersonalised property.

But not all directors correspond to this pattern; some are, in fact, the kind of entrepreneurial capitalists which the managerialist thesis claimed has disappeared. Over a half of the top 250 enterprises in Britain have dominant shareholders with majority or minority control, and in almost a half of these the dominant shareholder is an individual or a family. Many companies bearing a family name are still today under the direct ownership and control of that family: Baring and Rothschild in banking, Laing and McAlpine in construction, Sainsbury and W. H. Smith in retailing, and Guinness and Whitbread in brewing, to name but a few. And in many cases where control through a constellation of interests exists, founding families and individuals are to be found on the boards of directors and as substantial shareholders. This is the case, for example, in Cadbury Schweppes (the Cadbury family), Marks and Spencer (the Marks and Sieff families), and General Electric (Lord Weinstock).

Top corporate decisions, therefore, are taken by a group of directors with significant shareholding interests, often with controlling blocks of shares, and with interests which are closely allied with those of the financial intermediaries. Directors and top executives are the beneficiaries of the structure of impersonal share ownership, and through their membership of the boards of banks and insurance companies are actively involved in taking decisions about the use of this impersonal 'institutional' share ownership. Top directors are tied together through the 'interlocking directorships' which are created whenever one person sits on two or more boards. Through these interlocking directorships a web of connections is created which ties together a large number of enterprises and casts the

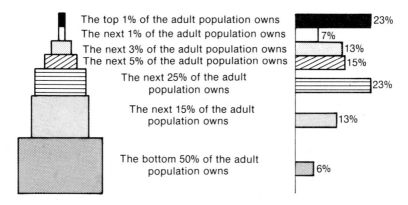

The top 1% of the adult population owns — 23%
The next 1% of the adult population owns — 7%
The next 3% of the adult population owns — 13%
The next 5% of the adult population owns — 15%
The next 25% of the adult population owns — 23%
The next 15% of the adult population owns — 13%
The bottom 50% of the adult population owns — 6%

Source: Adapted from Stanworth, P., 'Elites and Privilege', in Abrams, P. and Brown, R. (eds), *UK Society*, Weidenfeld and Nicholson, 1984.

Figure 1   The distribution of wealth in Britain (1980)

'multiple directors' in a key role as coordinators of the business system as a whole. Their power and influence spreads from individual enterprises through major sectors of the economy.

Top business controllers today, therefore, continue to show many of the characteristics of the prewar business class which earlier commentators believed had disappeared. While there may have been a shift in the balance between personal and impersonal possession since the 1930s, there has been no demise of the upper class as an economic force. One indication of its continued wealth is, perhaps, the continued importance of business enterprises as a source of personal fortunes. Millionaires dying in the 1970s and 1980s included, amongst many others, Viscount Rothermere (*Daily Mail* newspapers), who left £4.1 million; Sir Cyril Kleinwort (Kleinwort's bank), who left £2.4 million; Frederick Colman (Reckitt and Colman), who left £2.3 million; and Alan Pilkington (Pilkington's Glass), who left £1.5 million. As Figure 1 shows, the overall concentration of wealth is still such that 1% of the adult population owns 23% of the national wealth.

The development of political rule in Britain

Britain, then, still has an economically privileged *upper class* with substantial wealth and control over the levers of economic power. But does it still have a *ruling class?* That is to say, are those who

191

CLASS

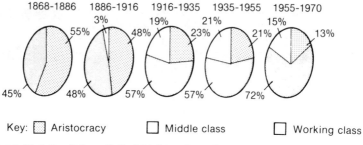

Sources: Adapted from Guttsman, W., The British Political Elite, McGibbon and Kee, 1963, p.79; and Johnson, R. W. 'The British Political Elite', European Journal of Sociology, 1973, pp. 50 and 52.

Figure 2   Class composition of cabinet (1868–1970)

make up the political 'elite' still recruited predominantly from this upper class? Research on the social composition of the political elite has shown the way in which the landed magnates and financiers who dominated eighteenth century politics were gradually joined in the late nineteenth century by the leading manufacturers. On this basis, writers such as Guttsman (1963) and Sampson (1982) made the further claim that the twentieth century has seen the rise of the middle classes to power. Just as the managers are supposed to have replaced the capitalists in the business enterprise, so the managerial and professional middle classes as a whole are supposed to have usurped the political power formerly held by the upper class.

Figure 2 is typical of the results produced by such research and it is clear that the proportion of titled and landed aristocrats in the political elite declined as the proportion of 'middle-class' politicians increased. But it is important to note that the category of 'middle class' was used by the researchers to include all those with business, administrative, or professional positions: it includes both the upper class *and* the salaried middle classes. Thus, the apparently increasing middle-class composition of the cabinet – and other sections of the 'elite' – masks any continuity that may be present in its upper-class composition. As I have shown, 'aristocracy' and 'upper class' are not identical terms, and the declining salience of the hereditary peerage does not, in itself, indicate the demise of upper-class rule.

The most sophisticated attempt to use the elite concept to study upper-class power in Britain is to be found in the work of Miliband (1969), who follows the same line of argument as Mills and Domhoff. The various parts of the 'state elite' – cabinet, parliament,

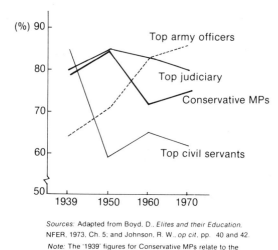

Sources: Adapted from Boyd, D., *Elites and their Education*, NFER, 1973, Ch. 5; and Johnson, R. W., *op cit*, pp. 40 and 42. Note: The '1939' figures for Conservative MPs relate to the period 1918–35, and the '1960' figures relate to 1959.

Figure 3   Public school background (1939–70)

judiciary, civil service and military – are recruited disproportionately from among the economically dominant upper class. This similarity of economic background is reinforced by the fact that they had studied at a small number of major public schools and at Oxford and Cambridge Universities. Figure 3 shows clearly that annual fluctuations in the numbers recruited from public schools vary around continuing high levels. Indeed, the top army officers showed a rising trend in public-school recruitment. It is these very same schools which supply the directors of many of Britain's largest enterprises; about three-quarters of the directors of large financial and industrial enterprises attended a public school, and about a half attended Oxford or Cambridge. The upper class and the political elite show a similarity of social background and are, in many cases, the same people.

But there is not a perfect association between membership in the upper class and membership in the political elite: not all capitalists are politically active, and not all leading holders of political power are drawn from a business background. This fact makes it difficult to sustain the conventional Marxist view of the 'ruling class'. The state cannot be simply the executive committee of the capitalist class if some of its members are drawn from outside that class. Mills was

193

correct, therefore, in rejecting the concept of 'ruling class' because it posited a simple correspondence between political and economic power. In this sense, Britain does not have a ruling class. But is the alternative 'elite' framework any more viable? It has been shown that elite research produces significant results only if related to the prevailing structure of class relations. The classical views of Pareto and Mosca fail to do this – indeed, their very *raison d'être* was the rejection of class analysis. To continue to use the terminology of elite theory, as even such a sophisticated writer as Miliband has done, is to run the risk of having research findings interpreted in the light of the arguments of the classic elite writers. This would result in a misunderstanding of the dynamics of political power in Britain today.

The 'power bloc'

Neither 'ruling class' nor 'elite' can be used as adequate descriptions of the British political structure. Historical patterns of class dominance must be understood in terms of the particular alliance of classes and sections of classes which constitute the 'power bloc'. A power bloc is an informal coalition of social groups, often under the leadership of one group, which actually holds the levers of political power in a society. An upper class may succeed in forming a power bloc in which it holds a dominant position if it is able to guarantee certain concessions to its partners. A dominant class must, therefore, accommodate itself to the interests of the other classes on whose support it depends. In such circumstances it is not necessary for *all* members of the upper class to be equally active in politics and so the composition of key political positions will show a relatively mixed social background. Of course, such power blocs are generally built in a less deliberate way than this definition implies: power blocs emerge as the partly unintended result of *ad hoc* and implicit agreements.

British society in the twentieth century has been ruled by just such a power bloc, headed by the upper-class members of the 'establishment' and having its political expression in the Conservative Party. Over the course of the century the cohesion of the power bloc has weakened, but it remains the basis of upper-class political dominance. To paraphrase the Marxist writer, Karl Kautsky:

Britain has an upper class that dominates government, but it does not have a ruling class.

Question

1. (a) Assess the evidence presented in the reading for the existence of a British upper class.

(10 marks)

(b) Why does John Scott conclude that the upper class is not a ruling class? Do you agree with him?

(15 marks)

25 John Rentoul and Andrew Lumsden: The Rich Inherit

Although this article could not be put forward as a model of unbiased analysis (it is written from a clearly socialist standpoint), it contains a considerable amount of hard information about the rich. Most importantly, it tells us that the majority of the rich are rich because they *inherit* their wealth.

Beyond this, in a happy go-muck-raking kind of way, the article provides data for a number of popular socialist-Marxist arguments. First, in illustrating that the upper class is alive and doing very well, it implicitly dismisses perspectives of the 'we are all middle class now' variety. Second, the authors show how ineffective taxation has been since 1970 in tapping the wealth of the rich for the public purse. Third, this article nicely sets up but does not quite ask the question dealt with in the next reading: how powerful are the rich?

Reading 25 From John Rentoul and Andrew Lumsden, 'It's Becoming Three Nations Mr Disraeli' in *New Statesman*, 4 April 1986, pp. 11–12.

There are now Three Nations, not Two, and Nigel Lawson's 18 March Budget was once again not just for the rich but for that other, discreet Nation, the super rich. The Three Nations are the *haves*, the *have nots* and the *have lots* – a social and economic elite now in its seventh consecutive year of reasserting itself.

We all know all about the other Two Nations: the underclass of the poor and the mass unemployed on low and no pay, and the comfortably-off majority in reasonably secure jobs whose pay has consistently outstripped inflation since 1980 as a group and, more substantially, as individuals.

But 'Two Nation' rhetoric, whether coded Wetspeak, Alliance flannel or full-blooded class hatred, has concealed the extent of the changes in British society since about 1979. It implies that any state-sponsored transfer of resources to the poor has to come from the *modestly* well-off. It implies that there is a continuity of interests between the middle class and the 'aristocracy' of the very rich – Two Nation rhetoric actually provides a cover for that 'aristocracy' to hide behind.

The Third Nation, as we're naming it, isn't precisely the same as the old aristocracy with its uneven jumble of titles and landed interests – though old titled wealth *is* having a boom. It's an inter-weaving of the old inheritors with the new capital owners from 'industry' and the City. And it is on a drip feed from above, as the Royals breed exponentially, creating a burgeoning cast of role models and status enforcers.

What distinguishes the 'Third Nation' from the nation below it is inheritance and the scale of its capital. Not since the 1920s has it been possible to talk of a leisured class, but what we're seeing is the reassembling of a culturally homogeneous grouping who own enough capital to live on. At today's rates of interest (on government securities) and – crucially – today's tax rates, a person needs to hold £111,000-worth of capital (in addition to their home) to secure an income equivalent to average earnings, and maintain the value of their capital against inflation. The sum is: average earnings in 1985 of £7,930 less £2,400 mortgage/rent, at interest rates of around 10 per cent with inflation at 5 per cent. In order to guess at the numbers of the potentially-leisured rich, try Inland Revenue estimates of the distribution of wealth in the UK, 1983, *Inland Revenue Statistics 1985*.

There are now at least 600,000 such individuals in Britain, and what is more, they can pass on their wealth – untouched by the tax person's hands – for generation after generation. Or as Mrs Thatcher put it last week, their wealth holdings will 'topple like a cascade down the line of the family'.

As the flow of apologist rhetoric might warn anyone – from Thatcher's 'cascade' to Heseltine's 'caring capitalism' – grotesque inducements are increasingly being offered not only to the recreation of a hereditary bourgeoisie or 'gentry' whose children will soon be leisured if they choose, but to the perpetuation *ad infinitum* of vast fortunes. Even the *Financial Times* following this March's Budget took the trouble to estimate that Earl Grosvenor, the Duke of Westminster's heir, 'will save a minimum of £600 million at a stroke as a result of Mr Lawson's statement'.

The gravy-train starts at the very top. Nobody in public life wastes any breath on the Queen's personal exemption from every inheritance tax on the presumption that she maintains her 'state' with it. It is less noticed that she's free to create brand-new wealthy individuals out of any of her relatives, and naturally does so. It must have been the untaxed fortune that paid for the Andrew-Fergie £25,000 engagement ring, and if it could do that, it will certainly do a great deal more for the couple after marriage. Major-scale tax-avoidance in Britain begins with the Head of State, 'by custom', and a millionaire-controlled popular press incites approval.

Nigel Lawson's abolition of Capital Transfer Tax (CTT) a fortnight ago, returning to an entirely avoidable death duty, was in fact mostly symbolic of cultural significance in asserting the soaring social value being placed on 'family money'. The Conservatives had already 'drawn the teeth' of CTT. Even in 1979, when its dismantling began, it only had dentures and a rather weak jaw, for when Denis Healey under Labour created it in 1975, he departed from his 'squeezing the rich until the pips squeak' prospectus by taxing lifetime transfers at a lower rate and allowing reliefs for farms, small businesses and anything else rich people might own.

Taxes on capital have not yielded significant revenue since the 1964–70 Labour government, although estate duty was once an important source of government income. In 1979 Capital Gains Tax and CTT produced only 1.3 per cent of total tax revenue (including rates). Last year they produced less than 1.2 per cent. As the indexation rules of 1982 and 1985 (which made capital gains taxable only if they exceeded the rate of inflation) take effect, the yield of CGT is expected to decline by up to 75 per cent, according to the Institute of Fiscal Studies. The replacement of CTT by Inheritance Tax will reduce yields from capital taxation further. Compare 1908: estate duty was then 29 per cent of Inland Revenue receipts. Even in 1928 it was 20 per cent, and as late as 1968 it was 7 per cent. Last year it was 1.5 per cent.

Even before Lawson abolished it, CTT could be regarded 'like an infectious illness' – advice of Professor Anthony Mellows in *Harpers and Queen*, January 1985. 'One only suffers if one fails to take precautions. A middle-aged couple can transfer to their children, grandchildren and others assets worth nearly £1 million without paying any Capital Transfer Tax. If they are particularly ambitious to defeat the Chancellor, they can increase that to a figure approaching £2 million.'

Professor Harbury and Dr Hitchens, in their definitive study of inheritance and inequality, conclude: 'Between 60 and 80 per cent of those who died rich in the third quarter of the present century owed their wealth to inheritances and the rest to entrepreneurship and luck.' (*Inheritance and Wealth Inequality in Britain*, 1979.) They conclude: 'Inheritance is the major determinant of wealth inequality. Regression analysis attributed some two-thirds of the inequality in the distribution of wealth in 1973 to inheritance. The proportions of top wealth leavers since the mid–1950s who were preceded by rich fathers was on what might be regarded as conservative assumptions in excess of 60 per cent . . .'

We have now had seven years (1979–86) of what Thatcher likes to pretend is a tax-shift away from 'socialist' refusal to let 'the people' be 'propertied' towards rewards for self-help and initiative. *Before* she began, the Royal Commission on the Distribution of Income and Wealth in 1977 and 1979 (reports 5 and 7), calculated what the distribution of wealth would be if it were only possible to own wealth through saving – but with existing unequal incomes. The share of the top 1 per cent would be between 3 and 7 per cent of total wealth (depending on assumptions about earnings and interest rates). As it is, the top 1 per cent actually owns nearly 20 per cent (including private pensions, which are a form of saving). The difference is the significance of inheritance. The *ancient regime* is coming back.

Question

1. (a) *What evidence is provided in the passage that 'the rich are getting richer'?* (10 marks)

   (b) *Do the rich constitute a ruling class in Britain?*

   (15 marks)

(Refer also to Reading 24.)

26 Anthony Giddens: The Problem of the 'New Middle Class'

The development of a 'new', salaried group between the old capitalist class and the traditional working class raised many issues of class analysis and theory. In the following reading, Anthony Giddens refers to several of these issues and attempts to resolve some of them.

Although not essential to an understanding of the extract(s), it helps to know something about Giddens' own theory of class *structuration* (as he calls it). He distinguishes between *mediate* and *proximate* factors in the formation of classes. The former are broad factors producing market capacity (i.e. saleable goods or services). They are:

1. Ownership of property in the means of production.
2. Possession of educational and technical qualifications.
3. Possession of manual labour power.

These broad factors underlie 'a basic three-class system in capitalist society: an "upper" (1), "middle" (2), and "lower" or "working" (3) class' (my brackets). The proximate factors are the immediate circumstances of class structuration. They are the:

1. Division of labour within the productive enterprise.
2. Authority relations within the enterprise.
3. Influence of distributive groupings.

Whereas 1 and 2 refer to the effect of the organisation of production on class formation, 3 indicates that the unequal capacity of groups to consume goods and services also contributes to class formation (e.g. there are 'cheap' and 'expensive' neighbourhoods reflecting differences in house-purchasing power).

Several of these six factors are more or less apparent in Giddens' analysis of the 'new' middle class extracted below. Broadly, the possession of educational and technical qualifications is the basis of the structuration of the middle class. According to Giddens, the middle class is generally affected differently than is the working class by the proximate factors of the division of labour (1) and in its members' relationship to authority (2). In discussing the latter points, Giddens draws heavily on the work of David Lockwood. Though interesting, Giddens' discussion of the third proximate factor using the example of class and neighbourhood is now somewhat dated in view of the extent to which the class-based patterns of residence have been complicated by the growing number of 'working class' owner occupiers.

Two other points are worth mentioning in relation to Giddens' general theory of class structuration. He gives great emphasis to 'consciousness' and suggests that members of the new middle class tend to have an individualistic rather than a collectivist image of society. He also stresses that social mobility can change the 'shape' of class structure – his is a dynamic model.

The passage in which Giddens refers to Marxist interpretations of the 'new middle class' is highly abbreviated. However, it helps to locate his own theoretical position. Clearly influenced by both Marx and Weber, he denies he is a Weberian, does not claim to be a Marxist nor a synthesiser of the two traditions. Perhaps his is a complex analysis for complex times. Marxists might find it too complex in certain respects. Arguably, it is the varied factors in his own model that force him to the conclusion that the middle class itself is so varied or 'heterogeneous'.

Reading 26 From Anthony Giddens, *The Class Structure of the Advanced Societies* (Hutchinson, 1981), pp. 177–8, 301, 307.

There is a now famous short passage in the 'fourth volume' of *Capital, Theories of Surplus Value*, in which Marx criticises Ricardo for having neglected 'the constantly growing number of the middle classes, those who stand between the workman on the one hand and the capitalist and landlord on the other'. These middle classes, Marx declares, 'are a burden weighing heavily on the working base and increase the social security and power of the upper ten thousand'. The statement is an enigmatic one, in spite of some recent attempts to make it appear otherwise, because it does not accord with the main weight of Marx's theoretical thinking, either on class in general, or the 'middle class' in particular. It must be attributed to the remarkable prescience of a man whose insights not infrequently broke the bounds of the theoretical formulations whereby he sought to discipline them. That it describes a fundamental aspect of modern social reality is unquestionable; and the same is true of the more characteristic Marxian conception that the tendency of capitalist development is to diminish the proportional significance in the class structure of those whom he normally designated as the 'petty bourgeoisie'. I shall henceforth refer to this grouping, however, as the 'old middle class', using the term 'middle class' without qualification to refer to propertyless non-manual, or 'white-collar', workers.

The decline of the old middle class, while a definite and identifiable phenomenon in the capitalist societies since the nineteenth century, has not proceeded in quite the radical fashion which Marx probably, and later Marxists certainly, expected. Not only are there, even today, important differences between the contemporary societies in terms of the relative size of the old middle class, but its decay has taken the form of a slowly declining curve, rather than a progressive approach to zero. Bernstein and Lederer, two of the first self-proclaimed Marxists to attempt systematically to confront the problems posed for orthodox Marxist theory by the burgeoning of the white-collar sector, were almost as perturbed by the stubborn persistence of the old middle class as by the growth of the new. But, however important the old middle class may remain in certain countries, there can be no doubt that the phenomenon of overwhelming consequence since the turn of the century is the massive relative enlargement of the white-collar sector.

In spite of general agreement upon the decline of the old middle class, statistical comparisons between different countries are extremely difficult to make. Modern economists have not been greatly interested in very small enterprises, and the relevant statistical materials are extremely patchy and incomplete. The figures do, however, suggest a general pattern which applies, although with quite wide discrepancies, to most of the capitalist societies: a pattern of a steady relative diminution of small businesses (including within this category small farms, manufacturing and retailing enterprises) from the closing decades of the nineteenth century up to the early years of the 1930s; whence the decline continues, but at a considerably reduced gradient. Compared to larger enterprises, however, small businesses typically manifest a very high rate of turnover.

There are also problems in making comparisons between different societies in the overall growth of white-collar labour, but the general trends are so striking that these can be overlooked for present purposes. The relative advance of the white-collar sector has proceeded furthest in the United States, which has recently been hailed as the first 'middle-class society'. Whether or not this is so, in the sense of manual workers being outnumbered by white-collar workers, depends upon the criteria used to make the relevant discriminations between occupational categories. Thus one recent estimate (1969) places them at parity, each composing 48 per cent of the total labour force; if, however, only the male labour force is considered, manual workers outnumber non-manual employees by 54 to 41 per cent. Certainly, in terms of the proportion of white-collar workers in the labour force as a whole, few other capitalist countries come near to matching the United States. Figures for Britain for the year 1959 show 29 per cent of the total labour force as non-manual workers, a rise of only 1 per cent over 1951, and 7 per cent more than 1921. In Japan, in 1963, white-collar workers numbered 27 per cent of the non-agricultural labour force, an advance from 24.5 per cent in 1944. It has been commonly assumed that the differences between the United States and countries like Britain and Japan are simply a matter of 'lag', indicative of the lower level of technical development of these countries – and that therefore in this case it is the United States which shows to the other societies 'the image of their own future'. But there are some indications that this may be a mistaken, or at least an oversimplified, conclusion. For there seems to have occurred a levelling off of the relative growth of the white-collar sector in the United States over the past decade; and a similar phenomenon seems also to have occurred in other societies, but at the considerably lower ratios of non-manual workers which characterise these societies as compared to the United States. An illustrative case is that of Britain, quoted above; another is that of France, where the ratio has barely changed over the last dozen years.

But, of course, it is misleading in itself to treat 'white-collar labour' as an undifferentiated category, and the overall expansion of the white-collar sector in the capitalist societies conceals differential rates of growth in various occupational sub-categories. Whereas the relatively early enlargement of the white-collar sector mainly concerned the growth of clerical and sales occupations, in neo-capitalism those occupations usually grouped by census statisticians as 'professional and technical' labour show the highest recent rates of development – although these nowhere comprise any more than a fairly small minority of white-collar workers as a whole.

The conditions of middle-class structuration

The differentiation between the market capacities conferred by educational and technical qualifications, as compared to manual skills or pure labour-power, in the capitalist societies has everywhere taken the form not only of quite clear-cut divergences in income, but also in other modes of economic reward. In terms of income alone, while there have been certain important internal changes within the general category of white-collar labour as a whole, there has been an overall stability in the differential between the mean incomes of non-manual versus manual workers – that is to say, if real income distributions at the turn of the century are compared to those of today, since there have been substantial fluctuations in interim periods. Thus, in both Britain and the United States, the differential between non-manual and manual workers was reduced during World War I, and again in the subsequent war, and has since re-established itself.

The significant changes which have occurred, now well-documented, concern, first, a relative diminution of the income of clerical workers within the white-collar sector, and, secondly, the development of some degree of 'overlap' at the margins between non-manual and manual labour. But out of these changes in the gross income statistics an enormous mythology has been built, in much of the technical literature on class as well as in the lay press. The apparent merging in the economic returns accruing to manual as compared to non-manual labour looks very different if the facts of the matter are inspected more closely. In the first place, the traditional superiority of the white-collar worker in terms of job security has by no means disappeared: in general terms, non-manual workers continue to enjoy a greater measure of security, even if, for reasons which I shall discuss in subsequent chapters, there is some cause to suppose that certain categories of manual workers will increasingly enjoy more favourable contractual conditions in the future. Secondly, typical patterns of overall career earnings are quite different in the two categories. It is not only the oft-quoted fact of the range of promotion opportunities which are potentially open to white-collar workers, but are largely denied to manual workers, which is at issue here. Even leaving this aside, the latter characteristically experience a 'declining curve' of earnings which the former, often having guaranteed annual increments, usually do not encounter. Thus Fogarty shows that, in Britain, unskilled manual workers reach peak income at an average of 30, and thence drop some 15–20 per cent to retirement age; skilled workers tend to reach their peak earnings some ten years later, and subsequently drop about 10–15 per cent. In addition, the length of the working week of manual workers is longer than that of non-manual employees: in 1966, in Britain, the former averaged 44 hours a week, as compared to 38 hours for white-collar workers. Thirdly, a considerably larger proportion of those in non-manual occupations are in receipt of fringe benefits of various kinds, such as pension and sick-pay schemes: in most countries these workers also gain disproportionately from tax remissions as a result of participation in such schemes.

It is perfectly clear that, since the first origins of the modern large-scale factory, there has come into being a generic disparity between white- and blue-collar labour – suggested by those very terms themselves, as well as by the terminology of 'non-manual' and 'manual' work – in terms of task attributes in the division of labour. As Lockwood has stressed, the clerical worker, with a relatively weak market capacity, has typically shared conditions of labour which have far more in common with higher-level managerial workers than with the workers on the shop-floor. Clerical employees work in the 'office', which is normally materially separated from the shop-floor and often is elevated above it, such that the office workers may physically 'look down upon' the workers. Whereas the nature of manual work-tasks frequently involves strenuous and exhausting labour in conditions which soil the hands and clothing, the clerk normally works in a relatively clean environment, at a task which simply involves the manipulation of symbolic materials. Even clerical workers, quite apart from higher-level management, may have little or no direct contact with the manual workers, since the foreman normally is the principal channel of communication between office and factory-floor. In Lockwood's words: 'The converse of the working cooperation of clerks and management is the social isolation of the office worker from the manual worker. The completeness of the separation of these two groups of workers is perhaps the most outstanding feature of industrial organisation.' Obviously the degree to which this is so varies, both in relation to size of enterprise and to the particular industrial sector involved; but the general principle holds good . . .

Differences in neighbourhood organisation are directly bound up with the exploitative connotations of class relationships, apart from those pertaining to the economic sphere itself – particularly in so far as these differences influence the distribution of educational chances. The mechanisms which govern the process whereby 'vicious circles' of underprivilege are set up in this respect are by now well understood. Working-class families are larger in average size than those of the middle class, and the amount of direct parental contact is lower – a phenomenon which, in so far as it influences the verbal facility of children, may have lasting effects upon intellectual abilities. Parental attitudes to education among the working class, moreover, often tend to be unfavourable. As regards the schools, poor equipment and poor facilities in the underprivileged areas are associated with badly qualified teaching staff and an educational environment in which problems of control assume precedence over intellectual development as such.

A number of fairly recent, and well-known, studies in the European countries have demonstrated that class awareness, rather than class consciousness, is the typical cognitive perspective of the middle class. The 'image of society', as Willener calls it, of the white-collar worker involves a hierarchical perception of occupational levels distinguished by differences of income and status – an evident generalisation from the hierarchical system of authority in which the non-manual worker is located. Movement up or down this hierarchy is perceived to be decided by the initiative and energy shown by any particular individual. Consistent with this 'individualism' is a general willingness to accept 'deferred gratification' as a necessary investment to secure anticipated future rewards. Such an 'image of society' does not inevitably preclude the possibility of subjective class identification, but it very definitely inhibits the formation of certain levels of 'class consciousness', as I have defined this term previously. Conflict and struggle play a part in this imagery, but primarily in terms of the striving of the individual to secure a social position which accords with his talents and zeal, not as any sort of class confrontation.

Sources of differentiation within the middle class

We may distinguish two major sources of differentiation within the middle class as a whole: that having its origin in differences in market capacity, and that deriving from variations in the division of labour. The most significant type of difference in market capacity is undoubtedly between the capacity to offer marketable technical knowledge, recognised and specialised symbolic skills, and the offering of general symbolic competence. The marketability of specialised symbolic skills has normally been protected or enhanced by the systematic enforcement of controlled 'closure' of occupational entry, a particular characteristic of professional occupations. The growth of professional occupations has been particularly marked in neo-capitalist society. In the United States, for example, the proportion of professional workers in the male labour force almost trebled between 1950 and 1970, and a similar trend can be observed in other societies, even if the total proportion of professionals in the labour force does not approach that of the United States (about 15 per cent). While the professions obviously share certain elements in common with other occupational associations, notably the trade unions, which attempt to impose control over the distribution of market capacities, in other respects they are quite distinct from these. The professional association functions not only as a medium of occupational control, but seeks also to establish ethical prerogatives governing general 'standards of conduct'.

Although there certainly are controversial problems of sociological analysis posed by the existence of the professions, professionalisation does not offer major difficulties for class theory. The same cannot be said, however, of other sources of differentiation within the middle class, which have caused many authors to doubt the applicability of any such generic term as the 'middle class' altogether. The term appears to have a definite usefulness in relation to white-collar workers within organisations, where these workers are part of a definite 'office', and consequently of a bureaucratic hierarchy of authority. But what of workers whose tasks are not primarily 'manual', but who are not so clearly involved in any such clearly identifiable hierarchy, and who, while they may often be connected with the professions, are not of them? As C. Wright Mills puts it: 'The old professions of medicine and law are still at the top of the professional world, but now all around them are men and women of new skills. There are a dozen kinds of social engineers and mechanical technicians, a multitude of Girl Fridays, laboratory assistants, registered and unregistered nurses, draftsmen, statisticians, social workers. In the salesrooms, which sometimes seem to coincide with the new society as a whole, are the stationary salesgirls in the department store, the mobile salesmen of insurance, the absentee salesmen – the ad-men helping others sell from a distance . . .

The problem of the 'new middle class'

Questions concerning the 'new middle class' have brooked large in discussions of class analysis ever since the debates over Marxist revisionism in the German Social Democratic Party. In the book I distinguished three main interpretations of the relative expansion of 'white-collar' occupations. One such interpretation, particularly favoured by some American authors, was that the relative increase in white-collar work heralds the arrival of a 'middle-class society'. This kind of view was linked to the idea that established forms of class conflict progressively disappear as the process of *embourgeoisement* becomes more complete. It stood in direct contrast to a second interpretation, the attempt of Mallet and others to appropriate some of those in these intermediate occupations to a potentially revolutionary 'new working class', rather than to a 'new middle class'. The third view was that of orthodox Marxism: that most of those in white-collar occupations are being downgraded rather than upgraded, in a process of proletarianisation, so that neither a new middle class nor a new working class exists at all. I rejected all of these views, although not *in toto*. Both of the first two, it seemed to me, derived in some part from over-generalisation from specific societies, one of the tendencies I was concerned to criticise throughout *CSAS*. The very same occupational categories supposedly involved in the revolutionary vanguard of the 'new working class' in France, where that conception originated, were taken by writers in the United States to be among the most stable and quiescent sectors of the 'middle-class society'. The third view simply seemed to fly in the face of the evidence, which just does not conform to traditional ideas that white-collar workers are (finally!) becoming thrust down into the proletariat.

Marxist authors however have in recent years devoted consider-

able attention to developing accounts of the distinctive characteristics of a white-collar middle class. Among writings worthy of
mention are those by Carchedi, Wright and Poulantzas . . .

. . . I do not think their work would lead me to make substantial
alterations in the analysis of the new middle class offered in *CSAS*.
The sources of class structuration of the new middle class are more
heterogeneous than those of either the dominant or working classes;
and, as I emphasised, the new middle class rarely features promi-
nently in manifest class struggles. But in all the advanced capitalist
societies, its social and political significance is considerable: that this
is so is at least more widely acknowledged today by Marxist authors
than was the case some years ago.

Question
1. (a) *What distinguishes the 'new' from the old middle class?*
(5 marks)
(b) *Critically review Giddens' analysis of the 'new middle class'.*
(20 marks)
(You may need to re-read my introduction before attempting (b))

27 Mike Saks: Professionals

'The professions' is perhaps not the most popular sociological
topic. Yet, its relevance to sociology students – most of whom
hope to end up 'in the professions' – is unquestionable. This
article reviews two major perspectives on the place of the
professions within the broader social structure.

In the earlier part of his article, not included here, Mike Saks
deals briefly with 'taxonomic' perspectives (functionalist and
trait accounts) on the professions. He reiterates the familiar criticism that these approaches tend to be based on descriptions of
the attributes or 'traits' of professionals – largely as presented
by professionals themselves. Recent, neo-Weberian and Marxist
perspectives on professions subject these traditional approaches
to radical analysis.

Central to the Neo-Weberian approach is the concept of social
closure: the practice of a given group preventing others from
gaining access to its position of advantage and prestige. Instead
of 'the public interest', 'self-interest' is regarded as the likely

motivation of organised professions. Marxists are more concerned to locate professionals as precisely as possible within the class structure. A particular focus of debate is the extent to which a profession helps to foster the interests of capital or is more closely allied to labour.

Saks criticises much of both neo-Weberian and Marxist writings on the professions for lack of empirical rigour. Nevertheless, he regards their common perspective, that professions are organised primarily in their own interest rather than to 'do good', as a potentially fruitful orientation.

Reading 27 From Mike Saks 'Removing the blinkers? A critique of recent contributions to the sociology of professions' in *The Sociological Review*, Vol. 31, No. 1, pp. 5–7, 11–14, 16–18.

The new orthodoxy in the sociology of professions in the contemporary Anglo-American context is now rooted in the contributions of neo-Weberian and Marxist writers. But have such contributors succeeded where their taxonomic and interactionist predecessors failed – namely, in developing and adequately applying a suitable theoretical framework for the analysis of the function and behaviour of professions in modern Western societies? The remainder of the paper will be devoted to the task of outlining and evaluating existing work deriving from the neo-Weberian and Marxist perspectives respectively against this historical backcloth.

The neo-Weberian approach

The term the 'neo-Weberian approach' to the professions will be used to denote recent work which has attempted, directly or indirectly and explicitly or implicitly, to apply the Weberian concept of social closure to the consideration of professional occupations in society. The notion of closure, introduced by Weber in Economy and Society, broadly refers to the process by which given social collectivities seek to regulate market conditions in their favour, *in face* of actual or potential competition from outsiders, by restricting access to specific opportunities to a limited group of eligibles. Although closure in Weber's own account can take many different forms, in general terms neo-Weberian writers on the professions tend to regard such occupations as legally privileged groups which have managed to monopolise to a considerable degree social and economic opportunities.

Amongst sociologists who most strongly exemplify this approach must be included Parkin and Parry and Parry. Parkin's latest work contains one of the more interesting recent applications of the concept of social closure. Parkin argues that two major generic forms of closure can be identified – that of usurpation which is oriented towards improving the position of a subordinate group at the expense of a dominant group and that of exclusion which is associated with the exercise of power in a downward direction through the subordination of socially defined inferiors. Professionalisation is said to be a particular type of exclusionary closure based on credentialism and is viewed as 'a strategy designed, amongst other things, to limit and control the supply of entrants to an occupation in order to safeguard or enhance its market value. In this respect, the crucial distinction between professions and manual trades seeking occupational exclusion is held to be that the former groups have generally been able to effect legal monopolies by means of state licensure. Parry and Parry also stand very much in the Weberian tradition in that they too regard professionalism as an occupational strategy to control the market for particular services – involving the establishment of self-governing associations of formally equal colleagues, restrictions on recruitment and, ideally, legal sanction in the field in question. Other sociologists working within the neo-Weberian mould are not always so firmly linked to the mainstream of Weberian thought. Johnson, for instance, sees professionalism as one way of resolving the structure of uncertainty which exists in the relationship between producer and consumer in an era of growing specialisation. Accordingly, he claims professions are occupations in which 'the producer defines the needs of the consumer and the manner in which these needs are catered for.' Freidson, on the other hand, argues that the main distinguishing feature of professions is legitimate, organised autonomy in the spheres of technical judgement and the organisation of work. However, although such conceptualisations emphasise control over clients and work respectively rather than the market *per se*, they are clearly notions related to the concept of closure and thus lie within the general spirit of the neo-Weberian approach.

Basing the definition of a profession exclusively on the idea of closure or some associated concept offers important advantages over the taxonomic contribution. Foremost of these is that, as with symbolic interactionism, the perspective enables sociologists to investigate empirically the assumptions about the current nature and role of professional groups which are built into the very heart of the trait and functionalist models of professions. Freidson very clearly describes the way in which the claims of taxonomic authors and, indeed, professions themselves are exposed to rigorous inquiry when he states that 'by defining a profession structurally, as a position in a division of labour, one can, without embarrassment and apology, deal with the difference between what a group typically claims its members to be as opposed to what they actually are, and between what is generally believed about a group by others and what is actually the case'. It follows, therefore, that the

conformity of the real characteristics of an occupation with all the beliefs about them is not presumed . . . and is a matter for empirical determination . . . Once we define the profession primarily as a special status in the division of labour supported by official and sometimes public belief that it is worthy of such status, we are liberated from the confusion and special pleading which permeates most discussions of professions.

It is also worth mentioning in this context that the neo-Weberian approach has the additional advantage over the taxonomic perspective of opening up the opportunity to examine adequately the historical dynamic of professionalisation; freed from the intellectual strait-jacket of taxonomy sociologists from the neo-Weberian school are able to consider empirically the socio-political conditions under which groups become professions. Since such historical analyses would not preclude a macro-sociological consideration of the process of manipulation of political power to promote professionalisation, the theoretical merits of the neo-Weberian perspective as compared to interactionism should be obvious too at this stage . . .

The Marxist approach

The Marxist view of the professions is centred on the relations of production as opposed to those of the market as in the neo-Weberian perspective. Much of the academic interest which this approach to the professions has attracted in the last few years has arisen from a general concern of Marxist writers to locate the position of the middle strata in the class structure under conditions of monopoly capitalism. A broad range of theorising has taken place in this regard – particularly in respect of the relationship of this group to the class cleavage between the bourgeoisie and proletariat. Parkin has helpfully classified this work according to the extent to which restrictive or inclusive criteria are applied in the assignment of proletarian status. In terms of Parkin's categorisation it is evident that professions, and especially dominant segments of professions, have rarely been seen in a very favourable light. Baran is perhaps amongst the more generous Marxist authors in that he does at least suggest that elements of the professional middle class like scientists and physicians form part of a diverse group with interests objectively opposed to the bourgeoisie; although he recognises that such strata are supported by the economic surplus in capitalist societies, it is claimed that the demand for their services would not only continue, but also be greatly increased under a socialist regime.

The majority of Marxist accounts, though, take a more cynical stance. An extreme view which is often adopted regards all members of professional occupations as politically suspect. Poulantzas, for example, firmly locates professions within the ranks of the new petty bourgeoisie. He argues that far from sharing a proletarian class situation, professional agents of the state apparatus like social workers and teachers in fact perform the tasks of ideological inculcation and political repression of dominated sectors of society while such occupational groups as engineers are often directly involved in the management and supervision of the working class under capitalism. Poulantzas's position has parallels in – although it is by no means synonymous with – Ehrenreich and Ehrenreich's claim that professions make up an important part of the 'Professional-Managerial Class' which is composed of salaried mental workers who do not own the means of production but exist in a mutually contradictory relationship with the working class by virtue of their role in reproducing capitalist culture and class relations. This argument is taken still further, moreover, in the field of health care where Navarro holds that professional elites like the Royal Colleges in Britain are actually segments of a dominant capitalist class.

Another school of Marxist thought, though, has rejected the notion that professionals are broadly lodged in an objectively antagonistic relationship to the working class and asserted that the fundamental line of class cleavage really lies within the petty bourgeoisie in general and the professions in particular. Braverman, for instance, suggests that the middle class draws its characteristics from both sides of the class divide; he believes that this stratum not only receives 'its petty share in the prerogatives and rewards of capital, but it also bears the mark of the proletarian condition.' This apparent paradox concerning the intermediate social positions has also been taken up in a celebrated article by Carchedi. For Carchedi, the two major classes are distinguished by the extent to which their activities are linked to either the 'global functions of capital' or the 'collective labourer'. On this analysis, specialists carrying out the former functions are associated with the process of exploitation as they are involved in control and surveillance activities designed to ensure that surplus value is appropriated, realised and the means of its production reproduced. Agents performing the functions of the collective labourer, on the other hand, are seen to be involved in tasks in the complex and cooperative labour process which are more heavily tied to the production of surplus value. Significantly, it *is* held that any particular occupation in the contemporary middle class can embody both aspects of the duality to differing degrees and polarise along such lines.

Carchedi's contribution is extremely relevant in this context given that Esland, amongst others, has argued that the paradoxical position of the intermediate strata is mirrored in the professions. More specifically, Esland contends that the new professional workers created by the growth of corporate capitalism and the rise of the welfare state along with, to a lesser extent, the older established practitioners of law and medicine 'have become both agents of capitalist control and also the professionally trained servants of capitalism' . . .

Certainly, Marxist authors can scarcely be accused of failing to consider the relationship between professions and the wider social structure; they do indeed link professions to the broader distribution of power in society and their explanations of the dynamic of professionalisation assuredly transcend the potential limitations of accounts based simply on occupational strategies or the logic of mere technique. But, these points notwithstanding, Marxist studies of the professions to date, like those of the neo-Weberian school, have largely proved deficient – again mainly because of the scant regard displayed for empirical evidence.

This can probably be most starkly revealed with reference to

Navarro's recent book *Class Struggle, the State and Medicine*. In this study the author pursues his familiar claim that the primary forces controlling health services in Western industrialised countries are to be discovered outside medicine in the class relations of capitalism. Applying his analysis to Britain, he argues that the National Health Service is not a sphere heavily influenced by quasi-autonomous professional elites, but merely a ruling class dominated sector contributing to capital accumulation by, amongst other things, treating the alienation and disease generated by life in advanced capitalist societies. Yet to see the medical profession as little more than an element of the ruling class in this way is plainly inadequate. In particular, it underplays the complexity of the relationship between professions and capitalism, ignoring the existing power base of professional groups involved in health care. It is especially difficult to square Navarro's ill supported study with Eckstein's careful inquiry which clearly demonstrated that medical policy in Britain in the years immediately following the inception of the National Health Service was, to a very large extent, British Medical Association policy. Despite Navarro's introductory critique of those who adopt a negative attitude to empirical research, his own analysis simply consists of the reiteration of a rigid framework of ideas which are not altered to encompass the specific historical and contemporary features of the British health care system.

Similar deficiencies have been apparent in the common Marxist theme concerning the alleged proletarianisation of professional workers in capitalist societies. Braverman, for example, holds that such groups as draughtsmen, technicians, nurses, engineers and accountants are undergoing an erosion of their position in terms of income and work control. But the argument that these personnel are in the midst of a process of proletarianisation paralleling the deskilling of manual craft workers earlier this century by dint of their role as sellers of labour power within the capitalist mode of production is highly dubious. As Parkin notes, it

> assumes the existence of a golden age of semi-professional inde-
> pendence now abruptly shattered by newly imposed external
> controls. In fact, of course, many of the lower professions were
> virtually the creation of bureaucracy, having been set up as
> government agencies for the administration of the welfare state.

Were Marxist writers associated with this line of argument to show just a little more understanding of the historical evidence, they might deserve to be treated with more respect.

Conclusion

The way forward, though, is not difficult to discern. Although there is no universal agreement about the precise definition of a profession amongst neo-Weberian and Marxist contributors, they do largely concur that they are at root occupational groups characterised by some configuration of concrete, usually legally sustained, privileges. This restricted conceptualisation carries important advantages over the outmoded taxonomic model in that it creates the possibility of opening up to rigorous empirical analysis the historical conditions under which professionalisation has occurred and the current nature and role of professions in society. Sociologists of professions should in future grasp this opportunity with both hands for only in this way will deeper insights be gained into such pressing issues as the explanation of state involvement in supporting strategies of professionalisation, the role of specialised knowledge in both securing and maintaining professional status and the extent to which an altruistic orientation does indeed distinguish professions from other occupational groups. It should be stressed, however, that, in making these recommendations, a plea is not being made for a crudely positivistic stance to be adopted to undercut the long-standing debates between sociologists who have addressed themselves to areas of inquiry of this kind. Of course, the differing theoretical presuppositions of neo-Weberian and Marxist writers will continue to influence the type of problems selected for investigation and the way in which these problems are handled. But this does not mean that sociologists of professions cannot move beyond the sphere of assumption and rhetoric to a far greater degree than hitherto – by both producing theories which are in principle testable within the bounds of the specific perspectives from which they emanate and being more prepared to evaluate them carefully in the light of what is held to count as evidence.

For the moment, however, it remains highly ironic that neo-Weberian and Marxist writers, having liberated themselves from the blinkers of the taxonomic perspective and the theoretical limitations of interactionism, should have little improved on the traditional practice of reifying elements of professional ideologies and turning them into objective definitional attributes of professions; their work, just as that of the previous trait and functionalist orthodoxy, has, so far, and with too few exceptions, tended to close off *a priori* sociologically interesting and socially worthwhile issues from systematic empirical scrutiny.

Question

1. *(a) Summarise recent neo-Weberian contributions to analysis of the professions.*

(5 marks)

(b) Summarise recent Marxist contributions to analysis of the professions.

(5 marks)

(c) Evaluate these two approaches.

(15 marks)

28 David Lockwood: The Privatised Worker's Image of Society

In a highly influential article, David Lockwood offered a three-part typology of 'working class images of society'. According to Lockwood, the work and community experience of the working class fell into three broad categories reflected in associated images of society. His three-part division of the working class is as follows:

1. 'Proletarian' traditionalist
2. 'Deferential' traditionalist
3. 'Privatised' worker

The extract included here describes only the outlook of the privatised worker but it will be helpful briefly to describe that of the other two. The proletarian traditionalist is 'solid' working class: socially, politically, and in terms of strongly supporting the unions. He or she sees society in antagonistic 'us' and 'them' terms. By contrast, the deferential worker accepts a lowly position in the hierarchy as legitimate and does not usually aspire beyond it.

The 'new' (in 1966) privatised workers have an instrumental (practical, self-interested) attitude to work and are committed to the immediate family rather than the community. They consider that earning a reasonable income is the key to a comfortable standard of living and to acceptance by the majority of 'ordinary people' who appear to be doing the same. Lockwood terms this a 'pecuniary model' of society. Workers who tend to see society in this way regard themselves as members of a vast 'central class' which they might variously refer to as 'the working class' or 'the middle class'. Above are the rich and below, the poor.

Three comments can be made on Lockwood's analysis of the privatised worker. First, the privatised worker's image of the class structure is broadly compatible with that presented twenty years later by Rentoul and Lumsden in Reading 24 (see also my introduction to that reading). Perhaps this view of society has become even more credible over the last two decades. Second, it is certainly true that in spotting the emergence of the privatised worker, Lockwood brought to attention an actor who has become ever more influential in social and political life in recent years. Whether because of isolation from traditional working class community (as Lockwood suggests) or, increasingly, because of relative affluence, the privatised worker typically appears to have no great commitment either to socialism or to the Labour Party. Indeed, Margaret Thatcher has made a powerful play for the privatised worker vote (see Reading 69). These developments have had immense cultural and political implications. Third, as a Weberian, Lockwood gives great emphasis to what people themselves think. Whether or not one likes what others think, this does seem to be a most helpful point at which to start analysis.

Reading 28 From David Lockwood, 'Sources of Variation in Working Class Images of Society', reprinted in Anthony Giddens and David Held eds., *Classes, Power and Conflict: Classical and Contemporary Debates* (Macmillan, 1982), pp. 370–2.

The social isolation of the privatised worker reflects itself in his ideology of a 'de-socialised' class structure. The single, overwhelmingly important, and the most spontaneously conceived criterion of class division is money, and the possessions, both material and immaterial, that money can buy. From this point of view, for example, education is not thought of as a status-conferring characteristic, but rather simply as a good that money can buy and as a possession that enables one to earn more money. In general, power and status are not regarded as significant sources of class division or social hierarchy. Power is not understood as the power of one man over another, but rather as the power of a man to acquire things: a purchasing power. Status is not seen in terms of the association of status equals sharing a similar style of life. If status is thought of at all it is in terms of a standard of living, which all who have the means can readily acquire. It may not be easy to acquire the income requisite to a certain standard of living and hence qualify for membership in a more affluent class; but given the income there are no other barriers to mobility.

Within this pecuniary universe, the privatised worker tends to see himself as a member of a vast income class which contains virtually the great mass of the population. This class may be called 'the working class' or 'the middle class'. Whatever it is called, it is a collection of 'ordinary people' who 'work for a living' and those who belong to it include the majority of manual and non-manual employees. They are united with one another, not by having exactly the same incomes, but by not having so much or so little income that their standard of living places them completely beyond the upper or lower horizons. A minority of persons in the society have either so much wealth or such an impoverished existence that they lie outside the central class. They are the very rich and the very poor. Since the main criterion of class membership is money, the lower and, especially, the upper limits of the central class are hard to define, and are consequently defined arbitrarily or regarded as indeterminate. In general the 'upper' or 'higher' or 'rich' class is not perceived as wielding power or deserving of respect. It is simply a vague category of 'all those up there' who have incomes and possessions and a standard of life that are completely beyond the bounds of possibility as far as the ordinary worker is concerned. The rich, however, are different from the rest only in the sense of Hemingway's rejoinder to Scott Fitzgerald: that they have much more money.

Finally, the central class with which the privatised worker identifies himself is seen as a relatively new phenomenon, brought about by the incorporation of the old middle class into the new 'working class', or, alternatively, by the incorporation of the old working class into the new 'middle class'. Whether the end result of the change is seen as a 'working class' or a 'middle class', its identity is basically an economic one; people are assigned to this central class because they have roughly similar levels of income and possessions. Because the convergence of the 'old' working and middle classes is seen in essentially economic terms, the designation of the new central class as 'middle' or 'working' would seem to be largely a matter of how the change is perceived as having taken place rather than an expression of status- or class-consciousness. Indeed, the logic of a purely pecuniary model of society leads to neither class consciousness nor status consciousness but to commodity consciousness. Class and status models entail a perception of social groups whose boundaries are identifiable by acts of power and deference. But the pecuniary universe is one in which inequalities are not expressed through social relationships at all. Income and possessions may be the marks of persons, but unlike power and status they do not involve persons in relationships of inequality with one another. Inequalities take on an extrinsic and quantitative, rather than an intrinsic and qualitative form. In fact, compared with power and prestige, money is not inherently a divider of persons at all; it is a common denominator, of which one may have more or less without its thereby necessarily making a difference to the kind of person one is.

In so far as the privatised worker thinks in terms of the pecuniary model, he has, of course, a somewhat distorted view of the class structure. All available evidence indicates that the amount of informal social interaction between the lower middle and upper working classes is very small and that, in this sense at least, class boundaries are still quite distinct. The privatised worker's idea of a vast central class, differentiated only by marginal differences in income and possessions, is not, therefore, an accurate sociological picture. At the same time, it must be noted that the boundary between the middle and working classes is probably maintained as much by work and residential segregation as by personal exclusion. Thus, from this point of view, the mechanisms of class dissociation operate in a way which is not entirely incompatible with an image of a 'de-socialised' class structure.

There is, finally, no suggestion that the pecuniary model of society is to be thought of as a direct product of working class affluence. The pecuniary model is an outcome of the social rather than the economic situation of the privatised worker; and he is only able to hold such a theory of society in so far as his social environment supports such an interpretation. His relative privatisation, his lack of a sense of class cohesion and his isolation from any system of hierarchical social status are the conditions under which he can view his society simply in pecuniary terms.

A purely pecuniary ideology is, of course, just as much of a limiting case as a purely class or purely status model of society. But it may be that it is at least as relevant as the other two in understanding the social and political outlook of the increasingly large section of the working class that is emerging from traditionalism.

Question

1. (a) What does Lockwood mean by a 'pecuniary model' of society?

    (10 marks)

    (b) How is the privatised worker's image of society (particularly class structure) influenced by his own experience? How misleading do you think this experience is about the privatised worker's position in society?

    (15 marks)

29 Sara Arber, Angela Dale and G. Nigel Gilbert: Problems of Classifying Women by Social Class

The following extract is clearly laid out and is an excellent introduction to the inadequacies of existing social class classifications in relation to women. More than that, it offers a new classification, the Surrey Occupational Class, specifically designed to do justice to the class position of women.

The opening and longest section of the extract, 'Problems of Classification', is divided into two parts: first, the limitations for women of classifications developed for men; second, the difficulties that arise from classifying women on the assumption that their primary function is domestic and that their occupational status is derived from that of their husbands. There follows a summary of the main points under both these headings.

SARA ARBER, ANGELA DALE AND G. NIGEL GILBERT

The limitations for women of classifications developed for men

1. The Occupational Unit Groups (OUGs) within which most occupational classifications are placed better differentiate male than female occupations.
2. The criteria by which men's occupations are divided into classes may not apply equally to women – for instance, in personal service work.
3. When men and women are categorised in the same social class, differences remain *within* these classes – women usually occupying inferior positions.
4. The same occupation may mean different things for a male than a female, e.g. a position as a clerk is more likely to provide a route to management for the former.

In dealing with the problems arising from classifying women in terms of their husband's occupation, Arber *et al* present and then refute the objections to classifying women by their own occupations.

Objections against classifying women by their own occupations

1. Women exit and re-enter the labour market more often than men.
2. Women change jobs more frequently than men.
3. A large minority of women are not in the labour force – 41 per cent of married women between 16 and 59, in 1981.

The second section of the extract presents and explains the Surrey Occupational Class (SOC) which, it is argued, has major advantages for understanding the occupational position of women. It classifies part-time and unwaged as well as full-time working women.

The Surrey Occupational Class is given at the end of the reading.

Reading 29 From Sara Arber, Angela Dale and G. Nigel Gilbert, 'The Limitations of Existing Social Class Classifications for Women' in Ann Jacoby *ed.*, *The Measurement of Social Class* (Social Research Association, 1986), pp. 49–58, 84.

Problems of classification

There are two distinct and somewhat conflicting strands to the debate about occupation-based classifications of social class for women. The first starts from the premise that it is worthwhile to use women's occupations as a basis for classification, but criticises the inadequacy of existing classifications because they have been derived for men's occupations, and the second focuses on the relationship between the sexual division of labour in the family and in the labour market. We shall discuss each in turn.

Existing classifications were devised for men's occupations; for example, the Registrar General's social classes and Socio-Economic Groups were constructed on *a priori* grounds for men, and Goldthorpe's classes were developed to provide theoretically relevant distinctions between men's occupations (see Catherine Marsh's paper in this volume for a discussion of these class measures). Empirically-derived class schemes, such as the Hope-Goldthorpe scale and the Cambridge scale were based on ranking the 'social desirability' of men's occupations and the friendship patterns of men respectively (see Catherine Marsh's paper). There are a number of reasons for being sceptical about taking classifications developed for one section of the population, men, and applying them wholesale to another section, women:

1 Occupational Unit Groups (OUGs) are the building blocks on which most occupational classifications are based; in 1970, 20,000 occupational titles were grouped into 223 OUGs (OPCS, 1970). The basis of classification was changed in 1980 to the Key Occupations for Statistical Purposes (KOS), which contains over 500 categories. Although there are differences in detail as to how specific occupational titles are classified, in broad outline in 1980 classification presents the same problems as the 1970 classification.

OUGs provide less differentiation for women's than men's occupations. For example, fifty-two percent of women are concentrated in *only five* of the 223 OUGs (Dale, Gilbert & Arber, 1983), and nearly a quarter of all women working full-time are classified in one OUG, number 139 – clerks and cashiers – compared to five per cent of men. This OUG contains a wide range of occupations, for example, receptionists, proof readers, library assistants, stock control clerks, postal and telegraph officers, persons issuing tickets at theatres and taking readings from meters. These occupations reflect diverse labour market relations and are likely to be related to different life styles. Had the classification been devised with women in mind then without doubt OUG number 139 would have been disaggregated. Similarly, nurses of all levels from untrained nursing auxiliaries to Ward Sisters and Chief Nursing Officers are coded in the same OUG – number 183 (in RG class II), yet they have very different pay and promotion prospects; and maids and air hostesses are classified in the same OUG – number 164 (in RG class IV).

An underlying problem is therefore the impossibility of further analysis of occupations within OUGs, or of grouping occupations in any other way, because of the indivisibility of the OUG. We understand that the Classification of Occupations for 1990 is being revised to take greater account of the distinctions between women's occupations.

2 The criteria used to divide men's occupations into classes may not be equally relevant when considering distinctions between women's occupations.

There is an extensive literature on class categorisations for men, which argues that there is a fundamental difference between manual and non-manual work (eg. Elchardus, 1981), but we have found no comparable literature for women. Much of women's work cannot be neatly split into a non-manual/manual dichotomy, since it involves various types of 'people servicing work'. Such work is not adequately dealt with in existing classifications. For example, a shop assistant and supermarket check-out worker are in Registrar General's class IIIN (non-manual), while a telephonist and waitress are classified in class IV (semi-skilled), together with semi-skilled factory workers. Allen (1982), in a wide ranging critique of the shortcomings of existing social class schema for women, questions the applicability to women of occupational classifications based on traditional divisions between non-manual and manual work.

A major defect of existing classifications is that they do not deal adequately with personal service work, perhaps because of the small proportion of men engaged in such work. Women, particularly women who work part-time, are heavily represented in personal service work. Murgatroyd (1984) suggests that personal service work differs from either manufacturing or clerical work in such a way that it is inappropriate to apply the same skill distinctions to all three groups of occupation, and that employees in personal service work may have a lower social standing than employees of equivalent 'skill' levels in other sectors, as suggested by their lower rates of pay.

Skill level is another area where distinctions drawn for men's work cannot be simply applied to women. The Registrar General's classification is primarily based on skill level, yet women are largely excluded from apprenticeships on which designation of skill is mainly based. The level of skill accorded to an occupation tends to be greater if an apprenticeship is required, irrespective of whether the tasks being performed require such a lengthy training period; a greater level of skill is also attributed to occupations with a strong union structure which can command relatively high rates of pay. These features all tend to favour placing men's occupations in a more skilled category than women's. There is evidence that many jobs performed by women are classified as semi-skilled or unskilled despite needing considerable expertise (Coyle, 1982; Armstrong, 1982). Thompson (1983) discusses the social construction of skills for bargaining purposes; skill designation may primarily be a market strategy used by trade unions to obtain and justify higher wages. Because of women's weaker trade union position they have been largely excluded from such market strategies. Among women manual workers there are much smaller differences in the level of pay and fringe benefits between women working in 'skilled' manual, 'semi-skilled' and 'unskilled' occupations than among men in these three classes (Arber, Dale and Gilbert, 1984; Heath and Britten, 1984), which suggests that skill distinctions may be less relevant when considering the class of women.

Goldthorpe (1980) emphasises the importance of employment status in conceptualising and measuring class. He argues that class schema should categorise the self-employed and own-account workers as distinct occupational classes because they have a different relationship to the means of production to that of employees. However, women who are self-employed are much less likely to have any employees than men, and are more likely to be peripherally related to the labour market, working only a few hours per week, and to be in a disadvantaged position, for example, as home workers (Hakim and Dennis, 1982; Hakim, 1984). Therefore, self-employment has very different meanings for men and women, and cannot be treated in the same way in class schema. In addition, a much smaller proportion of women are self-employed – under a fifth of the self-employed were women in 1981 (CSO, 1983).

3 When men and women are categorised in the same class in existing class schema, it is generally assumed that they share common occupations and common labour market or work situations. However, this is generally not the case because the composition of occupations *within* social classes varies markedly for men and women. One or two examples will suffice: 85% of women categorised in Registrar General's class V (unskilled) are cleaners (OUG number 166), but only ten percent of men in class V are cleaners (Dale, Gilbert and Arber, 1983). Men in class V are primarily labourers, railway porters, dustmen, road workers, road sweepers, lorry drivers' mates and messengers, occupations which contain virtually no women. Within class IIIN (routine non-manual) women comprise ninety-nine percent of typists and secretaries (OUG number 141) and ninety per cent of sales assistants (OUG number 144) (Dale, Gilbert and Arber, 1983). However, men in class IIIN are predominantly clerks, or, where they are in sales occupations, they tend to be sales representatives. For example, over 95 per cent of commercial travellers, OUG number 148, are men. These occupations have considerably higher incomes and promotion prospects than sales assistants. Thus, where the same classifications are used for men and women, they give the appearance of comparing like with like, but in fact each class contains quite different occupations for men and women, with women generally occupying inferior labour market positions.

4 The same occupation may have a different meaning and market potential when occupied by men and women. Stewart, Prandy and Blackburn (1980) have demonstrated this point with regard to clerks. For the majority of men the occupation of clerk provides a career route to management and higher paid non-manual jobs, whereas for women the same occupation is a destination from which there is little possibility of career advancement.

The second strand of the argument about women's class is premised on the assumption that their primary attachment is to the family and that attachment to the labour market is secondary. Nissel (1980) and Hunt (1980) discuss many of the deficiencies of government statistics on women which derive from this premise. One of them is the convention of classifying married women according to their husband's occupation. Thus in the Annual Reports of the General Household Survey married women are categorised by their husband's occupation, and single, divorced, separated and widowed women are categorised by their current occupation, or last occupation if not in paid employment (OPCS, 1978, Appendix A). The practice of classifying married women according to their husband's occupation began in 1911, when Stevenson introduced the precursor of the Registrar General's classification. This convention may have been justified in 1911 when only 10% of married women were in paid employment, but the situation is clearly quite different today when nearly 60% of married women aged 16 to 59 are economically active (Beacham, 1984).

Despite the increased participation of married women in the labour force, Goldthorpe (1983, 1984) still argues that a woman's attachment to the labour market is marginal and conditioned by her husband's class, and that wives are dependent on their husbands for the determination of their life chances, and therefore, their class position should be derived from their husband's occupation. However, data presented by Heath and Britten (1983; 1984) make this position increasingly untenable.

We will discuss issues related to women's secondary attachment to the labour market, focusing on the applicability of arguments which support the continued use of the husband's occupation rather than the wife's own occupation as an indicator of her class position.

1 One argument against using women's own occupation as a measure of their class is that the majority of women have a discontinuous work profile and their re-entry jobs after child-bearing are frequently of a lower occupational level than the job held before their first child's birth. The assumption is, therefore, that women with children 'under achieve' and their occupation does not reflect their market potential.

Martin and Roberts (1984) were able to quantify the extent of occupational mobility associated with child-bearing and rearing. They found that the major factor leading to a reduction in occupational level was taking on part-time work. Among women whose most recent job was part-time, nearly half (48%) were in a lower occupation than the job held prior to the birth of their first child, a third (34%) were in a job on the same level, and 18% were in a job at a higher level.

However, among women whose most recent job was full-time, only a fifth (20%) were in a lower occupation than the job held prior to their first child's birth, half (53%) were in a job at the same level, and over a quarter (28%) were in a higher level job. Thus, re-entry jobs after child-bearing are only likely to be of a lower occupational level if they are part-time. Martin and Roberts conclude 'Downward mobility was strongly associated with returning to part-time work' (1984, p 152). Elias (1983) also found that women returning to part-time work after having children do so at a lower level than those who are in full-time work.

The main constraint therefore for married women is where family commitments limit the number of hours a woman can work. The downgrading in occupational level is because part-time work tends to be available only in certain lower status occupations, such as semi-skilled domestic and catering work, as sales assistants and in unskilled work (Martin and Roberts, 1984).

These findings suggest that researchers should be sceptical about using the occupations of women working part-time as a measure of their class position and market potential. If this is the case, it means that for a large and growing proportion of employed women their occupations do not reflect their class position, since 39% of women in the labour force in 1981 had part-time jobs, compared to 22% in 1951 (Beacham, 1984). However, the occupation of married women working full-time is likely to be an adequate indicator of class.

2 A second argument, used by Goldthorpe (1983) and others, against using women's own occupations as a measure of their class is that women are said to change jobs frequently and therefore their present job is less likely to represent their class position. Although Greenhalgh and Stewart (1982), using work history data from the National Training Survey, found that women changed jobs somewhat more frequently than men, Martin and Roberts (1984) reject the assumption that women are unstable employees. 'It is often suggested that women are not stable employees; our evidence seriously challenges this.' (p. 151). They found that women had on average worked for under 5 employers, and women who had worked for 20 or more

years had an average of 6 employers, working on average for 6.2 years per employer.

Further work is necessary before precise statements can be made about the relative levels of job changing among different age groups of women working full-time, women working part-time and men, but it seems likely that a high level of job changing cannot be used as a justification for not using a woman's own occupation as a measure of her class, at least for women working full-time.

3 The most powerful argument against using married women's own occupation as a measure of their class is that 41% of married women between 16 and 59 were not in the labour force in 1981. They defined themselves as 'keeping house' and were unwaged. In common with the growing proportion of other unwaged groups – the unemployed and the retired – it is necessary to decide how to treat these women in class terms. It is unsatisfactory to treat them as a separate class of housewives, or as unemployed, or retired, since although each group may have a common employment status, within each group individuals differ very considerably in their market position and life chances. For the retired, their main occupation during their working life will have influenced the accumulation of assets which affects their current life style. Their previous occupation will also have determined whether the retired person has an occupational pension and, if so, the size of that pension. Similarly, the last occupation of the unemployed not only predicts their likelihood of obtaining another job, but whether their unemployment was cushioned by a redundancy payment and its size, and in addition, the level of assets accumulated while in paid employment.

For unwaged women, their most recent occupation does not usually have the same long-term financial effects on life style – women who leave work to have a baby rarely receive large lump sum severance payments or pensions – although it will have influenced their accumulation of assets. Nonetheless, the woman's last occupation prior to her first child's birth is related to her educational level and her market potential for obtaining jobs of a specific occupational level in the future. Unfortunately, surveys rarely collect data on a woman's last occupation prior to the birth of her first child; generally the only information collected is the woman's most recent occupation. This is a less satisfactory indicator of class position, especially if there is no indication of whether the most recent job was full-time or part-time, or when it was held. For these reasons, it is unlikely that a woman's most recent occupation will be a satisfactory measure of her class.

In summary, we would suggest that a woman's full-time occupation provides as good a measure of class as occupation does for men, but that for women working part-time, their current occupation provides a less adequate indication of class position. For unwaged women, when only the most recent occupation is available this provides a poorer indication of class position than the occupation held prior to their first child's birth.

Table 1 Surrey occupational class by employment status and sex

Surrey Occupational Class	Men Full-time	Women Full-time	Women Part-time	Women Unwaged
1. Higher Professionals	6.1	1.2	0.4	0.6
2. Employees and Managers	13.4	5.3	1.7	2.5
3. Lower Professionals	5.3	13.3	9.2	8.1
4. Secretarial and Clerical	9.1	39.4	19.8	29.2
5. Foremen, Self-employed Manual	12.0	3.5	3.8	1.6
6. Sales and Personal Service	3.2	13.8	35.2	25.2
7. Skilled Manual	32.2	5.1	3.0	6.3
8. Semi-Skilled	15.2	16.2	9.7	20.3
9. Unskilled	3.4	2.1	17.2	6.0
Total	100%	100%	100%	100%
N =	(7498)	(2967)	(2379)	(3418)

Question

1. (a) Summarise the arguments for and against categorising women according to social class scales primarily developed for men.

(10 marks)

(b) What evidence for the existence of patriarchy (the domination of females by males) do you find in the data and arguments presented in the above extract?

(15 marks)

SECTION 6

Inequality and Poverty

Readings 30–32

To consider the rich in the section on stratification, and the poor, separately, is arbitrary. However, it reflects the widely held view that the problem of poverty has taken on a new dimension since about the late nineteen seventies. First, there has been an increase in relative poverty, mainly because of the greater numbers of unemployed and low-paid. Second, the accelerating use of mechanised and automated rather than human labour has raised the possibility that a substantial minority of the population may remain unemployed in the long-term. This is a new and depressing prospect, especially for those facing it. Third, at a time when the main causes of poverty are clearly socio-economic, the contrary view that it is the result of individual failure or inadequacy has been strongly canvassed in the press and among some political groups. This is likely to have a demoralising effect on the poor.

The first reading in this section, by Mack and Lansley, seeks to establish a relevant basis for assessing the nature and extent of poverty in modern Britain. The brief piece from Jeremy Seabrook, makes perhaps the key theoretical point in this section. He argues that the capitalist system itself perpetuates poverty. Marxists such as Westergaard and Resler might prefer the term inequality to poverty, but the point is clear enough. Other than including Seabrook's article, I have chosen not to explore the debate about whether the causes of poverty are primarily structural (eg. caused by capitalism) or cultural (caused by the values, attitudes and lifestyle of the poor). In fact, the concepts of structure and culture are now generally seen as complementary rather than in opposition – as Tony Bennett explains in another context (Reading 98).

Finally, the reading by Frank Coffield and his co-authors describes the experience of poverty of one young woman in the nineteen eighties. This case study provides an important dimension of authenticity. There is much else of interest in their research, as I have tried to show in my lengthy introduction to this extract.

30 Joanna Mack and Stewart Lansley: Measuring Poverty in Britain

The opening section of this reading gives an account of the search for an 'absolute' or 'primary' standard of poverty in Britain, i.e. a minimum standard of living required for physical health. Seebohm Rowntree hoped to establish such a measure as a basis for policy towards the poor. The second section describes the development of the perception that poverty is a relative concept, i.e. what is regarded as poverty will vary in time and place. By 1936, even Rowntree had partly incorporated this concept into his definition of poverty. In contemporary Britain there is considerable disagreement about the best use of these terms. In particular, some find the concept of relative poverty altogether too elastic whilst others regard it as necessary to precise and humane analysis.

The third section very briefly describes the aim of the *Breadline Britain* survey. The survey was carried out by MORI and commissioned by London Weekend Television. Its purpose was 'to establish whether there is, in fact, a public consensus on what minimum standard people living in Britain in the 1980s should be entitled to'. In February 1983 MORI took a quota sample of 1,174 people, designed to be representative of the population as a whole. Respondents were asked to decide which in a list of 35 items are necessary to achieve a minimum standard of living on socially accepted criteria. Section 4 gives the responses to this list. (*Note:* The numbering of sections of the text is mine.) Table 1 gives detailed data and the accompanying text picks out main points. The item perceived as a 'necessity' by most respondents (97 per cent) was 'heating to warm living areas of the home if it is cold'.

Reading 30 Joanna Mack and Stewart Lansley: *Poor Britain* (George Allen and Unwin, 1985), pp. 16–19, 26–9, 49–50, 53–5.

1 The search for an 'absolute' poverty line

Throughout this century there have been proponents of the idea that it is possible to draw up an absolute minimum standard of living on the basis of what is required for physical health or fitness. It is this kind of concept that lies behind the view that there is no real poverty in Britain today. Although this view would have few adherents in academic circles, it is none the less highly influential, being a popular notion and more specifically carrying weight among the present Conservative Party leadership. For example, Sir Keith Joseph, Secretary of State for Education and one of the leading figures on the 'New Right', has argued:

> An absolute standard means one defined by reference to the actual needs of the poor and not by reference to the expenditure of those who are not poor. A family is poor if it cannot afford to eat. (Joseph and Sumption, 1979, pp. 27–8)

While the political right is on its own in tending to view 'poverty' exclusively in these 'absolute' terms, others, too, have found the concept of 'absolute' poverty useful. For example, Tony Crosland argued in *The Future of Socialism:*

> Primary poverty has been largely eliminated; the Beveridge revolution has been carried through. . . . It is true that considerable areas of social distress, not mainly due to primary poverty and of a character not always foreseen by pre-war socialists, still remain. But that is a new and different question. (Crosland, 1964, p. 59).

The concept of 'absolute' or 'primary' poverty was developed during the last century. Though it is now associated with attempts to limit the needs of the poor, at the time it was seen as a way of drawing attention to the plight of the poor. Seebohm Rowntree, in his classic study of poverty in York in 1899, defined 'primary poverty' as an income 'insufficient to obtain the minimum necessaries for the maintenance of merely physical efficiency'. He ruled out spending on 'the maintenance of mental, moral or social sides of human nature'. Spending on food, clothing and shelter was all that he allowed:

A family living upon the scale allowed for must never spend a penny on railway fare or omnibus. They must never go into the country unless they walk. They must never purchase a halfpenny newspaper or spend a penny to buy a ticket for a popular concert. They must write no letters to absent children, for they cannot afford to pay the postage. They must never contribute anything to their church or chapel, or give any help to a neighbour which costs them money. They cannot save nor can they join a sick club or trade union, because they cannot pay the necessary subscriptions. The children must have no pocket money for dolls, marbles or sweets. The father must smoke no tobacco and drink no beer. The mother must never buy any pretty clothes for herself or her children, the character of the family wardrobe as for the family diet being governed by the regulation 'nothing must be bought but that which is absolutely necessary for the maintenance of physical health and what is bought must be of the plainest and most economical description'. (Rowntree, 1922, p. 167)

Rowntree's aim in adopting such a stringent definition was to demolish the view that poverty was due to fecklessness and not to low wages. He felt he had established his case when he found that 15 per cent of the working-class population of York were, in 1899, living in 'primary poverty'. However, his findings in themselves posed contradictions and problems. Clearly the 15 per cent in 'primary poverty' were surviving. They may have been hungry, they may have faced ill-health, they may even have suffered a relatively high death rate, but none of these concepts provides a clear-cut line on which to base an absolute minimum living standard. Throughout the nineteenth century, some did die directly from poverty through starvation, but in general the results were less dramatic. Friedrich Engels, writing about a harsher period some fifty years earlier, describes the effect of poverty on those at the bottom of the pile:

To what extent want and suffering prevail among the unemployed during such a crisis, I need not describe. The poor rates are insufficient, vastly insufficient; the philanthropy of the rich is a raindrop in the ocean, lost in the moment of falling; beggary can support but few among the crowds. If the small dealers did not sell to the working people on credit at such times as long as possible – paying themselves liberally afterwards, it must be confessed – and if the working people did not help each other, every crisis would remove a multitude of surplus through death by starvation. Since, however, the most depressed period is brief, lasting, at worst, but one, two, or two and a half years, most of them emerge from it with their lives after dire privations. But indirectly by disease, etc., every crisis finds a multitude of victims. (Engels, 1969, p. 121)

This poses an intractable problem for Rowntree's concept of 'primary' poverty. There is no doubt that poor health stems from low living standards and that this makes a person susceptible to dying from disease, but others too die from disease. The susceptibility to disease and the level of life expectancy that are acceptable depend not on some absolute criterion but on the standards and expectations of the day. If this is true of Rowntree's aim of the 'maintenance of physical health' in relation to the simple question of survival, it is even more so of his aim of 'physical efficiency'. Concepts such as 'good health' and 'fitness' are nebulous. Although Rowntree followed closely the contemporary developments in dietetic science, his nutrition levels remain not the absolute scientific statement he presumed but a level determined by the assumptions and judgements of the day. Professor A. H. Halsey summarised the unsolvable problem of the search for an absolute poverty line for the *Breadline Britain* series:

There are some people who would want to make poverty entirely objective by seeking a measure of it outside people's heads and outside people's expectations and outside society's norms. And they sometimes think that death might do the trick for them. But it is not like that. Because of course the expectation that people have of how long they will live will always depend upon their expectations of others. It will depend on a socially created idea of life and death. And so even the use of mortality statistics is itself an essentially relative approach to poverty.

2 Viewing necessities as socially determined

There has been a long tradition that has tried to define poverty narrowly in terms of health, aiming either for a universal standard or for a standard relative to a particular moment in time. There has been an equally long tradition that has seen a person's needs as being culturally and socially, as well as physically, determined. It is a view that recognises that there is more to life than just existing. Two hundred years ago the economist Adam Smith wrote:

> By necessaries, I understand not only commodities which are indispensably necessary for the support of life but whatever the custom of the country renders it indecent for creditable people, even of the lowest order, to be without. A linen shirt, for example, is strictly speaking not a necessity of life. The Greeks and Romans lived, I suppose, very comfortably though they had no linen. But in the present time . . . a creditable day-labourer would be ashamed to appear in public without a linen shirt, the want of which would be supposed to denote that disgraceful state of poverty. (Smith, 1812, p. 693)

This theme was adopted and first used for a more practical purpose by Charles Booth in his pioneering surveys of poverty in London from the late 1880s to the turn of the century. He defined the very poor as those whose means were insufficient 'according to the normal standards of life in this country' (Booth, 1888).

Even Seebohm Rowntree, the man who had developed the idea of 'primary' poverty, had, by the time of his second survey of York in 1936, incorporated into his definition of poverty some needs that were not related in any way to the maintenance of physical health. His 1936 definition allowed for items such as a radio, books, newspapers, beer, tobacco, presents and holidays. Although the amounts allowed were small – and largely arbitrary – Rowntree had conceded the importance of a wide range of aspects of a person's standard of living – from consumer durables to leisure activities and social participation.

The essentially relative nature of poverty is immediately obvious when viewing people's standards of living in these broader terms. Purchases of consumer durables are specific to each generation, or even each decade, and activities involving social participation have no meaning outside the society in which people live. This has long been recognised; Karl Marx wrote in 1849:

> Our needs and enjoyments spring from society; we measure them, therefore, by society and not by the objects of their

satisfaction. Because they are of a social nature, they are of a relative nature. (Marx, 1946, p. 269)

To view necessities as socially determined is explicitly to view poverty as relative. For this reason this concept is often called 'relative poverty'. In practice, there has been a great deal of confusion about the concepts of 'absolute' and 'relative' poverty. In part this stems from a recognition that the living standards of the poor have risen considerably during this century and that it is important not simply to dismiss this. It also stems, however, from a failure to come to terms with the fact that, above starvation level, an 'absolute' definition of poverty cannot be sustained; that, for example, Rowntree's definition of 'primary' poverty was in fact a rather narrow definition of 'relative' poverty at the turn of the century.

The upshot has been that a body of opinion has persisted that places emphasis only on 'absolute' poverty. The fact that the poor in Britain today are better off than the poor of the past, and than the poor of other countries today, is seen to devalue their problems. Dr Rhodes Boyson, as Minister for Social Security, gave his view of 'relative' poverty to the House of Commons in a debate on the rich and the poor called by the opposition:

Those on the poverty line in the United States earn more than 50 times the average income of someone in India. That is what relative poverty is all about. . . . Apparently, the more people earn, the more they believe poverty exists, presumably so that they can be pleased about the fact that it is not themselves who are poor. (*Hansard*, 28 June 1984)

Others, in contrast, have argued that the facts of starvation in the poorest countries of the world and the intense deprivations suffered by the poor of the past are not relevant to the problems of the poor of the industrialised world today. Tony Crosland, for example, argued not just for the importance of a concept of 'primary' poverty but also that:

Poverty is not, after all, an absolute, but a social or cultural concept. . . . This demands a relative, subjective view of poverty, since the unhappiness and injustice it creates, even when ill-health and malnutrition are avoided, lies in the enforced deprivation not of luxuries indeed, but of small comforts which others have and are seen to have, and which in the light of prevailing cultural standards are really 'conventional necessities'. (Crosland, 1964, p. 89)

During the 1960s this view became widely accepted, as a result – at least in part – of the work of Professor Peter Townsend. For the last thirty years, Townsend has argued that poverty can only be viewed in terms of the concept of 'relative deprivation'. In his studies of poverty he has refined this concept, culminating in his 1969 survey of living standards. In his report of this comprehensive and influential study, Townsend defined poverty as follows:

Individuals, families and groups in the population can be said to be in poverty when they lack the resources to obtain the types of diet, participate in the activities and have the living conditions and amenities which are customary, or are at least widely encouraged or approved, in the societies to which they belong. (Townsend, 1979, p. 31)

Although something like this definition of poverty would now be widely accepted, there remains immense room for debate about what exactly it means.

3 The survey's purpose

The central brief given to MORI, the survey specialists commissioned by London Weekend Television to design and conduct the *Breadline Britain* survey, was as follows:

The survey's first, and most important, aim is to try to discover whether there is a public consensus on what is an acceptable standard of living for Britain in 1983 and, if there is a consensus, who, if anyone, falls below that standard.

The idea underlying this is that a person is in 'poverty' when their standard of living falls below the minimum deemed necessary by current public opinion. This minimum may cover not only the basic essentials for survival (such as food) but also access, or otherwise, to participating in society and being able to play a social role.

4 The public's perception of necessities

The survey established, for the first time ever, that a majority of people see the necessities of life in Britain in the 1980s as covering a wide range of goods and activities, and that people judge a minimum standard of living on socially established criteria and not just the criteria of survival or subsistence.

Table 1 *The public's perception of necessities*

Standard-of-living items in rank order	% classing item as necessity	Standard-of-living items in rank order	% classing item as necessity
1. Heating to warm living areas of the home if it's cold	97	19. A hobby or leisure activity	64
2. Indoor toilet (not shared with another household)	96	20. Two hot meals a day (for adults)	64
3. Damp-free home	96	21. Meat or fish every other day	63
4. Bath (not shared with another household)	94	22. Presents for friends or family once a year	63
5. Beds for everyone in the household	94	23. A holiday away from home for one week a year, not with relatives	63
6. Public transport for one's needs	88	24. Leisure equipment for children e.g. sports equipment or a bicycle	57
7. A warm water-proof coat	87	25. A garden	55
8. Three meals a day for children	82	26. A television	51
9. Self-contained accommodation	79	27. A 'best outfit' for special occasions	48
10. Two pairs of all-weather shoes	78	28. A telephone	43
11. Enough bedrooms for every child over 10 of different sex to have his/her own	77	29. An outing for children once a week	43
12. Refrigerator	77	30. A dressing gown	40
13. Toys for children	71	31. Children's friends round for tea/a snack once a fortnight[a]	37
14. Carpets in living rooms and bedrooms	70	32. A night out once a fortnight (adults)	36
15. Celebrations on special occasions such as Christmas	69	33. Friends/family round for a meal once a month	32
16. A roast meat joint or its equivalent once a week	67	34. A car	22
17. A washing machine	67	35. A packet of cigarettes every other day	14
18. New, not second-hand, clothes	64		

Average of all 35 items = 64.1

[a] For families with children only.

Table 1 lists the thirty-five items that were tested, ranked by the proportion of respondents identifying each item as a 'necessity'. This ranking shows that there is a considerable degree of social consensus. Over nine in ten people are agreed about the importance of the following basic living conditions in the home:

- heating,
- an indoor toilet (not shared),
- a damp-free home,
- a bath (not shared), and
- beds for everyone.

The right of everyone, regardless of income, to exactly these sorts of basic minima was a key objective of postwar housing policy until the recent sharp cutbacks in public sector housing investment.

The survey also found a considerable degree of consensus about the importance of a wide range of other goods and activities. More than two-thirds of the respondents classed the following items as necessities:

- Enough money for public transport
- A warm water-proof coat
- Three meals a day for children
- Self-contained accommodation
- Two pairs of all-weather shoes
- A bedroom for every child over 10 of different sex
- A refrigerator
- Toys for children
- Carpets
- Celebrations on special occasions such as Christmas
- A roast joint or its equivalent once a week and
- A washing machine

This widespread consensus on what are necessities clearly reflects the standards of today and not those of the past. In Rowntree's study of poverty in York in 1899, for a family to be classed as poor 'they must never spend a penny on railway fare or omnibus'. In Britain in the 1980s, nearly nine in ten people think that such spending is not only justified but a necessity for living today.

POVERTY

Question
1. (a) Distinguish absolute from relative poverty. Give the advantages
   and difficulties of a relative measure of poverty.

   (10 marks)
   (b) The Conservatives, Keith Joseph and Rhodes Boyson take a
   different view of relative poverty than the Socialists Tony Crosland
   and Peter Townsend. Describe and account for this.

   (15 marks)

Activity
1. List what you consider to be ten 'necessities' to achieve a minimum
   standard of living on socially accepted criteria.
2. Carry out a small social survey to establish a consensus on a range
   of 'necessities' to achieve a minimum standard of living on socially
   accepted criteria.

31 Jeremy Seabrook: Beveridge's Five Evils Return

Want, Disease, Ignorance, Squalor and Idleness are the five
'giant evils' which Beveridge hoped to defeat through the
welfare state. According to Jeremy Seabrook they have returned
to haunt us, albeit in some cases in different guises. As well as
material poverty, Seabrook finds massive cultural impoverishment: ignorance perpetuated by the advertising industry,
squalor generated by sections of the popular press. He refers to
this as 'cultural and ideological sewage'.

Seabrook explains the continuation of poverty and degradation in terms of the needs of capitalism. The system requires
'losers' to remind the 'winners' what it is they are working so
hard to avoid. Less obviously impassioned commentators, such
as Westergaard and Resler, have also argued that poverty or,
more precisely, inequality, is intrinsic to capitalism. Capital and
labour mean profit and exploitation. The welfare state is unlikely
to achieve more than minor mitigation of the extremes.

Reading 31 From Jeremy Seabrook, 'Beveridge's Five Evils Return' in
New Society, 28 February 1985, pp. 320–2.

Behind the current questioning of the nature and purpose of the
welfare state significant anniversaries loom. Not only, this year, the

fortieth anniversary of the coming to power of the reforming Labour government of 1945, but also, last year, the more sombre celebration of the Poor Law Amendment Act of 1834, for which some members of the present government may well retain considerable affection, even though they forbear to display it too openly. Long-term re-appraisals are in the air. The social security reviews initiated by Norman Fowler are to be 'the most substantial examination of social security since the Beveridge report,' which was published in 1942. In a report, *Of Benefit to All*, the National Consumer Council called for a drastic overhaul of the social security labyrinth. In the words of its chairman, Professor John Hughes, 'Beveridge's dream of a simple national insurance scheme has become a nightmare.'

Other, perhaps even more unsettling questions need to be asked, which go beyond the present re-assessment. In the celebrated para-graph 465 of the original report, Beveridge identified 'five giant evils.' These were Want, Disease, Ignorance, Squalor and Idleness; and the means whereby these were to be eliminated were then set forth. The 1945 government duly achieved what was believed to be necessary to lay to rest, once and for all, these scourges of the poor.

It now appears that these giants were by no means eradicated. They may have been transformed; metamorphosed even. But they haven't gone away. They have adapted themselves to the existence of the welfare state, and have re-emerged in our time – not always in the same guise, it is true, but modified in ways that fit the altered landscape of our lives, the changed decor of capitalism. Their re-appearance raises a disturbing possibility. Perhaps they remain the necessary and inseparable attendants of a system that defies all attempts of reformers to destroy them.

They may be less easy to recognise in the new forms they assume. But their presence is unmistakable, a blighting and destructive force in lives that were to have been delivered from them for ever.

Most people have little difficulty in acknowledging the recurrence of *Idleness*. Mass unemployment, for a long time felt to be politically intolerable, has proved remarkably acceptable, even to large numbers of those required as the human sacrifice. And as for *Want*, well, that certainly exists, with our seven million people in Britain dependent on supplementary benefit. But the common wisdom is that, like unemployment, it has been much mitigated by the welfare state.

Unhappily, this takes little account of the lived experiences of contemporary unemployment and modernised poverty. Far from being assuaged by welfare, these experiences have been aggravated by the insistent and aggressive images of plenty, by a culture which ceaselessly advertises its desire to shower all that is good and desirable upon its people.

The Child Poverty Action Group has expressed concern at its difficulty in bringing home to people the curiously harrowing pressures of present-day poverty. It couldn't find an image that would convey the feeling. This is not surprising, because the vast majority of images of our society are of remorseless luxury and abundance. The very presence of these ubiquitous scenes of comfort and ease reinforces the idea that, if there are people who fail to avail themselves of the cornucopia, it must be because they are failures as individuals. It must be their own fault.

What of the other horrors that Beveridge sought to banish? Surely they have been effectively dealt with. *Disease*, for instance. If there is one thing we can be proud of, it is the health service, the reduction of infant mortality, the elimination of TB and rickets, the enhanced life expectancy. The old afflictions have gone. That is plain for all to see.

But it may be that the continuities are to be found elsewhere. For instance, it was significant that the Lord Chief Justice, animadverting to the problem of heroin, said that it was 'worse than cholera or typhoid.' At a British Medical Association conference last year, a psychiatrist said that heroin addiction is 'not an epidemic now, it is a plague.'

We sometimes talk in metaphors that give us a sense of ugly recurrences and correspondences. We refer to 'outbreaks' of violence, 'epidemics' of crime. There has been a 'rash' of crimes against the elderly in one area, 'waves' of outrages against migrants in another. The urban riots of 1981 were felt to have been intensified by a copycat effect; in other words, they were contagious.

Revisiting the past

In this way we can understand how the system can have been transformed, and yet remains the same. The consequences of contemporary diseases are no different from those earlier visitations: a young person destroyed by glue or drugs, or left ·bleeding on a suburban pavement after a knifing at a party, suffers no less than those who went to paupers' graves in the cholera epidemics of the early 19th century. The fevers of today take their toll in stress and heart disease and cancers; they have their analogue in a past long familiar. Thatcherism has deep cultural resonances. There is the eerie impression of revisiting the first industrial revolution in spite of the glittering and refurbished appearances.

Ignorance seems an unlikely characteristic of 'information-rich' societies, where there have never been so many people busy 'communicating' with each other. But the spread of industries based on information – that landlordism of knowledge – depends, for its success, on the manufacture of ignorance, a special kind of unknowing. The advertising industry, for example, claims to teach and inform. But in a society in which surfaces are paramount, scepticism is essential if we want to be able to read accurately what is presented. This frequently means taking things at the opposite of their face value.

Advertising is really in the business of creating an ignorance that is necessary to the consumer economies of the west.

It spirits away public concern with the origin, content or suffering involved in the production of any commodity, service or bought thing. Advertising doesn't just encourage people to buy what they don't want. It also sanctifies the moment of purchase, any purchase. It blesses the act of buying by all the noise, show and excitement that are created around each fresh-marketed item. A cloud of unknowing envelops the mysterious communion between vendor and buyer, conjuring away all the awkward questions, such as whose mouths have been denied food to provide succulent milk-fed chickens or corn-raised beef in the supermarket, or who might have walked 200 miles to gain the privilege of working in a sweat shop for the sake of some fashionable garment destined to be tomorrow's rags, or who has crawled underground in a mine guarded by the military to fetch the metal that will make some trifling adornment? The mystic bond between promoter and purchaser is all that matters.

Creating ignorance

This modernised unknowing is not incompatible with people being 'better informed' than ever before. It is a carefully wrought artefact, admirable in its intricacy. Like poverty in the richest societies in the world, its production is a minor miracle.

And what of *Squalor?* The dismantling of 'classic' industrial areas
– the 19th century slums and tenements, mills and factories – was
to have done away with all those cruel sites of suffering, fixed so
indelibly by Dickens and Engels and Booth and Mayhew and Jack
London. But this has been the mere landscaping of capitalism. The
squalors of contemporary life aren't to be found in the infested
interiors, with their orange-box furniture and sacking at the
window, the empty cupboard and dry crusts and guttering candle.
Nor even are they to be found in the stinking breath of open drains
and offal-strewn canals. We should look perhaps at a different flow
of pollutants. There is one stream that can be traced from the ugly
graffiti in the poor estates, denouncing the prosses and divs and
wankers. Another is the violation in the marketing of images of
women, and the ruined relationships of people caged and goaded
by poverty until they tear each other apart, all gloatingly chronicled
in the popular and local press. Yet another stream flows through
what is mis-named the entertainment industry (which should more
accurately be called the ideology industry), where any evening's TV
viewing will yield a sequence of human beings being mangled,
destroyed, murdered and blasted apart.

This cultural and ideological sewage has its effect on humanity
in ways that appear different from Engels's Manchester, yet are so
evocative of the overflow from that poisoned and fetid environment.
For all the altered scenery, old patterns are reconstituted. The
lineaments of Beveridge's giant evils have been modified by the
beautified and re-worked surfaces, but the ugly familiar shapes can
be discerned again – transformed by welfarism, but intact. It
requires only small imagination; a quality, alas, disdained by a left
which thinks that all the horrors of capitalism are known, and have
been revealed for all time.

How would it be possible for these giants not to survive? They
are indispensable to the perpetuation of a society in which poverty
and its grisly attendants are essential. They are essential because of
the overriding need that people should be goaded on to the
continuing accumulation of a capitalist version of riches. Without
the spur of poverty, we might be content to rest in the certainty
that there is enough for all – not only those of us in the rich world,
but also for those suffering more absolute privations all over the
world. If poverty really had been mitigated, made less horrible and

less violent an experience, all the relentless striving might be seen for the driven, tormented absurdity that it is.

There have been curious and unforeseeable consequences in the mingling of welfare with capitalism. The result is a strange mutation, which has a life and dynamic of its own. The spectres of the classic moment of capitalism still haunt this new creation. They continue to do their work of impoverishment and loss, as they always did.

In this context, a review of Beveridge is certainly overdue. That it is Norman Fowler and not the left who is undertaking it comes as no surprise. But is it in order to slay, or even to chain up, those ghostly giants that a fundamentalist government has embarked on such a project? Hardly.

Question
1. (a) In what ways does Seabrook consider that the five 'giant evils' survive?

(10 marks)
   (b) Critically consider his explanations for their survival.

(10 marks)

32 Frank Coffield, Carol Borrill and Sarah Marshall: Poppy's Story: A Personal Experience of 'Shit Jobs and Govvy Schemes' in the North East

Poppy's story speaks for itself. It is a story full of her individual character but the circumstances she faces are typical of those confronted by many young people, particularly in the economically recessed areas of Britain. As the authors of *Growing Up at the Margins: Young Adults in the North East*, from which this extract is taken, say:

> Her experience . . . epitomises the choices open to young adults which in their own words were: shit jobs, govvy schemes and the dole. Poppy illustrates the fundamental point that the women and men who were in employment and on schemes were the same women and men who at other times were unemployed.

Poppy experienced all three alternatives – jobs, schemes and dole. Others in the sample of 48 young adults experienced a

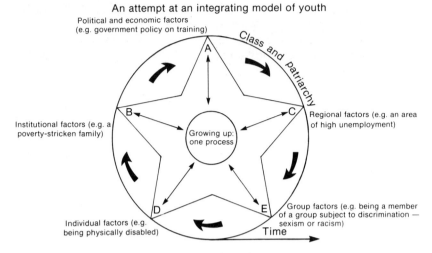

An attempt at an integrating model of youth

different 'mix' of the three alternatives but none was in full-time employment for the full period of the survey (January 1982 to August 1984). The sample was drawn from three sources: two from training schemes and the third was a 'natural group' of eight unemployed men aged between 16 and 28 who all lived on the same estate. Whilst the sample's representativeness of other young adults cannot be quantified, millions are in similar situations. Indeed, the single case of Poppy encapsulates much of what could and did happen to these young adults: the high hopes of a new job; the growing sense of exploitation and unused ability; the sheer boredom; niggling conflict with an employer or 'superior'; the 'dole' or a scheme again.

The authors of *Growing Up at the Margins* offer an integrated 'model of youth' which is presented here in a form adapted for the purpose of brief explanation. Class and patriarchy are considered to impact on all aspects of the lives of their sample. This broad model is especially useful given the limited and biographical quality of the extract below.

On the strength of their research, and reflecting their own opinions and values, the authors conclude their book by suggesting the following 'Charter for Youth':

FRANK COFFIELD, CAROL BORRILL AND SARAH MARSHALL

A Charter for Youth

1. A strong regional dimension to all aspects of government policy.
2. Linking training to jobs and jobs to training, wherever possible.
3. A comprehensive system of 16+ education, training and employment.
4. The closer involvement of employers in the training of young people.
5. Change the model of learning at the heart of the new initiatives by the MSC and DES.
6. Community education to combat racism and to promote social awareness and health education.
7. Programmes of positive discrimination in favour of young women.
8. Involve young adults in the formation of social policy about young adults and give them the freedom to develop alternatives.

Reading 32 From Frank Coffield, Carol Borrill and Sarah Marshall, *Growing Up at the Margins: Young Adults in the North East* (Open University Press, 1986), pp. 86–7, 92–4.

Letters from Poppy

Extract from Letter – January 1984.
Well, I got the job as a receptionist!! The pay's not very good at the moment 'cos I'm on three months trial, but it gets better after that! . . It's a dead responsible position – I do all the cash and organisation so if things go wrong it's on my head!!! I'm starting to settle in now though and don't make *too* many mistakes so life's looking up at last – I feel much more contented now and part of the human race once again!

2 March 1984

Hiya Carol,

It's bad news I'm afraid – well, (deep breath. . . .) I got the sack!!!
It was exactly 2 weeks before my three months trial period was to end and my good pay rise to start! I was totally devastated to say

the least . . . I felt as though someone had kicked me in the teeth. It was last Saturday when Tony (the manager) told me . . . he was really embarrassed and told me the decision had nothing at all to do with him as he thought I was really good at my job and had built up the appointment book well! Really Carol . . . I loved that job and worked damned hard at it but there's not a thing I can do about his decision. The reason the proprietor gave was that he needed someone either engaged or married with a settled outlook – what a load of shit!!! Anyway, his decision was final and on Monday morning I trudged back to my second home (the dole). Once again I'm a useless bloody number! However I was dead surprised when Tony (the manager) phoned my house on Monday evening to say that he was really sorry the way things had turned out and that there had been dozens of receptionists before me who they'd sacked after only a few weeks! He felt really awful about it and said that if it hadn't meant his job – he would have risked telling me a little sooner! So I felt loads better after that!!!

After one week I'm dead bored. I can't even get my job back at the Cock and Bull cos they've cut the staff's hours by ½. I've been to the Job Centre every day at 9 a.m. but there's nothing going! It's the first time for ages I've been really depressed!

I haven't been seeing much of Steve lately – him and his best mate have decided to go into business together. Terry was working for the Council in the offices and Steve packed in college. They're going into the music business – promoting local bands and things. I'll tell you more about it when I see you again!!!

Well, Carol, just as I thought my life was beginning to look good I've been pissed on again!

See you soon (I'm gonna cheer up now cos its off my chest!?!).
Loads of love
Poppy

Poppy, whose letters were quoted at the beginning of this chapter, left school in 1980 at the age of sixteen with four 'O' levels. Soon afterwards she started a YOP scheme working in an office. She did well and the firm wanted to keep her on, but the union objected and she finished at the end of her six months. She commented at this stage that she thought this was fair enough, considering older workers had more to lose than her.

Poppy's next scheme was at a post office. She hated it and left after one day. Poppy's first taste of unemployment followed. In June 1981, after four months on the dole, Poppy was interviewed for and offered a job as a trainee hairdresser in Shipton. She found that the heat in the shop gave her headaches and the hours were longer than she realised. After two days, she determined to find a better job, but there was nothing to apply for.

When we met Poppy early in 1982, she had started her third WEEP scheme, as a receptionist with a private Temping agency. She was led to believe that she would be kept on, but eventually told that there would be no job for her at the end of the placement. Poppy was furious because she had worked extremely hard, practically running the agency when the owner was away. She took her grievance to the Careers Officer who advised her to leave at once and she did.

In May 1982, the Careers Officer sent Poppy for a job as a clerical assistant in an accountant's office. She got the job, but very quickly found it boring. All she had to do was take photocopies, answer the phone and make cups of tea: 'I'm the lowest of the low'. In July, though, she felt brighter about her prospects as she was being given a wider variety of tasks, including using the computer on her own and supervising a lad who had started there on a WEEP scheme.

By August, Poppy had reverted to her original feelings about the job and was applying for new ones. She was eighteen now and went to the Jobcentre which, she said, had far more jobs to offer than the Careers Service. She felt at this time that being eighteen had opened up a lot of opportunities for her. None of her interviews came to anything, however.

It was the general atmosphere in the accountants' office that affected Poppy even more than the menial tasks she had to do. She reported that no one was allowed to speak, not only while they were working but during their breaks as well. The senior clerk was a middle-aged woman who had been with the firm for years. She ruled the office staff with a rod of iron. Poppy responded to this atmosphere by avoiding it: she took days off whenever she could. She did not want to leave the job because if it was her decision, she would be ineligible for unemployment benefit for the subsequent six weeks. Neither did she want to be sacked because it might have affected her employment chances afterwards. But, in September, Poppy could take no more and handed in her notice. She said it felt like a weight lifting from her shoulders. On her second to last day, the senior clerk told her she could not come into the office dressed as she was. Poppy explained that she was dressed as she always had been and had one full day left to do and so the long standing differences between the two women ended in confrontation. Poppy admitted to us: 'Well, I'll tell you what I told her. I told her she needed a good fuck'. She left the job with her pride and her dress sense, but suffered the penalty of six weeks with no income.

Poppy had been employed at the accountants' office for five months. After leaving, she was on the dole again for six months, until March 1983 when she announced that she had started what she called a WOC scheme. She did not know what the initials meant: we later learnt they stood for Wider Opportunities Course, one of the options under the TOPs programme. She heard about it through a friend of her dad's. It was for twelve weeks: 'I go every day to Brownwell Skillcentre' where she could try anything she wanted: motorbike maintenance, sewing, handicrafts, painting, basic electricals. She also went on two placements, one to a residential home and one as a receptionist in a local hospital. At the end of the twelve weeks, though, Poppy was back on the dole and said she felt worse than before and that it would have been better never to have done the scheme in the first place. Particularly, in the hospital, she considered she had worked harder than anybody else, but after paying her bus fares, she had come home with £23. This was less than she had been getting in unemployment benefit.

Poppy undertook her WOC course in the belief that it would improve her chances of getting a job. The MSC leaflet describes Wider Opportunities Courses as follows:

> These courses are open to men, women and unemployed young people who either cannot get the job they would like or want to try something different and are unsure of what sort of work would suit them. Under guidance, they try themselves out on a number of skills to identify what they like and do well. They are also taught social skills, such as applications for jobs and conduct at interviews.

Poppy had, however, already succeeded in interviews, had landed jobs and schemes with no problem and subsequently worked well at them, but she had not been given permanent employment. She knew from her experience what she liked and did well. She knew what sort of work would suit her, but it was simply not available, at least not in any secure or well-paid form.

Questions
1. *As far as the data in the extract allow, relate Poppy's experience to the 'integrated model of youth' given in the introduction to this extract.*

(10 marks)
2. *To what extent and in what way would you use the terms 'poverty' and 'disadvantage' to describe Poppy's situation?*

(15 marks)

(To answer this question, you will need to be familiar with the concepts presented in Reading 30)

Gender

Readings 33–37

This section begins with a review of 'current trends in feminist theory' by Mary Maynard. Simple but comprehensive, it might be helpful to return to this article at the conclusion of this topic. Talcott Parsons may well be thought of as 'the odd man out' in this section. He does not oppose patriarchy, indeed, he does not use the term. What he attempts to do is explain the functional nature of differential gender roles for American society (and presumably other industrial/capitalist societies). He argues that it 'works better' for modern society if women are domestically orientated and men work in the paid economy. It is precisely this functional relationship – seen by Parsons as more or less necessary – which feminists attack as oppressive to women. For them, differential gender roles are functional not for 'society' but for men and, in the view of Marxist-Feminists, (although they also consider working class men are exploited in their own right as wage-workers). Anna Pollert's article 'Girls Wives Factory Lives' describes sexual stereotyping in the workplace, specifically a factory. Highly empirical in nature, it illustrates in practice some of the theoretical points made in the survey of feminist theories by Maynard.

Anna Coote's article is concerned with politics and policy. Directing her arguments towards the Labour Party, she sets out what she believes are the measures necessary to achieve real progress towards gender equality. Finally, Juliet Mitchell gives a thought provoking assessment of the recent past and possible future of the feminist movement.

There are many other articles which deal with gender in this Reader – as a brief look at the table of contents will show. Two which capture something of the practice and practical problems (as opposed to the theory) of feminism are those by Gillian Pascall (Reading 82) and by the Glasgow Media Group (Reading 94).

33 Mary Maynard: Current Trends in Feminist Theory

This article makes the complex area of feminist theory relatively simple. Before examining various feminist theories, Maynard first argues the need for such a body of theory. Patriarchy – male domination of women – is what needs to be explained. There are broadly two strands of feminist theory indicated by Maynard: Marxist influenced and radical feminist. The former owe something to the legacy of Marxism and all, in one way or another, relate female oppression to capitalism as well as to male domination. The latter focus primarily on male domination in its various forms but particularly 'in the family and in sexual and personal relations'. Radical feminists seek to raise the *consciousness* of women to the public and structural causes of their oppression.

Although perhaps the most lucid and comprehensive short treatment of feminist theory available, Maynard's article leaves some areas untouched. She herself mentions that the problems of black women require particular analysis and one might also add for consideration the challenges facing many women in the Third World.

Reading 33 Mary Maynard, 'Current Trends in Feminist Theory' in *Social Studies Review*, Vol. 2, No. 3, January 1987, pp. 23–7.

Introduction

Since the re-emergence of the women's movement in the late 1960s, and particularly in recent years, feminism has had a major impact upon sociology. Initially, feminist sociologists were very critical of the neglect of gender issues and the invisibility of women within the major sub-areas of sociology. They pointed out, for example, that most of the research on education focused only on boys; that when 'work' was studied, the daily routines and tasks of the house-wife were ignored; and that a woman was put into the social class of her father or husband regardless of the nature of her own occu-pation or educational qualifications.

As such criticism mounted, feminists extended their work and began to conduct their own studies of women's lives. Their success can be seen today in the number of books and research projects directly concerned with women. For instance, the sexism of the education system has been explored, women's position in the sexual division of labour at home and at work has been described, and the ways in which women are portrayed in the media have been documented. In addition, some new areas of significance to women have been opened up. Studies of women and health, for instance, have looked at the ways in which the medical profession deals with female complaints and with childbirth. Largely as a result of feminists' efforts, it is now widely acknowledged that gender divisions are an important aspect of contemporary society and that their study should be given a prominent place in sociology. It is no longer acceptable for sociological research by men on men to be treated as if it also applies to women.

The need for feminist theory

At the same time as feminists have been making women visible in *empirical research*, they have also been developing their own particular brands of feminist *theory*. This, it is argued, is necessary for a number of reasons. Although it is very important to conduct empirical research which describes women's lives and feelings, this is not sufficient on its own. Feminism is not just a perspective which seeks to see *particular* areas of the world from a woman's point of view. It also aims to understand the structure and organisation of a society which appears to keep women as a disadvantaged, subordinate and dominated group *overall*, i.e. in most aspects of life. In order to do this feminists look for explanations as to how the social differences between males and females have arisen, why women are systematically disadvantaged in a whole range of social institutions, and what might be necessary to bring about social change, greater equality and freedom. It is impossible to tackle such questions without a framework which focuses on the links between different areas of social life and women's position within them.

Feminists claim, however, that mainstream sociological theory is unable to provide a useful framework for considering women's overall position in society. This is because all such theories are *gender-blind*. In other words, they do not take account of the differences between men and women and are unable to consider issues relating specifically to women. Most Marxist, functionalist and interactionist writing, for instance, says nothing about women at all. Feminists argue, therefore, that the claims to scientific detachment made by conventional sociological theory in fact mask a male political bias. Sociology is not, and cannot be, 'value-free'. The alternative theoretical positions formulated by feminists, therefore, seek an explicit union of sociology and politics in which theory and research must actively promote the views and interests of women.

For these reasons, then, feminists have begun to develop their own *feminist* theory. Feminist theory is concerned not only with the analysis of women's disadvantaged position in society but with women's *oppression*. Women are denied economic, social and political power and are the likely targets of sexual assault and other harassment *because they are women*. The concept of *patriarchy* is used to analyse the principles and structures underlying this oppression. Patriarchy is usually defined as the power relationship by which men dominate women. However, although most feminists are concerned with both oppression and patriarchy, there are differences in their focus and emphasis. Most texts divide feminist theory into two kinds: Marxist Feminism and Radical Feminism. This is a useful starting point but, as will become clear, some important differences within these two broad categories are hidden behind the labels. I will use my own terminology in teasing out these distinctions.

The Marxist legacy

Many feminists are developing their own analysis of women's oppression from within a Marxist framework, which means that it has to be seen as rooted within the capitalist economic system. In the early 1970s this often involved taking concepts which Marx had developed to analyse the workplace and trying to make them 'fit' women's experience in the family and at home. Most feminists, however, object to adopting Marxist terminology and forms of argument lock, stock and barrel, suggesting that ideas developed to explain the conditions of male workers cannot easily be applied to women. Accordingly, they have begun to alter and extend the Marxist approach, particularly by focusing on the family and women's dependent position within it.

Marxist feminists

This term refers to those feminists who, following Marx, regard the *economic* position of women as crucial to their oppression. Of particular interest to such writers is the way in which women's position within the family makes them a special target for capitalist exploitation. It is argued that because women are regarded as being financially dependent on their husbands, they can be given poorly paid, low-status, part-time jobs. This can be done without challenge because both husband and wife, as well as the employer, regard the woman's primary role as that of unpaid home-maker.

Veronica Beechey, for example, has argued that married women are advantageous to capitalism because it is not expected that the money they earn has to be sufficient to fully keep themselves (Beechey 1977) – the additional wages of the husband will do that. She suggests that because of their dependent position in the family, married women workers can be seen as semi-proletarianised workers. They are, in fact, economically below the working class. Other writers have argued that married women's economic dependency on their husbands makes them a useful industrial reserve army which can be moved in and out of the economy as needed (Breugal 1979). Although the effects of this may be tempered – for example, in all-female workplaces or in a recession, when keeping on badly-paid women makes economic sense – women's place in the home and their dependency on men mean that they can be regarded as marginal workers.

Thus, for Marxist-Feminists, women's oppression has an economic base which is most clearly reflected in their financial dependency on their husbands. This dependency has been created by capitalism to fulfil two needs. Firstly, it provides cheap female workers who can be exploited even more than men. Secondly, because housewives are not paid, it ensures that household chores are done cheaply. If housewives were paid, employers would have to raise wages so that the population could afford to employ someone to do the housework for them. Because of these important connections between women's oppression and capitalism, Marxist Feminists argue that the interests of women lie with the liberation of the working class and the overthrow of capitalism.

Feminist Marxists

Feminist Marxists also work within the Marxist tradition, but they are critical of the narrow economic focus of both Marx and Marxist Feminists. Although they argue that an understanding of the nature of the capitalist economic system must retain an important place in the analysis of women's contemporary position, it is suggested that other non-economic factors should also be taken into consideration. For example, they claim that more emphasis should be given to *ideology* in maintaining women's oppression and male power.

Michèle Barrett argues that an analysis of ideology, especially that concerning the family, helps us to explain why women continue to get married and live in conventional families when these are the very things that oppress them (Barrett 1980). She suggests that because ideology presents the nuclear family as natural, inevitable and as a major place in which females will be fulfilled, women are not encouraged to look for alternative ways of living. Ideology is, therefore, a powerful factor in encouraging women to accept family life. Barrett is not arguing that human beings do not need the emotional fulfilment of intimacy, sexual relations and parenthood. Rather, she claims that the assumption that these needs can be met only through the family as it is today is oppressive for women. This is because it makes them dependent on men and limits their activities and achievements. Unlike the Marxist Feminists, Feminist Marxists such as Barrett do not believe that women's liberation will occur *just* by overthrowing the economic system of capitalism, because other non-economic factors, such as the ideological factor, would be likely to remain. Changing the economic system is only one aspect of what is required. Another is a change in the relationship between the sexes. Barrett suggests that the liberation of women would require not only the removal of women's economic dependence on men but also the sharing of childcare between men and women and the transformation of the ideology of gender, so that men and women are free to behave as they wish without having to conform to masculine and feminine stereotypes.

Feminism and Freud

Some feminists have followed the link between oppression and ideology even further. In the 1970s Juliet Mitchell turned to the work of psychoanalyst, Sigmund Freud, to answer the question of why women are prepared to accept institutions and ideas which oppress them (Mitchell 1975). She uses Freud's notion of the unconscious to argue that ideas about females and femininity have become so taken for granted that we almost unconsciously take them as correct. They are deeply rooted in our personalities and therefore very difficult to dislodge.

At the time, many feminists were sceptical of Mitchell's use of Freud, whose writings about penis envy and female sexuality were regarded as sexist. Recently, however, some Marxist Feminists have also begun to use Freud's work. They claim that while Marxism is useful for describing the economic and social structure of society, psychoanalytic thought helps us to focus on individuals and their consciousness of gender. For example, Nancy Chodorow has used this approach to ask questions about mothering and motherhood (Chodorow 1978). Although women give birth to children, she wanted to understand why, in capitalist society, they reared and looked after them, often without help from men. What makes women want and expect to do this? Chodorow, like most feminists, rejects the idea that mothering is innate. Instead, she argues that in the family children learn to be men and women and that women *learn* to be mothers. They learn this role so intensely that it becomes built into their personality. A woman cannot be forced to take on the behaviour of a mother, says Chodorow, unless she has accepted at some conscious or unconscious level that this is part of how she sees herself. Although the use of psychoanalytic theory is still controversial among feminists, growing numbers are using it to explore the psychology of womanhood and femininity.

Materialist Feminism

The work of Christine Delphy is a major example of Materialist Feminism. Delphy calls her work materialist rather than Marxist, since she claims that Marxism cannot explain women's oppression and that most feminists who use Marxism give too much attention to a 'genderless proletariat' and not enough to women. She uses the methods of Marxism but alters the content of its theory.

Delphy says that there are two modes of production, the industrial and the domestic (Delphy 1984). The industrial mode of production leads to capitalist exploitation and the formation of the two classes, proletariat and bourgeoisie. The domestic mode of production leads to *patriarchal* exploitation and the formation of the two 'classes', men and women. In this a husband exploits his wife by receiving domestic and sexual services for which he does not pay and in return for which he simply provides her keep. For Delphy it is this exploitation in the home which enables men to dominate and control women. She argues that, from a woman's point of view, men and not capitalism are the 'main enemy' because most women get married and become domestic slaves. From a feminist point of view, therefore, the patriarchal exploitation of women in the home should be looked at and treated completely separately from the capitalist economic system.

Capitalism and patriarchy

We have seen that, whereas Marxist Feminists see the economic system of capitalism as most important in explaining women's oppression, Materialist Feminists emphasise patriarchy and men's domination and control of women as being most significant. Others, however, have argued that *both* capitalism and patriarchy must be taken into account. For example, Zillah Eisenstein uses the term *capitalist patriarchy* to indicate that women are oppressed through both the economic system and by men (Eisenstein 1979). She emphasises that capitalism and patriarchy are not two separate and unrelated systems of exploitation. Rather, they are linked and dependent on each other. Heidi Hartmann uses the term *patriarchal capitalism* to make a similar point that patriarchy and capitalism feed into each other (Hartmann 1979).

Radical Feminism

The Radical Feminist position began to develop in the early 1970s. It was started by women who wished to understand their inferior and secondary role in society and who felt that existing theories, especially traditional Marxism, did not give sufficient emphasis to the particular position of women. Radical Feminism focuses on patriarchy and the role of men in oppressing women. Two important features of Radical Feminist analysis were introduced at this time. The first was the idea that the *personal is political*. This called attention to the fact that it is not just a set of institutions which keeps women oppressed. Private lives and relationships can be oppressive and should not remain hidden and secret. If politics generally is about power and influencing people, then all relationships are to do with politics. Politics occurs in families and between individuals when one person attempts to control or dominate another. For Radical Feminists the most important power relations are between men and women. This is known as *sexual politics* and refers to the ways in which men individually, and as a group, dominate women and control their lives, particularly in the family and in sexual and personal relations.

The second important feature of Radical Feminism is its emphasis on *consciousness-raising*. Women are usually encouraged to see their problems as private and personal. However, through discussion, they are able to see that other women have similar worries and concerns. Through sharing experiences in consciousness-raising groups, they become aware of the situation of *all* women instead of simply being concerned with themselves.

When most textbooks discuss Radical Feminism they focus on the work of Shulamith Firestone (1971) and Kate Millett (1971). Their books were undoubtedly important in developing a non-Marxist feminism. Firestone focused on male control of women's child-bearing abilities as a source of oppression. Millett, who first coined the term *sexual politics*, examined the ways in which institutions such as the family, the state, ideology and culture continue to produce patriarchy. However, since these books were published, the focus of Radical Feminism has changed significantly. Millett and Firestone gave only minor attention to violence and sexuality. The active involvement of feminists with women who have been physically or sexually abused means that the analysis of sexuality and violence is now central to Radical Feminist theory and politics.

Sexuality

Sexuality refers to those feelings which arouse us and give us pleasure, how we wish to satisfy such feelings and with whom we enjoy fulfilling them. Feminists argue that sexuality is not simply biologically given, but that the form it takes is socially constructed. Indeed, it is constructed by men in a particular kind of way to satisfy their own desires. For instance, women are regarded as sexual objects, penetration is seen as *the* major source of sexual pleasure and men are expected to take the initiative in relationships. Women, on the other hand, are simply expected to be passive and pretty. They become the playthings of men. Adrienne Rich has referred to this as *compulsory heterosexuality* (Rich 1981). She argues that women are forced into a narrow form of sexual behaviour by men from which they themselves derive little erotic pleasure. They are forced into heterosexuality because this is the only form of sexuality considered socially acceptable. Lesbianism, for example, is regarded as deviant and abnormal behaviour. However, some feminists regard lesbianism as the only means through which women can experience sexual pleasure in a way which is not oppressive (Anon 1981). They argue that sexual intercourse with men involves women colluding with their main enemy. They also refer to intercourse as man's colonisation of a woman's body. It is regarded as an act through which he is able to control her body and ultimately the rest of her life.

Sexuality, male violence and the social control of women

Radical Feminists argue that men's role as the initiator in sexual and other relationships has led them to develop an aggressive masculine behaviour which is directed towards women. Men who rape, molest, or harass, for example, are not ill or mad. Rather, such acts are simply extensions of what is considered normal and acceptable behaviour by men. If men are encouraged by the media, pornography etc., to see women as sexual objects for their pleasure, we cannot be surprised if some men take this to the extreme.

Radical Feminists see the social construction of sexuality and male violence against women as inextricably linked, and as oppressive to women in two ways. Firstly, current views of sexuality denigrate women and encourage men to view them as sexual objects. Secondly, men can and do use violence against women to get their own way in a variety of different situations. However, it is not just the use of violence itself which is oppressive. The threat or fear of violence is sufficient to ensure that women have to modify their behaviour, for example by not going out at night for fear of being attacked. In this way men are able to control women's activities and oppress them.

In exploring the links between sexuality, violence and the social control of women, Radical Feminists have focused attention on several specific areas. For example, it has been argued that rape is significant in men's control of women because it helps all men to keep all women in a state of fear. This is because it is impossible for women to tell which men are safe and which are the rapists (Brownmiller 1976). Some writers have concentrated upon domestic violence and the widespread use of physical force by men to control their women. Others have claimed that pornography lies at the heart of male dominance because it portrays women as inferior and humiliated beings and distorts the true nature of womanhood (Dworkin 1981).

Thus, Radical Feminism views men and women as opposing groups, with one controlling the other. Society is divided by gender in such a way that men and women constitute two separate social 'classes'. Those feminists who follow Marx define class on the basis of ownership of wealth and private property, so that men and women are to be found amongst both the proletariat and the bourgeoisie. Radical Feminists, on the other hand, see all women as linked together in the same class position because of their social control and abuse by men. Women's liberation is, therefore, to be achieved by actively challenging the system of patriarchy. However, challenging 'the system' is not enough, for Radical Feminists argue that change is important for individuals as well as for society overall. Individuals should be encouraged to become aware of women's oppression and to live their lives in a way which is not based on exploitation. It is assumed, however, that men will not willingly give up their power over women. Radical Feminists therefore emphasise the importance of women forming groups and organisations apart from men. For some, such separate women's groups are simply an addition to their lives with men. Others try to have as little to do with men as possible, and live apart from them. This is known as *separatism*.

Conclusion

This article has described the various forms of feminist theory. However, it should not be thought that such theory is fully formulated, complete or static, for it is constantly being challenged and changed. Black feminists, for example, have criticised feminist theory as a whole for its lack of concern with, and relevance to, black women (*Feminist Review* 1984). Not only are black women invisible in most feminist theories, but their stress on patriarchy ignores the fact that for black women racial oppression may be of equal or greater significance. Feminist theory is also oriented to Western society and ignores Third World women. Such criticism must be taken on board if feminism is to be meaningful to all women.

Many sociologists now admit that much of the recent impetus for major changes in social theory has come from the growth of feminist theory. But such theory does not stand on its own. Its development has been closely linked to both empirical research into gender inequalities and consciousness-raising and political activities with the women's movement. Feminist theory is, therefore, a dynamic force which is constantly confronting new issues and debates concerning gender. All social scientists would do well to pay close attention to its progress in the years to come.

Question

1. (a) *Distinguish between Marxist Feminism and Feminist Marxism.*

(7 marks)

(b) *Distinguish between Marxist Feminism and Radical Feminism.*

(7 marks)

(c) *Briefly present what you consider to be the best analysis of patriarchy. Say why.*

(8 marks)

34 Talcott Parsons: The Functional Nature of 'Sex' Roles

The term 'gender roles' is now generally used to refer to patterns of *learnt* behaviour considered culturally appropriate to members of a given sex. Parsons uses the term 'sex' roles in this way. Here he makes the argument that sex roles have developed in a way that is highly functional for American society. It is a fair assumption from his writings that he would make the same case for most *modern* societies. He presents his analysis as follows.

He sharply (if rather verbosely) contrasts the values and needs of the American occupational system with those of the family. The former is characterised by achievement, universality (e.g. general rules of competition and selection) and impersonality, whilst the latter is based on mutual personal acceptance. Despite these differences, the two 'structures' of the occupational system and the family work reasonably harmoniously because only the male 'plays a full competitive role in the occupational system'. The rest of the family, including his wife, derives its status, income and class position mainly from his career 'achievements'. He describes the paid work of women as either temporary or marginal and considers that direct competition for occupational status between husband and wife would create 'intolerable strain'. He sees women's role, therefore, as primarily within the family although in his later writings he acknowledges the complementary trends to smaller families and greater career orientation among women.

Although Parsons sees differential sex roles as functional, he does recognise that women may be limited and frustrated by their situation. Since he wrote in the late fifties many women have expressed this sentiment far more strongly than Parsons. More recent research has also explored some destructive aspects of family life, including wife battering and child abuse – points not raised by Parsons (see Reading 14). Wife battering, in particular, may be part of the price of 'functional', but arguably oppressive, sex role differentiation. Parsons shows his own basic sympathy with the family and sex roles as he describes them in 'modern' America in his concluding paragraphs.

Reading 34 From Talcott Parsons, 'The Family: Its Function and Destiny' in Ruth Nanda Anshen *ed.*, *The Social Structure of the Family* (Harper and Row, 1949), pp. 189–201 – edited.

The American family is in a delicate state of balance and integration with the rest of the social structure, notably the occupational structure. A somewhat fuller treatment of this is necessary as a basis for discussing some of the dynamic problems of the family. The most essential feature of our occupational system is the primacy of functional achievement as an ideal pattern which is highly institutionalized. This fact has a variety of implications . . .

The patterns of behavior institutionalized in the modern occupational system run counter to many of the most deep-seated of human needs and motivations, such as relatively unconditional loyalty to groups, sentimental attachment to persons as such, the need for security against competitive pressures, and the like. The functioning of our occupational system, therefore, is possible only by virtue of a relatively severe discipline, which involves both motivation to maintain a high level of performance under difficult conditions and adequate resistance to the types of behavior and attitude which, if allowed to develop far enough, would seriously interfere with functional efficiency.

Broadly speaking, there is no sector of our society where the dominant patterns stand in sharper contrast to those of the occupational world than in the family. The family is a solitary group within which status, rights, and obligations are defined primarily by membership as such and by the ascribed differentiations of age, sex, and biological relatedness. This basis of relationship and status in the group precludes more than a minor emphasis on universalistic standards of functional performance. Similarly, the patterning of rights and obligations in the family is not restricted to the context specific to a positively defined functional role; rather, it is functionally diffuse. The family is treated as if entitled to call on any one of its members for any contribution within his power so long as it does not conflict with a higher obligation. Finally, instead of being defined in impersonal, emotionally neutral terms, the family is specifically treated as a network of emotionally charged relationships, the mutual affection of its members in our society being held to be the most important basis of their solidarity and loyalty.

Clearly for two structures with such different patterns to play crucially important roles in the same society requires a delicate adjustment between them. The direct integration of occupational function with the kinship system, as it occurs in many non-literate and peasant societies, is quite impossible. To an important degree their different patterns can be upheld only by mechanisms of segregation which prevent them from getting in each other's way and undermining each other. Yet they must be articulated.

Broadly this problem of structural compatibility is solved in the United States by making sure that in the typical case only one member of the effective kinship unit, the conjugal family, plays a full competitive role in the occupational system. This member is the husband and father, who is responsible for the status and support of his family, and it is noteworthy that his familial and occupational roles are sharply segregated from each other. He lives and works at different places. In his occupational role he functions and is treated as an individual on his own responsibility; his status in the organization is not shared by other members of his family.

It is clear that articulation with this type of occupational system and its structural correlates in the society places severe limitations on the kind of kinship structure which is compatible with such a system. Mobility on an individual basis is incompatible with such a kinship system as that of the Chinese, for example, which places a primary emphasis on the continuity of general social status through kinship from generation to generation. The isolation of the conjugal family emphasized above as a primary characteristic of the American system is the mechanism for freeing the occupation-bearing and competing member of the family from hampering ties which would both inhibit his chances and interfere with the functioning of the system. This applies, of course, both to his emancipation on maturity from his family of orientation and to the segregation of his own family of procreation from those of his brothers.

But not only mobility of status is important. The mobility of the occupational system also requires a great deal of shifting in place of residence. Since it is the individual, as such, who is in demand for new jobs in such a way as to necessitate his changing his residence, it is essential that his family be able to change with him, and this would not be possible if it were not an isolated conjugal family which was not bound to a particular residential location by the occupational, property, or status interests of other members.

Indeed in our status system, with certain qualifications, the family status is overwhelmingly bound to the occupational status of the husband and father. This works out primarily through two inter-related channels, income level and prestige. Except in the highest groups, family income is overwhelmingly derived from occupational earnings. Furthermore, without neglecting the sheer utilitarian aspect, what income buys has a fundamental aspect of status symbolism as a part of the way of life appropriate to the members of a family occupying a particular status. Thus, both through the status made possible by occupational income and through the direct prestige or lack of it of the breadwinner's job, the status of the family itself is primarily determined.

If there are rather definite functional requirements for the kind of kinship system which is compatible with our particular type of occupational system, conversely, within the broad structural pattern of the kinship system, there are functional requirements for the maintenance of the solidarity of its essential unity, the conjugal family. What a crucially important structural role is played by the marriage relationship – far more so than in most kinship systems – has already been pointed out. As a structurally unsupported relationship resting largely on emotional attraction, it must be protected against the kind of stresses that go with severe competition for prestige between the members. It is well known that segregation of role is in general one of the main mechanisms for inhibiting potentially disruptive competition. The functional importance of the solidarity of the marriage relationship to our kinship system may therefore be presumed to be a major factor underlying the segregation of the sex roles in American society, since sex is the primary basis of role differentiation for marriage partners. Indeed it is suggestive that, with the further development of the American occupational system in the last two generations, there seems to have been a tendency to increased emphasis on the segregation of the sex roles, as evidenced by the greater stress on the glamour pattern, rather than the reverse. This seems to be true in spite of strong forces operating in the opposite direction and connected with tendencies toward an identical treatment of the sexes, particularly in education and in the sphere of personal freedoms.

Structurally the most fundamental aspect of the segregation of the sex roles seems to be with reference to the occupational system. Especially in the structurally crucial middle-class area of our society, the dominant mature feminine role is that of housewife or of wife and mother. Apart from the extremely important utilitarian problems of how adequate care of household and children are to be accomplished, the most important aspect of this fact is that it shields spouses from competition with each other in the occupational sphere, which, along with attractiveness to women, is above all the most important single focus of feelings of self-respect on the part of American men. In this sector of society the largest part of the gainful employment of women is that of unmarried girls and of women living outside normal family relationships. There has been a notable check in the tendency for women to enter the higher occupational careers; for example, the proportion of women in the professions of medicine and law has remained approximately constant for more than a generation. Only a minority of such career women carry full normal family responsibilities, including the care of young children. Finally, when in the middle classes married women are gainfully employed, in a large proportion of cases it is in a job rather than in a career. Such employment is ordinarily not in competition with that of men of the same class status and ordinarily does not produce a comparable proportion of the family income.

Since the problems of the adult sex-role structure in the United States have been mentioned at a number of points, only a few remarks in summary need be added here. To take the feminine role first, the dominant element seems to be a basic ambivalence and instability. In so far as the functions of wife and mother are the structurally predominant ones in the fundamental American family type, it would seem to follow that what may be called a domestic pattern of the feminine role was the most appropriate one. This is true except for one fundamental function, the wife's role in the maintenance of the solidarity of the marriage relationship through appeal to the husband's sexual interests. It has been shown above that, in our family system, boys tend to grow up in a state of ambivalence about the feminine role; the mother tends to be defined as asexual and 'good' and is the prototype of the domestic woman. There is felt to be a deep conflict between this pattern and that of the sexually attractive woman. The latter pattern, that of the 'glamour girl,' has a tendency to predominate in the relations of the sexes in the premarital period, being deeply rooted in the youth culture. The fact that in our family system the stability of marriage must rest mainly on personal sentiment creates a tendency for this to carry over into marriage and into the adult feminine role. There is therefore a deep ambivalence and sense of conflict in both sexes over these two roles of the married woman. Too much emphasis on the glamour role may lead to a sacrifice of the domestic virtues and above all to an emotional rejection of the role of mother, with the most serious consequences for children. Given the psychology of American men, on the other hand, too heavy a leaning toward domesticity may threaten the emotional interests of the husband and the all-important emotional quality of marriage. Even if there is no tendency for a husband to stray, it may be unhealthy in that it appeals to his immature dependency needs and makes the wife more a mother to him than really a wife. A constructive synthesis of these too often conflicting tendencies in the feminine role is one of the most urgent needs of the American family.

The two tendencies, however, do not stand alone. Women in this country tend conspicuously to receive the same formal education as men, up to the professional levels. This fact expresses another major theme, that of the woman as a serious, intelligent, responsible human being who shares these qualities with men, in a context in which sex as such is often irrelevant. In many respects American society has gone farther than any other in the Western world in developing these possibilities, and in this direction seems to lie the most promising road to an escape from the dilemma of the domesticity-glamour impasse. Reference to our social structure, however, affords some understanding of the formidable obstacles to a major development in this direction. Generally speaking, men get their most important outlets of this sort in the occupational sphere. But the structure imposes on women very severe pressures against taking the same direction, as shown above. The problem then is to ascertain what opportunities exist for such development where the major status-giving role of the typical married woman is that of housewife. The activities of women's clubs, various kinds of good works, book clubs, and the like represent attempts in this direction, but they seem to fall far short of adequacy. Above all, there is relatively little that can be taken seriously and importantly rewarded in terms of the American system of achievement values.

The American masculine role does not seem to display a structural ambivalence at all comparable to that of the feminine. Its firm anchorage in the occupational structure seems to be the principal explanation of this. Virtually the only way to be a real man in our society is to have an adequate job and earn a living. As has become evident above, however, involved in the masculine role there is a set of deep psychological tensions which seem to be inherent in the American family structure. The essential problem seems to be that there is a compulsive element in our pattern of masculinity which covers over an undue and unfortunate type of dependence on women. On the one hand, this seems to be responsible for much of the aggressively self-assertive tone of the American masculine world and for some of our over-sensitivity to competitive threats. On the other hand, it is responsible for much of the dilemma which American women face, as analyzed above. The whole complex represents a vicious circle of mutually reinforcing parts . . .

In conclusion, a few general remarks are in order which may be relevant to the balance of judgment about the American family and its present situation. In the first place, structural analysis clearly shows that, if the United States is to remain and develop further as a democratic, urbanized, industrial society, with a large measure of equality of opportunity, the range of possible family structures which are compatible with its type of society is very narrow. As it is, our family system is responsible for serious limitations on the

269

ideal of equality of opportunity. But any considerable shift in the direction, for instance, of the family types found in peasant societies would undoubtedly entail serious consequences for the rest of the social structure. Such a family type may well be more stable than our own, but, if this stability must be purchased at the expense of drastic reduction in the productivity of our economy and drastic limitations on the realizability of our democratic values, is it worth the price? That some such consequences would in fact be the price of the realization of some current programs for the restoration of the strong family seems scarcely open to doubt.

There is some legitimate doubt whether the American type of family system is in the long run capable of sufficient stability to perform its extremely essential functions on behalf of our type of society. Sentiment plays such a prominent role in the judgment of such matters, however, that the social scientist is well advised to be cautious about the acceptance of such a view. Furthermore, from a practical point of view it would seem that Americans have little choice. By their commitment to a particular type of general society they are automatically committed in broad terms to the appropriate family type. Their dedication must be to making this work if it is at all possible; there is no other course.

Psychology and sociology can contribute something to the problem of judging what type of attitudes and measures are most likely to help in making it work. This is especially true of the judgment of what can be expected not to work. It seems quite clear, for instance, that the sources of ambivalence concerning the feminine role go so deep that any attempt to force or persuade an overwhelming majority of American women to accept a role of pure and virtuous domesticity alone is probably doomed to failure. Indeed, if it did succeed, it would probably have a seriously unsettling effect and create more problems than it solved.

Finally, it should not be forgotten that there is a bright side of the picture as well as a dark one. Ours is a society in which unprecedented demands for the responsible management of complex affairs are placed on large numbers of people. The evidence seems to be that, with all its strains and difficulties, our family system does a better job than most others in developing character traits which are relatively adequate to these demands. It also permits a kind of freedom for the development of personal feelings and attachments which is rare in the much more narrowly controlled systems of many other societies. At its best it seems to provide, in the intimate and private sphere, a highly appropriate pattern and environment of life for the enlightened citizens of a free society.

Question

1. (a) What reason does Parsons give for differential gender roles in the 'modern' American family?

     (5 marks)

     (b) What problems does he consider that differential gender roles can cause for women?

     (5 marks)

     (c) Critically discuss Parsons account of differential gender roles.

     (15 marks)

Note: You will need to refer to Reading 33 to answer part(c).

35 Anna Pollert: Girls, Wives, Factory Lives

The factory 'girls' of Anna Pollert's description experience a double subordination. They are working class and they are women. Like most factory workers their working conditions are disturbingly stressful and potentially unhealthy and their wages are likely to be lower even than those of men doing the same or a similar kind of work. It is clear that the productive means (i.e. technology and work organisation) by which the cigarettes are produced exert an exhausting and impersonal discipline on the women. The need to achieve high production quotas on which wage bonuses depend is an added worry. The author explains how the women's sexuality is used – sometimes humiliatingly – as an additional means of emphasising their subordinate and controlled position. The study bears comparison with Huw Beynon's *Working for Ford* and Jason Ditton's account of work in a bakery, *Absent at Work: or How to Manage Monotony*, both of which describe how workers deal spiritedly with the tedium of repetitive labour.

Pollert's account of alienating work is entertaining only because the women themselves 'manage' their work situation with humour and imagination. Daydreaming, even taking a quick sleep, are ways of combating monotony and fatigue. To catch

271

this detail, the author employs observational and tape-recording techniques. The result is an interpretive study of considerable human sensitivity but one which also conveys an awareness of the structure of inequality at work and in society.

Reading 35 From Anna Pollert, 'Girls, wives, factory lives' in *New Society*, 22 October 1981, pp. 139–41.

When I began my study of Churchmans, a tobacco factory in Bristol, I was met with astonishment from management; what could I possibly want to know about 'factory girls'? Was I, then, a 'troublemaker'?

On the shopfloor I was met with a mixture of suspicion and curiosity. I was not an employee and had to explain that I felt many people had no idea what factory life was like and I wanted to listen, learn and write about it. Slowly, I became a familiar figure, with notebook and cassette recorder in hand, and suspicion turned to amusement, even sympathy: 'Go on, my love'; 'I think it's a good thing: people ought to know how people live – not just think about themselves.'

Churchmans was a declining part of Imperial Tobacco, producing pipe and loose tobaccos. Rationalisation and insecurity were accepted parts of life, like the din of machinery, the sweet sickly smell of *rag* (the loose, shredded tobacco) and the unyielding pace of work. And indeed the factory is now shut.

It was a small factory. Most of the 140 women worked in the weighing and packing departments, the labour-intensive areas. The largest of these, the machine weighing room, was filled with long weighing machines with conveyor belts to the labellers and baggers.

Each machine contained six scales, each with a little light which went on to register the correct weight of tobacco. Machine weighing needs finger-tip precision and flying speed. Each weigher picks up tiny lumps of rag which she drops into a hole – sometimes taking back a few shreds – until the exact weight is reached. A counter records her performance. The machines clatter all day from 7.30 am to 4.30 pm, except for a 15–minute breakfast break and an hour for lunch, recording all the time.

Failure in performance standard or speed leads to a warning, and downgrading to a lower 'proficiency pay rate.' Each minute, ten empty foil packs pass below the scale inside the machine's belly; one weighing per woman every six seconds.

It is rowdy and pacey here. But it is also good for a laugh, and that counts in factory life. Most of the younger women are in the machine weighing room. There are other young women in the smaller, quieter hand-packing rooms, and the distinction between the 'crowds' in each came up again and again:

PATTI: (from the machine weighing room): They take their work seriously, whereas we don't. If you go in there, you can't talk. *They* all keeps themselves to themselves, whereas *we* all mucks in together.

Upstairs in the stripping department, and downstairs in the spinning room, are concentrated the older women – the long-term workers, women with children, women with grandchildren.

Stripping can be done either by hand or by machine. Hand-stemming means stripping the tobacco leaf from the stem between forefinger and thumb. Fingers get cut, calloused and bent. The dust catches the back of the throat; but it isn't a noisy job. There is an intimacy of years of shared experience, with quiet talk or, sometimes, group discussion about children and families, news and personal experiences.

Machine stripping makes a regular clacking noise. It looks like feeding washing through a mangle, as tobacco leaf is fed between two rollers operated by a foot pedal. A blade cuts out the stem, and the stripper carefully stacks the left and right halves of the leaf, avoiding tearing it, but always fighting time, and fighting to keep up to her proficiency standard.

In the spinning room, concentration was so intense that I was frankly told not to interfere by interviewing. There was no time to talk and keep up at the same time.

The air here is thick with oppressive fumes from the ovens which cook speciality tobacco. One woman describes it wrily as a 'slave camp.' In fact, work here is the most skilled task in the factory. You have to carry out the seemingly impossible feat of joining 'wrapper' leaves together, while twisting them round a 'filler' to produce a long roll of tobacco. But spinning wasn't paid at craftsman's rates.

Keeping up with the machines or the performance rates and coping with monotony – that was what factory work was about.

Geoff, the training supervisor, thought he really 'knew' the 'girls' at Churchmans:

'They're quite happy. They're in a fool's paradise. They've got the money coming in. They've never had it so good.' And indeed it *was* the money that kept them there. It was very good – *for a woman:*

PATTI: We get good wages. I think I'm lucky to be working here. We ought to be grateful for having jobs.

But 'good for a woman' did not mean it was a living wage:

SANDRA: You know, I thought it was good wages in here. Well it is, I suppose, except for the price of flats and food and bus fares.

And the money didn't mean that they were not bored:

PATTI: I'd like to see them here. I'd like to see the manager on a weighing machine for a week.

MARY: Not a week! An hour would be enough!

Finding escapes made factory life tolerable. You had to pretend it wasn't happening, or steal a break:

VAL: You gets used to it, though. I think it's imagination a lot of the time.

SUE: Some girls'll sit up all day and weigh. But with me, well, I gets me hair off. I mucks about. I gets so fed up, I goes out the back.

Twice a day there is music. In the hand-packing room, there is an encyclopaedia under the supervisor's desk for quizes. Some machine weighers read books while their hands continue 'on automatic.'

Most important of all, however, is companionship and collective life. As the women talked to me, it became clear that a 'good' factory was one where you found mates. The *work* could never be 'good':

JENNY: You've just got to be friends with everyone. Like it's terrible if someone's not talking to you. But if you're talking to them, and friends with them, it's all right.

Mucking in together, and having a laugh, are what make a 'good' day. There are jokes, sing-songs, teasing. In the hand stripping room, sits Vi, almost 60, single, bent and quite deaf:

PEARL: Vi's got the nice voice, haven't you, Vi? Come on, Vi!

VI (in a croaking voice, the others listening solemnly): We was walzing together, and the stars began to fall . . . In this wonderful moment, something's happened to my heart, We was once changing partners till I'm in your arms and then . . . So we'll keep on changing partners till I hold you once more.

PEARL: (shouting): Look, Vi, over there, your boyfriend's coming.

VERA: (pointing to a chargehand in his glass cubicle): Ooh. Here's your boyfriend coming. Here's Jo coming. You'll have a kiss now, Ivy.

PEARL and VERA (calling): Jo! Jo! (then like doves) Joey! Joey!

VERA: Ah, he didn't hear, Vi. Never mind, eh.

Some of the best laughs are from turning the tables on supervisors, especially getting the upper hand with men:

PEARL: Vi, sing *Robinson Crusoe!* Come over here, Stan (calling over to the chargehand).

VI (singing):

He's a dirty old man, called Crusoe, He sat on the rock and played with his sock,

(roars of laughter among the women, Stan looking hot under the collar)

Oh dear old Robinson Crusoe.

Higher management, who quite often visited the shopfloor, were not exempt from older women's mockery. While a visiting party of salesmen comb their hair before a photograph next to a hogshead of tobacco, the hand stemmers taunt them through a glass partition:

STELLA: He's combing his hair! If we combed our hair in the factory, he'd go out of his mind.

VERA: Well, go and tell him, Stan, manager or no.

At this point the salesmen pose with their arms round each other:

ALL THE WOMEN: Ah! Ah!

VERA: Wish they could hear us! AH! Everybody together. AH!

ALL THE WOMEN (even louder): AH! AH!

VERA: I'm glad he had a sauna. He's slimming; Nicholson, he's on a diet.

ME: Which one is he?

STELLA: The manager. With his hand here. He's always got his hand down his trousers.

Chargehands have to 'deal with' the build-up of boredom and frustration:

VAL: I goes to sleep. I daydream. But when we don't talk for two hours, I start tormentin the others, pulling the rag about, muck about sort of thing. With the Irish, you know, I picks on them. About Ireland – take the soldiers back, the bombings, all that –

only mucking about like I don't mean it. But then we has a little row, but we don't mean what we says. But I get so bored, I got to do something, or I start going out the back and have a fag. (Music comes on.) It's the best part of the day when the records come on.

Older women find the younger generation 'more defiant' than they used to be. 'Good thing, too, though sometimes it can go too far.' Shopfloor humour is aggressive, often sexual. 'Who were you in bed with last night?' – '*Me?* In bed with someone? Don't be disgusting.' There are quick-witted insults, jibes, competition. Sometimes there are uproarious sessions of jokes.

Once I was called over to a group helpless with splutters of laughter, red faces and watery eyes:

CHERRY: What do you think of polo?

ME: Polo?

CHERRY (shrieks up a pitch): Yes! The mint with the hole!

(Uproar.)

ANN: Want a banana? (shrieks)

CHERRY: Oh yeh – a banana!

ANN: Can I have it peeled, please?

Then they turn on Cherry, who has a face burnt red by a sun lamp:

RENE: You've got radiation.

ALL: Radiation! Radiation! Radiation!

RENE: Only three weeks to live! Never mind, eh. What are you going to do?

CHERRY: I don't want to be a virgin all my life. (A good minute's solid ribaldry.)

RENE: Ssh. Not so loud.

ME: What else are you going to do?

CHERRY: Two weeks left? Must see the changing of the guards. Ooh aah.

The supervisor's job is to contain these outbursts, to maintain work discipline. They find it hard to handle:

STEVEN (chargehand, machine weighing room): The environment of the girls has changed. This permissive society – now these girls are changing with it. Well, I'm afraid they're not so mature, not so reliable as they used to be. That makes our job harder. I mean, when you talk to them, they give you such daft answers. I say, 'If you want to act like children, I shall have to treat you like children.'

Treating them like children means wheeling out stock sexist

coaxes, 'Do us a favour, love,' 'Hey, gorgeous,' 'Come on, sexy.' When Kathy was trundled off on a trolley by a lad, causing a general giggle and skirmish, the chargehand had to get things back into line in a 'friendly' way: 'What are you up to there? It's your sexy looks that always does it.' And the others collude:

BRENDA: Ooh aah! Mind him, back there. I wouldn't trust him on my own.

Sexual banter was a laugh. But it was also the language of cloying control which went with touching girls' hands and shoulders as they worked – 'only being friendly, like.' Being treated like children is part of factory life, part of relations with men – including union men:

AILEEN: When he [John] came in to us about electing him for shop steward, he said, 'Will you vote for me? Thank you,' and went out without waiting for an answer.

Others recall the local union official's reaction to the stemmers' arguments about their grading scheme:

IDA: Well, he wouldn't listen. He didn't want to know. He said we didn't know what was good for us. We always get shouted down, like. He never ever gave us a straight answer. He always went on to something else, bla, bla, bla.

Some women don't mind: 'Some men in here are as good as gold; some are as miserable as sin – they never smile; some are two-faced bastards. It all depends on the individual.' Some resent having to 'please' and 'play the game':

'You've got to be blue eyes in a factory, you know what I mean? Your face has got to fit, or else that's it. Well mine don't fit, that's for sure.'

For most, feeling small and silly is one of the factors which keeps them out of union life: 'I won't do it 'cos I feel soft in front of all those people. When you've got to go in the office, makes you feel soft.'

Factory life is about getting on with It:

KATE: I grin and bear it. If you want money, you have to work.

Stella describes her 30 years at Churchmans as 'a humdrum, day-to-day nothing.' But as well as the monotony and the pressure to keep up, as *women* they have to face up to the men around them – like their cheerful and kindly supervisor who confidently asserts: 'The simple thing is, they're quite happy if they're allowed to chatter all day about the more ordinary things.'

Humour and comradeship *are* vital. But they provide only one level of interpretation of factory life. As I watched, listened and debated, I uncovered the complexity and contradictions which made the quality of *women's* experience as workers distinctive – because they were both workers and women.

Acceptance and rejection

There was *both* acceptance *and* rejection of sexist assumptions about the woman's place being in the home. There were illusions about marriage as an escape from the factory, *and* resignation to staying. There was a stoical endurance towards shouldering the double burden of home and work, *and* a sense of injustice. There was 'satisfaction' with the job, *and* revolt against the work itself.

Talking to the women cold seemed to confirm their passivity and fatalism:

IDA: When you're young, you think you'll stop some time, and the years slip by. Things don't work out like that. Time flies when you get older.

But when I talked to them after an unsuccessful strike, I found that things were not entirely static, even here in an 'uneventful' factory. Many reacted with disillusionment and cynicism. But there were some, who had always claimed flippantly 'not to bother' about things, who now expressed a frustrated desire for change:

JENNY: It's all right talking about it. But it's different doing it. What we need is a spark here to set it off. That's all we need. Then we'll all join in.

The fact that no radical break with the past did take place at Churchmans, was bound up not with apathy, or with 'being perfectly happy,' but with the vicious circle women found themselves in. They began by believing a job was temporary and ended in the 'double shift' of work at home and work at the factory.

Far from being in a fool's paradise, they lived in a perpetual conflict of time, priorities, identities and ideas. But conflict is unstable. It is also what provokes change.

Question
1. (a) *Describe the working conditions of the women.*

(10 marks)

(b) *How did they cope with these conditions?* (10 marks)

36 Anna Coote: Social Policy and the Needs of Women

The extracts so far in this section suggest considerable maturity in feminist thought – maturity enough, perhaps, to provide a theoretical basis for a programme of practical policy measures to advance substantially the position of women. In the following reading, Anna Coote does rather more than that. Shrewdly, she adopts a powerful instrument – the male-dominated Labour Party – as a vehicle for the reforms she proposes. This is not just a matter of convenience because she clearly believes that a programme of reforms beneficial to women can achieve the broader socialist purpose of helping men – especially poorer men – as well. Many of the measures she proposes would help both sexes. These include a flexible retiring age for both sexes between 60 and 65, a massive public building programme for nurseries and day-care centres, and a statutory minimum wage.

Coote's theoretical starting point reveals the strength of the feminist aspect of her socialist-feminism. Her strategy is concerned with both reproduction and production but 'starts with the former'. There is a powerful logic and appeal in this starting point: 'how can we best care for and support our children?'

Help for the children, particularly in the form of nurseries and day-care, will release mothers onto the labour market where they have the opportunity to earn the income and wealth necessary for equal power and status with men. But the jobs have to be there in the first place and radical suggestions for job creation are an essential part of her policy package. If fully adopted, Coote's proposals might go a long way to dealing with the oppression of women described in Mary McIntosh's analysis.

Reading 36 From Anna Coote, 'Labour: the Feminist Touch' in *Marxism Today*, November 1985, pp. 10, 11–14.

In the fresh faced future that is William Morris's socialist ideal, there are many interesting features: clean rivers, abundant green fields and forests, free children, high quality goods . . . and serving wenches. These 'comely' women are found 'flitting to and fro . . .

decently veiled with drapery'; they set roses on the dining table and present 'delicately cooked' food with 'much daintiness'.

In *News From Nowhere*, Morris explains through the elderly character Hammond that when there is no class tyranny, 'women do what they best can do':

> It is a great pleasure to a clever woman to manage a house skilfully . . . and then, you know, everybody likes to be ordered about by a pretty woman . . .

Five out of ten to the man in the cabbage-flowered waistcoat. Housework is highly skilled and valuable. But it is not our natural calling and we will not be segregated, even under socialism; we will share all kinds of work with our non-tyrannical brothers. Nor do we like your 'everybody', meaning men alone. We are part of this universal identity – subjects, not objects.

Sadly, the serving wench phenomenon survives to this day, lodged like shrapnel in the disabled imagination of the male Left. They don't celebrate her any longer, or even try to justify her existence. But as they conjure up their visions of the future with their burgeoning investment banks and their sleek computer systems and their teaming construction sites, and even their resuscitated health and welfare services, she is always there: woman as object and afterthought, flitting daintily to and fro in the domestic margins of the working class.

Labour's new start

The Left has an opportunity now that it has never had before. It could, through the flawed but suitably-poised mechanism of the Labour party, develop a genuinely modern radical programme. One that could begin to reverse the long-term decline in the party's appeal, where statesmanlike speeches from its leader can only bring temporary respite. I mean the kind that doesn't suffer delusions about serving wenches . . .

Meanwhile, we women have reached an important new stage in our long revolution. Not only are we in better control of our fertility (despite Gillick and co) than at any point in our history; not only are we claiming, more consistently than ever, our economic independence from men (as single parents, and as sole or joint breadwinners) – but we have also staked out our ground in the paid labour force and *held on to it* through a recession. We are the poorest workers still, but the figures suggest that we are no longer a 'reserve army of labour'; we are regulars. This signals a significant shift in the economic and social roles of men and women.

At the same time, we have created our own cultural revolution. We have rediscovered our history, learned the value of female solidarity and carried a range of ideas into popular currency. We have developed a political perspective that has challenged the traditional view of the male Left. It begins with personal, everyday experience and spreads outwards from there. It demonstrates the political centrality of the sphere of 'reproduction' – all the life and work that goes on in the home and the community. The sphere where women predominate, where the young, the sick and the elderly are cared for, where people without paid jobs spend all their time and people with paid jobs spend most of their time. It insists that the liberation of women is a precondition for any kind of socialism worth having – and that means transforming economic relations *within* as well as *between* classes.

It challenges the orthodoxy of the Left on the best means of working-class organisation – showing that groups based in the community are as vital to the political process as those based at the workplace. We have achieved some changes in public attitudes and in the law. Some of the more offensive signs of male privilege have disappeared from the practices of the state as well as the labour movement. But now we are pushed against the limits of our own achievements. We have built our body of theory, written our own political agenda, and face the implications of putting it into practice.

We have learned that it isn't enough to get laws passed which give women 'rights'. They may create a more favourable climate, but they confine the conflict to territory where men are safely in control: courts, tribunals, a 'quango' appointed by the Home Office. They are designed to deal with outcroppings of male privilege, not to shift the balance of power between women and men.

We know now (if we didn't know before) that women are not a 'problem' to be solved at some stage of the main 'socialist' enterprise. We are at the centre of the struggle. We understand it better than men do. We are the key to its success. We cannot just be a pressure group; we must engage with power directly, as equal participants – subjects, not objects.

Which brings us back to the Labour party, potentially powerful but caught in a time-and-gender warp, with heavily blurred political vision. The opportunity it has now is to learn from the women's movement and put women at the centre of its policy-making process.

Passive resistance

Labour's leaders and planners have better access to feminism than ever before. Women have had time to crystallise their own ideas about how to turn policy into practice, and find out what they want from the political mainstream. They are better organised within the Labour party and have built up a stronger presence – not in parliament, but in some policy-making circles, such as social security and poverty. Labour is at last committed to a statutory minimum wage – a change due in no small part to the weight of the feminist critique of collective bargaining. Women's committees in local and metropolitan authorities have begun to demonstrate what can be done when political and financial resources are put at women's disposal.

But Labour seems able to accommodate the female perspective only in piecemeal ways, around the periphery. When it comes to its basic approach to major policy areas, the party is stuck in its old rut. Take economic planning, for example: this area has probably had more time and effort put into it than any other, yet it remains profoundly conservative, sorely afflicted by serving wenches.

The real problem is shifting the weight of power within the party. No matter how much its leaders may wish to look forwards, they are doomed to look backwards as long as men continue to control the institution. While they do, the party sees with men's eyes only. Men have traditionally focused their politics around the point of production – concentrating on the world of paid jobs and industry, trade and finance. From this perspective (which reflects the main focus of their own lives), men imagine the future and determine their priorities. So Labour suffers from a kind of institutional blindness: it does not see, with anything like equal clarity, that part of human experience which revolves around reproduction. Without which there could be no life, let alone production.

This blindness is not simply a problem for women. It renders incompetent any attempt to move towards an equal and democratic society. It makes nonsense of any claim to a modern socialism. There are several reasons why this is so. The unpaid labour of women is a critical factor in relations between labour and capital. It underpins and determines the character of paid labour. The subordination of women within the family is a critical factor in the continuing subordination of the working class; a class divided by conflicting interests is fatally weakened. A political party with socialist aspirations cannot hope to develop a clear political vision unless it understands the needs and concerns and contradictions that arise in the sphere of reproduction, just as well as those in the sphere of production.

Labour's institutional blindness persists in spite of our efforts to make it see. Commonly these days, men in the party appear to listen and agree with what women say – and then do nothing about it (or as near to nothing as they can get away with). This is *passive resistance* – a highly effective strategy employed by men to resist women's liberation. It works, because most of the changes we need require movement on the part of institutions and organisations they control. Their inaction guarantees the *status quo*. It is a slippery kind of antagonism, harder to tackle than outright opposition.

A fine example is the response of the Labour party to women's demands for fair representation in the party and in parliament – not in the margins, but in the mainstream. Few men would openly dispute the need for women to be better represented. Yet they won't give practical support by voting for constitutional changes that could break the deadlock of women's powerlessness. They won't agree to the Labour women's conference electing the woman's section of the NEC, or putting resolutions straight on to the agenda of the main conference. They have gone on selecting men for parliament – so far, in all but 10 of Labour's 170 safest seats – as though they bore no responsibility for acting on the principle to which they had agreed.

But why?

We can see *how* men resist. But *why?* There are layers of reasons. At one level, they benefit from women's subordination. If women had more power, more opportunity, more pay, more time, more choice, men would have less. It is rare for any group or class of human beings to give up power voluntarily – unless convinced it is in their own best interests to do so. Men have not yet understood that their interests as men do not coincide in every respect with those of their class.

At another level, they cannot or will not recognise the need to shift their ground and change themselves in order to improve conditions for women. They have not understood that socialism begins at home. Consequently, many well-intentioned men on the Left still believe that the business of getting equality for women is quite unproblematic. Just let them get rid of the Tories and sort out the economy and maybe appoint a women's minister (in an advisory capacity) and the rest will fall into place. A law here, a nursery there, a few training schemes, jack up the odd benefit – and Bob's your uncle.

At yet another level, there are historical and institutional reasons why passive resistance is so widely practised by men in the labour movement. These concern the character of the trade unions and their relationship with the Labour party.

In Britain, trade unionism is essentially about people who share specific interests related to the workplace joining together to defend those interests – against the employer and, inevitably, against other workers. Its character was formed in the early period of craft unions, when the main purpose was to control entry to skilled jobs and regulate pay and conditions for elite groups. Even after the general unions were formed, the pattern remained largely unchanged, based on division of labour and inequality within the working class. Semi-skilled and unskilled workers have had to defend their interests in relation to skilled workers, women in relation to men. And since the unions are concerned primarily with the workplace, their political priorities relate to production. They are not geared up to represent or defend interests arising out of the sphere of reproduction.

Building new links

The Labour party was formed with the declared purpose of providing parliamentary representation for 'working class opinion by men sympathetic to the aims and demands of the labour move-ment' – in effect, to represent the unions at Westminster. It has since broadened its brief, but it has always looked to the unions to provide its primary link with the working class. The vehicle of this link has been the block vote and the strength of the block vote has been determined by the size of each union's financial contribution.

Not surprisingly, Labour has adopted and maintained the political priorities of its paymasters. Taking the block vote as a guarantee of its working-class credentials, it has never assumed responsibility for building up a primary political organisation by and for working-class people. Women are the main losers: we have marginal status in the unions because of our role in the reproductive sphere, and Labour provides no alternative focus for us. A small elite of predominantly white, male trade unionists vote at the Labour conference each year on behalf of hundreds of thousands of 'dead souls' – rank and file members who take little part in the political process by which they are represented.

These union votes outweigh the votes of constituency parties. The CLPs might have made up for the unions' limitations, had they not always had second-class status and second-rate power. They've been marginalised by their lack of financial clout and, ironically, by the fact that they are not seen as true representatives of the working class.

Labour needs its links with the unions – preferably more open and democratic ones. It also needs strong, organic links with working-class women and men who are not in paid, organised work, with young people, pensioners and the unemployed. Until it constructs these links, the political culture of the party will go on denying the central importance of the sphere of reproduction; the party machinery will continue to entrench the dominant view, instead of exploring other perspectives. The vicious circle of female powerlessness, male resistance and institutional inaction will keep on turning.

A different perspective

What hope of breaking it? There are no simple answers, of course, but one step in the right direction would be for women to identify male strategies of resistance, and confront men with their knowledge, so that it can be the subject of open political dialogue. We shall have to make alliances with men. We shall have to show them that it is in their best interests to make alliances with us. We shall have to teach them – if they will not teach themselves – that you can't win mass support for a political programme that overlooks the experience of more than half the people. We shall have to keep trying to persuade them to abandon their conservatism, face the

1980s, and radically reassess their approach and priorities from a female perspective.

For more immediate purposes, we shall have to supply the Labour party with an alternative strategy. Some feminists (myself included) have argued for a strategy that would begin by asking *not* 'how can we regenerate the economy to create full employment?', but 'how can we best care for and support our children?' (This is not, of course, a matter of private domestic choices, but of our collective responsibility to the next generation.) The strategy focuses on the spheres of reproduction *and* production, but starts with the former, on the grounds that this is the primary sphere, from which production springs.

The strategy would give priority to breaking down the traditional division of paid and unpaid labour, so that responsibility for children could be shared equally among men and women, and between home-based parental care and community-based collective care. It would mean a much shorter working week for men and women, vastly improved childcare provision outside the home, and a restructuring of family income, by increasing female earning power and child benefit, and improving the 'social wage'.

Suppose this strategy were adopted by Labour: how might it affect the party's programme? In fact, it is already committed to *most* of the policies (suggested below) that would be needed in the short term, in order to create the right conditions for full implementation in the long term. The first four are new – although Labour is committed in principle to shorter working hours. Of the rest, some are already destined for the manifesto; others have been widely discussed and accepted. What's missing so far is a coherent approach, which treats the policies as a package, designed to achieve a clear set of objectives – *and gives them priority*.

A new deal for women

- All new jobs in the public sector limited to 30 hours a week.
- Incentives to private employers to create new jobs at 30 hours a week.
- Flexible retirement age for men and women between 60 and 65, with a maximum 30-hour week for those over 60.
- Introduce a staged programme to reduce all jobs to 30 hours, over a fixed period of years.

- Statutory restrictions on overtime.
- Full employment rights for all part-time workers on 16 hours a week or more.
- Extended parental leave, on an equal basis for men and women.
- Massive public building programme for nurseries and day-care centres.
- Full implementation of the EEC directive on equal pay for work of equal value.
- National and local government to operate positive action programmes to improve training and job opportunities for women, and to offer contracts to private employers on condition that they do the same.
- Statutory minimum wage.
- Reinstate and strengthen wages councils.
- Voluntary incomes policy, designed to favour the low-paid.
- Abolish married man's tax allowance and use proceeds to increase child benefit – as a first step towards making this benefit cover the basic cost of a child.
- Uprate benefits for single parents and those looking after sick or elderly dependents.
- Priority in public spending on new housing, modernisation and repairs of existing housing, local public transport, education after-school and holiday facilities for children, home helps, meals on wheels, community nursing – and similar services designed to ease the burden of domestic labour.

The job-creating possibilities aren't bad. Even though the shorter working week would not guarantee a pro rata increase in new jobs, it would certainly help, and the expansion of childcare and social services involves labour-intensive work that could never be computerised into redundancy. The Labour party clearly intends to start a large programme of public works, to create jobs in construction and related industries: again, it's a question of priorities – it could make a world of difference whether motorways or nurseries were at the top of the agenda.

Until now, Labour's politicians and economic planners have tended to say: 'Let's work out what we can do with the economy, and then see what we can afford.' If they saw through women's eyes, or (better still) if they *were* women, they might be more inclined to say: 'Let's find out what people want and need, and then work out how to pay for it.' The economy, like the state – to borrow a phrase from Neil Kinnock – would be under the feet of the people, not over their heads.

Question

1. (a) Discuss the practicality and possible consequences of implementing Anna Coote's 'new deal for women'.

(10 marks)

(b) How important for the liberation of women do you think it is to establish a comprehensive, national system of nurseries and day-care centres?

(10 marks)

37 Juliet Mitchell: Working for Progress

In this reading, Juliet Mitchell reviews twenty years of feminism and asks some penetrating questions about the movement's relationship to the profound economic and social changes of recent years.

She states that the movement went through two stages. First, was the period of righting obvious wrongs, mainly in terms of discrimination in employment and in the exploitation of women's sexuality for commercial gain. Second, was a reassertion and positive revaluation of qualities of womanhood and being female, e.g. it is alright to care for people (though not to be hopelessly exploited as a result). Although some progress has been made in these areas, particularly the first, Mitchell observes in retrospect a possible unintended role of the movement – to facilitate change from an industrial to a service economy.

How can this have happened? The demands of feminists for paid work coincided with the demands for labour of a changing economy. As many men lost jobs in heavy industry, many women acquired jobs in service industries. Mitchell suggests that this development would probably have happened without the feminist movement and that its broader social effects are by no means all positive. In time, it may be that women will be edged out of work in these newer areas as men move in. To give credibility to this pessimistic scenario, Mitchell cites the earlier historical example of the legal removal of women and children from heavy industry after they had helped lay the basis for it. She implies that feminists might better have understood all this if they had thought more in class terms rather than of women as a single entity.

Reading 37 From Juliet Mitchell, 'Reflections on Twenty Years of Feminism' in A. Oakley and J. Mitchell *eds.*, *What is Feminism?* (Blackwell, 1986), pp. 42–8.

I believe that our feminist attacks on the system, despite our intentions, were highly complicit with the present changes. This is not to castigate ourselves (though certainly self-criticism is involved), but rather to demonstrate once more that a radical politics, indeed any radical thought, must bear the marks of its origin which may not be perceived until it is too late.

Looking back, for the sake of an organising schema, we can divide our recent feminist history into two stages. To characterise the two stages I would invert the title of a preceding anthology of essays which I edited with Ann Oakley in 1976. It was called *The Rights and Wrongs of Women*, itself the title of a seminal essay by Margaret Walters on, among others, Mary Wollstonecraft who, as well as writing *The Vindication of the Rights of Woman*, wrote a novel called *Maria, or The Wrongs of Woman*.

The first stage of our movement was directed to putting right the wrongs of women, the second to an emphasis on the values, the importance of the qualities of womanhood and femininity – peace, caring, nurturance . . .

First the wrongs. In England, our demands were two-pronged: on the one hand, for equal pay and work opportunities and, on the other, for a change in the sexual image and status of women. Both were badly needed.

If we examine critically our struggle for equal pay and work opportunities (again, within the ethics of our society, perfectly proper aims in themselves), the nominal achievement of these facilitated future male unemployment and the debasement – temporarily – of the condition of workers in general. To go back once more to 1844, Engels had commented on the role of the cheap labour of women and children: its task was to introduce a lower standard of living and lower wages for men. In the intervening period the trade union movement to protect the rights of workers had been established and the threat to the male worker's wage of women's cheaper labour had been recognised. Once, in the late sixties, women had been awarded the right to equal pay (in fact only achieved today in Britain, nearly eighteen years later, in the police force and among butchers), there could no longer be any union opposition to their employment. However, women's real pay is always lower and women predominantly work part-time and hence are largely unprotected. Women are poorly unionised at a time when union strength was to be assailed from all sides; lacking job security and health and old-age benefits, women have no reason, therefore, not to move jobs or move out of jobs should the need arise. Our aim was equal pay; a tragic effect of our achievement was to remove pay as an obstacle and then to erode the conditions of employment, to help lower the expectation of social security, state benefits, trade union support . . . workers' solidarity . . . to make way for a mobile, flexible worker and the self-employed. In fighting for equal pay, in no way was this our intention, but the passing of the law did facilitate the change.

Consciously we were attacking a consumer society and the place of women within it. We slapped stickers over the Underground – 'this ad. insults women', attacked 'Miss World' contests and challenged the treatment of women as sex objects. In America the epiphany, whether truth or fiction, was the bra-burning in Washington.

Twenty years ago in Europe, women were used as sexual objects in advertising and in the media in a far more blatant way than was the case in the USA. I can remember how appalled American feminists were by our bill-boards. I have done no statistical survey but, as a lay observer, I believe we have far fewer advertisements using women as their sales object today in Britain; instead there is a proportionate increase in appeals to minority groups such as Blacks and above all to children (again America was far ahead of us in this). The child, not the housewife, is today's consumer. Is this removal of women from advertising to be chalked up as a success for feminist campaigns, or as something more complex over which we had no control?

I wonder, though this does not invalidate the protests, whether in fact we are not attacking something already on the way out. Were we giving a helpful shove to an ideology that was already inappropriate? In the late sixties and early seventies we were attacking women as objects of consumer campaigns at exactly the time when women were wanted back into the workforce. It was precisely the housewives who a decade earlier had had to vie for the whitest wash of all who were now wanted for the part-time labour force – their children could be compensated by more and more toys. Women were not to be sex objects but service workers. In attacking the place of women in consumer society and in simultaneously promoting the employment of women, unwittingly, we were perhaps assisting a change already taking place.

In the second phase of our movement we attacked the idealisation of women by men in territories occupied by women only: the home, reproduction and caring for others. This 'pedestal' treatment, like all idealisations, was rightly seen to contain its negative, denigratory side.

It is interesting that after attacking the pedestal treatment of women as earth-mothers, after fighting and showing that we could do what men could do, we then discovered that for our vision of equality, we needed them to do what we could do. Motherhood and domesticity having been negatively appraised, we re-valued them. And so with the wrongs nominally righted, the way was open for the positive aspects of womanhood to be rediscovered. In discovering our values, we made the social and the psychological areas traditionally occupied by women fit for occupation by men – the home was a place for men to inhabit while the women went out into the world of work – for the time being. We facilitated a social shift: if women were to become more like men, men were also to be more like women: 'Men and women cannot be equal partners outside the home, if they are not equal partners inside it', wrote Ann Oakley. For the middle classes this was, and is, very acceptable; a four day week for the professional man with paternity leave and the real pleasures of comfortably off child-care and domesticity; for the woman, a part-time job in which the lack of security presents no hazards. For the working-class couple it is another story: an unemployed coal-miner and his wife bringing in the earned income from cleaning or clerical work. In theory, women, unified as a group, could do similar service jobs, whatever their class, but with very different effects.

However, something yet more important than our facilitation of women into the work-force and out of an old-style, consumer-oriented femininity seems to have been going on.

Challenging the wrongs of women – at work, as sex objects, in education – we were comparing ourselves with men. We could then assert our discrete and independent value. To do this we created or recreated a new unity: women. With tortuous arguing in the early days, we tried to see whether we could call ourselves a class, a caste, a social group and so on. The point is that, calling ourselves 'sisters', we created ourselves once more as a category.

When I started working on the topic of women in 1962, it was virtually impossible to get the differential information on the sexes – I remember how particularly hard it was in the field of education. Everything was broken down into socio-economic groups. Today I find the reverse: it is easy to obtain information on male/female differences but not on social class achievements and positions.

In forging a concept of women as a unity, we promoted a situation in which old class antagonisms would shift through a period of chaos into something new. In recognising on paper the class and race distinctions of women but being unable, by definition, to make them the focal thrust of our movement, we contributed to an ideology that temporarily homogenised social classes and created a polarity that disguised other distinctions by the comprehensive, all-embracing opposition – men/women.

We aimed to erode, and indeed did in part erode, the old distinctions between men and women, yet to do so we helped create a major opposition between the sexes. The paradox is only apparent.

By setting up the opposition of the sexes as dominant, we helped to produce the ideological notion of a 'classless' society by which, in this instance, one may mean a society in which the transition to new class lines, or a new class composition, has not yet solidified.

I am left with the two questions with which I started out. What is the meaning of the changed position of women in the last two decades? And, what is the relationship of feminism to this change?

If it is true, as the statistics assert, that women's employment has increased in the wake of male unemployment, what is the cause and what is the effect of this? In the first instance, it would seem that women at work serve to debase the standard of living, to create a new poor from the conditions of the industrial working-class family. Despite 'equal' pay acts, women are used to lower pay and lower conditions of work, to lower expectations; when men, in the future, take over the new jobs from women, the snail of progress will have slithered a foot back down the well. With men's future re-employment firmly established, the snail will struggle up again until the next crisis. But is there something less cyclical going on? Is there more of a linear progression in process, with less backwards slides? Through women's marginality and hence through our flexibility can humankind as a social being move for ever upwards? Do women put the future on trial? The one possibility does not exclude the other.

Both the forward-looking and the complicit aspects of feminism would seem to echo these two possibilities. But first the statistics of change must be looked at more closely. Feminist historians are starting to question Engels's portrait of the increased employment of women in 1844 and, today, even as in this essay I try to construct a picture, its prime colours start to decompose. The very statistics of women's entry into production are subject to both class and sex bias.

There is a massive labour force of working-class and immigrant women which is hidden – I am not here referring to the vexed issue of unpaid labour of childcare and housework – but to the paid, undeclared 'casual' labour and to the home-based production in the myriad forms of 'outwork'. Most women in England always work for wages of some sort. Is the claimed increase of women into production a largely middle-class phenomenon that casts its hegemonic mantle over other women's invisibility? Has one of feminism's unconscious tasks in getting woman out of history's hiding places been to turn her, for the time being, into a legitimate wage-earner for a family with an unemployed man? Does the creation of an umbrella category, 'woman', falsely suggest that middle-class entry into and exit from production which is sporadic, applies to all classes? Is my very argument in this essay trapped in the trammels of the class and sexist assumptions that it is trying to analyse?

In one women's liberation group in which I participated around 1970, we set ourselves the task of charting the amount and nature of the work and the conditions of women 'outworkers' in the area of London where we lived. The result of our enquiry was to uncover an extensive mycelium which only occasionally mushroomed above ground into legality and hence statistics. Today, we have national statistics on 'outwork'. As a further ironic twist of our type of enquiry, a family is less eligible for state benefits where the woman is known to be working.

What we can probably say with some confidence is that, overall, there is a large increase in the number of women seen to be working both in absolute terms and in relation to men. I think also that it is quite likely that women who worked in invisible jobs have for the time shifted into recognised work; maybe this is in addition to their previous work becoming recognised. Certainly it would seem that there is a real increase in middle-class, middle-aged women working for the first time since motherhood.

If we look back at the history of feminism, to its fits and starts, its uneven development over the past 300 years, do its times of efflorescence coincide with a particular type of social and economic transition that temporally places women in a vanguard position either through their new entry or newly acknowledged entry into production? This possibility makes sense to me. It was the eminent feminist Elizabeth Cady-Stanton who encouraged the advance of women, not into production but into a new relationship to circulation, that of consumption, with these words, to an imaginary congressman's wife: Go and buy a new stove! Buy what you need! Buy while he's in Washington! When he returns and flies into a rage, you sit in a corner and weep. That will soften him! Then when he tastes his food from the new stove, he will know you did the wise thing. When he sees you so much fresher, happier in your new kitchen, he will be delighted and its bills will be paid. I repeat – GO OUT AND BUY.

Feminism does emanate from the bourgeoisie or the petit-bourgeoisie, the social class which, in capitalist society, where it is dominant, gives its values to the society as a whole. It represents its particular interest as universal interest, its women as 'woman'. To see this is not to turn aside from feminism, but to note that as yet it has not transcended the limitations of its origins. We should use any radical movement or thought as an early warning system to make us aware of changes already in process.

In arguing as feminists for an end to the sexual division of labour, for social bisexuality, were we promoting an ongoing process of capitalism, a process whose triumph could only be enjoyed under socialism?

Many have argued that the process of capitalism (leading, indeed, to the communism envisaged by Marx and Engels) reduces the distinction between the sexes to the point of disappearance. Lyotard, for instance, suggests that the creation of a social-psychological androgyne (again an ideological contribution from, among others, the women's movement) is the ultimate goal of an economy driven towards a final point which is organised solely around the circulation of exchange objects.

Certainly the thrust of our movement's intention was to overcome the opposition we had perceived and highlighted – to make men and women more alike. Whatever our positions, whether as socialist-feminists coming with Marxist traditions (more typical of England) or as radical feminists (more typical of the United States) our visions of the future eroded the division of labour within the family, de-structured generational divisions and dispersed the family tasks of reproduction and nurturance into myriad alternatives.

However, I do not believe we are simply involved in a straight-forward and inevitable progression to an ultimately androgynous society. If women are the vanguard troops of change, it is not only because the whole society is becoming feminised or androgynised – though that is partly true. It is also because, as women, we occupy a socially marginal and hence shiftable position.

At each crisis of change, I believe, we imagine this androgyne and this endless circulation and free play of multifarious differences; with each period of stabilisation, something has to occupy the new points of opposition. In periods of intensified social change, men and women, the masculine and the feminine, come closer together; a new unity is created, a new man, and something different has to confront him. For the time being, we should note that, between the sexes, this new point of difference is called 'woman'.

I would suggest, then, that feminism is an ideological offspring of certain economic and social conditions. Its radicalism reflects the fact that it comes to prominence at points of critical change. It both abets this change and envisages it with an imagination that goes beyond it.

There was nothing wrong with our visions; they just reflected a shift already in process – as indeed they must, but we should have been conscious of this and (a matter for self-criticism) we were not. Again we can return to 1844. Like the machinery that replaced the gruelling labour, the leisure that could replace a long work week, the new technology and a sexual equality that was freed from the conditions of a class society would all be positive changes. This was our vision. As feminists we conceived yesterday's future.

Question
1. *(a) What were the goals of the feminist movement?*
(12 marks)
(b) How successful do you consider it has been in achieving them?
(13 marks)

(The reading from Juliet Mitchell is a starting point but not sufficient for this question).

SECTION 8

Race

Readings 38 – 44

This section opens with a brief discussion by Bhikhu Parekh of racism and of the three main pillars of British race relations strategy up to about 1980. Some readers may want to read the second part of this extract, the review of race relations strategy/policy, at the end of the topic.

Readings 39 and 40 present two sides of a debate about the location of blacks within the stratification system. Marxist writers, Castles and Kosack integrate race and racism within a class framework of analysis. By contrast, Douglas Glasgow gives decisive emphasis to racism and argues that, primarily as a result of it, a 'black underclass' has developed in the United States. The most distinguished theorist of the black underclass in Britain is John Rex who gives the concept a Weberian tinge (for a brief summary of his main points see my textbook, *A New Introduction to Sociology* (Nelson, 1987, pp. 346–7). Although the term underclass is now used by most writers, the theoretical differences mentioned above persist.

Ken Pryce offers a more personal and descriptive account of what certain black males think of 'slave labour'. By contrast, Simon Field's article, 'Trends in Racial Equality', is very much of the social survey variety. Ellis Cashmore provides an informed and concerned analysis of the 1985 urban disorders in Birmingham, and John Pilger describes the ordeals of an Asian family in East London.

It is important for the reader to pick up on other extracts dealing with race in other sections of this book. Reading 67 discusses apartheid and, in Reading 96, Bhikhu Parekh attacks what he considers to be the racism of sections of the British press.

38 Bhikhu Parekh: Racism, and Race Relations Strategy in Britain

This reading falls into two quite distinct parts. First, Parekh discusses the meaning of the term racism. Second, he describes 'official' race relations strategy in Britain from the late nineteen fifties to about 1980.

Parekh attributes three meanings to the term racism of which the third is perhaps most important from the sociological point of view. First, racism is the division of human beings into distinct races on the basis of scientific attempt rather than moral judgement or personal prejudice. Second, racism is the division of human beings into a *hierarchy* of races – this does involve moral and political judgements. Third, is the attitude of preferring one's own race to others without necessarily considering it superior. It is probably racism in the second sense that causes most conflict. Parekh goes on briefly to discuss the tendency to confuse racial and ethnic/cultural judgements and it is true that in practice racists often do not make nice distinctions. In sharply rejecting the view that capitalism causes racism, Parekh indicates his own non-Marxist position.

The second part of the reading deals with the three main government (and in Parekh's view, conflicting) race relations strategies. The first has been to control immigration, the second, to prevent discrimination, and, the third, to bring about the assimilation (absorption) of ethnic minorities into the mainstream of British society. In criticising the assimilation strategy, Parekh implies that the alternative approach of mutually accepting differences (cultural and otherwise), as well as similarities, is preferable.

There is inevitably much of importance both in respect to definitions and policy that Parekh does not discuss in this short extract. For instance, he does not define the difference between institutional and individual racism (the former refers to the seemingly 'fair' norms on which an organisation operates which in practice have a discriminatory effect). In the policy area, the 1981 Nationality Act continued the strategy of 'tight' immigration. Beyond that, it is perhaps fair to characterise government approach as 'laissez-faire'. By contrast, certain local authorities have adopted a vigorous anti-racist stance. Two major aspects of this approach have been efforts to recruit blacks to the public services and to teach anti-racism in schools and root out racism from the curriculum.

Reading 38 From Bhikhu Parekh, *The Experience of Black Minorities in Britain* (Open University Press, 1982), E354,3,10. pp. 5–6, 12–14.

An important preliminary task in assessing the experience of Britain's black minorities is to clarify the concepts of race and racism. It is pertinent to begin by asking if race is even a useful concept. Essentially it is a biological term and rests on the assumption that mankind can be divided into different groups on the basis of specific biological properties. It is generally recognised that all such biologically based modes of classification run into difficulties. It is also admitted that, as a result of racial intermingling over the centuries, no pure races can be found. Further, biological properties such as colour of skin, texture of hair and shape of nose or cheek bones obviously do not *cause* the behaviour of the people these properties belong to. Therefore race cannot be a basis for explaining or inferring human conduct. In the light of these and other difficulties do we need the concept of race at all? It has no explanatory value and only creates confusion and muddle.

Racism is also a dubious concept. It is, of course, true that while rejecting the concept of race we may nevertheless retain the concept of racism. It is not inconsistent to say that although mankind cannot be objectively divided into races, some people *think* that it can be so divided. The point, however, is that racism is an ambiguous concept and is generally used in a loose manner. It is used in at least three related but different senses. In the first sense, it maintains that mankind is divided into distinct races, each with its own peculiar genetic structure, psycho-physical make-up and a set of innate tendencies and dispositions. Each race is therefore believed to give rise to a distinct culture, way of life, way of looking at the world, type of human being, and so on. Racism in this sense claims to be a scientific and not a moral doctrine. It does not say that some races are superior to others, only that races are radically different in their constitution and destiny.

In the second sense, racism is a moral and political doctrine. It asserts that different races can be hierarchically graded, and that some races are inherently superior and fully human whereas others lack the basic capacities that constitute humanity. This type of racism takes many forms. It may suggest that some races are inherently and incorrigibly inferior and can be used and exploited, or that they can be 'educated' and 'civilised', or that they are a danger to 'superior' races and should be exterminated. The first two senses of racism are obviously related. Historically speaking, racism in the first sense has led to the latter. From saying that races are inherently different it is easy to slide into saying that some are superior. However, the two senses are logically separate and should not be confused.

Sometimes racism is used in a third sense, of dislike for or antipathy to another race. Racism in this sense is not a scientific or a moral theory, but an attitude. A person need not hold that race determines character or that other races are inherently inferior, but may simply prefer his or her own race and dislike either all other races or some particular race. It is possible to be a sinophile but an anti-Semite, or to like Jews but dislike blacks. Dislike need not be based on any kind of judgement as to the worth of different races, but may simply be an emotional attitude. A racist in this sense may not wish to maltreat other races or even to discriminate against them, but may simply wish to avoid close contact of any kind. (For a good discussion of the different kinds of racism see Baxter and Sansom, 1972, and Parekh, 1974.)

The reason for taking a close look at the concept of racism is that writers have used it to explain Britain's treatment of its black minorities without always clearly stating what they mean by the term or adequately differentiating it from xenophobia, ethnocentrism or cultural antipathy. Those who stress racism often have difficulty in explaining its origin and continued existence. For some racism is 'inherent' in human nature. For others it is 'inherent' in European culture – but they do not explain how European culture came to be racist, whether others' cultures are free from racism, and so on. For yet others it is a product of colonialism. While plausible it is hardly an adequate explanation. The British colonised both India and Africa, and yet treated the peoples involved very differently. For example, they had no hesitation in buying and selling blacks as slaves, but did not subject the Indians to this state of degradation.

Some scholars argue that racism is a product of capitalism. Again, the explanation highlights an important point, but remains inadequate. Racism preceded capitalism, as is evident in the history of

Greece and Rome, and it survives in Communist societies. Further, racism is not always in the interest of capitalism, as is evident in the opposition expressed to it by some South African and American capitalists; nor do the racially motivated immigration controls in Britain or the massacre of the Jews in Nazi Germany seem to have an overriding economic logic. An economic explanation cannot account for the different types of racism developed in different capitalist societies.

Racism is too complex to be explained in terms of isolated factors. In this unit I propose to concentrate on the specific case of racism in Britain by examining the manner in which it evolved a way of defining and responding to its black immigrants. . . .

Over a period of time, then, a consensus emerged concerning the best way to deal with the 'race problem'. It pinned its hopes on a tripartite strategy: first, immigration control; second, race relations legislation; and third, assimilation of the ethnic minorities into the mainstream of British society. The consensus was inherently contradictory, for the three policies did not all point in the same direction. It was also grounded in a false analysis of the 'race problem'.

Britain had convinced itself that the blacks brought problems and that their number must therefore be drastically curtailed. Successive governments went about the task with great vigour and determination. The story of how the Immigration Acts of 1962, 1968 and 1971 were passed has already been well told by Charles Husband in Units 5–6 and Ann Dummett in Unit 7, and need not be repeated here. Two points are, however, worth making. First, in historical terms the story of immigration control makes fascinating reading. It is striking that the secret plans for restricting black immigration were made the moment it began to occur, that within five years of the arrival of blacks in noticeable numbers strident calls for restriction were heard, and that within about eight years a law drastically restricting black immigration had already been passed. The speed with which Britain moved to restrict black immigration is unprecedented in her long history. Even the Jewish immigration from the 1870s onwards had continued for over thirty years before attempts were made to restrict it. Blacks could not help wondering why they were singled out for unusually harsh treatment, why more black immigrants had been locked up and deported than any other previous group of immigrants, and why their presence should have caused so much intellectual and moral panic.

Once successive British governments had convinced themselves that the presence of 'too many' blacks was a threat to the British way of life, government officials involved with immigration or immigrants began to see themselves as nationally authorised guardians of the British way of life, and pursued their task with almost a missionary zeal and in a spirit of self-righteousness. The Entry Clearance Officers in Britain's diplomatic missions in the New Commonwealth, and especially on the Indian sub-continent, subjected prospective tourists and immigrants as well as the dependants of those rightfully settled here to a most degrading form of interrogation. Those who managed to survive it were subjected to a further detailed scrutiny by the immigration officials at Heathrow Airport. Even if allowed in they were kept under scrutiny by the police, and sometimes social workers and National Health Service officials were asked to look out for illegal immigrants and over-staying tourists and students. Once black immigrants came to be perceived as a mortal threat to Britain's identity, stopping them at all cost became a task of supreme moral and practical importance. Every means to this end was fair and justified. This led to a gross coarsening of the nation's moral sensibility and almost blunted its capacity to appreciate the enormity of the actions done in its name. The virginity tests, the radiological tests of minors, the shunting back and forth of British passport-holders, the detention of innocent men and women at Heathrow Airport, the prolonged separation of families, and deportation of children, became common practices. The bulk of the nation could hardly be persuaded to take notice of what was going on, let alone feel outraged by it.

The second plank in the national strategy to deal with the 'race problem' was the enactment of race relations legislation. The logic of this legislation worked in opposition to that of immigration control. While successive Immigration Acts increasingly restricted the number of immigrants, including those in possession of British passports, the successive Race Relations Acts involved increasingly stronger action against racial discrimination. Once a government passed an Act which explicitly recognised the reality of discrimination and affirmed the nation's collective commitment to eliminate it, it could not arbitrarily stop at a convenient point. If one legislative Act does not effectively deal with discrimination, consistency demands that another, more effective, Act must be passed. The attempt to deal with the more obvious cases of discrimination uncovered others that had not hitherto been noticed or considered important. The very attempt to deal with discrimination aroused expectations and generated a momentum that could not be easily disregarded.

Assimilation was the third plank in the generally agreed national strategy of dealing with the 'race problem'. The argument for assimilation is fairly simple. If you are an immigrant and want the British to treat you like one of them, it is common sense that you must become like them. If, on the other hand, you insist on remaining different, you must expect to be treated differently. You cannot have it both ways. If you refuse to assimilate, you are bound to invite discrimination, a wholly natural and understandable response. Although never clearly defined, assimilation basically consists in requiring immigrants to give up almost all that is distinctive about them, be it dress, manners, lifestyles, systems of marriage or modes of bringing up children, and for all practical purposes to become like the British.

Question
1. (a) *Critically discuss the various definitions of racism given in the above passage.*

(10 marks)
(b) How, according to Parekh, was the 'race problem' dealt with in Britain? What is your opinion of this strategy?

(15 marks)

39 S. Castles and G. Kosack: Immigrant Workers and Class Structure

After discussing a number of alternatives, Castles and Kosack place immigrants, including black immigrants, firmly within the working class. Given their Marxist theoretical framework, this is not surprising. Like the rest of the working class, the vast majority of immigrants do not own the means of production and have to sell their labour to survive. Thus they conclude 'Immigrant workers and indigenous workers together form the working class in contemporary Western Europe ...'. However, they add significantly, 'but it is a divided class.' They describe how this division manifests itself in economic, social and political terms. They suggest that, at root, the division is a false one as it is produced by capitalists in their own interests and at the expense of the working class. Accordingly, they imply a fourth area of division among the working class, i.e. that of consciousness or cultural attitudes. They conclude that 'false consciousness can only disappear . . . when it is supplanted . . . by a class consciousness which reflects the true position of all workers in society.'

Reading 39 From S. Castles and G. Kosack, *Immigrant Workers and Class Structure in Western Europe* (Oxford University Press, 1973), pp. 474–82.

The impact of immigration

We may now return to the questions of immigrant workers' position in the class structure and the effect of immigration upon society in general. Our study has shown that immigrant workers in all the countries concerned share the same basic position; they have the poorest conditions and lowest status in every social sphere.

On the labour market, which is the key area for determination of class position, immigrants are highly concentrated in a limited range of occupations and industries: those offering the lowest pay, the worst working conditions, and the lowest degree of security. An analysis of socio-economic status showed that immigrant workers are considerably overrepresented in the lowest categories. The overwhelming majority are manual workers – mainly unskilled or semi-skilled – and very few are employed in white-collar occupations. Immigrant workers tend to suffer more severely than their indigenous colleagues from unemployment at times of recession.

Immigrants have a similar disadvantageous position outside work. They experience great difficulty in obtaining housing, and generally have to pay high rents for run-down accommodation seriously lacking in amenities. In some countries, there are special housing schemes for immigrant workers. These are insufficient to meet the demand, and often do not provide satisfactory material conditions, particularly when the housing is provided at the expense of the employer. Moreover, such housing tends to segregate immigrants from the rest of the population, and may expose them to the risk of pressure from the employer during industrial disputes. In France the housing situation is so acute that large shanty-towns have developed. Despite the atrocious conditions prevailing, these form the only refuge for tens of thousands of immigrants. Here there is a clear tendency to ghetto-formation, but elsewhere as well immigrant enclaves are becoming established in the older slum areas of large cities, and in the cellars, attics, and shacks which form typical immigrant habitations.

Such housing conditions are reflected in serious health problems. Tuberculosis, rickets, and other diseases associated with poverty are much more prevalent among immigrants in all four countries than among the rest of the populations. Other difficulties encountered by immigrants, with regard to education, leisure activities, and family life, are also closely related to their economic and social conditions.

Low income, insecurity, bad housing, social problems; these characteristics of immigrants were also regarded as typical of the nineteenth century European proletariat. Does this justify classifying immigrant workers as a separate class, a new sub-proletariat or *lumpenproletariat?* The answer depends on the concept of class structure which is adopted. In the functionalist model, in which classes are replaced by a profusion of 'status groups', immigrant workers would form one such group. Because of their inferior occupational position, the low material standards which characterize their 'life-style', and their lack of prestige, they would be regarded as one of the lowest status groups. In terms of functionalist theory, the presence of an immigrant group occupying such a subordinate position could be regarded as a rational feature of society. Immigrants would fulfil a necessary societal function by providing essential labour for menial tasks. Their remaining in this position could thus be seen as a necessary and more or less permanent feature of social stratification, although upward social mobility might be possible for the most talented individuals.

A representative of the *embourgeoisement* theory might regard immigrant workers as a new proletariat. While the indigenous workers have achieved incomes comparable to those of the middle class, and have accordingly taken on middle-class consumer habits, values and aspirations, the immigrants have characteristics similar to those of the proletarians in the period immediately following industrialization. But for the *embourgeoisement* theory, the inferior position of immigrants is only an irregularity in the overall process of the workers' advancement and integration into the middle class.

Immigrants fill the gaps left by indigenous workers who have gained promotion out of low-paid and unpleasant jobs. Technological progress may be expected to eliminate such jobs, and the type of labour at present provided by immigrants will cease to be necessary. Large-scale immigration may then be expected to stop, and those immigrants already present who decide to stay will participate in the general upward mobility.

But according to the concept of class structure which we have argued to be the correct one, immigrant workers cannot be regarded as a distinct class. A group which makes up 10, 20, or even 30 per cent of the industrial labour force is neither marginal nor extraneous to society and certainly does not constitute a *lumpenproletariat*. Nor are immigrant workers a 'new proletariat' or a 'sub-proletariat'. The first term implies that the indigenous workers have ceased to be proletarians and have been replaced by the immigrants in this social position. The second postulates that immigrant workers have a different relationship to the means of production from that traditionally characteristic of the proletariat. All workers, whether immigrant or indigenous, manual or non-manual possess the basic characteristics of a proletariat: they do not own or control the means of production, they work under the directions of others and in the interests of others, and they have no control over the product of their work. The basic long-term interests of immigrant and indigenous workers are common ones: the collective improvement of the living and working conditions of all workers, and the abolition of a capitalist system which creates distinctions between different categories of workers which assists in maintaining its own domination.

Immigrant workers and indigenous workers together form the working class in contemporary Western Europe, but it is a divided class. The immigrants have become concentrated in the unskilled occupations and the indigenous workers have tended to leave such jobs. Immigrants have lower incomes and inferior housing and social conditions. The two groups are more or less isolated from each other, through differing positions and short-term interests. This objective split is reproduced in the subjective sphere: a large proportion of indigenous workers have prejudiced and hostile attitudes towards immigrants. They lack solidarity with their immigrant colleagues and favour discriminatory practices. Often immigrants find themselves isolated and unsupported when they take collective action to improve their conditions. We may therefore speak of two strata within the working class: the indigenous workers, with generally better conditions and the feeling of no longer being right at the bottom of society, form the higher stratum. The immigrants, who are the most underprivileged and exploited group of society, form the lower stratum.

It is not to be expected that immigrants will rapidly gain promotion to better occupations and thus cease to form the lowest stratum. The labour market developments of the last two decades show that modern industrial expansion creates demand for both skilled and unskilled workers. Many menial jobs cannot readily be eliminated by mechanization. Even where this possibility exists, it may be more profitable to continue labour-intensive forms of work-organization, particularly where immigration tends to keep down the wages for unskilled labour. In this situation, promotion is most likely to be offered to indigenous workers, partly because of their better education and greater industrial experience, partly because of discrimination. As we saw previously, discriminatory laws and practices are important in maintaining the inferior occupational position of immigrants in all four countries.

The key to promotion for immigrants is therefore twofold: firstly promotion requires the end of discrimination. Secondly, it presupposes the provision of adequate educational and vocational training facilities for immigrant workers and their children. But the educational opportunities offered to immigrants are extremely restricted. Immigrant workers rarely get any vocational training permitting promotion beyond the semi-skilled level. Immigrant children also face educational difficulties, and most of them are unlikely to reach the same educational standards as the majority of indigenous children. Most immigrant children thus become manual workers. Obviously, it is not in the interests of the ruling class to follow policies which would encourage the promotion of immigrant workers and their children, as this would remove the supply of cheap unskilled labour which is at present so profitable.

The restructuring of the working class into an indigenous stratum and an immigrant stratum is immigration's most important impact on society. It is through this restructuring that the principal societal effects of immigration are mediated. These effects may be divided into three categories.

Firstly, there are economic effects. The existence of an industrial reserve army in underdeveloped areas, which can be brought in to

307

take unskilled jobs in Western Europe, tends to hold back increases in the wages for unskilled work. This effect may be great enough to hold down the general wage rate for the whole economy. In this case, immigration brings considerable gains for capitalists; in a situation of expansion, stagnant wage rates are matched by growing profits. In the long run, however, it is possible that indigenous labour may also benefit from the dynamic expansion allowed by immigration.

Secondly, there are social effects. By coming in at the bottom of the labour market, the immigrants have allowed many indigenous workers to move out of unskilled jobs and to achieve real social promotion. The number of white-collar workers has grown, while the number of indigenous manual workers has shrunk. This promotion has had important effects on the consciousness of indigenous workers. Those who have obtained better jobs no longer feel that they belong to the lowest group of society and that improvements can only be achieved collectively. Their advancement is taken as a sign that individual merit can bring gains, while the real causes for the upward movement are not perceived. At the same time, such workers tend to distance themselves from the immigrants, who might in the long run threaten their newly-won privileges if allowed equal opportunities. Moreover, even those indigenous workers who have remained in unskilled occupations do not feel solidarity with immigrant workers. This group fears competition from immigrants and is afraid – not without justification – that they may be used by employers to put pressure on wages and conditions. At the same time the attempt to stigmatize immigrants as intrinsically inferior is an effort by such unskilled workers to maintain a higher social status for themselves, even though no objective basis for this exists. Analogies may be found in the well-known 'poor white' mentality in the Southern states of the USA, and in the attempts of low-level clerks to maintain their higher status position against blue-collar workers who often have higher earnings. The main roots of working-class prejudice towards immigrants are to be found in these relationships of competition. The result is that class consciousness is weakened, and tends to be replaced by a 'sectional consciousness', based on real and apparent conflicts of interest between the two strata within the working class.

Thirdly, immigration has political effects. The change in consciousness among indigenous workers lessens the political unity and strength of the working class. André Gorz has drawn attention to an additional factor:

> Recourse to foreign workers leads, in particular, to the exclusion of an important part of the proletariat from trade-union action; a considerable decrease in the political and electoral weight of the working class; a still more considerable weakening of its ideological force and cohesion. In a word, it achieves the 'denationalization' of decisive sectors of the working class, by replacing the indigenous proletariat with an imported proletariat, which leads a marginal and cultural existence deprived of political, trade union and civil rights.

Except in Britain, the overwhelming majority of immigrant workers are foreigners, who lack civil rights in the countries where they work. This means that a considerable proportion of the working class in contemporary Western Europe is disenfranchised. Not only do such immigrants lack the right to vote: their trade union rights are also restricted in some countries. Even where immigrant workers do in theory enjoy certain political rights, these can be eroded by repressive use of labour market legislation. If an immigrant only has a residence permit for a specific job – and this is usually the case – he is liable to deportation if dismissed by his employer. In Chapter IV we described how this special means of pressure is used by employers and authorities to discipline immigrant workers who take industrial or political action. Immigrants form a particularly vulnerable section of the working class, and their weak position may be used to undermine the strength of working-class organizations in struggles for better wages and conditions.

Even where immigrant workers are not deprived of civil rights, as in Britain,* their presence may cause serious problems for the labour movement. Differences in language, culture, and traditions make it difficult to bring immigrants into the unions, and the problem is worsened by the anti-immigrant feelings of many indigenous workers. The unions have not been altogether successful in overcoming these difficulties. There can be little doubt that they

*Under the new immigration legislation introduced by the Conservative Government in 1971 the situation of immigrants in Britain will become similar to that prevailing in the other countries. Recruited for specific jobs, immigrant workers may be subject to deportation if dismissed.

have been weakened by immigration, particularly in those branches where immigrant workers form a large proportion, or even the majority of the labour force.

The economic, social, and political effects of immigration which we have outlined are not separate phenomena but rather aspects of the general impact of immigration on society. To sum up this impact: immigration has brought about a split in the working class of Western Europe. This split weakens the working class and hence increases the power of the ruling class.

A division of the working class based on the granting of privileges to one part of it is nothing new. In *Imperialism, the Highest Stage of Capitalism*, Lenin described how a section of the British working class had 'become bourgeois' and was willing to 'be led by men bought by, or at least paid by, the bourgeoisie'. Britain's monopolistic position on the world market made possible the imperialist domination of underdeveloped regions and the exploitation of cheap labour in such areas through capital export. This allowed the creation of privileged sections among the British workers. The results of this situation were the growth of opportunism and the 'temporary decay of the working class movement'.

If today some of the workers of the underdeveloped countries are brought to Western Europe because it is more convenient for the capitalists to exploit them here than at home, this alters nothing in the basic situation: the ruling class gains both through the possibility of utilizing cheap labour, and through giving privileges to indigenous workers in order to encourage the development of false consciousness. The immigration of manual workers to Western Europe has been described as colonization in reverse. The immigrants are given the jobs which no one else will do. This encourages the indigenous population to take on a colonialist mentality, regarding it as the inevitable destiny of the newcomers to carry out all the menial tasks. Immigration helps to give large sections of the indigenous working class the consciousness of a 'labour aristocracy' which supports or acquiesces in the exploitation of another section of the working class. In this way immigration helps to stabilize the capitalist order, not only economically, but also politically.

The change in the class consciousness of indigenous workers has gone further than the changes in actual conditions would justify: it has affected the majority, while improvements in wages, conditions, and status have only been experienced by a section. Indeed, as we have seen, many workers have actually lost through immigration. But by bringing in workers from outside and compelling them to accept social and economic conditions inferior to those of other workers, it has become possible for the ruling class to promote the feeling of being in a privileged position among the majority of the working class. Workers who think that they have gained something and that they are no longer the lowest group in society are less likely to take militant actions which might endanger their privileges. The split in the working class allows one section to be played off against the other, weakening the whole.

Workers who regard immigrants as inferior to themselves and who tacitly support their exploitation are victims of a false consciousness. Their behaviour is seriously detrimental to their own interests because it weakens the labour movement and reduces the political strength of the working class. The fight to secure civil rights and equality in economic and social matters for immigrants is important for all workers. It is a struggle for their own future, because only a united working class will be able to achieve any basic changes in social conditions. But the false consciousness which gives rise to prejudice and discrimination will not be destroyed by humanitarian pleas. It can only disappear when it is supplanted not merely by a correct understanding of the position of immigrant workers, but by a class consciousness which reflects the true position of all workers in society.

Question

1. (a) According to Castles and Kosack, what are the effects of 'restructuring' the working class into 'an indigenous stratum and an immigrant stratum'?

(15 marks)

(b) Why is it that some workers 'tacitly support. . . .' exploitation of immigrants?

(10 marks)

40 Douglas G. Glasgow: The Black Underclass

The following extract gives full consideration to, and illustration of, the controversial concept of a black underclass introduced into Britain mainly by John Rex. Marxists, of course, reject the term: they see immigrants, including black immigrants, as belonging overwhelmingly to the working class – though some immigrant groups do contain a middle-class minority.

Here Douglas Glasgow attempts to explain the development of the underclass and to describe its characteristics. He is specifically concerned with America, but his analysis could also be applied to Britain. The major characteristic is lack of social mobility. In his view, this distinguishes it from the lower class generally (although it is worth noting that, in any case, only a small amount of social mobility, particularly long-range, takes place out of the lower class). Lack of social mobility accounts for the inter-generational nature of the underclass. Second is the lack of effective connections with a range of institutions, such as unions and educational establishments, which would improve access to the job-market. Third, the fact that industry is expanding much more slowly than in the recent past reduces opportunity for work. Even so, dead-end jobs, when they are available, do not in themselves secure exit from the underclass.

Glasgow minces no words in suggesting the main cause of the existence of the underclass: it is racism (although he does discuss alternative explanations). John Rex would broadly agree with this view.

Marxists tend to dislike the term underclass because it separates a group on racial grounds from the rest of the working class. However, Marx's term, lumpenproletariat, which describes the 'residue' beneath the working class, will not do, nor will the Marxist term surplus labour force or population, which is usually used with specific reference to groups that are employed in, or laid off from, ancilliary industries as the capitalist economy expands and contracts. Indeed, there is an argument for extending the use of the term underclass to include the growing numbers of unemployed, low-paid and otherwise disadvantaged groups in contemporary capitalist society. Or, if we retain the specifically racial connotation of the term underclass, what term can we then adopt to refer to these millions and their families? It needs to be a powerfully descriptive word because their situation demands it.

It might be a useful exercise to discuss the suitability of the concept of the underclass to the situation of the blacks in Britain.

Reading 40 From Douglas G. Glasgow, *The Black Underclass* (Vintage Books, 1981), pp. 3–11.

The young firebrands of Watts were (and nearly all still are) part of what has recently been dubbed the *underclass*, a group whose emergence as a permanent fixture of our nation's social structure represents one of the most significant class developments in the past two decades. The term *underclass* has slowly, almost imperceptibly eased its way into the nation's vocabulary, subtly conveying the message that another problematic group is emerging that needs society's help. While still somewhat unclearly defined, and even thought by some not to be deserving of serious attention, a permanently entrapped population of poor persons, unused and unwanted, accumulated in various parts of the country. Although Myrdal early cited the existence of an underclass, little serious attention had been given to the idea that such a group would become a fixed part of the American economy, since upward social mobility was alleged to be the norm for those who participate in a free enterprise economy. For this reason, even when in the sixties the plight of the nation's poor once again surfaced, it was viewed as involving some isolated 'pockets of poverty' whose populations required some programmatic interventions to move them from poverty to a stable income earning state. In fact, a war against poverty was launched with the view that in a few years the condition would be eradicated. However, as the sixties waned and the seventies developed, the war was assessed to be an abominable failure as social analysts, sociologists, and social workers pondered why had the poor not been eliminated, and why were there poor people in the seventies, and most disconcerting, why were there to be, and who were to be, the poor in the eighties?

As the seventies drew to a close, an examination of the populations that constitute the nation's poor discloses some important new relationships. Whereas the traditional groups that made up the poor were usually identified as the immigrant, or new migrant who moved from one area of the country to another seeking work, or as the aged, the disabled, and handicapped, currently the ranks of the poor are not being swelled by newcomers or the traditionally socially needy groups, but rather by the children of previously poor families. Therefore, poor families of the fifties and sixties were more likely to have offspring who were poor in the seventies. And Blacks, who have consistently represented a disproportionately high percentage of the nation's poor over the past three decades, not only continue to hold this unenviable distinction, but the children and offspring of their families constitute the poor in the seventies and are the projected poor of the eighties. Structural factors found in market dynamics and institutional practices, as well as the legacy of racism, produce and then reinforce the cycle of poverty and, in turn, work as a pressure exerting a downward pull toward underclass status. . . .

A real problem reflecting the economic crisis facing Blacks is found in the large numbers of long-term, persistently poor, and immobile Blacks that persist from one generation to the next. Although reports note a decrease in Black unemployment during the past decade (1959–1969), improving a condition where better than one out of every two Blacks (55 per cent in 1959) were poor, nevertheless, in 1969 one of every three Blacks still remained poor. Also, the proportion of Blacks remaining in poverty showed little or no change between 1969 and 1974. As indicated earlier, the ferocity of unemployment, joblessness, and abject poverty affects Black youth the greatest. For example, in the period 1967 through 1977, the Washington office of the Urban Coalition charted unemployment rates for Black youth between the ages of 16 and 19, showing an increase from 25.3 per cent to 35.2 per cent during this period. The National Urban League (NUL) has also pointed to the severe crisis among Black youth, noting 'the most serious problems confronting Black America are its intolerably high level of unemployment, especially among young Blacks' (Williams, 1979, p. 1). In 1978, employing the NUL Hidden Unemployment Index, their survey showed that 'business in general has not been responsive to the employment needs of minority youth, despite the grim statistics that show black youth unemployment at over 50 per cent in 1978' (Williams, 1979). Clearly, then, joblessness and unemployment have become for so many youthful Blacks a way of life, a daily condition rather than a temporary one. The lack of opportunity to work and to gain a regular and sound income in the primary labor market results in many young Blacks being locked permanently into the underclass.

Escaping underclass entrapment is not determined simply by having a job or income. The many Black working poor who remain in poverty exemplifies the contradiction where one fulfils the work ethic, holds a job, and yet remains immobile and poor. The type of job – whether it provides for continuous full-time employment, upgrading, seniority protections, or other provisions aiding mobility – and the amount of pay have much to do with the ability to withstand the structural, induced downward pull toward underclass status which surrounds the Black poor.

Further, the underclass entrapment of poor Blacks is furthered by their lack of connections with standardized institutions that act as feeder systems to the primary labour market. That is, the lack of ties to unions, private industry, civil service or social agencies (professional, civic, or quasi-socioeconomic), or sanctioning institutions (education, banking, and crediting) results in the Black poor having to negotiate the labour market as individuals, ones who at best receive only partial information about its operations and openings. This is why so many Blacks who made it into the mainstream in the 1940s and 1950s, when asked how they did so while other colleagues and classmates did not, explain the occurrence by citing 'chance'. 'I was lucky, just happened to be leaning on the door when it opened.' This does not mean that they did not prepare, or did not have some organisational affiliations (usually Black), were not trying, but rather the factor of chance, more than systemal connections, was at work. The problem of today's even poorer, inner-city youth is somewhat different, as they are even less connected to any institutional network to help them 'enter' the job market. They are, therefore, easily programmed 'out', particularly in a market where the demand for unskilled entry-level manpower has significantly diminished. Inner-city youth represent the weakest applicants in the job world, since the labour market as a system holds no obligation to them as individuals.

The underclass is distinguished from the lower class principally by its lack of mobility. According to classical definitions, the lower-class experience is a variation of middle-class adaptation and striving. The perennial expressions 'I did better than my father' (who in turn did better than his) and 'My sons and daughters will do even better than I' typify this experience. It is precisely the inapplicability of such statements to underclass people that sets them apart; for most are the sons and daughters of previous generations of the poor, and their children will predictably remain in the grip of poverty. Many members of this class, in fact, can be considered the failures or dropouts of the lower class, persons who because of disability, age, race, or ethnicity have been able to obtain only marginal or part-time work for many years or often no work at all.

315

They formed what were called in the early sixties 'pockets of poverty', which were not actually small isolated groups in a temporary condition of want, as the phrase suggests, but the permanent nucleus of a swiftly growing underclass. Harrington (1966) referred to them as the poverty culture population. Its members are not exclusively Blacks or other ethnic minorities, nor are they exclusively city dwellers: They can be found in the isolated mountain valleys of Appalachia and across the rural South. But a disproportionately large number are Black men ranging in age from fourteen through twenty-seven who inhabit the rotting cores of nearly every major city. And these are my subjects – the youngsters with no saleable skills and no attachment to any system that might help them advance; the young who at best have access only to low-status jobs and more often are unemployed with no legitimate sources of income. They are the ones often identified as the dropouts and social deviants.

The term *underclass* does not connote moral or ethical unworthiness, nor does it have any other pejorative meaning; it simply describes a relatively new population in industrial society. It is not necessarily culturally deprived, lacking in aspirations, or unmotivated to achieve. Many of the long-term poor, those who have been employed for most of their productive lives but who have never moved from the level of bare subsistence living, are essentially part of the underclass. They try to keep body and soul together and maintain a job, but they remain immobile, part of the static poor. Others who could make this adaptation fail to do so, often preferring to remain unemployed rather than accept a job that demands their involvement for the greater part of each day but provides only the barest minimum of financial reward. They seek other options for economic survival ranging from private entrepreneurial schemes to working the welfare system. Hustling, quasi-legitimate schemes, and outright deviant activity are also alternatives to work. And still there are those who do wish to work but cannot find any meaningful employment. They spend a large part of their time hunting for jobs. They try many different low-level jobs, some seasonal, others part-time, but always for a limited period. They may also seek alternatives for survival, sometimes unemployment insurance or welfare when they can meet the eligibility criteria.

The youth in my study had tried many of the above ways to adapt to underclass confinement but were nevertheless a unique section of the underclass. They were first and foremost young, strong, and physically healthy Black men, who despite their desire to achieve, to become something, and to find a job were at a very early age of fourteen, fifteen, or sixteen well on the way to permanent underclass status. As young inner-city men, and a part of the Black urban experience of the fifties, they responded to their rejection with explosiveness; they used fire to bring a nation to a standstill, forcing it to examine their condition.

How did they arrive in this condition? Are they immobile because they are genetically inferior, mentally impoverished, or lacking in motivation or aspirations as many have claimed? Is it that they are just plain lazy, have no desire to work or hold a job, and just prefer to receive handouts? Any such thesis is an oversimplification, if not a distortion, of the complex relationship between ghetto youth and the traditional institutions of society. Their entrapment into under-class status is clearly affected by many factors, primarily the lack of real opportunities to succeed and the limited alternatives provided by socialisation patterns of the inner city. Although the 'school of the streets' prepares them for specific and often highly functional roles in that social context, these attributes do not necessarily prepare them to achieve effective roles in mainstream life. And the price they pay for potential entrance into that life is quite extraordinary; for in addition to demanding attributes and capacities different from those acquired in the ghetto, society's institutions systematically block and restrict access by their processes, criteria, and demands.

So much of the ghetto youths' anger and despair arises from contact with mainstream institutions, which, almost imperceptibly and very impersonally, reject them. This rejection, especially by such agencies as the schools, often maims and breaks them; it denies their individuality and integrity. To circumvent these consequences, they seek alternatives; however, many of these devices result in even greater loss and failure. And they need not do so repeatedly in order to become downwardly mobile, since failing in only one institution, and sometimes mere contact with only one social agency, is enough to start the decline. In particular, if the failure-inducing institution is supposed to provide primary socialization, as the schools are, the young men's inability to successfully negotiate this system also impedes their access to the other opportunities and social institutions needed for achievement. For them, the survival behaviour that many

317

persons consider destructive is the one great protection they have against a system in which failure is almost assured.

Another major cause of their entrapment has been a gradual alteration in the nation's economic development. In contrast with the mid-forties and fifties, when much of the nation's lower class gained steady employment along with rising incomes and upward mobility, the current period offers lower-class and marginal-income groups a rather bleak future. Because of industry's limited expansion and increased use of technology, rather than people, to improve productivity, entry-level and blue-collar jobs – the traditional means of absorbing new and less experienced workers – have dwindled considerably. No substantial change in this trend appears imminent, since industry continues to seek profit through automation, computer technology, and the like. Thus as the need for the vast unskilled work force of earlier periods diminishes, those on the bottom of the ladder become unneeded labour and therefore permanent members of the underclass.

Racism is probably the most basic cause of the underclass condition. Racism in the sixties was different. The 'for coloured' and 'whites only' signs of the thirties and forties had been removed, but the institutions of the country were more completely saturated with covert expressions of racism than ever. The exclusion was carried out now by computers, which ostensibly rejected people on the basis not of 'race' but of 'social profile'.

Question
See end of next reading.

41 Ken Pryce: Hustlers and 'Slave' Labour

Ken Pryce's book *Endless Pressure* was published some months before the Bristol riots of April 1980. Anyone reading it before then, however, would have had a shrewd idea of what was coming. Not that Pryce deals in prophecy: he is too good a scholar for that. Rather, he describes in great detail the various frustrations and humiliations that characterise the lives of many blacks in Britain. The book is theoretically literate and shows an awareness of class as well as racial factors but it is essentially a description of the life-styles of members of Bristol's black community. He relates how they variously adjust to and survive difficult material and cultural conditions.

The following passage describes the experience of work of a number of black men and how that experience persuades some of them that the life-style of the hustler is a better alternative. Several factors help to explain their alienation: the sheer tedium of 'slave labour'; racism at work; the frustration of ambition; and the insistent desire to do something more interesting. If, in some cases, sociology seeks to 'tell it like it is', Pryce comes as close to doing so as any recent academic writer.

Reading 41 From Ken Pryce, *Endless Pressure*, (Penguin, 1979), pp. 55–62.

What are the factors responsible for the hustlers' estrangement from legal work? What are the strains that give rise to the demotivation process which, as we shall see, is a major determinant of attitudes in the expressive-disreputable orientation?

Many critics of the capitalist, industrial system have been concerned with the alienating effect menial work tasks have on the typical industrial worker, and with the universality of this experience. It has also been pointed out, as far as Britain is concerned, that because racism in British society restricts and narrows the scope in which he can rise and improve himself, the problem is much more acute for the black worker. The fact remains, though, that despite all this the majority of West Indians have devised ways of coping with the situation rather than opting out. It would seem, therefore, that to understand the attitude of rejection expressed in the hustler's response we have to take into account the specific hopes and aspirations that the hustlers, as individuals, first brought with them to the British work situation, and how the shattering of these hopes is related to the erosion of 'ambition' in the conventional and West Indian sense of this word. (It is also worth noting at this stage that though the hustlers' interest in work has shifted away from stable law-abiding employment within the structure of the dominant society, they have conspicuously not abandoned the traditional West Indian motivation to achieve some kind of success, nor their own desire to make 'bread'. Hustlers have retained a materialistic interest in all the things that money can buy.)

It is evident from much of what the men say about their reasons for becoming work-shy that they experience strains caused by cultural definitions that predominate in their West Indian background, and these they bring with them to the job situation in England. The definitions they are most sensitive to are the ones related to the West Indian male's conception of manhood and masculinity and those based on the West Indian's fear of the 'whip' and distaste of having a white man as 'bossman' over him. All these attitudes should be understandable in terms of what has been said in chapter 1 about the historical roots of slavery in the West Indies and about varied attempts on the part of individuals to overcome it. Further on, we shall see how, during the 1963 bus dispute in Bristol, it was openly acknowledged that no white person wants to work under a coloured man. There is a tendency either to ignore or disregard the *subjective* feelings of members of the West Indian minority. It would appear that we are convinced either that the West Indian will finally settle down to his ascribed status, however much he may appear displeased with his present situation, or that he really does not mind being the white man's subordinate. (Seen in the long term perspective, these are really very dangerous assumptions to make.) We never bother to discover just how the black man feels about his situation of subordination. We get a glimpse of his feelings and reactions in the hustler's orientation to legal work.

The hustler's response is one in which is expressed a dread of having to work as a menial; abhorrence of having to take orders from a 'cheeky white man' indifferent to him as an individual; and resentment because these experiences hurt his pride as 'a man'. The terms 'slave labour' and 'shit work' are used interchangeably here to mean monotonous work which the hustlers all say they can never put up with. The attitude they adopt is: 'Who wants to do de white man's work anyway? Let dem keep it! I will die before I stoop to any white man!' These attitudes are not unrelated to the image the Jamaican cultivates of himself as being tough and aggressive and capable of fighting back and standing up for his rights. Both dispositions – the rejection of work associated with subordination to the white man and the readiness to fight for one's rights – are highly exaggerated in the overall response of the hustler (and other West Indians in the expressive-disreputable orientation).

Once again let's get back to the men themselves and hear how they explain their own predicament. Let us retrace our steps a bit and go back to Percy's autobiographical account of how he became a hustler. In the process of drift and alienation that finally made him into a hustler, he reminded us that 'the white man play a few parts in it as well'. At one place where he worked his boss and his workmates were 'more or less bugging' him: he always tried to dress as smartly as possible and they didn't like it, and 'they tried to show me who is the boss and that's the reason why I stopped working'. In one job, he was such a good worker that the foreman asked him to stay on; in his last job he got 'fed up' and decided to leave because the boss's son had been unnecessarily rude in telling him off for arriving late one day. Percy also explains that:

> I don't want to go to the whiteman's place, because I have a dedication to choose my work. I might have to go and take certain work, which I myself don't want to do – because I don't want to play on my friends' pockets, [but having to accept work he doesn't like doing] is not a thing I want to do every day. But I'd rather go around stealing if I can and saving up some money to do a business.

(Note that Percy wants to get a 'start' through hustling to do his own business.)

I asked Percy if there were any alternatives between working as a labourer in a factory and being a hustler. He replied that:

> I could get things and sell it. I am not confined to stealing. I like electrical work and I could go and toil, like take a job as a labourer in a factory. And I could even just put up with the whiteman if I have to work with him because I like working. I like working really. But 'is jus' the conditions of work. But I don't find it easy to get on with the whiteman, O.K.? – and I haven't got the money to set myself up, you understand. The only way out is to ask my people [relatives] and I don't want to ask them . . .

Harry Saunders was sent to prison for his attempt at trying to pull off what is considered in Shanty Town the greatest hustle. One day he and I were engaged in a long conversation in which he spoke of his 'great awakening' in prison. He is a deeply religious man and the awakening he described was a religious experience. I was interested to know how, with all this spiritual rebirth, he still wasn't able to hold down a job for very long. At the time of the conversation, Saunders had just lost his last job as an unskilled worker in a factory. The story as to why he was given the sack was by then common knowledge in in-betweener circles. In the conversation we had I referred to this story and the rumour that he had knocked down the foreman.

Well [he replied], this is showing how a man's soul is in conflict with the coarser elements of life: because here is a whiteman pushing me about in a way – and this is the thing I hate most, I don't like weaklings for a start and I don't like to be pushed by people who feel . . . because consciously I say to myself: 'Well I'm not a weakling and if I let myself be pushed then I am behaving like a weakling' – but here was a whiteman who is saying to me, who brings back to my mind . . . because I'm one of dem Negroes who is always conscious of the whip, you see, that sort of thing, perhaps it comes from reading too much history of slavery – I mean I know I can drive a lorry, I drive lorries for a living and I was pushing a little trolley [at the time of the flare-up between him and the foreman] and I decided: 'Right, I won't pull the thing, I'll push it so I can see where I'm going,' and this man [the foreman] came behind me and say: 'E . . . e . . . em, em, you ought to pull it, don't push it,' and I turn round and says: 'Well, it more convenient for me pushing it . . .'

. . . this man turned round and said to me: 'Well, I'm the foreman and I'm telling you to pull it . . .' So this man now is a slave-master to me! So I turn round and I say: 'Well, am I doing the work or am I not doing the work?' He says: 'You do the work how I ask you to do the work.' I says: 'Look, I don't mind if you give me the whole factory to move, but leave me alone, because I enjoy working, but I don't enjoy working under your terms like this.' He says if I don't like it I know what I can do.

Now that brings back many things to mind, don't it? [he asked me pejoratively, using the patois expression 'don't it', rather than 'doesn't it']. I say: 'What can I do?' He said: 'You can go and get your card.'

At the same time, I know this woman has this little baby coming [his common-law wife was pregnant by him] . . . now because of these things I will kill! . . . I don't like to be worried . . . perhaps if I didn't have problems I wouldn't hit the man, I'd probably just go and get my card and walk out. But what's facing me now?!! – I have this woman who's bringing this baby at the time, and rent to pay, and all this sort of thing and this man is saying to me: 'If I don't like it, you know what you can do, you can get your card!' I said: 'Is that all I can do?!' [demonstrating how he was poised to knock the man down]. He said: 'You can go and get it.' 'Well,' I said, 'Well, you go and fucking get it!' [shouting in front of me to demonstrate the rage he was in]. And when I hit him, I see blood and I said right and I decided to go the whole hog.

In the case of Joe, the problem is more complex: he brings with him a variety of attitudes to work. He speaks about them in what follows. It is around 2 a.m. in the Sea-Island Café. He is speaking to me and two others from the clique of 'conscious' people (another name for some in-betweeners).

Man, you got to know how to take care of yourself. It's just like sometimes when you were just a little boy growing up, there are some people who try to bully you and make you look on dem as above you. Like the other day I was working at this place and I went in late and this guy tried to bully me. You see, I don't believe in going in dead on time. I don't believe in it and I don't encourage anybody to do it. If I am to go in at 8.30 from the very first day I try to go in five or ten minutes late – I must always have a few minutes to play with. For if you always go in dead on time, when you are just one minute over the time, they will want to know why you are late. So I always go in a few minutes late. Anyhow, this morning I went in late and this foreman guy come and ask me why I am late. So I don't answer him. So the next day I say 'Good morning' and him don't answer. So I just say to myself: 'Fuck off, rarse-clawt, if you don't want to answer, fuck off. Keep you' work to yourself, I must survive.'

You see, I don't care . . . I do as I like. I am free. Of course, when dem put on the pressure too much, I leave and go home [back to Jamaica]. Man, I don't even mingle with the authorities. Dem don't have any tabs on me. I *don't* go to the Labour Exchange. Dem send me papers every day in the post and I don't even open it! I *don't* even use dem hospital! In fact sometimes I believe dem don't even know I am in dis country!

[Laughter from everybody.] When I ketch a 'dose', I don't even go to the hospital – what you call the place – the clinic. I just open the telephone directory and ring up a private doctor, because as soon as you get involved with dem people, dem can trace you – and you don't want that . . .

Some of the men in Shanty Town believe that because it is so hopelessly difficult either to derive intrinsic satisfaction from work or reap high remunerative rewards, there is no purpose in conforming to the model worker ideal of getting up early, clocking in on time every morning, doing overtime and remaining loyal to one's employers. Once this decision is taken, legal work then comes to be seen as a kind of ordeal, a kind of unprofitable restraint that restricts the full enjoyment of life. One Shanty Town denizen, who was not himself a hustler, expressed this attitude well when he said: 'I must enjoy life now and not when I am too old either. I believe in the other life, but I want to spend my money in this one.' He believed, he said, that the best solution to work was to have a woman on the street hustling for you. But he had to admit he was his own hustler. When he said this to me he had just quit his job as a factory labourer and was just feeling his way, trying to run a little garage of his own in Shanty Town. He described to me how he was a factory worker, but explained that he did not like the idea of having to do everything by the clock. He explained also how he used to do piece-work and how sometimes he could take home a possible £30-odd per week. However, he could only achieve this by working 'very, very hard'. Moreover, at the factory, 'everything is done by the clock'. He found this a strain, he said: You had to 'talk by the clock and even piss by the clock'. One day he went to work and his foreman wanted him to go out in the rain and do a piece of work that entailed digging up the ground with a drill. Ordinarily he wouldn't have minded, but it was raining that day and he thought it was unfair of the foreman to expect him to work outside, even when the rain was still pouring down. So he said to the foreman, 'Is dis what you want me to do?' The foreman replied: 'Yes.' After insisting to the man that he wouldn't do it, he got up and walked off the job. He got the idea straight away that he could set up his own garage business. He had the experience for this, since he had worked for a long time as a mechanic before he took the job as a labourer in the factory. The beauty of having one's own business, he said, is that 'you haven't got to clock in.'

Questions
1. *Explain, with examples, why 'hustlers' often do not like working for white men.*

(15 marks)

2. *Is there a black underclass in Britain? If so, what are its characteristics?*

(25 marks)

(See also Readings 39 and 40 for Question 2).

42 Simon Field: Trends in Housing and Employment among Afro-Caribbeans and Asians

Simon Field's text and accompanying diagrams are a model of clear presentation and organisation. He gives data on housing, unemployment and employment trends and, in a final section, offers explanations for them.

Housing trends in the reduction of overcrowding and of the numbers in shared dwellings show notable improvement. To an extent the problems associated with 'being new to the country' have been overcome in this area. Nevertheless, 'real inequalities . . . remain' between blacks and whites at the top, as well as the bottom, of the housing market. A point not noted by Field is the reported difficulties of many council house tenants in getting repairs done. Further, the selling off of generally better council houses and lack of funds for repair has reduced the quality of council housing stock. However, these comments apply equally to whites and blacks.

Unemployment among black ethnic minority members of both sexes is high compared to whites. In the inner cities, these figures are often much higher, sometimes in excess of 50 per cent among Afro-Caribbean youth. Lord Scarman linked high levels of unemployment and associated social deprivation with the urban disorders of the nineteen eighties. Certainly, these disorders coincided with a steep rise in unemployment. In contrast to the unemployment situation, the percentage of blacks in high status jobs has tended to increase and the percentage in low status jobs marginally to decrease. Within these trends, the situation of Afro-Caribbean females gives least cause for optimism. Overall, the trends in employment and unemployment are mixed. Field comments that recent research shows that racial discrimination still disadvantages blacks in the job market. The recession of the eighties has exacerbated the situation by putting proportionately more blacks than whites out of work and by reducing opportunities. This might well seem a recipe for the development of a black underclass, though Field does not use the term.

Reading 42 From Simon Field, 'Trends in Racial Inequality' in *Social Studies Review*, Vol. 1, No. 4, March 1986, pp. 29–34.

The relative deprivation of ethnic minorities living in Britain – their worse jobs, higher rates of unemployment and poorer housing – has been widely documented, most recently in the 1982 survey of racial minorities by the Policy Studies Institute (Brown 1984). A topic which is discussed less frequently is that of whether this inequality between whites and ethnic minorities is diminishing. The present article looks at this issue.

Changes in the position of a whole social group (like ethnic minorities) are usually examined by comparing data from two points in time – like the 1971 and 1981 censuses. It is important to recognise that people may join or leave the group in question during the period under review, and this will affect the results as much as will changes in the position of individual members of the group. This is a particularly important consideration when looking at trends in the position of ethnic minority groups over the last few decades, because the composition and size of this population has changed significantly. Two factors are particularly important. First, the second generation of immigrants from the New Commonwealth is now coming of age, entering the labour and housing markets, and therefore making their presence felt in statistics covering the ethnic minority population. Second, new immigration has added sufficiently to the ethnic minority population to affect the data.

Housing

In the early years of New Commonwealth immigration, the housing conditions of these immigrants were very poor. In 1961, half of these immigrant households were in shared dwellings, and two-fifths of the Afro-Caribbeans and just over 10% of the Asians were 'over-crowded' according to the official census measure of more than 1.5 persons per room. The new immigrants were unable to obtain council housing, often because of discrimination, and were forced into poor quality and often expensive private rented housing, or equally poor quality owner-occupation.

There is little doubt that the housing conditions of ethnic minorities have improved dramatically since that time, both absolutely and relative to that of whites, as illustrated in Figures 1 and 2.

To a great extent, the improvement in housing standards has resulted from dramatic changes in tenure patterns. In the last twenty years the private rented sector of the British property market has declined gradually from about one-third of all households in 1961 to slightly less than 10%. The proportion of households in owner-occupied and council-rented accommodation has increased gradually during the same period, although the proportion of households in

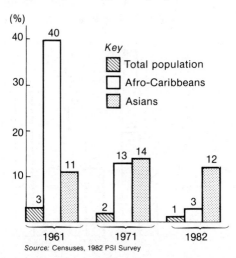

Figure 1 Overcrowding: Percentage of households living at more than 1.5 persons per room

327

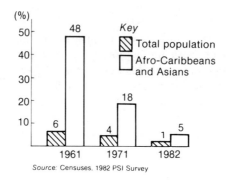

Source: Censuses. 1982 PSI Survey

Figure 2   Percentage of households in shared dwellings

council accommodation is now no longer increasing. Changes in the tenure pattern of ethnic minority households have mirrored these changes, but in an exaggerated fashion. Among Asians, the fall in the proportion in private rented accommodation has led to a rise in owner-occupation, while among Afro-Caribbeans it has led to a rapid increase in the proportion of households renting from the council. These changes are illustrated in Figures 3 and 4.

Asians and Afro-Caribbeans have therefore tackled their housing problems in different ways, and among both groups there has been a reduction in overcrowding and an improvement in facilities.

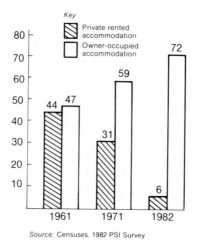

Source: Censuses. 1982 PSI Survey

Figure 3   Changes in the tenure pattern of Asian households (%)

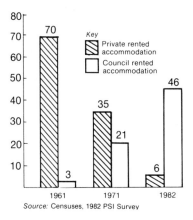

Figure 4 Changes in the tenure pattern of Afro-Caribbean households (%)

Between 1974 and 1982 the proportion of ethnic minority households lacking exclusive use of bath, hot water or inside WC shrank dramatically from nearly two-fifths to just 7%, a figure only marginally in excess of the white figure of 5%. Almost certainly this is a direct result of the move away from private rented accommodation, where about a third of households have to share such facilities. Moreover, it is almost certainly financially advantageous to leave the private rented sector, given that in the British housing market both council accommodation and the owner-occupied sector are in different ways (and to different extents at different times) subsidised by central and local government.

Real inequalities do, however, remain in housing conditions, many of them, no doubt, in turn related to the economic situation of ethnic minorities. Nearly 20% of white households live in detached houses or bungalows, compared with 5% of ethnic minority households. Five times as many Afro-Caribbeans and Bangladeshis (who are also well-represented in the council sector) live in high-rise flats in comparison with whites. One-third of all Bangladeshi households are overcrowded according to the measure of 1.5 persons per room. More than one-third of Asian households, and one-sixth of Afro-Caribbeans, have more than one person per room, compared with a miniscule 3% of white households. The real progress which has been made in housing conditions should not disguise the extent of inequality which remains.

Unemployment

The rising unemployment of the last decade has had a severe impact on blacks and Asians, worsening their position both absolutely and relatively. In 1974 (a time of relatively full employment) unemployment rates among ethnic minorities were about the same as among whites. However, by 1982 unemployment was higher among all ethnic minority groups than among whites. The decline in the textiles industry has had a severe effect on Pakistanis and Bangladeshis, and on other Asian women, as Figure 5 records.

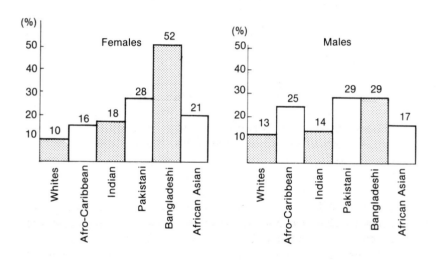

Figure 5 Percentage unemployment by ethnic group

The main reason why rising unemployment bears especially heavily on ethnic minority workers is that redundancies are most frequent in the low status jobs in which Afro-Caribbeans and Asians are concentrated. During better times employment in these types of job also expands more rapidly, and so ethnic minority workers would also benefit disproportionately from any fall in the overall level of unemployment. Youth unemployment is high at present, and therefore especially high among young blacks and Asians – nearly half of the blacks and Asians aged between 16 and 20 were unemployed in 1982, compared with about one-quarter of their white counterparts. Moreover, a larger proportion of blacks and Asians are in these vulnerable age groups than in the white population. For school leavers, direct discrimination is likely to be a more important factor than redundancies in creating unemployment. When vacancies outnumber job-seekers, the fact that *some* employers discriminate will not stop a determined ethnic minority school leaver from obtaining a job. When vacancies are few, racial discrimination by employers will express itself more directly in the unemployment of blacks and Asians, especially the young job-seekers.

Employment

How have the ethnic minorities *with* jobs fared over the last decade? One way of looking at this trend is to compare the distributions of workers in the standard socio-economic groups. A problem with this approach is that it is difficult to say whether the better manual jobs (which can be well paid) are more or less desirable than junior white collar jobs. The problem is perhaps best avoided by looking only at the top and bottom parts of the socio-economic spectrum, avoiding this confusing 'middle' part. Figure 6 shows the changing proportions of workers in the highest status jobs.

Black and Asian men, and Asian women, appear to be gaining entry into professional and managerial jobs, and in the case of men, seem to have significantly 'narrowed' the gap between their own position and that of whites. Afro-Caribbean women have achieved much less. Part of the reason is the relative success of those ethnic minority school leavers – particularly Asians – who *have* obtained jobs. Among male workers under 25, more than twice as many Asians as whites are in professional and managerial jobs.

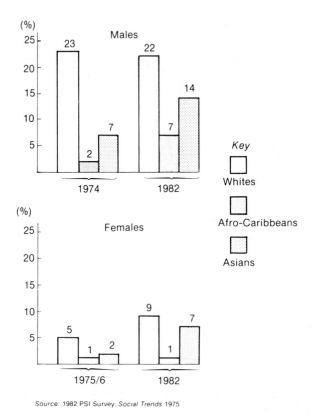

Figure 6 High status jobs: percentage of workers in professional and managerial work

A somewhat different picture emerges when the lowest status jobs are considered (see Figure 7). With the exception of Afro-Caribbean men, the proportion of all ethnic groups in these low status jobs fell during the period under review. However, there is little indication that the 'gap' between whites and ethnic minorities in respect of these jobs has narrowed. Moreover, these figures may be deceptively rosy, for the burden of rising unemployment has fallen heavily on those in low status jobs. This means that some ethnic minority workers who were in these kinds of work until recently have 'disappeared' from the 1982 figures because they have become unemployed. If unemployed workers are included in the data on the basis

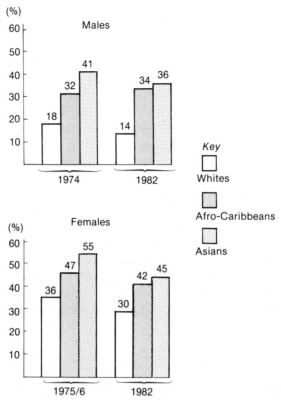

Figure 7 Low status jobs: percentage of workers in semi- and unskilled work

of their last job, the proportion of both Asian and Afro-Caribbean men in these less skilled manual jobs has actually increased.

In these summary statistics, the different Asian ethnic groups have been aggregated together for ease of presentation. This procedure needs to be qualified by a recognition of the wide variations in the occupational status of the different Asian ethnic groups. Bangladeshis are the most disadvantaged group in the labour market, and over two-thirds of Bangladeshi men are employed in semi- and unskilled manual work, a figure far in excess of any other ethnic group and one which partly explains the very high rates of unemployment suffered by this group. At the other extreme, African Asians of both sexes are distributed between socio-economic categories in a manner only slightly different from white workers.

Earnings are a rather different indicator of occupational status. High earnings do not necessarily reflect desirable work. There are many jobs where physical unpleasantness, unsocial hours or shift-work are partly compensated by higher pay, and ethnic minority workers have often been employed in such work. Bearing this in mind, full-time ethnic minority male workers in Britain earned about 10 or 15% less than whites in 1982, and there is no sign that the difference in earnings between whites and ethnic minorities has diminished since 1974. However, it is worth contrasting the position with that which obtains in the United States, where black workers earn about one-third less than whites.

Part of the reason why the earnings of ethnic minority workers are lower than those of whites is that they are more likely to be in the lower socio-economic categories. For women, socio-economic distribution, combined with the relative youth of the Afro-Caribbean and Asian working populations, appear to provide a full explanation of earnings differences. This is not true of men, where there are substantial earnings differences between white and ethnic minority workers within each socio-economic category – suggesting equivalent differences in occupational status. In 1974, only one-third of the gap in earnings between white and ethnic minority men could be explained through the differences in their socio-economic distributions.

Changes in the earnings of men in different socio-economic categories are very revealing. In 1974 the variation in earnings among Asian and Afro-Caribbean men was quite small, so that those in professional and managerial jobs did not earn a lot more than those in manual work. By 1982 the spread of earnings among ethnic minorities was much wider. In 1974 the median earnings of those in the highest socio-economic group were just over one-third more than those in the lowest, but by 1982 they were more than half as much again. The spread of earnings is becoming much more like that of whites, among whom in 1982 median earnings in the highest socio-economic group were 85% more than in the lowest. At the top end of the job spectrum there now appears less difference in earnings between whites and ethnic minorities. This suggests that Afro-Caribbean and Asian men are obtaining better types of non-manual work. At the lower end of the spectrum, the difference has increased, suggesting that ethnic minority men are less able than before to compensate for the poorer manual jobs they perform by working long hours or shifts.

This trend of an increasing spread of earnings within the male ethnic minority working population is reinforced by the process described previously – the penetration of the best professional and managerial jobs by Asian and Afro-Caribbean workers. However, this is proceeding without much sign of movement out of the lowest status manual jobs. In fact both trends probably reflect the same underlying process – a movement towards employment in a wider range of jobs, in other words a gradual integration into the economy of workers who were previously far more homogeneous in their pattern of employment.

This whole process would be much more encouraging if, overall, there were clearer indications of a narrowing gap in occupational status between white and ethnic minority workers. However, the picture is very patchy. If attention is confined to the top end of the job spectrum – say one-third of men with jobs – racial inequality appears to have diminished markedly. Within this top third, the socio-economic profile of Afro-Caribbean and Asian men improved and became more similar to whites between 1974 and 1982, and within each category of job, the earnings gap narrowed. Looking at the bottom third, the opposite result emerges. The socio-economic profiles remain distinct, and an earnings gap has opened up in manual work. Moreover, ethnic minority workers in these lower status jobs have borne the brunt of the rise in unemployment. Racial inequality in the labour market has become an increasingly working-class phenomenon.

Explanations: newness, discrimination and social mobility

All newly arrived immigrants are at some disadvantage relative to the indigenous population, particularly if their language and previous experience differ markedly from that indigenous population. Their unfamiliarity with the receiving country will make it difficult to recognise and make use of all the opportunities which might be available, and they may lack the right kind of experience, qualifications and linguistic skills. Research has shown that many immigrant groups, after initially being placed in a poor economic position, gradually approach the position of indigenous groups over a period of years. In the 1950s and 1960s it was widely assumed in academic and government circles that most racial inequality was attributable to the recent arrival of New Commonwealth immigrants in Britain. Although measures might be required during the transitional phase, it was felt that time alone would resolve many difficulties and that the second generation would be in a strong position.

In the field of housing, 'newness' has clearly been a major cause of inequality. Newly arrived immigrants with small financial resources had few options apart from private rented accommodation, with its attendant disadvantages. For this reason, the housing circumstances of ethnic minorities have shown considerable improvements with time. In employment the position is rather different, for, as we have seen, inequality in occupational status remains significant. Poor English is certainly related to low occupational status, but the research which has been carried out has tended to show that the earnings and socio-economic status of immigrants from the New Commonwealth are not related to the length of time immigrants have lived in Britain (Smith 1976; Chiswick 1980).

What can explain the relative presence of racial inequality in employment? A major factor must be racial discrimination. Such discrimination has been rendered unlawful in most areas by progressively more extensive legislation, and the 1976 Race Relations Act also made *indirect* discrimination unlawful. Direct discrimination occurs when, say, a job applicant is not recruited simply because he is black. Indirect discrimination occurs when a condition is applied which is unfairly detrimental to any ethnic group. In the case of employment, for example, it would be unlawful for an employer to insist that all recruits are Christians, given that this would exclude most Asians, in a case where an employee's religion had nothing to do with the job.

Most research on discrimination has involved the use of tests where pairs of real or fictional black and white job applicants (or applicants for a service) are chosen so as to be similar in most respects apart from their ethnic origin. Both members of each pair then apply for the job, or try and obtain a service, and the responses to the applications (which might invite a job applicant to interview) are compared. This is an elegant research design, but it imposes limits on the areas in which discrimination can be investigated. It cannot be used to investigate discrimination in promotion or dismissals, or indeed any case where the suspected discriminator would be already acquainted with the person against whom he or she discriminates.

Research on discrimination has been influential, most notably three studies carried out by Political and Economic Planning (now the Policy Studies Institute) in 1967, 1973/4 and in 1984/5. The first study showed that direct discrimination was widespread in many aspects of employment, housing and the provision of services. This research was one of the factors which led to a broadening of anti-discrimination legislation in the 1968 Race Relations Act. Together with later research, it was made clearly apparent that such discrimination is very largely based on skin colour, since white immigrants did not receive nearly such adverse treatment as did blacks and Asians. The second study, conducted around the end of 1973, found that discrimination against ethnic minorities seeking accommodation had decreased considerably since 1967, and probably also in the field of employment (although an exact comparison with the previous study was not possible in this field). However, discrimination remained substantial and was greatest in the treatment of applicants for unskilled jobs, where nearly half of all Asian and West Indian applicants faced discrimination. The most recent research, designed to replicate the 1973–74 study, was conducted in 1984 and 1985, and published very recently. It found that discrimination in recruitment has not diminished in the last decade.

In the absence of any decline in recruitment discrimination, the economic gap between ethnic minorities and whites may decline marginally as a result of diminishing problems of 'newness', but their position cannot be expected to converge with that of whites unless the level of discrimination falls.

It is important to recognise that racial inequality can be the result of a history of discrimination. For example, many black people are now unemployed because the jobs they previously held were insecure and vulnerable to economic recession. In turn, their concentration in these types of jobs is, at least in part, a result of discrimination experienced many years ago. By the same token, a reduction in discrimination will have a slow and incremental effect in reducing racial inequality. If the special barrier of discrimination were removed overnight, it would still take some time for ethnic minorities – like any group with a comparatively lowly social status – to gradually attain a spread of jobs distributed similarly to those of the population as a whole. The speed of this mixing-up process will depend on the amount of movement in society as a whole – social mobility.

Lieberson and Fuguitt (1967) carried out such a calculation in respect of American blacks. The index of occupational dissimilarity between blacks and whites in America was 40 in 1960. This means that 40% of one or other race would have to change occupational categories if the two races were to have identical occupational distributions. On the assumption that discrimination disappeared overnight (and some other idealising assumptions), the index of dissimilarity would, it was predicted, fall to 13 for the children of the 1960 workers when they were in employment. In other words, in the absence of discriminatory barriers racial inequality would fall to one-third of its previous level after one generation. The British situation is rather different, but it illustrates the kind of time scales which might be involved.

The essential point here is that changes in the economic position of ethnic minorities depend not only on the disadvantage of 'newness' and the effect of discrimination, but also on the opportunities available for economic advance – the extent and pattern of social mobility. The changing occupational distribution of ethnic minorities results from the interaction of all these factors together.

These considerations allow some tentative explanations of increasing inequality *within* the ethnic minority working population. At the lower end of the scale, the lack of job opportunities means that the Asians or Afro-Caribbeans may find it difficult to find an alternative employer when faced with one who discriminates. At the upper end, the excess of job-seekers over vacancies may be much less, and Asians may have found in self-employment and small business an opportunity for advance which is less subject to discrimination than employment.

Whatever the level of discrimination, the pace of economic growth is likely to affect the economic status of ethnic minority workers, both absolutely and relatively. In America the gap in income between blacks and whites has narrowed at a rate dependent in part on the pace of economic growth. During a period of declining discrimination, the mechanism for this process may well be the kind of 'forced' social mobility associated with economic growth. Such forced mobility occurs when, as in the postwar period, a large number of professional, technical and administrative jobs are created, and some at least of these posts must be filled by persons of humble origins. This forced mobility allows ethnic minorities to take advantage of any diminution in discrimination, but it is naturally vulnerable to changes in the economic climate.

Conclusion

Ethnic minorities in Britain have substantially improved their housing circumstances over the last twenty years, although real problems remain. In the field of employment, there are few signs overall of any substantial narrowing of the gap between their position and that of whites. The general rise in unemployment has opened up a new inequality between whites and ethnic minorities, discrimination has not declined, and working-class ethnic minority workers are, if anything, more disadvantaged in comparison with their white counterparts than previously. On the positive side, there are clear indications that Asians and Afro-Caribbeans are obtaining more of the better white-collar jobs and that the young who are in jobs have a socio-economic profile more similar to that of whites than their parents. The wide variation in fortunes of the different segments of the ethnic minority population, and in particular of the different social classes within that population, is a factor of increasing importance. Looking to the future, it is clear that the fortunes of ethnic minority workers will depend as much on the opportunities generally available for economic advance in British society as on the special barrier of discrimination.

References

Brown, C. (1984) *Black and White Britain: The Third PSI Survey*, Heinemann.

Chiswick, B. R. (1980) 'The earnings of white and coloured male immigrants in Britain', *Economica*, 47, pp. 81–7.

Lieberson, S. and Fuguitt, G. V. (1967) 'Negro-white occupational differences in the absence of discrimination', *American Journal of Sociology*, 73, pp. 188–200.

Smith, D. J. (1976) *The Facts of Racial Disadvantage*, PEP.

Question
1. (a) *Compare and explain the housing tenure patterns of Asians and Afro-Caribbeans.*

(10 marks)

(b) Present and explain employment and unemployment trends among Afro-Caribbean males and females.

(15 marks)

43 Ellis Cashmore: Why Birmingham's Blacks Rioted

Ever since the Brixton disorders of April 1981, there has been a widespread sense that 'it might happen again'. In 1985, it did, and on a wider scale. Major disorders occurred in Brixton, Tottenham, Toxteth and in Handsworth, Birmingham. Ellis Cashmore's article is about what happened in Handsworth. It is a response very close to the event but Cashmore has the long-term background of a researcher into race relations in the city.

He begins by quoting the bitter opinion of a black owner of a taxi-cab firm that 'the police wanted this'. Briefly, it seems as if Cashmore himself might be entertaining an anti-police bias but as the article develops he gives the issue of police relations with blacks a fair airing and goes on to consider other possible contributory factors to the disorders. These factors include rivalry between ethnic minorities; the inadequacies of government policies to deal with racism, unemployment and other inner city problems; and the hopelessness of many young people, especially blacks. Many black and white youth share conditions of disadvantage but the blacks have the added burden of racism. Racism and all the difficulties, demoralisation and conflict that flows from it is seen as the key issue.

Well before the 1985 disorders, Cashmore, like many others, had warned of the possibility of 'another Brixton' and urged the adoption of policies to combat racism and improve job opportunities. In a milder way, the report on the Brixton disorders of 1981 by Lord Scarman had said the same thing.

Reading 43 From E. Ellis Cashmore, 'What Lay Behind The Birmingham Riots' in *New Society*, 13 September 1985, pp. 374–6.

'The police *wanted* this,' claims the black owner of a taxi-cab firm situated next to the Villa Cross bingo hall in Birmingham. He points along Lozells Road, a stretch of smoking ruins, burnt-out cars and shattered glass. 'This is exactly what they wanted; the area's been so quiet lately that they haven't had any overtime pay. Now they can have as much as they like. As well as that, they can control us better. Nobody'll mind if they smash into our houses, lock us up or mash us. They'll say, "That's cool: we don't want another riot." '

It's a cynical explanation but, when conventional ones fail, you look to alternatives and, in the stupefied confusion that permeates Birmingham in the aftermath of Monday night's disturbances, the view seems as plausible as any of the others on offer. The blacks' latest allegations against the police may have a ritualistic ring to them. But there is some substance to the argument that matters have, as one black youth puts it, 'roughened up' over the last few months, with the arrival of the new Chief Constable of the West Midlands, Geoffrey Dear. He is said to favour a 'no nonsense' approach to cleaning up his patch, particularly with regard to drug trafficking (the Villa Cross pub was recently raided, as was a nearby cafe, with 27 arrests; two weeks ago £300,000 of heroin was seized in Handsworth). His apparent disregard for the softly-softly community policing developed over the past six or seven years – which he denies – has, in the words of a black resident of the Lozells area, 'upset the harmony.' Harmony doesn't strike this writer (a Handsworth resident) as an entirely appropriate term; still, it does indicate a sense of cohesion in the area.

Birmingham generally, and Handsworth in particular, have been held up as virtual models of community relations over the past five years. The concept of the 'bobby on the beat' was introduced at the behest of the previous Chief Constable, Sir Philip Knights, with acclaim from all sections of the community. The 1981 incidents were minor and containable compared with the events at Toxteth and Brixton. In their wake, a mood of revival swirled about the city.

The Handsworth Festival, originally an attempt to engage blacks and police in a joint activity, has become an annual fixture and this year's, held on 7–8 September, was regarded as the most successful to date. Yet, within 22 hours of the last steel band leaving the stage and the final float being parked, Lozells Road was ablaze. A 300-yard strip of shops, mostly Asian owned, was devastated and two people were killed there.

As in all disturbances of this kind, precipitating incidents are isolated. In this case, the black driver of a vehicle was apprehended after a routine fixed-penalty parking offence at the junction of Villa

Road and Lozells Road. An animated crowd assembled as the driver (reputed to be a 'madman' by locals) protested. After the arrival of police reinforcements, a struggle resulted in a black woman being knocked to the ground. Two arrests were made between 5 and 6pm on Monday.

The action seems to have subsided by the time of the next stage in the sequence. After almost two hours, black youths congregated at the site of the arrests and proceeded to petrol-bomb the disused Villa Cross bingo hall, which has stood since 1912 as one of the most impressive buildings in the area and which was shortly to be transformed into an amusement arcade. (It changed from a cinema to a bingo hall in 1970.) Up to 300 police managed to force the gathering crowd eastwards along Lozells Road, where the attacks then switched to garages and shops. The first visible evidence of the rage is a wrecked service station which stands opposite an advertising hoarding for *Rambo*, bearing the legend, 'No man, no law, no war can stop him,' and depicting Sylvester Stallone against a background of fire.

'They could have stopped it any time after it started here,' a Lozells Road resident told me. 'I was here at 8 o'clock, and I saw the police just watching as they smashed the places and looted the shops – grown men, black and white.' He won't go all the way with the cynical argument, but he ponders the possibility. 'You've got to wonder why they stood back and watched it.' He's not the only one to wonder. Criticisms about the police's failure to intervene at the earliest possible point have been raised, the riposte from Geoffrey Dear being that the police had difficulty in approaching the area because of the burning buildings and the barricades that were erected.

Whatever the police's reasons for not engaging their forces earlier, the result was the almost total destruction of the Lozells Road shopping area. The vast majority of shops along the street are owned by Asians. Food City is gutted, as are many Asian clothing stores, Islamic book stores and travel agents. Asian businessmen steer clear of attributing a strong motive to this. They prefer to emphasise the soundness of their relations with the local black community. There are other interpretations, of course, and the spectre of Watts in 1965 and Miami in 1980 emerge. Jewish-owned stores were early targets for rioting blacks in Los Angeles, and Miami blacks were known to be incensed by the preferential treatment they believed had been granted Hispanics in the city. Minority groups often measure their own success by that of other minority groups and inter-ethnic rivalries can often result.

Certainly, if the testimonies of local blacks are anything to go by, such rivalry was a contributory factor in the disturbance. 'You think blacks aren't ambitious, you think they haven't got brains?' asks a young black, currently on a Youth Training Scheme. 'The Asians around here started with the same as us: nothing. Look at them now. Why? Because they can get loans, grants and funds for business. If a black man goes in for a loan of some money to start himself up, they laugh at him . . . There's racism all right, but it's just against blacks.' In this perspective, Asians, instead of opposing the system, have burrowed their way inside the system – the one black youths call 'Babylon.' They may not have been accepted by whites, but they have at least established a presence. 'We're not even part of the system,' shouts one black youth over the rest of the arguing. 'We're being pushed out. Give us *something* to do: I don't even care if I can't get a job at the end of it. At least, it'll keep my head and hands working.'

The catalyst in this and, indeed, all the recent disturbances involving black youths in substantial numbers has been a police-related incident. But the blacks' aggression has not been directed at the police officers as much as the system they personify. In Birmingham, blacks have destroyed houses in which they live, shops on which they depend for provisions, environments in which they live. These don't seem politically intelligible targets, but the aggression is directed at symbols: institutions attacked are symbols of a system blacks see exploiting them. They've burned and looted the actual community they exist in, a community which stands as a testament to their impoverished lives. They haven't destroyed property and wrought havoc because they want a new colour TV, ghetto-blaster or video, but because they've lost faith in the capacity and will of establishment institutions to take into account their interests.

Drip-fed with pointless schemes

The government has, over the past six or seven years, been trying to rein back local authority spending. It has sidestepped some of the implications of Scarman's minimalist package. It has enacted racist legislation to restrict immigration further. It has drip-fed black youth with pointless YTS and analogous schemes. It has shown itself not only lacking in moral commitment, but totally out of touch with forces in modern society. It was not just Home Secretary Douglas Hurd's culpable ignorance of what is actually going on in the inner cities which took him into Birmingham and a hail of stones from affronted youths, but also his apparent insulation from the upsurge in feeling as a 'new' crisis looms; in fact, it is a continuation of an existing crisis.

Barry Troyna and I were roundly criticised for predicting more disturbances in our recent book, *Black Youth in Crisis*, and both of us reflect on certain inadequacies of our analysis. Yet, at least, we were sensitive to the scope and nature of the crisis. The Scarman report acknowledged that, in 1981, 'the common strands in many of the major disorders for which there is much evidence, are to be found in shared social conditions, in economic insecurity and perceived deprivation, in enforced idleness because of unemployment, and in the hostility of at least a section of young people to the police.' It was a rare insight in an otherwise insubstantial report. So why should anyone be surprised by the latest outbreak? Those 'shared conditions' are still there. As a black youth remarks, 'If anything it's worse than it was in '81. Now, nobody believes that the police are racialists.'

I was mindful of this when a BBC radio interviewer rang and asked me, 'Why has this happened?' 'Let's invert the question,' I replied. 'Why haven't we had *more* riots since 1981?' The basic social conditions are more or less the same and unemployment is worse (about 50 per cent amongst males in the Lozells area). 'But burning and looting is no answer,' I heard a reporter ask a black man in his thirties in Lozells. His retort, delivered with steely conviction, was a question, 'Oh really? And how did you arrive at that conclusion?' Troyna and I were making a similar point when we argued that the central question that should be asked of black youth is: 'What is the advantage of *not* rioting?' Such is the widespread loss of confidence in the future, that young blacks will take any option available to them.

In the eyes of many – including some Birmingham MPs and senior police officers – the Lozells rioters were 'criminals' bent on destruction. Blacks in the area take a different view, encapsulated by one youth's phrase, 'Something will happen now.' Well, it will certainly heighten the problem's visibility, and the arguments will be enlivened all over again. Once more, we will have the tedious denial of racism from the police force, and the usual attempts to depoliticise the affair by claiming that racism was not an issue. What has to be faced is this: racism is *the* issue. Blacks know it. Asians know it, although they don't advertise it so much. So why can't whites, especially power-holding whites? My present research (part of which concentrates on the Newtown area, which is adjacent to Lozells) strongly suggests that racism is rife amongst the working class whites. Yet it's over in west Birmingham, in places like Edgbaston or in Solihull, south of the city, where the racism of real consequence lies. In middle class areas such as these, decisions *aren't* made to recruit more blacks into industry or to implement procedures for boosting blacks' promotion chances or arranging changes in education to ensure a more satisfactory schooling for children of all colours and backgrounds. These non-decisions manifest themselves in the form of institutional racism.

Certainly many of the 'shared conditions' spoken of by Scarman are not exclusive to blacks. White working class youth also faces the prospect of 'no future'. There is a difference, however. Blacks have their problems compounded by racism. When they react as vigorously as they have done this week, they do so against a racism they feel is locked into the very institutions of this society. Rastas have been saying it for years. It's not so much whites who are evil and oppressive, but the system of which they're part. Rastas now speak to a general condition.

Monday night's Birmingham *Evening Mail* carried a story: 'A multi-million pound five-storey hotel may be built at Birmingham airport in advance of the 1992 Olympics.' Birmingham is proposing to host the games. The airport is in the south. Just a fraction of that money would help in the north of the city, where recent attempts to spruce up areas like Lozells, Newtown and Handsworth are seen by locals as the cosmetic devices they are. Their ambitions for the future might just as well depend on a sign posted outside the Ebenezer Bible Institute at a church facing the Villa Cross hall. It reads: HOPE FOR BETTER THINGS.

Question
1. *Critically discuss the causes of the 1985 inner urban disorders.*

(25 marks)

(You may want to draw on other readings in this section to answer this question.)

44 John Pilger: Victims of Racism

A colleague suggested that, as well as academic material on race, I include, in this edition, a personal experience of racism. This is it. Here journalist, John Pilger, records the prolonged racial torment of an Asian family in East London, through the testimony of a teenage girl. The story requires no comment from me.

There are particular reasons for including a personal piece on racism which are not specifically sociological. First, it gives an account of the horror and suffering of unprovoked racial abuse and attack. Second, it condemns such behaviour as shameful and disgusting. Third, it reminds us that racism is part of British culture and of what kind of society Britain would become if racism were to become more widespread and tolerated. These reasons are moral rather than sociological.

Clearly, this reading is a piece of journalism rather than sociology. But what is the difference? The main difference relates to the use of theory and methodology. Sociologists employ a variety of recognised, formal theories and methodologies which help them to understand data more 'objectively'. By contrast, a journalist confronts 'material' more directly and personally, unconstrained by the rules of an academic discipline. For this reason, journalists can be freer to write with greater passion and subjective conviction. Although, like journalism, interpretive sociology confronts the subject more directly, the researcher is still required to 'see' the subject through usually quite complex methodological apparatus. So, whilst sociologists are entitled to employ moral motives in choosing their subject of research and in commenting on their findings, it is not surprising that in looking for an anti-racist statement, I should have come up with a piece of journalism. Equally, journalism provides many examples of racism (see Reading 96,).

Reading 44 From John Pilger, 'Nasreen, voice of outrage from a house under seige' in *The Independent*, 2 February 1987, p. 17.

Last week, Nasreen phoned me to say: 'We have a new neighbour who is being nice to us. We are taking down the barricades and we are hoping for the best; but we are frightened.'

I have known Nasreen and her family for four years and this is the first good news. Almost every night since 25 January 1983 they have stayed together in their one large room, overlooking their street in the East End of London. They seldom go out after seven o'clock at night, neither do they go downstairs after dark.

Only their dog, a worrying beast called Soldier, is downstairs, in the front room that was to be the father's tailor's shop and which they barricaded four years ago on the urging of the police, who said, in effect, they could do nothing about the attacks.

When I was there the other night, Nasreen's mother was sitting beside the window as she has done for four years, rarely moving from this watching position. Her bed has been moved there, and when she talks her eyes remain fixed on the street below. Beside her is a plastic box filled with anti-depressants and sleeping talets and others for the relief of chronic asthma. As each siege has begun or appeared imminent, she has called out names that are familiar to all the family. They are the names of their tormentors.

'At first they'd go in circles,' said Nasreen, who is 19. 'They'd go round and round. Or maybe they'd just sit and do nothing at all. Or maybe they'd just smash the door and throw rocks. . . .'

'And shit,' said her father, trying to smile. 'And shit,' said Nasreen, '. . . through the letterbox, all over the hallway.'

Britain in the 1980s is a society in which large groups of citizens, and the fate allotted to them, are virtually invisible. That is to say, extraordinary and often terrible events can happen in people's lives and there is little or no news about them; and there is official indifference. Racist attacks on Asian people – relentless and unchecked – are part of this pattern of silence.

Of course there will be an occasional piece in the papers or on television; more likely it will be in the ethnic press. Most journalists live in places of suburban privacy, not in streets from which the Home Office six years ago drew its statistic that Asians were *50 times* more likely to be attacked than whites. That figure is thought to be much higher today. People seldom report racist attacks to the police because, according to one report by the London Race and Housing Forum, 'all too frequently' the attitude of the police is to blame and even threaten to prosecute the victim. Certainly, I know of few Asian families who will dare to call the police.

In spite of their public statements, the police are loathe to recognise racism as a motive for attack or harassment. They complain about the lack of 'hard evidence' and the difficulty of pinning charges on 'juveniles'. It is apparently so difficult that in the Borough of Newham, where Nasreen and her family live, the local monitoring project has recorded a prosecution rate of less than 5 per cent – in contrast with police statistics that tend to lump racial motives together with strictly criminal intent.

So widespread are racist attacks that on the Barking Road, a major artery of the capital, Asian shopkeepers are terrorised almost casually by those who appear to be members of the same gang. In his takeaway chicken shop, Ezaz Hayat keeps an axe handle on the counter. He has been fire-bombed and threatened, and he and those who work for him 'know the faces'. Three arrests have been made.

Police officers once kept a vigil at the shop, but most nights when Mr Hayat is under siege he has rung the police who, he says, have told him: 'We can't do anything now. You'll have to shut up shop.' At least two Asian restaurants and a shop within a mile have been terrorised. Last November, an Asian man and his son were subjected to an horrific attack in daylight in Barking Road.

The father was slashed in the face with a knife, his nose was broken and he has spinal injuries. The son suffered head injuries and a broken hand as he tried to protect his father. What was unusual about this was not the nature of the attack, but that the police arrested four of the gang, several of whom were found 'celebrating' in a nearby pub, with blood on their clothes.

Two weeks ago, not far away, a young black man, Trevor Ferguson, went to confront a gang of whites outside a house his friends were having a party. The gang was chanting: 'Kill the niggers!' and reportedly hurled teargas through the letterbox. Trevor was beaten so badly with bottles he was left with one eye hanging out and has now lost the eye. The police told the family they did not consider the attack racist. No one has been arrested.

It is hardly surprising that people have turned to groups such as Elwar (East London Workers Against Racism) for help and protection. Keith Thompson, of Elwar, says the pattern of attacks has changed from those inspired by organised fascist groups to marauding gangs and individuals. 'The assumption now,' he said, 'is that you can get away with it.'

Nasreen's family has known all kinds of attacks. The recent calm, and the interest of the police, are undoubtedly due to her efforts. For almost all her teenage years, she has been the protector and voice of her parents, who came here from Pakistan 22 years ago.

She phones me often, several times a week. In the beginning she would say, in her Cockney accent: 'They're at the door now. Hear 'em? I've called the police and we're waiting. That's all. Bye.'

She would phone back to say they were all right, or she might ask me to phone the police or the council, or she would ask nothing at all: she was merely making contact with the world outside her barricades. She reminded me of Anne Frank, the Jewish girl who hid from the Nazis in the attic of her Amsterdam home. She is Anne Frank with a telephone.

The diaries Nasreen has kept are surely material for future historians who wish to look beneath the surface of Britain in the 1980s. The first entry was during the week they moved into their house. A gang of 40 attacked on the 25 January 1983. The gang threw stones, smashing the shop windows and gave Nazi salutes. They shouted: 'Fucking Pakis out!' They were able to do this, undisturbed, for six straight hours. Nasreen wrote in her diary: 'When the trouble started we phone the police, but they never came. Then again we phone the police, but they never came. Then my father went to the police station to get the police . . . we had a witness. The police said they didn't need a witness.'

The entries in the diary for the weeks that followed, often written by candlelight in freezing darkness as the family huddled in an upstairs room, were repetitive and to the point: 'Trouble. Got no sleep. Had no telephone . . . three or four of them throw stones at our window.'

One night when she phoned me, Nasreen described her life as 'sort of like living under a table.'

At that time Newham police told me they had given the family 'special attention', but that it was impossible to mount a '24-hour guard'. They suggested the family move from the 'trap' of the cul-de-sac they live in. Two auctions have failed to sell the house. Alongside Nasreen's diary is a growing file of correspondence with the police, the Home Office, the local authority, local MPs and the

Prime Minister. Soon after the attacks began, the then MP for Newham North West, Arthur Lewis, asked the Prime Minister to do something about a family that were being 'smashed about by skinheads'.

Mrs Thatcher replied that the Home Secretary was 'taking up the matter'. The matter was never taken up. So Nasreen wrote to Mrs Thatcher this letter:

Dear Margaret Thatcher,

I am sorry to say you don't understand our matter . . . you don't care if we get beaten up, do you? My mother has asthma and she has to stay to 11am watching through the window because me and my brother and sister has to go to school. I can't stay home to look after my mother because I got exams to worry about. We have no money to repair our house since the kids in the street have damaged it. We are asking for your help, not your money, Mrs Thatcher.

Yours sincerely,

Nasreen

An extraordinary reply came, not from Mrs Thatcher but from a Mr C.D. Inge at the Home Office. Mr Inge urged the family to keep reporting every attack to the police 'even if the police are unable to take effective action'. He then apologised for not being 'able to give you a more helpful reply'.

Last year the Home Affairs Committee of the House of Commons published a report which was severely critical of police failure to prosecute in racist attacks. No doubt in response to this, the Metropolitan Police have set up a small Racial Incidents Squad and two weeks ago they issued a glossy brochure at a press conference, with the message that racist attacks were now being given the 'highest priority'.

The brochure advises potential victims to 'get plastic windows . . . take the washing off the line . . . buy a dog . . .'

Community workers who know the reality and scale of racist attacks have described the gap between the theories of senior officers, who have done the police media course, and 'local practice'. It is a gap frequently filled by the racism of police officers themselves. They also point out that if the 'highest priority' equalled half the determination shown by the police, and the Government, during the miners' strike and at Wapping, law and order might begin to return to streets few of us see.

Question
1. 'The diaries Nasreen has kept are surely material for future historians who wish to look beneath the surface of Britain in the 1980s.'
   (a) Explain and comment on this statement.
   (10 marks)
   (b) To what extent, if any, does sociology teach us to condemn racism?
   (15 marks)

SECTION 9

Age and Generation

Readings 45–49

The basic sociological perspective on age is that it is socially 'constructed'. This means that biological age is perceived and responded to differently in different cultures. The most obvious example of this is the general decline in status of the elderly from traditional to modern society. Changes in the cultural perception of an age group in turn reflect social, economic and technological factors.

The first reading, from Neil Postman's *The Disappearance of Childhood*, illustrates the above points. The invention of the printing press provided the technological means to increase book production. In turn, this stimulated the growth of schools which gradually led to the separating off of children into a social group which came to be perceived as having distinct characteristics. Although most of these characteristics were socially created they were often thought to be biological in nature. Postman goes on to argue that, just as printing caused childhood to appear, television is causing it to disappear.

S.N. Eisenstadt's analysis of youth also employs an historical and comparative perspective. He argues that in certain societies, including modern ones, it is functional for the young to be separated off as an age group. In modern societies this leads to youth operating as a stage of transition (a 'stage that in some cases can be extended well beyond biological youth'). John Clarke's piece on skinhead subculture injects a necessary element of class analysis into this section.

Bob Coles' review of contemporary trends in the analysis of youth shows the limits of subcultural analysis (of which Clarke's is an excellent example) but also suggests that in certain ways it can be built upon.

The reading on old age by Chris Phillipson combines Marxist class analysis with the social construction of age approach. He concludes by indicating how old age could be constructed differently and, in his view, better.

45 Neil Postman: The Rise and Fall(?) of Childhood

One of the rewards of compiling this collection of readings has been to come across Neil Postman's brilliant book, *The Disappearance of Childhood*. It is well worth persisting through the occasional complex section in this reading in order to get an overall appreciation of a highly creative piece of social analysis.

Postman's basic thesis is that a revolution in communications created modern childhood and that another communications revolution threatens to end it – if, indeed, it has not already done so. The first revolution was precipitated by the invention of the printing press and the spread of books. To gain access to the new world of print, children had to learn to read and write (though, at first, this was true mainly of upper and middle class children). In order to acquire these skills, children were *separated* off into schools. This separation was crucial in establishing children as what Postman calls a distinct class or, as I would prefer it, group. Once separate, a variety of characteristics were generated around childhood, as Postman describes.

In arguing that modern childhood is socially created, Postman is able to cite support from a range of authorities, not least Philippe Ariès from whose book, *Centuries of Childhood*, he borrows freely. The view that modern childhood is disappearing is, however, much more original and controversial. According to Postman, what is causing it to disappear is the effect of television in providing uncensored and unfiltered communication to children as well as adults. The 'messages' – news, views, sex, violence – do not differentiate among their audience but are equally available to all. In the frequent absence of adult guidance, or control, children are largely unprotected from the media. 'Adult' images implode into their consciousness and mould their behaviour: they become like adults although perhaps a little more confused. Postman interprets a variety of trends around this central perspective. Children are becoming more like adults in their criminality, their sexuality and their dress. What they see on television they imitate for themselves in 'real' life. A complementary trend is apparent among adults. They are closing the age gap between themselves and children by fudging adult responsibility and behaving like children them-

353

selves. A selfish pursuit of eternal youth leads to neglect of the old, abuse of the young and the cult of self.

Clearly, not everybody is going to agree with the above analysis. Those who regard much television watching as harmless 'escapism' are likely to regard Postman's view of its effects as exaggerated and even naive. They would want to consider other factors in explaining the undoubtedly disturbing trends he describes. Yet, his thesis on the disappearance of childhood provides a simple explanatory focus for a variety of data that previously lacked connection. His ideas merit further consideration and, where possible, testing.

Reading 45 From Neil Postman, *The Disappearance of Childhood: How TV is Changing Children's Lives* (W.H. Allen, 1985), pp. 37–8, 41–2.

1 Printing, schools and the development of childhood

The first fifty years of the printing press are called the *incunabula*, literally, the cradle period. By the time print moved out of the cradle, the idea of childhood had moved in, and its own incunabula lasted for some two hundred years. After the sixteenth and seventeenth centuries childhood was acknowledged to *exist*, to be a feature of the natural order of things. Writing of childhood's incunabula, J. H. Plumb notes that 'Increasingly, the child became an object of respect, a special creature with a different nature and different needs, which required separation and protection from the adult world.' Separation is, of course, the key word. In separating people from one another, we create *classes* of people, of which children are a historic and humane example. But Mr. Plumb has it backward. Children were not separated from the rest of the population because they were believed to have a 'different nature and different needs.' They were believed to have a different nature and needs because they had been separated from the rest of the population. And they were separated because it became essential in their culture that they learn how to read and write, and how to be the sort of people a print culture required . . .

What all of this led to was a remarkable change in the social status of the young. Because the school was designed for the preparation of a literate adult, the young came to be perceived not as miniature adults but as something quite different altogether – unformed adults. School learning became identified with the special nature of childhood. 'Age groups . . . are organised around institutions,' Ariès remarks, and just as in the nineteenth century, adolescence became defined by conscription, in the sixteenth and seventeenth centuries, childhood became defined by school attendance. The word *schoolboy* became synonymous with the word *child*. Ivy Pinchbeck and Margaret Hewitt express it this way:

> Whilst under the traditional system [of apprenticeship], 'childhood' effectively ended at the age of seven . . . the effect of organised formal education was to prolong the period during which children were withheld from the demands and responsibilities of the adult world. Childhood was, in fact, becoming far less a biological necessity of no more than fleeting importance; it was emerging for the first time as a formative period of increasing significance.

2 Television and the disappearance of childhood

One must *qualify* for the deeper mysteries of the printed page by submitting oneself to the rigors of a scholastic education. One must progress slowly, sequentially, even painfully, as the capacity for self-restraint and conceptual thinking is both enriched and expanded . . .

Television, by contrast, is an open-admission technology to which there are no physical, economic, cognitive, or imaginative restraints. The six-year-old and the sixty-year-old are equally qualified to experience what television has to offer. Television, in this sense, is the consummate egalitarian medium of communication, surpassing oral language itself. For in speaking, we may always whisper so that the children will not hear. Or we may use words they may not understand. But television cannot whisper, and its pictures are both concrete and self-explanatory. The children see everything it shows.

The most obvious and general effect of this situation is to eliminate the exclusivity of worldly knowledge and, therefore, to eliminate one of the principal differences between childhood and adulthood. This effect follows from a fundamental principle of social structure: A group is largely defined by the exclusivity of the information its members share. If everyone knew what lawyers know, there would be no lawyers. If students knew what their teachers know, there would be no need to differentiate between them. Indeed, if fifth graders knew what eighth graders know, there would

355

be no point to having grades at all. G.B. Shaw once remarked that all professions are conspiracies against the laity. We might broaden this idea to say that any group is a 'conspiracy' against those who are not in it by virtue of the fact that, for one reason or another, the 'outs' do not have access to the information possessed by the 'ins.'

Of course, not every instance of role differentiation or group identity rests on access to information. Biology, for example, will determine who will be a male and who a female. But in most instances social role is formed by the conditions of a particular information environment, and this is most certainly the case with the social category of childhood. Children are a group of people who do *not* know certain things that adults know. In the Middle Ages there were no children because there existed no means for adults to know exclusive information. In the Age of Gutenberg, such a means developed. In the Age of Television, it is dissolved . . .

In the face of all this, both the authority of adulthood and the curiosity of childhood lose ground. For like shame and manners they are rooted in the idea of secrets. Children are curious because they do not yet know what they suspect there is to know; adults have authority in great measure because they are the principal source of knowledge. The delicate balance between authority and curiosity is the subject of Margaret Mead's important book *Culture and Commitment: A Study of the Generation Gap.* In it she contends that we are moving into a world of new, rapidly changing, and freely accessible information in which adults can no longer serve as counselors and advisors to the young, leading to what she calls a crisis in faith. 'I believe this crisis in faith,' she writes, 'can be attributed . . . to the fact that there are now no elders who know more than the young themselves about what the young are experiencing.'

If Dr. Mead is right – if the elders can no longer be relied on as a source of knowledge for the young – then she has misnamed her book, and, indeed, missed her own point. She has not made a study of the generation gap but a study of the disappearance of the generation gap. For in a world where the elders have no more authority than the young, there is no authority; the gap is closed, and everyone is of the same generation.

3 Evidence for the disappearance of childhood

All of the foregoing observations and inferences are, I believe, indicators of both the decline of childhood and a corresponding diminution in the character of adulthood. But there is also available a set of hard facts pointing to the same conclusion. For example, in the year 1950, in all of America, only 170 persons under the age of fifteen were arrested for what the FBI calls serious crimes, i.e., murder, forcible rape, robbery, and aggravated assault. This number represented .0004 percent of the under-fifteen population of America. In that same year, 94,784 persons fifteen years and older were arrested for serious crimes, representing .0860 percent of the population fifteen years and older. This means that in 1950, adults (defined here as those over and including fifteen years of age) committed serious crimes at a rate 215 times that of the rate of child crime. By 1960, adults committed serious crimes at a rate 8 times that of child crime; by 1979, the rate was 5.5 times. Does this mean that adult crime is declining? Not quite. In fact, adult crime is increasing, so that in 1979 more than 400,000 adults were arrested for serious crimes, representing .2430 percent of the adult population. This means that between 1950 and 1979, the rate of adult crime increased threefold. The fast-closing difference between the rates of adult and child crime is almost wholly accounted for by a staggering rise in child crime. Between 1950 and 1979, the rate of serious crimes committed by children increased 11,000 percent! The rate of nonserious child crimes (i.e., burglary, larceny, and auto theft) increased 8,300 percent . . .

This unprecedented change in both the frequency and brutality of child crime, as well as the legislative response to it, is no doubt attributable to multiple causes but none more cogent, I think, than that our concept of childhood is rapidly slipping from our grasp. Our children live in a society whose psychological and social contexts do not stress the differences between adults and children. As the adult world opens itself in every conceivable way to children, they will inevitably emulate adult criminal activity.

They will also participate in such activity as victims. Paralleling the assault on social order *by* children is the assault by adults *on* children. According to the National Center on Child Abuse and Neglect, there were 711,142 reported cases of child abuse in 1979. Assuming that a fair amount of child battering goes unreported, we may guess that well over two million instances of child abuse occurred that year. What can this mean other than that the special status, image, and aura of the child has been drastically diminished? It is only half an explanation to say that children are beaten up because they are small. The other half is that they are beaten up because they are not perceived as children. To the extent that children are viewed as unrealised, vulnerable, not in possession of a full measure of intellectual and emotional control, normal adults do not beat them as a response to conflict. Unless we assume that in all cases the adult attackers are psychopaths, we may conclude that at least part of the answer here is that many adults now have a different conception of what sort of a person a child is, a conception not unlike that which prevailed in the fourteenth century: that they are miniature adults.

Question
1. (a) What caused childhood, as a social category, to develop?
(10 marks)
(b) Critically discuss Neil Postman's argument that childhood is 'disappearing'.
(15 marks)

46 S.N. Eisenstadt: Modern Youth as a 'Separate' Age-Grade or Class

Eisenstadt's book *From Generation to Generation* is a classic of Functionalist analysis. It is fascinating to see Parsons' social systems model unfolding in the context of generational analysis as the book progresses. The extracts selected do no more than give a flavour of Eisenstadt's approach, and it is necessary to say a little here about his theoretical framework.

The essence of Eisenstadt's 'hypothesis' is that the nature and demands of modern society have, to some extent, separated young people from their parents in a way that youth in primitive and traditional society was not separated. He suggests that in the latter types of societies the values of family and kin tended to be those of the immediate community, and that no formal education was needed to prepare young people for work. Indeed, the family itself often provided work for all or most of its members. In terms of Parsons' pattern variables, much used by Eisenstadt, the values of ascription (status given at birth), particularism (treating people on a personal rather than an objective or neutral basis), collective or community orientation, role diffuseness and affectivity pervade not only the family but traditional community as a whole. The family is therefore sufficient training ground for social life generally. Although age-grades exist in many traditional societies, they rarely tend to be a source of conflict. They have clearly allocated status, rights and duties, and succession to adulthood is invariably accompanied by certain rituals or rites of passage. Oversimplifying somewhat, age-grades tend to be manifestly functional, and seldom dysfunctional, in traditional societies.

In modern societies different values, reflecting the different needs of the social system, prevail. Important amongst these are achievement, universalism, role specificity, affective neutrality and self-orientation. Eisenstadt argues that these values, and the behaviour they indicate, are to a large extent learnt in schools. A process of secondary socialisation is necessary to prepare the young for the demands of a competitive, rationally-organised and occupationally-specialised society. The family is not competent to do this but, in the Functionalist model, it remains the major institution of personal expression and early socialisation. Eisenstadt considers that generally schools and institutions of higher and further education do successfully fulfil their functions. However, he also describes (in a section not included here) circumstances in which strain develops between the young and older generations. He refers to youth groups of this kind as 'deviant', and includes among them juvenile delinquent gangs and rebellious youth movements (often student based). He follows Merton broadly in analysing the former. The delinquents continue to share the materialistic goals of modern society, but because they are cut off from legitimate means of achieving them, adopt deviant ones. His comments on rebellious youth movements are relevant to the student movements of the 1960s to which similar analyses were applied. He considers that such movements tend to produce a romantic 'consciousness and ideology' which rejects the impersonal and bureaucratic nature of the modern world. He suggests that they are particularly likely to occur during times of rapid change when the young feel torn between traditional and modern values, although this explanation would not entirely explain the movements of the 1960s.

For a neo-functionalist account of delinquent youth gangs, see Albert Cohen (Reading 51).

Reading 46 From S. N. Eisenstadt, *From Generation to Generation: Age Groups and Social Structure* (Collier MacMillan, 1956), pp. 22–4, 30–4, 162–6.

An 'age grade' is usually defined in the broad terms of a general 'human type', and not of any specific, detailed trait or role. The vigorous young warriors of a primitive tribe, the 'wise old men', do not refer to any detailed, specific activities, but to a more general, diffuse pattern of behaviour that is proper to a man at a given stage of life. It is true, of course, that sometimes specific activities are thought to be characteristic of a given age, such as excelling in the warlike courage of the young, exhibiting physical prowess, etc. These activities, however, are not the only specific traits which by themselves define the 'nature' of a given age; they serve rather, as symbolic, sometimes even ritual, expressions of a more general pattern of behaviour. A cultural definition of an age grade or age span is always a broad definition of human potentialities and obligations at a given stage of life. It is not a prescription or expectation of a detailed role, but of general, basic role dispositions into which more specific roles may be built, and to which they may be ascribed. At the same time it is not merely a classificatory category as it is sometimes used in statistical censuses. However explicit its formulations, it always involves an evaluation of the meaning and importance of the given age for the individual and for society, thus giving it a fully ideological connotation. It contains certain definite expectations of future activities, and of relationships with other people at the same or at different stages of their life career. In terms of these definitions people map out, as it were, the broad contours of human life, of their fellow-men in various positions, ascribing to each a given place within these contours.

This brings us to the second basic characteristic of the role expectations of age grades, namely, that no such single expectation stands alone, but always constitutes part of a series. The characteristics of one age grade cannot be fully understood except in their relation to those of other ages. Whether seen as a gradually unfolding continuum or as a series of sharp contrasts and opposed characteristics, they are fully explained and understood only in terms of each other. The boy is seen to bear within himself the seeds of the adult man; or else he must, as an adult, acquire new patterns of behaviour sharply and intentionally opposed to those of his boyhood. The adult either develops naturally into an old man or decays into one. (But the one can be understood only in terms of its relation to the other.) Only when taken together do they constitute the entire map of human possibilities, of the potentials of human life; and as every individual usually has to pass through all of them, their complementariness and continuity (even if defined in discontinuous, contrasting terms) become obvious.

The same holds true – although perhaps with a somewhat different meaning – for the age definitions of the two sexes. Each age grade is differently defined for each sex, and these definitions are usually related and complementary, as the 'sexual image' and identity always constitute a basic element of man's image in every society . . .

The crucial importance which age differentiation and the interaction of members of different age grades possesses for the continuity of the social system can be most clearly seen in the fact that in most societies the attainment of full membership is defined in terms of transition from one age grade to another. As is well known, the exact age spans, which are defined in a unitary way and differentiated from other age spans, vary from one society to another, both in their age coverage and in the number of age grades between which they differentiate. There is, however, one focal point within the life span of an individual which is to some extent emphasised in most known societies, namely the achievement of full adult status, or full membership in the social system. Within all societies there is some definition – whatever the degree of its formalisation – of the 'adult man' or full member of society, and of the point at which the individual may acquire all of the paraphernalia of full status and enter the first stages of the adult age span. This entrance usually – and, it seems, necessarily – coincides with the transition period from the family of orientation to that of procreation, as it is through this transition that the definite change of age roles, from receiver to transmitter of cultural tradition, from child to parent, is effected. One of the main criteria of adulthood is defined as legitimate sexual maturity, i.e., the right to establish a family, and not merely the right to sexual intercourse. This crucial change of the individual's age roles, when the two age definitions still interact within him, is emphasized – more or less strongly – in practically all human societies. At the various ceremonies enacted at this point – *rites de passage* of different kinds – the interaction between different age grades and generations is intensified in various symbolic or ritual ways. Here also the basic characteristics of the age definition are brought sharply into focus: its relation to the total 'human image' in which the individual's appreciation of himself is stressed by the juxtaposition and integration of bodily (sexual) images and of evaluative norms; it is here that the double complementariness of sex-age roles finds its most articulate expression.

The best concrete examples of the ritual dramatization of this period or span of transition are the initiation ceremonies of various primitive tribes (or, with somewhat different emphasis, nuptial ceremonies of peasant folk societies). As anthropological literature abounds in detailed descriptions of these ceremonies, we shall not go into details; we shall merely attempt to analyse their most salient features. These may be summarized as follows:

(a) In these rites the pre-adult adolescents are transformed into full adult members of the tribe, the transformation being effected through

(b) A series of rites in which the adolescents are symbolically divested of the characteristics of youth and invested with those of adulthood from a sexual and social point of view. This symbolic investment, which has deep emotional significance, may have various concrete manifestations: bodily mutilation, circumcision, taking on of a new name, symbolic rebirth, etc.;

(c) the complete symbolic separation of the adolescents from the world of their youth, and especially from their close status attachments to their mothers; i.e., their complete 'male' independence and autonomous male image are articulated (the opposite usually holds true of girls' initiations);

(d) dramatisation of the encounter between the different generations, a dramatisation which may take the form of a fight, competition, etc., and in which the basic complementariness – whether of a continuous or discontinuous type – is stressed; thus, in all initiation rites the members of different generations must act together, the ones as teachers, the others as 'students'. The elders sometimes assume frightening forms and stress that without them the adolescents cannot become adults. Quite often the discontinuity between adolescence and adulthood is symbolically expressed in the 'rebirth' of the adolescents – in their symbolic death as children and rebirth as adults;

(e) transmission of the tribal lore and generalised patterns of behaviour and attitudes, both through formalised teaching and through symbolic ritual activities of different kinds. This transmission of the lore and role dispositions is combined with

(f) relaxation of the concrete control of the adults over the erstwhile adolescents, and its substitution by more generalised, internalised and symbolic controls; and with

(g) investment of the new members of the adult age span with authority-exercising roles; i.e., the substitution of concrete external controls by more internalised ones is clearly connected with the individual's changing position in the authority scheme.

Most of these dramatic elements can also be found, although in a somewhat more diluted form, in various traditional folk festivals of peasant communities, especially those (such as rural carnivals) in which youth and marriage are emphasised.

While this dramatisation of the period of transition to adulthood is not found in all human societies (especially not in those of the more 'modern' type), wherever it does exist, it brings into very sharp focus all the basic elements and functions of the differential age definitions and their crucial role in social continuity; the same holds true also of the general emphasis on the period or stage of transition to adulthood.

Here, the problem alluded to earlier is further clarified: the expectations which are directed towards individuals with respect to their age constitute one of the strongest, most essential links between the personality system of individuals and the social systems in which they participate. On the one hand, they are among the major criteria by which an individual defines his rights and obligations in relation to others; they also serve to define the types of units within the social system, to which various tasks and roles are allocated. The importance of differential age definitions, both for the individual's self-perception and for the continuity of the social system, can be most clearly seen in negative cases, i.e., when this continuity is broken in one way or another such as in delinquent and revolutionary youth groups of various kinds. Whenever this happens, the difference between various generations and age groups may become accentuated and sharpened to the breaking point, and the younger generation may develop a self-image completely opposed to the complementary image of the adult generation and rebel against it. One of the best examples of this is the German youth movement, or even, in broader terms, the whole modern Romantic movement, in which the extreme opposition between generations was stressed by means of an emphasis on a new type of man. . . .

Our analysis has shown that the interaction of members of different age grades is essential for the working and continuity of the social system. It is not only that people of different ages act together in the social system, but that their interaction is, to some extent at least, couched and defined in terms of their relative ages. This may take on a variety of forms. First, certain roles may be allocated on the basis of age, e.g., various roles in the family, in the sphere of authority, or in the economic and occupational spheres. The general division of labour in a society is necessarily based to some extent on age differences, and various social units may be regulated according to the criteria of age. Thus the right to take up a given occupation may be conditioned on the attainment of a certain age, and the same may apply in other social spheres and roles.

Moreover, even when age does not serve as an explicit criterion of allocation of roles, it very often influences it to a considerable degree, e.g., in the rules of seniority existing in many formal organisations, in the general assumption that for certain occupations and professions, like medicine, law, etc., experience is of great importance, etc.

In addition, age grading obviously implies that those belonging to a given age grade usually have some similar and common experiences; they may be required to behave in many respects in a similar way and to have similar relations with members of other age grades. They have, on the one hand, many common values, interests and expectations, while on the other hand they have many common points of contact with members of other age grades . . .

Unlike, however, in all the primitive and most of the historical (with the exception of Athens and the Hellenistic cities) societies, no one unitary organisation of age groups can be found in modern societies. We may distinguish between three main types of such groups and agencies which develop within modern societies. The first is the educational school system, the second are various adult-sponsored youth agencies and the third are spontaneous youth groups. These three types usually develop concurrently, although in some cases they (especially the second type) may be absent. All of them develop in relation to the various problems stemming from the development of modern economic and political, etc., systems and their repercussions on family and youth life. From that point of view they may be seen as one system. But at the same time there exists a significant differentiation between them. Some are organised by adults, and aim at the preparation of children for their adult roles and the smooth transference of the social heritage; others are more spontaneously developed by the children themselves to satisfy their own needs. While there is a constant interaction and interdependence between these various types of youth groups and agencies, there does not always exist a full complementarity and harmony between them. It is highly significant that in modern societies, unlike even in the historical societies, there is a great dissociation between the educational system and other forms of youth groups and agencies. The analysis of the relations between them, and the factors which influence these relations – and foremost among them the family – is one of our main concerns in this section, as well as in other places in the book.

This transition to the universalistic sphere of adult society is, however, here much more difficult and complicated than in other societies. These difficulties are inherent in the structure of family relations and may often be accentuated because this transition involves, in particular, severance from the mother and her image – attachment to whom has necessarily been very strong, albeit at the same time ambivalent – because of her relative confinement to the family sphere and formally lower position in the authority structure.

The school system. Economic and professional specialisation in modern societies is based on an accumulation of technical knowledge, the transmission of which lies beyond the powers of any family, and also necessitates a period of learning and preparation, the length of which is usually directly related to the extent of specialisation. This also holds true of many aspects of ideological, philosophical and religious knowledge, the acquisition of which constitutes a necessary prerequisite for the performance of many roles and for the attainment of full membership and status within the total society. The transmission of this knowledge is effected in special, institutionalized, educational organisations – the schools.

While various types of professional and educational schools exist in many societies, it is only in modern societies (and perhaps to some extent in certain sectors of the societies of classical antiquity) that they have gradually become an almost universal institutional device for the transmission of knowledge necessary for the attainment of full social status. Their first distinct characteristic is that, unlike the so-called initiation schools of the primitives, they organise the life of children for a long period of time, usually for several years. The second basic characteristic is their very strong technical-preparatory emphasis.

Their universal institutional importance clearly bears witness to the shrinkage of the family's scope of activities, and to the inadequacy of the family as the sole educational agency. In other words, they arise because family and kinship age-heterogeneous relations cannot ensure the smooth and continuous transmission of knowledge and role dispositions. The social structure and the sphere of the school is obviously distinct from that of the family, and necessarily involves a different way of organising relations between the various generations. The school society, becoming more formalised, is organised on the basis of age homogeneous groups, which interact with each other and particularly with representatives of the adult society (teachers) more or less corporately, in an organised way. The world of the school is a world of clearly defined age groups (grades, classes) which form a unitary heterocephalous hierarchy directed and oriented by specialised representatives of the adult world. Thus age grading within the school has, as it were, a dual differentiation. There is, first, the internal differentiation between different classes within the total hierarchy, and secondly, juxtaposition of the total organisation of children and adolescents with adult society and its representatives who are the bearers of power and authority within the system.

Questions
1. (a) Explain the importance of the rites of transition to adulthood in 'simple' societies.

(7 marks)

(b) How does the school manage the transition to adulthood in modern societies?

(8 marks)

2. *Why is the transition to adulthood in modern societies not always smooth?*

(25 marks)
(You will also need to refer to Sections 4 and 6 to answer this question, particularly Readings 19, 21 and 32).

47 John Clarke: An Example of Working Class Youth Sub-culture: Skinheads

In an article that appears in the volume *Resistance through Rituals*, John Clarke works together three basic concepts: youth, class and community. Like Paul Corrigan (see Reading 8) he sets age-specific factors such as being at school and having an interest in certain kinds of leisure activity in a much broader class context. He describes how the skinheads tend to dislike and oppose the various authorities that attempt to control and organise their activity. Similarly, many working-class men 'don't like being told what to do all the time' and, if they accept the necessity of authority, they often still seek to express their own independence, freedom and power at work and otherwise (see Willis, Reading 20). Such attitudes are quite rational in the sense that it is the role of the authority to ensure that the manual working class continues to perform hard, physical toil at rates of pay generally less than those of the rest of the community.

As Clarke explains, the defensiveness of the 'skins' is intensified by the feeling that their 'territory' and social community is being 'attacked' from several directions. Mistakenly, they sometimes perceive immigrants as a major source of this attack. Both their defensive-aggressiveness and working class identity is apparent in their life-style, including their clothing. The 'bovverboot', for instance, is symbolic of menace, as well as quite functional. Like Anna Pollert (Reading 35), Clarke produces a sensitive interpretive account which also lacks nothing in its awareness of structural realities.

Reading 47 From John Clarke, 'The Skinheads and the Magical Recovery of Community' in Stuart Hall and Tony Jefferson *eds, Resistance Through Rituals* (Hutchinson, 1976), pp. 13–16.

Note: *In this extract from his longer study of 'Skinhead culture' John Clarke describes the way this sub-culture focuses around the notions of 'community' and 'territory'. Skinhead culture selectively reaffirms certain core values of traditional working class culture, and this affirmation is expressed both in dress, style and appearance, and in activities. The reaffirmation is symbolic, rather than a 'real' attempt to recreate some aspects of the 'parent' culture. The preoccupation in Skinhead culture with territory, with football and 'fanship', and with a particular kind of masculinity thus represents what Clarke calls their 'magical recovery of community'. See also the use of this example in Clarke's MA Thesis, 'Reconceptualising Youth Culture' (CCCS. Birmingham) and in 'Skinheads and Youth Culture' (CCCS Stencilled Paper No. 23).*

Our basic thesis about the Skinheads centres around the notion of community. We would argue that the Skinhead style represents an attempt to re-create through the 'mob' the traditional working class community, as a substitution for the *real* decline of the latter. The underlying social dynamic for the style, in this light, is the relative worsening of the situation of the working class, through the second half of the sixties, and especially the more rapidly worsening situation of the lower working class (and of the young within that). This, allied to the young's sense of exclusion from the existing 'youth sub-culture' (dominated in the public arena by the music and styles derived from the 'underground') produced a return to an intensified 'Us-Them' consciousness among the lower working class young, a sense of being excluded and under attack from a variety of points. The resources to deal with this sense of exclusion were not to be found within either the emergent or incorporated elements of youth sub-cultures, but only in those images and behaviours which stressed a more traditional form of collective solidarity. Material from *The Paint House* illustrates this sense of oppression:

> Everywhere there are fucking bosses, they're always trying to tell you what to do . . . don't matter what you do, where you go, they're always there. People in authority, the people who tell you what to do and make sure you do it. It's the system we live in, it's the governor system.

Schools, you 'ave to go, doncha? The teachers and the head-master, they're the authority, ain't they? They're telling you what to do and you're glad to get out and leave and that, aren't ya? They think because you're young and they pay you and that, that they can treat you how they like and say what they want. Then there's the 'old bill' and courts . . . they're all part of authority. Official and all kinds of people in uniforms. Anyone with a badge on, traffic wardens and council and all that . . . yeah, even the caretaker at the flats, they even 'as a go at you. Then when you finish at work or at school, you go to the clubs and the youth leaders are all just a part of it.

(Daniel and McGuire, eds., 1972: 67).

But the skinheads felt oppressed by more than just the obvious authority structure; they resented those who tried to get on and 'give themselves false airs', people from within the neighbourhood who had pretensions to social superiority; they resented the 'people on our backs':

All these dummoes at school, who always do what they're told . . . they're the ones who end up being coppers and that. I hate them do-gooders who come to "elp the poor in the slums . . .' They're all nice and sweet and kind, they pretend to be on your side and by talking nicely find out about you but social workers and people like that, they ain't on your side. They think they know how you should live. They're really authority pretending to be your friends. They try to get you to do things and if you don't do them, they've got the law on their side. With all this lot against us, we've still got the yids, Pakis, wogs, 'ippies on our backs. (ibid: 68).

The sense of being 'in the middle' of this variety of oppressive and exploitative forces produces a need for group solidarity, which though essentially defensive, in the Skinheads was coupled with an aggressive content, the expression of frustration and discontent through the attacking of scapegoated outsiders. The content of this solidarity, as we shall see in our consideration of the elements of the skinhead style, derived from the traditional content of the working class community – the example, *par excellence*, of the defensively organised collective.

However, the skinhead style does not revive the community in a real sense; the post-war decline of the bases of that community had removed it as a real source of solidarity; the skinheads had to use an *image* of what the community was as the basis of their style. They were the 'dispossessed inheritors'; they received a tradition which had been deprived of its real social bases. The themes and imagery still persisted, but the reality was in a state of decline and disappearance. We would suggest that this dislocated relation to the traditional community accounts for the exaggerated and intensified form which the values and concerns of that community received in the form of the skinhead style. Daniel and McGuire claim that:

> Rather than a community spirit, the Collinwood gang tends to have an affinity with an image of the East Enders, as being tough, humorous and a sub-culture of their own . . . The gang sees itself as a natural continuation of the working class tradition of the area, with the same attitudes and behaviour as their parents and grandparents before them. They believe that they have the same stereotyped prejudices against immigrants and aliens as they believe their parents have and had, *but they play these roles outside of the context of the community experienced by their parents* . . . (ibid: 21–22. Our emphasis).

These observations are reinforced by comments from the Skinheads themselves about the gang and its relation to the locality:

> When people kept saying skinheads, when they're talking about the story of us coming up from the East End, this has happened for generations before, past . . . I mean where does skinhead come into it? It's a community, a gang, isn't it?, it's only another word for community, kids, thugs, whatever . . . (ibid: 21; 31).

The kids inherit the oral tradition of the area from the parent culture, especially that part which refers to the community's self-image, its collective solidarity, its conception of masculinity, its orientation to 'outsiders' and so on. It is perhaps not surprising that the area with which the Skinheads should be most associated should be the East End, which from a sociological standpoint has been seen as the archetypal working class community. Its internal self-image has always been a particularly strong one, and has been strengthened by its public reputation as a 'hard' area, a reputation which in the mid-sixties was further increased by the glamorous careers of the Krays.

Finally, we would like to exemplify this relation between the Skinheads and the image of the community through some of the central elements of the skinhead style. One of the most crucial aspects is the emphasis on territorial connections for the Skinheads – the 'Mobs' were organised on a territorial basis, identifying themselves with and through a particular locality (e.g. the 'Smethwick Mob', etc.). This involved the Mobs in the demarcation and defence of their particular 'patch', marking boundaries with painted slogans ('Quinton Mob rules here', etc.), and maintaining those boundaries against infractions by other groups. This territoriality, like the community, has its own focal points around which interaction articulates – the street corner meeting place, the pub, and the football ground. Although the football ground did not necessarily coincide with the mobs' patches, its own local identification and the already existent activities of the Ends provided a particular focal point for the Mobs to organise around.

Football, and especially the violence articulated around it, also provided one arena for the expression of the Skinheads' concern with a particular, collective, masculine self conception, involving an identification of masculinity with physical toughness, and an unwillingness to back down in the face of 'trouble'. The violence also involved the Mobs' stress on collective solidarity and mutual support in times of 'need'. This concern with toughness was also involved in the two other most publicised skinhead activities – 'Paki-Bashing' and 'Queer-Bashing'. Paki-bashing involved the ritual and aggressive defence of the social and cultural homogeneity of the community against its most obviously scapegoated outsiders – partly because of their particular visibility within the neighbourhood (in terms of shop ownership patterns, etc.) by comparison with West Indians, and also because of their different cultural patterns (especially in terms of their unwillingness to defend themselves and so on) – again by comparison with West Indian youth.

'Queer-Bashing' may be read as reaction against the erosion of traditionally available stereotypes of masculinity, especially by the hippies. The Skinhead operational definition of 'queer' seems to have extended to all those males who by their standards looked 'odd', as this statement from a Smethwick Skinhead may indicate:

Usually it'd be just a bunch of us who'd find somebody they thought looked odd – like this one night we were up by Warley Woods and we saw this bloke who looked odd – he'd got long hair and frills on his trousers.

We may see these three interrelated elements of territoriality, collective solidarity and 'masculinity' as being the way in which the Skinheads attempted to recreate the inherited imagery of the community in a period in which the experiences of increasing opposition demanded forms of mutual organisation and defence. And we might finally see the intensive violence connected with the style as evidence of the 'recreation of the community' being indeed a 'magical' or 'imaginery' one, in that it was created without the material and organisational basis of that community and consequently was less subject to the informal mechanisms of social control characteristic of such communities. In the skinhead style we can see both the elements of continuity (in terms of the style's content), and discontinuity (in terms of its form), between parent culture and youth sub-culture.

Question
1. (a) Why did the skinheads 'need . . . group solidarity'?

(10 marks)

(b) Discuss the relationship between the skinheads' style and their image of community.

(10 marks)

48 Bob Coles: Recent Developments in the Sociology of Youth

The nineteen eighties saw a change of direction in the sociology of youth. A major reason for this was a change in the situation of youth itself. A sharp rise in youth unemployment and a corresponding decline in the job prospects of many students generated a more sombre mood among the young and the sociologists who surveyed them. Emphasis shifted from the 'spectacular', stylish subcultures – mods and rockers, skinheads, hippies and the rest – to more practical matters of work, training and education. Bob Coles notes these changes of direction.

First, the new sociology of youth is increasingly about females as well as males (Reading 95). The work on young males of Clarke (Reading 47), Willis (Reading 20), Corrigan (Reading 8) and others is now complemented by a growing body of writings on young females. Second, a considerable literature on black youth has now emerged. A major early contribution to this was the chapters on black youth in Ken Pryce's *Endless Pressure*, first published in 1979 (see Readings 9 and 41). Third, youth studies have recently concentrated on 'ordinary' kids and their 'ordinary' problems – not least of which is getting a job. This has involved consideration of the policy of vocational training adopted by the government (see Reading 32). Coles' review of the research suggests that the responses and subcultural solutions of the young vary not only regionally but even by locality.

Whilst poking fun at the 'old' sociology of youth, Coles more seriously suggests that current work should build upon rather than disregard it. Contemporary cohort studies can gain depth and texture by employing techniques such as the semiotic analysis of style and ritual so brilliantly pioneered by Clarke and Willis and others at the Contemporary Centre for Cultural Studies.

Reading 48 From Bob Coles, 'Gonna Tear Your Play House Down: Towards Re-constructing a Sociology of Youth', in *The Social Science Teacher*, Vol. 15, No. 3, pp. 78–80.

The sociology of youth has had a somewhat chequered career. In the 1970's it was one of the most popular areas to teach. The subject matter was topical, interesting and guaranteed to raise an informed and lively debate. But the studies produced in the 60's and 70's are now regarded by many students as something of an embarrassment, as the sociology of youth has stubbornly refused to grow up. It still struts around in the empirical gear it purchased way back in the 1960's and 70's, and to the fashion conscious kids of the 1980's, this renders it faintly ridiculous, and about as topical, recognisable and relevant as Doc and his Street Corner Society. The mods may have managed a resurrection and given Stan Cohen as well as Pete Townsend a new lease of life, but many of the other creatures around which youth sub-culture theory developed its conceptual apparatus have long since grown up and settled down. Youth itself, of course, is still with us. But many of the pictures of youth given to us by sociology are now, if we are honest, a little faded and out of date.

Sociologists of youth are sometimes very aware of this state of affairs and have spent melancholy evenings bemoaning the lack of contemporary studies, frankly admitting that there is little that they can directly do as greying academics whose research heyday was in previous decades. But much of this melancholia is unjustified, and a review of the full range of recent writings on youth indicates that a considerable body of research has been produced in the last few years. It is just that this body of literature has a different shape and focus, and the cut of its intellectual clothes is less glamorous and eye catching. For if the obsession of the sociological studies of the 1970's was with style and the meaning of style, the sociologists of this decade are concentrating their gaze upon the impact of youth unemployment and the transition to adulthood. The semiology and sociology of scooters and safety-pins has been replaced by the social demography of post-16 progression and the epidemiology of YTS. But despite the apparent differences of these approaches, they still constitute sociological studies of youth. This article will argue that there is much to be gained from putting the two streams of thought together in a revised and less partial sociology of youth. For just as not all the young of the 70's were mods, rockers or punks, nor do most of the young of the 1980's find themselves conscripted into the sullen and colourless standing army of the long term unemployed. Glamorous youth culture studies of the 70's ignored most youth. The YTS obsession of the 80's runs the same risk. This article argues for the reconstruction of a sociology of youth around the social world of 'ordinary kids'.

Filling the gaps

Many of the important studies in youth in the 1980's were developed as a counterpoint to some of the obvious absences in earlier studies. They filled in the three major gaps in our knowledge about youth. The first and most obvious criticisms of the youth studies of the 70's was that, with a few notable exceptions, they fulfilled the worst features of sexist sociology. Youth was male, and when young women were included as research subjects they were either confined within bedrooms or consigned to the role of male lookalike or hanger on. Style was male, a sophisticated repertoire of resistance, through which macho youth engaged in symbolic guerrilla warfare against the repressions of class society. Alienation was male. This was not so much experienced through coercion, since the lads were seen as developing glorious patterns of resistance to school on their way to dead-end working class jobs. But resistance did have its other side in the objective constriction of career possibilities. Macho anti-school cultures acted as a suitable apprenticeship to working class jobs in the days when such jobs still existed. But we are left in the 1980's wondering about what happens to 'the lads' now, as well as being aware that this 1970's version of working class reproduction also missed out half the story, for it almost completely ignored young women.

Recent studies have served to counteract that bias. Female youth has been discovered, and discovered to be conscious, sub-cultured, and resisting, rather than passive, isolated, and uncultured. Whilst they appeared only on the fringe as sex objects in the social worlds described by Willis and Corrigan, the young women described in 1980's ethnography are not merely feminised cultural dopes into which 'Jackie-culture' is unreflexively poured. The women described by Christine Griffin and Beverley Skeggs in separate studies are, for example, just as much sub-cultural schemers as the lads described by Corrigan or Willis. Girls may be seen as less *troublesome* than boys by those in authority and they can be seen to operate smaller 'gangs'. But Griffin and Skeggs describe distinct sub-groups with distinctive value systems. Women have sub-cultures too and they have become established topics for investigation in the study of youth in the 1980's.

The second major addition to the 70's studies has been the study of 'black' youth. Generic studies of Rasta-youth were of course in evidence in research but this has been substantially expanded and enlarged by CCCS and PSI studies, Cashmore and Troyna, Mary Fuller, Sheila Allen and others. We are now much more knowledgeable about black youth and Asian sub-cultures. The youth subcultures of the 1980's are thus clearly documented in the literature as male and female, black, white and brown. But whilst these dimensions of difference have become important items on the agenda, there is still some way to go in completing the picture.

The third area in which youth studies have concentrated their attention in recent years has been on 'ordinary kids'. Richard

Jenkins' ethnographic study of working class youth in Belfast was one of the first recent studies to question the bi-polar model developed by Willis. 'Ordinary kids' did not neatly fit into the rough/respectable dichotomy, or fall within the social networks which supported the contrasting life styles and social aspirations of either the 'lads' or the 'ear 'oles'. But importantly they constituted the majority of Jenkins' sample, which, in marked difference to the earlier studies by Willis and Corrigan incorporated male and female youth. Phillip Brown, in a recent study of comprehensive schooling in South Wales, also found he had to abandon the old sub-culture dichotomy and use a tripartite division between 'Rems' (anti-school culture), 'Swots' (pro-school culture) and (again, the largest category) 'ordinary kids'. The majority of young people in both Jenkins' and Brown's research developed a complex sub-cultural response to the social and economic worlds which faced them. Brown's ordinary kids had a definite *instrumental* orientation to education and qualifications.

Whilst they would not sacrifice leisure time by working as hard at school as the 'swots', especially if this meant never going out at night, they were prepared to 'make an effort' at school. This they did partly out of 'self respect' and partly in the belief that it made some difference in the search for jobs afterwards. Jenkins, in his study illustrates that a different orientation towards dress, leisure, crime and courtship distinguishes the 'ordinary kids' from the tough male culture of the 'lads'. In a third study based on the Isle of Sheppey, Clare Wallace emphasises the importance of the domestic and the public sphere for both male and female youngsters as they attempt to make the transition to adulthood. Aspirations to be 'breadwinners' and 'homemakers', socially settled, symbolically secure, became significant as the cohort she studied reached 21. What is clear from all three research projects is that working class culture does not clearly polarise into the rough rebels and the conforming respectables. Instead the majority of young people develop a complete framework of motives as they struggle to find their footing in an adult world.

Cohort studies

Much youth unemployment research is based upon cohort studies, which take as a sampling frame all young people in a particular year group. The Brown and Wallace studies, whilst broadly ethnographic in approach, contain important differences when compared to the earlier 1970's style ethnographies. They involve the study of the full range of youth sub-cultures which are manifest within a local community. Once a full age cohort becomes the focus of a study, it is hard to ignore the importance of 'ordinary kids' or the ways in which male and female sub-cultures interrelate and influence each other. The cohort study is also becoming a common form of approach in 'youth unemployment' research. But much of the latter work has been concerned simply to monitor the different progression routes being followed by young people in the turbulent world of the YTS-generation. The increase in youth unemployment at the beginning of the 1980's has brought about a complete transformation of the educational, training and economic institutions which structure the transition to adulthood. In recent years we have witnessed an enormous growth in publications which have described the new structures, attempted to diagnose the impact of the 'new vocationalism' foisted on the education and training machine, and monitored how young people are scrambling through the various tentacles of the MSC. But much of this research has been descriptive and demographic, informing us about the range of the changes which have re-routed the transition to adulthood in a way which keeps the unemployment figures within politically acceptable limits.

However, youth unemployment has meant not only the 'disappearance of the youth labour market, the growth of post-16 further education, and a new training industry, but also a new series of barriers between the 'childhood' status of school, and the 'adulthood' symbolised by full time work. In short, it has elongated the status of 'youth' and made its outcome and termination less predictable. Willis has described this as the 'fractured transition' and local labour market studies make it clear that the nature of the transition and the degree to which it is 'fractured' is very dependent upon local economic conditions. The most recent Ashton and Maguire study, for example, reported that 1 in 33 of their sample of young people in St. Albans were unemployed, compared with 1 in 3 of an equivalent sample in Sunderland. They also make it clear that regional differences are so significant that class-based variations in employment opportunities are disappearing under a tidal wave of regional factors. Thus Roberts may be correct when he argued that it is 'the bottom' which has dropped out of the youth labour market in the North, the Midlands and the South. It must also be recognised that there are vast regional differences in the economic world confronting working class young people in different parts of the country.

Local labour markets and subcultural responses

My own research, conducted with Robert MacDonald, indicated that local labour market differences also occur within regions with major differences in conditions occurring within a distance of 20 or 30 miles. But more important, from the point of view of the argument being developed here, are the ways in which this is leading to differences in sub-cultural responses to local labour market conditions. We have been examining the ways in which the 'career paths' followed by young people are informed by locally based youth sub-cultures. In doing this we have focused our attention on several interrelated dimensions of aspiration, involving both positive and negative feelings about school, work, training, as well as social, domestic, and leisure life. The dimensions we have examined include: the importance and significance of 'adult' status; the significance of money – the symbolic as well as material value it has for young people (wage/dole/pocket money/allowance); the concern for security and the sources of security; the conceptualisation of time – time invested/time wasted/time-on-one's-hands (boredom); the institutional basis of friendship patterns and sub-cultures – school, work, scheme, club, neighbourhood gang; and the ways in which 'success' and 'failure' are attributed and the locally based reference groups used in this attribution. What is clear from our research is that whilst these dimensions of life style aspiration may help to organise our understanding of locally based youth sub-cultures, the particular shape of sub-cultural responses is dependent upon local differences. Thus whilst the collapse of the labour market in one of our areas, Whitby, has resulted in a swelling of the ranks of male 'swots' (getting on in Whitby means getting qualified and getting out – of the area), twenty miles down the road in Malton 'swots' still form only a small minority of the boys as most of them leave school in droves willing to risk their fortunes in a more buoyant local labour market. Nor is it sufficient to see this as simply a 'labour market effect', with high unemployment resulting in higher staying on rates. For Ashton and Maguire report exactly the opposite pattern in Sunderland. Rather it is apparent that locally based youth sub-cultures are responding in different ways to the local economic and social conditions they experience.

It is not without significance that youth unemployment research has taken the form that it has. It would have been quite possible for sociology to have produced a new crop of ethnographies featuring the glamorous fringe whose response to the absence of jobs for the young has been to eke out an alternative status system through non-work-based life styles. Certainly, there are such alternatives 'out there' to be 'discovered' and possibly glamorised. The media has certainly tried to foster a belief that amongst the ranks of the young unemployed there are substantial groupings of the tattooed and nihilistic, the sniffers, the surgees, the park-based cider drinkers, the beach bums and the workless 'casuals' conspicuously consuming mysteriously acquired wealth. But by and large sociologists have rightly resisted returning to their former role as scholarly sidekick to the media myth makers. The overwhelming findings of youth research in the age of unemployment is that joblessness is a serious blight upon the economic, psychological and social maturation of the Thatchered young and that the young unemployed who find worklessness a lark and an opportunity for fun are, to use an over-worked phrase, 'a tiny minority'. Unemployment research has at least resisted the temptation to slander 'ordinary kids'.

But the time is now right for uniting sub-culture theory and unemployment research. Sub-culture research may have been richly ethnographic, and at times highly theoretical, but it was often based upon dubiously unrepresentative, and sometimes remarkably small, groups of the young. Unemployment research whilst often based upon more representative samples is sometimes aridly descriptive, and often narrowly focused upon the economic dimension of life. If we were to summarise the best of both worlds we could produce a sociology which was richly ethnographic but based upon a representative survey of all youth: male, female, black, brown and white, and encompassing the full range of cultural responses within social class groupings. Given the vast regional differences of the 1980's it would also be wise to pay due regard to locally based youth sub-cultures rather than the media-hyped, nationally famous trendies. The Economic and Social Research Council is just about to launch a research initiative to study the social and psychological progression processes experienced by 16 to 19 year olds. Perhaps this is the opportunity to bring traditions together, and for the sociology of youth to come of age.

Question

1. *(a) What changes in direction have occurred in the sociology of youth, and how do you account for them?*

(10 marks)

(b) To what extent do recent developments in the sociology of youth contradict or complement the work of the nineteen seventies?

(15 marks)

(You may want to refer to other readings mentioned in the introduction to this extract in answering this question).

49 Chris Phillipson: Capitalism, Socialism and the Construction of Old Age

It will now be clear to those who have systematically been working through this section what the 'social construction' of age means. It refers to how the position and experience of an age group is structured in a particular society.

Chris Phillipson takes a strongly socialist view on the social construction of old age in capitalist society. Citing Westergaard and Resler, he contends that inequality is basic to capitalist society and that the working class aged are particularly at risk of poverty. He gives four reasons in support of his view:

1. The old tend to come off worst when capitalism is in crisis and there is generally less to go round.
2. Other matters have priority over their needs – such as defence and law and order.
3. Capitalist economic decline and the decline of facilities for the old tend to go hand in hand.
4. Capitalism remains a system of labour exploitation and does not provide adequately for 'ex' workers.

Social reformers would find Phillipson's arguments both pessimistic and deterministic. They would contend that measures have been passed (including the state pension) to improve the situation of the old and might point out that between 1971 and 1982 pensioners dropped as a percentage of those in poverty from 52 to 27 per cent. This relative improvement may reflect the increased political strength of the elderly – as their numbers have increased, so have their votes!

Part of Phillipson's response to such criticisms is given elsewhere in his book. He indicates that, limited by its concern for profit, capitalism lacks the commitment and values to ensure security, purpose and identity for the old in a long-term and systematic way. By contrast, he believes socialism could achieve these goals and he suggests the key issues around which a socialist social policy for the elderly could be developed. These include the possibility of making available more cultural and educational facilities for the old and of revitalising their relationship with the young.

Reading 49 From Chris Phillipson, *Capitalism and the Construction of Old Age* (Macmillan, 1982), pp. 1–5.

This book has been written in a period of crisis for elderly people. Health and social services are being substantially reduced; questions are being raised about the ability of society fully to protect pensioners against price increases; older workers are urged to retire as soon as possible as a means of reducing high unemployment amongst young people. At the same time, a tremendous expansion is taking place in the number of people aged 60 and over, a development which will require significant increases in resources to the welfare state, if health and living standards are to be maintained. The broad dimensions of these demographic changes are well understood, and are not the object of detailed scrutiny in this book. Instead, it aims first to develop a critical account of the position of elderly people in a capitalist society, and second to analyse the responses of the state to the emergence of retirement.

In placing the emphasis on the elderly and capitalist social relations this study is less concerned with old age as a biological and psychological problem. We are rather more interested in old age as a problem for a society characterised by major inequalities in the distribution of power, income and property. Westergaard and Resler have written that:

Subsistence poverty is indeed common among old people, the sick, the handicapped, and so on; but only because the majority of the old, sick and handicapped have previously been dependent on jobs that provided them with few or no other resources to fall back on than meagre benefits from public funds. Rank-and-file wage earners – manual and routine non-manual – live with the risk of poverty over their heads. They face a likely prospect of poverty on retirement. And they face a threat of poverty even before that: on redundancy and if forced to work short-time; on transfer to low-paid work in the later years of working life; in sickness, in widowhood, and through loss of subsidiary household earnings. The risk of poverty at two stages of the working-class life cycle – in childhood and the child-rearing phase of working life – has been markedly reduced during this century: this for the simple reason that families are now much smaller than they were, and child-bearing is compressed within a short span of years. But poverty in old age is more common than it was, because more workers live on to experience it. To the bourgeoisie, by contrast, the risk of subsistence poverty is remote. High earnings, fringe benefits, greater job security, the incremental rise of the typical life cycle, the consequent relative ease of individual 'planning' and saving – all these confer relative immunity. And property ownership gives total immunity.

(Westergaard and Resler, 1975, pp. 124–5)

Hitherto, class and gender relations have been given inadequate treatment in studies on the elderly. Despite the development of more radical approaches by French and North American researchers (see, for example, Guillemard, 1977; Marshall, 1981; Myles, 1981), British research has only recently begun to explore the interaction between social and economic inequalities and experiences in later life (the work of Peter Townsend is an obvious exception). I would argue that undue weight has been given to biological and psychological changes in old age (and the deterioration seen to accompany them), in contrast to the role played by the economic and political environment.

The neglect of issues associated with a political economy of old age has had some important repercussions. In most commentaries on the elderly, it has usually been assumed that the types of problem associated with old age can easily be resolved within the framework of a capitalist society. Research on the elderly invariably comes to the conclusion that with more government aid, additional family support and voluntary help, adequate services will emerge. This book will question that viewpoint. There is little evidence that, given an expanding economy, capitalism would contribute the massive resources which elderly people require (the historical picture to emerge in Chapters 3 and 6 supports this view). Moreover, when capitalism is in crisis, the speed with which resources are removed, both from the elderly and from other groups, indicates the tenuous hold of any legislation which is conceded. Yet this book will maintain that, regardless of the state of the economy at particular periods, *the logic of capitalism as a productive and social system is irreconcilable with meeting the needs of elderly people.* We can see this in four very obvious ways:

(1) Whenever capitalism is in crisis – as in the 1930s or in the early 1980s – it is inevitably working-class people (particularly those who become unemployed and/or are forced into retirement) who suffer most. Indeed, what we see is an attempt by capitalism to solve its problems through cuts in the living standards of working people. The expansion in, for example, the number of people entering early retirement is a thinly disguised attempt to reduce the social impact of unemployment. Many of those who retire early, once their 'golden handshakes' have been exhausted, experience many years of poverty, with no chance of re-entering the labour market, except in the most menial of jobs. Certainly in terms of the sacrifices which are constantly being urged upon working people, the price can be very high.

(2) Capitalism has a distinct set of priorities which almost always relegates social and individual needs behind the search for profits and the maintenance of defence and of law and order. In a 1979 interview in the magazine *Social Work Today*, Patrick Jenkin (then Secretary of State for Social Services) was asked: 'You would put defence spending as a higher priority above the elderly, the infirm and other disadvantaged?'

JENKIN: Of course. If we did not defend ourselves with the three per cent growth target which is the NATO target to which we are committed, then whether it is the elderly, the mentally handicapped or the ill or Uncle Tom Cobley and all, our lives would be at great peril.

SWT: You personally believe in that?

JENKIN: Yes, of course I do.

(*Social Work Today*, October 1979)

In line with this philosophy, while social services have been cut back, defence spending has increased as a percentage of Gross Domestic Product (GDP). The £7,500 million programme on Trident missiles is the clearest illustration of this trend.

(3) Capitalism as a social system can have a disastrous impact on the lives of elderly people. Through the decline of major industries, areas which were once prosperous fall into decay, creating substandard housing, loss of jobs and the migration of younger workers with families (Community Development Project, 1977). Elderly people find themselves caught in a 'scissors' between their own need for better services, and the steady decline of facilities within their neighbourhood (a decline being accelerated by the early 1980's expenditure cuts).

(4) Capitalism remains a system of exploitation: a ruling class still appropriates and controls the wealth produced by the working class. For Marx:

> The free labourer . . . sells himself and, indeed, sells himself piecemeal . . . the worker belongs neither to an owner nor to the land, but 8, 10, 12, 15 hours of his daily life belong to him who buys them. The worker leaves the capitalist to whom he hires himself whenever he likes and the capitalist discharges him whenever he thinks fit, as soon as he no longer gets any profit out of him, or not the anticipated profit. But the worker, whose sole source of livelihood is the sale of his labour power, cannot leave the whole class of purchasers, that is the capitalist class, without renouncing his existence.

> (Cited in Blackburn, 1976, p. 17)

When the older worker steps permanently outside the wage system he or she becomes reliant on personal savings, an occupational pension or the state pension. In fact, most older people (over 70 per cent) rely on the state pension as their main source of income. Yet, at the present time this pension (for a married couple) is equivalent to just 50 per cent of the average take-home pay of an industrial worker. For those without significant additions to their income, the most devastating experiences can follow:

Lack of finance for other things means lack of choice in housing (and the elderly certainly figure largely amongst those in poor housing), in consumer goods, in recreational and other facilities. The value of increased free time in retirement is restricted when, at the same time, income is diminished. All this too at a time when the need for expensive items has perhaps never been greater – a washing machine to help arthritic hands, a refrigerator to save daily trips to the shops on shaky legs. And how does it feel to be in this position? In a survey of elderly workers many revealed that it had been the feelings of poverty that had been the hardest thing to bear about retirement, the inability to participate in social life as a normal member of society, simply to be able to ask people to 'Have a drink'. Current trends towards early retirement will mean for many a very long time in this disadvantaged position – even with retirement at 65 this period can exceed 30 years.
(Trade Union Studies Information Unit, 1979, p. 14).

Questions
1. *The extract describes some differences between the material security of working class and middle class old people. What are these differences?*
(5 marks)
2. *Critically evaluate Phillipson's analysis of the position of the old in capitalist society.*
(10 marks)

Questions on Stratification (Class, Gender, Race and Age)
1. *(a) Consider the view that the working class is now divided into two main groups: a better paid 'core' in regular work and a low paid or unemployed 'reserve pool' of labour.*
(8 marks)
(b) Compare the position of part-time and temporary women workers, school-leavers and blacks in the paid labour force.
(9 marks)
(c) Lord Scarman has argued that the development of a black middle class should ease racial tension and conflict. What evidence is there

that a black middle class is developing? Do you agree with Lord Scarman's analysis?

(8 marks)

2. (a) In what ways does the role of domestic worker help to maintain society?

(8 marks)

(b) Most domestic work is carried out by women. Compare the position of women in paid work to the position of women in domestic work.

(8 marks)

(c) Consider the view that the occupational and class categorisation of women should be based on their own work (domestic or paid) rather than that of their husband.

(9 marks)

3. (a) Give two explanations for the highly unequal distribution of wealth in Britain.

(6 marks)

(b) Discuss the evidence that the very wealthy share a common upper class culture.

(6 marks)

(c) Is the upper class a ruling class?

(13 marks)

SECTION 10

Organisations, Work and Non-Work

Readings 50–56

Richard Brown begins this section by defining work (not necessarily as one might expect) and by sketching out changing occupational trends. Reading 51 is a classic statement by Max Weber on the nature of bureaucracy – an organisational form he found particularly characteristic of modern society. Stephen Wood critically but sympathetically summarises Harry Braverman's immensely influential 'deskilling thesis' in which the latter attacks the division of labour under capitalism (particularly Taylorism) as intentionally manipulative and belittling. After concentrating on hierarchically organised forms of work, it is important to be clear that there are alternatives. John Cunningham describes one in the form of the workers' co-operative movement (Reading 53). In Reading 54, Tom Keenoy argues, moral panics to the contrary, that strikes are an ordinary part of the industrial bargaining process and not always 'caused' by workers.

In Reading 55, Sue McIntosh and co-authors comment sharply on Stanley Parker's now much criticised theory of work and leisure, mainly from a feminist perspective. Chris Rojek puts leisure in a socio-economic context and suggests, in effect, that our leisure is perhaps not as 'free' as we may think.

50 Richard Brown: The Changing Shape of Work

The changing nature of work and the relationship between work and non-work are currently areas of intense interest and concern both within and beyond sociology. It is important, therefore, to begin this section with a definition of work which adequately embraces current understanding of the nature of work – including, for instance, housework and work in the community. Richard Brown does this in the opening section of this extract.

Just as usefully, the reading goes on to discuss recent changes in the social organisation of work and some of the economic developments that underlie them. He suggests that over the last twenty years or so the following are the most important changes: the decline in the number employed in manufacturing industry; the expansion of the service sector; the continuing decline in the relative importance of manual work; the increasing importance of the state as an employer; the massive increases in unemployment; and the continuing rise to economic domination of large corporations, many of them multi-nationals. Undoubtedly, as Brown says, 'all these changes represent major shifts in the nature of work in our society'. I would add that currently unpaid work in the home and the community, and paid but untaxed work in the informal economy, are areas of comparable significance.

The concluding part of the extract deals with the future of work. Brown focuses on the effects of the new technology and gives fair consideration to the optimists – who see it as a potentially liberating force – and the pessimists who are more impressed with the loss of jobs and great inequalities of income and wealth it is likely to bring. Finally, Brown leaves us with the question that, if work does become less important and time-consuming, what will replace it at the centre of human affairs?

Reading 50 From Richard Brown, 'Work: Past, Present and Future' in Kenneth Thompson *ed.*, *'Work, Employment and Unemployment: Perspectives on Work and Society'* (Open University Press, 1984) pp. 262, 266–8, 270–2.

As will be apparent from the discussion in other contributions to this volume, there is no universal agreement among social scientists as to the definition of 'work'. Clearly it cannot be defined solely in terms of the activities to which it refers, but must also include reference to the purposes for which and the context within which such activities are performed. Thus, for example, for some people to 'work' is to play games to entertain spectators, games such as football, tennis, golf or snooker, which many others play for pleasure or relaxation; reading a book for interest is a different activity from reading it to prepare a lecture or write a review; the significance of digging the garden, driving a car, or even walking, all vary depending on the purpose for which they are done, for their own sake or in order to produce goods or provide a service. Work activities are instrumental activities; this does not mean that they cannot be enjoyable, but whatever intrinsic rewards they offer to those who perform them, they are carried out in order to achieve some extrinsic purpose and not just for their own sake. Within that limitation, however, almost any activity can be 'work'. This wide scope of work activities is perhaps adequately contained if they are defined as any physical or mental activities which transform materials into a more useful form, provide or distribute goods or services to oneself or others, and/or increase or improve human knowledge and understanding of the world.

Many work activities, and certainly the ones we most commonly think of as 'work' are performed in order to provide something – goods or services – either for which others are willing to pay, or for which others would have to be paid if one did not provide them oneself. In the first case, we are talking about work within the context of employment, or self-employment, leading to the sale of the product of one's labour directly, or indirectly in return for a wage, salary or fee. In the second case, we are referring to work within the household and for consumption by the household – domestic work, do-it-yourself, care of the elderly and sick, and so on. Thus work can be and is performed both when conventionally 'at work' (during one's employment, typically located away from the home) and during one's own time (typically spent at home) (see Parker *et al.*, 1972; Parker, 1983, ch. 1; Brown, 1984). Even this broad definition does not exhaust the contexts within which work occurs; some work (e.g. voluntary work, help to neighbours) may be communal, in that its products are not sold or bartered, nor do the producers themselves consume the results of their labours; the benefits go to third parties or to society in general (Gershuny and Pahl, 1980).

The adequacy of the conception and definition of work suggested here should be judged against the discussion which follows, and the discussions of the nature of work in this volume and elsewhere. As we shall see, it has at least the merit of being considerably more broad and more inclusive – and therefore, in my view, more satisfactory – than the taken-for-granted conceptions of work which have characterised most popular and social scientific discussions in the past. . . .

The roots of recent changes in the social organisation of work in Britain can undoubtedly be traced back a long way. It is predominantly during the past twenty years or so, however, that the impact of these changes has become clearly apparent so that laymen and academics alike have been forced to reconsider their understanding of 'work', a fairly painful process which is still going on (see, for example, Chapter 1 of this volume). Without attempting any sort of comprehensive account of causes or consequences, it is possible to indicate something of the nature and scale of the changes which have occurred.

As Littler and Salaman argue (in Chapter 2), the changes which have occurred in Britain reflect developments in the world economy specific to a particular stage in the development of capitalism. Britain in particular, despite the benefits of North Sea oil, and Western industrial nations more generally are relatively less powerful; manufacturing industry in both traditional (e.g. shipbuilding, textiles and clothing) and modern (e.g. vehicles, electronics) sectors has increasingly been relocated in 'Third World' countries, for example, in South-East Asia or Latin America, where labour is plentiful and cheap. This new 'international division of labour' has been possible partly due to the fragmentation of work processes, making them 'suitable' for unskilled labour, and to the development of means of communication and transport. It reflects also the activities of multinational corporations which operate on a world-wide basis without allegiance to any one national economy or nation-state (though states may be expected to intervene in national economies to provide, through education and social welfare provision and through measures of economic management, conditions within which modern capitalist corporations can flourish). In Britain's case, the impact on employment of these trends, and of others such as increasing productivity in manufacturing and some service industries and the introduction of microelectronic technology, has been intensified by government economic and fiscal policies.

The most striking effect on employment has been the decline in the number employed in manufacturing industry. Between 1961 and 1981, the numbers employed in that sector (an increasing proportion of whom were in non-manual jobs) fell by 2½ million, from just over 38 per cent of the occupied population to just over 28 per cent; and the numbers have fallen further by more than half a million since 1981. The decline was perhaps especially notable in those industries which had been of greatest importance during the earlier years of industrialisation – textiles and clothing, metal manufacture, and engineering and allied activities. During the same period, employment in the service sector grew, especially in insurance, banking and finance, in education and health services, and in miscellaneous services such as catering and personal services. In the past three years, however, this growth has been halted and has been reversed as a result of the recession and cuts in public-sector employment (*Social Trends*, 1982; Department of Employment, 1983, p. 58; for a powerful commentary on these changes, see Beynon, 1983).

Secondly, associated particularly with the expansion of the service sector, there has been an absolute and relative increase in the number of women who are 'economically active'. Whereas the male labour force (employed, self-employed and registered unemployed men) in the United Kingdom fell from 16.3 million in 1961 to somewhat less than 15.7 million in 1981, the female labour force increased in the same period from 8½ million to 10 million, most of this increase occurring after 1971. As a result, women represented nearly 40 per cent of the civilian labour force at the start of the present decade, as compared with less than 35 per cent twenty years earlier. Much of this increase reflected two trends: the increased participation of married women in the labour force (nearly two-thirds of all economically active women in Great Britain in 1981 were married, and nearly six out of every ten married women were economically active outside the home); and the growth of part-time work especially for women (nearly 42 per cent of economically active women worked part-time in 1981, when less than 6 per cent of men did) (*Labour Force Survey 1981*, quoted in Equal Opportunities Commission, 1983).

Thirdly, the decline in the relative importance of manual work has continued, although it has had less effect on men's work than on women's. The numbers and proportions in all the main categories of white-collar work have grown – managers and administrators, professionals, salespersons, and (especially) clerical workers. According to Price and Bain (1983, p. 51) the proportion of employees in non-manual work was just over 30 per cent in 1948: in the next twenty years it grew to just over 41 per cent; and in the following decade to nearly half (49.2 per cent in 1979). Because of their heavy concentration in clerical work, selling and lower professional and technical occupations, however, and their under-representation in skilled manual work, women were much more likely to be in non-manual work than men. In 1981, for example, whereas some 45 per cent of all those economically active were in one of the main categories of white-collar work (Socio-Economic Groups 1–6), the proportion of women so categorised was well over half (59 per cent) and the proportion of men only just over a third (36.5 per cent) (*Census 1981*, 1983, p. 25). Thus, though manual work remains the typical lot of the male worker, male manual workers now represent a minority of the labour force as a whole.

Fourthly, in one form or another the state has become increasingly important as an employer. Employment in national and local government, the armed forces, nationalised industries, and so on totalled 26.5 per cent of all employees in 1979, over 700,000 more than in 1968, despite declining employment in many of the nationalised industries during the same period (Price and Bain, 1983, p. 52).

Fifthly, in recent years, and especially since the end of the 1970s, there has been a massive increase in unemployment. The numbers recorded as unemployed in the United Kingdom reached a million in the post-war period in 1975, 1½ million in 1980, 2 million early in 1981 and 3 million in 1983, when it represented more than 12 per cent of the labour force. The impact of unemployment has been very uneven; recorded unemployment (much women's unemployment may go unrecorded) is particularly severe for the young and those over 55 years old, for men, for manual workers generally and for unskilled manual workers especially (Department of Employment, 1983; Sinfield, 1981). It is significant that neither politicians nor academic forecasters expect the level of unemployment to change in the near future, and some suggest that it may well get a lot worse. One of the consequences of increasing unemployment has been that even greater emphasis has been placed on education and on qualifications as prerequisites for employment, in many cases in jobs where the credentials demanded bear little or no relationship to the tasks to be performed.

Finally, the size of industrial organisations has continued to increase so that private-sector economic activity is dominated by a relatively small number of large corporations, many of them multi-nationals, and a considerable proportion of them based outside the United Kingdom. The ultimate control of work has become increasingly further removed from the shop or office floor.

Clearly all these changes represent major shifts in the nature of work in our society. Paid work is more likely to involve manipulating symbols or processing people than dealing with things; it is much more likely to be providing a service than making a product; it is increasingly likely to be done by a woman rather than by a man (though there is still clear segregation between most men's and women's work) (Hakim, 1979); and whereas paid work was readily available for nearly thirty years to all who wanted it, except a small residual minority, it has now become scarce. The changing shape of paid work during the last decade has necessitated fairly radical changes in sociological approaches to the study of work. What were the predominant characteristics of employment in the early 1960s, and what was problematic about work then, are no longer an adequate agenda for research work in the 1980s.

Work: the future

Comments on the future of work are inevitably speculative. At least in the short to medium term, however, it seems likely that many of the trends outlined in the previous section will continue. As previously mentioned, high and possibly even increasing levels of unemployment are widely forecast, so that we may soon come to see the 1940s–1960s as the 'exception', a time when a fortunate conjecture of circumstances permitted successful full-time employment politics, rather than regarding three million unemployed as a temporary phenomenon which will soon go away. It is unlikely that the balance of employment in Britain will swing back towards manufacturing industry or manual work, even less likely towards male manual work in large-scale manufacturing plants. Employment in the public sector may decline as a result of privatisation and policies to cut public expenditure, but state involvement in regulating work and workers directly and indirectly shows no sign of diminishing. Temporary work, part-time work, work under short-term contracts (perhaps interspersed with periods of unemployment), work (for pay) outside the 'formal economy', home-based work (as home-workers and on a 'self-employed' basis), job sharing and households with multiple 'breadwinners' all seem likely to increase. Patterns of employment have never been as neat and uniform as the dominant images of work assumed, but they are likely to become messier, more varied and more complex. This will have implications for trade union membership and organisation; by and large unions have thrived where large workforces with relatively stable employment faced bureaucratic employers (Price and Bain, 1976). It seems likely that most women will spend nearly (or even equally) as large a proportion of their lifetimes 'gainfully occupied' as men do.

All these possibilities are overshadowed and may be significantly affected by the development and application of microelectronic technology. What the silicon 'chip' (and parallel technical developments, e.g. fibre optics) make possible is the very rapid processing of large quantities of information, its storage, retrieval and transmission, all using electronic devices which are increasingly compact, increasingly versatile, and reducing in cost all the time. Attached to electromechanical devices (as in robots), physical tasks such as handling goods or using tools can be carried out automatically. Attached to visual display units, printers, graph plotters, and so on, words, numbers and pictures can be displayed and reproduced. The storage facilities of computers make it unnecessary to keep 'hard' copies (papers, files, books, etc.) and electronic storage of such materials has the advantage that it can be available virtually simultaneously to a large number of people, in different locations and at a distance. It can also be amended, updated, sorted, rearranged and deleted without any handling of physical copy. Current developments include attempts to give robots, effectively, the senses of sight, touch and/or hearing so that they are able to cope without operator intervention with irregular and unexpected situations; and to make computers increasingly 'user-friendly', accessible to the untrained and the inexpert, including making them responsive to speech, rather than instructions or questions typed in at a keyboard.

Clearly, if the full potential of these developments were to be realised immediately, it would have enormous repercussions for the nature and organisation of work. It seems unlikely that the alarmists' worst fears (or the technological utopians' best dreams) will be realised. All our earlier experiences of technical changes would suggest that the adoption of technological innovations, which are 'available', is uneven and takes place over a considerable period of time. Indeed, technologies of clearly different 'generations' may well coexist in the same situation (for example, the situation described in Nichols and Beynon, 1977). The reasons for this are partly economic: even if the cost of the microelectronic hardware –

computers, etc. – is falling, there are still considerable costs involved in its adoption and installation, in devising appropriate programmes, retraining staff and so on; and the costs of abandoning investments in previous generations of equipment, and of compensating employees made redundant. They are also partly social and psychological, such as the resistance to innovation which derives from considerable collective and individual investment in existing systems.

Nevertheless, national and international competitive pressures alone are likely to mean that much of the potential of the 'new technology' will be realised in time, and as a result much existing paid work will become unnecessary. This is, of course, already happening. Robots weld car bodies at Longbridge and elsewhere; computers are programmed to set up type so that the skills of the compositor are no longer needed; cash points dispense banknotes without the intervention of a bank cashier; and computers and word processors now do much of the work previously done by large numbers of clerical and secretarial workers.

On an issue which clearly arouses extreme hopes and fears – the employment implications of microelectronic technology – there could be said to be two polar positions (with a range of others in between). Some argue that, as in the case of technological innovations in the past, there may be temporary dislocation, structural unemployment and hardship, but in the longer term the productivity and wealth creation made possible by the new technology will generate demands for goods and services at the moment unknown and possibly unknowable, and this demand will lead to the creation of new jobs which will absorb those who have been displaced. We can then go on much as before, though with a higher standard of living.

Others hope or fear that the changes are qualitatively different from any in the past, there is no possibility of new demands which will generate enough jobs to replace those lost due to adoption of the new technology. This could be due to a number of reasons: such demand will itself be met using microelectronics and therefore with minimal new jobs; finite world resources – and increasing competition for them – will set limits to what can be consumed in any one society like our own; human consumption of goods and services is inherently limited; and so on. The new technology will, however, allow existing levels of demand to be met with very much lower levels of employment and of human effort, so that the existing gross national product and therefore existing standards of living could easily be maintained, or increased. Here, the proponents of the view that the new technology will permanently reduce the need and opportunities for paid work divide into optimists and pessimists. For the optimists, the future holds the possibility of everyone spending a much smaller proportion of their day, their week and/or lifetime in paid work, and consequently all having greatly increased leisure *and* the means to enjoy it. The pessimists fear that the necessary changes in the social organisation of work, the (re) distribution of incomes, and so on, will not take place for such an idyllic solution to be realisable. Instead, developments will lead to a situation where a proportion have well-paid jobs requiring skills and education, another proportion may have low paid unskilled jobs which have not been or cannot be automated, and the remainder, possibly even the majority, are permanently unemployed and without the resources, both material and cultural, to utilise their 'leisure'. In such a society, the prospects of social conflict and disorder are clearly considerable, with the danger that authoritarian solutions will be adopted to meet them.

Whichever of these or other possible scenarios is more likely to be realised, what does seem likely is that the combination of the trends already discussed with the developments made possible by the new technology will alter the meaning and significance of work, and especially of employment, very considerably. Already, as Kumar's contribution to this volume indicates, there is advocacy of a reduction in emphasis on the Protestant work ethic, and of a search for and recognition of other sources of social status, of structure and purpose in life, and of other social contacts outside the home than are provided by an occupation. As the contributions to this volume by Pahl and by Roberts, Noble and Duggan show, there are some signs of 'alternative' life-styles, in which employment plays a much smaller part. Clearly, there will be no shortage of questions and problems for researchers interested in the sociology of work – broadly defined – even if they are unlikely to be the same ones as have so far attracted most attention.

Whether or not current theoretical perspectives will prove appropriate for the study and analysis of the new situations must also be uncertain. It is, however, already clear that the focus on the capitalist labour process, which has done so much to give a fresh impetus to the sociology of work, has limitations. These arise, especially with regard to Braverman's formulation, from the assertions within it as to the inherent tendencies of the labour process to deskill work leading to an increasingly unskilled, powerless and alienated workforce dominated by capital. This view has justifiably been criticised as inadequate on both theoretical and empirical grounds: it attributes an omniscience and omnipotence to capitalists or to a management which is in any case far from monolithic, as Chapter 7 above shows; and it denies the possibility of any effective opposition by workers, thus reinforcing a highly deterministic view of the course of social development. Empirical, especially historical, studies have shown that there were considerable variations in the nature of the labour process in the past, that the developments have been equally varied, and that the outcome in the case of any particular industry or enterprise has been the result, at least in part, of the actions and interactions of specific managements and sets of workers, constrained by particular historical circumstances (see the contributions to Wood, 1982 and also Chapter 9 above). Once such a more varied set of possibilities is recognised, then some of the approaches and research which predated the focus on the labour process, and may have appeared to be superseded by it, become of relevance to help account for such variation – for example, the concerns with orientations to work, with the influence of technology on organisations, with social relations within management, and between workers, and with payment systems. The end result should be a sociology of work which is more coherent and more adequate. Such a sociology of work must also be open to the possibility that in the future work within an employment relationship may be less important as a form of work, and indeed less central to an understanding of society in general, than it has rightly been seen to be for the past 150 years. In any case, the social relations and social processes which make such work possible, and work outside the 'formal' economy and outside employment of any sort, must continue to be regarded as worthy of the sort of attention which they have only received comparatively recently.

Question
1. (a) *Briefly define and discuss the concept of work.*
                                                                    (5 marks)
    (b) *Summarise recent changes in the social organisation of work,
    and discuss the implications of these changes for the future.*
                                                                    (20 marks)

51 Max Weber: The Characteristics of Bureaucray

Weber's ideal type of bureaucracy has often been considered to capture the essence of modern organisation. Even more than that, his description of the rule-governed, centrally-directed organisation seems to embody the rational spirit of modernism itself. The strength of his organisational analysis is partly in that it can plausibly be applied to the immense bureaucracies that have emerged in the Eastern European socialist societies as well as those of capitalist societies.

In contrast to Weber, Marxists argue that the major repressive features of capitalist organisation – particularly business organisation – are the product of capitalism itself and will only be removed with the abolition of that system. We examine one element in this position in the reading following this one and look at an alternative to capitalist control – workers' control – in the reading after that.

Reading 51 From Max Weber, 'Bureaucracy' in H. H. Gerth and C. Wright Mills *eds., From Max Weber* (Routledge and Kegan Paul, 1948), pp. 196–8.

Modern officialdom functions in the following specific manner:
I. There is the principle of fixed and official jurisdictional areas, which are generally ordered by rules, that is, by laws or administrative regulations.
1. The regular activities required for the purpose of the bureaucratically governed structure are distributed in a fixed way as official duties.
2. The authority to give the commands required for the discharge of these duties is distributed in a stable way and is strictly delimited by rules concerning the coercive means, physical,

sacerdotal, or otherwise, which may be placed at the disposal of officials.

3. Methodical provision is made for the regular and continuous fulfilment of these duties and for the execution of the corresponding rights; only persons who have the generally regulated qualifications to serve are employed.

In public and lawful government these three elements constitute 'bureaucratic authority.' In private economic domination, they constitute bureaucratic 'management.' Bureaucracy, thus understood, is fully developed in political and ecclesiastical communities only in the modern state, and, in the private economy, only in the most advanced institutions of capitalism. Permanent and public office authority, with fixed jurisdiction, is not the historical rule but rather the exception. This is so even in large political structures such as those of the ancient Orient, the Germanic and Mongolian empires of conquest, or of many feudal structures of state. In all these cases, the ruler executes the most important measures through personal trustees, table-companions, or court-servants. Their commissions and authority are not precisely delimited and are temporarily called into being for each case.

II. The principles of office hierarchy and of levels of graded authority mean a firmly ordered system of super- and subordination in which there is a supervision of the lower offices by the higher ones. Such a system offers the governed the possibility of appealing the decision of a lower office to its higher authority, in a definitely regulated manner. With the full development of the bureaucratic type, the office hierarchy is monocratically organised. The principle of hierarchical office authority is found in all bureaucratic structures: in state and ecclesiastical structures as well as in large party organisations and private enterprises. It does not matter for the character of bureaucracy whether its authority is called 'private' or 'public'.

When the principle of jurisdictional 'competency' is fully carried through, hierarchical subordination – at least in public office – does not mean that the 'higher' authority is simply authorised to take over the business of the 'lower'. Indeed, the opposite is the rule. Once established and having fulfilled its task, an office tends to continue in existence and be held by another incumbent.

III. The management of the modern office is based upon written documents ('the files'), which are preserved in their original or draught form. There is, therefore, a staff of subaltern officials and scribes of all sorts. The body of officials actively engaged in a 'public' office, along with the respective apparatus of material implements and the files, make up a 'bureau.' In private enterprise, 'the bureau' is often called 'the office.'

In principle, the modern organisation of the civil service separates the bureau from the private domicile of the official, and, in general, bureaucracy segregates official activity as something distinct from the sphere of private life. Public monies and equipment are divorced from the private property of the official. This condition is everywhere the product of a long development. Nowadays, it is found in public as well as in private enterprises; in the latter, the principle extends even to the leading entrepreneur. In principle, the executive office is separated from the household, business from private correspondence, and business assets from private fortunes. The more consistently the modern type of business management has been carried through the more are these separations the case. The beginnings of this process are to be found as early as the Middle Ages.

It is the peculiarity of the modern entrepreneur that he conducts himself as the 'first official' of his enterprise, in the very same way in which the ruler of a specifically modern bureaucratic state spoke of himself as 'the first servant' of the state. The idea that the bureau activities of the state are intrinsically different in character from the management of private economic offices is a continental European notion and, by way of contrast, is totally foreign to the American way.

IV. Office management, at least all specialised office management – and such management is distinctly modern – usually presupposes thorough and expert training. This increasingly holds for the modern executive and employee of private enterprises, in the same manner as it holds for the state official.

V. When the office is fully developed, official activity demands the full working capacity of the official, irrespective of the fact that his obligatory time in the bureau may be firmly delimited. In the normal case, this is only the product of a long development, in the public as well as in the private office. Formerly, in all cases, the normal state of affairs was reversed: official business was discharged as a secondary activity.

VI. The management of the office follows general rules, which are more or less stable, more or less exhaustive, and which can be learned. Knowledge of these rules represents a special technical learning which the officials possess. It involves jurisprudence, or administrative or business management.

The reduction of modern office management to rules is deeply embedded in its very nature. The theory of modern public administration, for instance, assumes that the authority to order certain matters by decree – which has been legally granted to public authorities – does not entitle the bureau to regulate the matter by commands given for each case, but only to regulate the matter abstractly. This stands in extreme contrast to the regulation of all relationships through individual privileges and bestowals of favor, which is absolutely dominant in patrimonialism, at least in so far as such relationships are not fixed by sacred tradition.

Question

1. *(a) What does Max Weber mean by bureaucracy?*

(5 marks)

(b) Critically consider the advantages and disadvantages of bureaucratic organisation.

(20 marks)

(You will need to use additional material to answer this question).

52 Stephen Wood: Braverman's 'Deskilling Thesis': The Control of Labour under Capitalism

Harry Braverman's *Labour and Monopoly Capital* has had immense influence on the analysis of the organisation and control of work under capitalism. In this book, he presents his thesis that work under capitalism has deliberately been made less skilful and that control over production has been increasingly taken out of the hands of the workers. Here, Stephen Wood's summary of Braverman's thesis and various critiques of it are given. Many responses to Braverman's work have often been highly worthwhile in their own right. However, if the 'deskilling' debate has progressed beyond Braverman's initial propositions, the interest and controversy he has raised indicate the originality of his insight.

Braverman's main target is not Weber but the American architect of scientific management, F. W. Taylor. Nevertheless, in

Braverman's few references to Weber, it is clear that he opposes the same point in both their work: the assumption that 'modern' work organisation is determined by considerations of efficiency rather than by the need of capitalists to control and exploit labour. Taylorism – roughly what Weber refers to as bureaucracy – was based on the view that the labour process could be made more efficient by 'rationalising' it into smaller and smaller parts which the individual worker would perform as quickly as constant repetition allowed. In contradiction, Braverman argued that Taylorism destroyed craft-skills and deskilled the work process, primarily to enable capitalist management effectively to gain control over workers. It is this thesis, and comments on it, that Stephen Wood reviews below.

It should be noted that Braverman applied his deskilling thesis not only to manual workers but also to white collar and the majority of professional employees as well. He also saw these 'workers' as losing autonomy and flexibility at work. Braverman considers routine office work as essentially the same as manual work, for example.

He writes of the computer operator:

The computer operator runs the computer in accordance with a set of rigid and specific instructions set down for each routine. The training and education required for this job may perhaps best be estimated from the pay scales, which in the case of a Class A operator are on the level of the craftsman in the factory, and for Class C operators on about the level of the factory operative.
(Braverman, *Labour and Monopoly Capital*, Monthly Review Press, 1974).

Two criticisms of Braverman – and Wood gives several more – are that, on the one hand, he overestimates the conscious planning of capitalists to control labour by means of the organisation of work and that, on the other, he does not consider the conscious opposition of labour to Taylorism and kindred tendencies. However, what he clearly does do is raise awareness of the 'threat' of organisational control and so perhaps improves the possibilities that alternative organisational forms will be pursued (see Reading 53).

Reading 52 From Stephen Wood, 'Work Organisation' in Rosemary Deem and Graeme Salaman *eds.*, *Work, Culture and Society* (Open University Press, 1985), pp. 77–84.

Introduction

Discussions in British sociology of work organisations have in the past ten years been dominated by the labour process debate. The expression, the labour process, refers simultaneously to a conception of the nature and origins of work within capitalism, and a theoretical tradition which explains this sort of work. Both derive, ultimately, from Marx and, more recently, Braverman.

The emphasis in Marx was on the development of manufacturing; with the increasing use of machines, capitalism developed from handicraft production to what he called machinofacture. Braverman's *Labor and Monopoly Capital* (1974) has followed this development; he stresses that, especially with the advent of monopoly capitalism and large-scale industrial organisation, capitalism involves a complete subordination of labour to capital. In this process all possibilities of initiative, direction and control are wrested from the worker. Whereas the old style artisans/craftsmen were responsible for a large part of their work, including at least some part in the design of the product and the production process, capitalists scientifically regulate all production through increasingly hierarchical management control.

As Brown (1984, p. 269) says, 'What was important about his [Braverman's] approach . . . is that within a coherent theoretical framework it directed attention to a variety of issues and topics which had previously been seen as largely unrelated'; and central to this, he continues, 'are the processes of production and reproduction of labour itself'. For example, there is a need to ask, 'where does the labour force come from? . . . How are workers socialised?' The broader issues are dealt with in Chapter Three. The emphasis in this chapter will be primarily on the questions of skill and control.

The four issues which will *not* be explored in great depth here are: worker resistance; the question of the similarity between capitalist and socialist labour processes; the location of changes within the labour process and the intensification of work within the context of other forms of rationalisation and internationalisation of the economy; and finally, the relationship between employment and domestic labour.

403

This chapter is concerned with the design and nature of jobs. With the development of mass production methods and systematic managerial control in the twentieth century, have jobs increasingly become devoid of skill and intrinsic meaning? If so, why? Does this reflect changing technology, or is it, as Braverman suggests, more a reflection of a scientific management inherent to the capitalist enterprise? If there is a trend towards deskilled jobs, is it inevitable? What of counter tendencies, or attempts to reverse the trend through the use of humanistic methods largely derived from social sciences?

Section one introduces Braverman's deskilling thesis, in which emphasis is placed on the specificity of the capitalist labour process and the importance of Taylorism in it. This is followed by a section on skill, which ends with a brief discussion of the problems involved in assessing the changing trend in jobs. Section three discusses the role of technology and the extent to which jobs reflect it. Section four looks at the question of alternatives to scientific management and attempts to 'humanise' work.

A major concern of this chapter is to introduce the readers to some of the methodological and empirical complexities involved in the development of work organisation. Attention will focus mainly on factory work, partly because as we saw in Chapter One it is treated as the stereotype of all work, but also because of its centrality in both economy and past writings about it and in the labour process.

The deskilling thesis

We have seen in previous chapters the centrality accorded, in much recent discussion on work organisation, to the domination of capital and the need for control. There has been what P. Thompson (1984) calls a rediscovery of the labour process and Garnsey (1984), a rediscovery of division of labour. Central to these rediscoveries, as both authors note, is Braverman's work which is an attempt to *renew* Marx's theory of the labour process and apply it to subsequent historical development, taking a fresh look at skills, technology and work organisation. The argument is that it is the logic of capitalist accumulation, and not the imperatives of technology, which dictate work organisation. There is, within this Marxist perspective, a fundamental conflict between workers and capitalists, and this, coupled with the economic efficiency of specialisation, dictates that capital, through the process of management, eliminates the scope for workers' control or discretion for the individual worker. The importance of the notion of a labour process is, as Garnsey (1984, p. 38) says, that it provides a more direct focus on the division of labour itself in contrast with analyses which treat the 'prevailing state of technology' as given. As Garnsey also stresses, Braverman directs attention away from a technological determinist interpretation of Marx, arguing 'that the capital intensive deskilling and labour displacing features of modern industrial technology are to be accounted for with reference to the structure of constraints and incentives created by the property relations of capitalism'. As such Braverman, and other recent followers of Marx, 'analyse division of labour as the outcome of a given distribution of power, they reject the premise that technology is neutral, and inquire into the ways in which the direction of technological development has served specific interests' (Garnsey, 1984 pp. 38–40).

Deskilling and Taylor's scientific management

Central to Braverman's thesis is the importance of managerial control – the merciless directions from the control room (Kamata, 1982, p. 200) – rather than technology. On the deskilling process F. W. Taylor's famous work *Scientific Management*, first published in 1912, emphasised the need for systematic study and the planning of work. His central concept was the distinction between conception and execution, between designing tasks and carrying them out. Taylor argued that professional managers should take full responsibility for conception, thus: 'The art of management is knowing exactly what you want men to do, and then seeing that they do it in the best and cheapest way' (see 1947 edn., p. 21).

Taylor's proposal for scientific management involved three important tasks:

1. the development of a science for each element of a man's work, which replaces the old rule-of-thumb method;
2. the scientific selection and training and development of workmen;
3. the co-operation with the men so as to ensure that all of the work is being done in accordance with the principles of the science which has been developed.

Taylor contrasted this proposal with existing styles of management which were either highly authoritarian (the workers being driven or coerced by their bosses) or *laissez-faire* (the worker being 'left to his own devices'). He argued that most experienced and enlightened managers were adopting the *laissez-faire* approach and, by so doing, were leaving the task of management to the workers. They were thus placing 'before their workmen the problem of doing the work in the best and most economical way'. Under this system success depends almost entirely upon getting the 'initiative of the workmen', and this is attempted by incentives. It was management by incentive in as much as management was through the payment system; to Taylor it was management by neglect. As Taylor says (1947, p. 62), 'Under the management of "initiative and incentive" practically the whole problem is "up to the workman".' By contrast, under scientific management, management takes on new, and previously neglected duties such that 'fully one-half of the problem is up to the management' (Taylor, 1947, p. 38).

> The management must take over and perform much of the work which is now left to the men; almost every act of the workman should be preceded by one or more preparatory acts of the management which enable him to do his work better and quicker than he otherwise could. And each man should daily be taught by and receive the most friendly help from those who are over him, instead of being, at the one extreme driven or coerced by his bosses, and at the other left to his own unaided devices. (Taylor, 1947, p. 26)

The significance of Taylor for Braverman is that he was the first management theorist to acknowledge the necessity of management control. Taylor outlined the theoretical justification and the practical means whereby this process could be set in motion: as such, according to Braverman, Taylorism is 'the explicit verbalisation of the capitalist mode of production'. Braverman takes the core of Taylorism to be his usage of the distinction between conception and execution. Applying this in practice would divorce mental from manual work and would reduce the jobs of the mass of workers, including what are termed white-collar workers, to degrading tasks lacking any responsibility, knowledge or interest. The degradation to which Braverman refers can be seen to encompass a number of processes:

1. a process whereby the shop-floor worker loses the right to design and plan work;
2. the fragmentation of work into meaningless segments;
3. the redistribution of tasks amongst unskilled and semi-skilled labour, associated with labour cheapening;
4. the transformation of work organisation from the craft system to modern, Taylorite forms of labour control.

Technology, for Braverman, is less important than the growth of managerial control: for mechanisation goes hand in hand with the advance in Taylorism, which is concerned with and appropriate to any level of technology. As P. Thompson (1984) implies, this is seen by Braverman as one of Taylorism's great strengths. It has increasingly pervaded work organisation in the twentieth century, and attempts to introduce alternatives to it – for example, through the application of social science such as the human relations theory developed since the 1930s (to be discussed in section four) – are significant, in Braverman's thesis, only in so far as they 'habituate' workers to the dictates of Taylorist systems. There is thus a big gulf between the rhetoric and the reality of modern 'human relations' whose significance is essentially ideological: 'Taylorism dominates the world of production; the practitioners of "human relations" . . . are the maintenance crew for the human machinery' (Braverman, 1974, p. 87).

The deskilling debate

Braverman's work has been subjected to a great deal of examination, much of it critical (for full details of this, see Thompson, 1984; Wood, 1982). Central to it is Braverman's self-imposed limitation to what he terms the objective aspects of capitalist development. This, as Thompson (1984) notes, amounts to a 'deliberate exclusion of the dimension of class struggle and consciousness', or as Braverman puts it, 'the modern working class on the level of its consciousness, organisation and activities'. Accordingly, Braverman (1974, pp. 26–7) claims that his argument is 'about the working class as a class *in itself*, not as class *for itself*'. This has attracted the criticism that in so following this procedure he neglected the role of class struggle in history, and its manifestation in industrial conflict. There are at least three possible implications one can draw from this:

1. Braverman's work needs to be extended to take account of the consciousness of the working class and its struggle against the dictates of capitalism;
2. when developing their control strategies, especially with the increasing unionisation of workers in the twentieth century, managements have to take account of potential worker resistance;
3. work organisation is partly the outcome of struggle between capital and labour, and subjective and ideological assumptions, for example about gender, also influence it.

Whilst it may be misleading in certain cases to identify an author too rigidly with a particular one of the above arguments, it is possible to suggest authors to illustrate each type. Zimbalest (1979), introducing a set of interesting cases on the labour process, is illustrative of the first. He defends Braverman on two counts: first, that where workers have resisted they have not been able effectively to limit managerial control, and second, that Braverman is talking about a long-term tendency.

Both Friedman (1977) and Edwards (1979), who emphasise the importance of resistance by workers, for example to Taylorism, in relation to *managerial* behaviour illustrate the second of arguments. In the twentieth century, managements have had to come to terms with resistance, especially in times of full employment. As a result, they have had to adopt more liberal methods than Taylorism: what Friedman terms 'responsible autonomy' strategies. Methods such as the gang system, human relations, job re-design, are all treated by Friedman as genuine alternatives to Taylorist methods, or 'direct control' strategies, as he prefers to call them. In certain circumstances management has to come to terms with human needs and potential recalcitrance of workers, by building real autonomy and discretion into jobs or by allowing groups of workers to run themselves. This contrasts with Braverman's position, according to which such methods merely represent an alternative *style* of management rather than a genuine change in the position of the worker. For Friedman, the collective organised strength of work groups can force management to adopt strategies other than direct control, or Taylorism.

The third of the three implications listed above points to the omniscient, almostly overtly conspiratorial, model of management in Braverman's work, in which he presents the reorganisation of the labour process as the outcome of a conscious design rather than as the product of the struggle of contending groups (Zeitlin, 1979; Cressey and McInnes, 1980; Littler, 1982; Wood, 1982). While it may be necessary to have hierarchical modes of management and specialised divisions of labour, strategic groups of workers often play a crucial role in the determination of the structure of these hierarchies and in the division of labour. Moreover, the struggle is not simply a battle between autonomous and free-floating policies of management and workers, for these policies themselves are forged out of the changing technological and market opportunities available to enterprises.

Any solutions to management's problem of control are, in this view, temporary and precarious. Management is not omniscient, nor does it have an absolute prerogative over the design and conception of work. A minimum of consent and co-operation has to be gained for management's plans and rights, and this need is rooted in the collective nature of the labour process. Even consent based on the 'dull compulsion' of the labour market and the coercion of economic necessity is necessarily precarious and has to be supported by ideologies concerning the importance of employment and economic efficiency. Furthermore, management may not acord absolute primacy to the problem of control. Even within Braverman's terms, control is for profit, and not necessarily for its own sake. This latter point goes beyond Friedman's argument that employers may seek to avoid conflict with highly organised work-forces, and cede control over task performance, provided the work group attains a minimum level of productive efficiency. The maximisation of productive efficiency cannot be reduced to labour intensification. Goods are produced for sale on the market, and profitable production presupposes past investment decisions that secure the 'right mix' of production processes. Very often the labour process debate takes place in the vacuum of the shop floor, and can fall prey to a kind of thinking which values above all else production for production's sake. But the structure of the market can limit the kind of labour process used, and, on the other hand, the market itself is not totally independent of managerial initiatives. For example, in the early 1980s British car components manufacturers attempted to lift this market constraint by reducing their product range and securing access to foreign markets, thereby creating the conditions for volume production.

In appraising Braverman we should focus not so much on what he neglects, as on his treatment of what he does deal with; as P. Thompson shows, Braverman acknowledges opposition to Taylorism, but treats it as having little or no significance or effect. Furthermore, Braverman makes certain assumptions about working-class consciousness and organisation that can be questioned: essentially, that workers' aims are purely to secure economistic objectives such as high wages and job security, aims which mirror the dominant profit motive of capitalists.

We might also question Braverman's particular use of Taylorism. At the fundamental level his treatment of it as expressing the logic of capitalism and as providing an adequate language with which to describe the objective side of the development of the capitalist enterprise can be challenged. Certainly Braverman relies very heavily on Taylor's own account of scientific management when outlining the development of the capitalist labour process: he does not examine in sufficient depth actual work situations or conscious applications of Taylorite principles, and consequently relies excessively on the theorisation offered by management theorists or organisations. At least four consequences follow from this. First, Braverman does not pay sufficient attention to the problems attached to the implementation of Taylorism. Second, he ignores the resistance that some workers and managers have offered to inhibit its introduction or transform its effects. Third, he does not examine empirically the effects of Taylorism in practice. Fourth, human relations and other forms of management cannot, by definition and not by analysis, be genuine options – for Taylorism is *the* labour process of capitalism.

There is also the problem of Braverman's conception of Taylorism. For example, Taylor (1947) was conscious, and increasingly so, of the problem of co-operation and gaining consent, legitimacy and shared understandings: 'Without cooperation there is no scientific management', he wrote. He struggled to arrive at an answer, and to convince managers of the need for a change in their attitude. This 'mental revolution', as he called it, would involve treating workers with care and consideration as opposed to the more normal tyrannical approach. Ultimately Taylor fell back on the authority of science to legitimise his ideas and management's role.

Rather than assuming the supremacy of Taylorism, it is more useful to start from an appreciation of the limits of, constraints upon, and contradictions within scientific management. For example, an individualised work organisation may not always be feasible. It is perhaps not surprising that the Tavistock Institute's attempt to develop an alternative to Taylorism's socio-technical theory (to be discussed later) – with an emphasis on autonomous groups without supervisors and flexible working arrangements – began in coal mining (Trist and Bamford, 1951) and not manufacturing. More generally, we should be aware of the variety of labour processes which exist. In some cases, it may not be technically or economically possible to specify closely all the tasks to be performed, especially in small batch production.

As was stated at the beginning of the chapter, a full treatment of all issues is beyond the scope of the present context. Having concentrated on Braverman's highlighting of Taylorism at the expense of technology, we shall now concentrate on three problematic features of the deskilling thesis: the content of skill, the role of technology and the nature of work humanisation.

Question

1. (a) What is Braverman's 'deskilling thesis'?

(5 marks)

(b) Discuss its strengths and weaknesses.

(20 marks)

53 John Cunningham: The Workers' Co-operative Movement: A Third Way?

There are alternative forms of industrial organisation to the corporations of public and private enterprise. The bureaucratic principles described by Weber (Reading 51), applied by Taylor, and so sharply criticised by Braverman (Reading 52) are not eternal truths. The alternative principles of equality and democracy have been applied economically as well as politically. As with all basic principles the *degree* to which they have been implemented varies greatly with individual cases.

In understanding the degree to which an organisation is more or less egalitarian or democratic, it helps to distinguish between worker participation and worker control. Participation usually involves partial involvement by workers in the running of an enterprise, decisive power being left in the hands of ownership and management. Germany and Sweden are far ahead of Britain in establishing participatory institutions in industry. Workers' control means that the workers run the enterprise, either directly or by representatives. During the nineteen seventies there were over 100 factory occupations by workers in Britain, usually to prevent or protest closure, some of which resulted in workers' co-operatives being formed. The best known of these was at the Norton Villiers Triumph (NVT) motorbike factory at Meriden which survived for several years against tough Japanese competition. In fact, a problem for many workers' co-operatives has been that they have been founded in weakness rather than strength. Further, some Marxists have argued, with Mandel, that 'the fundamental principle underlying self-management . . . is unrealisable in an economy which allows the survival of competition . . . in the present economic system, a whole series of decisions are inevitably taken at higher levels than management'.

Nevertheless, in the nineteen eighties there has been something of a flowering of workers' co-operatives. The following article is merely descriptive and not at all sociological. However, it provides the necessary empirical prompts for some interesting sociological questions. Most important is to contrast co-operative working with working in a hierarchical context. Done imaginatively, this exercise could change your life! The article does not explore the different reasons of the political parties for supporting the co-operative movement, though this matter certainly merits consideration. Does the movement betoken a turn to egalitarian, democratic and organic principles of organisation, more appropriate, perhaps, to our times? Or is it trifling compared to the enormous control, power and wealth of capital? In any case, Mandel's comment of 1975 now seems unduly pessimistic. The mood of the late eighties seems to be to give it a try.

Reading 53 From John Cunningham, 'Why Workers' Co-op Movement Wins New Political Friends' in *The Guardian*, 6 November 1986, p. 24.

Will workers' co-operatives grow into a third sector of the economy – a junior partner alongside public and private enterprise – as its devotees hope? This week, senior Conservative and Labour politicians are making pledges of support to a tiny but growing movement which they hope will help vindicate their different employment policies.

At a conference in Birmingham on Saturday, a campaign called Co-ops for Labour is being launched, parallel in intent, but obviously much smaller in scale, with the effort made by the unions to promote a Labour victory in 1983. However, the gathering will be just as much about Labour's commitment to worker co-ops.

Amid much razzamatazz, the shadow trade and industry spokesman, John Smith, is expected to confirm that three initial thrusts of the next Labour government's economic policy will be re-nationalisation, – starting with British Telecom; a National Enterprise Board; and a big push to fund and foster more co-ops.

No figures will be mentioned, but then there weren't any either when, for the Tories, Kenneth Clarke, Paymaster General, confirmed that worker co-ops were by no means outside his party's thinking. Indeed, such experiments were to be encouraged because they generated jobs, and operated without management–shop floor barriers.

So long as co-ops raised their capital in the City, without relying on central or local government subsidy, they had a place in capitalist Britain.

If co-operatives had a bad name, that was due to Tony Benn, who had been responsible as Industry Minister, Clarke said in a speech at Manchester University. He was out to score points, for the shadows of the ill-fated Scottish Daily News and the Meriden motorbike co-ops no longer haunt the movement. It has out-grown its other image, too, of co-ops being run by the muesli and sandals brigade, of the mid-70s.

In fact, it is really since 1980 that growth has been dramatic, paralleling the recession. There are said to be some 1,200 co-ops. But an authoritative survey by Keith Jeffries of the Open University located 900, of which 750 had started in the last six years. 1984 and 85 were spectacular years, with 210 and 190 new ventures starting.

The new breed of co-ops have little to do now with alternative life-styles, or union-run take-overs of bankrupt manufacturers. It is true that about 15 per cent of new starts arise out of redundancies or closures of existing factories, but the big majority, 67 per cent, the OU survey shows, start from individuals wanting to get together on a new project.

They tend to cluster in particular sectors. Those with between 60 and 80 co-ops are building, entertainment (everything from music to video); food retailing (which has had the highest number of failures at 50 per cent) and printing. An average co-op has four workers and an annual turnover of £80,000. Keith Jeffries guesses that the total turnover of the sector is £150 million.

Some massive expectations surround what is proving to be a small, fragmented but valuable method of job creation. Aside from the hopes of the political heavyweights, David Ralley, of Industrial Common Ownership Finance, the fund which has loaned about £1 million of local and central government money to co-ops, has an optimistic target of co-ops eventually accounting for 5 per cent of the economy.

But there is a fundamental question, still unanswered, ten years after the Industrial Common Ownership Act, a Labour measure, paved the way for co-ops. 'How much of a worker co-op sector do we want?', asks Peter Clarke, research officer of the Co-operative Party.

There are several other unresolved matters. While there was broad political support for the ICO Act, subsequent practice has been for Tory ministers to give grudging shoe-string financial support. To supplement this, about 70 local co-operative development associations have been set up, many by Labour councils, to help good ideas turn into viable co-ops.

Those involved have developed their own ethos; the full and part-time workers, and the two organisations – the Network of CDAs, and the Industrial Common Ownership Movement – are politically independent, there to help any group which wants to start up, whether it is in catering or transport. There can be tension between the need to preserve this independence, and the political flavour of a local authority providing funds for projects.

There is also the matter of a larger political tie-in. Co-ops for

Labour is being presented as a pre-election pact, mutually benefiting movement and party. Not all members of worker co-ops vote Labour, of course. The Alliance claims some support among them and, after Kenneth Clarke's initial foray, the Tories will probably firm up some pre-election commitments.

Even the movement's links with its most natural ideological ally – the Co-operative Party – are not always unfraught. The party, which sponsors seven MPs, took the worker co-ops under its wing, by starting a national network of CDAs, and keeping them going, because, as Peter Clarke says, 'our retail masters wanted it.'

The relationship has not always been smooth, and the Co-op Party, according to Peter Clarke, defines its role to the movement thus: 'We are a campaign resource for them. But there's been this problem: do they want to be independent? ICOM has an all-party policy group and wants to retain its independence.'

There is a significant SDP presence on ICOM, Clarke acknowledges. It might seem that the co-operators have an embarrassment of political friends. Clarke points out that, as well as the Co-operative MPs, they have seven peers, and 400 local councillors. 'And this year, the opportunity to create co-ops for Labour has arisen.' He is involved in that, too.

If worker co-ops and Labour signal on Saturday that they can do business, then both ought to recognise that only a small deal is involved. After all, Tony Benn was not alone on the Left in being unrealistic in his expectations.

The first Labour working party on the issue was chaired by Leslie Huckfield, who put forward the notion that any factory in which at least 51 per cent of the workforce voted for a workers' co-op should be turned into one.

That proposal did more harm than good. The present reality is that – and estimates vary considerably – perhaps 10,000 people work in co-ops; and that even a government investment of £100 millions would do very little to turn the country into a nation of co-operators.

Questions

1. (a) *Discuss with examples the concept of workers' participation.*

(5 marks)

(b) *Is workers' participation possible under capitalism?*

(10 marks)

2. *Is democracy in organisations possible?*

(25 marks)

54 Tom Keenoy: Strikes as an 'Ordinary' Part of the Industrial Bargaining Process

Throughout his book, *Invitation to Industrial Relations*, Tom Keenoy seeks to lay to rest the 'myth' of trade unions and shop-stewards as industrial spoilers. He argues that in the past 25 years every symptom of Britain's industrial malaise has been blamed on the unions – 'low productivity, reluctance to accept new technology, strikes, balance of payment deficits, poor competitiveness, low morale, unemployment, or whatever'. It is the issue of strikes that is examined in this extract. Elsewhere in his book, Keenoy establishes key statistical facts – that the British strike record is not 'bad' in comparison with other countries and that far more 'working' days are lost through both absenteeism and unemployment than strikes. Here he presents the case that, in general, strikes are a normal part of the industrial bargaining process even though their incidence will vary from year to year with circumstances.

Keenoy suggests that the industrial bargaining process (concerning wage and working conditions) is usually seen as involving three major stages: preparation, negotiation and settlement. The brief opening section in the reading argues that the strike may be used in the bargaining process at any time up to settlement.

The second section of the reading suggests that employers and government, as well as employees, can and do 'cause strikes'. This section, the 'meat' of the reading, carries further the argument that strikes should not be seen in terms of what Keenoy scathingly refers to as the 'red moles and blue meanies' model. Rather they should be seen in terms of the interests of those involved and within the social, political and economic contexts in which they are generated.

Reading 54 From Tom Keenoy, *Invitation to Industrial Relations* (Basil Blackwell, 1985), pp. 127–8, 181–5.

Going on strike is one of the many tactics available to the two sides in their collective bargaining. It can occur at various points in the overall process. Sometimes a strike is necessary in order to persuade management to *start* bargaining. We frequently read that management refuse to open negotiations until the strike is called off – what we are not told is that it was management's refusal to negotiate in the first place which led to the strike. Everyone goes back to work having convinced management that they were serious about whatever issue is in dispute; or, in other instances, the strike is a result of management making what are deemed to be totally unacceptable proposals. Other times a strike may occur during the negotiations at that point where the term 'deadlock' is used to describe the state of play. This may result from the two sides making insufficient progress and the union negotiators decide to call a strike just to prove to the other side that they are serious about their demands. On yet other occasions there is too big a gap between the fall-back position of the two sides and neither side is prepared to make any further concessions. In this situation it may take a strike to convince one side or the other that their position is unrealistic. What is common to all these strikes is that they are an integral element of the bargaining process – their function is to persuade one of the two sides to revise their expectations. Thus, even when a strike is taking place, the process of bargaining has not actually stopped: both sides have merely retreated to prepared positions from which they not only shout at each other – as Messrs Scargill and McGregor ably demonstrated – but attempt, through various offers and counter-offers, to persuade the other side to resume the employment relationship. Collective bargaining – in that it *necessarily* involves the actors in exercising their bargaining power – could not take place unless both sides are 'free', on occasion, to fully express that power . . .

The widespread belief that those who call a strike are also the cause of strikes has become an almost unquestioned truism. It is understandable but deeply misleading, for it completely neglects the fact that strikes occur in the context of an employment relationship and, as such, can only be understood as a product of that relationship. This does not mean trade unions and shop stewards do not call for strike action, but they do so in response to something which the employer has or has not done. Technically, this could be taken to mean that virtually all strikes are caused by employers since they are formally in control of the terms and conditions of employment: it is they who decide whether changes to the existing practices will be made. However, this is to walk down exactly the same blind alley as those who insist all strikes are caused by trade unions or shop stewards.

Initially, it seems useful to briefly reiterate some of the analytical points made earlier. The key actors – employers, employees and governments – have their own particular interests, and their own frames of reference in which they come to decisions about what action they will take. They calculate the consequences of such decision and, on occasion, are aware that one of the possible consequences will be conflict of some kind. This may be resolved through bargaining or it may produce overt conflict in the form of a strike. Any one of our actors can miscalculate and face unwanted but, perhaps, unavoidable strike. During pay negotiations an employer, in making the 'final' offer, could underestimate the determination of the employees to insist upon more. But the 'final' offer has been publicly declared and it would be unwise to revise it too quickly because this might lead the employees to hold out for an even greater increase. Trade union officials can argue themselves into similar corners either by raising the expectations of employees to an unrealistic level or by misjudging the real position of the employer. But not all circumstances involve miscalculations or errors of judgement.

Some strikes occur over what are called 'perishable' issues. This refers to those situations where, if the employees do not take immediate action, they will lose the issue by default. For example, if an employee or a shop steward is sacked and escorted off the premises, sometimes the only way to secure their reinstatement is to take immediate strike action. This only occurs when the employees regard the dismissal as victimisation or grossly unwarranted. To take such cases to an industrial tribunal is by no means a guaranteed route to reinstatement. Even if the case is won, employers sometimes refuse to reconsider such decisions – which may have been made in the heat of the moment. Employees may respond in a similar frame of mind and down tools until the decision is reversed.

418

Similar action is often thought necessary when – as has been known to occur in car-assembly plants – management increase the speed at which the assembly line is moving without prior consultation. Such action may be in contravention of an existing agreement on line speeds and, once discovered, is likely to produce an instant protest strike in order to reverse the decision. Such covert changes in the production process not only produce an outraged reaction but also do little to breed confidence and trust in the employer–employee relationship. Many of the instant strikes over piecework prices are also of this perishable and almost bloodless variety.

Establishing clear-cut proof of management or the employer deliberately provoking a strike is by no means easy. No employer would admit to such seemingly irresponsible behaviour and, in terms of public opinion, it is clearly not in the employers' interest to be seen as the obvious cause of a strike. Despite this, there is, occasionally, very powerful circumstantial evidence to suggest that, even if employers do not actively instigate a strike, they sometimes do very little to discourage strike action. In a now famous analysis of strikes in the motor-car industry in the 1950s and 1960s it was demonstrated that, for the employers, strikes function as a means of suspending production at times when there were adequate stocks to supply the market demand. Analysis of the strike patterns showed that the greatest loss of working days tended to occur when the demand for new cars was low – precisely when any 'lost' production could not have been sold. The researchers suggested, that at such times, management did not pursue solutions with any great degree of energy until existing stocks had been depleted. Such episodes, to anticipate the next section, may have distinct advantages for management. They make financial savings on wages, raw material costs and overheads; they avoid all the problems associated with short-time working – which is administratively complex; and they retain their workforce through not having to declare redundancies, which, apart from its financial costs, means that former employees who have been trained, once stocks are depleted or the market picks up, may not return to the plant because they have found more secure employment elsewhere. Hence, not all the allegations that management have provoked a strike should be dismissed as red mole rhetoric – for there are clearly situations in which a strike may be of advantage to managerial objectives.

By far the clearest evidence of management starting strikes comes

419

from the rare occasions on which somebody grasses. This occurred, for example, in 1980 following the 13-week national strike in the steel industry. The strike was called by the steel unions after abortive wage negotiations in which the BSC (British Steel Corporation) decision-makers – headed by Mr Ian McGregor who subsequently presided over the national coal strike of 1984–85 – made a final offer which even the traditionally non-militant steel workers could not accept. After 13 weeks the employees returned to work on terms which were hardly victorious. Not long afterwards, *The Times* – on information provided by a managerial employee who, not without irony, came to be known as the 'steel mole' – revealed that BSC management must have known that their initial final offer would almost certainly cause a strike. At that time – for reasons we shall come to – the strike suited managerial purposes.

Governments too, given their extensive and sometimes intensive involvement in industrial relations, may also be regarded as the causal agents in some strikes. Decisions to pass new laws which will have the effect of restricting trade unionism are often accompanied by demonstration strikes – in 1971 there were two 1-day national strikes against the proposed Industrial Relations Act. Leaving aside the question of whether or not workers ought to strike for such 'political' purposes, the analytical point is that had the Government not announced its intention to pass the Act against the collective wishes and advice of the TUC and virtually all the trade unions, these strikes would not have been called.

Similarly, governmental decisions about their direct involvement in the regulation of industrial relations may be a cause of industrial stoppages. In their detailed statistical voyage in search of an explanation for the increase in strikes in Britain after 1950, one of the conclusions reached by Durcan, McCarthy and Redman is that some of the increase was due to deliberate governmental decisions to reduce the availability of independent conciliation and arbitration. This is not to say there was a deliberate provocation of strikes but – in the pursuit of wage-restraint – governments decided to restrict the use of arbitration since this was seen as one of the mechanisms through which wages were increased. In effect, government were prepared to exchange more strikes for lower wage increases. Similarly, the same study also established clear links between government attempts to directly regulate wages and the level of strike activity. They conclude: 'all the evidence indicates that on balance incomes policy has both provoked particular strikes and done a great deal to raise the general level of strike activity'.

On other occasions the inadequacy of union representation may be the most important cause of a strike. This was the case in the 1970 strike at Pilkington's Glass Works in St Helens referred to in the story of the laggers. On the surface, the cause of this strike – which lasted 7 weeks and spread to most of the company's plants elsewhere – was a small number of miscalculated wage packets. Within hours, however, the dispute escalated into a substantial wage claim and within days became a strike against the union itself for failing to provide effective representation. At the time the strike was celebrated by some on the political Left as a great act of working-class self-liberation, an explosion of working-class consciousness; and there was much dark and irrelevant talk of political subversives. It undoubtedly reflected a range of long-suppressed and deeply felt frustrations about the employer and the union but, once the grievances had been aired and, to some extent, remedied, work life once again settled to its peaceful, hard-working routines. Virtually nothing has stirred at Pilkington's since that time.

The purpose of the foregoing examples has not been to allocate blame to any specific individuals or any particular organisations. Indeed, all attempts to specify such responsibilities are likely to be no more than expressions of our own preferred political frame of reference. The point which this chapter seeks to secure is that any analysis of strikes in these terms will produce nothing but crude stereotypes; a social world peopled by red moles, blue meanies, wicked capitalists and a manipulative, all-pervasive State. Sadly, such caricatures are not unknown in the industrial relations literature and, like the media images, do little to enhance our understanding of the employment relationship. The first step in this process is to stop looking for someone to blame and start by examining the social, political and economic contexts in which strikes are generated.

Question

1. (a) What purposes can a strike serve during the industrial bargaining process?

(5 marks)

(b) Who causes strikes?

(15 marks)

55 Susan McIntosh: A Feminist Critique of Stanley Parker's Theory of Work and Leisure

In this reading, Sue McIntosh first succinctly analyses what she sees as lacking in 'conventional' contributions to the sociology of leisure: an adequate application of the concepts of class, race and gender. In developing the third point, she makes a penetrating critique of the patriarchal assumptions that she argues underlie Stanley Parker's analysis and, in particular, his division of work–leisure into a five-part spectrum: work, work-obligations, existence time, non-work obligations and leisure. She contends that these divisions usefully apply to men in full-time work, but not to women. Likewise, she is critical of the irrelevance to many women of the model Parker adopts to show the relationship between work and leisure. He suggests 'three typical ways in which people tend to relate their work to their leisure': the extension, neutrality and opposition patterns. Thus, a businessman's 'work' may extend into leisure time whereas a miner is likely to seek leisure activities in sharp opposition to work. A clerk may seek relaxation in leisure, perhaps making family the centre of life – an example of the 'neutrality' pattern. For many mothers, particularly with young children, and whether in paid work or not, these 'patterns' just do not fit.

McIntosh makes a powerful case and it is interesting that in a reply to her criticisms Parker agrees that leisure theory has concentrated too exclusively on people in full-time employment (i.e., mainly men). He suggests that McIntosh's points apply chiefly to full-time housewives but it can be argued against him that his theory also inadequately conceptualises the situation of women in both part- and full-time employment. The traditional commitment of women, whether in employment or not, to 'domestic responsibilities' means that the fifth category of leisure may be seldom completely applicable to most of them. Such is the effect of patriarchy.

Reading 55 From Susan McIntosh, 'Leisure Studies and Women' from Work Group (Susan McIntosh, Trisha McCabe, Chris Griffin and Dorothy Hobson), 'Work and Leisure', in Alan Tomlinson *ed.*, *Leisure and Social Control* (Brighton Polytechnic, 1981), pp. 93–9.

First, then, we look at work in the field of leisure that may be described as 'conventional'. The field itself is a large one encompassing, in Tony Veal's terms, both 'macro' and 'micro' approaches, and employing economics, philosophy, sociology, social psychology and ethics as contributory disciplines. Nonetheless, its history seems to be one of ad hoc development, rather than theoretical clarity or debate. Thus definitions of leisure of an empirical kind currently available within the discourses of dominant ideology are not questioned; one might even say that the academic contribution has tended to be one of systematising and sophisticating the currently held definitions of leisure. This has serious implications from the point of view of any analysis attempting a critique, rather than a reinforcement, of the current economic, political and social order. Three dimensions of this critique may be referred to.

Firstly, class. A Marxist critique of the leisure field would want to expose the middle-class bias inherent in much existing work, and the politics of current concern about leisure. The title of this conference, indeed, indicates awareness of the class nature of this concern. The possibility of provision of leisure facilities being elided into planned control of unemployed people is a real one.

The second critical perspective we should mention is the anti-racist one. As yet relatively young in the field of theoretical studies of culture, the 'race' perspective might want to put the question of leisure in a world perspective, connecting to questions of levels of economic development and ways of life of different classes and racial groups within this. Black people as providers, or objects, of leisure (as in jazz, cricket), would also be of interest, as would ways in which leisure may represent styles of resistance for blacks within white culture.

The third critical perspective we refer to here, and around which this contribution is centred, is that of feminism. As such we are interested particularly in the male orientation of almost all the literature we have studied, the empirical absence of women in studies on leisure, and the poverty of conceptualisation as a result of this absence.

There are ways in which clearly these three dimensions are insufficient. Other dimensions exist – age, physical ability, level of education, and so on. More than this, there are complex ways in which the dimensions interweave. On our first three dimensions alone, there are groups (such as black women) whose position demands that we articulate two or three dimensions at once. Indeed if we do this for oppressed groups we should also do it for powerful groups. Thus, the white, bourgeois male should also be seen in relation to class and gender.

We have attempted a critique, and an analysis, of leisure from the point of view specifically of feminism. While the best analysis would articulate gender with at least race and class, we cannot apologise for not doing so here. Studies focussing on race, while growing rapidly, are still small. Those analysing class have, of course, a longer established tradition behind them. However, they have severe problems themselves on the question of recognising the specificity of women. Marxist work in the field of leisure is still new, but we shall indicate the reproduction of some of these problems later.

Perhaps, since there is such a wide variety of interests and backgrounds represented here, we should very briefly spell out what we mean by a feminist perspective. We have ourselves experienced the fog that besets the mind when words like 'the family', 'gender relations', 'sexuality' are mentioned. The areas seem vast and deep, unmapped and unplumbed. Here at the Centre, however, as of course elsewhere, women have been gradually mapping some of this territory, and while recognising that we have no monopoly of the truth here, we hope it is useful to summarise our own views.

Patriarchy we see as a total dimension structuring all levels of society. It describes a situation of dominance by men over women. It is *based* on at least two major facets: control over women's sexuality and fertility: and the sexual division of labour; that is, the allocation of women to a *primarily* reproductive role, through which all their other roles are mediated. Patriarchy also operates at an ideological level, influencing women's perceptions of themselves and men's views of what is appropriate for them.

Patriarchy articulates in some way with other structures – with capitalism, with racism, with age, etc. Exactly how this articulation works is a matter of keen debate; we can say with certainty that it varies historically and is affected by struggle. At this stage in the academic story there is a need to maintain its outline over and against the overwhelming presence of class as the major and only dimension. This does not deny the need to hold (at least) both dimensions in mind for the ultimate, definite analysis.

Here we intend to move from a critique of existing studies, through an indication of the patterns of women's leisure, to the implications at the level of theory for future work on leisure.

We take as an example of the conventional literature on leisure that doyen of the field, S. R. Parker – in particular his study of work and leisure, and specifically the assumptions in that book on the definition of leisure. Parker's earlier work has been chosen because, as his Ph.D. thesis, it concentrates on definitions, spelling out the definitions of leisure in real detail. Also because, as he said himself yesterday, he sees work as the prime determinant of leisure patterns and this whole study concentrates on that connection: the later book looks at other institutions in more detail.

Why Parker? His work not only represents something of a back-bone to the study of leisure in Britain, but its broad perspective is fairly representative of the mainstream British sociological tradition.

This perspective emerges clearly in the first chapter. Parker goes beyond the empiricism of the discrete category – he insists that leisure must be seen in its relation to work. This promise is fulfilled later in the book – both work and leisure are placed in historical and cross-cultural perspective, and the final categorisation of leisure for which he is widely known, relies entirely on its relation to work. Indeed, two sorts of person are delineated (in Ch. 8) according to the very degree to which they connect work and leisure. The 'holists' are likely to have an *extension* pattern of work and leisure, and this is likely to be true also of the society in which they live. The 'segmentalists' are likely to have either an opposition or a neutrality pattern of work and leisure – the tendency again being reflected in the society. As a theorist, then, Parker may be seen as – in his own terms – a 'holist'. The total model of society that he holds, however, seems to be a fairly strongly functionalist one. He says: 'Sociology is concerned with relationships, and there are two kinds of relation-ships to be studied: that between society's need for work to be done and for the benefits that its members may collectively derive from leisure; and that between the functions of work and leisure to individuals themselves' (p. 14). This view is consistent with his mildly social democratic view of practice: he aims (p. 15) 'to change

425

society so that more people are afforded more opportunities for a creative and satisfying work and leisure life'. Parker is thus clearly using a functionalist view of society and individuals, of a loose pluralist sort, and with broad reforming aims. He is not, however, beyond taking the odd leaf from the book of a somewhat more critical approach. He considers (on p. 18) that 'the evolution of society through various forms of social production and ownership of property progressively breaks down the direct link between individual productive effort and consumption of goods and services'.

Clearly, however, we are not here dealing with someone who identifies himself in any sense with a Marxist perspective. Neither indeed are we dealing with someone who has considered feminism – or the situation of women – in any depth.

Parker spells out his assumptions in defining 'leisure' as a concept, in his second chapter. Here he summarises existing definitions of both work and leisure before giving his own. His final categorisation of the work–leisure spectrum is both a summary, and a systematisation, of work that has gone before, and as such is useful for our purposes here.

The broad distinction in the definition of *work* that emerges is that between work done for its own sake, and that done for the purposes of earning a living. In fact, in his own categorisation, Parker sticks to the latter version of work as employment. In considering existing definitions of leisure, it is clear that Parker draws on a tradition of antecedents who 'write out' the connection between women and leisure. Take, for example, the definition of the International Group of the Social Science of Leisure (1960): 'Leisure consists of a number of occupations in which the individual may indulge of his own free will – either to rest, to amuse himself, to add to his knowledge, or improve his skills disinterestedly, or to increase his voluntary participation in the life of the community after discharging his professional, family and social duties'. The linguistic male bias is the least of the problems here; we are given a picture of rational economic man outside his work, doing specific things, and acting as a citizen. This is perhaps the pure utilitarian definition: as he improves himself with skills, he does so in the knowledge that his family duties are out of the way. The realm of the wife and children is thus clearly dealt with from the point of view of the husband.

Parker's final categorisation of the work–leisure spectrum is cross-

426

classified according to time and activity. When we have looked at this scheme, we shall see how neither the dimensions of time nor activity, as assumed by Parker, apply to women. The divisions here apply usefully to men in full-time work, but not so to women.

What, then, is this final scheme? Its basic rationale is one of full-time work giving way by five stages to total leisure – and it thus also clearly relies on a fundamentally male definition of work. Parker's five main points on the work/leisure spectrum are: work, work-obligations, existence time, non-work obligations and leisure. He outlines the meaning of each clearly (on p. 27) and we wish to take this definition, stage by stage, as indicative of his assumptions. We shall be interrogating each stage of this schema with reference to the situation of women working in the home – not because we wish to deny the reality of work both inside and outside the home for many women – but in a heuristic sense, to provide the polar opposite case to full-time employment.

'In this scheme', he begins, 'work may be defined as the activity involved in earning a living, plus necessary subsidiary activities such as travelling to work'. This is the first category and is, in fact, the one by which the others are defined. The assumption here is that work is what is done for money, that it takes place outside the home, and that it is a distinct area, capable of producing subsidiary categories. For women at home, however, work is not done for money, but for 'love' or maternal duty; it takes place in the home; and it is not a distinct area: it takes place all day – often during the night (getting up to see to the kids), and its boundaries are not at all clear. Thus Parker's first category immediately places itself within the terrain of male full-time employment.

The second category is that of 'work obligations'. 'These', says Parker, 'include voluntary overtime' (a strange categorisation), 'doing things outside normal working hours associated with the job or type of work, that are not strictly necessary to a minimum acceptable level of performance in the job, or having a second job'. Once again we have here the use of full-time employment as the yardstick – even to the point of relegating overtime or a second job to the category of 'work obligations' (something, I suspect, few workers doing overtime would agree with). The fact that 'women's work' in the home is not so clearly defined means that for them the boundary between work and work obligations is very blurred. Is ironing a clean shirt for your child to wear at school actually work

427

or work obligation? Is refusing to leave the house till the beds are made and the sink clear, work or work obligations? The distinction is fairly meaningless for women: we shall see why later. In a sense, everything that women do in the house is 'work obligation'.

The third category of Parker's is the first of his 'leisure' categories. This is 'existence time', or 'the satisfaction of physiological needs'. Of this Parker says, it 'follows the conventional definition of these needs'. In elaborating, he gives 'sleep, eating, washing, eliminating' as examples. There is an immediate problem here for a woman. That is, she is not simply doing these things for herself, but facilitating them in other people: feeding her husband, washing her invalid mother-in-law, changing the baby's nappies. It is unclear here whether these things should be differently categorised for women – category 3 for eating the meal, category 2 for preparing it and serving it to the family? A further problem Parker *does* see: the possible overlap with leisure. Eating may be for pleasure, sexual activity may be 'beyond the call of purely physiological need' (p. 26). By-passing the somewhat quantitative mentality of this latter distinction, it is worth noting that the ambiguity may be considerable for women. Recent and not so recent research indicates that heterosexual intercourse is largely male-defined, and that sexual activity of this sort does not always mean 'leisure' or the 'satisfaction of physiological need' for women.

It is in general clear that this category of 'existence time' 'works' only for men; the distinction between ensuring one's own existence, and perpetuating that of others breaks down in the case of women. Further, the subsuming of this whole category under the rubric of 'leisure' is not appropriate for women. It seems that there is a real danger of the reproduction of men and their labour power being conflated with 'leisure' in this definition – and thus the whole workload of women at home being placed within this category.

The fourth category is that of 'non-work obligations'; Parker says they are 'roughly what Dumazedier calls semi-leisure plus the domestic work part of work obligations'. Here again the category clearly refers to men. Discharging domestic duties is an activity seen as marginal to work, but constituting an obligation on otherwise 'free' time. Elaborating (p. 26), he makes this clearer. 'The obligations are usually to other people, but may be to non-human objects, such as pets or homes or gardens.' (Who, one asks, are the 'human' objects?) The husband presumably plays with the children, visits the relatives, listens to his wife's problems with the children, mows the lawn, takes the dog for a walk. Apart from the dangers of slipping into a bland white middle-class picture, this category is clearly male in assumptions. For women, the content of this category fills a large part of her day: 'discharging domestic duties' is, after all, the sum total of her work in the home. Is women's work therefore to be equated with male 'semi-leisure'? Or is it that this categorisation can only be used for men?

Finally, we have 'leisure' – with a mental sigh of relief. He's been to work, done the overtime, eaten and eliminated, taken the wife and kids for a run, and now at last he's free. To do what? Parker says: 'Leisure is time free from obligations either to self or to others – time in which to do as one chooses'. This is the place for enlarging the mind, doing one's hobbies, becoming a full human being, and so on. The problem for women is that they have very little of this time. So little, in fact, that it may become a threat when it exists, pointing up in relief the *lack* of autonomy and time for herself in the rest of her life. It is to be free from obligations – so no kids or grannies to look after. It is 'time in which to do as one chooses'. Anything at all? Take a day off for a walk? (What about the meals? Kids after school?) Go for a drink on your own in the evening? (What about the money? What about women alone in pubs? What about your husband's attitude to your mixing with other men?) Take a couple of hours off at lunchtime for a swim? (Who'll take care of the kids? How to stop thinking about your 'obligations' in so short a space of time?) The facilities don't exist for women's leisure: the crèches, the proximity to home, the cheap entry fees.

Women may well (or may not) accompany men on some of their leisure activities. The 'night out' may well be constructed as such for both the man and woman. However, the freedom truly to choose where to go, who to talk to, and how to enjoy the evening may not be there for the woman having time off with her husband. The culture of the 'night out' makes it difficult for the woman to see herself as the *definer* of the entertainment. In the pub, for example, she is distinctly 'with her man' – and owes her presence in such a male culture to being with him.

In all five categories, therefore, Parker has in mind not simply 'a person' as presented, but 'a man' quite specifically. On p. 29, at the end of the introduction to the whole analysis, Parker says, somewhat disarmingly: 'One important qualification must be made

429

to the analysis of life space. In considering the various categories, we have had in mind men in full-time employment. Certain modifications to the scheme are necessary if it is to fit the cases of other groups.' However, this male bias is not made explicit in the analysis itself, as it is assumed that it forms the *general* case, while women form *one particular instance* containable within a modified version of that scheme. It is precisely this assumption (that women form a specific offshoot from the male category which is synonymous with the neutral, general category) that constitutes what has been described as masculine hegemony.

Some of these assumptions become clear at a more general level when we consider the dimensions along which Parker cross-classifies work and leisure. He considers *time*, in the sense of being at work or not, and *activity* in the degree of freedom or constraint involved. Neither of these dimensions works for women. The work/non-work split doesn't exist in the same way for women. All time is potential working-time, the home is workplace *and* living-place. And for the women the freedom–constraint dichotomy is also false; 'pure' freedom seldom exists for women in the way that it can (and is institutionalised) for men. (Though this concept is itself based on the idea of a free-floating individual, regardless of historical (class) specificity and limitations.) 'Constraint' in the sense of full-time employment is not the same for the woman at home. She has, it is true, more choice about the content and timing of her work – but that is within strong constraints, both material and ideological.

Question
1. *How convincing do you find the relationships between work and leisure given by Parker and criticised by McIntosh?*

(25 marks)

56 Chris Rojek: The Organisation of Leisure in Modern Capitalism

Chris Rojek attempts to outline the 'deep-rooted historical tendencies which give contemporary leisure relations their specific organisational form'. These are:
1. privatisation
2. individuation

3. commercialisation
4. pacification.

These charateristics reflect the nature and needs of modern capitalism. The privatised individual is the commercial target of a system which also largely controls him or her. This sounds sinister and, indeed, the view that we are 'buying' subordination under the guise of pleasure is disconcerting. Whether one agrees with Rojek or not, his analysis merits careful consideration.

Reading 56 From Chris Rojek, *Capitalism and Leisure Theory* (Tavistock, 1985), pp. 18–23.

Throughout this book I shall exploit and develop two minimal methodological positions. First, it is fundamentally wrong to study leisure as an immediately given datum of human experience. Leisure shapes, and is shaped by, history and the interplay of social interests. Second, all views of leisure which devote themselves to uncovering universal laws which enshrine timeless qualities of leisure behaviour must be abandoned. Leisure practice must be thought of in terms of dynamic relations, i.e. relations that change over time.

The stress on process and change can easily lead to the conclusion that leisure relations are all too dynamic: they can never be pinned down. Accordingly, the purpose of this section is to forestall such a construction by itemising the deep-rooted historical tendencies which give contemporary leisure relations their specific organisational form. I believe that four key tendencies should be differentiated: privatisation, individuation, commercialisation, and pacification. Let us consider them in turn.

Privatisation

The home is now the major site of leisure experience in capitalist society. The main catalyst behind this process has been the mass production of cheap home entertainments in the shape of television, radio, audio, and video equipment. If one looks closely at the design and marketing trends in these entertainment forms, two things rapidly become apparent. First, there has been a persistent tendency to miniaturise the unit size of equipment. Second, and at the same time, there has been a tendency to design units where entertainment functions are combined, e.g. music centres, radio cassette receivers, personal stereo equipment, etc. The microchip has revolutionised the scope available to producers and designers for accelerating these tendencies. Nowhere is progress more evident than in the case of television. Small compact sets are now widely available. They combine a number of leisure functions. For example, they can be used to: (a) receive commercial and public service broadcasts, (b) process information via the various teletext systems, (c) play back video-recordings, (d) receive cable transmissions, and (e) act as monitors for computer packages. One corollary of privatisation is the increased capital intensity of leisure activity. I shall return to this point when I consider commercialisation and leisure.

Individuation

Individuation refers to the historical and material processes which demarcate the individual as a specific person who is publicly recognised as separate and distinct from others. Forms of individuation include name, date of birth, nationality, marital status, home address, national insurance number, club membership, and academic qualifications. The groundwork of the individuated personality is laid in the socialisation process which begins in the family and the school. The registration of birth, christening, school registers, and school reports are, *inter alia*, devices for differentiating individuals and 'distilling' their essence in standardised systems of retrievable information. Turner (1983:163) has commented on the double-edged character of individuation. 'By making people different and separate,' he writes, 'it makes them more subject to control.' How is individuation expressed in modern leisure relations? Two related points need to be made. First, the specialisation and differentiation of persons find a corresponding reference point in the specialisation and differentiation of leisure pursuits. The institutionalisation of leisure, in the shape of members' rules, newsletters, festivals, and competitions, has extended the power of discipline throughout leisure activities. The individual pays homage to the obligations of his chosen leisure enthusiasm almost as a condition of participation. This is obvious where the voluntary consent of the individual is given to the rules of a particular sport or leisure association. But some authors argue that even in privatised forms of leisure, such as TV watching, the choices that an individual may exercise are very few. For example, Adorno submits that,

'We are all familiar with the division of television content into various classes, such as light comedy, westerns, mysteries, so-called sophisticated plays and others. These types have been developed into formulas which, to a certain degree, pre-establish the attitudinal pattern of the spectator before he is confronted with any specific content and which largely determine the way in which any specific content is being perceived.'

(Adorno 1954:226)

For Adorno, the individuation of content, which is represented in the enumerated classes of programmes, exploits and develops the individuated attitudes and inclinations of the viewers. In 'the totally administered society', the production and scheduling of broadcasts is calculated to achieve a planned response. Perhaps Adorno exaggerates the passivity of viewers. Even so, his work does highlight an important point about individuation and leisure: the leisure industry can manipulate people's emotions even in contexts where they feel most free, e.g. the home.

This leads on to the second point. The leisure industry encourages and reinforces the narcissism of the individuated identity. Mass-produced leisure commodities are presented to the individual as unique and exciting accessories of personal lifestyle. For example, Chambers (1983) has investigated some of the marketing ploys of the luxury motor-bike industry. The motor bike, she argues, is advertised and sold as a personalised, symbolic expression of the 'transcendental woman'. Bikes are, for example, 'long legged and easy to live with' (Moto Guzzi); 'full of mounting excitement' (Kawasaki); and a pure 'thoroughbred/racebred' (Honda). From a Marxist standpoint, the individuation of commodities penetrates to the heart of alienation in capitalist society. Thus our consumption of commodities has the effect of separating and differentiating us further as individuals; this masks shared life conditions, and also marginalises the whole question of how these conditions are materially produced and reproduced.

Commercialisation

Leisure is increasingly run on business lines. Roberts (1978:20) argues that the top five leisure pursuits in Britain today are television, alcohol, sex, tobacco, and gambling. These are not only pursuits that engage people's faculties and energies; they are also multimillion-pound industries which are organised to produce a continuous profit for the social interests who own and control them.

The leisure industry consists of the conglomerate of business units which aim to produce and reproduce consumer demand for leisure goods and services. Its branches include tourism, catering, sport, outdoor recreations, and the huge area of mass communications, including pop music, video, television, radio, magazines, and books. The leisure industry seeks to organise leisure activities on strict market principles, i.e. in pursuit of the accumulation of profit rather than the satisfaction of social need.

Pacification

Modern capitalist society is based on the complex division of labour. This is associated with distinctive forms of power bonding and social integration. It would be wrong to say that we live in 'unexciting societies'. The revolutionary breakthroughs made in science, industry, and communications bring with them new opportunities for excitement and pleasure in work and leisure relations. However, they also presuppose degrees of administration and surveillance which make our experience of excitement and pleasure qualitatively different from the experience of people who lived in societies where the division of labour was less complex. Elias and Dunning describe the deep change which has occurred in the emotional drives and bonds of people in the advanced industrial societies as a decline in 'the spontaneous, elementary and unreflected type of excitement, in joy as in sorrow, in love as in hatred. The extremes of powerful and passionate outbursts have been dampened by built-in restraints maintained by social controls, which, in part, are built-in so deeply, that they cannot be shaken off' (1969:60). In short, a comprehensive pacification of violent emotions has occurred.

Elias (1978a, 1982a) explores this idea more fully in his theory of 'the civilising process'. This is considered in detail in Chapter 7 of this book (especially pp. 166–69). At this point, it is enough to state that the civilising process refers to long-term changes in the social organisation of deep emotions. Standards of restraint and thresholds of repugnance at the public display of naked physical aggression have risen. Similarly, in private life, most people feel embarrassed and self-conscious if their emotions get the better of them. The dominant inclination is not to express intense emotions but to keep them imprisoned in the garrison of the self.

Few theories in modern sociology have been so widely misunderstood as Elias's theory of the civilising process. The theory does *not* argue that intense and violent emotions have disappeared from society. What it does submit is that, in adult life, the face of physical aggression has become more calculating and discreet. As regards leisure practice, Elias and his followers have used the theory to make two related propositions. First, they argue that in a long time-scale of over half a millennium a clear, demonstrable tendency can be discerned for leisure forms to become less violent. For example, Dunning and Sheard's (1979) study of the development of rugby football shows that the institutionalisation and professionalisation of the game correlate with a marked reduction in aggressive outbursts. Second, they suggest that in the relatively pacified societies of today, certain leisure forms may perpetuate mock violence and so, in a relatively peaceful and controlled way, arouse the intense emotions in human beings that are necessary for vitality.

Questions
1. *Define and illustrate each of Rojek's concepts of privatisation, individuation, commercialisation and pacification.*

(12 marks)
2. *How useful do you find these concepts in understanding the organisation of leisure in modern capitalist society?*

(8 marks)

Urbanisation and Community

Readings 57–61

There are two notable traditions of urban theory: the Chicago School and recent Marxist urban sociology. In the first reading in this section, Malcolm Cross summarises the former. As Cross makes clear, Louis Wirth, perhaps the major figure in the Chicago School, was greatly influenced by Durkheim. The latter's influence is also apparent in Reading 58, from Robert Nisbet, which presents a core pair of concepts in urban–rural analysis – *Gemeinschaft* (community) and *Gesellschaft* (society/association). Howard Newby introduces the concept of conflict into the topic; in this case, class conflict and the potential conflict between agricultural and environmental interests. Reading 60 from Friend and Metcalf is a Marxist analysis of how the workings of the capitalist system change not only the urban–rural landscape but people's lives. Stuart Lowe overviews the enormously influential work of Manuel Castells in this field, particularly his analysis of urban social movements.

57 Malcolm Cross: The Rural–Urban Continuum

The main approach to community/urban analysis prior to the Marxist revival of the nineteen seventies was based on a contrast of rural and urban characteristics. Louis Wirth, referred to in the extract, produced the most influential version of this approach. Although useful at a descriptive level, the 'rural–urban continuum' perspective (as Cross refers to it) does not convincingly explain the development and functioning of modern cities. Manuel Castells' work perhaps comes closer to explaining the urban dynamic (Reading 61). Reading 63 presents the rural–urban continuum approach projected onto a global context where, in the form of modernisation theory, it acquires a more explanatory character.

Reading 57 From Malcolm Cross, *Urbanisation and Urban Growth in the Caribbean* (Cambridge University Press, 1979), pp. 15–16.

The rural–urban continuum

The first point about this simple device is that it is essentially descriptive and not explanatory. The object is to define the nature of 'rural' and 'urban' types (usually ideal types) of social relation or of culture. Devices such as this have a long and time-honoured history in sociology, ranging from Sir Henry Maine's legalistic distinctions between pastoral ties of 'status' and urban bonds of 'contract', to Emile Durkheim's separation of mechanical and organic forms of social solidarity or Ferdinand Toennies' famous classification of social relations dependent on either 'natural' or 'rational' will (*Gemeinschaft/Gesellschaft*) (cf. McKinney, 1966; Loomis and McKinney, 1963). It is hard to overestimate the degree to which these or similar classifications have infiltrated our thought; the very separation of pre-industrial from industrial society, or of modernity from traditionalism inevitably connotes ideal type forms or patterns of social relation.

In most cases the key differentiating factor, upon which changes in cultural or social relationships are thought to depend, is simply the demographic change resulting from concentration and increased density of population. Two examples may demonstrate this common view. For Durkheim the change towards a greater role for *organic* solidarity or social cohesion is dependent upon greater complexity and interdependence of the constituent parts of a social system, and this itself is a necessary consequence of numbers and the 'density' of social relations. As Durkheim wrote in the *Division of Labour in Society:* 'From the time that the number of individuals among whom social relations are established begins to increase, they can maintain themselves only by greater specialisation, harder work and intensification of their faculties' (Durkheim, 1964: 336–7). The style of life and pattern of inter-relations is thus dependent upon the concentration of population. As Durkheim was at pains to point out, the pressures associated with the increased 'intensity' of life may produce patterns of development which we associate with the growth of cities and emergent civilisation, but they often produce pathological reactions as well.

It is the way of thinking and acting that gave rise to these unwelcome concomitants of urban growth that Louis Wirth was later to label 'urbanism'. Wirth argued that three variables (numbers, density, and heterogeneity) could 'explain the characteristics of urban life and . . . account for the differences between cities of various sizes and types' (Wirth, 1938: 18). These characteristics were thought to be many, but included a distinct personality type, the primacy of secondary relationships, formal organisations, anonymity, greater social and spatial mobility and weakened bonds of kinship and neighbourhood. It is true that not all aspects of urbanism were perceived as regrettable, but the central thrust of this typology is upon the association between 'urbanism' and social problems, which are themselves conceived in a pathological vein.

The major difficulty with these kinds of approach is not that differences of culture and social relationships are described as they are, because it is useful to demarcate the characteristics of 'rural' and 'urban' living. The problem is that the only theory which is developed is one which suggests that 'urbanism' is the result of concentrated population. This is not a theory of *how* populations came to be concentrated, and thus it cannot be a theory of urbanisation; it is a theory which is dependent upon correlations between social phenomena and spatial variables. Unfortunately, there does not appear to be any very powerful relationship between the two. It is quite possible to discover 'rural' kinds of primary or *gemeinschaft* relationship in city centres, while the 'country' may reveal many instances of 'urban' relationships. This is especially true of smaller societies with easier communications, like those that are the subject of this study, since here there may be even more opportunities for *urbs in rure*, to use Pahl's phrase (Pahl, 1965; Pahl, 1975).

It is probably true to maintain that there are features of urban life which are particularly important in the sociology of urban growth. As R. Dewey suggested there are structural features associated with greater complexities in the division of labour and peculiar forms of inequality that do demand our attention (Dewey, 1960). However, for understanding urbanisation, it is the inequalities and divisions *between* city and countryside that have to be understood. Concentrations of population are the effects of such relationships, not their cause. We can elaborate typologies of this kind as freely as we wish, and they may thereby be more useful in accurately identifying significant features of the variables we want to relate, but contrary to the views of some (see McGee, 1971: 47), they will not aid the main theoretical task.

ROBERT A. NISBET

Question

1. *(a) What characteristics are considered typical of the city in this approach?*

(5 marks)

(b) According to Louis Wirth, what variables explain these characteristics? How convincing do you find his explanation?

(10 marks)

58 Robert A. Nisbet: Community (*Gemeinschaft*) and Society (*Gesellschaft*)

A major feature of the theoretical approach of Durkheim, Tönnies and Cooley (see Reading 12) was to contrast the characteristics of traditional with modern society. They considered that a sense of community (*Gemeinschaft*) was typical of traditional and/or rural society, whereas in modern and/or urban society relationships tend to be more impersonal and instrumental. This contrasting typology inspired a number of community studies on both sides of the Atlantic, but has recently been widely criticised, particularly because it tends to romanticise the traditional-rural and to give an unduly negative view of the modern-urban. (See the readings by Cross (57) and, especially, Newby (59) in this section.)

In the concluding paragraphs of this brief extract, Nisbet usefully indicates that these two concepts have a wider application than simply within the above contrasting typology of social development. He says, in effect, that the two terms indicate types of relationships: *Gemeinschaft*-like, close, supportive and affective (involving feeling), and *Gesellschaft*-like, distanced, often contractual and rational (involving practical interests). These types of relationships are similar to informal and formal group relations and both can exist in virtually any type of society, although *Gemeinschaft*-like relationships are considered more typical of traditional society, and *Gesellschaft*-like of modern society.

Reading 58 From Robert A. Nisbet, *The Social Bond: An Introduction to the Study of Society* (Alfred A. Knopf, 1970), pp. 105–7.

Gemeinschaft and Gesellschaft

I used the German words for the two types of social aggregate which are the subject of this section because there is no single English word that expresses the distinctive nature of either one. The nearest we can come is 'community' for the first and 'society' for the second, but in neither case is the full meaning expressed by the English word. We owe to Ferdinand Tönnies primarily the sociological interest in these types of relationship.

When we refer to groups of a *Gemeinschaft* character, we have in mind relationships encompassing human beings as full personalities rather than the single aspects or roles of human beings. These are relationships characterised by a high degree of cohesion, communality, and duration in time. The most obvious and historically persistent types of *Gemeinschaft* are kinship groups, village communities, castes, religious organisations, ethnic groups, and guilds. In each of these the whole personality of the individual tends to be involved, and in each of them the claims of the social unity upon the individual tend to be nearly total. *Gemeinschaft* types of social aggregates may spring from personal or territorial attributes, be religious or secular, small or large. What is essential is the quality of strong cohesiveness of persons to one another and the quality of rooted, persisting collective identity. The kinship group serves as the archetype of *Gemeinschaft*. It is by all odds the oldest form, and its spirit, its sense of communal membership, even its nomenclature, tend to become the image of other, nonkinship types of *Gemeinschaft*. In any genuinely *Gemeinschaft* type of social grouping there is a profound ethic of solidarity, a vivid sense of 'we *versus* they', and of commitment of the whole self to the *Gemeinschaft*.

If we speak in moral terms, it would be a great mistake to label *Gemeinschaft* as necessarily 'good'. Bear in mind that examples of genuine *Gemeinschaft* include the ethnic ghetto as well as the village community, the totalitarian nation as well as the family, extreme social caste (as in India) as well as the guild or religious parish. *Gemeinschaft* is a neutral, descriptive term so far as ethical preference is concerned. *Gemeinschaft* cannot be subsumed under any of the types of social aggregate we have thus far considered, for it may be either small or large, open or closed, personal or territorial. Like each of these, it is a distinctive perspective for examining social behaviour and a social order.

Gesellschaft may also be either small or large, open or closed, personal or territorial. What is crucial to this type of aggregate, irrespective of anything else, is the fact that, whether small or large, personal or territorial, it engages the individual in only one of the aspects of his total being, or, at most, only a few aspects. From the individual's point of view his relationship with others in *Gesellschaft* is more tenuous, loose, and less deeply rooted in his allegiances or commitments. *Gesellschaft* is commonly founded around a few specific interests or purposes, whether religious, economic, recreational, or political. In contemporary Western society there is a vast abundance of *Gesellschaft* types of relationship among individuals, types in which human beings are to be found linked more or less casually or else contractually, in terms of some specific interests. Such types do not and, by their nature, cannot command depths of loyalty or become the focus of motivations, as do those in *Gemeinschaft* groupings.

Just as the shift from personal to territorial types of human relationships is a momentous one in history, so is the analogous shift from *Gemeinschaft* to *Gesellschaft*. A given period in history, or a given area of the earth's surface, may be rich in *Gemeinschaft* groupings – whether personal, such as kinship, or territorial, such as village community or town. Then, through profound events and changes, that historical period or area may see the number of *Gemeinschaft* groups diminish relative to the number of *Gesellschaft* types. Or, as is common in periods of change along this line, *Gemeinschaft* groups may become altered by the rise within them of motivations, ties, and incentives which are more of a *Gesellschaft* character. In business, a generations-old family form of enterprise, one in which employees are either literally or symbolically members of the family, may become, as the result of competitive pressures, more and more of a *Gesellschaft* type. As a result, the spirit of contractualism, individual competition, self-interest, and loose, specific-interest-orientated motivations will replace the older ones. The same kind of change is witnessed in the history of the school, the university, the church, the village or town, the guild, and so on. It is one of the most universal types of social change to be found in the history of human society.

Sometimes, of course, the change works in reverse fashion. A relationship that begins as a *Gesellschaft* type – whether a business enterprise of the modern age, a military bond in early feudalism, or a political association – may in time become increasingly characterised by *Gemeinschaft* relationships among the members. The history of the modern political state is a striking example of an association that in the beginning encompassed very little of the ordinary human being's life and was limited to the sole functions of military defense and civil order. Gradually, through the growth of modern nationalism, a more and more *Gemeinschaft* type of social relationship arose. Today the political nation commands from most persons an allegiance, a sense of rooted membership, that a few hundred years ago was given to kindred or church.

Question
1. (a) *Define and illustrate* Gemeinschaft *and* Gesellschaft.

(5 marks)

(b) *Do you consider that* Gemeinschaft-*like relationships are declining?*

(5 marks)

59 Howard Newby: Stratification and Change in Rural England

The following passage from Howard Newby's 'Green and Pleasant Land?' implicitly rejects the urban–rural continuum as an adequate theoretical framework. Instead, he stresses that changes in the rural economy have created new divisions and inequalities in the rural population itself. Essentially, the growth of large-scale, highly mechanised farming has created a class of wealthy, rural farmer-businessmen at the expense of the small farmer and farm labourer. Middle-class commuters or second-house owners are another major high status group. The second part of this brief extract, however, concentrates on the rural poor rather than the rural wealthy.

Although Newby concentrates on the new forces of stratification and inequality brought about by the capitalisation and 'modernisation' of agriculture, he acknowledges that these forces eroded the old 'occupational communities' of rural England. As he rightly points out, however, the *value* that one attributes to traditional community life is, in the last instance, a personal matter. He certainly does not subscribe to the rural romanticism apparent in the *Gemeinschaft-Gesellschaft* model. As he would be the first to acknowledge, inequalities in feudal England – for instance, those between lord and serf – could be as great as those in capitalist society. Indeed, the focus of Newby's analysis is, finally, on inequality, both past and present. He sees the causes of it within the nature of the socio-economic system (whether feudal or capitalist) rather than as a product of either rural or urban society as such.

Reading 59 From Howard Newby, *Green and Pleasant Land? Social Change in Rural England* (Penguin Books, 1980), pp. 271–4.

The outflow of labour from agriculture has brought about some radical and decisive changes in the social life of the English village. Few villages these days contain a population which is solely, or even predominantly, dependent upon agriculture in order to earn a living . . . the village as an occupational community, centred upon farming, has therefore declined. This transformation has occurred within a single generation in most rural areas and has been so rapid and far-reaching that it is not surprising that it has received so much attention from writers and commentators on English rural life. Most of these observations have been elegiac in tone, concerned to document the 'decline of the English village' and enunciate the last rites over any lingering 'community spirit'. As we have seen, whether the rural village has indeed declined as a vigorous community is something of a moot point and one which is ultimately dependent upon the value judgements of the individual concerned: it all depends upon what is meant by 'community'. In this respect the debate about the quality of life in rural England has paralleled the arguments concerning the landscape changes wrought by modern farming methods, where an objective standard of 'beauty' has proved as elusive as that of 'community' and where even quite widely held judgements can be regarded as ultimately a matter of personal aesthetic taste. It has, perhaps, been the very subjective basis of these assessments as much as the intrinsic importance of the issues which has caused so many words to be written about them and which has allowed the arguments for and against these changes to continue for so long and yet be so inconclusive.

A more worrying aspect of this public discussion is that by

concentrating on the more subjective perceived aspects of rural change it has tended to obscure some of the underlying objective realities. For example, although the appreciation of changes in the rural landscape is dependent upon aesthetic judgements, they also have objectively measurable effects in their impact upon the rural ecology. If the removal of a hedgerow or a copse involves the destruction of a unique wildlife habitat, that is something which is objectively calculable: it either is or is not unique; it either will or will not be destroyed. Although the *value* which we place on this destruction is not, of course, an objective matter, at least the precise ecological consequences are. In a similar fashion the long and inconclusive discussion over whether there has or has not been a decline of 'community' in the English village has tended to obscure some of the underlying, objectively assessable changes. This is not to say that the subjective feelings of rural inhabitants are unimportant or should be disregarded; but it is a plea for a little more balance and a good deal more realism in this discussion. For it *is* possible to identify in a reasonably objective manner the important social changes which have occurred in rural England over the last three decades. Indeed the two most important changes are quite obvious, despite not having always been granted the attention which they have deserved. The first concerns the extensive social polarisation which has occurred in the rural population since the war, between what is by now an affluent majority (of both newcomers *and*, in many cases, local farmers and landowners) and a poor and *relatively* deprived minority. The second major social change involves the gradual absorption of rural life into the mainstream of English society as a whole. The autonomy and distinctiveness of rural life have gradually but progressively been eclipsed by nationally inspired social, economic and political developments. This has not only narrowed the gap between 'rural' and 'urban' life-styles, but has made it increasingly difficult to understand recent discontinuities in rural life by examining only the indigenous sources of social change.

The social polarisation of the countryside has been a slow but inexorable process since the end of the Second World War. Within agriculture the large-scale landowner and farmer has generally benefited at the expense of the small marginal producer and the farm worker. At the same time a stark contrast has arisen in most villages between a comparatively affluent, immigrant, ex-urban middle class and the rump of the former agricultural population tied to the locality by their (low-paid) employment, by old age and by lack of resources enabling a move. The former group lives in the countryside mostly by conscious choice (and this includes the majority of farmers and landowners) and has the resources to overcome the problems of distance and access to essential services. The latter group, by contrast, has become increasingly trapped by a lack of access to alternative employment, housing and the full range of amenities which the remainder of the population takes for granted. While there can be little doubt that the material conditions of the rural poor, the elderly, the disabled and other deprived groups have undergone a considerable improvement in absolute terms since the war (in the sense that they are better fed, better housed, better clothed and better educated), in relative terms they have encountered little improvement and in many cases in recent years an alarming deterioration. Their poverty is often submerged – socially, and even literally, invisible – and there is a danger that, as rural England increasingly becomes middle-class England, their plight will be ignored and their needs overlooked.

In the previous two chapters an outline has been given of this polarisation process through a brief examination of planning policies in the areas of housing, employment and land use. A similar process can be observed, however, covering the whole range of social services, especially health services, and even the provision of apparently mundane amenities from shops to sewerage. The affluent sections of the rural population can, of course, overcome any problems which arise by stepping into their cars and driving to the nearest town, whereas the poor, the elderly and the disabled are particularly vulnerable to any decrease in the provision of local public and private services in rural areas, and especially of public transport. It therefore makes little sense any longer to contrast the poverty of rural areas with the prosperity of the towns, for the major divisions lie *within* the rural population between those in need and suffering multiple social deprivation and those who have benefited from living in the countryside in recent years and for whom access to a full range of services and amenities does not present a problem. Numerically it is the latter group which has consistently been in the ascendancy over the last thirty years and which has achieved a firm grasp on the levers of local political power. As a result the deprived section has found it increasingly difficult to obtain recognition of its requirements, let alone feel capable of diverting a larger proportion of resources in its direction. Many rural planning policies concerned with housing and employment have, either deliberately or unintentionally, discriminated against this group. Elsewhere the economics of public service provision have suffered from the fact that the newcomers to the countryside have possessed the means to be self-reliant. As a majority of ratepayers they have demonstrated an understandable reluctance to foot the rapidly rising bill on behalf of their less fortunate neighbours.

Question
1. *Discuss Newby's view that 'the major divisions lie* within *the rural population' (rather than between town and country).*

(*10 marks*)

60 Andrew Friend and Andy Metcalf: London: Manufacturing Decline and the Pattern of Capital Investment

Perhaps the best known Marxist urban sociologist is Manuel Castells. For him, the city in capitalist society is essentially a capitalist convenience. Above all, it centralises labour as well as a variety of other commercial and financial factors necessary for production, marketing and, ultimately, profit.

Friend and Metcalf's analysis of de-industrialisation and the resulting social and population decline is similarly within the Marxist tradition. They begin by referring to the long period of industrial development and population expansion characteristic of major urban areas in Britain, including London, which is their major focus of analysis in the following passage. They argue that, just as this period of widespread urban growth was generated by the needs of capitalist production, so, too, is the urban decline beginning in about the mid-1960s, and still continuing. They contend that the traditional, skilled industrial labour force concentrated in the inner city was increasingly not wanted or even needed in the newly expanding areas of the economy, such as electrical and service industries. Capital sought to by-pass heavily unionised and expensive (male) urban labour, and to employ less organised, less skilled and, above all, less expensive (frequently female) labour in less urbanised localities. They see a largely 'deskilled' rather than a better trained workforce emerging. They consider government housing and local, regional and national development policies as being broadly led by capital, rather than vice versa. The possibility that many individuals and families may have deliberately 'opted out' of the inner city in pursuit of some hoped-for suburban or rural alternative is not substantially considered. Whether or not one gives the same balance to the various factors associated with urban decline and decay as Friend and Metcalf, their analysis is consistent, challenging and currently (1988) quite influential.

Friend and Metcalf do not here analyse the social effects of urban de-industrialisation. However, they indicate elsewhere that poverty or, at least, a drop in living standards and demoralisation are among them. These particularly affect what they refer to as 'the surplus population' – the chronically unemployed or low-paid among whom the young particularly are now numbered.

Reading 60 From Andrew Friend and Andy Metcalf, *Slump City: The Politics of Mass Unemployment* (Pluto Press, 1981), pp. 91–8.

From the first throes of industrialisation to the middle of the present century what are now the London, Clydeside, Merseyside, West Midlands, Tyneside and South-East Lancashire conurbations gained population in each successive decade. Accounting for less than 3 per cent of the total land area they still house roughly a third of Great Britain's population – but since the mid-sixties the cities on which they are centred have all been losing population quite rapidly. In the decade to 1976 this population decline ranged from 22 per cent in the case of Liverpool to 8 per cent in that of Birmingham as people moved to the fringes of the conurbations or well beyond into the surrounding regions.

But this migration was not a uniform one in terms of class; effected largely through the operations of the private house market, and to a lesser extent through state decentralisation policies it was households with skilled manual male wage earners that tended to move out and those with 'unskilled' and 'semiskilled' heads of household that tended to stay behind. It is the people who have remained in the older working class areas of the major cities, together with new entrants to the British labour market and those excluded from it for reasons of age and family responsibilities, who

447

have borne the brunt of the changes that have overtaken the urban economy. From these groups is drawn the surplus population of the older urban areas, which – as we are arguing – is both swelling in size and becoming an increasingly distinct social group within society.

It is a characteristic of long waves that patterns of development and underdevelopment that have been laid down (or continued to exist in muted form) during the expansionary phase register with full force at the surface of industrial, social and political life during the succeeding phase of stagnation . . . Here we are going to concentrate on how the mobility of capital has interacted with the changing social and detailed division of labour to affect the industrial structure and class composition of London. What follows analyses this in terms of large-scale manufacturing, the small firm, office and 'growth service' work, and other service sector employment . . .

The decline of large scale manufacturing

In 1951, when manufacturing accounted for 35.5 per cent of total employment in Greater London, there were over 1.55 million people at work in the sector. By 1966 the number had declined to just under 1.33 million, accounting for 29.5 per cent of all jobs, but this fall had been more than compensated for by increasing employment in other sectors. As a result total employment in the conurbation had actually risen from 4.29 million to 4.43 million despite a decline in population from 8.80 million to 7.81 million. Since then, however, employment in London manufacturing has fallen precipitously. Between 1966 and 1974 – a period in which the city's population fell by 9.4 per cent and manufacturing employment nationally declined by 8.4 per cent – the conurbation lost 27 per cent or 370,000 of its manufacturing jobs. And the available evidence suggests that the trend has continued – the GLC for example, (in an assessment made before the extent of the 1980–81 recession became apparent) estimated that in 1981, of a total 3.70 million jobs in London only .74 million or 20.1 per cent would be in manufacturing.

It is worth noting that the decline has not been localised in terms of London's 'inner city' areas. Detailed analysis has shown that there was only a couple of percentage points difference between the average rate of job loss in the inner and outer boroughs over the

1966–74 period. This major rundown of manufacturing employment is a process affecting the whole conurbation – and all the major conurbations in the UK. Between 1971 and 1976, for example, Liverpool lost 14 per cent of its manufacturing jobs and this was followed by 20,000 notified redundancies (equivalent to 22 per cent of the 1976 workforce) between 1977 and 1979.

TV and press – drawing selectively on snippets of specialised reports and freely on the pronouncements of business pressure groups – have popularised a highly distorted understanding of this process. We are told that high rates and hostile planning decisions have killed off enterprises and that firms have been forced to leave because of the unco-operativeness of their existing workforces. A more accurate picture emerges if we look at the way monopolisation and technological transformation have altered the locational and labour requirements of leading firms and sectors.

During the nineteenth century industrialisation went hand in hand with urbanisation as industrial investment was drawn towards existing towns and cities or towards areas with special advantages (such as proximity to raw materials) which thereafter were rapidly built up. In these centres the higher costs of land – a reflection of market pressure – were offset by economies arising from other factors: the availability of labour, access to the market and – in an era when transport costs were relatively high and most enterprises were relatively small – proximity to other independent enterprises forming part of the chain of production. The interaction of all these ensured that while firms often moved to the fringes of urban areas in search of cheaper sites they rarely detached themselves from existing industrial centres. The very process of industrialisation led to urban 'agglomeration'.

During the twentieth century, however, particularly since the war, the advantages of operating within the major conurbations have been eroded and in many sectors the balance has tipped decisively against it. As monopolisation has advanced there has been a strong tendency for corporations to integrate complex chains of production on a more highly automated basis within a single plant. A prime locational requirement of these new high productivity plants is horizontal space for conveyor belts, machine to machine linkages, storage, container lorry docking, staff parking and steady expansion. But parcels of land on a scale sufficient for such major investments are not easily assembled in already built-up areas. And the most modern technology cannot be installed or profitably operated in plants cobbled together out of old multi-storey buildings which are cramped and have difficult access. (70 per cent of industrial buildings in Greater London are multi-storeyed compared to 15 per cent in the rest of the South-East.) At the same time as monopolisation has reduced the need to be near clusters of suppliers, land prices have encouraged dispersal, not only because land is cheaper outside the cities but also because of the value of the urban sites if sold for redevelopment. Such asset stripping has been a factor throughout the post-war period, but became a major influence on company planning during the property boom of the early seventies.

The growth of new transport systems, and access to them, has had a decisive bearing on the location of certain types of investment. In the case of the petrochemical industry, for example, the development of seaborne bulk transport and the need for these highly capital-intensive ships to achieve a quick turnaround time determined a move from the fringes of conurbations like London to often remote deep water access ports. But across a broad range of manufacturing activity it has been the dramatic shift from rail to road haulage and the differential development of the motorway system that has been the most important influence.

Britain's motorway building programme began late in 1957, but by 1970 trunk routes running through open country and linking the outskirts of most major industrial centres had been completed. The South-East Lancashire and Birmingham conurbations had the beginnings of a system of urban motorways as well, but little progress had been made on the 1964 plan to build three concentric motorways linking areas inside built-up London to the national grid. The high cost of urban motorway building, cutbacks in capital expenditure programmes and increasingly organised opposition to the necessary clearances and the prospects of pollution, interacted to stall the plan. As a result the motorway system petered out at the edges of the capital and, at the few points where it penetrated further, merely served to feed a growing volume of traffic on to an already congested road network.

In 1973, at the beginning of a period which also saw the axing of Maplin superport-airport and the Channel tunnel, plans for the two inner ringways were finally scrapped. Thus throughout the post-war period there has been a generally widening gap between the effective one day operating radius of lorries based in London and those based in other smaller cities and towns with easy access to the high speed trunk routes. And this gap has had a proportionately greater influence on location – especially for transnational companies – as the older transport systems (the railways and the upstream ports) based on the nineteenth century conurbations have decreased in importance and as traffic to and from Europe across the 'motorway bridges' provided by the east coast ports has increased.

Although some areas in the north and west of London are not as badly isolated as inner urban areas in its south and east (and proximity to Heathrow is a positive advantage in the west), there is little doubt that higher transport costs have combined with higher land prices to generally repel investment in new high productivity plants.

In terms of the availability and pliability of labour the advantages offered by London in the inter-war period were steadily eroded during the post-war boom. The growth industries of the thirties had been attracted to the metropolis by its reserves of craft labour, the size of the unskilled labour market and the comparatively low level of unionisation. By the end of the thirties some of the difficulties facing the unions in the vast city had been overcome, but even so major factories like Ford at Dagenham were not effectively organised until the fifties. During the long wave of expansion, however, demand for workers in other sectors of the capital's economy and an unemployment rate consistently below the national average combined to produce periodic shortages, encourage unionisation and raise wages. And although no precise London figures are available it is probable that by the beginning of the seventies – when over 60 per cent of the manufacturing workforce nationally were organised – the below average level of unionisation that had previously attracted investors had been transformed into an above average one.

The demise of the London docks provides a clear example of how labour organisation has often spurred both technological change and spatial reorganisation. In 1967, after eighty years of struggle, the dockers finally achieved 'decasualisation' and a guaranteed minimum wage, so bringing to an end a system of employment that had provided companies with a cheap flexible labour force easily shed during slack periods. While this system had survived the employers had judged investment in 'containerisation' to be uneconomic. Now it followed on a massive scale and, when combined with removing the work of stuffing and stripping the containers to inland depots, resulted in the registered dock labour content of handling

451

cargo being reduced by up to eighteen times from its previous level. In addition employers began to divert freight through ports where the Dock Labour Scheme did not apply and where companies retained unilateral control. Throughout the seventies the tonnage handled by these ports increased vastly, while the London port found itself trapped in a spiral of falling traffic and rising debt which had resulted in the near total closure of the upstream docks by the end of the decade.

For industrialists generally, the effects of increased unionisation were compounded by shortages in London of tappable reserves of married female labour. As we saw in Chapter 2 the incorporation of married women into the labour force was a major feature of post-war expansion throughout the capitalist economies – in Britain over the twenty year period to 1971 a 10.6 per cent rise in the total labour force was largely the result of a 115 per cent rise in the number of economically active married females, whose numbers increased from 2.7 to 5.8 million.

In London, however, the level of women's employment was much higher than elsewhere; sufficiently large reserves of married women wishing to work, and have the childcare facilities to do so, simply did not exist. In 1951 the Greater London activity rate for married women was 39.8 per cent at a time when it was 17.3 per cent for Great Britain outside the major conurbations. By 1971 the decentralisation of manufacturing employment and the expansion of the service sector in the rest of the country had narrowed the gap; the London rate had crept up to 48 per cent, but the rate for the rest of Great Britain outside the big cities had leapt to 40 per cent. And there is strong evidence from the intervening period that it was shortages of women workers that motivated relocations triggered by labour shortages – the Department of Industry inquiry into locational attitudes during the 1964–67 period, for example, revealed that one firm in nine considered that a shortage of female labour was the 'outstanding' reason for moving: shortages of male labour were rarely mentioned despite the fact that 40 per cent of respondent firms cited labour shortages as a 'major reason' for investing in new areas.

On the other hand the now frequently heard assertion that shortages of skilled labour have been a major long-term influence on the decline of manufacturing in London does not bear serious examination. One of the most thorough empirical analyses of recent changes in a given branch of British industry provides useful evidence on this. For their *Industrial Restructuring Vs. The Cities* Doreen Massey and Richard Meegan surveyed firms involved in the 1966–72 IRC-encouraged reorganisation of the electrical, electronic and aerospace equipment sectors. By the beginning of the period many of these enterprises had lost markets to overseas competitors, profits were falling and overcapacity was beginning to manifest itself. A series of major takeovers took place and all the surviving firms were faced with the need to reorganise production on a more modern basis. Generally, this involved moving towards mass production techniques via the substitution of less skilled labour and semi-automatic machinery for craft labour wherever possible. Total employment declined by 16 per cent – but this figure masks a much bigger shift from skilled to semi-skilled work on the shop floor and an extensive relocation of mass production from older urban areas to greenfield sites outside the conurbations. Greater London, Liverpool, Manchester and Birmingham – which, at the beginning of the period, accounted for 32 per cent of total employment – experienced 84 per cent of the total job loss as the labour-intensive inner city plants employing a high proportion of skilled labour were axed. In this case industrial capital was not moving on because of a shortage of skilled labour – indeed it would seem that investment was often being decentralised in the expectation that the old workforce would resist the necessary deskilling. Shortages of specific types of skilled labour may well now be acting as a barrier to expansion in some inner city areas because of the long-term effects of population dispersal, the collapse of the apprenticeship system and the destruction of pools of craft skills – but to cite this as a major cause of the decline of manufacturing in the conurbations is plainly wrong. The dominant thrust of the post-war redivision of labour within manufacturing has had the effect of deskilling the workforce and it has been the search for malleable unskilled labour, not the pursuit of elusive craft skills, that has motivated the typical post-war industrialist.

Since 1976 government attempts to stem the tide in inner urban areas have involved the reversal or cancellation of policies intended to encourage the decentralisation of population and employment. These moves, and the attendant publicity, have had the effect of deflecting public attention from the degree to which the decline of the manufacturing sector in London has resulted from a process of restructuring determined by market forces and controlled by monopoly capital rather than the state.

Question

1. (a) Describe and illustrate the decline of major inner city areas.
(8 marks)
(b) Critically discuss Friend and Metcalf's analysis of this decline.
(12 marks)

61 Stuart Lowe: Manuel Castells' Analysis of the City and Urban Social Movements

There are now few, if any, more significant figures in urban theory than Manuel Castells. Castells first 'fitted' urban analysis within a Marxist framework and on this basis has gone on to develop a genuinely original and dynamic theoretical approach. Arguably, he makes more sense of the city than any other contemporary sociologist.

This highly edited reading from Stuart Lowe describes the three phases of his urban theory. Central to all these phases is the urban social movement. Basically, urban social movements organise around urban issues – particularly those related to collective consumption (e.g., housing, the enviroment) – although the precise use of the term is debated. As his theoretical perspective has developed, Castells has increasingly seen these movements as autonomous from established political parties and pressure groups and as capable of defining their own meanings and goals. Several examples of urban social movements are given in the reading.

Briefly, the three phases of Castells' theoretical development are as follows:

1. The *primary* contradiction in capitalist society is that between capital and labour. Labour is centralised in the city. Urban social movements based on consumption (e.g., of welfare, of public housing) are of *secondary* importance to the primary class conflict, to which they need to ally themselves for maximum effect.
2. Urban social movements based on consumption arise inde-

pendently of the class system. They deal with 'a new source of inequality', mainly produced by welfare policy and bureaucracy which can cut across class lines. Correspondingly, in this phase, Castells sees urban social movements as potentially autonomous from established political parties.

3. Castells now recognises urban social movements as varied and *primary* sources of change. These movements are concerned with 'needs', 'inter-personal communication' and, in certain respects, 'self-government' as opposed to profit, mass communication and political manipulation. Castells sees them as a rich and creative source of change. Perhaps the London squatters' movement of the nineteen sixties and seventies and the various local movements against nuclear waste dumping (though not strictly urban) exemplify the characteristics indicated by Castells.

The strength of Castells' work is that it connects theoretically areas usually left unconnected. Government bureaucracy (including the 'capitalist' welfare state) is presented as a target of urban movements and both are related to a wider analysis of capitalism. This is 'grand theory' of the scope and imagination of Marx or Durkheim and just as appropriate to the times as were theirs. Whether Castells idealises urban social movements and exaggerates their potential remains to be seen.

Reading 61 From Stuart Lowe, *Urban Social Movements: The City After Castells* (Macmillan, 1986), pp. 2–5, 17–21, 33–5.

Among the research workers and writers who fashioned the new urban politics, the figure of Manuel Castells is dominant. His book, *The Urban Question*, remains the most discussed and influential work of the new literature because in it are the foundations of a distinct 'urban' sociology: a field divorced from the institutionally contained urbanism thesis of the Chicago School (Park, Burgess, McKenzie, 1925; Wirth, 1928, 1938), which was the only other school of sociology to have identified a distinctively urban subject matter. Writing initially from within a continental neo-Marxist school, associated with the structuralist philosopher Althusser, Castells condemned all previous urban sociology as ideological, and reconstructed a new subject field which saw the urban system not as the location of geographically contained social processes, but as the focus of political conflict based on state intervention into the provision of key public services. The 'urban' was defined as the arena of the 'collective consumption' process. The significance of this at the political level was, as Castells saw it, that the urban was a focal point of a range of new challenges to the dominant capitalist order, matching the industrial class struggle as a fundamental source of social change. Within this conflictive process, Castells pointed particularly to the significant role of 'urban social movements' as harbingers of the transformation of the social relations of society. In its initial formulation, urban social movements, in alliance with the advanced sections of the working-class movement, were to create a revolutionary change in the distribution of power away from capitalist interests and towards socialism. Urban sociology was thus no longer a small, if influential, sub-discipline of academic sociology but was the theoretical basis for new schools of thought and urban practices at the centre stage of social transformation.

Over a decade on from his radical text of 1972 (published in English in 1977), Castells produced a new English language work in which he candidly renounces his early position, particularly the idea that class struggle is the motor force of social change, and adopts a new set of propositions concerning urban social change. But in *The City and the Grassroots* (1983), Castells retains at the core of his analysis the concept of urban social movements as the originators of alternative political and cultural systems: indeed, urban social movements are disengaged from association with political parties as initiators of change and stand as autonomous organisations constantly generating the possibility of new 'meaning systems'. Since Castells is a founding father of the new urban sociology, tracing the evolution in his thinking is likely to be productive as a means of exploring and reviewing the debate about the urban system and process.

But what are urban social movements? There has been some discussion about the precise meaning of the phrase. In this study, the meaning adopted is different from the relatively specialised usage of Castells. It is important at the outset to be clear about definitions. The term is used here to mean organisations standing outside the formal party system which bring people together to defend or challenge the provision of urban public services and to protect the local environment. The implication of these organisations as 'social movements' is that their objectives are undertaken collectively by the mobilisation of a distinct social base and that the momentum of their activity is towards changes in policy direction. The definition suggested by Dunleavy fits closely to this notion: 'The important elements here are the stress on collectivity and on the push towards change of some kind. An urban social movement must display these characteristics in organising around urban issues of collective consumption' (Dunleavy, 1980, p. 156). Dunleavy goes on to draw attention to the distinctive organisational style of these groups – their grassroots orientation and unhierarchical mode of organisation, their distance from and non-involvement in formal party politics, and their emphasis on direct action and protest tactics. It is on these grounds that it is possible to distinguish urban social movements from conventional pressure groups and voluntary associations. The pattern of genesis of urban social movements in this definition is characteristically the creation of an issue around a particular social base, that is to say an objectively identifiable population targeted by an urban policy agency or policy issue. Mobilisation around these bases by no means always occurs, and one of the key themes in the analysis of urban social movements is the uncovering of forces and processes that operate at the institutional level to screen out social conflict; the theme of non-action is most readily approached in the analytical field of urban protest movements.

There has been an upsurge of urban social movement activity in Britain over the last two decades. Specific organisations of this type include the council house tenants' movement (dating from the late 1960s), which opposed government restructuring of rents towards market levels and the introduction of means-tested rebates; the ratepayer organisations that emerged in the mid-1970s to promote private sector provision of urban services and the abolition of rates; a range of groups opposing public spending cuts, giving rise to organisations concerned to save village and local schools, to defend smaller hospitals against mergers into large-scale district hospitals; redevelopment action groups that emerged in every major population centre where urban renewal and slum clearance programmes threatened stable communities and good quality housing; the squatters' movement that developed, particularly in London, in the late 1960s and reached a peak in the mid-1970s, housing thousands of single young people and families in empty public and private sector property; organisations to defend and promote public transport;

groups against road-widening schemes and the building of trans-urban motorways; groups emerging at the time of the Health and Safety at Work Act (1974) that had gained a new understanding of the effects of industrial pollution on local residents. The list is by no means comprehensive but it does indicate the range of groups in Britain that fall within our adopted definition of urban social movements. This range and intensity of movements marked a significant upsurge of political activism in the British context. However, it is also clear that what happened in Britain was but a small part of a much wider post-war escalation of urban protest throughout the world, with an intensification in the 1960s and 1970s. Chapter 6 is directed specifically towards discussing comparative urban social movements and explores the evidence for the existence of cross-national structuring of urban protest. As will be shown in Chapter 2, the core of Castells's 1983 text is directed towards developing a comparative, cross-cultural theory of urban social change which has urban social movements as its central mechanism.

In *The City and the Grassroots*, Castells completely reorientates his use of the theory of urban social movements. They are still at the centre of his ideas on urban-based social change, but now, among other things, must be autonomous from political parties and be more involved in creating new cultural settings and urban 'meaning'. The consistent element in Castells's usage is this ability to achieve some fundamental type of social change.

Urban social movements – phase one

In his early articles and texts, we must recall again, Castells locates his theoretical position within formal structuralism. The dominant level is the economic and the primary contradiction in society is between capital and labour at the point of production. In this context it follows that urban social movements – organisations that consciously and materially alter the balance of class forces in society – can only be generated if they can be linked to the dominant level. As secondary contradictions there is no possibility of urban movements, on their own, being able to produce 'effects' that change the structure of social relations.

there is no qualitative transformation of the urban structure that is not produced by an articulation of the urban movements with other movements, in particular (in our societies) with the working class movement and the political class struggle. (Castells, 1977, p. 453)

At this stage Castells is arguing that urban movements are only capable of becoming urban social movements if they are drawn into the advanced sections of the working-class movement.

Urban social movements – phase two

The problems associated with the structural determination of social change, and in particular the way in which Castells theorised secondary contradictions (and the 'urban' within that level) began to produce significant changes of emphasis in his position in the mid-1970s. His view of urban social movements entered a completely new phase that had been, to some extent, prefaced in Part Five of *The Urban Question*. The key text in this period is his *City, Class and Power* (1978a), which is a collection of articles and essays written between 1971 and 1977. But in new material – the Introduction and concluding chapter – Castells updates his general perspective and begins to look forward to a major re-working of his analysis of the urban system.

There are two main areas of development in the text. These concern, first, adaptations to his general theorisation of the urban, and, second, a new formula for the politicisation of the revised urban system. Under the first heading the key change involves the identification of new forms of social cleavage arising from collective consumption but *not* dependent on the class system *per se* for their existence in the social system, or as a source of political conflict.

> our hypothesis is precisely that . . . there is a new source of inequality in the very use of these collective goods which have become a fundamental part of the daily consumption pattern. (Castells, 1978a, p. 16)

This makes quite explicit the point that was emerging towards the end of *The Urban Question*. In an article from 1975, Castells uses this analysis to upgrade his initial reading of urban issues within the structural level of secondary contradictions. They do not supplant the primary capital/labour contradiction, but he now reaches a point where there is much greater parity between the two levels:

> we are not proposing the replacement of the labour/capital

contradiction which defines the working class by a new principal contradiction defined in the sphere of socialised consumptions; rather, it is the deepening of a secondary structural contradiction and the new historical role it can play through social movements and the processes of change it can potentially provoke. (Castells, 1978a, p. 127)

This position points also to the second area of development in the 1978 book, concerning the politicisation of the urban. Here Castells suggests that urban-based movements may have an *autonomous* role in social change, a role that his earlier model of urban political conflict (based solely on the linkage of secondary contradictions to the working-class movement) vigorously denied. It clearly follows that if there are non-class-based consumption stakes, then there can equally as well be consumption-based political movements that do not depend on the mediation of a vanguard party to achieve political 'effects'; although at this stage Castells does not in fact draw out the complete logic of this position.

Urban social movements – phase three

The whole of Castells's previous position, certainly as it appears in *The Urban Question* based on urban issues as secondary contradictions in the social system, now gives way to a plurality of other primary sources of change. Castells goes on to classify these movements for social change into three main types arising from the particular goals that each pursues:

1. Groups involved in collective consumption issues that seek to build a notion of urban living based on the city as an entity concerned with need (use value) rather than for profit (exchange value).

2. Groups that fight to defend or create communities with a particular cultural identity; arising from historic or ethnic sources. The defence of 'inter-personal communication' is contrasted to the hegemony of the mass media in the arena of personal and community association. Movements orientated to this goal are called 'community movements' by Castells.

3. The goal of attempting to achieve local self-government and the decentralisation of service provision from the central state, the 'struggle for a free city', is undertaken by groups called 'citizens' movements'.

These three themes, of the relationships of consumption, of communication and of power are the new core of Castells's urban political analysis, and it is around them that he constructs his third phase urban social movements.

As with his original specification of urban social movements – organisations that can effect social change – so in their most recent form they are singled out for their ability to create a qualitatively new balance of relationships within the social system. But in this case the change that is required concerns the impact that can be made on 'urban meaning'. Organisations that achieve this do so as a result of synthesising in their practice the three elements of collective consumption demands, community culture and political self-management. Only organisations that interconnect these themes are capable of accomplishing a change of urban meaning. Urban social movements are defined as

> a collective conscious action aimed at the transformation of the institutionalised urban meaning against the logic, interest, and values of the dominant class. It is our hypothesis that only urban social movements are the urban-orientated mobilisations that influence structural social change and transform the urban meaning. (Castells, 1983, p. 305)

The political strategy on which these movements are based extends the 1978 position by insisting on the *separation* between urban social movements and political parties:

> while urban social movements must be connected to the political system to at least partially achieve their goals, they must be organisationally and ideologically autonomous of any political party. (Castells, 1983, p. 322)

The reasons for this insistence on political autonomy arise from his new reading of the social system reliant on social process, meaning here personal and group interaction, to achieve changes in values and meaning systems. To be able to implement value and meaning changes urban movements must be ideologically untainted by party programmes. Castells sees that political parties are bound into the 'political level', which refers in this text to the area defined previously by Castells as the theme of urban planning; broadly, it is the state apparatus operating in the terms of dominant social interests. On the other hand urban social movements relate to 'civil

461

society', which is a separate level of the social structure in which dominant values and institutional norms are not necessarily accepted. This is why social movements are the genuine source of social change whereas political parties remain only at the level of political bargaining. But Castells is careful to argue that an open political system is necessary in order to permit the innovations proposed by urban social movements to be carried through.

> Without political parties and without an open political system, the new values, demands, and desires generated by social movements not only fade (which they always do, anyway) but do not light up in the production of social reform and institutional change. (Castells, 1983, p. 294)

Unfortunately this leads to an ambiguous conclusion that although urban social movements can innovate social change, they themselves cannot carry it through to a transformation of society because this depends on adaptations at the political level.

Question
1. (a) *What is an urban social movement?*

(5 marks)

(b) *How does Castells relate urban social movements to his analysis of capitalist society?*

(10 marks)

(c) *Do you consider that Castells idealises urban social movements and exaggerates their potential?*

(5 marks)

SECTION 12

Development/Underdevelopment (Industrial Society versus Marxist Interpretation)

Readings 62–67

The first reading in this section, by Robin Cohen, is an excellent overview of the area. Cohen gives due emphasis to the methodological importance of the comparative approach (see also Reading 99) as well as to the theoretical debate around the development/underdevelopment issue. In the second reading, Malcolm Cross critically summarises modernisation theory, including an important contribution from Bert Hoselitz. The brief reading from Gunder Frank outlines underdevelopment theory and Frank Gaffikin and Andrew Nickson (Reading 65) give a clear outline of the international role of multi- (or trans-) national corporations. The two examples given of the operation of multinationals in the Third World give practical illustration of many of the points raised more theoretically by Frank and by Gaffikin and Nickson.

The final reading in this section by Christian Rogerson is on apartheid. It probes the economic and, to a lesser extent, the racial roots of this notorious system of exploitation.

62 Robin Cohen: An Introduction to the Methodology and Scope of the Sociology of 'Development'

This reading is a highly authoritative overview of the sociology of development/underdevelopment. If there are any lingering doubts about the relevance of this area to introductory sociology courses, this extract should remove them.

Cohen's arguments cover two areas: methodology and content. He fully illustrates that the comparative sociology of development was a central part of the methodological equipment of the major nineteenth century sociologists and, in the twentieth century, of Max Weber. Comparative sociology partly fulfils the function of the experiment in the natural sciences. Pursued systematically, comparative sociology seeks to establish different types of society and explanations for the differences between them (a full account of comparative sociology is given in Reading 99). Even those for whom these goals seem too ambitious would hardly deny that comparative data can usefully support a theoretical position. Cohen concludes this section by giving some explanations for the decline of comparative sociology in the post-second world war period. It can be added by way of emphasis that this decline has reached the point where there is widespread ignorance about the methodological application of comparative sociology.

The next section in the reading deals with the period between 1945 and 1970, when Western sociology of Third World societies was rather weak but general academic interest in them high. Economic theories of development, such as Rostow's, tended to dominate, and social and cultural aspects of the kind that sociology might have explored tended to be crudely interpreted. As a result, development policy and planning was often narrowly conceived and inadequate in scope.

Since the seventies a revival of the sociology of development has taken place which, if anything, transcends its original conception. Cohen describes four features of current studies of development:

1. comparative sociology
2. the growth of holistic sociology
3. the revival of Marxist political economy
4. an increased appreciation by development agencies of the application of sociology.

To these, it is possible to add a fifth aspect, more apparent perhaps after the Ethiopian famine of 1985 than when Cohen wrote. That is the moral imperative to know something about and perhaps do something about the problems and progress of Third World societies.

Reading 62 From Robin Cohen, 'The Sociology of Development and the Development of Sociology' in *Social Science Teacher*, Vol.12, No.2, Spring 1983, pp. 52–6

Introduction

The sociology of development is a specialism that has gained an increasing place in the syllabi provided by 'A' level examiners, particularly those of the AEB and Cambridge boards. Though this article is in no sense an attempt to provide a summary account of the provisions of the syllabi (I've had nothing to do with their framing or examination), I attempt nonetheless to situate and interpret some of the contrasting positions in the field. The article may therefore be of some use as a guide to teachers unfamiliar, or only partially familiar, with the relevant literature.

Early concerns and the disappearance of the sociology of development

The fairly sudden interest shown in the Sociology of Development by those who have been responsible for drafting our new syllabi might lead some teachers to assume that this is yet another example of the proliferation of sociologies 'of' that we've had to cope with in recent years. In addition to the established sub-fields of the sociologies of industry, law, religion, education and medicine, in recent years there have either been revivals or freshly constructed sociologies of – knowledge, race relations, deviance, literature, leisure, communications, culture, and so on. In its origins, the sociology of development was not like one of the sociologies 'of' just mentioned, but rather constituted a vital element in the provenance of the discipline itself. By this I mean, that the classical 19th century sociologists, the so-called founding fathers of the discipline, were in fact much preoccupied with societal development as a whole. They did not confine their sociological theory or their sociological observations to any one set of problems – like crime, social stratification, the family structure – nor again were they inhibited in addressing the question of social development in societies other than their own.

Indeed, Durkheim explicitly laid the ground for work in comparative sociology by warning his fellow-sociologists, first in 1893 in the

Division of Labour and again in the next year in his *Rules of Socio-logical Method* to:

> . . . *renounce* the method all too often followed by sociologists who, to prove their thesis, are content with citing without order and haphazardly a more or less impressive number of favourable facts . . . One cannot explain a social fact of any complexity except by following its complete development *through all social species*. Comparative sociology is not a branch of sociology, it is sociology itself. (Cited Payne 1973 p. 14)

Again, on this side of the Channel, John Stuart Mill, who can perhaps be counted as a fraternal cousin, if not a founding father of the discipline, had insisted on what he called 'the study of concomitant variation' as one method of inductive enquiry in his *System of Logic*. (See Payne 1973.) Durkheim's observations, though methodologically and theoretically exciting, didn't mean that he entirely practised what he preached. He derived his theory of religion, *The Elementary Forms of Religious Life*, from one case, that of the Australian aborigines, and *that* was not based on direct fieldwork. On the other hand, his study of *Suicide* was remarkably widely based for his time, covering as it did some 26,000 records in Central Europe, France, Britain and Denmark, classified by age, sex, religion, number of children and marital state – all hand-tabulated, one might add, for those who have the modern convenience of a computer or calculator.

Comparative work on societal development in the 19th century was, however, limited in two essential respects. One I've already mentioned in referring to Durkheim's work on religion. The 19th century sociologists relied on the characteristically prejudiced or fanciful ethnographic accounts collected by missionaries and travellers. And where that did not suffice, 'haphazard favourable facts' (to use Durkheim's terminology) were assembled from classical history, the Bible or from a fictive 'state of nature'. The second limitation is that with only rare exceptions 19th century theorists were trapped in the great precognition of the Enlightenment – that man was destined to escape 'barbarism' and to establish higher and higher planes of 'civilisation'. In sociology, as in biology (at that time a kindred subject), the specific form this precognition took was in the development of evolutionary theory. The supposed 'law' of evolution was shared by Maine, McLennan, Morgan, Taylor,

Spencer and Frazer and with some important qualifications, Marx, to mention only some of the adherents of this view. This position was shared also by Darwin who in praising his contemporary, the English sociologist Herbert Spencer, saw in Spencer's work the foundation for 'far more important researches' than his own. Darwin indeed concludes *The Origin of Species* by espousing a typical evolutionary statement.

'We may look' he says 'with some confidence to a secure future of great length. And as natural selection works solely for the good of each being, all corporeal and mental endowments will tend to progress towards perfection'. (Darwin 1958 edition pp. 449–50)

For sociologists the equivalent theory was to establish an historical chain from early 'primitive' or acephelous societies, to civil or 'modern' society. Though this implied a study of the full range of variation, few 19th century sociologists (Marx being a notable exception), were able to use their classificatory schemes to specify the middle ground between the two poles with any degree of precision. The result was normally a naive optimism about the inevitability of social progress, which was seen as a unilinear process, combined with a set of crude and over-simplified dualisms – which dogged sociological reasoning for many years afterwards. Dualisms like traditional-modern, agrarian-industrial, folk and urban cultures, Gemeinschaft-Gesellschaft, mechanical and organic forms of solidarity became commonplace.

While the limits to classical sociological discourse are clear and real, in a sense I don't want to attack it too fiercely because it had the redeeming virtues of holism and at least the beginnings of a comparative method. This concern for societies in the round, for world societies if you like, survived, but not all that vigorously, into the 20th century – it survived in particular in the work of Max Weber. Weber's discussion of the complex relationship between religious belief and economic practice did not only involve – as even some sociologists are wont to believe – his justly famous study of the *Protestant Ethic and the Spirit of Capitalism* in Western Europe. Rather, he paid considerable attention to the connection, or absence of a connection, between religion and entrepreneurship in India, China and ancient Palestine. He had even sketched, but not completed, some comparative work on Islam. However, Weber's wide vision did not stimulate other sociologists to undertake detailed empirical accounts of countries outside the advanced industrial societies. Instead, I think it could be fairly argued that from the 1920s and continuing into the post war period, there is a major rupture with the concerns of the early sociologists, a rupture which had the effect of narrowing the range of societies under investigation quite dramatically. Ultimately, 'sociology' became little more than the sociologies of Britain, France, the United States and Germany. Even within the much reduced sub-set of 'all social species' sociology acquired a national flavour with all too little cross-societal comparison.

The reasons that can be adduced for this rupture are numerous and I do not propose to go into them too deeply on this occasion. Let me, however, provide some brief suggestions. Within the USA, for example, the new-found preoccupation with quantitative verification led to the desire to use statistical data that was easily accessible and qualitatively superior to that which could be assembled for far-off places. The survey method also was more easily applicable to samples drawn from a convenient and culturally familiar environment. In the case of Britain, sociology became institutionalised very much within the ambit of indigenous social philosophy – post-utilitarianism, liberalism and Fabianism. In both countries, the demand for relevance meant the discipline became involved (or more accurately, enmeshed), in social policy – social policy, moreover, that was linked to welfarist objectives close to the areas of visible social deprivation. Also of great significance was the parallel development (at first unique to Britain) of social anthropology. The subject grew up very much in tandem with colonial administration and in general, the study of the non-British world, outside the US, France and Germany, became the preserve of social anthropologists. Some, like Radcliffe-Brown, made notable contributions to the emergent functionalist perspective in sociology. But his own work tended to stress static normative structures and types of society rather than to examine patterns of change or actual behaviour. Other anthropologists firmly embraced a notion of cultural relativity, arguing that societies had to be assessed very much within their own terms: that alone permitted an appreciation of the specificity of kinship, ritual, language and social structure. The worst anthropologists engaged themselves in an ever more frantic search to find their micro-anthropological zoos – societies that had evaded the most dramatic effects of the universal processes of urbanisation, industrialisation and exposure to the world market.

The cumulative effect of these tendencies was to make inimical the study of underdeveloped areas and regions from a comparative or holistic standpoint.

The post-war period, 1945–1970: the underdevelopment of sociology

This period can be characterised as a period of general academic interest in the societies of what came to be called the Third World, but a partial or weak response from inside the mainstream of sociology itself. Some comparative theoretical work was presaged in the formulations of structural functionalists like Parsons, Levy, Bellah and Eisenstadt who saw development in terms of the increasing differentiation of structure and the increasing specialisation of function. For Parsons, this could be expressed in terms of his well-known five paired pattern-variables: (a) Universalism/Particularism, (b) Achievement/Ascription, (c) Affectivity/Affective-neutrality, (d) Specificity/Diffuseness and (e) Self-orientation/Collective-orientation. Though obviously a more comprehensive schema showing greater theoretical sophistication and rigour, the elaboration of the supposed universal pattern variables mediating social action, still echoed the more prosaically expressed dualisms of an earlier period. And again, there was initially little interest shown in providing detailed sociological accounts of societies outside the major metropolitan countries. This can, for example, be documented in the case of the US, where Marsh found that of the 1,479 doctoral dissertations presented in the 23 most productive Departments of Sociology between 1950 and 1960, only 12% were concerned with societies other than the US and only 8% dealt with societies other than the US, Canada and Western Europe. (Marsh 1976 p. 6.) Equivalent quantitative data for Britain is less easy to come by, but Krausz's survey of research in British sociology covering the early fifties to the late sixties, simply ignored all empirical work not directly concerned with British data. He rather piously hoped, however, that this editorial decision would not 'be interpreted as a narrow attitude *per se.*' (Krausz 1969 p. 3.)

The growth of interest in developing societies thus took place predominantly outside the discipline and was essentially a reflection of the real world into the academic consciousness. India became independent in 1947 while an even greater mass mobilisation was evident in China where the communists came to power in 1948. As the old European empires collapsed, the whole continents of Asia, Africa and Latin America were increasingly seen by Western leaders as an ideological battleground where the natural appeal of communism to the poor and underprivileged was to be countered by the new magical word 'development' – conducted of course under the aegis of the West's new hegemonic power, the United States. Characteristically, John F. Kennedy caught the mood of the times. In a speech defending the Alliance for Progress in 1963, two and a half years after his disastrous decision to back an invasion of Cuba at the Bay of Pigs by Cuban exiles, he maintained:

> . . . the hard reality of life in Latin America, will not be solved simply by complaints about Castro, by blaming all problems on Communism or generals or nationalism. The harsh facts of poverty and social injustice will not yield merely to promises and goodwill. The task we have set ourselves in the Alliance for Progress – the development of an entire continent – is a far greater task than any we have ever undertaken. It will require difficult and painful labor over a long period of time. (Kennedy 1964 p. 160)

In assessing the academic work of the period, it is impossible to escape the political context within which it was generated. This extended even to the personalities involved. The economist Walt Rostow, author of *The Stages of Economic Growth*, subtitled a *Non-Communist Manifesto* (Rostow 1962 and 1967), was director of Policy and Planning in the State Department and President Johnson's advisor on Vietnam. The political scientist and government advisor, Samuel Huntington, likewise combined policy and scholarship in his *Political Order in Changing Societies*. (Huntington 1961.) There he attempted to alter the principal criterion for being a recipient of US aid, from being anyone who maintained an anti-communist posture, whatever the nature of their internal policies, to one which stressed the capacity of a third world government to maintain internal order, more or less irrespective of its declared ideological preference.

If the political context was all important to understand why the US government and its allies were now vitally concerned with the process of development, it was at first to the economists that the governments and the development agencies turned for advice and succour. The answer that emerged was disarmingly unproblematic – a massive injection of capital was needed – state capital in the form of foreign aid, private capital channelled through the multinationals, investment brokers and banks and multi-lateral capital channelled through the international agencies and the World Bank. The solution found a ready response in many third world governments. As a self-declared socialist politician in a small francophone West African state plaintively but accurately remarked: 'How can we be capitalists, if we have no capital?' (Modiba Keita – cited from memory, source unknown).

The theoretical support for the capital injection solution was poorly articulated. Rostow, for example, advanced a five-stage model which claimed that all societies in their economic dimensions, lay within five categories: the traditional society, the preconditions for take-off, the take-off, the drive to maturity, and the age of high mass consumption. Thus was the unilinear development path of the 19th century theorists re-established. But whereas the 19th century theorists worked with rather abstract categories of what advanced or backward societies looked like, now a more specific and more ethnocentric version of modernisation theory was propagated by Rostow, *et al*. The US was the most advanced industrial country, with the highest levels of technical and scientific achievement, and the highest per capita income: *ergo*, any country which sought development was destined to follow the trail-blazing path of that country. As the decade of the 1960s, the UN's Development Decade, progressed, there appeared some cruel shocks to the hope of a capital injection solution. Even where statistically high rates of growth were achieved, there were self-evident problems of redistributing the new wealth to those who most needed it. Further, rates of illiteracy remained distressingly high while poverty, ill-health, and shanty-housing were everywhere in evidence. It was in response to the perceived failure of development strategies, that some sociologists and social psychologists were, as it were, called in as nurses to wrap a few band-aids around the suppurating wounds of economic development theory. The social psychologist David McClelland advanced the notion that the peoples of the underdeveloped world from their early years lacked *n.ach.* (the need for achievement). Their folk-tales and patterns of socialisation stressed cooperation, not competition, youthful entrepreneurs were inhibited from achieving their aims by family responsibilities, while short-term financial pursuits were preferred to deferred gratification. Other sociologists and anthropologists pronounced on the negative effects of the extended family system, or the supposed 'culture of poverty' which allowed people to accommodate to their conditions of deprivation or the contradictory family planning decision taken by agricultural communities to have more children to increase the numbers available for family labour, but at the same time produce more mouths than their agricultural produce could possibly feed. Somehow it seemed, if there was poverty, it was 'all their own fault'.

Of course, there were a few dissenting voices to the picture of fixated economists and their handmaiden sociologists. Gunner Myrdal had talked in terms of the theory of 'the cumulation of backwardness'. On the right, Peter Bauer had rejected all forms of aid as a viable economic strategy, while on the left, Baran and Sweezy had propounded a theory of monopoly capitalist development which stressed the production of waste at the centre and the extraction of 'surplus' from international trade (i.e. in the sphere of circulation) as well as at the point of production. (Baran and Sweezy 1966.) But these voices remained at the periphery of the academic debate and very far from the critical centres of decision-making. (Cohen *et al* 1977.) It was into this vacuum that certain radical, so-called 'structuralist' or dependency theorists, mainly based in Latin America, stepped. One in particular, Andre Gunder Frank, made a quite critical intervention in his essay – *'The Sociology of Development and the Underdevelopment of Sociology'* first published in 1967. To anticipate my argument a little, I believe that while Frank was largely correct in the characterisation of contemporary writings, most of the authors he cites were not in fact sociologists, nor was the pessimism he expressed there justified when we look at the strength of subsequent theoretical work. Frank basically indicted three approaches common to American social science at the time – all of which he argued were empirically invalid, theoretically inadequate and ineffective at the level of policy. These he characterised as (a) the Index or Gap Approach, which set up supposedly ideal-typical characteristics of development against which third world societies were found wanting. In criticism of this approach, Frank scornfully declared that the Parsonian-type pattern variables like universalism, were as much or more absent in the US as they were in Latin America. Where else could Robert McNamara, the President of Ford Motor Co., become Secretary of Defence – in succession to 'Engine Charlie' Wilson who gave the world the *bon mot* of 'what's good for General Motors is good for the country'. (b) The second approach, the Diffusionist Approach, concerned itself with how these assumed typical characteristics were diffused into the underdeveloped countries. The underdeveloped were told to wait until capital, knowledge, skills, technology and modern values reached them, but in fact, so Frank argued, the flow happened the other way. Over the period 1950–1965, $9 billion of investment went to the underdeveloped countries from the US, but $25.6 billion in profit flowed back to that country. (c) The third approach, the Psychological Approach, concentrated on how the diffused values were to be accelerated within the 'underdeveloped' centres by reorganising fantasy and family life to promote, in McClelland's formulation, a higher degree of the need for achievement. In this way, great cultures of the third world were told to bow down to the two great gods of American society, Santa Claus and Sigmund Freud. Frank concluded that in all three approaches, underdevelopment was wrongly understood as a natural *condition* (something like original sin), and needed rather to be conceived as an *outcome* of the relationship underdeveloped zones had with the metropolitan zones they were linked to. Underdevelopment was thus a *process*, one zone *became* underdeveloped because of the development of another.

In Frank's terminology history showed a 'development of underdevelopment' initiated by metropoli over their satellite regions. Now clearly this was an important breakthrough, and when Frank cast about for sociological analyses that would ground his critique, he found none of any consequence. His work was really predicated on a radical trade theory, continued Baran's idea that surplus could be extracted through trade and drew very little on sociological reasoning. As I've argued, sociology had retreated behind national barriers, while the exception, modernisation theory, was often crudely ethnocentric or blindly evolutionary. Frank was thus correct in attacking the failings of sociology at that time.

The decade 1970–1980: the development of sociology

During the 1970s, by contrast to the earlier period, a number of major advances in the sociology of development were observable.

473

These were made partly by restructuring and regrounding older theory, partly by elaborating and criticising dependency theory and partly also by sociologists gaining a significant voice in development agencies and institutions.

Once again it was changes in the external world that served to crack the political hegemony on which the ideological pre-eminence of modernisation theory had rested. Let me identify here only two major shifts in consciousness. First, a largely peasant nation, Vietnam, had stood up to the global power of the United States, and not to put too fine a point on it, had defeated it. Technological and material superiority was henceforth to be thought of as inferior to 'winning the hearts and minds of the people' to use a phrase of the times. Second, within the core industrialised societies, there was a spiritual and moral crisis popularly referred to as the growth of a counter-culture or the 'greening of America', which questioned the trajectory and purpose of a society based predominantly on the cash nexus. Interestingly enough, the models that were assembled for cultural recognition and reference, were those characteristic of pre-industrial societies like those of the native Americans, together with eastern religious models which stressed spiritual awareness, and a certain directness and frankness in social relationships which were firmly distinguished from the desire for material improvement. Under the impact of these and other changes a unilinear modernisation theory now became impossible to sustain.

A variety of fresh approaches to the study of development now became possible. While the strands of theory-building are complex and intertwined, perhaps four predominant approaches or trajectories are discernable: (a) the movement back to a genuinely comparative sociology, (b) the growth of holistic sociologies, (c) the revival of Marxist political economy and (d) a recognition from within the development agencies themselves of the importance of a sociological perspective. The first is in a sense a reaffirmation of Durkheim's original vision and has a particular importance for methodology. Durkheim had established three levels of comparison: (a) variations within one society at one time (a study commonly undertaken by practising sociologists), (b) variations in several similar societies (either at one time or at several times) and (c) variations in several dissimilar societies (either by time or place) which contain some similar features. The last two had never been systematically pursued even though this provides immense methodological advantages for sociology and allows us to mitigate the disadvantages we have in being unable to use the experimental method as a basis for research. (I might add that sciences sharing a common problem include geology, seismology, astronomy and genetic engineering.) Like these other sciences, instead of artificially inducing variations in phenomena in the laboratory, we can study and observe the variable phenomena themselves. (Nadel cited in Payne 1973 p. 16.) In this respect, the sociology of development is making a crucial contribution to the development of the discipline itself, by extending the range and scope of comparison. This task has also been much aided by the recent growth of indigenous sociologies in certain third world countries, notably Mexico and Brazil.

Second, and this trajectory really follows the insights of dependency theorists, practitioners of the sociology of development have recognised that it is no longer possible to treat the undeveloped countries as objects of study separable from the central societies with which they are symetrically but inescapably linked – through aid, trade, investment, migration and political and ideological fealties. In its original form, Raul Prebisch and the other economists working for ECLA (the United Nations Economic Commission for Latin America) saw their structuralist analysis as a way of arresting underdevelopment by isolation. Instead of opening their economies to unrestricted investment from the metropole, a strong interventionist government with a strong nationalist thrust could mitigate their economic dependency by, for example, import substitution behind high tariff walls. Some would take this process much further. Richard Gott, the journalist and editor, in attacking the *North-South Programme for Survival* (the Brandt Commission's report) in a recent article argued that if accepted, the report would only serve to patch up the existing world system:

> . . . just at the moment when there are signs all over the Third World that peoples and nations are beginning to envisage breaking loose from the existing one. Never before has the system been so questioned. The mindless pursuit of international trade, the soulless promotion of industrialisation, the persistent destruction of local agriculture is at last being held up to criticism and ridicule. (Gott 1980)

The statement envisages a degree of autarky that is clearly now impossible, but it does open the question of what are the benefits

475

and disadvantages conferred by pushing a national economy more tightly into the net of the world system. Unlike the simple-minded versions of capital injection, the issues at stake now are what form of capital investment is acceptable, from whom and to what end? What form of export-oriented commodity should be produced, to whom should it be sold and on what terms? What balance can be established between industry and agriculture, rural and urban sectors, growth and redistribution – in the end, between *social* and *economic* development? As to the overall global system of dependency Gott rails against, of course it exists and is likely to persist. But at least in one case it is clear that the talons are not only reaching out in one direction. If the system operates by cartels, monopolies and price fixing in the Bourse, the City of London or Chicago then it could also be fixed in Riyadh and Caracas, as OPEC demonstrated. The same manoeuvre was attempted though with much less success in the case of cocoa, coffee, copper and other commodities. Sociologists of development are centrally engaged in understanding the social processes that underlie these shifts and realignments of contemporary world economic and political power. Another version of world sociology seeks to examine, not present-day attempts at self-development, but rather recovers an historical, but firmly holistic perspective. This has involved, at least in the version dominated by Immanuel Wallerstein, an eclectic combination of a cybernetic analogy (the world as a system, with core, semi-peripheral and peripheral zones), a link with the historians of the grand vision, in particular Braudel and the *Annales* school, the historical economics of Weber, Schumpeter and Poulantzas, the Marxism of Lenin and Mao Zedung, and the third-world perspectives of Fanon, Balandier, and the 'structuralists' or dependency theorists – already referred to. (Goldfrank 1979 p. 10.) Wallerstein's *The Modern World System* (1974) has already become the *locus classicus* of this trajectory, even though only the first two volumes covering the growth of the capitalist system in the sixteenth and seventeenth centuries have been published. Further volumes are anticipated from Wallerstein's home base in the Fernand Braudel Center for the Study of Economics, Historical Systems and Civilizations (no less) at Binghamton.

The third approach is basically a revival of the classical Marxist debates, sometimes organised under the rubric of 'political economy'. This, of course, presents some irony as Marx himself had constructed his economic theory largely as a critique of Scottish political economy. Another source of confusion, is that both the dependency and world systems approaches have been narrowly and falsely conflated with a Marxist conception by these theorists themselves. Perhaps the most useful task here is not to give a detailed account of all Marxist positions on development (which range from official Russian, Chinese, Cuban, Albanian, North Korean, etc. models to Trotskyism and Althusserianism), but rather to indicate where the paths diverge. Firstly, the dependency and world-system approaches tend to use aggregated data from *countries* (which therefore become their principal units of analysis) rather than concentrating centrally on *classes* and how they are enplaced within a particular mode of production. Secondly, the dependency theorists concentrate essentially on the sphere of exchange and circulation (trade, investment, etc.) rather than, as Marxists would insist, the sphere of production. Thirdly, there was a common misunderstanding, not necessarily propagated by the central figures in the dependency and world-systems approaches, but rather by their followers, concerning Marx's original understanding of the process of underdevelopment. As Marx was to make clear in his writings on India, he does not see external capitalist penetration as wholly regressive and destructive (as dependency theorists believe). Rather, while he acknowledges the destructive force of the colonial intrusion into India, he believed that, 'England has to fulfill a double mission in India: one destructive, the other regenerating – the annihilation of the old society, *and* the laying of the material foundation of Western Society in Asia'. It was true that Macaulay's writings 'will bear comparison with the richest slang of highwaymen and cutthroats' but on the other hand: 'Has the bourgeoisie ever done more? Has it ever effected a progress without dragging individuals and peoples through blood and dirt, through misery and degradation?' (Marx 1969 edition pp. 132–3, 86, 137).

In short, the problem of 'underdevelopment' to be addressed was not that the colonialists exploited the third world (that much was evident and predictable) but that it exploited it insufficiently (exploitation now being used in the specific sense of raising the level of accumulation by a greater and greater expropriation of a surplus value). By drawing out these distinctions the lines are now sharpened between the Marxist current, and those of the world-system and structuralist theorists. The Marxist trajectory has taken two principal forms. At the macro societal level, with the aid of heavy doses of Althusserianism, 'the modes of production debate' (as it has come to be called) has been opened out. How does one characterise social formations on the periphery? If pre-capitalist, then how precisely is surplus value appropriated? – through the lineage (as Meillassoux argues for West Africa), through control of land apportionment (as theorists of the Andean mode of production have argued) and so on. How do modes of production differ from or resemble Marx's own typology – of primitive communalist, slave, feudal, Asiatic and capitalist modes? How, above all, do pre-capitalist modes articulate with the capitalist mode especially in the period when this becomes the dominant mode? (Taylor 1979.) At the level of the peripheral modes themselves, the Marxist debate has concentrated on the characteristics of other societies in terms of the evolving class structures – questions of peasantisation, proletarianisation and class formation amongst the strata close to the post-colonial state itself. What bonds link the ruling classes to their counterparts in the industrialised world? What sources of opposition exist to upset the post colonial order? Can one rely on the working class alone to act as an oppositional force, or is that itself enmeshed in a relatively privileged position? What political bonds can be effected between the potentially revolutionary classes and strata – progressive intellectuals, the peasantry, the working class and the huge army of unemployed and intermittently employed in the urban sprawls and *favelas* of Third World cities? (Cohen *et al* 1979 is a book of readings on these problems.)

The fourth and final trajectory in the post-1970 sociology of development that I wish to briefly consider is a far-reaching movement within the development agencies by advisors and policy-makers themselves. For me, the symbolic moment of arrival came in 1978 when the British Government Overseas Development Ministry (now Administration) advertised for Social Development Advisors in addition to their usual list asking for those with technological skills or economic expertise. Not of course that the agencies are about to embrace the questions addressed by the most radical theorists, but what is interesting, is how far they have moved to accepting that the development process is meaningless without some social (and even moral) content. Second, that participation in the development process must stem from below and not only involve the consent but also the active engagement of the supposed beneficiaries of development. Take for example this statement from the Third-

System Project, a project run by the International Foundation for Development Alternatives (sponsored largely by European social democratic funds). Here the project organisers argue:

> Development is the process of liberation of people and societies: it cannot be reduced to economic growth, as necessary as this may be when socially meaningful. . . . Power is exercised through the state and the market, but people have an autonomous power legitimately theirs, which they are increasingly asserting. Accountability of those who hold power – political, cultural, economic – must be established and mechanisms for its enforcement set up in all spaces of development. (IFDA 1980 p. 150)

The themes of accountability and participation are again stressed in a document entitled 'Social Development and the International Development Strategy' published by the United Nations Research Institute for Social Development:

> . . . the widely accepted objectives of self reliance require popular participation by definition. Popular participation, like meeting basic needs, is both a goal and a means of development. This is a fundamental socio-political issue, as it implies a redistribution of wealth and power among and within nations and social classes. The United Nations should do everything possible within its limitations to encourage participatory structures, processes, organisation and research. (UNRISD 1979 p. 15)

Maldevelopment in the centre: the relevance of development studies

Why do we in Britain need to study the sociology of the less developed nations, when we are ourselves in the midst of a prolonged economic crisis? Perhaps the first thing to emphasise is that the scale of the crisis is vastly different. We are not talking about mass poverty, food riots in the streets, unemployment which frequently exceeds one third of the male population, astronomically high infant mortality and illiteracy rates. There is every reason why our students should widen their intellectual and moral horizons to comprehend the full totality and degradation of the human condition. Sociologists should not devalue this essentially moral task of creating some bonds of international empathy by too cynical an outlook.

But, secondly, the sociology of development does provide an insight into our own condition. Of course this comparison can be exaggerated for dramatic effect, but I would like to at least mention in point form some of the analogies that I've found helpful pedagogically. (a) Wales, Scotland and Ireland can be analysed as 'internal colonies' of England – an analogy that is sometimes extended to the immigrant ghettos of the big cities. (b) Regionally, we have the problem of 'combined and uneven development' arising from sectorally overdeveloped areas like the South-East or the area affected by North Sea oil. (c) We also share the problems of maintaining an indigenous industry in the face of foreign capital, notably in the areas of consumer goods, cars and processed food. (d) Like peripheral societies, we too are having to learn to cope with the consequences of structural unemployment.

Though each one of these points can be unpacked and given detailed exposition, they all bear on one central critique. Much of our work in the social sciences is rooted too narrowly in a national outlook. We talk too quickly about the British economy, British politics or British society as if it is possible to disentangle the threads that link us – through economic ties, historical associations and political necessity – to other parts of the world. If we were, for example, to be crassly economistic, a quick glance at the financial pages of a quality newspaper will reveal that of the shares quoted on the British stock exchange, a large proportion are in foreign companies while many more are quotations for British companies with a substantial proportion of their operations overseas. If we then held to the rather crude view that our social structure is ultimately derivable from its economic base, how can we go on to describe the British social structure without reference to the fact that much of the relevant economy exists outside the formal boundaries of the state? Put at its minimum, what the study of the sociology of development should aim for is the understanding of Britain's place in world society.

This paper is adapted from Professor Cohen's inaugural lecture at the University of Warwick and from a lecture given to members of the ATSS at Loughborough University in October 1981.

Questions

1. *What is the comparative method and what are its applications and advantages?*

(10 marks)

2. *Account for the revival of the sociology of development.*

(15 marks)

63 Malcolm Cross: Modernisation Theory

Malcolm Cross introduces and then criticises modernisation theory. The theory is largely based on the view that to become 'modern', 'undeveloped' societies must adopt major Western cultural values (the 'culturalist' argument). Modernisation theorists vary on what precisely these values are but all reflect Parsons' analysis of the contrasting values of traditional and modern society. Parsons' emphasis on the need for the modern values of universalism (a system of rules equally applicable to all, e.g. equality before the law) and achievement is particularly apparent in the work of Bert Hoselitz discussed by Cross. It is the spread or 'diffusion' of modern values that fosters modernisation. (The city is the key entry point for Western values and ideas to undeveloped societies.)

There are some minor problems for the student with this extract, though they are more apparent than real. The opening paragraph is hard going, but after that the extract is well worth the mileage. Cross's criticisms of modernisation theory are particularly cogent but he nevertheless gives it a fair assessment. His occasional references to 'Caribbean societies' and 'plantation economies' can be ignored – the Caribbean is simply his area of specific interest.

Reading 63 From Malcolm Cross, 'Urbanisation and Urban Growth in the Caribbean' (Cambridge University Press, 1979), pp. 16–20.

Modernisation theory

There are numerous theories of social change that could be bracketed together as 'theories of modernisation'. Like the majority of rural-urban continua, they tend to focus the attention of the investigator on to patterns of social integration, where the urban or more

481

modern sector of the society is perceived as the independent or explanatory variable. Modernisation theories do have the advantage of stating a hypothetical relationship, but it is one which does not come to terms adequately with the colonial or postcolonial reality of Caribbean societies. The fundamental reason for this problem is that modernisation is conceived as the transformation of 'Third World' societies into liberal capitalist democracies, and urbanisation is seen as a concomitant of this process, since the city is the nucleus for the cultural penetration of the modernising society.

An essential ingredient of the modernisation approach is a 'culturalist' line of argument which maintains that social systems are organised and controlled in the last resort by the values, attitudes and beliefs of their social actors. It follows that if a society is attempting to undergo a social transformation from a 'traditional' to a 'modern' state then researchers should investigate these values and beliefs and, if they are required to give policy advice, they should suggest ways by which these may be replaced by others more conducive to change. Two examples may illustrate this perspective.

There is an extensive literature on the dimensions of value systems or 'value orientations' as they are sometimes termed. Most of the recent work originated with the contributions of Talcott Parsons and it is characterised by a functionalist approach to social change. One such study is that of J. A. Kahl on Mexico and Brazil who sought to measure 'modernism' by breaking this value component down into five variables. The 'modern' man was one who scored highly on a scale of 'activism' as opposed to 'fatalism', who betrayed a relatively low degree of integration with relatives but a high level of individualism, contact with the mass media and a pronounced interest in urban living. 'Modern' men also saw the occupational structure as open and regarded the sacrifices of occupational effort as worthwhile (Kahl, 1968: 18–22). The 'modern man' is stimulated by the city and urban life; 'he sees it as open to influence by ordinary citizens like himself'. Furthermore 'he sees life changes or career opportunities as open rather than closed; a man of humble origins has a chance to fulfil his dreams and rise within the system. He participates in urban life by actively availing himself of the mass media. He reads newspapers, listens to the radio, discusses civil affairs' (Kahl, 1968: 133). Not surprisingly, the thesis is advanced that the more modern one's men, the more likely a society is to develop and modernise, that is to converge towards the goal of 'development' reached by the United States. Another study illustrates the theoretical thinking that underpins this assumption.

An influential work by Bert Hoselitz suggests that the difference between an advanced economy (or the 'advanced' sector of an underdeveloped one) and others is that the former is characterised by:

1. Universalistic norms in determining the selection process for the attainment of economically relevant roles.
2. Roles that are functionally highly specific.
3. Norms for selection to these roles that are based upon achievement.
4. Elites that are oriented towards 'social objects of economic significance'.

(Hoselitz, 1960: 41).

Since the underdeveloped society has a predominant value system exactly opposed to this pattern, the problem becomes one of understanding the mechanism by which a transformation may take place. One crucial mechanism is the city itself because cities 'exhibit a spirit different from that of the countryside. They are the main force and the chief locus for the introduction of new ideas and new ways of doing things' (Hoselitz, 1960: 163).

The development problem is how to promote the natural 'diffusion' effect of the city so that it overcomes the 'resistance' of rural areas occasioned by their attachment to traditional or 'folk' ways of life. The cities have a cultural effect on the rest of society and by so doing they are able to provide a set of values and principles more conducive to the rationalism inherent in the modern business ethic, and thus to economic development. Hoselitz grants that, in the colonial context, a city or urban centre may have had a 'parasitic' effect on its hinterland, but this he regards as a short run phenomenon. In time, 'factors of change developed in and around the city which had the effect of turning the parasitic character of the city into a generative one' (Hoselitz, 1960: 193).

Hoselitz is aware of the fact that migrant patterns to urban centres differ in the underdeveloped society from the analogous processes in the West, in that the latter were accompanied by industrialisation. Migration here is seen as a response to the attractions of the city, not through employment but through 'the relatively strong pull of superior consumption patterns' (Hoselitz, 1960: 202), coupled with a decline of opportunities in rural areas. Again, the theory of urbanisation is dependent upon the effects of diffusion; as more and more people develop, or are socialised into, Western values, they will naturally migrate to that centre of these values – the city.

There are three main areas of weakness to the modernisation approach to urbanisation which seriously limit its application in the context of understanding Caribbean societies. First, all approaches, to a greater or lesser degree, betray strong ideological elements which manifest themselves most clearly in a rather blatant ethnocentrism. The 'modern man' discussed by Kahl is a well known figure, an individualised version of the American Dream. There is every reason to oppose a thesis of simple convergence based upon technological determinism. There is no reason to suppose that technology and industrialisation will mould advanced societies in the same fashion, let alone assume that the developments of capitalist societies in the West will be emulated by 'developing' countries. The very existence of the advanced societies is one of the crucial reasons why this will not take place. Second, the argument is based upon a 'culturalist' premise which inevitably produces two false, or at least partial, assumptions. One is that it is 'culture' which determines, rather than being itself fashioned by and responsive to other forces, and the other, which is closely related, is that social control through culture is more important than, say, constraint through differential access to scarce resources. It is often Max Weber's writing on the relevance of an individualised ethos, stressing the ascetic commitment to worldly success, that is advanced as support for the culturalist position, but Weber was insistent on defining the city as founded upon a 'market settlement'. He went on to qualify the definition by pointing to the difference between production and consumption cities, and those that subsequently developed major administrative or garrison functions, but it was the relationships of trade and exchange that separated the 'city' from other forms of settlement (Weber, 1958: 65–75).

The third ground for opposition to the modernisation perspective is that it perceives the process of change between the urban centre and the rural hinterland as one of *diffusion*. In fact this is a two stage process; the Western nation diffuses the culture of modernity to the 'developing' country or colony where it becomes concentrated in the city. The city then extends its influence throughout the land. If the previous criticism is granted some worth, then the process of diffusion of cultural traits as a theoretical perspective for under-standing colonisation processes loses some of its explanatory power. It must be based upon the premise that only cultural forces are important in structural change. However, there are other limi-tations. Diffusion is also an 'integrationist' approach because it can only throw light upon how the rural sector becomes more like the urban, and thus, perhaps, on why it is that rural dwellers are attracted to city living even when economic returns are not obvious. However, what if the relationship between the two appears to be one of growing inequalities and possibly incipient conflicts? One can certainly discuss *obstacles* to diffusion of 'modern' values but hardly understand the tensions and conflicts engendered by a growing impoverishment of rural economies. And yet, as we shall see, that is the *leitmotif* of Caribbean rural economy. The diffusionist thesis, therefore, is not an adequate theoretical perspective; it has the virtue of focussing attention on *relationships* between sectors of society, or between one society and another, but in common with all 'modernisation' approaches it presumes an autonomous determining role for 'culture' and is wedded to assumptions of gradual, consen-sual change which hardly tally with the poverty and burgeoning inequalities that are characteristic of the processes we seek to understand.

It must be stressed that no one is attempting to deny the differ-ences that exist between city and rural life or culture, nor indeed that reciprocal influences of one upon the other will be important in appreciating patterns of change. What is being argued is that urban culture is more properly viewed in the context of the relation-ship between metropolitan society and satellite, and that relation-ships between the urban 'core' and the rural 'periphery' within the dependent society must also be viewed in terms of what will later be termed 'plantation' economies. Before developing the main strands of that position, however, it is necessary to examine the two kinds of approaches to the urban-rural relationship that do indeed stress economic distinctions.

Question

1. *(a) Describe modernisation theory.*

(10 marks)

(b) Critically discuss its strengths and weaknesses.

(15 marks)

64 André Gunder Frank: Capitalism and Development/ Underdevelopment

The following is a basic statement of Frank's analysis of development/underdevelopment. It is as clear as one is likely to get, given his cumbersome style.

Frank begins by describing how, in his view, the various phases of capitalist expansion and domination have caused underdevelopment in other parts of the world – an effect of the 'capitalist world system' dating back to the sixteenth century. This is an example of his 'core'/'periphery' model: a developed capitalist 'core' and underdeveloped 'periphery'. Frank goes on to describe the same pattern within national states both in the developed and underdeveloped world, e.g. London develops at the expense of 'the North', Mexico City at the expense of rural Mexico. Thus, there is an unequal metropole/regional relationship *within* countries as well as *between* core and peripheral countries.

Frank then deals with objections and alternatives to his model. He refutes the views that underdevelopment is merely a temporary ('initial') problem, still less a given state, or that the developed countries simply 'took off' first and are now *'diffusing'* the means to 'catch up' (see Reading 63). He insists that the developed countries developed *at the expense of* the underdeveloped ones. Frank also takes to task certain Marxists who have given much more emphasis to the different systems of production (e.g. feudal as well as capitalist) within some underdeveloped societies. For them, these 'pre-capitalist' sectors still await development towards capitalism, whereas, for Frank, they are already (an exploited) part of the capitalist world system. A related debate occurs over the role of the indigenous elites in these countries. Frank sees them as easily manipulated by international capital whereas his Marxist opponents tend to regard them as exploitative and repressive in their own right. In practice, these arguments have been partly resolved in Frank's more recent writings as he has incorporated these more complex ideas into his world capitalist system theory (which he keeps essentially intact). Similarly, he now appears to acknowledge more forms and complex levels of development than previously.

In his more recent work, Frank makes two theoretical points

which are useful in understanding the wider context of the two newspaper articles which make up Reading 66. First is the concept of 'superexploitation' which simply means the extreme exploitation of labour. Superexploitation is characterised by easy hire/easy fire, long hours, a high level of work-related accidents, and the decline of real wages. Second, Frank links underdevlopment with superexploitation and with political authoritarianism. For superexploitation to occur it is 'necessary to have a political regime that allows it'. Frank cites as examples the former Marcos regime in the Philippines and the military dictatorship in Chile of General Pinochet.

Reading 64 From André Gunder Frank, *On Capitalist Underdevelopment* (Oxford University Press, 1975), pp. 95–8

Only the briefest summary statement of the analysis and thesis of this essay should now be necessary. Underdevelopment, no less than development itself, is the product but also part of the motive power of capitalism. Capitalist development everywhere has been a fundamentally contradictory development based on exploitation and resulting simultaneously in development and underdevelopment. Additionally, the growth and expansion of European mercantilism of the 16th century led to the development of a single, integrated, capitalist system of world-wide scope. Associated ever since the very beginning with the growth of powerful states, the expansion of mercantilism-capitalism led to the development of a metropole and, related to it through ties of commerce and force, of a periphery. Variously related to each other through colonialism, free-trade, imperialism, and 'neo-colonialism' the metropole exploited the periphery in such a way and extent that the metropole became what we today call developed while the periphery became what we now call underdeveloped.

At the same time, the same fundamental contradiction of capitalism led to a development/underdevelopment structure within the metropole and its regional and sectoral parts and within the various national and regional parts of the periphery. These national development/underdevelopment contradictions differ from the global one primarily in that, in addition to reflecting the inevitable exploitative structure of capitalism anywhere, they are additionally subordinate to, and in large part a consequence of, the contradictory exploitative-development/underdevelopment structure of the single world-wide capitalist-colonialist-imperialist system which came to dominate most of the globe. Capitalism, and more particularly the single world capitalist system and its various national sectors, has not changed, as it cannot change, its fundamental contradictory, exploitative structure and character. Accordingly, we may note, the development of development and the development of underdevelopment continues apace both on the global or international level and on the various national levels on which the capitalist system continues to operate. The only peoples who have been capable of escaping from underdevelopment are those who have substituted socialism for capitalism. Only the development of socialism has permitted any people already suffering from metropolitan produced peripheral underdevelopment to escape from the structure of the world capitalist system and from its consequent underdevelopment.

All serious study of the problems of development of underdeveloped areas and all serious intent to formulate policy for the elimination of underdevelopment and for the promotion of development must take into account, nay must begin with, this fundamental historical and structural cause of underdevelopment in capitalism. Indeed, all serious study of development must take into account the fundamental relation the development of development has had, and continues to have, with the development of underdevelopment. All serious study of capitalism, of its manifestation in the development of the metropole and of that in the underdevelopment of the periphery, and especially the study of the contemporary single world capitalist system and its development in the past and future, must begin with capitalism's unity and its fundamental internal contradiction, which has always and everywhere expressed itself in diffusion and exploitation, development and underdevelopment.

The conventional wisdom about underdevelopment, its causes, and its elimination are entirely inadequate. The reasons have been detailed above. Each of several central tenets of the conventional wisdom are quite out of keeping with past and contemporary reality. Thus, the conventional notion that underdevelopment is 'initial' and 'traditional' is evidently challenged by all historical fact and observation. Yet, whatever the differences among various branches or modes of conventional analysis, the notion of underdevelopment as an initial state is explicitly or implicitly common to it all.

Inadequate also is the idea that development is a process while

underdevelopment is a state of being. And erroneous is the associated supposition that development occurred essentially independently in that the now developed areas took off and left the now
underdeveloped ones behind where they were. The evidence is
that the development of the former occurred in conjunction with
underdevelopment and at the cost of the latter; both development
and underdevelopment were and are processes; more accurately,
they were and are both part of the same process. Similarly unsupported by the examination of the historical evidence is the popular
and in the conventional wisdom well nigh universal notion that
having taken off independently, the metropole now does or will
diffuse out or trickle down to the periphery the wherewithal
necessary for the underdeveloped countries to develop as well. The
evidence of the past and present is that far from diffusing down
development, the relation between the metropole and periphery
widens the gap between the two and generates ever deeper structural
underdevelopment in the periphery.

All of these tenets of the conventional wisdom neglect or deny
that there exists a single social and economic system which embraces
everybody in the non-socialist world, including the most 'isolated'
'subsistence' farmer, and that it is in the structure and operation of
this system that we must seek all the essentials of development and
underdevelopment. The conventional wisdom, and many would-be
Marxists as well, instead have adopted a dualist or multiple sociology
which claims to identify, especially in the underdeveloped
periphery, dual societies whose two or more supposed parts are
essentially independent of each other. One or more of these, then,
are termed as exhibiting the social, economic, political, cultural,
etc. 'structure' of underdevelopment *within* it, while another one is
termed 'developed' in that it exhibits some of the features of the
metropolitan economy and society. Development is then quite
erroneously and inadequately viewed as the diffusion of development from this national metropolitan centre out to the underdeveloped provincial periphery – or rather the re-diffusion of what has
already been diffused down or out from the global metropole. Sometimes, this process is regarded less in terms of diffusion than in
terms of the penetration of the capitalist metropole into the 'pre-
capitalist' or 'feudal' periphery, or again, the incorporation of the
pre-capitalist sector into the more developed capitalist one.

The evidence belies the existence of such a process. Far from being due to the existence and operation of the underdeveloped peripheral provinces of a feudal or pre-capitalist system, a careful reading of the historical and contemporary evidence demonstrates that what goes on there today is the result of these people's incorporation in the capitalist system long ago, albeit admittedly not into its developing but rather into its underdeveloping sector. Any 'development' policy will therefore surely and necessarily be inadequate if it rests on the supposition that underdevelopment can be eliminated in the peripheral area in question by eliminating 'pre-capitalism' or 'feudalism' and substituting capitalism instead – that is, more of the same capitalism which caused the underdevelopment and now maintains it. Serious study of the problems of development/underdevelopment will have to go well beyond the conventional wisdom.

Question
1. *What does Frank mean by 'underdevelopment'?*

(10 marks)

65 Frank Gaffikin and Andrew Nickson: The Contribution of Multinational Companies to Underdevelopment

This is a clear analysis, from a socialist point of view, of the effect of multinational or transnational companies (TNCs) on the countries in which they invest. The charge that the TNCs contribute to underdevelopment is made on five counts:

1. They remove more in profits than they invest
2. In their search for cheap labour they lend support to repressive regimes in developing countries
3. TNCs distort the development strategy of developing countries
4. TNCs promote inappropiate forms of consumption in developing countries
5. TNCs directly interfere in the politics of developing countries

The extract requires little explanation. Only point 3 is likely to cause any difficulty. The last paragraph in that section refers to the ways in which TNCs manipulate the different tax systems operating in the various countries in which they have companies. Basically, the purpose of the manoeuvre referred to is to achieve high profits in the countries where these will be taxed little or not at all, and to make low profits where there may be some compensation given.

This extract ought to provoke a response – in agreement or not. It is commited, even provocative, and yet as empirically well based as many academically more 'neutral' writings.

Reading 65 From Frank Gaffikin and Andrew Nickson, *Jobs Crisis and the Multinationals: The Case of the West Midlands* (Russell Press, 1984), pp. 43–50.

Transnationals and the developing countries

According to an ILO (International Labour Office) study, based on a sample survey of 250 companies employing 860,000 workers in 1977, TNCs account for only 4mn directly created jobs in the developing countries, which is a mere 0.5% of the total labour force in those countries. This job creation is highly concentrated in just 12 of the most 'advanced' developing countries with Latin America accounting for over 60% of the total. A national breakdown reveals that TNCs control 70% of manufacturing jobs in Singapore, 35% in Kenya and 20% in both Brazil and Mexico.

Apologists for the role of TNCs in developing countries argue that they add to, rather than subtract from, the local pool of skills, capital and other resources. Critics of their role, on the other hand, argue that they contribute to the underdevelopment of the poor part of the world in the following ways:

1 They remove more in profits than they invest

Profit repatriation ensures that much of the wealth produced by the developing countries is transferred to the rich industrialised West. In the period 1974–1977, net earnings from British overseas investment in developing countries (excluding oil and insurance) averaged £675mn p.a., whereas the annual net flow of new British investment to such developing countries was only £400mn. During this period the developing countries accounted for only 25% of new British overseas investment, while at the same time they were the source of 33% of repatriated earnings from overseas investment.

2 In their search for cheap labour they lend support to repressive regimes in developing countries

The so-called Free Trade Zones (FTZs) are the clearest example of the scope that TNCs have for exploitation in the developing countries. They are industrial estates set aside for TNC manufacturing plants which produce goods for export. These zones offer the TNCs the following: a pool of cheap non-union labour kept in check by harsh anti-strike legislation, a range of subsidies to their own capital investment and unrestricted repatriation of profits. The FTZs were first established in the mid-1960s. There are now over 80 operating in more than 30 countries.

> 'Almost one million people are now employed in FTZs around the world (70% of them in Asia) and the great majority are girls or young women between the ages of 15 and 25. Prized for their nimble fingers, supposed tolerance of boring yet strenuous work, their docility and lower expectations of workers' rights, they comprise at least 85 per cent of the workforce in such countries as Malaysia, the Philippines, Taiwan and Mexico.'

Investment by TNCs in the FTZs offers little prospect for the majority of the poor in the world. It diverts finance and energy away from development in rural areas where most of the people have to eke out a frugal living. Meanwhile the TNCs are free to make excess profits out of human misery, while remaining unaccountable for the social costs of their operations.

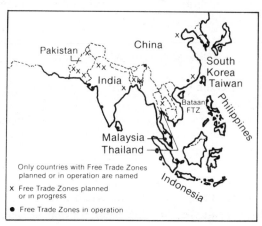

Only countries with Free Trade Zones planned or in operation are named

X Free Trade Zones planned or in progress

● Free Trade Zones in operation

Developing countries increasingly compete with each other to attract TNCs to their FTZs. An advertisement placed by the Philippine Department of Public Information in the *Times*, 12 June 1975, included the following statement:

'We like multinationals . . . the multinational company setting up its regional or area headquarters is now "exempt from all forms of local licences, fees, dues, imposts or any other local taxes or burdens" . . . In Manila your expatriate managers will enjoy Asia's lowest living costs . . . A cook starts at £12, a maid at £6 and a first-rate chauffeur at £22 . . . Recent Presidential decrees have simplified conciliation and arbitration of labour disputes (both strikes and lock-outs are prohibited), lifted work restrictions on Sundays and holidays, liberalised the employment of women and children, and expanded the scope of the apprenticeship programme . . .'

3 TNCs distort the development strategy of developing countries

Although TNCs may boost the level of exports, most of the raw materials or parts needed for assembly production are usually themselves imported and not domestically produced. When added to the outflow of foreign exchange due to the repatriation of profits, royalties and management fees by the TNCs, the net effect on the balance of payments is often negative. Nor does the presence of TNCs provide a major source of taxation for development because of widespread tax concessions. The transfer of technology is also restricted by the fact that although individual operations are transferred to developing countries, the overall technological package is jealously guarded by global headquarters.

Because such a large part of world trade consists of business within TNCs, there are considerable opportunities for 'transfer pricing'. This involves buying goods from a subsidiary at artificially high or low prices in order to reduce taxation on profits or to avoid any control on profits being sent back to the country of origin.

4 TNCs promote inappropriate forms of consumption in developing countries

TNCs tend to promote in developing countries those products for which they have already established a lucrative world market. In

Transfer Pricing at Work

Selling too cheap

METHOD: whereby an international company shifts profits from one national subsidiary to another to minimise tax payments. The products of the first subsidiary are sold to the second too cheaply, ensuring the first makes a loss or breaks even while the second makes an exceptionally high profit.

Commodity	Country	Date	% under-invoiced	Sum lost	Source
Copper	Chile	1956–71		$400mn	
Bauxite	Jamaica		100%		US import prices
	Greece	1976	9%	$4mn	Other export prices
Metal Products	Greece	1976	9%	$4mn	
Tea	Kenya	1976		$4mn	Tea price comparison
Bananas	Panama	1973	22%	$12mn	IMF

Buying too dear

METHOD: One subsidiary pays too high an import price from an overseas associated company. Unnaturally high profits are made abroad whilst the home subsidiary stands still.

Commodity	Country	Date	% over-invoiced	Sum lost	Source
Synthetics Textiles	Ethiopia	1967–71	46%	$2mn	Tariff Commission
Steel	Kenya	1976	6%	$4mn	Ministry of Industry
Metallurgical Products	Greece	1975–76	20%	$8mn	Comparative International Price Data
Pharmaceuticals	Iran	Late 1960s	varied		
	Colombia	1968	155%	$3mn/20mn	
	UK	1966–72	4000%–4500%	$32mn	UK Monopolies Commission
	Spain		880%		Foreign Market Prices (UNCTAD)
Rubber	Colombia	1968	440%		World price comparison

many cases these products can only be purchased by the rich minority whose consumption pattern is modelled on that of consumers in the developed countries. The excessive demand on foreign exchange needed to import such luxury items is usually borne by the poor rural majority of the population. They are the victims of a development strategy which emphasises cash crop production for export at the expense of food crop production for domestic consumption. At times the transfer of such inappropriate forms of consumption can actually damage health. Food TNCs like Nestle continue to promote powdered milk in developing countries, despite the well-proven medical dangers to babies when mothers use such products:

- where there is no access to clean/running water;
- where there is no facility for boiling water;
- where levels of literacy mean that instructions on the cans cannot be understood;
- where the high costs tempt users to dilute the product to stretch the milk.

Similarly, tobacco TNCs have vigorously exported a deadly habit to developing countries, where governments are encouraged to see tobacco as a source of taxation and export earnings. But this particularly labour-intensive cash crop yields little gain for the farmers who grow it. Consumers of cigarettes in developing countries are sold tobacco, usually with no health warnings, which 'packs twice the punch of cancer-causing tars as that of the rich world's cigarettes'.

The world's major agribusiness transnationals – such as Brooke Bond Liebig, Lonhro and Unilever – actively develop the export of cash crops like cotton, cocoa, coffee and tea throughout sub-saharan Africa. In so doing they take over the most fertile land which local people need for food production. In this way, they not only exploit the food crisis, but are significantly responsible for it in the first place.

But most important of all, by introducing the ideology of Western consumer society TNCs have neglected the pressing basic needs of the mass of underprivileged persons of the developing countries in favour of fostering and catering to the needs of a privileged elite in their own image, whose own economic and political interest then become identified with the preservation of the presence of TNCs in these countries.

5 TNCs directly interfere in the politics of developing countries

The revelations of ITT's involvement in the de-stabilisation of the democratically-elected government of Salvador Allende in Chile has drawn attention to the overt political behaviour of TNCs in subverting Third World governments which attempt to introduce policies detrimental to their interests. Other examples of underhand methods adopted by TNCs include: BP and Shell's breaking of sanctions against the then Rhodesia, and Lockheed's involvement in a bribery scandal in Japan.

The present world economic crisis is increasing the power of the TNCs. Most poor countries are now faced with crippling foreign debt burdens, and are consequently more amenable to offers of large-scale foreign investment. The rich countries are themselves beginning to compete with each other for such investment, as shown by the recent attempt by Britain and France to attract Timex, the electronics assembly company. The efforts of poor countries to impose controls over TNCs with regard to export levels, job creation, and profit destination, are in retreat.

In the developed countries there is also a growing realisation of the threat to national autonomy posed by the TNCs. In Britain the TUC is expressing concern at the 'de-industrialisation' of the economy as traditionally British-based TNCs cut back their operations in the domestic economy and expand overseas. In addition there is a growing realisation that the reverse flow of foreign investment into Britain by foreign-owned TNCs provides no panacea either. Indeed successive British governments have attempted to attract foreign investment to depressed areas of Britain by offering the same sort of tax holidays as developing countries. An Economist Intelligence Unit Special Report on 'The UK as a Tax Haven' (Spring 1982) stated that:

'The tax and exchange control changes of recent years, coupled with a superior range of financial services, make the UK one of the most attractive tax havens available.'

Yet there is growing disillusionment with the use of such tax holidays and development grants to attract investment to Britain. In many cases on the expiry of tax holidays, TNCs have closed down their subsidiaries in Britain and shifted their plant elsewhere. Such experience has revealed the vulnerability of the British economy to the decision-making process of TNCs, over which governments have little control. One classic example stands out of the lack of power of national governments facing TNC decisions in recent years – Chrysler's agreement with the British government, which was subsequently nullified by the sale of Chrysler's British holdings to Peugeot without consultation with the government.

British-based TNCs like their US, German or French counterparts bear no special allegiance to the national economy, let alone the working class of that country. It matters little whether these companies have their global headquarters in Birmingham, London or New York, since the viability of each production unit is constantly reviewed according to its contribution to the key objective of global profit maximisation.

Despite the difference in living standards and economic structure, in essence TNCs pose similar problems for developed and developing countries. The central problem is that the growth of these giant corporations has placed great power in few hands. This power is beyond, and usually against, the democratic wishes of people throughout the world.

Question

1. (a) *What evidence does the extract give that TNCs are economically disadvantageous to developing countries?*

(10 marks)

(b) *Explain, with examples, why TNCs sometimes get involved in the politics of developing countries.*

(15 marks)

66 **Geoffrey Lean, John Madeley and Lindsey Hilsum: Two Examples of the Relationship between Multinational Companies and Third World Countries**

There are two obvious aspects of the economic dependence of the poor countries on the rich in the contemporary world. First, many Third World countries, not least the more developed ones, are heavily dependent on the advanced countries for credit. Up to 30 or 40 per cent of the total value of the exports of some Third World countries are devoted to servicing merely the *interest* on debts. Brazil's debts of over 60 billion dollars and Zaire's debts of over 4 billion are equally punishing to both, given their relative wealth. As the advanced Western countries control not only the leading private banks but also the United Nations agencies, the International Monetary Fund and the World Bank, there is little hope that developing countries can avoid the tangling net of financial dependence. The second aspect of dependence lies in the generally unequal relationship between the multinational companies and Third World nations, and it is this we illustrate here. Liberal modernisation theorists tend to argue that, in the long term, the multinationals help to generate development, but the two newspaper extracts given below present a more exploitative picture. The first deals with the selling of pesticides to the Third World – and it would be equally easy to tell 'horror stories' about trade in other commodities, such as tobacco, and dried milk for babies. The second concentrates on the use of cheap female labour – provided courtesy of local Third World elites who, invariably, get their own 'kick back' from the favoured companies. It may be interesting to compare the working conditions of these women with those of the British female factory workers described by Anna Pollert (Reading 39). The concessions offered by the Mexican government to American companies effectively provide the latter with a free trade zone. Such zones are common in certain Third World countries, particularly the Philippines, and the conditions of labour described here are typical, if not somewhat better than is usual.

The articles below are produced solely as practical examples of the unequal relationship beween large multinational or trans-national companies and the Third World. The reading from Gunder Frank is more theoretical.

Reading 66(a) From Geoffrey Lean and John Madeley, 'Oxfam Split by Pesticide Row', in *The Observer*, 7 February 1982, p. 2.

Top British companies have been selling pesticides in the Third World, one with insufficient labelling and others with inadequate advertisements, according to a highly controversial Oxfam draft report.

The confidential report 'Pesticides and the Very Poor,' a late draft of which is in the hands of *The Observer*, has caused a long-running row at the Oxford-based charity. Senior officials and members of the council are split over whether to publish or suppress it.

A meeting of Oxfam's executive committee last summer voted in favour of publication in principle but set up an editorial panel to vet it. It comes back before the committee at the end of this month and will then go to the charity's council in March.

The draft, a 150-page study of pesticides in Third World countries, covers products made or marketed by Shell, ICI and Boots or their associates, as well as four European, five American and one Japanese company.

It accuses individual companies in Britain or abroad of selling pesticides banned or restricted in some Western countries, advertising hazardous materials without properly warning of their dangers, describing some dangerous chemicals as 'safe,' failing to print instructions in local languages and making 'impossible guarantees' of high profits and good harvests.

The Oxfam report follows the long international row over the marketing of baby food in the Third World which, partly because of the charity's pressure, has now led to a special code of conduct to restrain malpractice. The draft report calls for a similar code for the marketing of pesticides.

The draft makes a rough but 'conservative' estimate that there are more than 375,000 cases of pesticide poisoning from all causes in the Third World every year, and 10,000 deaths. But it acknowledges that no accurate or reliable figures are available.

The Third World is particularly vulnerable, says the draft, because Third World farmworkers, who make up nearly three quarters of the working population, are the poorest people on earth. They usually cannot get the protective clothing used in rich countries, get insufficient information from the rudimentary farmers' advice programmes, and often do not even have clean water to wash in after using pesticides.

The draft says that such factors make it particularly important that companies give farmers the right information.

In Sri Lanka a Shell company changed the formulation of a product without changing the information it gave in antidotes. Shell says the mistake was 'very regrettable' but had been rectified some time before the Oxfam inquiry.

The draft says that the International Chamber of Commerce code on advertising 'appears to be frequently infringed'. The code lays down that advertisements should be prepared with 'a due sense of social responsibility', and take into account that the consumer is usually motivated by the impression gained by a brief scanning of an advertisement.

Specifically, it says, advertisements should indicate 'the potential danger' of potentially poisonous products and not 'contain any visual presentation or any description of dangerous practices or of situations which show a disregard for safety'.

Two ICI advertisements shown in the draft appear to contravene the code. One for the pesticide 'Agrocide' in Malaysia shows a man in bare feet, short trousers, a short-sleeved shirt and a hat spraying the ground whereas, the draft says, 'people using any pesticide should wear at least some footwear, long trousers, long sleeved shirt and a hat'.

ICI told *The Observer* that the company agreed the advertisement was 'inappropriate' and that it was being discontinued.

The draft adds that a German company advertised a pesticide classed as 'highly hazardous' by WHO in Guatemala without mentioning any hazards.

Some advertisements go even further and call pesticides 'safe'. The draft report say that an American firm advertised an insecticide banned in the EEC and for most uses in the United States as 'safe'.

'In central America in July 1980,' the draft goes on, 'Boots advertised their product Mitac (amitraz) for use in integrated control programmes boasting of its "High degree of security for . . . the environment".'

'In Britain it has been recommended that amitraz be covered by the health and safety regulations, requiring the use of protective clothing. The UK recommendations stress that it is harmful to fish'.

A spokesman for the Fisons Boots Company, which now sells Boots pesticides, said: 'We won't be making any bald statements of this kind in the future'. He said the firm would make sure that in future advertisements made clear the product should be used only in accordance with instructions they supplied, and expressed gratitude to Oxfam for raising the issue.

Mr Brian Walker, director-general of Oxfam, said yesterday: 'The author of the draft report has privately sought comments from a large number of independent experts on the subject. He has asked for the views of companies on specific cases.

'Our interest, of course, is in the welfare of poor agricultural workers overseas. We would rather contribute to securing agreed remedies to unsafe practices than be pressed into a confrontation with the chemical companies.'

Reading 66(b) From Lindsey Hilsum, 'Uncle Sam's Jobs South of the Border', in *The Guardian*, 19 March 1982, pp. 8–9.

Ten years ago, when Dolores was 17, her family moved from rural Chihuahua to Mexico's booming border town of Ciudad Juarez. Her father had heard that there was work in the new factories which *los gringos* (the Americans) were building. Dolores's father was not the only one to hear the news. Thousands of Mexican peasants left their tiny, arid plots and flocked to Juarez.

New factories there certainly were, but not enough to absorb the influx. Moreover, they did not want to employ Dolores's father. The advertisement specified: 'We need female workers; older than 17, younger than 30; single and without children; minimum education primary school, maximum education secondary school; available for all shifts.' Dolores's father remained unemployed. Dolores got a job.

Dolores is typical of the 100,000 women who work in the mainly US-owned assembly plants on the northern Mexican border. Since 1965, when the In Bond Border Industrialisation Programme began, the seven major border towns have swelled. Ciudad Juarez, a town of some 150,000 in the 1950s and early '60s, now has a population of 650,000.

Mexicans who can no longer scrape a living off the land come in search of work. The US companies come in search of cheap labour. Ninety per cent of the *maquiladora* workers receive the official minimum wage; with all fringe benefits paid it costs the companies $2.10 per worker, per hour. In the USA the basic hourly wage is $3.55.

The Mexican and US governments arranged the *maquiladora* industrialisation programme to benefit both countries. The idea was to alleviate unemployment in Mexico and strengthen the economy, while enabling US transnationals to maximise profits.

The scheme has benefited the transnationals, which are exempted from the law which states that companies operating in Mexico must have a 51 per cent Mexican share. Most *maquiladoras* are 100 per cent US owned. The corporations import unassembled components duty free or 'in bond,' and re-export them, assembled, with only labour costs added. Operating in Mexico is cheaper than in other less developed countries because it is so close to home, and transport costs are minimal.

From the Mexican Government's point of view, too, the programme has been a great success. Last year it improved Mexico's balance of payments deficit by an estimated $980 millions. In 1981 the *maquiladoras* created 10,000 jobs, but this made little impact on unemployment figures. In fact, in Ciudad Juarez, the largest border town, unemployment rose 3.5 per cent and passed 24,000. By employing young women like Dolores who have never worked before, the companies are not reducing unemployment but creating a new workforce. Men remain unemployed, or migrate further north over the border into the USA.

Women are chosen for this work 'because they're damn good at this type of work. They have a certain manual dexterity and work consciousness,' as one American executive put it. Most of the plants are assembling electronic components – complex, fiddly processes requiring accuracy and attention to detail – or textiles, traditionally 'women's work.'

The personnel manager of one transnational explained his criteria for recruitment: 'I choose people with elegant figures and thin hands because they are more agile. . . . I take physical appearance into account; you can tell if people are aggressive by the way they look, so I try to choose people who seem more docile and can be managed more easily.' Mexican women will work for long, tedious hours assembling tiny components, whereas – as the American said: 'It goes against a man's macho pride.'

Mexican women are 40 per cent more productive than their North American counterparts. Taught all their lives to submit to male authority, they rarely object to the conditions imposed upon them. A US businessman whose job is to promote the *maquiladoras* to foreign firms, explained: 'there's no welfare here. You can punish Mexican workers. Also there's the 48-hour week. You don't see any horsing around here, no queues for the water-fountain or the bathroom. These girls work.'

Dolores does indeed work. She rises at 4 am to arrive at the factory for the 6 am shift. During her 8-hour day she will have one break of ten minutes and one of 20. She will solder a minimum of 4,400 'resistors.' The company organises competitions between production lines to see who can produce the most. When most of the lines have exceeded the minimum, the 'standard' is raised. What was once the goal becomes the minimum.

Consistently speeding up work causes strain and tension. In one factory fighting broke out when the girls' frayed nerves finally snapped. This is sometimes used to mask health hazards; in one factory where 32 people suffered ill effects from the escape of hydro-chlorine gas, the illness was attributed to a 'collective psychosis.'

That same factory displays a simple decree: 'Workers who try to join a union will be dismissed.' In other factories unions are toler-ated, but only those which toe the government line and do not negotiate the workers' demands.

Recently workers have been laid off, or put on a shorter working week. Many of those dismissed have been older women; the companies prefer younger women with more nimble fingers.

The future of the *maquiladoras* looks bright. This year European and Japanese firms are opening subsidiaries on the Mexican border, and the Government is allowing some firms to operate farther inside the country.

Their ability to do so depends on a docile and submissive labour force. However, the very fact that women are now earning and working together means that the workforce is becoming less docile.

Activity
Try to construct a defence of the multinationals, against the charge of exploiting the Third World consumer and Third World labour that could be made on the basis of the information in the above extracts.

67 Christian M. Rogerson: The Industrial System of Apartheid in South Africa (including the Use of Cheap Black Labour)

Theory is useless unless it helps us to understand individual cases. However, South Africa is a hard test of both development and underdevelopment theory because it is untypical. What makes it untypical is the extreme and complex form the 'race issue' takes there, particularly the system of apartheid.

This extract generally follows the theoretical framework of Frank. The latter now differentiates between various degrees of underdevelopment. In terms of the capitalist 'core' and exploited 'periphery', South Africa is 'semi-peripheral' with some of its development occurring more or less independently of the major capitalist powers. Frank also suggests that South Africa is 'sub-imperialist' in that it is important to the Western powers in providing a bulwark against the Marxist regimes to its north.

Rogerson divided his analysis of the industrial system of apartheid into three sections:

1. *The role of the state.* State involvement in industrial development has been substantial and direct and has included the setting up of parastatal (state directed) corporations. The term 'capital intensive' refers to production based on machines rather than labour (labour intensive).
2. *Foreign capital and technology.* South African industry is largely South African owned but foreign technology has played a key role in its development.
3. *Cheap Black labour.* The exploitation of Black labour for profit is the key to understanding the South African social system. Rogerson locates the Bantustans (Black homelands) firmly within his analysis of Black labour exploitation. If Blacks are used as a reserve pool of cheap labour, the Bantustans are the reservoir. Since this article was written, Blacks have obtained greater freedom of geographical mobility and residence but whether this will much alleviate the fundamentals of economic exploitation remains to be seen. The economic strategies currently being pursued by the South African state, succinctly summarised at the conclusion of the extract, suggest not.

This extract neatly lays the groundwork for the question, 'Is the exploitation of Black labour in South Africa primarily a race or class issue or are the two factors impossible to disentangle?'. In any case, we are probably too inclined to see the matter exclusively in racial terms.

Reading 67 From Christian M. Rogerson, 'Apartheid, decentralisation, and spatial industrial change' in David M. Smith *ed.*, *Living Under Apartheid* (George Allen and Unwin, 1982) pp. 47–53, 62–3.

An understanding of the industrial system of South Africa is central to an appreciation of the functioning and contemporary dynamics of apartheid. The policies and programmes which fall under the rubrics of apartheid or separate development represent, as Wolpe (1972, p. 427) argues, 'the attempt by the capitalist class to meet the expanding demand for cheap African labour in the era of industrial manufacturing capital'. The lives of at least one generation of black South Africans have been conditioned by the making of this apartheid industrial system . . .

The industrial system of apartheid South Africa

The Republic of South Africa, a 'semi-peripheral' country in terms of the capitalist world economy (Frank 1979, Wallerstein 1979), possesses the most highly industrialised economy on the African continent. In 1976 manufacturing engaged some 1.36 million workers (South Africa 1978) and contributed almost a quarter of the Gross Domestic Product. The tempo of growth is greatest within heavy industry, reflecting the increasing integration, sophistication and potential self-generating capacity of South African manufacturing. Historically there occurred in South Africa 'a much greater degree of genuine diversification than has been possible for most countries seeking to develop secondary industry' (Milkman 1977–8, p. 71). At the root of this substantive and relatively sophisticated industrial base are three interrelated factors: (a) the actions of the South African state, (b) the role of foreign capital and technology, and (c) the exploitation of large supplies of cheap black labour. The most distinctive facet of South Africa's industrialisation is the exclusion of the overwhelming majority of the country's black populace from the fruits of manufacturing progress and their concomitant relegation to the position of a source of low-cost labour.

The role of the state

Historically the state has assumed a pivotal role in the industrialisation of South Africa. In the 1920s and 1930s state power was used to resolve the conflicts between agricultural, mining and industrial capital such as to foster a 'national' alliance against foreign capital (Legassick & Hemson 1976, Bozzoli 1978). There was constituted in South Africa a 'national bourgeoisie sufficiently strong to uphold a "national interest" *vis-à-vis* the metropolitan countries' (Arrighi & Saul 1973, p. 55). This permitted the retention and accumulation within South Africa of capital which in other peripheral states simply drained off to the core countries. Because of the reluctance of private capital to invest in basic industry, the South African state intervened extensively in the economy channelling retained surplus (diverted from mining) into the creation and later sustenance of an industrial base. In this fashion 'South Africa, a country which experienced imperial conquest of a far-reaching and violent nature, "broke out" of the vicious cycle of underdevelopment and embarked on a path of comparatively independent capitalist development' (Bozzoli 1978, p. 41).

The major tools applied by the state to catalyse industry were direct investment through the establishment of parastatal corporations and the introduction of a panoply of import controls to stimulate import-substitution industrialisation (Seidman & Seidman 1977). The initial state ventures were in iron and steel in the late 1920s and energy in the 1930s. The numbers of parastatal corporations multiplied, particularly after the National Party achieved power in 1948 (Phillips 1974). State investment in manufacturing expanded both absolutely and as a percentage of total manufacturing investment; by 1974, the state contributed 45.6 per cent of total investment and 29.6 per cent of industrial investment. Through the operations of parastatal corporations such as ARMSCOR (military equipment), ISCOR (iron and steel), ESCOM (electricity), SENTRACHEM (chemicals), SASOL (the production of oil from coal) and NATREF (oil refining) the state enjoys a high degree of control over the commanding heights of the economy (Weiss 1975, Rogerson 1981). Moreover, the degree of state ownership and control over South African manufacturing is extended further by participation since 1948 in a host of 'private' enterprise concerns, especially those controlled by Afrikaner capital (Ehrensaft 1976).

In addition to the stimulus of direct investment in key economic sectors the state further encouraged South African industrialisation through a series of indirect supports, most importantly through the imposition of import controls and extensive tax incentives. The post-war expansion of manufacturing owes a great deal to a commercial policy which assured substantial protection to domestic manufacturers for a growing range of goods and preferences for the import of required capital goods and materials (Seidman & Seidman 1977). The general pattern of industrial expansion was of major growth until the 1950s in 'light' and comparatively 'labour-intensive' industrial activities, such as metals and engineering, textiles, clothing,

food and drink, and footwear. But in the aftermath of the Sharpe-
ville massacre and of threats of international sanctions against South
Africa, the state increasingly pursued the development of more
capital-intensive strategic sectors of manufacturing. The major
industrial 'growth poles' of the 1960s and 1970s have therefore been
motor-cars and auto accessories, chemicals, pulp and paper, military
hardware, capital goods equipment, and electronic and computer
manufactures (Legassick 1974a). The motor-vehicle industry illustrates the catlytic role of the state in South Africa's industrialisation:
initially this was based upon the local assembly of imported
components, but by introducing high taxation on cars with a high
percentage of imported components, the state has encouraged the
local evolution of backward linkage manufactures (Grundy 1981).
This pattern of industrial development is currently being repeated
in the newly introduced sector of television manufacture (Rogerson
1978).

Foreign capital and technology

Foreign capital began to move into South African manufacturing
only after 1945. British capital dominated inflows until the 1960s,
after which United States and EEC investment became considerably
greater (Seidman & Makgetla 1978, 1980). It is difficult to evaluate
the importance of foreign capital in South African industry quantitatively, especially with the emergence of monopoly capital and
the growing interpenetration of foreign with local private and state
capital. Nevertheless a recent investigation estimated that approximately 28 per cent of manufacturing employment in South Africa
is in foreign-controlled enterprises (Rogerson forthcoming). A study
of the leading 100 industrial companies quoted on the Johannesburg
Stock Exchange revealed that 17 were majority-owned by overseas
investors and that foreign holdings were registered in a further 29
firms (Savage 1978). Such data may still understate the full involvement of foreign capital in South African manufacturing. Suffice it
to note that foreign firms dominate motor-cars, oil, tyres, electrical
equipment, computers and pharmaceuticals as well as being strongly
represented in such areas as food and chemicals. Schollhammer's
(1974) investigation of the determinants of the international
locational strategies of multinational corporations shows that the
particular form of racial domination that lies at the heart of South

African society is of no particular concern to international capital except insofar as it presents certain operational difficulties. Indeed, it is commonly argued that the interests of the South African state and of international capital coincide concerning apartheid, in that the burdens of under-development are borne entirely by blacks whose exploitation enriches both South African whites as a group and the foreign concerns (Seidman & Seidman 1977, Seidman & Makgetla 1978, 1980; Milkman 1979, Seidman 1979).

The benefits of foreign capital to South Africa have been not so much quantitative as of a qualitative nature. As Legassick (1977, p. 189) notes: 'South African industrialisation has depended on the employment of more and more capital-intensive and "modern" methods in a succession of industrial sectors. And, in each case, it has been foreign capital which has financed the purchasing of the required machinery; and it has been foreign firms which have imported the expertise to initiate the handling of such machines'. Yet, notwithstanding the benefits of foreign technology in strengthening South Africa's industrial base, there exists another dimension to the country's traditional reliance upon imported technologies – the implications for employment.

The industrial system of South Africa is locked into the world economy, through linkages of finance, trade and, most importantly, technology. The patterns of these linkages determine the local techniques of production, types of product manufactured, marketing practices and so forth, which in turn determine overall levels of industrial production. For South Africa these linkages facilitate capital accumulation and increases in output, but without a corresponding impact upon levels of employment (Erwin 1978). That South African industry applies predominantly capital-intensive techniques is highlighted by a recent survey showing that 71 per cent of firms use manufacturing technologies embodying at least 90 per cent of foreign technology (Nattrass & Brown 1977), the overwhelming bulk of which originates in the USA or Western Europe where labour is often in short supply and relatively expensive. With production technologies and the types of products manufactured determined largely by foreign capital, South Africa has followed an increasingly capital-intensive trajectory of industrialisation, which is contributing little to solving the country's massive unemployment problems (Maree 1978). Moreover, South Africa suffers an added potential employment loss, typical of semi-peripheral countries in the world economy (cf. Taylor & Thrift 1981), as a result of the drain of repatriated profits and surplus to the 'core' capitalist countries (Samoff 1978, Milkman 1979). The full contemporary significance of this arrested industrial employment growth is apparent only in the light of South Africa's reservoir of cheap Black labour.

Cheap Black labour*

South Africa's rapid industrialisation has been underpinned by the creation of a system in which the Black majority participates only as a source of cheap labour (Seidman & Seidman 1977). The origins of this system, its elaboration or 'modernisation' to the conditions of an industrialising society and the lineaments of the present-day apartheid political economy are treated elsewhere (e.g. Legassick 1975, 1977; Magubane 1979). In relation to the present discussion it is important to recognise that the forms of integration, or incorporation, of South Africa's Blacks into the capitalist world economy 'have been consistently shaped by White political power and manifested in a system of racial differentiation' (Legassick 1975, p. 232). the combined apartheid apparatus of segregationist legislation, the industrial colour-bar, the perpetuation of migratory labour and, latterly, of programmes for establishing so-called 'independent' Bantustans or homelands† serves to insure that the mass of Blacks

---

* Black is capitalised from this point on in the chapter, as the discussion focuses on the African population; however, blacks in general (including Coloureds and Asians) serve as sources of cheap labour [Ed.].

† The term 'Bantustan' is preferred in this chapter to the official designations of homeland or Black state. Many Black South Africans, particularly those born in the 'white' area, deny that these poverty-stricken and mostly geographically fragmented territories, constituting 14 per cent of the area of South Africa, are their homelands. Moreover, they disavow also the notion that the South African government has the right to confer 'independence' on them, thus stripping them of claims to citizenship in the wealthier 86 per cent of the country. As pointed out by Kane-Berman ' . . . to use the term "homeland" is to concede a terminological victory to the ideologues of separate development. Although this may seem a small point at first, it . . . in fact (goes) to the heart of (South African) politics. For when government says that the homeland of the Zulus is KwaZulu or that of the Tswanas Bophuthatswana, what it really means is that *only* these areas are their "homeland" and that the rest of South Africa is not. Thus, *insidiously* with the term "homeland" gaining general currency, does language help to shape political thought' (Kane-Berman 1979b, p. 41).

are forced into a reservoir of low-skilled labour from which avenues of escape are few.

The much publicised 'improvements' to South Africa's labour legislation, as incorporated in the recommendations of the Wiehahn (South Africa 1979c) and Riekert (South Africa 1979a) Commissions of Inquiry, offer only cosmetic efforts toward de-racialisation. By granting limited rights the new legislation provides a means of co-opting the small but increasingly skilled group of urban Blacks at the expense of further tightening apartheid controls on the majority of Blacks (see Shafer 1979, *South African Labour Bulletin* 1979a, b; Hindson 1980). The proposals of Wiehahn and Riekert together constitute a broad attempt by the state to restructure capitalist social relations in order to make them more effective and to secure capitalist domination and exploitation of Black labour under the changed circumstances of class struggle which now characterise South Africa (Davies 1979, Hindson 1980). The recommendations of these two commissions represent no attack upon the essential structures of the cheap labour economy. The rural Bantustans are today the form in which the 'industrial reserve army' exists in South Africa (Legassick & Wolpe 1976). From these areas, industry augments its labour needs in times of expansion; to these areas workers return after completing the period of selling their labour in one of the metropolitan-industrial complexes of 'white' South Africa. The 'cheapness' of Black labour for South African industry is assured as the social costs of reproducing that labour – of caring for children, the unemployed, the aged and the non-working dependants – are transferred on to the Bantustan governments (see Ch. 2).

The imperatives of exclusionary industrialisation

Upon the advantages afforded by this system of cheap labour, the South African state, supported by foreign capital in the post World War II period, has constructed a modern and relatively independent industrial system. The industrial transformation of South Africa occurred in a time-span of just over 50 years during which living conditions for most Blacks improved only marginally, if at all (Legassick & Hemson 1976, Seidman & Seidman 1977). Herein rests the key structural feature of contemporary South African manufacturing, viz. its *exclusionary* character. This feature derives, in part, from the particular phase in the capitalist world economy during which South African industrial growth has taken place, a phase in which the linkages of South Africa to the core countries result in a limited employment impact in terms of an expanded industrial capacity. More important, however, is that the structures of racial domination in South Africa forged white workers into a classic labour aristocracy. Creating this relatively high-income group of whites, at the expense of the Black majority, allowed a market for early South African manufacturers. But as industry expanded, the sharp market limitations imposed by the country's exclusionary path of industrialisation and by the impoverishment of the Black masses had to be faced (Seidman & Seidman 1977, Rogerson 1981).

Seeking to resolve this contradiction, the South African state is currently pursuing simultaneously several economic strategies (Ehrensaft 1976, Milkman 1979):

1. *The growth of a military-industrial complex.* One partial solution to the constraints imposed by the narrowness of the domestic market is found in expanded state expenditures on defence. Nevertheless the emergence of a military-industrial complex (Seidman & Makgetla 1978) in South Africa provides only a temporary relief. It does nothing to alleviate the long-term structural problems facing South African manufacturing.

2. *'Sub-imperial' expansion.* The exigencies of searching for new outlets for domestic manufactures accentuates South Africa's 'sub-imperial' role in Africa and of its outward reach into surrounding countries, particularly Botswana, Lesotho, Namibia and Swaziland (Rogerson 1981). The much discussed programmes for a 'constellation' of Southern African states (Herbst 1980), and for a zone of regional economic co-operation, centre around the exchange of the labour and raw materials of the surrounding states for the manufactures of South Africa.

3. *Export subsidisation.* A third strategy is that of using export revenues to subsidise export industries, increasing their scale of production to the point at which South Africa's cheap labour costs yield competitive advantages, in the context of what Fröbel *et al.* (1980) style as the 'new international division of labour'. Together with this programme, the state seeks also to take advantage of the leverage afforded by world demand for South Africa's mineral resources and to force tariff concessions

from core countries upon the entry of South African manufactures.

4. *New high technology industries*. One final response centres on the use of state capital to develop new advanced technology exports in selected industrial sectors (e.g. uranium enrichment) that can be internationally competitive with the manufactures of core states.

In summary, the shaping of the apartheid industrial system is a product of the actions of the state, the contributions of foreign capital and technology and, most importantly, of the exploitation of cheap Black labour within the framework of South Africa's 'labour-coercive' economy (Legassick 1977, p. 190). Paralleling the country's industrial transformation, South Africa increasingly has assumed the role of a sub-imperial power within Southern Africa. Moreover, the continuing importation of foreign capital and technology strengthens the capacity of the minority-ruled white military–industrial complex to confront the struggles of South Africa's Blacks to secure their liberation from the apartheid system (Seidman & Makgetla 1978).

As part of the strategy for arresting the progress of Black liberation in South Africa the state operationalised the Bantustan programme for establishing a series of formally independent ethnic nations (Southall 1980). In attempting to provide these fledgling nations with at least a facade of economic viability, the policies of decentralisation and spatial industrial change assumed a new importance.

Conclusion

The exclusion of the Black majority from the substantive benefits of manufacturing growth is the most outstanding feature of South Africa's semi-peripheral pattern of industrialisation. Under the policies and programmes of apartheid, the institutions of the country's cheap labour economy have been progressively modernised and expanded to meet the circumstances of an industrialising economy. Supported by foreign capital and foreign technology, the South African state has forged the most integrated and sophisticated industrial system in Africa.

The consequences of excluding Blacks, except as a source of low-cost labour, find expression in the several contemporary strategies which seek to overcome the restrictions of the domestic market and open new markets for the products of South African industry. Not the least of these strategies is that which involves restoring the respectability of South Africa in the eyes of international opinion. This goal is sought by introducing a suite of policies and legislation which, superficially at least, afford the appearance of change. For example, the much discussed proposals contained in the Wiehahn and Riekert Commissions' reports foster an illusion of major changes in apartheid industrial legislation. But nowhere do these reports challenge the underlying institutionalised structure of white privilege and exploitation of Blacks (Seidman & Makgetla 1980) which lies at the heart of the apartheid industrial system.

The illusion of change is similarly apparent in the programmes for spatial industrial change in South Africa. Again, this sort of change is not one that threatens to recast the central function of Bantustans as cheap labour reservoirs. The programme of industrial decentralisation is often portrayed as progressive, bringing positive benefits in the form of new employment opportunities for South African Blacks. Nevertheless the strategy is one which first and foremost buttresses apartheid, seeking to contain the numbers of Blacks in the 'white' areas of South Africa. The proclaimed benefits of new job opportunities mask the poverty wage levels and poor working conditions in areas where the labour of a recently impoverished peasantry is tapped without imposing on capital the social welfare costs that accompany permanent urbanisation. Furthermore, it is argued that the employment creating effect of decentralisation for Blacks is a myth; rather, the chief effect of the implementation of the Environment Planning Act has been to contribute towards further raising levels of Black unemployment.

The considerable publicity and propaganda which surrounds the issues of 'developing' the Bantustans and 'improving' labour legislation affecting Blacks obscures a subtle yet potentially important change which is presently taking effect in the South African industrial landscape. Engineered by the provisions of the Environment Planning Act there is emerging a 'new spatial division of labour' (Massey 1979) in South Africa. The pattern in the metropolitan areas is one of the continuing concentration of high-order business functions alongside a progressively capital-intensive form of manufacturing production. To the border area and Bantustan growth points are being sloughed off certain low-wage and Black-labour-intensive industrial activities. Recent announcements of plans to establish new 'regional development axes' (Gordon 1981), growth areas situated between white areas and Bantustans, appear a further step towards such a new spatial division of labour in South African manufacturing. Nevertheless, as long as the objective of stemming Black influx into white areas remains the pivot of the whole programme for spatial industrial change, so long must Blacks suffer the continuing burdens of mounting unemployment, poverty-in-employment and miserable work environments under apartheid.

Questions
1. *(a) Critically discuss the role of the state in the development of apartheid.*

(5 marks)

(b) Critically discuss the role of foreign capital and technology in the development of apartheid.

(5 marks)

(c) Do you consider apartheid to be primarily a problem of class or racism?

(15 marks)

2. *Relate the particular case of South Africa to theories of development and underdevelopment. (To answer this you will need to be familiar with the main theoretical readings in this section.)*

(15 marks

SECTION 13

Political Sociology

Readings 68–71

Politics is the pursuit of public power in order to achieve goals. In modern societies these goals are often codified as policies. Political goals reflect ideologies (values and beliefs). Power may be achieved by either peaceful or violent means and it may be accepted as legitimate (rightful) or not.

A central feature of life in the 'Western democracies' is the belief that a political system has evolved which provides for the legitimate exercise of power. This system is known as representative democracy, though the terms liberal democracy or liberal pluralism are also used. Politics is conceived of, not in terms of fundamental class conflict, but as the conflict, negotiation and compromise of parties and pressure groups which reflect a variety of interests, including those of class. Jean Blondel gives a descriptive rather than theoretical account of the liberal-democratic system. It is worth noting that Margaret Thatcher has departed from the 'consensus' politics of the nineteen sixties. She has sought sharply to define the difference between her party and her political opponents. However, a liberal democratic system can accomodate such a change. There may be conflict within the system but consensus about the legitimacy of the system itself.

It is essential to know other perspectives than the liberal democratic in assessing which groups hold political power. In Reading 24, in Section 5, John Scott presents both elitist and ruling class theories of power – the latter in detail. Scott's article could equally be in this section and should be regarded as a core-reading on political sociology

The readings by Ivor Crewe and Hilde Himmelweit and her co-authors focus on contemporary voting behaviour although in very different ways. Soundly basing his arguments on electoral statistics, Crewe explains the decline of the Labour vote. Himmelweit offers an interpretive model of the contemporary voter which illuminates the trends Crewe discusses. Crewe describes the apparent decline of class as a basis for voting behaviour and Himmelweit argues that attitudes on particular issues now provide a better explanation (the 'consumer model'). According to Crewe's evocative phrase, used elsewhere as an explanation of voting behaviour, 'class gets cleaned out of the equation'.

Stuart Hall's *The Ideology of Thatcherism* provides a useful balance to the highly empirical trend of research discussed in the above paragraph. In effect, he reminds us that attitudes do not simply arise naturally within the individual but are socially suggested. In his view, if Thatcherism has won the minds of many voters, including working class voters, it is partly because they have been ideologically misled. He indicates how.

68 Jean Blondel: Parties and Interest Groups: Liberal Pluralism

Jean Blondel's account of parties and pressure or interest groups in the British political system needs to be read in the same critical spirit that it was written. Although Blondel does not use the term 'liberal pluralism,' it is this political philosophy – based on a belief in the effectiveness of parties and interest groups – that he, in fact, describes. The conviction that, whatever its limitations, Western democracy 'works' is passionately held by most Western politicians and by most of the journalists and academics who write about their activities. Broadly, this is a 'liberal' belief. It is pluralistic in the sense that it is committed to the view that the interests of *many* groups ought to be expressed and represented. It is deeply and irrevocably opposed to totalitarianism of either the right (e.g. Fascism), or the left (e.g. Stalinism). In the following reading, Blondel concentrates mainly on the issue of the 'representativeness' of interest groups.

The liberal-pluralist view of how British democracy operates should be contrasted with Scott's analysis of the British upper class, given in Reading 24. Scott does not, however, say that the political system cannot be used to achieve fundamental change: he merely points out that the upper class has great power and resources outside formal politics to stop this happening. Blondel himself hints at this possibility towards the end of this extract. The reader might well consider whether it *is* possible to achieve a radical redistribution of wealth and opportunity through existing political institutions – allowing that this might involve attempting to change those institutions themselves.

The statistics in the table showing various kinds of interest groups are now out of date but the information given is otherwise valuable.

Reading 68 From Jean Blondel, *Voters, Parties and Leaders: The Social Fabric of British Politics* (Penguin, 1969), pp. 87–9, 159–67.

The political parties

Political parties occupy a peculiar position in Western democracies. They are, almost everywhere, and in particular in Britain, private associations to which the law does not give more rights and duties than to other private organisations. However, neither Britain nor any other democracy could function without parties. They are the main link between electors and their M.P.s. Without them, elections would be meaningless for the vast majority of voters who know very little about the candidates. Without them, elections would decide nothing. Parties are part and parcel of the real life of elections and of Parliament. They are not really private bodies: they perform the public function of representation. The law says that the M.P.s are the representatives; but, since the candidates owe their loyalty and their seat to the parties, the reality of the function of representation is, nowadays, more in the parties than in the M.P.s.

Parties perform this function of representation in two main ways. They do so by selecting candidates for elective posts – in local government as well as in national politics. They also do so by adopting policies which these candidates, as well as the party as a whole, propose to the electors. In order to achieve both these aims, political parties have long ceased to be, in Britain more perhaps than elsewhere, loose federations of small committees constituted in each locality; they have become large machines, with hundreds of thousands of members, with hundreds of paid officials.

This transformation was inevitable. It came as a result of various causes, among which the growth in the size of the electorate, the loss of influence of prominent individuals in the constituencies, the development of nation-wide mass-media, the virtual ending of local issues, and the overriding importance of national problems played a part in varying degrees. Moreover, the appearance of mass parties was held by many to be the proof of the democratisation of politics: political organisations would no longer be run by small groups of self-appointed 'natural' leaders; the people at large – at least those who were interested enough to join the party of their choice – could play a part in the decisions.

This pious hope has not been realised at all, according to the cynics. Almost as soon as the mass parties developed in Western Europe, some observers asserted that even in the alleged democratic parties, like the Socialist parties, an 'iron law of oligarchy' prevailed. According to such critics, leaders are not really 'chosen' by the rank-and-file, but tend to be selected by a narrow group and often perpetuate themselves in office. Politics are not the result of the consensus of opinion of the local militants, but the fruit of the personal whims of these oligarchs.

Students of politics have since introduced nuances to both these theories and probably no one would seriously hold that either of these extreme models fits the British political parties . . .

The representation of interests

The centre of gravity of the study of British politics has slowly moved from parties to interests and to interest groups. Interests seem to work more in the open. Interest groups have greatly developed their action in the post-war period. Admittedly most interest groups were created before 1939: trade unions were already powerful before 1914; professional associations and trade associations had become active in the later part of the inter-war period. Yet, before 1939, the open action of many associations was not as common or as readily accepted as it has been since the war. Traditional theories of politics still prevailed, and they usually ignored interest groups either because they were too small or because they did not fit with the principles of representation on which British democracy was said to be founded.

Views have changed and a new theory of politics has emerged and indeed been widely accepted. Under the influence of American studies, interest groups have been analysed; they have been justified, instead of being criticised. The theory of representation has been enlarged to include them. Democratic government is now established on two columns, parties and interest groups, while it was, before the war, founded on the single column of the parties. Most theorists now consider that the representative system of government would neither be efficient nor really democratic without interest groups. An 'economic and social chamber' may not ultimately be created, although the National Economic Development Council leads the way and although the House of Lords has come to include a wider range of the interests of the nation than in the past. Yet, if that economic chamber is not formally created, it may simply be because interest groups will have found other and better channels through which to exercise their influence.

The importance of interest groups in the representative process is undeniable. We must examine them. But we cannot examine them in the same detail as political parties. Their numbers are vast; their structure, their size, their objects vary enormously. In the course of one chapter we can hope only to consider the one aspect of the life of interests which is most important for the political process, the problem of representation: it is in many ways different from the representation which is effected by political parties. Interest groups differ from political parties by their aim, which is not to take power but only to exert pressure. They differ from parties by their objects, which are usually limited in scope. They differ from parties by the nature of their membership, which is often limited to one section in society. There are so many difficulties in the field of the representation of interests that one can expect only to tackle even this problem alone in a general fashion.

Interests and the notion of representation

Interest groups must be divided according to their aims. The most important – at any rate the most effective ones – are the *protective* groups, which defend a section in society: trade unions defend the workers, professional associations defend members of the professions, trade associations and trade federations such as the Chambers of Commerce, the Chambers of Trade, and the Confederation of British Industry created by amalgamation of the National Union of Manufacturers and the Federation of British Industries, defend the interests of business. Local authorities or motorists are defended in the same way. The list is huge. All these associations, unions, federations, etc., have one thing in common: they each defend a certain group, a certain number of hundreds or thousands or hundreds of thousands of people who think that their interests, as a group, must be defended.

The other type of groups are the *promotional* ones. These are the ones which want to promote a cause by appealing, not to a section, to a special group, but to everybody. The Campaign for Nuclear Disarmament wanted to promote nuclear disarmament, the Royal Society for the Prevention of Cruelty to Animals wants animals to be better protected, the Council for the Preservation of Rural England wants rural England to be better preserved. Some of these societies may want to protect a special group, like the National Society for the Prevention of Cruelty to Children, but they do not do so by appealing to members of this group only. They appeal to the whole public: anyone in the British Isles can be a member of the N.S.P.C.C.

We already encounter one way in which the notion of representation varies among interest groups. Groups of the protective type represent each a section of society: one can find out the section which is covered by the group – or at any rate which the group aims to cover. If there are 10,000 university teachers in Britain, an Association of University Teachers can expect to have only 10,000 members, but, if it has 10,000 members, it will 'represent' the university teachers, at least from the point of view of their professional interests. Promotional groups do not have a predetermined sphere of representation. Their aim is, presumably, to have as many members as possible among the whole population of the British Isles. The maximum membership of the Association of University Teachers may be 10,000, the maximum membership of the R.S.P.C.A. could be, if not 50 million, at least 30 or 35 million. If one used the word 'representative' in the same sense, these should be the figures which the R.S.P.C.A., and C.N.D., etc., should aim at in order to become 'representative'. This is why it is, in practice, difficult to measure, and indeed even to examine, the 'representative' character of promotional groups. Admittedly, parties, like promotional groups, hope to obtain the support of the whole population and do not; however, we know through elections which proportion of the population supports each party. There are no elections enabling promotional groups to show their real strength. If we consider only the figures of membership, we probably underestimate the scope of their influence; yet there is usually no other criterion. In some cases, Gallup polls can be a guide: we have an

Some examples of interest groups

	Number of members (approx.)
Business	
Federation of British Industries	8,607 firms and 280 trade associations
National Union of Manufacturers (the above two organisations are now united in the Confederation of British Industry)	5,110 firms and 53 trade associations
Association of British Chambers of Commerce	60,000 members
National Farmers' Union	200,000 members approx.
Labour and professions	
Trade unions affiliated to the Trades Union Congress: 170 and 8,867,522 members (1965) of which the largest are:	
Transport and General Workers' Union	1,443,738
Amalgamated Engineering Union	1,048,955
National Union of General and Municipal Workers	795,767
National Union of Mineworkers	446,453
Union of Shop, Distributive and Allied Workers	349,230
National and Local Government Officers' Association	348,528
Electrical Trades Union	292,741
National Union of Railwaymen	254,687
Non-affiliated:	
National Union of Teachers	about 230,000
Professional associations:	
British Medical Association	about 70,000
Institute of Directors	about 40,000
Local authority associations	
Association of Municipal Corporations	County Boroughs and Boroughs
County Councils' Association	Counties (except G.L.C.)
Other	
Automobile Association	3,000,000 members approx.
Promotional groups	
National Federation of Old Age Pensioners	about 400,000
British Legion	about 850,000

(from Trades Union Congress Report, 1966; S. E. Finer, *Anonymous Empire*, Pall Mall Press, 1965, *passim*; H. Eckstein, *Pressure Group Politics* (the B.M.A.), Allen and Unwin, 1960; P. Self and H. Storing, *The State and the Farmer*, Allen and Unwin, 1962) idea of the proportion of the population which has the same aims as those of the R.S.P.C.A. In most cases, we just do not know. This difficulty limits the study of interest groups. When the 'representative' character of groups is considered, generalisations and comparisons can be made for protective groups, but they cannot easily be made for promotional groups. Since, on the whole, promotional groups are less influential and less successful, it may not matter so much that we should not be able to compare both types of groups. But the problem does exist.

There are other difficulties which concern protective groups as well. One comes from the difference in size between the social groups which protective organisations cater for. We have mentioned the Association of University Teachers. It has to be examined together with other groups, like the National Union of Mineworkers which has over 400,000 members, and the Association of Town Clerks which has a few hundreds. Generalisations are difficult to draw because the size of the membership has important repercussions on the structure of the organisation, on the relationship between the leadership and the rank-and-file; and on the 'bureaucratic' character of the machine of the organisation.

Yet this difficulty is perhaps dwarfed by two others which strike at the root of the nature of the 'representative' character of interest groups. In the first place, it is very difficult to compare the representative character of associations which are composed of individual members with that of associations composed, wholly or in part, of other associations or companies. Bodies like the Association of University Teachers or the National Union of Mineworkers have a certain number of members, each of whom is a single individual. One can count heads. Presumably, the views of the Association or of the Union are the views of the majority of its members. If one wants to examine the 'representative' principle at work, one examines, as for the parties, the local branches, the regional organisations, if there are any, and the national leadership. One can conclude from this analysis whether the organisation is democratic or oligarchical, whether the oligarchy is one of 'bosses', of 'natural social leaders', or of 'bureaucrats'.

One cannot as easily use these criteria when one considers associations which are partly or wholly composed of other associations or companies. A trade association is composed of member-firms. These firms are unequal in size, in assets, in staff. One cannot expect a straightforward majority rule to prevail: it is not clear whether such a majority would be a majority of firms, of assets, or of both. In fact these criteria are difficult to use: small firms will not easily submit to the domination of the few large firms which have big assets, and the few large ones cannot be expected to agree with the verdict of a majority made up of a host of insignificant firms. Neither of these systems would be 'democratic'. What 'democracy' might mean is therefore unclear and, as a result, what 'representation' would mean is equally unclear. It becomes difficult to define the notion of 'oligarchical' rule in such associations.

This situation would not be serious if one could decide, as we did earlier for promotional groups, that associations composed of companies or societies are not sufficiently influential to deserve being examined in detail. This is obviously not the case. Firstly, business associations and local authority associations are built on this model: they have to be and always will be. Secondly, associations of wage and salary earners also fall in this category when primary organis-ations come to be grouped into 'federations'. The T.U.C. is only partly an association of individual members, it is also – and indeed formally only – an association of trade unions. Admittedly, decisions are taken at the Congress on the basis of the total number of members of the T.U.C. In practice, however, the decisions are taken through the means of the block vote, which gives to the leaders of the large unions a greater weight than to the leaders of the small ones. Even in the General Council, unions do not receive seats in precise relation to the number of members of each union. A precise apportionment would clearly be impractical and too rigid. The result is that the organisation is not just composed of some millions of members, expressing themselves through delegates, but of a number of groups, the individual unions. The analogy with federal countries, which is sometimes used – and used in the very name of many organisations – is, in reality, misleading. Federations are based on a compromise between the representation of popu-lations and the representation of territories; the compromise is effected by the existence of two chambers, neither of which, usually, can impose its will on the other. There are no such distinctions in interest groups. In business or local authority associations, the basis of representation is usually left unclear, probably because no one ever found a satisfactory criterion. In organisations such as the T.U.C., the 'federal' principle is superimposed on to the representation of individual members in the primary units, the unions. The result is more like a 'confederation', or the United Nations, despite the maintenance of the majority principle at the Congress. Decisions are based on the relative power and prestige of some of the groups rather than on the sheer weight of the numbers of the individual members.

This difficulty is not the only one: another drawback comes from the fact that interest *groups* do not cover the whole field of interests. Earlier in this chapter, we divided interest groups into protective and promotional. We made this distinction as if we assumed that in our society the organisations devoted to the defence of certain sections were the only ones which fulfilled either of these functions. This is clearly not the case. One must sharply distinguish between wage and salary earners who have to constitute protective organisations in order to defend their interests, and other sections which can protect their interests without having to set up an organisation solely for the purpose of defence. Admittedly, unions and professional associations were not created to put pressure on the State; they were created to put pressure on private employers. Only later did they also come to be used in order to obtain certain concessions from the State, chiefly because the government became a large employer and because it began to regulate conditions of employment in many branches of the private sector. But both to put pressure on private employers and to put pressure on the State, wage and salary earners needed these organisations.

Question
1. (a) Distinguish, with examples, between protective and promotional pressure groups.

(10 marks)

(b) Discuss the importance of the concept of 'representativeness' in British politics.

(15 marks)

69 Ivor Crewe: Can Labour Rise Again?

Ivor Crewe's assessment of the electoral prospects of the Labour Party is so clearly set out that it requires no summary. He gives four reasons why Labour might recover from its 1983 debacle and ten reasons why it might have great difficulty in doing so. He then briefly analyses voting trends post-1983 and the issues of party leadership and image.

I will use this introductory space to draw attention to a key aspect of political sociology raised in this article – the relationship between class and voting (mainly, points 4 to 8 of the Pessimists' View). Two key variables in the decline of the Labour vote are the numerical decline of the working class itself and the trend to fewer members of the working class voting for Labour. Crewe clearly regards the latter factor as more important. This leaves him in seeming disagreement with A. F. Heath who emphasises the former factor. Heath argues that 'in focusing on class dealignment, political scientists have concentrated on a minor rearrangement of the furniture while failing to note a major change in the structure of the house' – the change in structure referred to is the decline in size of the working class. How can this apparent disagreement be reconciled? In fact, Heath uses a much narrower definition of the working class than Crewe which is based mainly on the traditional, manual working class. This group has remained more loyal to Labour than what Crewe refers to as the 'new working class'.

The 1987 election generally confirmed the analysis given below.

Reading 69 From Ivor Crewe, 'Can Labour Rise Again?' in *Social Studies Review*, Vol. 1, No. 1, September 1985, pp. 13–19.

The June 1983 election was by any standard a disaster for the Labour Party. Four years in Opposition to a government which had presided over Britain's worst recession since the 1930s gave it ample opportunity to recapture public support. Instead, the Conservatives were re-elected with a massive majority. Labour was reduced to 209 MPs, its lowest number since 1935. It lost a quarter of its 1979 vote in the sharpest collapse suffered by a major party at a single election since the Second World War. Labour was virtually wiped out as a serious political force across large tracts of Britain, notably the South (outside London) and the suburbs and countryside everywhere. In terms of vote per Labour candidate, the 1983 result was Labour's worst performance since the Party was founded in 1900.

Labour's electoral Everest

Labour's debacle in 1983 followed a decisive defeat at the previous election of 1979 when the Labour vote had already ebbed to its lowest level since 1931. Having slid twice in succession, the Labour Party must now climb an electoral Everest to win the next general election.

'Winning' an election can mean different things. At the minimum it means becoming the largest single party in the Commons, even if short of a majority over all the other parties combined. This might oblige Labour to form a coalition government with one or more parties but would at least enable Neil Kinnock to become Prime Minister. Yet, as Table 1 shows, even this minimal victory would require a uniform national 'swing' from Conservative to Labour of 7.7%. Since 1945 the largest swing at any general election has been 5.2% (in 1979).

Table 1   The swing and the number of seats that Labour needs to 'win' the next election

Outcome	Uniform national swing required (%)		Result (vote shown as % share of total)			
			Conservative	Labour	Liberal/SDP	Other
Labour win *safe* overall majority (340 seats)	11.5	vote: seats:	30.9 238	39.1 341	25.3 47	4.7 24
Labour win *bare* overall majority (326 seats)	10.5	vote: seats:	31.9 255	38.1 326	25.3 44	4.7 25
Labour become *largest* party	7.7	vote: seats:	34.7 293	35.3 300	25.3 33	4.7 24
Conservatives lose *bare* overall majority (325 seats or less)	5.3	vote: seats:	37.1 325	32.9 270	25.3 31	4.7 24

Notes: Figures are for the UK. The Alliance and other parties' share of the UK vote is assumed to be unchanged from 1983. 'Swing' is the conventional measure: the percentage point increase in the Labour vote plus the percentage point fall in the Conservative vote, divided by two.

What swing does Labour need to be sure of governing on its own? For a *bare* overall majority in the House of Commons Labour would need to double the postwar record with a swing of 10.5%; and for a *safe* overall majority of 30 (340 seats), which could withstand midterm by-election defeats and backbench defections, it would need to gain an additional 131 seats. This not only requires a massive 11.5% swing but it also means winning *every* seat in which Labour came second in 1983 – or winning at least some seats in which it came third. So: *can Labour rise again?*

The grounds for optimism

Despite the enormity of the task, optimists give four reasons for believing that Labour can regain its ground.

1 Historical precedent

Electoral catastrophes in the past have usually been followed by equally dramatic recoveries: the Conservatives' crushing majority of 205 in 1924 was followed by a minority Labour government in 1929; in 1959 Harold Macmillan ('Supermac') led the Conservatives to a 100 seat victory but in the following election Harold Wilson transformed it into a Labour majority of five. In fact, reversals are the norm: only once this century – in 1935 – has a single-party government enjoying a majority of over 100 secured re-endorsement with a *workable* majority at the following election. The further the electoral pendulum swings at one election, the further it swings back at the next.

2 1983 was an aberration

Optimists *expect* the electoral pendulum to swing back. Labour's dismal performance in 1983, they argue, was due to strictly short-term factors. The party's leader turned out to be completely implausible as an aspiring prime minister; its over-ambitious economic programme was not credible; its defence policies unravelled into incoherence; and its campaign disintegrated into division and confusion, reviving barely-faded memories of the party's internal battles between 'moderates' and 'extremists' over the previous four years. Not since 1931 have all the short-term electoral factors had such an adverse impact during a campaign. Such unusual misfortune is unlikely to strike twice in succession.

The impact of these short-lived factors is underscored by the fact

527

that Labour's vote of 28% fell well below its showing on various indicators of long-term support. The BBC/Gallup's election-day survey found that 33% of voters chose Labour as 'best for people like me' and 38% of voters described themselves as Labour identifiers. These measures of long-term allegiance are close to Labour's 35% vote in the local elections, held only a few days before election day was announced but when the local dimension made the party's defence policies and Michael Foot's leadership less relevant to the vote. Thus Labour's 'normal', underlying vote appears to lie between 35 and 40%.

3 The victory threshold has fallen

A vote of 35–40%, optimists argue, would have brought about disaster in the two-party era of the 1950s and 1960s but is enough for victory in the new three-party system of the 1980s. When three parties compete under the first-past-the-post rules, a 40% vote virtually guarantees victory. Moreover, the electoral system is particularly favourable to the Labour Party. For example, if the Alliance vote stays at 26% at the next election, Labour could deprive the Conservatives of their overall majority with as little as 34.5% of the vote, become the single largest party with 36% and win an overall majority with 38–39%. And if the Alliance vote rose at the expense of the Conservatives (as the 1985 mid-summer polls suggested), Labour could 'win' in these various ways with an even smaller vote (Reece 1985, pp. 15–17). Thus, according to this view, the electoral pendulum is not only expected to swing back to Labour but it also need not swing back as far as before.

4 Partisan dealignment

Over the past twenty years the British electorate has gradually lessened its commitment to *both* major parties and grown readier to switch votes between parties from one election to the next. The Conservative Party has not escaped this long-term erosion of partisanship: the proportion of the *electorate* voting for it in 1983 was the third lowest this century. The new volatility happened to hurt Labour more than the Conservatives in the 1979 and 1983 elections, but the reverse could just as easily occur next time. If many more voters are 'up for grabs', there is no reason why *Labour* should not do the grabbing next time.

The pessimists' view

For others, however, these are tiny crumbs of comfort in the grim electoral arithmetic of recovery. Pessimists place the 1983 result in long-term historical perspective, examine the trends, and reach much gloomier conclusions.

1 The historical counter-precedents

The pessimists match the optimists' reliance on historical precedent with one of their own. The Labour Party, they point out, has *never* managed to win a safe, overall, majority from a position of Opposition. In 1923, 1929 and February 1974 it formed a minority government; in 1964 its majority was only 5, and it was forced into another general election eighteen months later; in 1950, 1966 and October 1974 it was re-elected from office. Even its famous 1945 victory came after five years in a wartime coalition government.

2 Labour's decline is long-term

Granting that the immediate circumstances of the 1983 election were exceptional, pessimists nonetheless argue that they reinforce long-term forces which have gradually worked against Labour over the past 30 years.

It used to be thought that history was on Labour's side. Before the war the leading Fabian, Beatrice Webb, referred to the 'inevitability of gradualness' with which a Labour victory at the polls would come. This idea was echoed as recently as the late 1960s in David Butler and Donald Stokes's *Political Change in Britain* (Macmillan, 1969). It portrayed Labour as a party slowly coming into its full electoral inheritance as older generations, initiated into the pre-1914 party system in which Labour played little part, gradually died out.

More recently, however, the talk has been of *The Forward March of Labour Halted?* (Hobsbawm 1981). The proportion of the electorate voting Labour has fallen in all but one of the last nine elections and in each of the last five (see Figure 1). In 1951, its twentieth-century peak, the figure stood at 40.3%; by 1983 it had been halved to 20.1%. Labour's share of the *vote* has remained below 40% at every election since 1970. The vote for democratic socialist parties has drifted down in most European democracies since the early 1950s but in none so precipitously as Britain (Maguire 1983). By

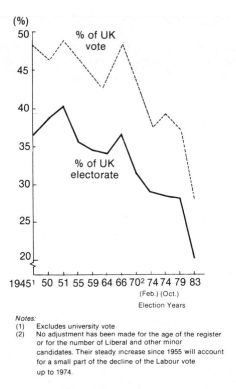

Notes:
(1) Excludes university vote
(2) No adjustment has been made for the age of the register
or for the number of Liberal and other minor
candidates. Their steady increase since 1955 will account
for a small part of the decline of the Labour vote
up to 1974.

Figure 1 The decline of the Labour vote at general elections 1945–83

1983 there were only three other European democracies (Eire, Belgium and Switzerland) in which the combined vote for parties of the Left was lower than in Britain.

3 Labour identification is declining

Identification with the Labour Party has likewise been reduced, falling from 43% of respondents (including non-voters) in 1964 to 32% in 1983. This erosion has not left a militant core: the proportion of 'very' or 'fairly strong' Labour identifiers has also dropped, from 37% in 1964 to 22% in 1983 (Table 2). Levels of identification with the Conservative Party, however, are unchanged and the proportion of very/fairly strong identifiers has only dropped slightly, from 34% to 29%. In 1983, for the first time, there were more Conservative than Labour identifiers in the electorate.

Table 2   Decline of Labour party identification 1964–83 (%)

% of respondents identifying with Labour	1964	1966	1970	Feb/Oct 1974 (combined)	1979	1983
Very strongly	19	23	20	15	10	10
Fairly strongly	18	19	17	18	19	12
Not very strongly	5	4	5	8	9	9
Total % identifying with Labour Party	42	46	42	40	38	32
% of respondents identifying with Conservative Party	38	35	40	35	38	38

Note: Figures rounded to nearest percentage so may differ slightly from total.

4 Labour's class base is declining

This inexorable erosion of Labour support, the pessimists argue, reflects the working of long-term social forces against the Labour Party. The most obvious is the gradual contraction and changing social make-up of the party's traditional electoral base – the manual working class. As the service sector and 'high-tech' light industry have replaced Britain's heavy smokestack industries, the proportion of manual workers in the electorate has slowly fallen, from 63% in 1959 to 54% in 1983. Thus even if manual workers' loyalty to Labour remained absolutely constant, Labour could expect to lose support gradually.

5 The working-class Labour vote is declining

In practice, the changing social composition of the manual working class has undermined its Labour allegiance. A telling illustration is provided by comparing the two Conservative landslide election years of 1959 and 1983. Had manual workers' loyalty to Labour been constant, the quarter-century decline in their numbers would have reduced the Labour vote by a slender 3.6 percentage points. In fact, over this period the Labour vote in the country as a whole fell by 16 percentage points, from 44% to 28%, and among manual workers it plummeted by 24 percentage points – half as much again – from 62% to 38%. Thus only a small part of Labour's decline is due to manual workers shrinking in number; a much larger part is due to manual workers shrinking from Labour.

6 *Labour's working-class base is fragmenting*

The collapse of the working-class Labour vote, the pessimists argue, is the most significant electoral change in postwar British politics. It arises from the changing social make-up of the working class, of which two aspects are particularly important: the spread of home ownership and the flight from the big cities.

In the mid-1950s only a fifth of all manual workers owned their homes; now the majority do (54%). The Conservative Party, which portrays itself as the home-owner's party of mortgage tax relief, pegged rates and council house sales, has benefited electorally as a result. The Labour Party, by contrast, has suffered electorally through its association with the interests of private tenants, whose numbers have rapidly dwindled.

Labour's electoral grip on manual workers has also weakened as they have moved from North to South, from inner city to suburb and from town to country. This migration has depopulated and dispersed old working-class communities with a tradition of Labour solidarity rooted in local trade unions, co-ops and working men's clubs. Many more manual workers now live in suburbs, small towns and commuter villages which are dominated by Conservative rather than Labour culture. The reverse migration of agricultural workers into towns and of the professional middle classes into fashionable inner city enclaves is numerically much less significant.

7 *The new working class has abandoned Labour*

Manual workers can therefore be divided into the 'traditional' and the 'new' working class. In 1983 these two groups voted very differently, as can be seen from Table 3. Among the traditional working class of trade unionists and council house tenants, and in the traditional strongholds of Scotland and the North, Labour remains the first, if not always the majority, choice. But among the new working class of manual workers who live in the South, who own their home and who do not belong to a trade union, the Conservatives have established a clear lead over Labour. Indeed, Labour trails in third place, behind the Alliance, in the first two categories. It is as if the two groups of manual workers belong to quite different social classes.

Table 3   The two working classes: percentage of three-party vote, 1983

	New working class			Traditional working class		
	Owner-occupiers	Lives in South	Does not belong to union	Council tenants	Lives in Scotland/North	Belongs to union
Conservative	47	42	39	19	32	28
Labour	25	26	33	57	42	49
Liberal/SDP	28	32	27	24	26	23
Con./Lab. majority	Con. +22	Con. +16	Con. +6	Lab. +38	Lab. +10	Lab. +21
Category as % of all manual workers	54	36	59	35	38	41

Source: BBC/Gallup Survey, 8–9 June, 1983.

8 The new working class is growing

Pessimists point out that the 'new' working class now outnumbers the traditional working class. There are more working-class home owners (54%) than council tenants (35%), more manual workers who do not belong to a trade union (59%) than do (41%), and almost as many living in the South (36%) as in Scotland and the North combined (38%).

Moreover, the pessimists go on, the new working class is likely to continue growing at the expense of the traditional working class. The migration of manual workers from Labour to non-Labour milieus will proceed inexorably. The spread of owner occupation, through tenants' purchase of their council houses, and the decline of local authority council house building, will widen. Trade-union membership will go on declining, especially among manual workers, as a result of unemployment, earlier retirement and a shift in the economic base from strongly-unionised heavy manufacturing to a weakly-unionised service sector. Labour support is stronger in the public than private sector, but the public sector will contract further as the Government implements plans for privatisation and cuts the number of civil servants and council officials. And, of course, the class ratio will continue to tilt towards non-manual workers. The social trends are not on Labour's side.

Nor, indeed, are the demographic trends. Medical advances and the drop in the 1960s birthrate are together producing an aging electorate – to the benefit of the Conservatives who are always better supported among the elderly than the young. The only counter-trend of note is the growth of the overwhelmingly Labour black electorate. But as blacks represent a tiny 4% minority of the total electorate and are in any case concentrated in safe Labour seats, their impact on an election result is bound to be limited.

9 Other electoral trends hurt Labour too

The task of recovery, the pessimists argue, is made even more Herculean by a number of additional electoral trends which will operate against Labour at the next election. The *first* is the falling number of marginal seats. Defined as a seat held by one major party over the other by under 10% of the two-party vote, the number has halved from 157 in 1959 to 80 in 1983 and, if current trends persist, will drop to below 60 by 1987–88 (Curtice and Steed 1982, 1984a). The causes are complex but the consequence is simple: an ever-increasing swing is needed for any given number of seats to change hands. Thus the 10.5% figure mentioned earlier might not be enough.

The *second* factor is the accumulating evidence that newly-elected MPs who assiduously look after their constituencies can earn a significant personal vote worth an additional 1,500 to their majority on the first occasion they seek re-election (Curtice and Steed 1984b). Up to 101 Conservative MPs are in this position at the next election, many nursing the marginal seats Labour needs to recapture if it is to win.

Thirdly, under the Representation of the People Act 1985, holi-day-makers and large numbers of British citizens working or resi-dent abroad will for the first time obtain the right to a postal vote in a British election. How many will exercise this right cannot be predicted, but it is highly probable that more will vote Conservative than Labour.

Only time will tell whether the optimists or pessimists are right. In the meantime it is worth looking for clues in the elections and opinion polls since 1983.

Local and Euro-elections

Table 4 sets out the parties' performances in the local elections of 1984 and 1985 and the Euro-elections of 1984. Mid-term elections

Table 4 The parties' performance in the 1984 district elections, 1984 Euro-elections and 1985 county council elections, as percentage share of the vote

	Conservative	*Labour*	*Liberal/SDP*	*Others*	*Swing to Labour since 1983*
General election[b] (GB) June 1983	43.5	28	26	2.5	—
District elections[a] May 1984	37	38	22	3	+8.3
European elections[b] June 1984	41	36.5	19.5	3	+5.5
County elections May 1985	33	36	28.5	2	+9.3

Notes: (a) *Estimates* of support for the three main parties in Great Britain. The author has adjusted the raw local election figures to take account of the fact that the Alliance fields fewer candidates than the Conservative and Labour parties and that local elections are only held in part of the country.
(b) Figures are rounded to nearest 0.5 per cent.

are notoriously unreliable predictors of future general elections. In the past the Opposition has usually surged into a commanding lead, as disillusioned government supporters cast a protest vote (or stay at home), but has seen that lead whittled away at the general election when most voters return to their normal loyalties.

In the three mid-term elections since 1983, however, Labour has failed to take a *decisive* lead over the Conservatives. It has recovered from 1983, but polled no more than its 'normal' vote. The Conservative-to-Labour swing at the European elections (5.5%), if repeated at a general election, would barely be enough to deprive the Government of its overall majority. If the swings of the local elections of 8.3% in 1984 and 9.3% in 1985 are repeated, this would make Labour the largest party but without an overall majority. The Alliance would hold the balance of power in a 'hung' Parliament and Labour could be forced to form a coalition government – or face one in Opposition.

Vote intention

Figure 2 traces the monthly fluctuations in vote intentions for the three main parties and confirms the results of the mid-term elections. Until October 1983 Labour support remained in its general election doldrums at barely more than 25%. Immediately after Neil

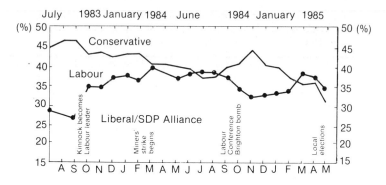

Note: Mean of Gallup, MORI, Marplan and NOP polls; vote intention question, don't knows, etc. excluded.

Figure 2 The parties' support in the monthly opinion polls since June 1983

Kinnock's election as the new Labour leader in October 1983 it rocketed to 35%, largely at the expense of the Alliance. Labour appeared to be recapturing its campaign deserters to the Alliance now that Michael Foot was no longer party leader.

Since then, Labour support has remained within a 35% to 40% range except for a four-month dip after October 1984, following the IRA bomb attack on Mrs Thatcher and Arthur Scargill's rapturous reception at the 1984 Labour Party Conference. As in the mid-term elections, Labour appears to have recovered lost voters rather than recruited new support. It has run ahead of the Conservatives in only five of the twenty-three months and never by more than 3.5%. And in no month has Labour support reached 40% – the level it touched in Great Britain when Labour last won an election, back in October 1974.

The labour leader

Neil Kinnock's election as Labour leader produced an overnight surge for Labour in the polls. But his modest and dwindling 'approval ratings' in the monthly Gallup polls suggest that so far he has not been a major electoral asset to the party (see Figure 3). In January 1984 43% considered he was 'proving a good leader of the Labour Party' while 23% did not, an approval rating of +20. A third were still undecided. A year later many of the 'don't knows'

Source: Gallup. The question is: 'Do you think Mr. Kinnock is or is not proving a good leader of the Labour Party?'

Figure 3 Approval rating of Neil Kinnock, October 1983–May 1985

had turned against Neil Kinnock: disapprovers outnumbered appro-vers by 49% to 36%, an approval rating of −13.

This is a relatively modest showing for an Opposition Leader after eighteen months in the job (see Table 5). Margaret Thatcher

Table 5   How Neil Kinnock's 'Approval Rating' compares with that of earlier Opposition Leaders

| | *Percentage saying:* | | |
	Is a good leader	*Is not a good leader*	*Balance of approval*
Harold Wilson (July–Sept 1964)	59	23	+36
Edward Heath (Jan–Mar 1967)	26	51	−25
Margaret Thatcher (July–Sept 1977)	45	41	+ 4
Michael Foot (April–June 1982)	18	69	−51
Neil Kinnock (Mar–May 1985)	37	47	−10

Source: Gallup Political Index. The question is: 'Do you think Mr. Wilson (Mr. Heath etc.) is or is not proving a good leader of the Labour (Conservative) Party?' *Note*: The figures are the average for the 18th, 19th and 20th month of each person's career as Opposition Leader.

was more popular at the equivalent stage of her career as Opposition Leader, having an approval rating of +4. And the last Labour leader to win an election, Harold Wilson, was far more popular (+36).

Too much should not be made of such comparisons. The figures can change rapidly and most voters do not choose parties on the basis of their leaders. Edward Heath's public stock after a year and a half was lower (−25) but he went on to win the 1970 general election. Yet the evidence suggests that Neil Kinnock does not yet appreciably add to Labour's electoral strength. So far his main asset in the public's eyes is that he is not Michael Foot.

The Labour Party's image

The party leader is a less persuasive factor with voters than the party's overall impression of governing competence. Here too Labour has recovered substantially (see Table 6). Between August 1983 and April 1985 there were drops in the proportions believing that Labour was 'split and divided' (−18%), that the economy

Table 6   Changes in the Labour Party's image, August 1983–April 1985

Percentage agreeing that:	August 1983	April 1985	Change
The Labour leadership is poor now	94	63	−31
The Labour Party is too split and divided	90	72	−18
The Labour Party's policy of getting rid of all nuclear weapons would be dangerous	82	74	− 8
It's not very clear what a vote for Labour means these days	80	70	−10
The economy will be in a worse state under Labour	67	52	−15
Percentage disagreeing that: Labour is the only party that can turn out the present Government	69	44	−25
Labour is the only party that looks after ordinary working people and their families	62	51	−11

Source: Gallup Political Index, Nos. 276 (August 1983) and 296 (April 1985).
Note: Percentages have been recalculated after excluding 'Don't knows'.

would be in a worse state under Labour (−15%) and, above all, that its leadership was poor (−31%).

But again it has not recovered sufficiently. On virtually every item making up Labour's 'image', the majority view has remained unfavourable: 72% continued to see Labour as split and divided, 63% considered its leadership as poor and 74% considered its nuclear weapons policy – which is unlikely to change before the next election – as dangerous. The party is no longer dismissed by the electorate as hopelessly inadequate, but it remains far from widely respected.

Labour's dilemma

A full recovery for the Labour Party involves two stages: first, winning back the voters it suddenly lost in 1983; and second, winning back the voters it steadily lost throughout the 1970s. Midway through this Parliament it has successfully completed stage one, thereby vindicating the optimists. But it has made little headway on the much more difficult stage two, and in that sense corroborated the pessimists.

Between now and the next general election Labour requires a strategy for attracting additional support, especially from the new working class and from the Alliance. In devising such a strategy the party faces difficult dilemmas. Should it abandon many of its traditional but electorally unpopular positions – nationalisation, trade-union power and unilateral nuclear disarmament, for example – at the risk of alienating its activists and provoking further internal divisions? Or should it stick to these positions, striving more strenuously to convert the uncommitted to them, at the risk of failing yet again? Should the Labour Party bring its socialism into line with the electorate, or the electorate into line with its socialism? Or should it forsake any planned strategy, fudge its policy dilemmas, and rely on a wave of anti-Government disillusion to waft it into office?

Question
1. (a) *Critically assess the arguments suggesting that Labour might recover from its 1983 defeat.*

(10 marks)

(b) Critically assess the arguments suggesting that Labour might not recover from its 1983 defeat.

(10 marks)

(c) In your view, can Labour rise again?

(5 marks)

Note: The major trends in the 1983 election were generally reinforced in the 1987 election.

70 Hilde T. Himmelweit *et al*; Is Social Class Still the Major Factor Associated with Voting Behaviour?

The following passage is from the conclusion of Himmelweit *et al, How Voters Decide: A Longitudinal Study of Political Attitudes and Voting Extending Over Fifteen Years*. As might perhaps be expected from a team of social psychologists, they argue that individual attitudes rather than class membership as such provide the best clue to voting behaviour. They are able to cite substantial empirical evidence in support of this thesis, although they also show that many individual attitudes are, in fact, class related. However, they argue that there has been a long term tendency for the class-basis of voting to decline and for voters to vote across class lines. Class membership has become a rather unreliable predictor of voting behaviour. The steady increase of the Liberal vote, which is drawn unpredictably from all classes, and the relative decline of the more class-based Conservative and Labour votes supports their argument. Should the Liberal–Social Democratic Alliance achieve sustained and substantial support from most classes, their analysis will seem well validated by events. In place of the 'class-propelled' voter, they offer a model of the voter as consumer. They suggest that most voters do make a rational choice on the basis of what the parties present to them. The various influences on this choice, including class-related ones, cannot diminish the fact that, in every case, it is made personally and unpredictably.

The authors' own survey covers the six elections between 1959 and 1974 but they also refer to other data on the 1979 and 1983 elections.

Reading 70 From Hilde T. Himmelweit *et al, How Voters Decide* (Academic Press, 1987), pp. 205–10.

Decrease in the role of social determinants in vote choice

Commentators in this country and abroad describe Britain as a class-ridden society, seeing in this an important reason for low productivity and industrial unrest. While reference is made to historical factors, the Empire, the early industrialisation of Britain, the structure of the trade union movement, and the lack of techno-logical training of management, equal prominence is given to the pervasive and continuing effects of class division. Indeed, at the launching of their party in March 1981, the Social Democrats cited as one of their principal aims, the 'healing of class divisions'. The implication is that class divisions in the more industrially efficient European countries are less pronounced and that as a consequence there is a more effective partnership between management and the workforce. Our research shows such analysis to be over-simplistic, as it fails to take into account the importance of people's current attitudes. Moreover, we found that it was possible to predict atti-tudes to political issues little better than by chance from knowing solely a person's social origin, education and social status. Only attitudes towards big business and Britain's membership of the EEC were linked to class (Chapter 4). In Chapter 6 we showed that the political views of people within a given social class varied a good deal, and that such social determinants as class, education, age, sex and even trade union membership discriminated between the voters less well than did attitudes. Adding the social determinants to the cognitions made no independent contribution to the accuracy of voter classification.

People's political attitudes, although important, are not, of course, by themselves sufficient for an appraisal of the strength of class divisions in society.

Education and social status also have a direct influence on an individual's general perspective on society, including his or her goals and values. These in turn help shape reactions to specific issues. Thus the middle class and the socially mobile were more concerned with personal success and less with societal betterment – an echo of Runciman's (1966) distinction between egocentric and fraternalistic aspirations.

Goldthorpe's (1980) study of social class and social mobility found

541

not only a good deal of upward social mobility, resulting from changes in the occupational structure in Britain, but also that many of those who remained in the working class described themselves, relative to their fathers, as having 'risen'. Perceived mobility, whether through change in status or living standards, increased personal as opposed to collectivist aspirations (Chapter 2). This would account not only for the growing reluctance of people to label themselves in class terms, but also for the marked decrease in class-linked voting compared with former times. Up to and including 1974 much of it was due to an increase of Labour voters among the middle class (from 17% in 1964 to 27% in 1974, in addition to the 19% Liberal voters drawn from all social classes). By contrast, in 1979 there was a marked swing to the Conservatives, particularly among the skilled and semi-skilled working class.

Our study provides some further clues about the development or absence of class-related attitudes and voting. Early political socialisation through parental examples was strong only where there was a consistency among the cues generated by the adolescent's environment. Imitation was also less where the father's vote was atypical of his social class or where parents disagreed. Parents' vote continued to exert an influence in adult life on the adults' vote choice. Where parents, whatever their social class, had voted Conservative, movement away from Labour was strongest, and weakest where the parents had voted Labour.

Class-linked voting still exists, of course. More of the middle class vote Conservative even though less than in the 1960s; in the working class, however, the decline in Labour's share of the vote has become almost a rout. In 1959 62% of the working class voted Labour, by 1983 only 38% did so. The decline was so steep that among working class voters, Labour had only a 5% advantage over the Conservatives. Crewe (1983b) suggests that it would be more accurate in the 1980s to describe Labour as a party of *a segment of the working class*, the segment that is engaged in the declining heavy manufacturing industries in the North and in Scotland. Among more prosperous members of the working class, particularly those owning their homes, or working in industries that are holding their own, Labour was often the third rather than the first choice.

We make a distinction between class-*linked* voting and class-*determined* voting, whose decline is unlikely to be reversed. While the historically determined relations between labour and capital are of course structured along class lines, what emerges from our studies is that the political views of individuals, or indeed their political actions, are to a much smaller extent influenced by their social class position or their social mobility than a view of them as members of a class-ridden society would lead one to suspect. Such a view fails to differentiate between the effect of economic and social structures and their history on *society* as a whole and the effects on *individuals* for whom these structural categories represent one experience among several that form their view of society.

The future relation of class to vote

The degree of class-linked voting is time bound and election specific except in socially homogeneous areas (the industrial North or the South) with a long and unbroken tradition of voting Labour or Conservative. In the absence of specific regional and traditional ties with one party, the greater the geographical mobility, the more socially varied the neighbourhood, the smaller the place of work, the looser the relation between class and vote (Rose, 1980). Increase in standard of living, home ownership, upward social mobility and a middle class occupation encourage individualistic rather than collective aspirations (Strumpel, 1976). In our study, where concern with personal success was high, this coloured the individual's reaction to political issues (Chapter 4). By contrast, reduction in living standards, fear of inflation, high levels of unemployment and a working class job with little security or prospect of advancement led to more collectivist aspirations and the support of policies which in the 1970s were closer to those of the Labour than the Conservative Party.

What matters are the priorities of the voters at the time of each election. Where economic conditions are bad and mobility at a standstill, where unemployment hits society differentially and hardships fall unevenly, and where the government, by word or deed, does little to correct the imbalance, class-linked voting could increase. These conditions prevailed in 1983. There was also an increase in the polarisation of the views of the two parties which should have yielded, at least among manual workers, more class-linked voting rather than less. We had expected that former Labour supporters from the working class who had voted Conservative in 1979, largely we thought as a reaction against the 'winter of discontent', would return to Labour in 1983. This did not happen. Disillusionment with a party's promises and performance would be a sufficient reason for change of vote *only* where there is trust in the leadership and the realism of the proposals of the opposition. Both were absent.

It is the economic conditions of a society and the performance of the government in office which make the potential for voting along social class determinants more or less likely. But it is the beliefs that individuals develop about the available alternatives which will largely determine how far disillusionment with the party for which they had voted is translated into a move away from that party the next time around.

In the last 15 years, voting has entered a new era in which once familiar landmarks no longer operate or have been reversed. For example, in the early 1970s, trade union membership proved a significant factor over and above other social determinants in favour of a Labour vote. Since 1979, this has not been the case; indeed, in 1983, more trade unionists than non-union members voted Conservative. This was only partly due to an increase in the membership of white-collar unions; above all, it is an indication that those joining a union do not necessarily share the same political views, nor that membership generates such similarity.

The relevance of age to vote choice has changed as well, at least among the young. In every election since World War II up to 1979 new voters favoured Labour over the Conservatives. In the 1964 and 1974 elections, which Labour won with a very small majority, it was in fact their votes which tipped the scale. In contrast by 1983, despite unprecedented levels of youth unemployment, no more than 18% of the new voters opted for Labour as their first choice.

In the period after World War II the Conservatives consistently attracted more women than men. By 1979, this difference too had disappeared, largely because of increased voting for the Conservatives by male manual workers. In 1983, the pattern was actually reversed, with more men than women voting Conservative.

Comfortable landmarks on which politicians and political scientists have relied are disappearing one by one. For how long no-one can tell. What is certain, however, is that such landmarks no longer indicate invariant or even a strong predisposition for one party rather than another, unless other favourable conditions are also present.

544

The increased importance of voters' assessments of policies, parties and their leaders

In the past voters were thought to have made their task easier by voting in line with party loyalty and significant reference groups. These supports, as we have seen, no longer have much force. Since the task of deciding has become more difficult, it is not surprising that the number of people who make up their minds during the campaign has increased, with a considerable percentage deciding only in the last few days. There has also been an increase in the number who change their vote intention during the campaign.* In voting as in any other decision making where previous guidelines have lost their force, individuals need increasingly to draw on their own assessments.

In Chapter 1, we outlined our cognitive model of vote choice which indicates the factors influencing the decision. We compared the way the voter decides how to vote with how he decides what goods to buy. Instead of buying goods, the individual purchases a party, in the manner we described in Chapter 10. We drew this particular analogy to highlight the extent to which the individual searches for the best fit or least misfit between his or her views and preferences and the parties' platforms. In doing this, he or she may also be affected by two other more variable and weaker influences. The first of these is the habit of voting for a party, like the loyalty people develop for a particular brand, which predisposes them in its favour. Where preferences between competing goods are evenly matched, brand loyalty – or in the case of voting, party identification – may well tip the scale. The second influence is the example of others. Here we draw an analogy to the influence of spouses, friends and colleagues whose purchases at times influence our own.

In the case of most purchases, the final choice is a compromise. The same is true of voting. Some preferences are met, others are incompatible and others not reflected in the stance of any party. There are other similarities between voting and the purchase of goods: in both cases individual preferences matter as does the voter's attempt to examine the realism of the claims made by the parties in competing for votes.

* In 1983, 17% changed their voting intention and 11% changed the party they wanted to vote for between two weeks before the election was called and a few days before election day (Worcester, 1983).

While the analogy between purchasing a party and purchasing goods is a useful one, there are aspects which make choosing a party that much harder. In the case of voting, options are few and the policies on offer are those generated by the parties, not the voter. The timetable too is fixed by government. *De facto*, there are few opportunities for the ordinary voter, only moderately interested in politics, to hear the parties' claims seriously challenged, except by the other parties' counter claims. There is also no Trade Description Act to limit the claims of the parties, nor is there a consumer guide like *Which?* to assess their realism. Relative costs and incompatibility of policies are rarely mentioned; for example, that it would be difficult to reduce government expenditure while improving the lot of the needy, health and education services, as well as provide help for the developing countries. Yet all parties claim these as their objectives.

Is it any wonder that there are wide fluctuations in the opinion polls and that the voter is particularly critical of the party for which he had voted last time or the one he tried 'for size' in the pre-election period? It is for this reason that a party which does very well early on in a campaign needs to be particularly on its guard. For some voters the final choice is as often as not dictated by a general wish for change or a growing *dislike* of some posture of one party about which the voter already felt ambivalent, rather than attraction for another party. With the loosening of party ties negative partisanship is becoming more prevalent (Crewe, 1984).

Even though we found certain of the attitudes to be remarkably stable over a 12-year period, the model itself does not require stability of attitudes since each election is like a new shopping expedition in which familiar and new goods are on offer – some perennials, others shop-soiled and others still pristine in their wrappings.

Finally, our model of the voter as consumer does not imply that a voter who is in favour of two apparently incompatible policies lacks political acumen. When we buy goods, for example furniture or clothes, we want cheapness, elegance and good workmanship, generally incompatible qualities, but then decide between the available options by giving more weight to one rather than to the other quality. On another occasion the priorities as to which qualities matter most might well be reversed. For example, in most Western developed societies, voters want a reduction in public expenditure but no reduction in welfare provisions for which government is

STUART HALL

generally responsible: two apparently incompatible requirements which stem from different considerations; the first is economic, while the second derives from a shared value orientation which accepts that society has some responsibility for its poor. In Victorian times, when the poor were deemed to be responsible for their own plight, such incompatibility of views would have been less frequent.

Question
1. *To what extent are contemporary voting patterns better explained by a consumer model rather than a class model?*

(25 marks)

71 Stuart Hall: The Ideology of Thatcherism

In the early nineteen sixties Daniel Bell published an influential book, *The End of Ideology: The Exhaustion of Political Ideas in the West.* Few observations about emerging trends have proved to be more incorrect. In the nineteen sixties a new radicalism of the Left emerged and, in the late nineteen seventies and eighties, the New Right achieved popularity and power in the United States and parts of Europe, including Britain. Thatcherism is the major form the New Right has taken in Britain. Hall's term 'authoritarian populism' neatly sums up its blend of strong leadership and mass appeal. His article is included here in recognition both of the importance of ideology in the political process and of the specific contemporary significance of Thatcherism which looks like being *the* crucial political development in Britain in the last quarter of the twentieth century.

Hall's brief article offers little in the way of a general framework for understanding the role of ideology in promoting or preventing change (but see Readings 89 and 92). Thus, the question of whether Thatcherism is basically an expression of deeper economic and social forces or is in itself a powerful, relatively independent force is not tackled. Clearly, however, Hall considers that Thatcherism has articulated the feelings of many Britons more effectively than has the Labour Party. It has spoken to their frustration with state interference, their irritation at economic decline, their anger at the rising crime rate, and their national pride. Thatcherism in practice may have done little about these 'problems', or may have even made them worse, but it remains a powerful and apparently appealing ideological rhetoric. A sub-theme of Hall's article is the failure of the Labour Party to achieve a comparable appeal to Thatcherism. Indeed, this article complements Ivor Crewe's 'Can Labour Rise Again?' (Reading 69), providing the consideration of ideological factors he omits. In analysing Labour's failures, Hall reveals his own ideological preference which is for a more genuinely democratic, popular, socialism.

Reading 71 From Stuart Hall, 'The Great Moving Right Show' in *New Internationalist*, No. 133, March 1984, pp. 24–5, 28.

There can be no doubt about it: the move to the right no longer looks like a temporary swing of the pendulum. On the national political stages of Britain and the United States and at the international meetings the spotlight has veered hard over to the ideas and rhetoric of the New Right.

Nowhere has this been more apparent than in Maggie Thatcher's austere kingdom. But it would be wrong to identify the success of the British radical right solely with the personality of Mrs Thatcher and her hard-nosed cronies. Although they have given the swing to the right a distinctive personal stamp, the deeper movement is a form of authoritarian populism which has great appeal to the average punter.

At the ideological level many of the key themes of the radical Right – law and order, the need for social discipline and authority in the face of a conspiracy by the enemies of the state, the onset of social anarchy, the 'enemy within', the dilution of British stock by alien black elements – had emerged well before the full extent of the recession was known. They emerged as a reaction to the radical movements and political polarisation of the 1960s.

The radical Right is engaged in a struggle for dominance against both social democracy and the moderate wing of its own party. The strength of its intervention lies partly in its commitment to break the mould. It takes elements of the prevailing philosophies, dismantles them and reconstitutes them in a new logic. Thatcherism succeeds by directly engaging the 'creeping socialism' and 'apologetic state collectivism' of the Conservative 'wets'. It strikes at the very nerve centre of consensus politics, which dominated and stabilised the political scene for over a decade. Whilst actively destroying consensus politics from the right, it aims for the construction of a new national consensus of its own making.

The contradictions within social democracy are one key to the whole rightward shift of the political spectrum. The contradiction can be put in simple terms: to win elections social democracy (Labour in this case) must maximise its claims to be the political representative of the working class and organised labour. This relationship of class-to-party has depended on the set of bargains negotiated between Labour and trade union representatives of the working class. This 'indissoluble link' is the practical basis for Labour's claims to be the natural governing party when there is crisis.

But once in government, social democracy is committed to finding solutions to the crisis which are capable of winning support from key sections of capital, since its solutions are always framed within the limits of capitalist survival. And this requires that the link between party and class be used not to advance but to *discipline* the class and organisation it represents.

The rhetoric of 'national interest', which is the main way that a succession of defeats have been imposed on the working class by social democracy in power, are exactly where this contradiction shows through. For people-to-government (the basis of Mrs Thatcher's appeal) dissects the struggle in a different way than class-to-party. At key moments of struggle – from the strikes of 1966 right through to the 1979 five per cent pay norm which was broken so disastrously – the Labour government was forced to come down on the side of 'The Nation' against 'sectional interests', 'irresponsible trade union power' etc – that is, against its own class.

This is the terrain on which Mr Heath played such destructive games in the lead-up to the Industrial Relations Act of 1971 and its aftermath, with his invocation of 'the great trade union of the nation' and the spectre of the greedy working class 'holding the nation to ransom'. Thatcherism, deploying the vocabulary of 'the nation' and 'people' against 'class' and 'unions' with far greater vigour and popular appeal, has homed in on this objective contradiction between Labour and the class which is the basis of its support. Considerable numbers of people – including many trade unionists – find themselves caught up in this rhetoric of 'the nation' and 'people', and swirled along in a rising wave of hostility to trade unions.

Closely related strands in the philosophy of the radical Right are the themes of anti-collectivism and anti-statism ('Big government is the problem'). Thatcherism has rejuvenated these traditional nineteenth century themes. On the economic front this has meant refurbishing the ideas of monetarism, and knocking away the Keynesian linch-pin at the centre of corporatist state intervention throughout the postwar period – pumping money into the economy to create jobs.

Neither Keynesianism nor monetarism, however, win votes in the electoral marketplace. But Thatcherism discovered a powerful means of translating the clichés of 'freedom of the marketplace' into the language of experience, moral imperative and common sense, providing an alternative ethic to that of 'the caring society'. 'Being British' became once again identified with the restoration of competition and profitability; with tight money and sound finance (you can't pay yourself more than you earn!); and the national economy became debated on the model of a household budget. The essence of the British citizen, the Tory message read, should be self-reliance and personal responsibility, not crippled by taxation, enervated by welfare state 'coddling', with their moral fibre irrevocably sapped by 'state handouts'. This assault on the very principle of social welfare – the corner stone of consensus politics from the mid 1950s onwards – was mounted through the emotive image of the 'scrounger': the new folk devil.

This populist language and the reconstruction of a 'free market' ethic has been given a sensitive public relations treatment to render it palatable. The excessively high-minded Sir Keith Joseph and the excessively broad-bottomed Rhodes Boyson, the 'disinterested' lead writers of *The Times*, *The Telegraph* and *The Economist* and the ventriloquists of populist opinion in the *Mail*, the *Express*, the *Star* and the *Sun* gave it their undivided attention. One of the country's top advertising agencies, Saatchi and Saatchi, were called in to polish up the popular appeal of the Leader and her policies. Gaining the support of the popular press was a critical victory in the attempt to redefine the commonsense of the times: from the 'caring society' to the 'by our own bootstraps' nation.

Thatcherite populism is a particularly rich mix. It combines the resonant themes of basic Toryism (nation, family, duty, authority, standards, tradition) with the aggressive themes of a revived neo-liberalism (self-interest, competitive individualism, anti-statism). 'Freedom of the people equals the free market' is once again in the foreground of the conservative ideological repertoire. Around this contradictory point the authentic language of 'Thatcherism' has crystallised. It began to define the crisis: what it was and how to get out of it.

When in a crisis traditional alignments are disrupted it becomes possible to persuade working people to align themselves with the formation of a new power bloc: an alliance with the new political forces of the Right in a great national crusade 'to make Britain "Great" once more'. The idea of 'the people' unified behind a reforming drive to turn back the tide of 'creeping socialism', banish the illusions of full employment without inflation from the state apparatus and renovate the power bloc is a powerful one. Its radicalism connects with popular sentiments. But it effectively turns them on their head, absorbs and neutralises their popular thrust and creates, in the place of a popular move toward radical change, a *populist unity*. It brings into existence a new coalition between certain sections of the dominant and the dominated classes. We can see this alliance between 'Thatcherism' and 'the people' in the very structure of Mrs Thatcher's own rhetoric: 'Don't talk to me about "them" and "us" in a company', she once told readers of Woman's Own: 'You're all "we" in a company. You survive as a company survives, prosper as the company prospers – everyone together. The future lies in co-operation and not confrontation.' This ousts the existing structure of opposites – 'them' vs 'us'. It sets in its place an alternative set of equivalents: 'Them' *and* 'us' equals '*we*'. Then it puts we – 'the people' – in a particular relation to capital: behind it, dominated by its imperatives (profitability, accumulation); yet at the same time yoked to it, identified with it. 'You survive as the company survives'; presumably you also collapse as it collapses. Company liquidations and bankruptcies totalled 40,019 in the four years of Mrs Thatcher's rule 1980–1983, compared to 21,393 in the previous four years of Jim Callaghan's office.

This process of absorption and neutralisation of popular sentiments has often been described as 'false consciousness', just a set of ideological con tricks whose cover will be blown as soon as they are put to the stern test of the real world. But this underestimates both the rational core of these populist sentiments and their real basis. 'Thatcherism' operates directly on the real and contradictory experience of the popular classes under social democracy: that when Labour comes to power as champion of the working class and trade unions, it turns round and forces them into a straight jacket of wage controls. On this basis it tars Labour with the 'burcaucratic statist' brush – and wins support amongs all freeborn Englishmen.

Labour's social democracy *did* increase state control. 'Statism' was a stifling force. That's why anti-statism has proved so powerful a populist slogan. The Labour party in government did set itself to *contain* and *reform*, instead of transform, British capitalism. What capital could not accomplish on its own, Labour's 'reformism' would do by using the state as representative of the 'general interest' to create the conditions for 'business as usual', the effective resumption of capitalist accumulation and profitability. Social democracy had no strategy other than massive state control and support for both private and public industry, plus a welfare tax for the working class. Hence the state has become a massive presence, inscribed over every feature of social and economic life. But, as the recession bit more deeply, so the management of the crisis required the Labour government to discipline, limit and police the very classes it claimed to represent.

The best index of this problem was the incomes policy, especially in its last and most confusing manifestation, the Social Contract. To the Labour government it represented the only way in which social and economic discipline could be 'sold' to the trade union movement. The glaring discrepancies between the redistributive language of the Social Contract and its actual disciplinary character was the best example of how the state, under social democracy, came to be experienced as 'the enemy of the people'. This contradiction bit deeper and deeper into the Labour/trade union alliance between 1976 and 1979 until it undermined the credibility and *raison d'etre* of Mr Callaghan's government itself.

The radical Right welcomed this trade union revolt against 'state interference in free collective bargaining' much the same way that the father welcomed the return of the Prodigal Son.

The problem stemmed from Labour trying to work within the capitalist system while expounding socialist policies. The expansion of the state machine, under the management of civil servants and experts, has often been defined in this tradition as synonymous with socialism itself. Labour has been willing to use the state to reform conditions for working people, provided this did not bite too deeply into the logic of capitalist accumulation. The fact is that 'statism' is not foreign to Labour socialism: it is intrinsic to it.

The Right has capitalised on the fatal hesitancy of the Labour party to identify itself with the emergence of democratic power at the popular level. Mrs Thatcher is guilty of exaggeration – but no more than that – when she identifies state bureaucracy and creeping state ownership with the Labour party's 'socialism'. Then she goes further and identifies this 'socialism' with the spectre of socialism of East European regimes: and contrasts this with the sweet sound of 'Freedom' which, of course, she and her New Model Conservative Party represent.

It is the New Right's further advantage that the experience working people have had under Labour has not been a great advert for more nationalisation. Whether in the growing dole queues, the waiting-rooms of the over-burdened National Health Service, or suffering the indignities of claiming Social Security benefits, people experience the corporatist state increasingly not as a benefit for them but as a powerful bureaucratic imposition on them. The state has become less a welfare agency, and more a benevolent dictator.

Instead of confronting this contradiction at the heart of its strategy, Labour has fallen back on stressing the neutrality of the state, incarnator of the National Interest and above the struggle between the contending classes. It is precisely this abstract state which has been transformed by Mrs Thatcher into the enemy. It is 'the State' which has over-borrowed and overspent; fuelled inflation, fooled the people into thinking there would always be more where the last handout came from; tried to regulate things like wages and prices which are best left to the hidden hand of market forces; above all, interfered, meddled, intervened, obstructed, instructed and directed – against the essence, the genius, of the British People. It is time, she says with conviction, 'to put people's destinies back into their own hands'.

So in any polarisation between state and people, it is Labour which is represented as undividedly part of the power bloc, en-meshed in state apparatus, riddled with bureaucracy, in short 'with' the State; and Mrs Thatcher, grasping the torch of freedom with one hand, who is undividedly out there, 'with the people'. It is the Labour Party which is committed to things as they are – and Mrs Thatcher who means to tear society up by the roots and radically reconstruct it. This is the process by which the radical Right has become 'popular', and Labour unpopular.

Question
1. *(a) What does Hall mean by 'authoritarian populism'?*

(5 marks)

(b) To what extent has ideology contributed to the success of the New Right in Britain?

(15 marks)

Social Order, Control and Deviance

Readings 72–78

Sociologists have given great attention to issues of social control and deviance but less so to social order. In part, this may be because social order is considered to be primarily a problem for political analysis. Certainly, one aspect of social order is who has the power to enforce it and by what right. But within sociology the emphasis has been more on how society 'hangs together' or 'functions' in an orderly manner or, to put the matter in ethnomethodological terms, how people create order in everyday life. In this broader social sense, Durkheim's study of social solidarity in *The Divison of Labour in Society* can be considered one of the first sociological studies of social order. Robert Nisbet (Section 11, Reading 58) treats the problem of order in a similar way to Durkheim.

The first extract in this section is from Durkheim's *Suicide*. In explaining suicide essentially in terms of the degree of an individual's 'social integration', Durkheim's basic frame of reference is again social order. Albert Cohen's subcultural theory remains close to the functionalist tradition but stresses class analysis more than Durkheim or Durkheim's major American interpreter, Robert Merton. The third reading in this section, from Howard Becker, is a classic of symbolic interactionism, and Stanley Cohen also uses concepts from that perspective in the following reading.

The first clearly Marxist influenced reading in this section is from John Lea and Jock Young's, *What Is To Be Done About Law And Order?* This reading bears the influence of both the radical criminology with which Young was formerly associated and of the Marxist subcultural theory of the Centre for Cultural Studies (see Reading 47). Stephen Savage summarises some recent work in the area of social control. He covers the sociology of the police, courts and prisons. Much of this work assumes that the social and political aspects of order and control cannot be fully separated and I would agree with this. Police, judicial, and penal power has important social dimensions.

The second reading in this section by Stanley Cohen overviews historical and contemporary developments in the area of social control. His book is titled *Visions of Social Control* and at times Cohen's analysis seems to verge on visionary pessimism. His grasp of the field certainly transcends the American derived symbolic interactionism of his earlier work (see Reading 75).

72 Emile Durkheim: The Social Element of Suicide

This extract from Durkheim's study, *Suicide*, presents his uncompromising view that the suicide rate and other rates of deviancy can be explained only in social terms. This analysis may be better understood in the context of a brief summary of his general perspective on deviance and, particularly, suicide.

Durkheim describes deviance as relative, normal and functional. It is relative in that what is regarded as deviant varies from society to society, normal in that every society has some deviance, and functional mainly in that the deviance of a minority enables the majority to reaffirm their moral conformity. According to Durkheim, each society has a normal rate for each form of deviance, including suicide.

He argues that major variations in the rate of suicide within a given society must be due to some important social factor – such as rapid economic change. In fact, he offers a model of three types of suicide – anomic, egoistic and altruistic – and relates each to the degree of integration ('connectedness') of the individual with society. Anomic and egoistic suicide occur when the individual is 'disconnected' from society, and altruistic suicide happens when an individual so identifies with society that s/he is prepared to commit suicide for it (e.g., *Kamikaze*).

The contention that a statistical norm can be established for any sort of behaviour within a given society and that deviation from it requires social explanation is typically positivist (though Durkheim did not use this term to describe his method). In the following extract, Durkheim strongly dismisses the view that the individual causes of suicide can explain variations in the suicide rate. By contrast, the phenomenologists, Maxwell Atkinson and

556

Jack Douglas, have approached suicide not so much as a social issue, but as a personal phenomenon. (For Douglas's comments on Durkheim's analysis of suicide, see Reading 100.)

Reading 72 From Emile Durkheim, *Suicide: A Study in Sociology* (Routledge and Kegan Paul, 1970), pp. 297–300.

Now that we know the factors in terms of which the social suicide-rate varies, we may define the reality to which this rate corresponds and which it expresses numerically.

The individual conditions on which suicide might, *a priori*, be supposed to depend, are of two sorts.

There is first the external situation of the agent. Sometimes men who kill themselves have had family sorrow or disappointments to their pride, sometimes they have had to suffer poverty or sickness, at others they have had some moral fault with which to reproach themselves, etc. But we have seen that these individual peculiarities could not explain the social suicide-rate; for the latter varies in considerable proportions, whereas the different combinations of circumstances which constitute the immediate antecedents of individual cases of suicide retain approximately the same relative frequency. They are therefore not the determining causes of the act which they precede. Their occasionally important role in the premeditation of suicide is no proof of being a causal one. Human deliberations, in fact, so far as reflective consciousness affects them are often only purely formal, with no object but confirmation of a resolve previously formed for reasons unknown to consciousness.

Besides, the circumstances are almost infinite in number which are supposed to cause suicide because they rather frequently accompany it. One man kills himself in the midst of affluence, another in the lap of poverty; one was unhappy in his home, and another had just ended by divorce a marriage which was making him unhappy. In one case a soldier ends his life after having been punished for an offense he did not commit; in another, a criminal whose crime has remained unpunished kills himself. The most varied and even the most contradictory events of life may equally serve as pretexts for suicide. This suggests that none of them is the specific cause. Could we perhaps at least ascribe causality to those qualities known to be common to all? But are there any such? At best one might say that they usually consist of disappointments, of sorrows, without any possibility of deciding how intense the grief must be to have such tragic significance. Of no disappointment in life, no matter how insignificant, can we say in advance that it could not possibly make existence intolerable; and, on the other hand, there is none which must necessarily have this effect. We see some men resist horrible misfortune, while others kill themselves after slight troubles. Moreover, we have shown that those who suffer most are not those who kill themselves most. Rather it is too great comfort which turns a man against himself. Life is most readily renounced at the time and among the classes where it is least harsh. At least, if it really sometimes occurs that the victim's personal situation is the effective cause of his resolve, such cases are very rare indeed and accordingly cannot explain the social suicide-rate.

Accordingly, even those who have ascribed most influence to individual conditions have sought these conditions less in such external incidents than in the intrinsic nature of the person, that is, his biological constitution and the physical concomitants on which it depends. Thus, suicide has been represented as the product of a certain temperament, an episode of neurasthenia, subject to the effects of the same factors as neurasthenia. Yet we have found no immediate and regular relationship between neurasthenia and the social suicide-rate. The two facts even vary at times in inverse proportion to one another, one being at its minimum just when and where the other is at its height. We have not found, either, any definite relation between the variations of suicide and the conditions of physical environment supposed to have most effect on the nervous system, such as race, climate, temperature. Obviously, though the neuropath may show some inclination to suicide under certain conditions, he is not necessarily destined to kill himself; and the influence of cosmic factors is not enough to determine in just this sense the very general tendencies of his nature.

Wholly different are the results we obtained when we forgot the individual and sought the causes of the suicidal aptitude of each society in the nature of the societies themselves. The relations of suicide to certain states of social environment are as direct and constant as its relations to facts of a biological and physical character were seen to be uncertain and ambiguous. Here at last we are face to face with real laws, allowing us to attempt a methodical classification of types of suicide. The sociological causes thus determined by us have even explained these various concurrences often attributed to the influence of material causes, and in which a proof of this influence has been sought. If women kill themselves much less often than men, it is because they are much less involved than men in collective existence; thus they feel its influence – good or evil – less strongly. So it is with old persons and children, though for other reasons. Finally, if suicide increases from January to June but then decreases, it is because social activity shows similar seasonal fluctuations. It is therefore natural that the different effects of social activity should be subject to an identical rhythm, and consequently be more pronounced during the former of these two periods. Suicide is one of them.

The conclusion from all these facts is that the social suicide-rate can be explained only sociologically. At any given moment the moral constitution of society establishes the contingent of voluntary deaths. There is, therefore, for each people a collective force of a definite amount of energy, impelling men to self-destruction. The victim's acts which at first seem to express only his personal temperament are really the supplement and prolongation of a social condition which they express externally.

This answers the question posed at the beginning of this work. It is not mere metaphor to say of each human society that it has a greater or lesser aptitude for suicide; the expression is based on the nature of things. Each social group really has a collective inclination for the act, quite its own, and the source of all individual inclination, rather than their result. It is made up of the currents of egoism, altruism or anomy running through the society under consideration with the tendencies to languorous melancholy, active renunciation or exasperated weariness derivative from these currents. These tendencies of the whole social body, by affecting individuals, cause them to commit suicide. The private experiences usually thought to be the proximate causes of suicide have only the influence borrowed from the victim's moral predisposition, itself an echo of the moral state of society. To explain his detachment from life the individual accuses his most immediately surrounding circumstances; life is sad to him because he is sad. Of course his sadness comes to him from without in one sense, however not from one or another incident of his career but rather from the group to which he belongs. This is why there is nothing which cannot serve as an occasion for suicide. It all depends on the intensity with which suicidogenetic causes have affected the individual.

Question

1. *What arguments does Durkheim present for the view that 'the social suicide rate can be explained only sociologically'?*

(10 marks)

73 Albert Cohen: Delinquent Sub-culture

Albert Cohen is one of several influential American sociologists who published work on delinquent sub-cultures between the mid-1950s and 60s. Others included Cloward and Ohlin and Walter Miller. With the exception of Miller, the major theoretical influence on these writers was the Functionalist Robert Merton's celebrated essay on nonconformity *Social Structure and Anomie*, published in 1938. Merton argued that much crime and delinquency can be regarded as a form of 'innovation' by which those who are shut out of the legitimate opportunity structure (i.e. the acceptable ways of achieving success) use nonconformist or deviant means to obtain their goals. In this extract, Cohen departs from Merton in suggesting that not only the means but some of the goals of delinquents are 'nonconformist'. However, the overall Functionalist design of Cohen's analysis is very apparent (even though he does accommodate a measure of class conflict analysis within it).

Cohen begins by suggesting that 'corner boys' or, more simply, working-class boys are influenced by two sets of norms and values, those of the middle and working class. They can seek status (which Cohen assumes everybody needs) within either class. He clearly regards this 'ambivalent' situation as potentially stressful and describes several modes of 'adjustment' to it. Some working-class children seek status by attempting to become middle class; others try to keep a foothold in both worlds; others identify with the stable (i.e. non-delinquent) working class, and a minority become delinquent. Cohen sees delinquency in terms of 'reaction-formation'. Deprived of middle-class means of achieving status, delinquents react against middle-class standards and seek identity and status by adopting opposite ones. Whereas the stable 'corner boy' retains some interest in middle-class values, the delinquent rejects them aggressively. Values such as aggression and cheating become positive virtues within delinquent sub-culture. It is, of course, the group nature of delinquency that makes it a sub-cultural, as opposed to an individual activity. Finally, in typical Mertonian fashion, Cohen locates the broad context of delinquency within the nature of American society as a whole.

There are a number of established criticisms of Cohen's analysis. First, Cloward and Ohlin's point that delinquents seek material or property rewards as much as status is surely correct. Perhaps more important, however, is the argument that delinquent sub-culture is not merely a reaction against middle-class values, but bears a very close relationship to the general values of the working class. Walter Miller forwarded this thesis and, to some extent, it has been taken up in the class-based analysis of youth sub-cultures made by various British sociologists from about 1975 onwards (see Section 6, Readings 29 and 30).

Reading 73 From Albert Cohen, *Delinquent Boys: The Culture of the Gang* (Collier Macmillan, 1966), pp. 127–37.

We have suggested that corner-boy children (like their working-class parents) internalise middle-class standards to a sufficient degree to create a fundamental ambivalence towards their own corner-boy behavior. Again, we are on somewhat speculative ground where fundamental research remains to be done. The coexistence within the same personality of a corner-boy and a college-boy morality may appear more plausible, however, if we recognise that they are not simple antitheses of one another and that parents and others may in all sincerity attempt to indoctrinate both. For example, the goals upon which the college-boy places such great value, such as intellectual and occupational achievement, and the college-boy virtues of ambitiousness and pride in self-sufficiency are not as such disparaged by the corner-boy culture. The meritoriousness of standing by one's friends and the desire to have a good time here and now do not by definition preclude the desire to help oneself and to provide for the future. It is no doubt the rule, rather than the exception, that most children, college-boy and corner-boy alike, would like to enjoy the best of both worlds. *In practice*, however, the substance that is consumed in the pursuit of one set of values is not available for the pursuit of the other. The sharpness of the dilemma and the degree of the residual discontent depend upon a number of things, notably, the intensity with which both sets of norms have been internalised, the extent to which the life-situations which one encounters compel a choice between them, and the abundance and appropriateness of the skills and resources at one's disposal. The child of superior intelligence, for example, may find it easier than his less gifted peers to meet the demands of the college-boy standards without failing his obligations to his corner-boy associates.

It is a plausible assumption, then, that the working-class boy whose status is low in middle-class terms *cares* about that status, that this status confronts him with a genuine problem of adjustment. To this problem of adjustment there are a variety of conceivable responses, of which participation in the creation and the maintenance of the delinquent subculture is one. Each mode of response entails costs and yields gratifications of its own. The circumstances which tip the balance in favor of the one or the other are obscure. One mode of response is to desert the corner-boy for the college-boy way of life. To the reader of Whyte's *Street Corner Society* the costs are manifest. It is hard, at best, to be a college-boy and to run with the corner-boys. It entails great effort and sacrifice to the degree that one has been indoctrinated in what we have described as the working-class socialisation process; its rewards are frequently long-deferred; and for many working-class boys it makes demands which they are, in consequence of their inferior linguistic, academic and 'social' skills, not likely ever to meet. Nevertheless, a certain proportion of working-class boys accept the challenge of the middle-class status system and play the status game by the middle-class rules.

Another response, perhaps the most common, is what we may call the 'stable corner-boy response.' It represents an acceptance of the corner-boy way of life and an effort to make the best of a situation. If our reasoning is correct, it does not resolve the dilemmas we have described as inherent in the corner-boy position in a largely middle-class world, although these dilemmas may be mitigated by an effort to disengage oneself from dependence upon middle-class status-sources and by withdrawing, as far as possible, into a sheltering community of like-minded working-class children. Unlike the delinquent response, it avoids the radical rupture of good relations with even working-class adults and does not represent as irretrievable a renunciation of upward mobility. It does not incur the active hostility of middle-class persons and therefore leaves the way open to the pursuit of some values, such as jobs, which these people control. It represents a preference for the familiar, with its known satisfactions and its known imperfections, over the risks and the uncertainties as well as the moral costs of the college-boy response, on the one hand, and the delinquent response on the other.

What does the delinquent response have to offer? Let us be clear, first, about what this response is and how it differs from the stable corner-boy response. The hallmark of the delinquent subculture is the explicit and wholesale repudiation of middle-class standards and the adoption of their very antithesis. *The corner-boy culture is not specifically delinquent.* Where it leads to behavior which may be defined as delinquent, *e.g.*, truancy, it does so not because nonconformity to middle-class norms defines conformity to corner-boy norms but because conformity to middle-class norms *interferes with* conformity to corner-boy norms. The corner-boy plays truant because he does not like school, because he wishes to escape from a dull and unrewarding and perhaps humiliating situation. But truancy is not defined as intrinsically valuable and status-giving. The member of the delinquent sub-culture plays truant because 'good' middle-class (and working-class) children do not play truant. Corner-boy resistance to being herded and marshalled by middle-class figures is not the same as the delinquent's flouting and jeering of those middle-class figures and active ridicule of those who submit. The corner-boy's ethic of reciprocity, his quasi-communal attitude toward the property of in-group members, is shared by the delinquent. But this ethic of reciprocity does not sanction the deliberate and 'malicious' violation of the property rights of persons outside the in-group. We have observed that the differences between the corner-boy and the college-boy or middle-class culture are profound but that in many ways they are profound differences in emphasis. We have remarked that the corner-boy culture does not so much repudiate the value of many middle-class achievements as emphasise certain other values which make such achievements improbable. In short, the corner-boy culture temporises with middle-class morality; the full-fledged delinquent sub-culture does not.

It is precisely here, we suggest, in the refusal to temporise, that the appeal of the delinquent sub-culture lies. Let us recall that it is characteristically American, not specifically working-class or middle-class, to measure oneself against the widest possible status universe, to seek status against 'all comers,' to be 'as good as' or 'better than' anybody – anybody, that is, within one's own age and sex category. As long as the working-class corner-boy clings to a version, however attenuated and adulterated, of the middle-class culture, he must recognise his inferiority to working-class and middle-class college-boys. The delinquent sub-culture, on the other hand, permits no ambiguity of the status of the delinquent relative to that of anybody else. In terms of the norms of the delinquent sub-culture, defined by its negative polarity to the respectable status system, the delinquent's very nonconformity to middle-class standards sets him above the most exemplary college boy.

Another important function of the delinquent sub-culture is the legitimation of aggression. We surmise that a certain amount of hostility is generated among working-class children against middle-class persons, with their airs of superiority, disdain or condescension and against middle-class norms, which are, in a sense, the cause of their status-frustration. To infer inclinations to aggression from the existence of frustration is hazardous; we know that aggression is not an inevitable and not the only consequence of frustration. So here too we must feel our way with caution. Ideally, we should like to see systematic research, probably employing 'depth interview' and 'projective' techniques, to get at the relationship between status position and aggressive dispositions toward the rules which determine status and toward persons variously distributed in the status hierarchy. Nevertheless, despite our imperfect knowledge of these things, we would be blind if we failed to recognise that bitterness, hostility and jealousy and all sorts of retributive fantasies are among the most common and typically human responses to public humiliation. However, for the child who temporises with middle-class morality, overt aggression and even the conscious recognition of his own hostile impulses are inhibited, for he acknowledges the *legitimacy* of the rules in terms of which he is stigmatised. For the child who breaks clean with middle-class morality, on the other hand, there are no moral inhibitions on the free expression of aggression against the sources of his frustration. Moreover, the connection we suggest between status-frustration and the aggressiveness of the delinquent sub-culture seems to us more plausible than many frustration-aggression hypotheses because it involves no assumptions about obscure and dubious 'displacement' of aggression against 'substitute' targets. The target in this case is the manifest cause of the status problem.

It seems to us that the mechanism of 'reaction-formation' should also play a part here. We have made much of the corner-boy's basic ambivalence, his uneasy acknowledgement, while he lives by the standards of his corner-boy culture, of the legitimacy of college-boy standards. May we assume that when the delinquent seeks to obtain unequivocal status by repudiating, once and for all, the norms of the college-boy culture, these norms really undergo total extinction? Or do they, perhaps, linger on, underground, as it were, repressed, unacknowledged but an ever-present threat to the adjustment which has been achieved at no small cost? There is much evidence from clinical psychology that moral norms, once effectively internalised, are not lightly thrust aside or extinguished. If a new moral order is evolved which offers a more satisfactory solution to one's life problems, the older order usually continues to press for recognition, but if this recognition is granted, the applecart is upset. The symptom of this obscurely felt, ever-present threat is clinically known as 'anxiety,' and the literature of psychiatry is rich with devices for combating this anxiety, this threat to a hard-won victory. One such device is reaction-formation. Its hallmark is an 'exaggerated,' 'disproportionate,' 'abnormal' intensity of response, 'inappropriate' to the stimulus which seems to elicit it. The unintelligibility of the response, the 'over-reaction,' becomes intelligible when we see that it has the function of reassuring the actor against an *inner* threat to his defenses as well as the function of meeting an external situation on its own terms. Thus we have the mother who 'compulsively' showers 'inordinate' affection upon a child to reassure herself against her latent hostility and we have the male adolescent whose awkward and immoderate masculinity reflects a basic insecurity about his own sex-role. In like manner, we would expect the delinquent boy who, after all, has been socialised in a society dominated by a middle-class morality and who can never quite escape the blandishments of middle-class society, to seek to maintain his safeguards against seduction. Reaction-formation, in his case, should take the form of an 'irrational,' 'malicious,' 'unaccountable' hostility to the enemy within the gates as well as without: the norms of the respectable middle-class society.

If our reasoning is correct, it should throw some light upon the peculiar quality of 'property delinquency' in the delinquent subculture. We have already seen how the rewardingness of a college-boy and middle-class way of life depends, to a great extent, upon general respect for property rights. In an urban society, in particular, the possession and display of property are the most ready and public badges of reputable social class status and are, for that reason, extraordinarily ego-involved. That property actually is a reward for middle-class morality is in part only a plausible fiction, but in general there is certainly a relationship between the practice of that morality and the possession of property. The middle-classes have, then, a strong interest in scrupulous regard for property rights, not only because property is 'intrinsically' valuable but because the full enjoyment of their status requires that that status be readily recognisable and therefore that property adhere to those who earn it. The cavalier misappropriation or destruction of property, therefore, is not only a diversion or diminution of wealth; it is an attack on the middle-class where their egos are most vulnerable. Group stealing, institutionalised in the delinquent sub-culture, is not just a way of *getting* something. It is a means that is the antithesis of sober and diligent 'labour in a calling.' It expresses contempt for a way of life by making its opposite a criterion of status. Money and other valuables are not, as such, despised by the delinquent. For the delinquent and the non-delinquent alike, money is a most glamorous and efficient means to a variety of ends and one cannot have too much of it. But, in the delinquent sub-culture, the stolen dollar has an odor of sanctity that does not attach to the dollar saved or the dollar earned.

This delinquent system of values and way of life does its job of problem-solving most effectively when it is adopted as a group solution. We have stressed in our chapter on the general theory of sub-cultures that the efficacy of a given change in values as a solution and therefore the motivation to such a change depends heavily upon the availability of 'reference groups' within which the 'deviant values' are already institutionalised, or whose members would stand to profit from such a system of deviant values if each were assured of the support and concurrence of the others. So it is with delinquency. We do not suggest that joining in the creation or perpetuation of a delinquent sub-culture is the only road to delinquency. We do believe, however, that for most delinquents delinquency would not be available as a response were it not socially legitimised and given a kind of respectability, albeit by a restricted community of fellow-adventurers. In this respect, the adoption of delinquency is like the adoption of the practice of appearing at the office in open-collar and shirt sleeves. Is it much more comfortable, is it more sensible than the full regalia? Is it neat? Is it dignified? The arguments in the affirmative will appear much more forceful if the practice is already established in one's milieu or if one senses that others are prepared to go along if someone makes the first tentative gestures. Indeed, to many of those who sweat and chafe in ties and jackets, the possibility of an alternative may not even occur until they discover that it has been adopted by their colleagues.

This way of looking at delinquency suggests an answer to a certain paradox. Countless mothers have protested that their 'Johnny' was a good boy until he fell in with a certain bunch. But the mothers of each of Johnny's companions hold the same view with respect to their own offspring. It is conceivable and even probable that some of these mothers are naive, that one or more of these youngsters are 'rotten apples' who infected the others. We suggest, however, that all of the mothers may be right, that there is a certain chemistry in the group situation itself which engenders that which was not there before, that group interaction is a sort of catalyst which releases potentialities not otherwise visible. This is especially true when we are dealing with a problem of status-frustration. Status, by definition, is a grant of respect from others. A new system of norms, which measures status by criteria which one can meet, is of no value unless others are prepared to apply those criteria, and others are not likely to do so unless one is prepared to reciprocate.

We have referred to a lingering ambivalence in the delinquent's own value system, an ambivalence which threatens the adjustment he has achieved and which is met through the mechanism of reaction-formation. The delinquent may have to contend with another ambivalence, in the area of his status sources. The delinquent sub-culture offers him status *as against* other children of whatever social level, but it offers him this status *in the eyes of* his fellow delinquents only. To the extent that there remains a desire for recognition from groups whose respect has been forfeited by commitment to a new sub-culture, his satisfaction in his solution is imperfect and adulterated. He can perfect his solution only by rejecting as status sources those who reject him. This too may require a certain measure of reaction-formation, going beyond indifference to active hostility and contempt for all those who do not share his sub-culture. He becomes all the more dependent upon his delinquent gang. Outside that gang his status position is now weaker than over. The gang itself tends toward a kind of sectarian solidarity, because the benefits of membership can only be realised in active face-to-face relationships with group members.

Question
1. (a) *What does Albert Cohen mean by the term 'reaction formation'?*
                                                                    (5 marks)
    (b) *How is this concept illustrated in the behaviour of the 'street-corner' boys?*

                                                                    (10 marks)
    (c) *Critically review the concept of 'reaction formation'.*
                                                                    (10 marks)
(You may prefer to answer 1 (c) after studying other sub-cultural perspectives.)

74 Howard S. Becker: Deviance and Labeling

Whereas Durkheim describes deviance in terms of breaking society's rules, Becker defines it as the public 'labeling' of an individual as a rule-breaker or deviant, whether or not s/he actually performed the act of which s/he is accused. In defining deviance in this way, Becker draws attention to the power of society and, particularly, of law enforcement agencies such as the courts or police to make labels 'stick.' He also stresses the consequences of labeling in terms of social stigmatisation and loss of personal esteem and opportunity. Both these points are apparent in the extract from Malinowski's research in the Trobriand Islands quoted by Becker. It is only when the youth is publicly labeled as a sexual deviant that he is fully regarded as such and only then do the consequences of 'being a deviant' come into operation. Although Becker is certainly not a Marxist, his analysis is quite compatible with the view that the wealthy and powerful can frequently avoid unwanted labels, whereas the less well off and powerless find this more difficult to do. Both interactionists and modern Marxists, therefore, go beyond Durkheim's rather simple concern with rules and rule-breaking to issues of power, control and enforcement.

Reading 74 From Howard S. Becker, *Outsiders: Studies in the Sociology of Deviance* (Collier Macmillan, 1966), pp. 8–12.

The sociological view I have just discussed defines deviance as the infraction of some agreed-upon rule. It then goes on to ask who breaks rules, and to search for the factors in their personalities and life situations that might account for the infractions. This assumes that those who have broken a rule constitute a homogeneous category, because they have committed the same deviant act.

Such an assumption seems to me to ignore the central fact about deviance: it is created by society. I do not mean this in the way it is ordinarily understood, in which the causes of deviance are located in the social situation of the deviant or in 'social factors' which prompt his action. I mean, rather, that *social groups create deviance by making the rules whose infraction constitutes deviance*, and by applying those rules to particular people and labeling them as outsiders. From this point of view, deviance is *not* a quality of the act the person commits, but rather a consequence of the application by others of rules and sanctions to an 'offender.' The deviant is one to whom that label has successfully been applied; deviant behavior is behavior that people so label.

Since deviance is, among other things, a consequence of the responses of others to a person's act, students of deviance cannot assume that they are dealing with a homogeneous category when they study people who have been labeled deviant. That is, they cannot assume that these people have actually committed a deviant act or broken some rule, because the process of labeling may not be infallible; some people may be labeled deviant who in fact have not broken a rule. Furthermore, they cannot assume that the category of those labeled deviant will contain all those who actually have broken a rule, for many offenders may escape apprehension and thus fail to be included in the population of 'deviants' they study. Insofar as the category lacks homogeneity and fails to include all the cases that belong to it, one cannot reasonably expect to find common factors of personality or life situation that will account for the supposed deviance.

What, then, do people who have been labeled deviant have in common? At the least, they share the label and the experience of being labeled as outsiders. I will begin my analysis with this basic similarity and view deviance as the product of a transaction that takes place between some social group and one who is viewed by that group as a rule-breaker. I will be less concerned with the personal and social characteristics of deviants than with the process by which they come to be thought of as outsiders and their reactions to that judgment.

Malinowski discovered the usefulness of this view for understanding the nature of deviance many years ago, in his study of the Trobriand Islands:

> One day an outbreak of wailing and a great commotion told me that a death had occurred somewhere in the neighborhood. I was informed that Kima'i, a young lad of my acquaintance, of sixteen or so, had fallen from a coco-nut palm and killed himself . . . I found that another youth had been severely wounded by some mysterious coincidence. And at the funeral there was obviously a general feeling of hostility between the village where the boy died and that into which his body was carried for burial.
>
> Only much later was I able to discover the real meaning of these events. The boy had committed suicide. The truth was that he had broken the rules of exogamy, the partner in his crime being his maternal cousin, the daughter of his mother's sister. This had been known and generally disapproved of but nothing was done until the girl's discarded lover, who had wanted to marry her and who felt personally injured, took the initiative. This rival threatened first to use black magic against the guilty youth, but this had not much effect. Then one evening he insulted the culprit in public – accusing him in the hearing of the whole community of incest and hurling at him certain expressions intolerable to a native.
>
> For this there was only one remedy; only one means of escape remained to the unfortunate youth. Next morning he put on festive attire and ornamentation, climbed a coco-nut palm and addressed the community, speaking from among the palm leaves and bidding them farewell. He explained the reasons for his desperate deed and also launched forth a veiled accusation against the man who had driven him to his death, upon which it became the duty of his clansmen to avenge him. Then he wailed aloud, as is the custom, jumped from a palm some sixty feet high and was killed on the spot. There followed a fight

within the village in which the rival was wounded; and the quarrel was repeated during the funeral . . .

If you were to inquire into the matter among the Trobrianders, you would find . . . that the natives show horror at the idea of violating the rules of exogamy and that they believe that sores, disease and even death might follow clan incest. This is the ideal of native law and in moral matters it is easy and pleasant strictly to adhere to the ideal – when judging the conduct of others or expressing an opinion about conduct in general.

When it comes to the application of morality and ideals to real life, however, things take on a different complexion. In the case described it was obvious that the facts would not tally with the ideal of conduct. Public opinion was neither outraged by the knowledge of the crime to any extent, nor did it react directly – it had to be mobilised by a public statement of the crime and by insults being hurled at the culprit by an interested party. Even then he had to carry out the punishment himself . . . Probing further into the matter and collecting concrete information, I found that the breach of exogamy – as regards intercourse and not marriage – is by no means a rare occurrence, and public opinion is lenient, though decidedly hypocritical. If the affair is carried on *sub rosa* with a certain amount of decorum, and if no one in particular stirs up trouble – 'public opinion' will gossip, but not demand any harsh punishment. If, on the contrary, scandal breaks out – everyone turns against the guilty pair and by ostracism and insults one or the other may be driven to suicide.

Whether an act is deviant, then, depends on how other people react to it. You can commit clan incest and suffer from no more than gossip as long as no one makes a public accusation . . .

Question
See end of next reading.

75 Stanley Cohen: The Amplification of Deviance

The following extract is taken from Stanly Cohen's book *Folk Devils and Moral Panics.* It further illustrates symbolic interactionist perspective on deviance and particularly reflects Becker's notion that deviance is socially created. The key concept in this piece is 'amplification.' This term refers to the way in which widespread or sensational media coverage of a deviant activity such as gang 'warfare', football hooliganism, or even terrorism can mould public response and also somewhat increase participation in them. Like the concepts of labelling and self-fulfilling prophecy, that of amplification indicates the power of certain individuals and agencies, in this case the media, to present and even define events in a way that greatly influences perception of them. Specifically, Cohen argues that the media 'amplified' the Mods and Rockers phenomenon of the 1960s by helping to trigger a series of 'riots', by helping to stimulate a hostile public response (including, possibly, by control agencies such as the police) and by attracting some youngsters to the confrontations who might not otherwise have become involved. It is the first of these aspects of amplification that he considers to be least generally understood. Cohen does not suggest that the media causes events such as the Mod and Rockers' riots – clearly other social factors are also relevant – but he does show that they play a part both in the way such events occur and how they are perceived.

Reading 75 From Stanley Cohen, *Folk Devils and Moral Panics: The Creation of Mods and Rockers* (Martin Robertson, 1980), pp. 161–3.

This is the point at which to analyse the more explicit on-the-spot role of the mass media which, as we have seen, operated from the outset in reinforcing and giving shape to the crowd's sense of expectancy and in providing the content of rumours and shared definitions with which ambiguous situations were restructured. Although popular commentators on the Mods and Rockers often blamed 'publicity' for what happened (and the press responded with indignant editorials about its 'duty' to publish the 'facts'), the term 'publicity' was used in a somewhat restricted sense. It either referred to the publicity immediately before the event (during the warning phase), which advertised the disturbances and pin-pointed the resorts where they would take place, or to the supposed gratification young people derived from the exposure to publicity during the event.

The first of these factors operated in the gross sense of publicising the event in such a way that it might look attractive, but it is unlikely to have directly influenced the choice of target: asked where they got the idea from (of going to Margate), 82.3 per cent of the Barker-Little sample mentioned friends as their source, only 2.9 per cent mentioned newspapers and 2.9 per cent television. Only a handful I spoke to at any stage said that anything in the press or television *initially* decided them on a particular resort. The media more likely reinforced rather than initiated rumours already current. There were certain exceptions, though, when during the weekend a sensational report or TV interview might have directly attracted new crowds. One notorious B.B.C. interview in which two Rockers said that reinforcements would be arriving was followed by a sudden influx of both Mods and Rockers, large numbers of whom might have been attracted by the excitement the interview promised.

There were also signs of direct publicity-seeking behaviour in the sense that on-the-spot attention from journalists, reporters and photographers was a stimulus to action. The following account is by one of the boys in the Barker-Little sample: 'By the railway station a cameraman asked, "Give us a wave". So me and a group ran about and waved some flags we bought. My picture was in the paper. We were pleased; anybody would be.'

If one is in a group of twenty, being stared at by hundreds of adults and being pointed at by two or three cameras, the temptation to do something – even if only to shout an obscenity, make a rude gesture or throw a stone – is very great and made greater by the knowledge that one's actions will be recorded for others to see. There is a tendency for the participant in such situations to exaggerate the extent of his involvement and to look for some recognition of it. Thus at every weekend, young people could be observed at newspaper kiosks buying each edition of the evening paper as it appeared and scanning it for news of disturbances. The exploitative element in this feed back is reflected in the rumours – which, at least in one case, I am certain were firmly based – that press photographers were asking suitably attired young males to pose kicking in a window or telephone kiosk.

The cumulative effects of the mass media, though, were at the same time more subtle and more potent than simply giving the events pre-publicity or gratifying the participants' need for attention. Through a complex process that is not yet fully understood by students of mass comunication, the mere reporting of one event has, under certain circumstances, the effect of triggering off events of a similar order. This effect is much easier to understand and is better documented in regard to the spread of crazes, fashions, fads and other forms of collective behaviour, such as mass delusion or hysteria, than in cases of deviance. The main reason why this process has been misunderstood in regard to deviance – particularly collective and novel forms – is that too much attention has been placed on the supposed direct effects (imitation, attention, gratification, identification) on the deviants, rather than the effects on the control system and culture and hence (via such processes as amplification) on the deviance.

The simple triggering-off or suggestibility type effects can be seen even in apparently individual forms of deviance such as suicide. A particularly vivid example is the spread in self-immolation as a form of suicide following the report in 1963 of a Vietnamese monk burning himself to death as an act of political protest. This is a form of suicide almost completely unknown in the West; in the period 1960–63, there was only one such case in England, yet in 1963, there were three and in 1964, nine. A similar progression in numbers occurred in America. In this case, the contagious or imitative effect was in the technique rather than the motivation behind the act. Cases where the motive as well as the technique is stimulated by mass communication, might be the spread of prison riots, prison escapes and racial and political riots. A particularly well-documented example is the Swastika Epidemic of 1959–60. The contagion effect could be clearly shown in plotting the curve of the epidemic.

An example closer to the Mods and Rockers is the spread during the fifties of the Teddy Boy riots and similar phenomena elsewhere in Europe. Most commentators on these events acknowledged the role of publicity in stimulating imitative or competitive forms of behaviour and some studies have been made on the mass media coverage of such events. At the same time, though, blame was put on 'publicity' in the restricted sense and there was little awareness of the complex ways in which mass communication operates before, during and after each 'impact'. The causative nature of mass communication – in the whole context of the societal reaction to such phenomena – is still usually misunderstood.

The common element in all these diverse examples of the amplification of violence is that an adequate medium of communication must be present for spreading the hostile belief and mobilising potential participants. The mass communication of the news of one outbreak is a condition of structural conduciveness for the development of a hostile belief which, in turn, has to sensitise the 'new' crowd (or individual deviant) to incipient or actual action and lower the threshold of readiness by providing readily identifiable symbols.

Question
1. *How does Stanley Cohen's example of deviancy amplification extend and develop Becker's approach to deviance?*

(20 marks)

76 John Lea and Jock Young: The Causes of Crime (including an Analysis of Crime Statistics)

The theory behind the analysis of the causes of crime given in this reading is not fully presented below. In fact, it is in the section preceding the one extracted here that Lea and Young explain why they consider certain groups are more likely to commit crime than others. They use three concepts to do this: subculture, relative deprivation, and marginalisation. A subculture is a way of life created by a group of people in response to common problems. The relative deprivation experienced by certain subcultural groups (e.g., young Afro-Caribbeans), will become part of their identity and awareness. When such a group is politically powerless (marginalised), then its members are more likely to turn to crime than otherwise.

Lea and Young organise their analysis in four sections:

1. The Causes of Crime – in which they argue that, while all social groups are influenced by the materialist ideals of capitalism, some are relatively deprived of the means to achieve them.
2. The Nature of Crime and Criminal Values – in this section they argue that criminal responses to deprivation are highly dubious and problematic.
3. The Nature of Crime Statistics – in which they suggest that,

575

although official criminal statistics are biased, they can provide useful indicators.

4. The Role of the State and Its Agencies – in this section they contend that, in upholding law and order, the state can help the working class as well as the middle class. Throughout their arguments, Lea and Young belabour both 'conventional criminology' and 'left idealism' which, they consider, misconceive crime albeit in contrasting ways.

Eleven years previous to the publication of the book from which this reading is taken, Jock Young co-authored *The New Criminology: For a Social Theory of Deviance* (Routledge and Kegan Paul, 1973). Here it was suggested that an adequate theory of deviance required to deal with the following seven points:

1. The wider origins of the deviant act.
2. The immediate origins of the deviant act.
3. The actual act.
4. The immediate origins of social reaction.
5. Wider origins of deviant reaction.
6. The outcome of the social reaction on deviant's further action.
7. The nature of the deviant process as a whole.

Obviously, a brief extract will not meet all those requirements, but perhaps it gives an indication of the extent to which Young is keeping faith with the agenda of radical criminology.

Reading 76 From J. Lea and J. Young, *What is To Be Done About Law and Order?* (Penguin, 1984), pp. 95–104.

1 The causes of crime

For orthodox criminology crime occurs because of a lack of conditioning into values: the criminal, whether because of evil (in the conventional model) or lack of parental training (in the welfare model), lacks the virtues which keep us all honest and upright. In left idealism, crime occurs not because of lack of value but simply because of lack of material goods: economic deprivation drives people into crime. In the conventional view-point on crime, the criminal is flawed; he or she lacks human values and cognition. In the radical interpretation of this, the very opposite is true. The criminal, not the honest person, has the superior consiousness: he or she has seen through the foolishness of the straight world. To be well conditioned is to be well deceived. The criminal then enters into a new world of value – a sub-culture, relieved in part of the mystifications of the conventional world.

We reject both these positions. The radical version smacks of theories of absolute deprivation; we would rather put at the centre of our theory notions of relative deprivation. And a major source of one's making comparisons – or indeed the feeling that one should, in the first place, 'naturally' compete and compare oneself with others – is capitalism itself.

We are taught that life is like a racetrack: that merit will find its own reward. This is the central way our system legitimates itself and motivates people to compete. But what a strange racetrack! In reality some people seem to start half-way along the track (the rich), while others are forced to run with a mill-stone around their necks (for example, women with both domestic and non-domestic employment), while others are not even allowed on to the track at all (the unemployed, the members of the most deprived ethnic groups). The values of an equal or meritocratic society which capitalism inculcates into people are constantly at loggerheads with the actual material inequalities in the world. And, contrary to the conservatives, it is the *well-* socialised person who is the most liable to crime. Crime is endemic to capitalism because it produces both egalitarian ideals and material shortages. It provides precisely the values which engender criticism of the material shortages which the radicals pinpoint.

A high crime rate occurs in precise conditions: where a group has learnt through its past that it is being dealt with invidiously; where it is possible for it easily to pick up the contradictions just referred to and where there is no political channel for these feelings of discontent to be realised. There must be economic and political discontent and there must be an absence of economic and political opportunities.

2 The nature of crime and criminal values

For conventional criminology, as we have seen, crime is simply antisocial behaviour involving people who lack values. For left idealists it is the reverse: it is proto-revolutionary activity, primitive and individualistic, perhaps, but praiseworthy all the same. It involves, if it is a theft, a redistribution of income, or if it is part of youth culture, symbolic and stylistic awareness of, say, the loss of traditional working-class community or the repressive nature of the system. In either case it involves alternative values.

We would argue that both of these interpretations of crime are superficial. It is true that crime is antisocial – indeed the majority of working-class crime, far from being a prefigurative revolt, is directed against other members of the working class. But it is not antisocial because of lack of conventional values but precisely because of them. For the values of most working-class criminals are overwhelmingly conventional. They involve individualism, competition, desire for material goods and, often, machismo. Such crime could, without exaggeration, be characterised as the behaviour of those suitably motivated people who are too poor to have access to the Stock Exchange. Crime reflects the fact that our own worlds and our own lives are materially and ideologically riddled with the capitalist order within which we live. Street crime is an activity of marginals but its image is that of those right in the centre of convention and of concern. As Jeremy Seabrook (p. 64) puts it:

> What we cannot bear, rich and liberals alike, is to see our own image in actions that are ugly and more stark reflections of transactions in which we are all implicated in our social and economic relationships: the universal marketing, the superstitious faith in money, the instant profit, the rip-off, the easy money, the backhander, the quick fiddle, the comforting illusion that we can all get richer without hurting anyone, the way in which individual salvation through money has become a secularised and man-made substitute for divine grace.

The radicals are correct when they see crime as a reaction to an unjust society. But they make a crucial mistake: they assume that the reaction to a just cause is necessarily a just one. On the contrary: it is often exactly the opposite. The reaction to poverty among poor whites, for example, may be to parade around waving Union Jacks: it may be the tawdry nationalism of the National Front. The reaction to relative deprivation may, as Paul Willis has so ably shown, be sexism, racism and anti-intellectualism. Crime is one form of egoistic

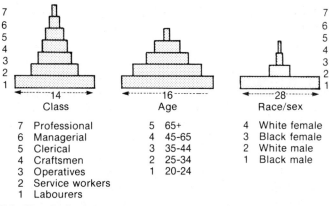

7 Professional	5 65+	4 White female
6 Managerial	4 45-65	3 Black female
5 Clerical	3 35-44	2 White male
4 Craftsmen	2 25-34	1 Black male
3 Operatives	1 20-24	
2 Service workers		
1 Labourers		

Likelihood of going to prison

Figure 1 Recorded and unrecorded crime

response to deprivation. Its roots are in justice but its growth often perpetuates injustice.

3 The nature of the crime statistics

If we look at the official crime statistics in any Western capitalist country we see a remarkable similarity: the young are consistently seen to offend more than the old, the working class more than the middle class, black more than white, and men more than women. In Figure 1 we have constructed a series of Aztec pyramids each representing the likelihood of going to prison dependent on class, age, race and gender. We have used American statistics rather than British, as they are more complete. The British figures, particularly in terms of class and race, are kept much more closely guarded. The shape of these pyramids is, however, constant across cultures and there are close parallels; for example, one British study showed that the chances of going to prison by class were exactly the same as in America.

As can be seen, a labourer is fourteen times more likely to go to prison than a professional; someone aged between twenty and twenty-four is sixteen times more likely than a sixty-five-year-old; a black male is twenty-eight times more likely than a white female. If one compounds these figures, of course, one achieves much higher ratios, the most extreme being the contrast between the chances of going to prison of an elderly, white professional woman compared to a young, black, lower-working-class man. This has some very dramatic results; for example, on an average day in the United States one in 450 Americans is in prison, but one black man in twenty-six between the ages of twenty-five and thirty-four. Offenders, like victims, are sharply focused in terms of social category; in fact, the same social attributes which tend towards high victimisation rates tend also towards high offender rates. We have talked about this so-called moral symmetry between the victim and the offender in Chapter 1. Serious crime, according to the official statistics, is a minority phenomenon within which certain social categories most marginal to society are vastly over-represented. The prisoner is thus on the fringe of the economy (unemployed or a casual labourer), has missed out on the educational system, and belongs to a minority group.

Now, these pyramids illustrate the major empirical problem for understanding crime. For conventional criminology it is scarcely a problem: the lower orders are much more likely to be badly socialised than the middle and upper echelons of society – hence the pyramid. For left idealists, however, this fact poses a considerable quandary. For, on the one hand, gross economic deprivation will surely lead to crime; but on the other, is it not true that the police pick on the poor, ignoring the crimes of the rich? Our response to this contradiction is simply to ask why either-or is a realistic analysis. There is no doubt that different social categories of people behave differently both in their degree of orderliness and criminality and that this relates to their position in the world; but there is also no doubt that the police react differently to different categories of people. If both these points are true, then the official statistics are a product of differences in the 'real' rates of crime between groups and differences in the police predisposition to arrest them. Thus the crime rate of old ladies is no doubt actually very low, but it probably appears *even* lower in the official statistics because of the police disinclination to suspect or arrest elderly persons. And as far as lower-working-class youths are concerned, the exact opposite is true: they commit more crimes and they are excessively harassed, the result being an augmented crime statistic. Moreover, different types of people commit different types of crimes. This point is put particularly well by Reiman (pp. 7–8). He writes:

There is evidence suggesting that the particular pressure of poverty leads poor people to commit a higher proportion of the crimes that people fear (such as homicide, burglary, and assault) than their number in the population. There is no contradiction between this and the recognition that those who are well off commit many more crimes than is generally acknowledged both of the widely feared and of the sort not widely feared (such as 'white-collar' crimes). There is no contradiction here, because, as will be shown, the poor are arrested far more frequently than those who are well off when they have committed the same crimes – and the well-to-do are almost never arrested for white-collar crimes. Thus, if arrest records were brought in line with the real incidence of crime, it is likely that those who are well off would appear in the records far more than they do at present, even though the poor would still probably figure disproportionately in arrests for the crimes people fear. In addition to this . . . those who are well off commit acts that are not defined as crimes and yet that are as harmful or more so than the crimes people fear. Thus, if we had an accurate picture of who is really dangerous to society, there is reason to believe that those who are well off would receive still greater representation.

In other words, (a) the pyramids we have constructed with regards to class and crime (and the same is true of race, gender and age) are quantitatively too dramatic: if middle-class people were equally subject to arrest and conviction the contrasts between each level could not be as steep. (b) Qualitatively, given the above provision, they are reasonably correct if one does *not* include white-collar crime and focuses, as Reiman outlines, on the 'normal' crimes which people fear. If people were arrested and imprisoned for white-collar crimes, then the pyramid would remain in shape but its gradient would be lessened even more. (c) To admit to a pyramid of crime by class is not, of course, to believe in a pyramid of impact. That is, the fact that lower-working-class males commit more crime than upper-class counterparts does not mean that the overall impact of such crimes is necessarily greater. As we have seen, it is probably less, although none of this suggests that we should concentrate on either one or the other, as criminologists, both radical and conventional, have done in the past. Both types of crime create considerable problems for the population.

4 The role of the state and its agencies

For conventional criminology the state is a neutral institution that protects the universal interests of all against problems such as crime. In parliamentary democracies it is an eminently re-formable institution where popular demand can be translated into legislative practice. For the left idealists, the state is the direct instrument of the ruling class. The various institutions – whether ideological (like education and the mass media) or directly repressive (such as the police and the judicial system) – exist in order to maintain capitalism. They mesh together in a seamless web of interrelating institutions which are explained by the function in which they contribute to the status quo. Reform in a progressive direction is an impossibility. The most that will happen is neutralisation – like punching into a beanbag; the worst, and more usual, the reform will be turned against the working class. Thus part of the explanatory task of such theoreticians is to explain how 'anomalies' such as Intermediate Treatment or Community Service Orders are, in fact, in the interests of the ruling class despite the fact that they look, on the face of it, eminently progressive.

As regards the explanation of the behaviour of the agents of social control, such as the police, there are parallel differences between the two positions. In the conventional model the police are seen as attempting to solve the problem of crime. They are faced with a problem and they do their best to deal with it within the limits of the law, and with a choice of action based on the pragmatic possibilities of resources and the science of detection of crime. For the radicals, the behaviour of the police is, at base, materially determined: it follows the logic of capital. The policing initiatives which Police Commissioners take and the notions of the rank-and-file police officers are in the end determined by the imperatives of maintaining a disciplined work-force and subdued population. Such policies follow a drift towards an increasingly strong state which is seen as inevitable and itself a product of the declining fortunes of world capitalism. Events which look like having a reasonably progressive content, such as the publication of the Scarman Report or the shift from McNee to Newman as head of the Metropolitan Police Force, are seen as cosmetic touches in what is an inevitably worsening situation.

This sheds light on the left idealist position on crime. The problem of crime – or, more correctly, working-class crime – is very largely an illusion, orchestrated by the ruling class in order to engender moral panic which distracts the population from the real problems which assail them. The fear of crime is a potent symbol in the armoury of mystification. For, by mobilisation of this fear, the powerful can literally replace the class war by the war against crime. The preponderance of crime-reporting in the mass media is no accident, for the spectre of crime is a central component of the mystification which besets us.

We reject the notion of conventional criminology that the state is a neutral institution acting in the universal interests of the population against, in this instance, 'the crime problem'. At the present moment the British state represents very largely ruling-class interests, but gains can be wrung out of it; reforms, however difficult to achieve, are possible and, in fact, relate to the state as in essence a site of contradicting interests.

The basis for the political support of bourgeois society among the mass of the population is closely entwined with their fears of crime and disorder. For the ruling class takes real working-class demands for justice and attempts to enmesh them in the support of a class-ridden society. The existence of a class society leads to desperation, demoralisation and a war of all against all, and the working-class community suffers immensely from the criminals in its midst. Law gains its support not just through mystification of the working class, an ability to render people spellbound by its paraphernalia of pomp and authority. Legal institutions partially represent, it is true, the interests of the ruling class but they are also much more than just this. As Herbert Marcuse put it (p. 101):

In Marxian theory, the state belongs to the superstructure in as much as it is *not* simply the direct political expression of the basic relationships of production but contain elements which, as it were, 'compensate' for the class relationships of production. The state, being and remaining the state of the ruling class, sustains *universal* law and order and thereby guarantees at least a modicum of equality and security for the whole society. Only by virtue of these elements can the class state fulfil the function of 'moderating' and keeping within the bounds of 'order' the class conflicts generated by the production relations. It is this 'mediation' which gives the state the appearance of a universal interest over and above the conflicting particular interests.

The class society which creates social disorganisation also creates its partial palliative. Law not only involves ruling-class domination: it has a legitimate component to it, in terms of the protection of working-class interests. It is not, therefore, just a mystification disguising the naked one-to-one interests of the powerful, as left idealists would maintain. Laws against vandalism do to some extent protect working-class property, those against rape are intended to protect women, however sexist the manner in which they are employed, and those against income-tax fiddling are there often to aid income redistribution, however tardily they may be invoked in practice. It is in the interests of working-class people that crime is controlled, and it is in their interest that the agencies of the state deal with crime in a just and effective fashion. The struggle for justice in the area of crime is a central part of a socialist strategy.

Questions

1. (a) Compare criminal values to the mainstream values of capitalist society.

(7 marks)

(b) What explanation of high crime rates is given in the reading? (Refer also to the introduction to the extract.)

(8 marks)

2. What can we learn from official crime statistics?

(20 marks)

3. According to the authors, to what extent does law and order help the working class?

(15 marks)

4. How convincing do you find sub-cultural explanations of working class crime?

(25 marks)

(To answer question 4, further reading in sub-culture theories of crime is required: see, for instance, Reading 73.)

77 Stephen Savage: The Sociology of Law and Order: Police, Courts and Prisons

This reading has the great merit of presenting in a clear way certain important areas of the subject that are often inadequately covered. The areas dealt with are the sociology of the:

1. Police
2. Courts
3. Prison

The literature surveyed in the reading generally rejects the view that the institutions of law and order are totally neutral. Police, judges and magistrates, and prison officers have values and attitudes which are formed in specific social contexts and which affect their behaviour at work. A major aspect of the sociology of law and order is to explore these connections.

The section on the police is the fullest. A summary is given of Robert Reiner's *The Politics of the Police* which analyses the rather inbred quality of police 'culture' and, in particular, tendencies to conservatism, racism and sexism. This leads to a useful discussion of police stereotyping. Finally, the policy of increasing the numbers of police officers is briefly evaluated.

The section on the sociology of the courts opens with an analysis of the class background of the judiciary and their sexual make-up. There follows a discussion of Pat Cohen's *Magistrates' Justice* which is an ethnomethodological survey of how 'the courts' arrive at their decisions. This harks back to work by the founder of ethnomethodology, Harold Garfinkel, who studied the 'commonsense' reasoning of jurors in arriving at their verdicts. The point is that reasoning and negotiation, rather than rigid adherence to legal guidelines, produce decisions and verdicts. A classic example of this – cited in the reading – is plea-bargaining. This section concludes with a reference to McCabe and Purves' *The Shadow Jury at Work* which gives a favourable 'verdict' on the quality of British courts.

The section on prisons raises two issues: inmate culture and the 'crisis' of the prisons. The discussion of inmate culture provides useful data on total institutions which supplements Goffman's *Asylums*. The multiple crises of the prisons leads

Savage to wonder whether it would be better to get rid of them. The trend, however, is in the opposite direction. Britain is one of the few Western European countries increasing the number of prisons and prisoners.

The conclusion of the reading suggests questions worthy of anyone's attention. Are the tough social control measures taken in response to Britain's economic problems and social unrest creating a drift towards 'a law and order society'? How did we get into a situation in which we *apparently* need more law and order? Could it be that in adopting an American-style economic system, we are also producing American-style problems of social inequality, unrest and control?

Reading 77 From Stephen P. Savage, *Law and Order* (Hyperion Press, 1986), pp. 1–12.

Introduction

The term 'law and order' is a politically loaded one. It has tradition-ally been identified with the Political Right – The Conservative Party has often been referred to as 'The Party of Law and Order'. More recently, however, it has become a label used to outline a very important area of academic interest. Sociologists and political scientists have become increasingly involved in studying the field of law and order and are using their concepts and theories to help develop a deeper understanding of the issues and questions surrounding it.

Law and order is also a very broad area. It covers many aspects of the long standing field of criminology and the sociology of deviance, together with the study of penology (which is concerned with an understanding of the penal system) – and it also includes aspects of public administration. For our purposes 'law and order' will be used to define processes of **law** and **law-enforcement** which includes three major stages: the **police**, the **court** and the **penal system** (prisons and other forms of punishment).

One reason for the increased interest in law and order in recent years has been the spate of inner-city disturbances and riots in major British cities – in St. Paul's in Bristol in 1980, Toxteth and Moss Side in 1981, and Handsworth, Brixton and Tottenham in 1985. These events have caused all sides to reconsider some basic questions about law and order in British society as well as wider questions of social policy (housing and education) in relation to our ethnic and racial minorities. Another reason has been a definite growth in public concern about a 'lawless' society. In 1984, the Observer published findings from in-depth interviews with a stratified sample of over 1,000 adults. This survey revealed a concern over the growth of crime in Britain when it asked respondents if certain crimes had become more of a problem over the previous 3 or 4 years.

Question:	Which have become more of a problem in the country as a whole over the last three or four years?	
Answers:	(Crime)	(Proportion of respondents)
	Mugging	54%
	Crimes of violence	51%
	Football hooliganism	46%
	Vandalism	37%
	Sexual offences	36%
	Drug abuse	36%
	Robberies from houses	32%
	Crime involving young	31%

The result of these two sources of concern has been some very interesting research and a variety of competing explanations and opinions about the way in which we maintain law and order in Britain . . .

The sociology of law and order

Sociologists interested in the field of law and order have mainly been involved in criminology and the study of deviance, i.e. the study of crime and the criminal. As well as looking at their major concern – explaining criminal and deviant behaviour – they have also begun to look in more detail at what happens to 'criminals' – how they are dealt with by the police, how they are processed by the courts, and what happens when they are sentenced, particularly if sentenced to serve a prison sentence. In other words, sociologists have been attempting to help us understand how law and order **works**. In order to outline some of the most important features of the law and order machine from a sociological point of view, let us follow the path taken in the law enforcement process, beginning with the police, through the courts, and finally the penal system.

After that I will make some general points about the way sociologists have viewed the law itself.

1 The sociology of the police

The number of police officers per head of the population has increased substantially in recent times. The present figure of one policeman for every 387 people in the population compares with one for every 602 in 1961. In 1961 there were less than 88 thousand police compared with over 145 thousand just 25 years later.

Table 1   Police in the UK (1984)

	Regular police			
	Number	Population per officer	Hectares per officer	% women officers
United Kingdom	145,608	387	168	8.5
England	114,656	409	114	9.3
Wales	6,347	442	327	6.2
Scotland	13,208	390	596	5.4
Northern Ireland:				
Royal Ulster Constabulary	8,003	194	176	8.5
R.U.C. Reserve	3,394	458	416	5.8

Source: Regional Trends 1985, HMSO.

Police in the UK are mainly white males. As Table 1 shows, women officers account for just one in twelve of the police force. Police recruited from the ethnic minorities account for an even smaller proportion of the force. According to **Social Trends 1986** there were only 680 black police officers in England and Wales by the start of 1985, 253 of whom were in the Metropolitan Police Force, 87 in the West Midlands (i.e. about one in every 180).

The police hold a key position in the total system of law-enforcement. To a great extent it is they who decide who shall enter the criminal justice system and under what charge. Given that those who do enter the process are only a small percentage of the total number of offenders in the community (see R. Hood and R. Sparks, **Key Issues in Criminology**), the type of people police officers are and the way in which they make their decisions become important issues in our understanding of law and order. Are they even-handed in their enforcement of the law, or are they inclined to apply the law differently to various social groups? In order to answer questions such as this we need to look first at sociological studies of police **attitudes** and police **culture**.

Robert Reiner in his book **The Politics of the Police** has collected together American and British Studies into 'Cop Culture' to outline some of the common themes running through police attitudes and types of behaviour. A central feature of police culture is the isolation of the police from the wider public – the product of the nature of their work and the way the police view themselves – and the solidarity which such isolation leads to and feeds off. Police officers tend to develop a strong 'them' and 'us' attitude, a belief that their work is linked to a 'mission', the 'thin blue line' protecting the public from the element which threatens people and property. They develop deeply ingrained attitudes of suspicion towards other groups in society, not just 'villains' but also 'do-gooders' and 'politicians' in general. Such attitudes are fostered not so much by police training, which in recent years has deliberately been aimed at broadening the officer's understanding of the wider society, but rather by the informal socialisation process within the force, particularly within the lower ranks. What is more, these attitudes tend to have particular consequences for some sectors of the community rather than others. Reiner's own studies, for example, have shown that the British police are an essentially conservative body, both morally and politically, leaning noticably to the Right on a broad range of issues, such as drug-taking and homosexuality. Their own involvement in policing public order problems in strikes and political demonstrations would seem to both influence and be affected by their conservative stance on political issues. Strikers, pickets and political protesters are often placed together with criminals as part of 'them', the threat to 'peaceful' society.

To conservatism we can also add two further dimensions of 'Cop Culture', highlighted by the recent report by the Policy Studies Institute (PSI) of their study into the Metropolitan Police **Police and People in London**. This report, made all the more effective because it was commissioned by the Commissioner of the Metropolitan Police Force himself, outlined widespread attitudes which reflected police sexism and racism. Sexism is the outcome of the 'cult of masculinity' or 'machismo' which pervades police work. As the report states, although 9% of officers in the Met. are women,

the dominant values of the Force are still in many ways those
of an all-man institution such as a rugby-club or boy's school.
(p. 372)

These values are expressed in bigotry towards sexual deviance, in
sexual boasting and horseplay, and in the denigration of women
(including women officers). Such attitudes and standards of behaviour may not in themselves always be damaging to the police task,
but in cases in which the police have to deal directly with women,
they may prove very harmful. An example of this was shown to TV
audiences in explicit fashion during the series 'Police' based on the
Thames Valley Police Force, shown during the early 1980's. In this
instance a rape victim was treated with immense suspicion and great
insensitivity by male officers on the case, a fact which caused a
political storm and which subsequently led to changes in police
methods in dealing with rape cases.

Police racism is even more potentially damaging. Both American
and British research has found extensive attitudes of suspicion and
prejudice towards ethnic minorities amongst police officers, often
linked to racialist stereotyping and expressed in abusive language.
The PSI study, for example, discovered racist abuse and racist jokes
daubed in graffiti in police lavatories, and found racist attitudes
expressed openly by officers in casual conversation. They did not,
however, find that such attitudes were expressed in actual police
behaviour in dealing with black or Asian people. Other studies have
been less reassuring. Paul Gorden in **White Law** has argued that
police racism goes further than language and belief, it is carried as
far as the policing task itself, in which the police victimise and
persecute blacks, particularly young blacks, for a host of 'street
crimes'. Any difference in arrest rates for blacks, argues Gordon, is
explained more by police racism than a higher rate of black criminality. Indeed, the PSI itself contains some evidence of this. In the
case of 'stop and search' police powers were often exceeded and it
was young 'West Indian' men who were most likely to be stopped.
This, says the report, has led to a 'disastrous' lack of confidence in
the police amongst young blacks. Among those aged 15–24, 41%
believe that the police fabricate records, 53% think they use
excessive force and 62% believe the police regularly use threats. The
Home Office report in 1985 indicated that 'stop and search' tactics
were used by police on blacks far more than whites and also that

between 30% and 40% of all arrests stemmed from such stops. On this basis, as even the report acknowledges, the over-representation of blacks arrested for street crimes will owe something to the extra frequency with which they are stopped.

Distrust of the police by the Afro-Caribbean population is now a fact more or less openly acknowledged by the Home Office both as a result of the **Scarman Report** on the Brixton and Toxteth riots in the summer of 1981 and as a result of a Home Office review of research on the topic which was published in August 1984 (**The Attitudes of Ethnic Minorities**, S. Field, Home Office Research Study No. 80). This review concluded that, whilst the Afro-Caribbean population has a positive attitude in general towards British society and its institutions – with attitudes to education, jobs, housing and health being much the same as the attitudes of the white majority – the one glaring exception is in attitudes towards the police. Amongst black youth in particular it appears that there is a distrust of the police which does not stem from any generalized hostility to authority or to British society (Rastas excepted), but from their **experiences** in contact with the police.

The debate on policing, race and crime goes on, intensified of course by the inner-city riots of the early and mid–1980's, but it is clear that racism is, at the very least, a part of low-rank police **attitudes**, a fact to which new police training methods (such as 'racism awareness training') draw attention.

This outline of sociological work on police culture allows us to make some general comments about the role of the police in the law and order process. It is a well-established fact that the police have, in each situation they face, wide choice as to how to proceed. They can ignore a crime altogether, they can caution a suspect and take it no further, they can choose to charge and if so can select from a number of possible offences which one to press, and so on. If that is the case then it is possible that their culture and attitudes may influence their decisions so that, for example, young working-class boys are more likely to be charged than mature middle-class women for similar offences (e.g. shoplifting). Dennis Chapman, in his book **Sociology and the Stereotype of the Criminal**, has documented how apparently similar types of 'criminal' behaviour may be 'explained' in very different ways by the police and lead to different conclusions. For example, whereas painting slogans on walls may be excused as part of a students' rag-day 'exuberance', when done by working-class football supporters it may be seen as 'vandalism' and lead to prosecution. It is likely that at least a part of the higher rates of convictions for working-class offenders may be due to such attitudes and stereotyping on behalf of police officers. Yet the police can never be 'neutral' as regards law and order. The attitudes they may hold are also widespread in the community as a whole, and they cannot be expected to operate without any preconceptions. Furthermore, some types of crime are more visible than others ('street crimes' such as minor drug trafficking) and as such they are more likely to act on those committing them (the young, particularly in inner-city areas). What sociologists have done is asked us all to be at least a little more attentive to the link between the police as 'people' and the sort of tasks they carry out, between police culture and attitudes and the enforcement of the law.

Finally, the sociological study of police behaviour serves to expose at least one of the contradictions within the present Government's approach to law and order. The Tories have made great play about the problem of crime in British society, talking frequently of the 'crime wave' and the threat to person and property posed by increased criminality. The major solution they have offered to this problem (as we shall see later), is to significantly increase the numbers of police officers on the street, and to improve their resources to respond to crime. But sociologists have shown that increased policing can actually lead to **increased** crime, in the sense of recorded crime (on which claims about a crime 'wave' are based). The greater the police presence, the more likely it is that crimes will be detected, again, particularly 'street' crimes. We should not be greatly surprised if the more police resources are pumped into areas the more crimes are recorded. There is almost something of a vicious circle in the relationship between policing and crime.

The 'clear up' rate is also of interest to sociologists. The British Crime Survey conducted in early 1984 revealed a marked difference between the actual amount of crime committed and the amount reported to the police (see Figure 1).

The 'clear up rate' for crimes is falling (see Table 2). The clear up rate is based on the number of crimes for which a person is charged (not necessarily convicted) compared with the number of crimes recorded by the police. As a percentage of crimes recorded the clear up rate has fallen from 45 per cent in 1971 to 35 per cent in 1984. This reduction has occurred despite the growing number

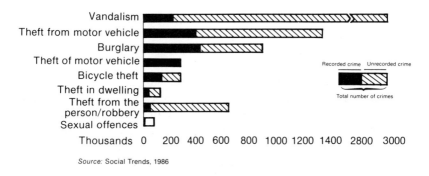

Vandalism
Theft from motor vehicle
Burglary
Theft of motor vehicle
Bicycle theft
Theft in dwelling
Theft from the person/robbery
Sexual offences

Recorded crime   Unrecorded crime

Total number of crimes

Thousands   0   200 400 600 800 1000 1200 1400 2800 3000

Source: Social Trends, 1986

Figure 1   Crimes reported to the police

of police. The question is, does it imply that people are becoming more prepared to report crime or does it mean the police are becoming less efficient?

Table 2   Clear up rates in the UK   Percentages

	England & Wales		Scotland		Northern Ireland	
	1971	1984	1971	1984	1971	1984
Notifiable offences recorded						
Violence against the person	82	74	87	80	28	57
Sexual offences	76	72	77	70	87	67
Burglary	37	28	26	18	27	26
Robbery	42	22	29	25	7	27
Theft and handling stolen goods	43	35	37	27	46	28
Fraud and forgery	83	69	80	70	84	67
Criminal damage	34	23	32	21	10	22
Other notifiable offences	92	93	85	94	89	46
Total notifiable offences	45	35	38	31	32	31

Source: Criminal Statistics 1985, HMSO.

2 *The sociology of the courts*

Sociologists have also made valuable contributions to our understanding of the next stage in the law and order process, the courts. In our courts the stress on 'neutrality' is even more important than in policing. The idea that everyone is 'equal before the law' is central to our system of justice. Yet here again sociologists have asked us to be cautious.

Firstly, research into the **social background** of those who run the courts – magistrates and judges – has raised the question of whether there is a possibility of **class bias** in the justice system. Magistrates, who deal with the vast majority of cases and who decide both on verdict ('guilty' or 'not guilty') and sentence, are selected as 'lay' members from the public. Yet as Hood has shown (**Sentencing in a Magistrate's Court**) almost 80% of them are from the professional classes I and II. This and other research has revealed an almost complete absence of unskilled working-class people on the bench. And while the balance of women to men is more representative of the community as a whole, there is also a marked under-represen-tation of black and Asian magistrates. **Judges** deal generally with more serious criminal cases and only decide the sentences; the verdict here is left to the jury (made up of members of the public). Research here points to an even stronger middle and upper-class background. As Griffiths has shown in **The Politics of the Judiciary**, not only are the vast majority of judges from Social Classes I and II, but up to 70% of them have been to 'top' public schools and either Oxford or Cambridge University. Furthermore, judges are with only a few exceptions male and white, not to mention rather old.

At the start of 1986, of the 357 Circuit Judges in England and Wales only 14 were women. Three of the 74 High Court judges were women and there were no women judges sitting in the Court of Appeal, nor was any of the Law Lords in the Home of Lords a woman.

Now none of these facts in themselves imply bias in the way magistrates and judges make their **decisions** (although Griffiths and others have collected evidence to claim that in fact at least judges do in the main exhibit their biases in this way). But they do raise the problem of the extent to which, coming from such backgrounds, they can adequately understand the situations and experiences of those, primarily working class and often black, who appear as defendants before them. At least when it comes to judges' attitudes about women, as Wilson has argued in **What can be Done About Violence Against Women?**, there do seem to be some remarkable examples of male eccentricity. This was shown in the recent rape trial in which a man convicted was given only a £2,000 fine because, in the judge's view, a woman hitch-hiker had shown 'contributory negligence' in her rape for hitching lifts! Perhaps the 'neutrality' of our courts should not be taken for granted.

Sociologists have also studied the courts as systems of interaction, and the effects of this on defendants. In Britain the most important study of this kind is Pat Carlen's **Magistrates' Justice**. Carlen undertook an in-depth observation of magistrates' courts in order to assess the quality of justice achieved in them and to grasp the interactional setting for the courtroom. She argued that behind the appearance of procedure and justice lay a complex informal pattern of interaction between the main personnel in the court – the police, solicitors, magistrates and probation officers. They knew each other and had developed an accepted (though silent) set of 'rules of the game' by which each hearing could be 'played'. Trials were thus a little bit like 'sausage-machines' producing regular verdicts (usually 'guilty') despite the differences between individual cases. In all of this the defendant became a 'dummy player', unaware of the rules and largely ignored by other players. Apparently the centre of attention in the trial, defendants were usually placed as, and often felt like, 'outsiders' in the whole affair. For Carlen the courtroom is like a mini-version of the wider society in which those with power decide on the future of the disadvantaged (usually working-class) members of the community.

The only way in which courts can cope with the volume of prosecutions brought before them is to ensure that most cases involve a plea of guilty and therefore do not take up time with the presentation of defence and prosecution in court. In the USA there is a fairly well developed practice of **plea bargaining** in which the prosecution and defence lawyers – with the agreement of the judge – negotiate the severity of the charge with a view to persuading the defendant to plead guilty rather than risk pleading not guilty to a more serious charge and having the case examined by jury in court. The process, though well established, remains informal, and has interested sociologists in the way the **rules of procedure** are learnt and used in the every day practice of lawyers.

In the UK the practice of plea-bargaining is not technically acknowledged by the courts. None the less, the majority (66 per cent) of criminal cases brought before the Crown Court lead to a guilty plea (see Figure 2).

Not all sociological studies of British justice paint a gloomy picture

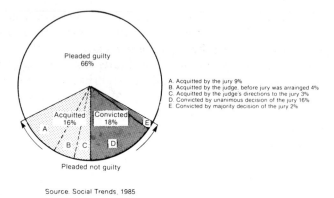

A. Acquitted by the jury 9%
B. Acquitted by the judge, before jury was arrainged 4%
C. Acquitted by the judge's directions to the jury 3%
D. Convicted by unanimous decision of the jury 16%
E. Convicted by majority decision of the jury 2%

Source: Social Trends, 1985

Figure 2 Pleas in criminal cases, Crown Court (UK)

of the quality of British courts. If we look at Crown courts where the more serious criminal cases are dealt with, we come across a body of great historical significance, the **jury**. The jury is made up of ordinary men and women, selected at random from the electoral register. It has long been held up as a way of protecting the ordinary citizen from the abuses of those in power, from arbitrary or malicious prosecutions. Perhaps somewhat surprisingly, sociological studies of the jury, such as McCabe and Purves' **The Shadow Jury at Work**, also conclude that the jury is a good decision-making body, which can be relied upon to reach rational and balanced verdicts according to evidence. In the main, sociologists see the jury as a fair and reasonable element in the system of British justice. Such conclusions may become very relevant in the light of recent famous trials, such as the Ponting case and the Cyprus 'spy' trial. In these cases the jury returned verdicts of not guilty, much to the surprise of the judges and to the horror of the Government which had clearly expected guilty verdicts. As a result the Government has set up an inquiry into the jury system which may well recommend restrictions on the powers of the jury. To those concerned with civil liberties, this would be yet another example of the erosion of the role of the jury, to add to those of 'jury-vetting' (which seeks to root out from the jury those with 'extreme' political views), and the shift of many criminal trials from the Crown courts to magistrates courts.

3 The sociology of the prison

The next stage in the law and order process is 'punishment'. If a person has been found guilty of a crime the courts can then impose a sentence. These range from an absolute discharge, with no further action, through to the most severe type of punishment, a prison sentence. Sociologists have understandably been more interested in the prison as a form of punishment. It can be seen as a 'mini-society', showing in clear form the pressures which are placed on individuals by the 'system'. Authors like Goffman, in **Asylums**, talk of 'total institutions', in which an organisation totally controls the inmates' lives – what they eat, when they sleep, how they organise their leisure time, and in the end, Goffman argues, much of what they think. From a 'law and order' point of view, sociology's main contribution in this area is to show how an informal 'inmate culture' is often built up within the prison which can act as a corrupting factor amongst inmates – what is often called a 'school of crime'. For Sykes, in **A Society of Captives**, this inmate culture arises as a way of coming to terms with the pains and deprivation of imprisonment, but its effect is to ensure that the 'official' aims of prisons – to reform the character and allow him or her to lead a good and useful life – cannot be achieved.

More recent studies of prison life have looked in a broader sense at the role of the prison within the wider society and the social context of the prison system. Mike Fitzgerald and Joe Sim in **British Prisons** have argued that we are faced with nothing less than a 'prison crisis', not just in terms of the issues most pressing on the authorities – the appalling living conditions inside our prisons – but more generally in relation to the role and function of the prison in British society. They have talked of five types of crisis facing the prison system. Firstly, conditions and overcrowding – lack of basic facilities, prisoners sharing with two or three others in cells designed for one, severe limits on physical exercise, educational time and work opportunities, and on prison visits. Britain's prisons are over-crowded more than ever before, yet Court appearances are more likely to lead to a prison sentence than they were ten years ago (**Non-custodial Sentences**, National Association for the Care and Settlement of Offenders, September 1985). Alternatives to imprison-ment (community service, probation day centres, intermediate treat-ment schemes etc) have grown in number but have not prevented

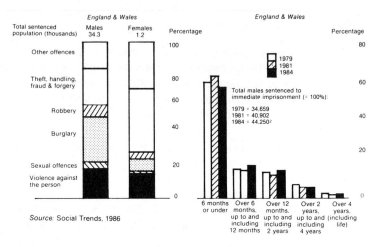

Source: Social Trends, 1986

Figure 3 Sentenced prisoners: by sex and type of offence, 1984

Figure 4 Male offenders aged 21 or over sentenced to immediate imprisonment: by length of sentence

an increase in immediate prison sentences for adult men from 16 per cent in 1973 to 20 per cent in 1983. According to NACRO, both in absolute numbers and in proportion to the population more people get sent to prison in the UK than in any other Western European country of more than 10 million people. The Government's call for harsher sentences for crimes of violence, football hooliganism, drug pushing and civil disorder will, of course, do little to ease the situation.

Secondly, there is a crisis of 'visibility', the veil of secrecy that surrounds the prison system and the tensions it creates for those working within it, all too aware of the potential hostilities which the system contains. Thirdly, a crisis of authority, concerning conflicts as to who controls the prison – the Home Office, prison governors, or the prison officers, all of whom often have different views on what the prison is there to do.

The fourth crisis is one of 'containment'. This refers to the problems of containing an increasing number of people serving long sentences, and the problems of security that entails. As a consequence, prisons have become more and more organised around the issue of security and control, at the expense of 'rehabilitation'.

598

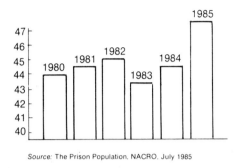

Source: The Prison Population, NACRO, July 1985

Figure 5   The number of prisoners

Finally, prisons are experiencing a crisis of 'legitimacy'. The culmination of all of the problems facing our prisons is that their very existence is increasingly being called into question – are they really the best way in which to maintain law and order in modern British society?

Concluding comments

We can see, therefore, that from sociological points of view the system of law and order is far more complex and controversial than official or traditional images imply. This is not to say that sociologists are in full agreement about law and order overall. On the contrary, as in other areas, this field has been covered both by conflict theorists – who see the law and its enforcement as a means by which certain groups exert their power and their interests over others – and by functionalists, who see the law as the reflection of a collective will and collective interests. What most sociologists stress however is the role of the informal and often unseen social processes underlying law and order (such as the role of police culture outlined earlier), and the wider social and political implications of law and order (its functions for the wider society and groups within it). One important study which combines both is that by Stuart Hall and his associates **Policing the Crisis: Mugging, the State and Law and Order**. This study combines the issues of crime, racism, policing and the State within a Marxist framework of social theory. What is most relevant from our point of view in this complex and compelling thesis is the claim that Britain as a whole is drifting towards a 'law and order society'. Hall argues that, as a result of social and economic crises facing Britain, law and order issues have developed as central concerns for the British State, partly to 'scapegoat' certain sectors of the community for Britain's decline (mainly the black community through the image of the 'black mugger'), partly in response to real threats to social order posed by class protest. The media, the police and the courts have both responded to and aggravated the crisis, bringing law and order ever more to the front of the political scene. It is not, therefore, just parts of the law and order process which reflect class and racial issues, but the very theme of 'law and order' as a political slogan and the policies it involves. It is at points like this that the sociology of law and order overlaps strongly with the **politics** of law and order.

Questions

1. (a) *How is the concept of 'police culture' useful in understanding police law enforcement?*

    (10 marks)

    (b) *How is the concept of 'prison culture' useful in understanding the effectiveness of prison in discouraging criminals from continuing further crime?*

    (5 marks)

2. *'Justice is impartial'. What problems does the sociology of law and order suggest in relation to this principal?*

    (25 marks)

    (The previous reading (76) contains information relevant to this essay.)

78 Stanley Cohen: Master Patterns of Deviancy Control

In *Visions of Social Control*, from which the following extract is taken, Stanley Cohen gives as good an overview of historical and contemporary trends in social control as I have read. It is certainly helpful to be well anchored historically in an area noted for the variety of its theoretical explorations or 'stories' as Cohen calls them. The key to this brief extract is the table, 'Master Changes in Deviancy Control'. It describes three phases in deviancy control: control in pre-eighteenth century society (not discussed in this extract); control from the nineteenth century to the present day; and the challenge to dominant ideologies and forms of control from the nineteen sixties.

The extract begins with a succinct summary of the centralised, 'scientifically' based systems of control which emerged during the nineteenth century (phase 2). Throughout his book, Cohen uses the prison as the typical example of these types of systems (the asylum is another). He then discusses the movement to 'destructure' the control mechanisms built up from the nineteenth century – a movement with which he himself was associated in the nineteen sixties (phase 3).

The last section of the extract carries a sting in the tail. Cohen suggests – shades of *1984* – that the 'impulse' behind phase 3 may not be strong enough to turn back or perhaps even radically modify the march of centralised, 'rational' control of the last 200 years. His attempt at an optimistic conclusion is not convincing: he clearly does not 'buy' the 'story' of 'uneven progress' from 'the heart of the system' but gives the impression that authoritarian trends predominate.

In adopting this extract, I have taken into account that the language level and range of reference may cause difficulty. However, the overall clarity and usefulness of Cohen's analysis outweighs this consideration. Cohen's brief summaries of the four groups of destructuring movements (phase 3) may cause problems – in particular, his summary of movement 4, 'Away from the mind'. This movement wants attempts to 'treat' (or 'change') the criminal's mind – by drugs, surgery or whatever – to be abandoned. But, as in earlier history (phase 1), the criminal (actor) must be 'judged' for the crime (act) against agreed standards (neo-classicism).

Although I have not opened Section 14 with this reading, it could well be used in teaching to introduce the topic of 'deviance and social control'. It might provide a refreshing alternative to the 'perspectives' approach.

Reading 78 From Stanley Cohen, *Visions of Social Control: Crime, Punishment and Classification* (Polity Press, 1985), pp. 12–13, 16–17, 30–3, 36–9.

There have been two transformations – one transparent, the other opaque, one real, the other eventually illusory – in the master patterns and strategies for controlling deviance in Western industrial societies. The first, which took place between the end of the eighteenth and the beginning of the nineteenth centuries, laid the foundations of all subsequent deviancy control systems. The second, which is supposed to be happening now, is thought by some to represent a questioning, even a radical reversal of that earlier transformation, by others to merely signify a continuation and intensification of its patterns.

The history and the 'revisionist' history of that original change has just about been written, and is not the subject of this book. The cumulative picture we have been given is of the following four key changes.

1. The increasing involvement of the state in the business of deviancy control – the eventual development of a centralised, rationalised and bureaucratic apparatus for the control and punishment of crime and delinquency and the care or cure of other types of deviants.
2. The increasing differentiation and classification of deviant and dependent groups into separate types and categories, each with its own body of 'scientific' knowledge and its own recognised and accredited experts – professionals who eventually acquire specialised monopolies.
3. The increased segregation of deviants into 'asylums' – penitentiaries, prisons, mental hospitals, reformatories and other closed, purpose-built institutions. The prison emerges as the dominant instrument for changing undesirable behaviour and as the favoured form of punishment.
4. The decline of punishment involving the public infliction of physical pain. The mind replaces the body as the object of penal repression and positivist theories emerge to justify concentrating on the individual offender and not the general offence.

There are, of course, differences of emphasis, detail, location and timing in the revisionist historiography of this transition, but there is agreement on the reality and clarity of these momentous changes. The really important disagreements, which I will soon examine, are about *why* these changes occurred.

The second master correctional change – the subject of this book – is considerably more opaque. The very essence of the transformation – just *what* is happening – is open to dispute as well as its supposed causes. For some of us there have indeed been real changes – the increasing extension, widening, dispersal and invisibility of the social-control apparatus – but these have been continuous rather than discontinuous with the original nineteenth-century transformation. Moreover, these changes run in almost every respect diametrically opposite to the ideological justifications from which they are supposed to be derived. In other words, if we are in the midst of a 'second transformation', it is not quite what it appears to be.

This chapter, then, moves from a story of change that we think is clear (but have some trouble in explaining) to another story whose very plot is ambiguous . . . Before the middle of the nineteenth century, the four major features of today's deviancy control system that I have outlined above had already been established in most industrial societies. These features are elaborated in *Table 1* in the column headed 'Phase Two'.

Beginning in the 1960s (so the story goes) those massively entrenched transformation of the early nineteenth century began to be attacked. These attacks were not altogether new in content – the prison, for example, had been criticised virtually from its inception and on the same grounds as those used by current reformers – but they became more radical, they emerged not just from the margins but from the actual centre of the crime control establishment itself and, moreover, they appeared to be successful.

I will conceive of the whole package of these attacks – criticisms, claims, visions, ideologies, theories, reform movements and all sorts of other talk – as taking the form of a profound *destructuring impulse*. There appeared to be a sustained assault on the very foundations (ideological and institutional) of the control system whose hegemony had lasted for nearly two centuries. An archaeology of post-1960s social-control talk would reveal a near complete ideological consensus in favour of reversing the directions taken by the system in the late eighteenth century. These supposed reversals are listed as Phase Three in table 1 and can also be expressed as four groups

Table 1   Master changes in deviancy control

	Phase One (Pre-eighteenth century)	Phase Two (From the nineteenth century)	Phase Three (From the mid-twentieth century)
1. State involvement	Weak, decentralised, arbitrary	Strong, centralised, rationalised	Ideological attack: 'minimum state', but intervention intensified and control extended
2. Place of control	'Open': community, primary institutions	Closed, segregated institution: victory of the asylum, 'Great Incarcerations'	Ideological attack: 'decarceration', 'community alternatives', but old institutions remain and new forms of community control expand
3. Focus of control	Undifferentiated	Concentrated	Dispersed and diffused
4. Visibility of control	Public, 'spectacular'	Boundaries clear, but invisible inside – 'discreet'	Boundaries blur and 'inside' remains invisible and disguised
5. Categorisation and differentiation of deviance	Hardly developed at all	Established and strengthened	Further strengthened and refined
6. Hegemony of law and criminal justice system	Not yet established; criminal law only one form of control	Monopoly of criminal justice system established, but then supplemented by new systems	Ideological attack: 'decriminalisation', 'delegalisation', 'diversion', etc. but criminal justice system not weakened and other systems expand
7. Professional dominance	Not at all present	Established and strengthened	Ideological attack: 'deprofessionalisation', 'anti-psychiatry', etc. but professional dominance strengthened and further extended
8. Object of intervention	External behaviour: 'body'	Internal states: 'mind'	Ideological attack: back to behaviour, external compliance, but both forms remain
9. Theories of punishment	Moralistic, traditional, then classical, 'just deserts'	Influenced by positivism and treatment ideal: 'neo-positivist'	Ideological attack: back to justice, neo-classicism, partly successful, though positivist ideal still present
10. Mode of control	Inclusive	Exclusive and stigmatising	Ideological stress on inclusion and integration: both modes remain

of destructuring movements or ideologies (table 2), each directed against one of the original transformations.

1. *Away from the state:* 'decentralisation', 'deformalisation', 'decriminalisation', 'diversion', 'non-intervention': a call toward divesting the state of certain control functions or at least by-passing them and creating instead innovative agencies which are community based, less bureaucratic and not directly state-sponsored.

2. *Away from the expert:* 'deprofessionalisation', 'demedicalisation', 'delegalisation', 'anti-psychiatry': a distrust of professionals and experts and a demystification of their monopolistic claims of competence in classifying and treating various forms of deviance.

3. *Away from the institution:* 'deinstitutionalisation', 'decarceration', 'community control': a lack of faith in traditional closed institutions and a call for their replacement by non-segregative, 'open' measures, termed variously 'community control', 'community treatment', 'community corrections' or 'community care'.

4. *Away from the mind:* 'back to justice', 'neo-classicism', 'behaviourism': an impatience with ideologies of individualised treatment or rehabilitation based on psychological inner-states models and a call to reverse the positivist victory and to focus instead on body rather than mind, on act, rather than actor.

Table 2   The Destructuring Impulse

Nineteenth-Century Transformation	1960s: Counter Ideologies/ Destructuring Movements
(1) Centralised state control	Decentralisation, deformalisation, decriminalisation, diversion, divestment, informalism, non-intervention
(2) Categorisation, separate knowledge systems, expertise, professionalisation	Deprofessionalisation, demedicalisation, delegalisation, anti-psychiatry, self-help, removal of stigma and labels
(3) Segregation: victory of the asylum	Decarceration, deinstitutionalisation, community control
(4) Positivist theory: move from body to mind	Back to justice, neo-classicism, behaviourism

My focus in this book is principally on the third set of slogans but, as we will repeatedly see, these movements often overlap with each other, draw on the same rhetoric and can invariably be traced to common societal origins. The prison–community contrast will work as a model for all the others.

The destructuring impulse here took the form of a radical attack on the very idea of imprisonment. The whole ideological consensus about the desirability and necessity of the segregative social-control institution appeared to break. The prison – we were widely assured – was an experiment whose time had come to an end, it had played out its allocated role, the long grim history of prison reform was over, alternative methods were at hand. This seemed to be not just the old 'monotonous critique', but something more total: the institution was 'necessarily always and absolutely a failure – a colossal mistake whose commission can only be redeemed by its abolition'. It was not just a matter of administrative mistakes, lack of funds, prejudiced custodians, but rather a fundamental flaw in the vision itself.

This assault on prisons became widespread from the 1960s, was found throughout the political spectrum and, initially at least, led to a decline in some rates of incarceration. The assault on mental hospitals was more dramatic and had more obvious results. At the end of the eighteenth century, asylums and prisons were places of the *last* resort; by the mid-nineteenth century they became places of the *first* resort, the preferred solution to problems of deviancy and dependency. By the end of the 1960s they looked like once again becoming places of the last resort . . . The gap between the rhetoric of the destructuring movement and the reality of the emerging deviancy control system is the subject of the rest of this book. For, indeed, something *was* happening. Instead of any destructuring, however, the original structures have become stronger: far from any decrease, the reach and intensity of state control have been increased; centralisation and bureaucracy remain; professions and experts are proliferating dramatically and society is more dependent on them; informalism has not made the legal system less formal or more just; treatment has changed its forms but certainly has not died . . .

Unevenly to be sure, and in some parts of the system much more clearly than others, there has been an intensification, complication and extension of these early nineteenth-century master patterns, not their reversal. Those original patterns – rationalisation, centralis-ation, segregation, classification – were not born fully grown. They were trends which are still going on and the more recent changes are also trends yet uncompleted. But it was as if the destructuring impulse revealed how deep were those original structures.

These sorts of doubts were to emerge almost simultaneously with the impulse itself. The very same intellectuals and reformers who had been apostles of the new order now cast themselves as prophets of doom. This language of doubt drew on many sources: the tend-ency of a self-reflective culture to immediately reflect on itself and then reflect on these reflections; the mood of scepticism in which good intentions no longer command automatic assent; a harsh mon-etarist economic climate looking for any excuse to cut back on 'innovations' in social policy; a gigantic research establishment obsessed with questions of evaluation; a distrust by political radicals of all reforms as disguised measures of coercion.

Later chapters will examine each of these sources. They combined to produce a series of unhappy new stories. Some gains were conceded, but the final status of the destructuring movements came to be seen as ambivalent, ambiguous or wholly negative:

1. Decarceration and community control were not being carried out for good reasons (revulsion against institutions or the search for 'reintegration') but mainly in response to fiscal pressures and a retrenchment of welfare policies.
2. In regard to crime and delinquency at least – if not mental illness – decarceration anyway was hardly even happening. Rates of institutionalisation simply were not diminishing as rapidly as they should have.
3. It has not been established that community alternatives are any more effective in reducing crime (by preventing recidivism) than traditional custodial measures.
4. These new methods are not always much cheaper.
5. They are not necessarily any more humane and, indeed, they might be less humane by disguising coercion, increasing invis-ible discretion or (for the mentally ill) simply dumping deviants to be neglected or exploited.
6. Overall, the system enlarges itself and becomes more intrusive, subjecting more and newer groups of deviants to the power of

the state and increasing the intensity of control directed at former deviants.

So it was not merely a question of reform 'going wrong'. The benevolent-sounding destructuring package had turned out to be a monster in disguise, a Trojan horse. The alternatives had merely left us with 'wider, stronger and different nets' . . .

But these first doubts, these second thoughts, however interesting intellectually, however rich theoretically, emerge from the margins of the correctional enterprise. At the heart of the system one message and one message alone can dominate – that from the 'uneven progress' story. There have indeed been advances and changes; things are going well, slow progress is being made, all such changes take time, mistakes will soon be rectified, more of the same is needed (more resources, money, patience, tolerance and, of course, research). All the signs are the same: 'business as usual'.

Question

1. (a) Describe, with examples, phase 2 of 'master changes in deviancy control'.

(7 marks)

(b) Describe, with examples, the 'alleged' phase 3 of 'master changes in deviancy control'.

(7 marks)

(c) With reference to the reading, analyse the problems associated with the 'destructuring' movements (phase 3).

(11 marks)

Social Problems and Policy

Readings 79–82

In Reading 79 Howard Becker argues that a 'social problem' only becomes a problem when it is defined as such. This perspective extends to social problems in his analysis of deviance. Indeed, he regards deviance as simply a major category of social problems (social disorganisation being another). Although aspects of Becker's analysis have been challenged, notably by Functionalist Robert Merton, it remains essentially intact and widely accepted.

Ramesh Mishra moves the section on to the issue of social policy. As he illustrates, support for given policies, like definitions of problems, reflects values. Mishra, seeking to avoid the so-called 'extremes' of Left and Right, summarises the ideological values underlying competing social policy positions. Similarly, Peter Townsend, writing from a more socialist position, stresses the political nature of social policy and specifically rejects definitions which regard it merely as

concerned with public administration of welfare, that is the development and management of specific services of the State and of local authorities, such as health, education, welfare and social security services, to remedy particular social problems or pursue social objectives which are generally perceived and agreed as such.

On the contrary, for Townsend, it is precisely the *disagreement* about social problems *and* about their causes and solutions which is the stuff of social policy. Social policy can raise questions about the very structure of society. As Townsend puts it: 'Social policy is, in other words, the institutionalised control of services, agencies and organisations to maintain or change social structure and values'. Ironically, in recent years, the most sustained attempt to achieve radical change has come from the political Right rather than the Left – the opposite of what Townsend would have wished (see Reading 81).

If social policy is an area of political commitment, Townsend sees a different role for sociology. By providing informed and accurate analysis of social structure it can provide a basis on which social policy decisions can be taken.

Reading 82 from Gillian Paschall invites us to think about, rather than take for granted, the domestic caring by women for children, the elderly and the handicapped. In reviewing the policy of 'Community Care' she implies that it might mean simply more work for women. This reading could usefully be read alongside the extract from Anna Coote on family/gender policy (Reading 36). Anna Coote also provides a succinct, policy-oriented analysis of class-related health problems (Reading 83).

For a reading on crime with policy discussion and implications, see Lea and Young (Reading 76).

79 Howard S. Becker: Social Problems: Definition, Development and Context

Basing his approach on Fuller and Myers, Becker here distinguishes between the objective and subjective aspects of social problems. The objective element is simply the factual 'reality' of a given 'problem', for example, race or poverty. Such things do not, however, become social problems unless a particular group or groups decides that they are – i.e., unless they are subjectively defined as such. But subjectivity cuts even deeper than this: different groups may define the same 'social problem' (e.g. race relations) in different ways. Such groups may then seek to persuade a wider public that their defination of the 'problem' is 'right'.

Becker's stress on the subjective aspects of social definitions is central to labelling theory and, in giving an example of an imagined social problem, he illustrates how the processes of defining and labelling can have consequences of their own, even if based on mistaken premises. He is deliberately trying to get away from the idea associated with Functionalism that, on any issue, there is typically a consensus around the norm, deviation from which is seen as a problem. Becker's rough sketch of the development of a social problem is consistent with his general approach that what emerges as a social problem is subject to a variety of forces including group interest and conflict.

Reading 79 From Howard S. Becker, *Social Problems: A Modern Approach* (John Wiley and Sons, 1966), pp. 1–14.

Sociology, indeed, social science generally, has a double perspective. Sociology concerns itself with current social ills. At the same time some sociologists are also interested in constructing general theories to explain human behavior. The tension between the drive for a deeper understanding of what is going on in the society we live in, what Robert E. Park called The Big News, and the thrust toward a deeper understanding of the nature of man and society in the abstract characterises the best of present-day sociology. The scientific study of social problems represents in some ways a merger of the two interests.

Sociologists investigating social problems are not content to make surveys of existing conditions, pointing to wrongs that need to be put right. They concern themselves with how problems come about and are perpetuated and in so doing necessarily attempt to reach conclusions that apply to a broader range of phenomena than the specific problem they study. They study classes of problems and the underlying social conditions that give rise to them.

But the student of social problems still retains an interest in present-day society as an object worthy of study because the problems are those of his own time and place, problems that his knowledge, insight, and skill may help solve.

What is a social problem?

We must first understand clearly what the term *social problem* refers to. At first glance the referent seems obvious – everybody knows what a social problem is. Indeed, the table of contents of this book is a common sense definition of social problems – social problems are problems like crime, poverty, and race relations. For scientific purposes, however, we need more than a list. We need an abstract definition.

Fuller and Myers, a generation ago, presented a definition of social problems that is implicit in much of this book. Though their examples are dated, their conception is as useful now as it was when first presented.

A social problem is a condition which is defined by a considerable number of persons as a deviation from some norm which they cherish. Every social problem thus consists of an objective condition and a subjective definition. The objective condition is a verifiable situation which can be checked as to existence and magnitude (proportions) by impartial and trained observers, e.g., the state of our national defense, trends in the birth rate, unemployment, etc. The subjective definition is the awareness of certain individuals that the condition is a threat to certain cherished values.

The objective condition is necessary but not in itself sufficient to constitute a social problem. Although the objective condition may be the same in two different localities, it may be a social problem in only one of these areas, e.g. discrimination against Negroes in the south as contrasted with discrimination in the north; divorce in Reno as contrasted with divorce in a Catholic community. *Social problems are what people think they are* and if conditions are not defined as social problems by the people involved in them, they are not problems to those people, although they may be problems to outsiders or to scientists, e.g., the condition of poor southern share-croppers is a social problem to the braintrusters of the New Deal but not to many southern landowners.

The central tenet of the Fuller-Myers approach is that a social problem consists of an objective condition in society that is defined by members of the society as a problem about which something ought to be done. There are ambiguities in this view that need to be clarified and implications that need to be explained.

One ambiguity concerns the role of the 'objective conditions' in the creation of a social problem. Some sociologists argue that the existence of a social problem can be detected objectively whether it is defined as a problem or not. If the members of a society have values and purposes negated by some social condition, then, even when they accept that condition and do not regard it as problematic, it is a social problem. A hypothetical example will help us.

The sex ratio of newborn infants normally runs about 105 to 107 males per 100 females. But women now live longer than men so that in the total population, according to the 1960 Census, there were only 97.8 men for every 100 women. And the proportion of men to women varies at different ages, with the excess of males persisting until age 24 when the excess shifts to one of women. The sex ratio in the population also varies from one time period to the next; in 1910 there were 106 men to every 100 women. But the changes are slow enough that the institutions of our society – kinship, marriage, education, work, housing, and so on – can adapt

themselves to the changing number of men and women p
the society.

Suppose that for whatever reason the sex ratio at birth chang
suddenly and that the proportion of women surviving increases. In
this hypothetical society the new excess of females would have far-
reaching consequences for social institutions. The proportion of
unmarried women might rise far beyond what it is now, creating
grave discontent with our institutions of courtship and marriage.
We are inclined to think of some kinds of work as 'men's work'
and others as 'women's work' and, if the sex ratio in the population
were to change so radically, there would be too many women for
the jobs identified as women's and not enough men to do all the
work defined as men's. Problems would rise about the allocation of
people to jobs; women would begin to invade men's occupations
and the repercussions might be felt in the organisation of the family,
the appearance of new problems of mental health, and community
politics.

In what sense could such a change in the distribution of the sexes
be considered a social problem? In what sense would the objective
condition in and of itself be problematic? Fuller and Myers suggest
that no objective condition is necessarily a social problem. The
condition may be troublesome, but members of the society can
adapt to it, changing their institutions and practices to cope with
the troubles the condition creates. They may change their values
and purposes, arriving at a compromise between society as it was
and society as it will be.

From this point of view, an objective condition becomes a social
problem only if we assume that society must be maintained as it is.
Insofar as a sociologist adopts this stance, he can indeed discover
objective conditions that will make it difficult to maintain society in
a state of equilibrium. But neither social scientists nor laymen agree
unanimously that society must be maintained as it is. And, if they
did, they might not agree on what in particular was to be maintained
without change.

This issue recalls a time when the study of social problems was
called 'social pathology.' The term evokes an analogy to medicine
which is appropriate to the view that social problems arise out of
objective conditions but which is inaccurate in one significant way.
When we speak of pathology in the human body, our knowledge
of human physiology allows us to identify the objective conditions

e normal functions of the organism. A tumor,
en bone, a derangement of the metabolism all
ay the body normally works.

ever, describe an analogous 'normal state' of
is true that all the data we would need for such
not yet been collected and all the research is not
yet done. Bu̶t ̶ knowledge of human physiology is not complete
either. In the case of physiology, however, we have reason to believe
that all the data, if they are ever gathered, can lead to a useful
description of the normal human organism; deviations from the
normal state can then be defined as pathological. We have no reason
to believe that any amount of research, no matter how much, can
produce a description of a 'normal society' that deserves to be
maintained as it is.

There is little essential disagreement, either among scientists
themselves or between scientists and laymen, about what constitutes
normal physical functioning, for it is commonly agreed that to be
'healthy' is to have no physical difficulty that interferes with carrying
out one's daily activities. But there are fundamental disagreements
among both scientists and laymen about what constitutes a 'healthy'
society, for people define the good society in various ways according
to their interests and values. And interests and values differ among
people placed differently in society. The interests of a rich man are
not those of a poor man, and the values of a man from one ethnic
or religious group may differ from those of a man from another
group. No amount of factual research can resolve these differences,
for they do not arise from a disagreement about facts but from
disagreement about how facts are defined and interpreted.

To return to our hypothetical example, a change in the sex ratio
would have consequences that scientific research could uncover. But
research could not identify the condition as a social problem, for
its problematic character would arise from how people defined its
consequences. Social scientists who think society is operating relatively efficiently as it is might view the consequences as upsetting
and troublesome and thus see a social problem. Others might think
the society was already in bad shape and welcome the changed sex
ratio because it made possible changes in institutions that were not
functioning well; they would not view the development as a social
problem.

In short as Fuller and Myers argued, no objective condition is necessarily a social problem; social problems are what people think they are. But where does that leave the role of objective conditions? Can people call *anything* a social problem? The question has two parts: can people define *any* condition that exists as a social problem, and can people define a condition that does *not* exist – an illusion – as a social problem? Let us consider the latter question first.

People clearly *can* define nonexistent conditions as social problems. The inhabitants of Salem, Massachusetts believed in witches and imagined that their community was infested with them. They took stern measures to deal with the supposed social problem. Today we know that there are no witches and, consequently, we cannot have that social problem. Many people have believed in more recent times that the earth is about to be invaded by flying saucers from other planets and consider this an important problem that needs to be dealt with; so far as we know, their belief is erroneous.

If people can define conditions that do not exist as social problems, it necessarily follows that they can also define any condition that does exist as a social problem. Think of the varied 'problems' that have bothered one group or another in the not-so-distant past: dancing on Sunday, dancing at any time, women smoking, anybody smoking, not enough highways, and too many highways in the wrong places. The examples may be frivolous, but they suggest that any set of objective conditions can, from some point of view, be defined as a social problem.

The development of a social problem

If we understand that social problems are what interested parties think they are, we must recognise that they become defined as problems as the result of a lengthy process of development which has identifiable stages. Fuller and Myers called attention to this when they spoke of *the natural history of a social problem:*

> Social problems do not arise full-blown, commanding community attention and evoking adequate policies and machinery for their solution. On the contrary, we believe that social problems exhibit a temporal course of development in which different phases or stages may be distinguished. Each stage anticipates its successor in time and each succeeding stage contains new elements which mark it off from its predecessor. A social problem thus conceived as always being in a dynamic

state of 'becoming' passes through the natural history stages of awareness, policy determination, and reform.

We need not accept the terms they use, or the stages they posit, to share Fuller and Myers' principal idea: to understand a social problem fully, we must know how it came to be defined as a social problem.

This idea of social problems sees them as the result of a basically 'political' process, a process in which opposing views are put forward, argued, and compromised; in which people are motivated by various interests to attempt to persuade others of their views so that public action will be taken to further ends they consider desirable; in which one attempts to have the problem officially recognised so that the power and authority of the state can be engaged on one's side.

Little research has been done on the stages of development of social problems, so we cannot present a commonly accepted scheme of analysis. Instead, we can indicate the kinds of questions that might be raised in exploring the process in the case of a specific problem.

The first step in the development of a social problem comes when some person or group sees a set of objective conditions as problematic, posing a danger or containing the seeds of future difficulties. To whom does the condition appear troublesome? What brings it to his attention as a potential problem? What kinds of conditions are likely to be problems to what kinds of people? What distinguishes conditions that come to be viewed as potential problems from others (from an objective standpoint equally problematic) which do not provoke that response?

After a problem has come to someone's attention, concern with it must become shared and widespread if it is to achieve the status of a social problem. The person who originally noticed it must point it out to others and convince them the situation is dangerous enough to require public action. We can raise the same kind of questions about the second step in the process as we did about the first. What kinds of people will the original definer of the problem be able to convince that his argument is sound? Who, on the contrary, will think his view foolish or mistaken? What tactics are most successful in winning support for the definition of a condition as a problem? What is the role of the mass media of communication – newspapers, magazines, radio, and television – in promoting widespread concern with a problem, and how does a person who wishes to define a new social problem get access to them?

When widespread concern has been aroused, it must be embodied in an organisation or institution if the problem is to achieve lasting existence as a defined social problem. An existing organisation may take the responsibility for dealing with the new problem, as the police were more or less forced to do when 'juvenile delinquency' was defined as a social problem, or a new organisation may be created, as the Narcotics Bureau was created to deal with the newly defined problem of drug addiction. In the first case, the problem will be redefined, so far as possible, by the personnel of the organisation to conform with their more general opinion of the character of social problems. If, for instance, a problem like alcoholism is made the responsibility of a mental health agency, its psychiatrically oriented staff will redefine it as a problem of mental health; the police, given the responsibility, will define the situation as a problem of law enforcement. If a new agency is created, it is likely to be staffed by members of one of the established professions, and the same process results.

Once some organisation takes charge of a problem, the group of aroused citizens whose collective concern prompted the development is likely to lose interest. They have, after all, turned the problem over to an organisation so that they need no longer worry about it.

One of the interesting features of this stage in the development of a social problem is that the personnel of the organisation devoted to the problem tend to build their lives and careers around its continued existence. They become attached to 'their' problem, and anything that threatens to make it disappear or diminish in importance is a threat. What can be said of 'rule enforcers' working in organisations dedicated to controlling deviance may be applied with equal justice to the staff of any organisation devoted to dealing with a social problem, even in fields such as race relations, housing, or education . . .

Questions
1. *Summarise the arguments Becker puts forward for the view that 'Social problems are what people think they are'.*

(5 marks)

617

2. *Try to apply the three stages in the natural history of a social problem – awareness, policy determination, and reform – to a social problem with which you are familiar (e.g., heroin use, the AIDS 'epidemic').*

(10 marks)

3. *What does Becker mean by 'the social context of social problems'? Briefly give the social context of one social problem with which you are familiar.*

(10 marks)

4. *What theoretical similarity is there between Becker's approaches to deviance and social problems?*

(5 marks)

80 Ramesh Mishra: Ideology and Welfare: The New Conservatism (Market Liberalism), Socialism and Social Democracy

Ramesh Mishra's *The Welfare State in Crisis*, from which this extract is taken, describes the breakdown of the post-second world war social democratic consensus on the welfare state. This consensus was founded on the view that the state would provide adequate security for all its citizens financed out of the wealth created mainly by private industry. Two 'breaks' from this consensus developed strongly during the nineteen seventies – one on the Right, the other on the Left. The former is referred to variously as the New Right, the New Conservatism, market liberalism and, in its British manifestation, simply as Thatcherism. The latter is socialism of a radical or Marxist kind.

Mishra reviews these two ideologies in terms of their normative values and practical (technical) achievements and finds them inadequate. Thatcherism lacks even a basic commitment to equity (e.g., to reducing extreme inequalities) and at a practical level has seen a steep rise in unemployment and bankruptcies. Marxism, for its part, fails to reassure both in terms of its uncertain commitment to democracy and in terms of organising production efficiently and flexibly.

Mishra's arguments lead him back to 'some form of centrist position', i.e. to a version of social democracy. He contends that public support for the welfare state still exists and that the 'worst' aspects of the Thatcher years show the necessity for it.

He then puts his case for a 'corporatist' form of the welfare state and draws on the Swedish and Austrian models. Corporatism involves recognising that economic and social planning must be integrated and that unions and business as well as government must be involved in doing this. Mishra sees in corporatism the possibility of achieving a balance of political freedom, economic planning and prosperity, and a decent, equitable society.

Reading 80 From Ramesh Mishra, *The Welfare State in Crisis; Social Thought and Social Change* (Harvester Press, 1984), pp. 164–71.

First then, the normative position. Generally speaking, I believe that the Welfare State – which combines a managed market economy, a plural polity and a developed social welfare system – represents a social formation, however hybrid and compromised, worth preserving. Why? There are two reasons. First, consider the alternatives. Essentially they seem to be either a return to free market, or a socialist revolution. Let us look at each briefly.

The free-market option is currently being tried in both Britain and the United States. Its logic is economic and social *laisser-faire* (with pragmatic departures from this principle if they help the business class), a return to the Social Darwinism of Spencer. The major normative issue here is that this approach would require the relatively powerless segments of the population (workers, blacks, women) to pick up the cost of change. If progress is predicated on the survival of the fittest, then the weak must by definition be allowed to go to the wall. This approach would enhance freedom (especially of the wealthy) at the cost of social justice. It attempts to put the clock back to the 1930s. However fitfully and partially the movement for social rights (understood in the broader sense) has established a foothold in liberal market society by committing the state, the government, to certain forms of action, to taking certain measures. A return to the free market, to deregulation, amounts to a counter-revolution. It means the disestablishment of a variety of rights which do something towards maintaining minimum standards and providing a context within which the struggle against inequities can be waged. It is above all the equity claims or entitlements that are largely inscribed in the welfare state. Take, for example, the right to work, informally recognised since the 1940s. Now in some ways it is an absurdity to claim such a right within a predominantly market economy. Indeed the guarantee of full employment itself changes the nature of the economy from a free market to a regulated one. It was the genius of Keynes to show that with only minor and indirect forms of state intervention a market economy could be made to provide full employment. And although the welfare state was more concerned with unemployment insurance, one of the assumptions of the Beveridge Report, for example, was that the government will try to maintain high levels of employment. In this sense the right to work and thereby also a fully legitimate entitlement to income has been recognised by the welfare state. The right to education, health care and a minimum level of living are other relevant examples. Attempts to create greater equity between citizens – discriminated against on sexual or ethnic grounds – through affirmative action are again measures to secure human rights.

The neo-conservative strategy is to discredit government and thus depoliticise, or rather desocialise, the market economy. Yet what the politicisation of the economy from below (full employment and the social services) has essentially achieved is a modicum of security which a society founded on pure market capitalism lacks and whose absence played such havoc in the 1920s and 1930s. Thus a return to unalloyed capitalism, even if politically feasible, without repression, would be a return to insecurity and grosser forms of injustice. It would be to return to a society in which basic social rights are denied and the costs of economic change allowed to lie where they fall. We must remember too that on all accounts technological developments and industrial restructuring of advanced capitalist economies might mean continuing large-scale unemployment. What does a *laisser-faire* or market economy offer in these circumstances? Even in terms of short-term economic recovery and growth Thatcherism and Reaganomics have little to show. At a purely technical level, the monetary medicine applied by these pro-market regimes has been so strong as to endanger the patient's life itself. Inflation has been tamed and wage demands lowered at an enormously high cost in the form of unemployment and bankruptcies. In short the neo-conservative solution has little to recommend either as a value-orientation, or even as a short-term technical fix. As Thurow has pointed out, perhaps the changes that are needed for some variant of a free market to restore economic dynamic and growth (profits, investments, etc.) would be so massive as to rule itself out on grounds of equity and justice, as well as political feasibility.

What of the socialist alternative? For the other major response to the current crisis is to move toward some variant of Marxist socialism so that the contradictions of capitalism are overcome once and for all and a social system based on the recognition of human needs at last becomes a reality. In a sense, this could be the realisation of a welfare society which would take the values of welfare much further. Although attractive from this viewpoint there are several problems with this socialist vision. Normatively speaking, socialism exalts the collective over the individual, distributive justice over liberty. Moreover, in Marxist socialism, which has so far taken a more or less élitist form, the whole question of democracy remains unresolved. At any rate 'actually existing socialism' does not inspire confidence as a model to be emulated. Thus to end up with such a regime would be to jump out of the frying pan into the fire. Individualism, liberty and the rule of law, of which I spoke earlier, constitute a valuable part of the modern western heritage and any progressive social system must incorporate these within itself. If it is conceded that collectivism and distributive egalitarianism are not the only desirable values then the socialist project must demonstrate that it can encompass libertarian values as well and carry forward the entire complex of values and institutions to a higher level of civilisation (as Marx for example seems to have envisaged). The problem of how to organise an efficient system of production without the use of coercion and material incentives also remains unsolved (at the level of both practice and theory). Post-revolutionary societies ('actually existing socialism') show that this could be the Achilles heel of socialism.

In short, both at the normative and technical levels, Marxist socialism, like neo-conservatism, fails to convince as a social theory of progress for advanced western societies. This does not rule out forms of transitional or gradual socialism (e.g. Eurocommunism, workers' fund socialism of Sweden) which in effect promise us that we can have our cake and eat it too. But if these have to be tried within a broadly democratic framework it remains unclear (as with Eurocommunism or the 'alternative economic strategy' in Britain) how they are to realise their major objectives and how they might reconcile liberty, equality, democracy and economic growth. It may well be that historically fortunate countries (e.g. Sweden) may yet surprise us by achieving this seemingly impossible objective. But at present no one seems to have a convincing enough model of transition to democratic socialism.

If we reject neo-conservatism and Marxist socialism, then we are left with some form of Centrist position. I would like to suggest that the corporatist form of the welfare state seems to offer the possibility of overcoming some of the major defects of the post-war welfare state. Whether and to what extent corporatism might succeed is a difficult question to answer. None the less, a corporatist approach seems worth a try. Let me explain why.

First, let us note that public support for state-provided services remains high in capitalist democracies. The responsibility for maintaining full employment and general conditions of equity are also seen as the government's sphere. In this sense the welfare state shows no sign of having lost its popular appeal or legitimacy among the masses. Taxation may not be popular, but right-wing expectations of Proposition 13-style tax revolts spreading throughout western countries have come to nothing. There is certainly no evidence of general support for the retrenchment of government and the privatisation of economic and social life. Admittedly, there are also some contradictory findings which suggest that conflicting tendencies may be at work. But on the whole the evidence in favour of continuing support for the basic social services and the maintenance of full employment is unmistakable. As I have argued above, the victory of the Right at the polls in several countries, notably the UK and the USA, does not by any means signify the repudiation of the objectives and values of the welfare state. Rather it suggests the search for an alternative route (with some temporary hardships on the way) to roughly the same destination.

Second, the recession, the fiscal crisis and other problems of the welfare state have also shown the importance of economic welfare, of full employment and economic growth, for the masses in capitalist democracies. The key objectives seem to be security – economic and social – and prosperity. True, the influence of the media, manipulation by élites, and the sheer weight of dominant ideology have to be borne in mind. However, popular surveys show that the masses do not follow blindly whatever is decreed from above – by the government of the day or by the ruling class. At least in the democracies the masses are exposed to some degree of plurality of viewpoints and beliefs and it would be well not to lose sight of the fact. In any case, as I have tried to explain earlier, my own standpoint is that the market capitalist system must meet equity claims and spread the risks and costs of social change evenly. In this sense I find my own preference for the role of government to be broadly in line with those of the masses.

If the welfare state both enjoys popular support (legitimacy) and also appears to have been effective in providing a measure of security and equity, then the next problem could be stated in the form: 'But can we afford it?' In short the problem is that of financing various services adequately and coping with the apparently negative consequence or externalities of the welfare state. Here key economic issues such as inflation, the trade-off between the economic and social wage, full employment (or some equivalent social arrangement), profitability and investment, efficiency and productivity, budget deficits, and the like have to be addressed. It is precisely the lack of an institutional framework for addressing such problems (outside electoral competition and a free-for-all interest group politics) that has brought the welfare state (DWS) into disrepute. For, as we have seen, underlying the Keynes-Beveridge model was the notion of a form of moderate collectivism that would manipulate demand to maintain employment and provide an underpinning of social security (in the wider sense) for all citizens. The assumption was that once these correctives were put in place the rest of the economy could be left, more or less, to the operation of market forces. This notion of moderate collectivism did not anticipate the possible effects of a pressure group polity on the state welfare system.

More important, the institutional separation between the 'social' (welfare) and the 'economic' (market economy) took a too static and 'social engineering' view of the social system. Social democratic reformism, typified by Richard Titmuss's approach, reinforced the idea of a sharp separation between the social (welfare and needs, etc.) and the economic (market, profits, efficiency, etc.) realms by emphasising the different values embodied in them. This emphasis had two unfortunate consequences. First, the importance of full employment and economic growth for the general welfare of the masses was obscured by the emphasis on social welfare and distribution. Second, and more important, the lack of a theoretical perspective on the social structure obscured the fact that the social and the economic were not only functionally related (interdependent) but both formed part of a larger reality (of values and institutions) of welfare capitalism. The perspective of piecemeal social intervention, based on a somewhat dramatised ethic of welfare and choice (in place of a focus on society, its dominant institutions and values), also encouraged a somewhat free-floating view of social welfare isolating it from the wider social structure of which it was a part. The connection with the social structure was chiefly made at a technical-administrative level (e.g. demography, family and household composition, urbanisation) in order to formulate needs and help with social planning. The macro-level connections with the economy and the polity (power relations, economic production, sectional interests) were on the whole missed out. The focus on the social welfare aspect of state activity has also encouraged the view in which public services, such as transport and government subsidies of various kinds to producers and consumers, were seen as lying outside the sphere of the welfare state. The upshot was that social policies were seen as unrelated not only to economic policies but to public policies as well. This may have been especially true of Britain, but a similar institutional separation in the analysis of these various sectors can be seen in other English-speaking countries.

The isolation of the social from the economic, of social welfare activities from other relevant activities of the state (e.g. subsidies, employment policy), has also inhibited the search for appropriate institutional forms through which the problem of interdependence among these spheres, especially between economic and social welfare, might be addressed. There is an important difference here between countries like Sweden with its Labour Market Board and centralised wage bargaining and Austria with its social partnership institutions on the one hand, and say Britain or Canada on the other. The corporatism of countries like Austria and Sweden, whatever its shortcomings, at least in principle takes the social services and social welfare out of the 'ghetto' and tends to relate them to the wider institutional and group context of society. It is due to the ability of countries like Sweden to address the problems of productivity, wage settlements, inflation and technological change through institutions which seek to arrive at a working consensus (consensus, as we saw above, has been stressed far more and quite explicitly in Austria) that potentially adverse economic consequences of full employment, wage militancy and rising public expenditure have been avoided for a long period. It should also be remembered that there is a good deal of voluntarism involved in wage bargaining as well as other forms of social co-operation between employers and trade unions in these countries. Corporatism, in short, must not be equated with the extension of government.

Question

1. (a) Describe the three ideological approaches to the welfare state presented in the reading from Mishra.

(10 marks)

(b) Present and evaluate Mishra's criticisms of the New Right and Marxist approaches to welfare.

(15 marks)

81 Peter Townsend: Policies to End Poverty

Peter Townsend is one of the leading experts on poverty in Britain. His massive book *Poverty* (Penguin, 1979) was the result of several years of research. He has never made a secret of his opinion that poverty is not just a matter for research but is a problem to be solved. Here he offers a critique of the limited welfare state policies of most of the post-war period and of the more openly elitist policies of the Thatcher government. He then goes on to suggest his own policies which he urges the Labour party to adopt.

Townsend gives a very useful definition of social policy and its potential scope:

If social policy is conceived as the institutionalised control of services, agencies and organisations to maintain or change social structure and values, then what is at stake is not just the social division of welfare or the management of public, fiscal and private welfare, but the allocation of wealth, the organisation of employment, the management of the wage system and the creation of styles of living.

In other words, social policy involves not only tinkering with the welfare state but fundamental economic and even cultural issues. Underlying social policy is the ideological debate and contest for control without which policies cannot come to fruition. Only the opening section of Townsend's article is given here – in which he presents the case for regarding economic and social policy as indivisible. The next section (not included) argues that the scope of social policy is very wide and can, indeed, involve a radical restructuring of society. After further criticism of other policy approaches, Townsend then goes on to detail his own suggestions. These include an annual wealth tax, a ceiling on the amount of wealth an individual can possess, community trust development funds, a maximum as well as minimum level of earnings, a relative change in the incomes of the non-employed and employed, and equal status and income with other forms of work for work in the home.

How can we differentiate Townsend the sociologist from Townsend the social policy advocate? In fact, his socialist convictions are likely to lead him to research some areas rather than others and may also predispose him to adopt certain theoretical concepts and models (neo-Marxist or, otherwise, radical) than others. However, his research itself is required to be reliable and valid if it is to be taken seriously by those who do not share his views or, simply, if it is to be good sociology.

Reading 81 Peter Townsend, 'Poverty in the 80s', in *New Socialist*, Sept–Oct 1981, No. 1, pp. 26–31.

Britain stands at a point of crisis in its history. I cannot recall a period in my lifetime when deprivation was more widespread, public attitudes less fair-minded or the prospects worse for reversing the indicators of not only economic and industrial but social decline. In a short span of years the spectres of mass unemployment, mass poverty and the disaffection and despair of racial minorities and other sections of society, including unemployed youth and people with disabilities, have turned into everyday realities. At the same time, attempts to limit the wealth of the wealthy have been aborted or stultified and the institutions representing the working class have been placed under sustained and hostile public examination.

The austere but fairer society of the 1940s and early 1950s is but a distant memory, though few people are as yet aware of the run-down of the relative incomes of the poor and of expenditure on the public social services, compared with the rest of Europe. According to the EEC, the percentage of gross domestic product devoted to the public social services in Britain in 1980 was smaller than in all but one other member of that community – Ireland. The Netherlands and Germany spend between a third and a half as much again, relative to their income. In Britain, specific kinds of benefits are smaller and services less generously financed, than in a number of other countries. Poverty is more widespread than in some other industrialised countries in the OECD and – at twelve per cent on an international definition – the present unemployment rate is exceptionally high.

Estimates from official surveys show that the numbers living on very low incomes – that is, below or only up to ten per cent above the supplementary benefit basic scales – increased from 4.6 to 8.0 million between 1960 and 1977. There remain marked inequalities in health: for example, while the mortality rates for both male and female manual workers over 35 have barely changed, the rates for professional, managerial and senior administrative groups have fallen steadily.

How did a nation committed to full employment in 1945 change into one reconciled to the numbers of unemployed rising officially to more than 3 millions and unofficially to over 4 millions by 1982? Why did redistribution and the expansion of the welfare state have so little effect as a strategy in changing a class-fractured society?

The problem began with the failure at national level to integrate social with economic policy. The management of an economy is inseparable from its social effects. It is impossible to have an economic policy, whether monetarist or Keynesian, which is not also a social policy. Economic policy inevitably specifies support for those in society on whom economic development is believed to depend – even if that has to be extracted with difficulty from the statements about policy. Certain groups are favoured. Policies on investment, taxation and public expenditure can be analysed to reveal who it is are believed by the government to be important and who to be unimportant.

The present government has declared its priorities by relieving the very rich of high rates of income taxation and doubling the threshold of capital transfer tax. Those in charge of the pension funds are pouring money into overseas investment at the rate of over £1 billion per quarter. The abolition of exchange controls makes it harder to tax the rich effectively, while encouragement to invest overseas will make more likely a further fall in both employment and wage levels.

But the government has also declared its social priorities by allowing the number of unemployed people, including unemployed people with disabilities, to increase, by reducing the relative share of income of many among the non-employed and by choosing to act in the detection of fraud against supplementary benefit recipients rather than those who evade tax.

Question

1. *(With reference also to the previous reading:)*
   (a) What arguments do Townsend and Mishra give for linking economic and social policy?

   (5 marks)

   (b) Compare and contrast their differing socio-economic policy 'prescriptions'.

   (20 marks)

   (You will need information from my introduction to Reading 81, as well as from the reading.)

82 Gillian Paschall: Women, Caring and Social Policy (with Special Reference to 'Community Care')

Caring is looking after people, some of whom need to be looked after, some of whom do not. As Paschall notes, it is mainly carried out by women. She argues that it should be given the serious analysis that its central position in social life merits. Drawing particularly on essays by Hilary Graham and Margaret Stacey, she contends that caring is essential *work* and needs to be reconceptualised.

She indicates two aspects that any reconceptualisation of caring work should involve. First, caring occurs at the juncture of the personal (family) and the public (economy/society). Some caring is carried out by public agencies, much more by the family (overwhelmingly by women). This stark reality could be the starting point of a fresh analysis of caring which could change both public attitudes and policy. Second, she asks that any analysis of caring fully considers its core emotional aspect. She implies that any change in policy should preserve rather than jeopardise this quality.

The brief section on 'Community Care' makes one essential point. The meaning of the concept has changed to reflect public attitudes, particularly those of governments. The current (1987) official use of the term invites close attention.

This article could usefully be read in combination with Reading 36 in the Gender Section.

Reading 82 From Gillian Paschall, *Social Policy: A Feminist Analysis* (Tavistock, 1986), pp. 70–2, 85–7.

In simple terms, caring is looking after people: people capable of looking after themselves but who choose not to – teenagers, husbands, perhaps – and people who need intimate daily care for health and life – babies, and the very old and frail. Such looking after involves work, often hard work, and it involves relationships which are likely to be profoundly important to those involved. It is often assumed that the state has 'taken over' a great deal of such work from the 'family', and that men have taken over much from women. This chapter is about the division of caring work, between state and family, and between men and women. And because caring work is mostly done by women, it is concerned with the meaning of such work in women's lives, the material context in which women accept it, and its material consequences.

Some of the most interesting recent work in feminist social policy has centred on caring, or 'human service' or 'people work'. Two particularly important essays are by Hilary Graham, on 'Caring: A Labour of Love' (1983), and by Margaret Stacey on 'The Division of Labour Revisited or Overcoming the Two Adams' (1981). Both these essays claim a central significance for caring work, in society and social policy. According to Graham, 'caring is not something on the periphery of our social order; it marks the point at which the relations of capital and gender intersect. It should be the place we begin, and not end our analysis of modern society' (Graham 1983:30). Graham goes on to quote Stacey: 'We shall never be able to understand the social processes going on around us so long as we tacitly or overtly deny the part played by the givers and receivers of "care" and "service", the victims of socialisation processes, the

629

unpaid labourers in the processes of production and reproduction' (Stacey 1981:189).

A second point shared by these authors is a critique of the ways in which existing conceptual categories and disciplines fragment and obscure the meaning and importance of caring. Stacey sees this in terms of reconceptualising the division of labour. She argues that the way sociology divides work from family, public from private, leaves us with inadequate means of understanding work that straddles the two. Work that takes place in the private domain tends to be uncounted and unanalysed; or if it is analysed, it is described in inappropriate terms borrowed from the world of industry. The whole division of labour is thus understood in terms of work in the public domain. We need, she thinks, to 'rethink what constitutes work' (Stacey 1981).

The point is followed up by Graham in her argument that we need a 'reconception of caring' (Graham 1983:23). Disciplinary boundaries, she argues, have fragmented our understanding of caring which demands 'both love and labour, both identity and activity' (Graham 1983: 13). Social policy has studied the work aspects of caring, the material constraints within which women make choices about caring, and the material effects on women's lives that flow from these responsibilities. Psychology, on the other hand, has focused on the emotional aspects of caring; it sees the responsibility for others as the key to female identity. Caring is what makes women women. Both approaches are inadequate. The account of caring as work fails to face up to the 'emotional component of human service' (Stacey 1981: 173). It 'tends to underplay the symbolic bonds that hold the caring relationship together. The roots of people's deep resistance to the socialisation of care is thus lost' (Graham 1983: 29). But analysis in terms of feminine identity and self-fulfilment neglects the material aspects of caring; it runs the risk of concluding that caring is an essential, natural, part of women's identity and of legitimising women's place in the material world. Instead of these separate accounts, we need an analysis which can contain both love and labour, which can take seriously both the emotional and material understandings of caring and of why women do it.

Unfortunately, for the present, we have to rely mostly on accounts that are conceived in traditional categories. However, these authors do point in important directions, which can be followed to some degree. First, Stacey points to the need to connect the division of labour at home to the division of labour in the public world; to understand social policy developments in terms which incorporate both, and which analyse the changing boundaries between state and family in caring for people. Such a look at the division of caring labour shows that a large part of state social policy consists in taking a small part of caring work into the public sphere. Health services in particular, but also education and social work, consist in turning some specialised aspects of caring work into 'professional' employment; and in their absorption into a masculine hierarchy, though with a large female labour force. At the same time, large parts of educational, health, and caring work are still undertaken within the family. Here they may not be thought of as 'health work' or 'education work' or even as work. Nevertheless, for children under five, the greater part of health and educational care is given by mothers; schoolchildren may spend 'fifteen thousand hours' at school, but they will spend more waking hours than that at home; and at the other end of life, the most dependent elderly people are more likely to rely on relatives than on social services:

> 'The extensive and intensive care provided by the family forms the basis on which the professional services have evolved. Professional health workers, like doctors and health visitors, do not provide an alternative to the family; rather, they have a range of skills which they employ in order to improve the quality of care that families provide. Doctors diagnose and prescribe treatments for the patients who come to them; they do not nurse the sick. Similarly, health visitors listen and advise; it is left to mothers to put their advice into practice.'
>
> (Graham 1984: 7)

The state has not, therefore, taken away the work of caring from families or from women. Males of all ages, and females young and old are likely to require care and to be looked after at home by women. The small percentage of children and elderly who are cared for out of families – at great expense – are still cared for mainly by women. Caring work cuts across the boundaries of family/employment and family/social policy; understanding its pattern is central to understanding social policy.

The second direction in which this writing points is to putting both love and labour aspects of caring in the balance, even where we lack the material for a more integrated account. The unsharing of caring can be counted and costed; but those who bear that cost are not clamouring to hand their children or their mothers over to the government. To count the very small part that social policy plays in the care of young and old is not to call for comprehensive institutional care for the under fives and over sixties. It should be assumed that caring relationships matter profoundly to those involved in them.

'Community care'

An ideology that romanticises caring for the elderly and handicapped seems more improbable than one that romanticises motherhood. However, the idea of 'community care', while less developed than romanticised notions of motherhood, fulfils a very similar function in legitimating minimal state activity in the private sphere of home and family. It also disguises minimal men's activity.

The notion of 'community care' belongs to social policy documents rather than to women. It does not have the widespread allegiance of 'maternal deprivation': nor is it in any sense 'needed' to persuade women to look after dependent relatives and friends. Its use has been in justifying low government spending on the elderly and handicapped, and in disguising policies whose real effects are to burden and isolate individuals. Irony is plentiful. For community one can read its virtual opposite. The heavier the demands of caring, the less likely the 'community' will care to be involved (Equal Opportunities Commission 1982a: 17–18). An expression which appears warmly to encompass everyone disguises the fact that, whether as paid workers or as relatives, it is generally women who do the 'caring'. And for 'care', when it comes to state activity, one may often read neglect.

'Community care' has been casting its warm glow over government documents for almost as long as we have had a 'Welfare State'. Titmuss found official use of the term in 1950 (Titmuss 1968: 107). He was probably the first to hint that it served an ideological function: 'And what of the everlasting cottage-garden trailer, "Community Care"? Does it not conjure up a sense of warmth and human kindness, essentially personal and comforting, as loving as the wild flowers so enchantingly described by Lawrence in *Lady Chatterley's Lover?*.' The concern of Titmuss's essay 'Community

Care: Fact or Fiction?' was to begin to uncover the reality which this 'comforting appellation' (Titmuss 1968: 104) so well disguised. The need for this exercise becomes more urgent as 'community care' is sprinkled ever more liberally through government documents, apparently to deal with an increasing population of dependent people.

The idea of community care would have no power but for its basis in widely shared values. Its use in the 1950s and 1960s in the critique of inhumane institutions was not altogether sham. And the ideal of people in general supporting the elderly and handicapped is hardly contentious. What is contentious is the implication of a state of affairs which has never existed (i.e. a comprehensive network of community service in support of work in the private world of home); and the disguising of a sexual division of labour disadvantageous to women.

The rhetoric of 'community care' has undergone some change. In the 1950s and early 1960s it was part of an assault on large-scale, isolated institutions. 'At that time the emphasis seemed to be mainly upon replacing large and often geographically remote institutional facilities with smaller units of residential provision, located in built-up areas which would, if possible, be familiar to individual residents' (Finch and Groves 1980: 489). By the late 1960s and 1970s the emphasis had shifted towards ideas of community involvement. By the 1980s care by the community was to take the place of state involvement. For example, a recent White Paper, *Growing Older*, takes community resources as its theme, with cuts in public services lurking not far below the surface. Chapter 1 concludes:

'Providing adequate support and care for the elderly people in all their varying personal circumstances is a matter which concerns – and should involve – the whole community; not just politicians and officials, or charitable bodies. It is a responsibility which must be shared by everyone. Public authorities simply will not command the resources to deal with it alone; nor, even if they did, would it be right or possible for official help to meet all individual needs.'

(DHSS 1981a:3, para 1.11)

And the very last remarks of the paper are:

'improving the lives of elderly people must involve the whole of society. The government hopes it will help people everywhere to take stock of the implications – for themselves and for others – of the growing numbers of elderly people, and encourage them to consider what they can do to meet the challenge and the opportunity it poses.'

(DHSS 1981a:64, para 9.23)

When such remarks are taken in conjunction with public spending plans, their implications are quite plain: 'community care' is a substitute for social services.

'Community care', then, has flexible meaning. It may be used to contrast with institutions; to imply publicly provided services in support of caring work; or to imply informal 'networks of provision'. While the rhetoric changes, the underlying meaning is more consistent. As Finch and Groves put it: 'in practice community care equals care by the family, and in practice care by the family equals care by women' (Finch and Groves 1980: 494).

Questions
1. *(a) In what ways does Gillian Paschall suggest 'caring' should be thought out again and re-defined?*

(10 marks)

(b) What does 'community care' mean? Why might it be a dangerous concept for women?

(10 marks)

2. *Why do women do most direct personal caring yet men more often occupy senior positions in welfare services?*

(25 marks)

(You will also need to refer to readings in the Gender section to answer this question.)

SECTION 16

The Sociology of Health

Readings 83–88

The sociology of health needs to be broadly contextualised. The quality of health reflects the nature of society. The first and second readings relate health in Britain to the nature of the country's social, economic and political system – in other words, to the political economy of British capitalism. The first reading is a useful introduction to the patterns of health inequality in Britain. Some policy suggestions are made to reduce this inequality. The second reading, from Doyal and Pennel, is a more specific and theoretical examination of the political economy of health, and is the key reading in this section.

The third reading is from Ivan Illich's *Limits to Medicine*. Illich offers a critique of the professional and organisational power and control of medicine rather than a more directly class-based analysis. To that extent, he is closer to Weber than Marx, although he does not write within conventional sociological limits. He is as much a polemicist as a theoretician. The reading from David Tuckett switches our attention from the structural to the interpretive level, but class-related factors continue to be raised.

The fifth and sixth readings show a change of emphasis. They are concerned with the relationship of general cultural beliefs and attitudes to health. Models or paradigms of health are seen to reflect the wider cultural environment. Thus, the Zande model of health is based on their belief in magic and sorcery. In effect, ill-health is just one example of misfortune and, like other forms of misfortune, is explained within a framework of magic, sorcery and consultation with oracles. By contrast, the dominant Western model of health is scientific. The commonly used metaphor of the body as a machine and health as a form of machine-maintenance illustrates the dominance of scientific ideology. Samuel Osherson and Lorna Amara Singham discuss the 'machine metaphor' in a fascinating, but by no means easy, reading. They contrast modern scientific medicine with the spiritually based medieval understanding of life (including health) and death. Thus, the final two extracts cover primitive (magical), traditional (religious) and modern (scientific) paradigms of health. They lead naturally into the next section on the sociology of knowledge and religion in which the basis of cultural beliefs and attitudes is discussed in detail.

83 Anna Coote on *Inequalities In Health* (Department of Health and Social Services Report): Social Class and Health (and Health Policy)

Anna Coote's article, originally entitled 'Death to the Working Class', is a succinct but informative summary of the government report *Inequalities in Health*, sometimes referred to by the name of its Chairman as the Black Report. Little disservice is done to the original report by presenting it at second-hand because it is substantially a straight-forward empirical exercise. A variety of existing data is brought together to illustrate the relationship between health and social class and, to a more limited extent, that between health and gender.

The facts are, indeed, startling and describe a situation of major inequality in health between the social classes. Coote usefully summarises the explanations offered by the Commission for this situation. Here it may be possible to detect the influence of sociologist Peter Townsend who sat on the Commission, particularly in the preference for explanations based on the working class's lack of 'material security and advantage' rather than cultural deficit. The policy recommendations of the Report are radical and were comprehensively ignored by the Conservative government to which the Commission reported. Apart from its usefulness in establishing the relationship between social class and health, this piece can also be studied as a further example of the relationship between sociology and social policy.

Reading 83 From Anna Coote 'Death to the Working Class' in *New Statesman*, 12 September, 1980, pp. 8–9.

Britain's Health Service doesn't work – especially for the working classes. The lower down the social scale you are, the less likely you are to be healthy and the sooner you can expect to die. Your children, too, will be at greater risk of injury, sickness and death. It is hardly surprising that Patrick Jenkin has been anxious to hush-up the official report from the Department of Health and Social Security which presents these embarassing findings. But *Inequalities in Health* (DHSS, £8) goes a great deal further than that.

The poorer health of the lower social classes, the report says, is a result not just of failings in the National Health Service, but of glaring inequalities in income, education, nutrition, housing and working conditions, as well as cultural differences. What is more, the gap in health standards between the upper and lower classes has increased steadily since 1949.

The Working Group which produced the report – commissioned by Jenkin's predecessor, David Ennals, in 1977 – was chaired by Sir Douglas Black, Chief Scientist at the DHSS and president of the Royal College of Physicians; with him were Professor J.N. Norris of the London School of Hygiene and Tropical Medicine, Dr Cyril Smith, Secretary of the Social Science Research Council and Peter Townsend, Professor of Sociology at Essex University. Hardly a bunch of dangerous radicals, yet they have shown, by analysing a vast range of data, that class divisions in Britain are, if anything, deeper today than they were thirty years ago. And they conclude that drastic shifts in social policy are needed to establish equal health standards.

Taking mortality rates as an indicator of health, the report shows that over the last half-century, men in occupational classes IV and V have made no improvement in their health, even in absolute terms. Between 1949 and 1972 the number of deaths per 100,000 working class men in the 45–54 age group dropped by only *one*, from 895 to 894, while in the 55–64 age group the death rate increased from 2,339 to 2,409.

Women have fared better than men: their health has shown an improvement in all occupational and age groups. But upper class women have been getting healthier a lot quicker than their lower class contempories; so, too, have their chances of surviving child birth and producing healthy babies. In 1972, the maternal mortality rate for class V women was nearly double that for women in classes I and II.

The length and degree of illnesses are hard to measure, as statistics often depend on people's own assessment of their state of health.

However, in 1972, semi-skilled and unskilled manual male workers lost nearly four times as many working days as men in the professional and managerial classes. And in 1976, there were nearly two and a half times as many women suffering from chronic illness in class V as in class I.

Although working class children are more vulnerable to fatal injury and illness (see Table and caption), their parents are less likely than those in the middle classes to take them to the doctor. This may have more to do with the quality of care and the costs (financial and otherwise) which the parents anticipate, than with any unreasonable response to sickness. For it is well-known that health services in predominantly working class areas are less accessible and of a poorer quality. The report suggests that working class adults may be 'typically *more* sick than are middle class ones before help is sought'. Middle class patients tend to get better care from their GPs, not only because they live in areas which are better served, but also because they are more skilled at eliciting the care they need.

Fatal accidents among children

			Social Class			
	I	II	IIIN	IIIM	IV	V
Boys	25.8	39	44.5	56.3	66.2	122
Girls	18.8	19	21.4	24.9	35.1	63.1

Child deaths in general have decreased in all age groups and social classes in the last 20 years, except in social classes IV and V in the 10–14 age group, where there has been a marked increase. Sharp differences remain between the classes. For example, boys are twice as likely to die aged 5–9 if they belong to social classes IV and V than if they belong to classes I and II. And girls in classes IV and V are almost twice as likely to die aged 1–4 than their contemporaries in classes I and II. Children who suffer the greatest risk are class V boys aged 1–4.

The Working Group was especially worried by the working classes' 'severe underutilisation' of preventive services. Among married women who make bookings for ante-natal care, 29.8 per cent of those in class II make them after the twentieth week of pregnancy, compared with 35.3 per cent in class IV and 40.5 per cent in class V. Working class women are less likely to be screened for cervical cancer 'even though mortality from this condition is much higher in these classes than in the non-manual classes'.

Other studies quoted in the report show that working class people make less use of dental services and chiropody, and receive inferior dental care. All this, it says,

> is a complex resultant of under-provision, of costs (financial, psychological) of attendance, and perhaps of a life style which profoundly inhibits any attempt at rational action in the interests of *future* well-being.

Class also determines the kind of institution in which elderly people end their days. Predictably, the middle class keep out of hospital more often, and stay in superior homes.

Class and mortality: who dies soonest?

Mortality rates of occupational classes III, IV and V, as a percentage of the rates for classes I and II

Occupational class	Age	Men			Women		
		1949–53	1959–63	1970–72	1949–53	1959–63	1970–72
Class III	25–34	119	123	125	134	125	121
Class IV & V		145	177	196	166	151	162
Class III	35–44	122	134	151	118	130	131
Class IV & V		146	171	180	133	151	164
Class III	45–54	114	130	132	112	124	128
Class IV & V		126	155	161	120	141	151
Class III	55–64	114	123	129	109	122	127
Class IV & V		112	135	141	112	138	135

The number of deaths per 100,000 in each group has declined over the years, but the decline has been much steeper in the upper groups, so that the class difference has shown a marked increase.

Comparing Britain's experience with other industrialised Western countries, the Working Group confirms that while adult mortality patterns are about the same, infant mortality is worse in Britain than elsewhere. There is evidence that infant death rates are lower where incomes are more evenly distributed. England, it turns out, has a more even regional distribution of doctors than other countries, but that doesn't seem to help: 'the extent of provisions of nurses and midwives, and of hospital beds, are more important than the provision of physicians'. The amount of emphasis placed on preventive ante-natal care and child health services is also considered more relevant.

The chief causes of unequal health are identified as poverty, and the relatively poor access of low-income groups to the knowledge and facilities which help to maintain physical fitness. The analysis is not a surprising one – except that it has been produced by such an august body, under instructions from a government department.

Working class children, the report says, are less able to acquire linguistic, cognitive and communicative skills which would equip them for jobs in the higher-paid and healthier occupation groups 'because of the *fit* which exists between middle-class norms of social-isation and the dominant structure of the educational system'. People with lower incomes eat – and feed their children – more harmful foods; they smoke more and take less exercise. These habits are not simply a product of working class culture, but reflect a relative lack of 'material security and advantage'.

Poverty and health

Numbers living below or just above the bread-line have increased over the last 20 years

	Britain (000s)		
Income	1960	1975	1978
Below supplementary benefit level	1260	1840	2020
Receiving supplementary benefit	2670	3710	4160
Up to 40 per cent above supplementary benefit level	3510	6990	7840

At today's rates, supplementary benefit is £42.20 a week for a married couple with two children aged 5–10; and £18.30 for a single householder. Income 40 per cent above that level amounts to £59.10 and £25.62 respectively.

Income and nutrition

Ounces consumed per person per week

Income group	Food			
	white bread	sugar	potatoes	fruit
A	18	11.3	29	33
B	25	11	39	24
C	28	13	49	20
D	31	15	52	17

Resources which improve the quality of parental care tend to be material – such as 'sufficient household income, a safe, uncrowded and unpolluted home, warmth and hygiene, a means of rapid communication with the outside world, e.g. telephone or car, and an adequate level of man or woman power'. Accidents and violence are the main causes of child deaths:

> Among child pedestrians, for example, the risk of death from the impact of a motor vehicle is multiplied by 5–7 times in passing from class I to class V; for accidental death caused by fires, falls and drowning, the gap between the classes is even greater. These differences demonstrate the *non-random* nature of accidents as a collective class of events.

The report also quotes the Camberwell study of Brown and Harris which concludes that one reason for the greater prevalence of accidents in working class homes 'is the higher incidence of stressful life events experienced by mothers'.

High death rates among working class adults are attributed to the risks of accidental injury and damage to vision, hearing and breathing which commonly accompany manual work and 'which, it must be said, are in no way compensated for by financial reward'. The report insists that higher levels of smoking among working class men and women cannot be dismissed as a wilful, self-destructive habit when it 'depends on a multi-million pound industry, is sanctioned by Parliament, treated as an important source of taxation income and freely permitted in public places, even on premises owned by the National Health Service'. Moreover, smoking habits are related to feelings of satisfaction and security – and these are often improved by material advantage.

A determined shift in resources is recommended by the working group – towards community care and greater provision for mothers, young children and the disabled. The group wants non-means-tested free milk for infants, an enlarged programme of health education, better facilities for physical recreation in the inner cities, the establishment of 'National Health Goals', and strong anti-smoking measures including an invitation to tobacco companies 'to submit plans in consultation with trade unions for the diversification of their products over a period of 10 years'. The government should spend £30 million on a special health and social development programme in selected areas – and the ten with the highest death rates are South

Tyneside, Tower Hamlets, Durham, Bolton, Wirral and North Tyneside.

The reports' most radical proposals are in the field of social policy. It recommends that child benefit be increased to 5.5 per cent of average gross male industrial earnings (£5.70 in November 1979). This could have an interesting impact on the current debate about the role of 'the family wage' in collective bargaining. It proposes, too, that the maternity grant be quadrupled from £25 to £100. Disappointingly, it makes no suggestions about increasing parental leave and extending it to fathers (along Swedish lines), which would help eliminate health *and* sex inequalities. Instead, the working group wants to pay women to stay at home, 'to strengthen the mother's role', by introducing an infant care allowance, equivalent to child benefit, for mothers of children under five. Its proposals on child care are more helpful: it wants a statutory obligation to be placed on local authorities to ensure adequate day care for the under-fives, with a minimum number of places laid down centrally. But it stops short of recommending statutory facilities for children who are not in special need. Free school meals should be provided for all children – and the report explains that the cost of these measures could be met by withdrawing the extra married man's tax allowance from men who have no dependent children or elderly relatives.

Policy on housing, employment and other factors which affect health should be co-ordinated at Cabinet level, with an independent Health Development Council to 'play a key advisory and planning role'.

Question
See end of next reading.

84 Lesley Doyal and Imogen Pennell: The Political Economy of Health

Like the last reading, the subject of this extract is inequality in health. However, it offers more detailed illustration and explanation than the last piece.

Doyal and Pennell stress repeatedly that patterns of health and illness must be understood in the context of the social and economic system as a whole. In Britain this system is a capitalist one. It is true that the nature of industrial production tends to cause certain problems – such as pollution and noise – but Doyal and Pennell point out that the toleration and regulation of these problems is a matter of power and choice. They suggest frankly that in certain instances ill-health is the result of the pursuit of profit, the basic motive of capitalism. They give a number of examples relating to industrial accidents and disease. They suggest that the two major potential defenders of workers – trade unions and the state – have not been particularly effective. They criticise especially the inadequacy of health and safety law enforcement, and suggest that the power of capital to pursue profit, even at a high price in health, is greater than any counter-vailing power.

The authors also briefly discuss the relationship between modern working conditions, stress and rates of sickness absence. They conclude by examining stress and unemployment, and stress and housework.

Elsewhere in their book, Doyal and Pennell examine other aspects of the political economy of capitalism and health in addition to industrial accidents and disease. These include consumption and health and pollution and health. The classic example of the production of a dangerous consumer item for profit is, of course, tobacco. It is, however, in the selling of various dangerous or, at least, unhealthy products to the Third World, including particularly high-tar quality cigarettes, powdered milk, and sub-standard or inappropriate pesticides, that capitalist enterprise has most shown its 'unacceptable face' (see Reading 66(a)).

Reading 84 From Lesley Doyal and Imogen Pennell, *The Political Economy of Health* (Pluto Press, 1979) pp. 66–75.

Production and the health of workers

The most direct relationship between the process of commodity production and the destruction of health is obviously to be found in industrial accidents and industrial diseases. In these cases, ill health, disability or death are directly produced through the victim being at work. During the twentieth century, technological change and a different attitude towards the conservation of labour power have meant that some industrial diseases have been eliminated, or at least reduced in their incidence. Industrial accidents have also declined from the extremely high rates of the early nineteenth century. But new, and often more serious hazards, have been generated in their place, and work still remains for many an extremely dangerous activity.

Accurate statistics on the number of people who are killed or injured at work, or who contract industrial diseases are difficult to obtain, but the 1972 *Report of the Committee on Safety and Health at Work* (the Robens Report) suggested that,

> Every year something like one thousand people are killed at their work in this country. Every year about half a million suffer injuries in varying degrees of severity. Twenty-three million working days are lost annually on account of industrial injury and disease.

There are cogent reasons however for assuming that these figures seriously underestimate the real numbers involved. This is due (among other things) to the under-reporting of accidents, to the failure of doctors to recognise industrial disease, and to the large number of work-related illnesses which are not classified as such – i.e. are not 'prescribed'. Patrick Kinnersley has argued in *The Hazards of Work* that a realistic assessment of the annual figures for industrial accidents and disease would be about two thousand dying from injuries received at work, one thousand dying from industrial diseases, one million injured or off work with an industrial disease for at least three days, and at least ten million injured and needing first aid. In addition, any such annual reckoning leaves out those disabled and bereaved people left behind by previous years of production, as Kinnersley indicates. In 1975, 203,000 former workers were receiving an industrial disablement pension, while 31,000 widows were in receipt of industrial death benefit.

Whichever set of figures we take, it is clear that industrial accidents are still very common in Britain, affecting at least half a million workers each year. Certain industries have particularly high accident rates (e.g. the mining and construction industries, and the railways). During the year 1975–76, 59 miners were killed at work, 538 were seriously injured, and 52,946 were injured and off work for more than three days, and any miner still has approximately a one in five chance of being injured at work in any particular year.

The incidence of industrial disease is even more difficult to estimate than the number of industrial accidents – the causes are often very complex and the presence of a particular pathological process difficult to identify. Industrial diseases are contracted through the entry into the body of various toxic substances – chemicals, dusts, fumes or gases. The ingestion can be by a variety of routes – lungs, skin or stomach – and the ingested substances can be harmful in several different ways. They can cause direct poisoning (e.g. lead or mercury); an allergic response (e.g. industrial dermatitis); abortions or congenital abnormality (e.g. over-exposure to radiation); or specific diseases such as cancer (lung, skin and bladder cancer are all prescribed diseases *under certain circumstances*). Some of these processes can be illustrated in more detail through looking at the health problem produced by dusts and chemicals.

Dusts have been known to cause serious illness and even death for as long as there have been miners. About thirty thousand miners in Britain still suffer to some degree or other from lung disease. In 1973, 367 deaths were officially declared to be due to pneumoconiosis (although this is likely to be an underestimate), and about seven hundred *new* cases are still being diagnosed by pneumoconiosis panels each year. Dusts of a different kind produce byssinosis, asbestosis, and silicosis. Byssinosis was very common in the textiles factories of the nineteenth and early twentieth century, and was produced by the coarse dust and fibres accumulating in factories without adequate ventilation. Improved conditions were assumed to have wiped out the disease by the 1940s, but it has since been 'rediscovered'. Its apparent disappearance illustrates some of the problems involved in isolating industrial diseases from other environmentally-produced ill health. It seems that cases of byssinosis have often been confused with bronchitis, which is commonly found in those manufacturing areas where byssinosis could be expected. Moreover, any respiratory disease such as byssinosis will be aggravated by smoking and by the atmospheric pollution which is common in industrial areas. Therefore, its specific occupational origin may often go unnoticed, particularly where there is such a marked absence of health services in the workplace and when many factory doctors identify with the interests of employers rather than workers.

A very wide range of chemical substances can also be taken into the body while a person is at work. Lead and mercury are still among the most dangerous and since both are being used increasingly frequently, they represent a growing health hazard. In addition, new substances are coming into use all the time, and many of these are receiving very limited toxicity testing. The relative ease with which potentially dangerous chemicals are introduced into the workplace, is a particularly serious problem because many industrial hazards only produce diseases after a long latency period. By the time their pathogenic effects have been realised it is often too late to do anything for the workers who were exposed to them many years earlier. This problem has been highlighted recently by experiences with two chemicals – beta naphthylamine and vinyl chloride monomer.

Beta naphthylamine was widely used in the rubber and cable industries in Britain until 1950, but medical evidence now shows that exposure to it can cause bladder cancer some forty or fifty years later. Vinyl chloride monomer is the major ingredient of PVC and it has now been discovered that exposure to this chemical can eventually cause a very rare form of liver cancer known as angiosarcoma. But it is the 'epidemic' of asbestosis and mesothelioma (cancer of the chest lining) which has occured during the 1970s which illustrates most vividly the long-term effects of exposure to industrial hazards. Despite the fact that new regulations to control asbestos were introduced in 1969, figures published in the second annual report of the Employment Advisory Service showed an increase in cases of mesothelioma of at least sixty-eight per cent between 1970 and 1976. The latent period for this type of cancer may be anything from five to thirty-five years, and since the worst industrial exposures occurred between 1935 and 1970, the peak incidence still seems some years away. This same problem was examined by the US National Institute of Environmental Health Sciences. Their official report published in 1978 estimated that more than two million American workers will die prematurely of cancer over the next thirty years, because of exposure to asbestos in the course of their jobs. It further argued that as many as fifteen per cent of all cancer cases in the United States are work related, rather than the one to five per cent often quoted.

It is clear that it will often be in the economic interest of employers not to inquire whether their workers are at risk from accident, disease or death. Firms tend to operate on the basis of 'acceptable risks' for a given return on investment but it is often the lives or health of workers which are at stake. It is assumed that in this situation, workers have two basic defenders who are concerned to protect their health – the state and the trade unions. However, it is clear from the incidence of industrial accidents and disease that these safeguards are not operating very effectively in Britain.

Work is generally assumed to create no dangers to health, unless there is clear evidence to the contrary. The health and safety of people at work is, therefore, ultimately dependent on their own awareness of hazards and potential illnesses. However, most medical and legal knowledge is concentrated in the hands of 'experts' and, as a consequence, workers usually have to rely on their unions both to obtain such information, and also to initiate any necessary action. Despite this, most unions have given low priority to working conditions in general, and to health and safety issues in particular. Thus, an almost exclusive concentration on levels of pay has often detracted from important (possibly life or death) aspects of the physical environment of the workplace. Moreover, when health risks have been identified, unions have tended to demand danger money rather than changes in working conditions. Recently, there has been evidence of growing awareness among unions of the importance of health and safety issues, but much remains to be done. It is clearly difficult, however, for such concerns to be brought to the fore, when attempts to make the workplace safer can so easily be countered with threats of unemployment.

Whatever the priorities of the trade union movement, it is usually assumed that it is, in the final analysis, the responsibility of the state to protect the health of all of its citizens. The history of health and safety legislation, however, shows that this protection has been provided only within certain very narrow limits, and on a frag-mented and pragmatic basis. When pressure has been exerted, the state has introduced limited health and safety regulations, and also minimal levels of compensation for those who 'deserve it'. Such legislation has had only a limited effect on employers, and two basic deficiencies are evident in the existing state machinery for dealing with industrial accidents and disease. The first concerns the arrange-ments for inspection of workplace and the sanctions that can be imposed on those who endanger the lives of workers; the second concerns the absence of any national industrial health service.

The administrative machinery for enforcing health and safety legislation has always been very cumbersome, and until recently, responsibility was dispersed between several different departments. Following the report of the Robens Committee in 1972, the system was rationalised and improved by the Health and Safety at Work Act, which came into force in 1975. The act did a number of things. It improved the bureaucratic efficiency of the administrative apparatus by setting up a unified health and safety executive. It allowed inspectors to make immediate closures of dangerous premises. It required that all firms with more than five employees should provide them with written statements about the new legislation, and very importantly it required that employees should be appointed as safety representatives. Above all, it extended health and safety provisions to about eight million workers who had not been covered before. Yet the act has very severe limitations, which reflect the underlying philosophy of the Robens Report.

In preparing the way for the act, the Robens Report made its own position very clear.

> Our present system encourages rather too much reliance on state regulation and rather too little on personal responsibility and voluntary self-generating effort. This imbalance must be redressed. A start should be made by reducing the sheer weight of the legislation.

Thus the emphasis in the act was on the rationalisation of the legal situation so that individual workers could look after their own health better, rather than on any strengthening of legal controls. Indeed, the Robens Report effectively depoliticised the whole issue, suggesting that there exists, 'a greater natural identity of interest between "the two sides" in relation to safety and health problems than in most other matters'. Moreover, it assumed that the single most important cause of accidents is apathy or carelessness on the part of the workers, rather than negligence or lack of concern on the part of employers. The emphasis in the act was, therefore, placed firmly on persuasion and education and the means of enforcing the legislation remained severely restricted. There are still, for example, very few factory inspectors for all the workplaces to be visited, and even when prosecutions do take place, the penalties imposed by magistrates are often derisory – the average fine paid by an employer in 1975 was £75.

The relative ineffectiveness of the health and safety law enforcement machinery is exacerbated by the lack of a national occupational health service. It has always been a major criticism of the NHS, that it did not include an industrial health service – those industrial health provisions which do exist are organised by individual employers. As a consequence, it has been estimated that only about thirty per cent of workers have access to such services. Relatively efficient emergency services are provided by the NHS, so that the lack of an industrial health service is significant not so much in terms of the treatment of accidents but because of the potential role of such a service in the prevention of accidents, and in the identification and prevention of industrial disease.

Industrial health strategies have been developed within the limits set by a capitalist economy and the overall thrust has been towards the adjustment of workers to the pace and the physical conditions of the production process, rather than the reverse. An extremely apt illustration of this is provided by the recent trend towards genetic screening. Since the 1960s, it has been known that a relationship exists between the possession of certain genetic characteristics, and the likelihood of developing particular diseases. As a result, discussions have been going on for some time about the need to identify those workers with a genetic susceptibility to particular industrial chemicals, in order to exclude them from particular jobs. While this may appear on the surface to be a very sensible proposition, it is of course no substitute for the more desirable alternative of making the workplace safer for *all* workers. There is no evidence to suggest that hypersusceptibility is responsible for any significant proportion of occupational disease, but genetic screening continues to be hailed in many quarters as the way forward for industrial health programmes.

So far we have examined some of the more physical dimensions of industrial ill health, but it is also important to look more broadly at the relationship between health and work. It is now relatively commonplace to suggest that workers are bored and alienated by assembly line work, and that many aspects of the labour process are stressful for both workers *and* managers. The existence of a link between an individual's health in the broadest sense, and the nature of his/her work is increasingly accepted. As yet, very few attempts have been made to look at this relationship in more detail, but it is illuminating to consider patterns of sickness absence in this connection. In Britain, rates of sickness absence have been rising continuously since the early 1960s, and by 1972 the annual number of working days lost through illness had risen to over three hundred and twenty million. This rise is difficult to explain, since during the same period, there was a decline in the number of days lost through those diseases such as TB, penumonia and stomach and duodenal ulcers, which have traditionally produced a significant volume of sickness absence. However, other causes such as 'sprains and strains', 'nerves, debility and headache' and 'psychoneuroses' have increased. Thus the 'harder', more objectively identifiable causes of sickness absence have been replaced by more subjective psychosomatic ones, and it is the presence of these new ailments which needs to be explained.

It is often suggested that these new illnesses are 'excuses' which workers consciously use because they are lazy, or wish to avoid unpleasant work situations. Increased sickness absence is also said to be a direct consequence of the availability of sickness benefit under the social security system. However, for most workers sickness absence still involves considerable financial loss – only very few (i.e. those with large families and very low wages) are actually better off on sickness benefit than they are at work. Moreover, benefit is payable only *after* the first three days of absence. It seems unlikely then, that conscious and calculated 'malingering' would be a widespread phenomenon. An alternative interpretation of the statistics is that for many, work has become not only physically but also psychologically dangerous. Thus the demands of boring repetitive and deskilled work performed at very high speed, combined with increased rates of over-time and shift work, may well be producing an increasing amount of stress which for many workers is exacerbated by job insecurity. This stress is reflected in an increased incidence of 'psychoneuroses' and of 'nerves, debility and the headache' and may also be a precipitating factor in what appear to be more straightforward physical illnesses.

Any attempt to explain present trends in sickness absence more fully must, therefore, take into account the more qualitative aspects of work and the working environment. It appears, for instance, that the less control workers have over their work, and the less satisfied they are with their job, the greater the number of days that are likely to be lost through sickness absence.

So far, our discussion has concentrated on the situation of waged workers (both male and female). However, the organisation of work in a capitalist society threatens health on an even broader basis. In the first place, employment is not available to everyone who wishes or needs it. As a consequence the experience of unemployment is a source of severe stress for many people, and often undermines their health. Secondly, many women risk their health, both physically and psychologically, in the performance of domestic labour. Women at home have a high accident rate, and the undercapitalised and isolated nature of housework is an important contributory factor in this. In 1971, 6,245 people died in home accidents – 35.3 per cent of whom were men and 64.7 per cent women – while many more were injured. Naturally, none of these figures appear in the industrial accident statistics since domestic labour is not officially counted as work. More importantly, perhaps, full-time housewives experience their own version of occupational disease in the form of depressive illness. Obviously there are several factors which could be important in explaining the high rate of psychiatric illness among housewives. Not only is housework unpaid, but the work itself is of low status – it is menial labour. It is hardly surprising that in a society where an individual's value is measured by what they can command on the labour market, anyone doing manual work without pay may have difficulty in maintaining a reasonable level of self-esteem. Moreover, housework is both isolated and extremely repetitive, while the care of young children can be both exhausting and demoralising. Many women respond to these pressures created by the nature of their labour with feelings of depression and anxiety – a widespread if unacknowledged form of occupational ill health. Much research remains to be done in understanding the relationship between work and health, but Marx's classic description of the nature of wage labour remains an important philosophical starting point for such an analysis.

> What constitutes the alienation of labour? First, that the work is external to the worker – that it is not part of his nature; and that consequently he does not fulfill himself in his work, but denies himself, has a feeling of misery rather than well-being, does not develop freely his mental and physical energies, but is physically exhausted and mentally debased.

Question
1. (a) *Work is 'often both a physically and psychologically dangerous activity which is undertaken only in order to earn the means of survival' (Doyal and Pennel). Discuss.*

(15 marks)

(b) Explain the limited effectiveness of legislation to improve working conditions.

(10 marks)

2. Why do the middle class tend to be healthier than the working class?

(25 marks)

(See also Reading 83.)

85 Ivan Illich: The Power and Control of Organised Medicine: Social Iatrogenesis

Neither Illich's style nor the precise nature of his analyses is always absolutely clear. Nevertheless, his passionate attack on all forms of self-interested power, particularly that of professional bureaucracies, has reached a world-wide audience. If he had perhaps phrased his arguments in the terms of conventional academic sociology, he would have had fewer readers.

A key concept employed by Illich is 'iatrogenesis' which means illness caused by medicine itself. We are all aware that 'accidents can happen' in medicine as in any other activity, but Illich means more than this. He describes three types of iatrogenesis against 'defenceless patients'. The first is clinical iatrogenesis: this occurs where medical prescription is itself dangerous, as in ill-advised drug use or surgery. The second, social iatrogenesis, is dealt with in the following extract. This refers to the way in which the medical profession has taken over the definition, administration and control of health – to the profit of practitioners and, so Illich argues, at the expense of the public ('clients' of the 'system'). Third is cultural iatrogenesis which occurs to the extent that 'managed health' becomes accepted as health itself, so that a 'paralysis of healthy responses to suffering, impairment, and death' occurs. Thus, the ideology as well as the organised practice of the 'engineering' or 'machine' model of medicine triumphs.

Illich does not offer a coherent class-based analysis of medical practice. He recognises, almost in passing, that medical practitioners are middle class and that their power is a form of class power. He observes that the same is true of other professions. He would like to see medicine and other professions, such as education and the law, 'repossessed' by the people who could then meet their own needs in a more democratic, decentralised and organic fashion. What Illich's relationship to Marxism is on these matters is perhaps worth pondering.

Reading 85 From Ivan Illich, *Limits to Medicine: Medical Nemesis: The Expropriation of Health* (Penguin, 1977), pp. 49–56.

Social iatrogenesis

Medicine undermines health not only through direct aggression against individuals but also through the impact of its social organization on the total milieu. When medical damage to individual health is produced by a sociopolitical mode of transmission, I will speak of 'social iatrogenesis', a term designating all impairments to health that are due precisely to those socio-economic transformations which have been made attractive, possible, or necessary by the institutional shape health care has taken. Social iatrogenesis designates a category of aetiology that encompasses many forms. It obtains when medical bureaucracy creates ill-health by increasing stress, by multiplying disabling dependence, by generating new painful needs, by lowering the levels of tolerance for discomfort or pain, by reducing the leeway that people are wont to concede to an individual when he suffers, and by abolishing even the right to self-care. Social iatrogenesis is at work when health care is turned into a standardised item, a staple; when all suffering is 'hospitalised' and homes become inhospitable to birth, sickness, and death; when the language in which people could experience their bodies is turned into bureaucratic gobbledegook; or when suffering, mourning, and healing outside the patient role are labelled a form of deviance.

Medical monopoly

Like its clinical counterpart, social iatrogenesis can escalate from an adventitious feature into an inherent characteristic of the medical system. When the intensity of biomedical intervention crosses a critical threshold, clinical iatrogenesis turns from error, accident, or fault into an incurable perversion of medical practice. In the same way, when professional autonomy degenerates into a radical monopoly and people are rendered impotent to cope with their milieu, social iatrogenesis becomes the main product of the medical organization.

A radical monopoly goes deeper than that of any one corporation or any one government. It can take many forms. When cities are built around vehicles, they devalue human feet; when schools pre-empt learning, they devalue the autodidact; when hospitals draft all those who are in critical condition, they impose on society a new form of dying. Ordinary monopolies corner the market; radical monopolies disable people from doing or making things on their own. The commercial monopoly restricts the flow of commodities; the more insidious social monopoly paralyses the output of non-marketable use-values. Radical monopolies impinge still further on freedom and independence. They impose a society-wide substitution of commodities for use-values by reshaping the milieu and by 'appropriating' those of its general characteristics which have enabled people so far to cope on their own. Intensive education turns autodidacts into unemployables, intensive agriculture destroys the subsistence farmer, and the deployment of police undermines the community's self-control. The malignant spread of medicine has comparable results: it turns mutual care and self-medication into misdemeanours or felonies. Just as clinical iatrogenesis becomes medically incurable when it reaches a critical intensity and then can can be reversed only by a decline of the enterprise, so can social iatrogenesis be reversed only by political action that retrenches professional dominance.

A radical monopoly feeds on itself. Iatrogenic medicine reinforces a morbid society in which social control of the population by the medical system turns into a principal economic activity. It serves to legitimise social arrangements into which many people do not fit. It labels the handicapped as unfit and breeds ever new categories of patients. People who are angered, sickened, and impaired by their industrial labour and leisure can escape only into a life under medical supervision and are thereby seduced or disqualified from political struggle for a healthier world.

Social iatrogenesis is not yet accepted as a common aetiology of disease. If it were recognised that diagnosis often serves as a means of turning political complaints against the stress of growth into demands for more therapies that are just more of its costly and stressful outputs, the industrial system would lose one of its major defences. At the same time, awareness of the degree to which iatrogenic ill-health is politically communicated would shake the foundations of medical power much more profoundly than any catalogue of medicine's technical faults.

Value-free cure?

The issue of social iatrogenesis is often confused with the diagnostic authority of the healer. To defuse the issue and to protect their reputation, some physicians insist on the obvious: namely, that medicine cannot be practised without the iatrogenic creation of disease. Medicine always creates illness as a social state. The recognised healer transmits to individuals the social possibilities for acting sick. Each culture has its own characteristic perception of disease and thus its unique hygienic mask. Disease takes its features from the physician who casts the actors into one of the available roles. To make people legitimately sick is as implicit in the physician's power as the poisonous potential of the remedy that works. The medicine man commands poisons and charms. The Greeks' only word for 'drug' – *pharmakon* – did not distinguish between the power to cure and the power to kill.

Medicine is a moral enterprise and therefore inevitably gives content to good and evil. In every society, medicine, like law and religion, defines what is normal, proper, or desirable. Medicine has the authority to label one man's complaint a legitimate illness, to declare a second man sick though he himself does not complain, and to refuse a third social recognition of his pain, his disability, and even his death. It is medicine which stamps some pain as 'merely subjective', some impairment as malingering, and some deaths – though not others – as suicide. The judge determines what is legal and who is guilty. The priest declares what is holy and who has broken a taboo. The physician decides what is a symptom and who is sick. He is a moral entrepreneur, charged with inquisitorial powers to discover certain wrongs to be righted. Medicine, like all crusades, creates a new group of outsiders each time it makes a new diagnosis stick. Morality is as implicit in sickness as it is in crime or in sin.

In primitive societies it is obvious that in the exercise of medical skill, the recognition of moral power is implied. Nobody would summon the medicine man unless he conceded to him the skill of discerning evil spirits from good ones. In a higher civilisation this power expands. Here medicine is exercised by full-time specialists who control large populations by means of bureaucratic institutions. These specialists form professions which exercise a unique kind of control over their own work. Unlike unions, these professions owe their autonomy to a grant of confidence rather than to victory in a struggle. Unlike guilds, which determine only who shall work and how, they determine also what work shall be done. In the United States the medical profession owes this supreme authority to a reform of the medical schools just before World War I. The medical profession is a manifestation in one particular sector of the control over the structure of class power which the university-trained elites have acquired. Only doctors now 'know' what constitutes sickness, who is sick, and what shall be done to the sick and to those whom they consider *at a special risk*. Paradoxically, Western medicine, which has insisted on keeping its power apart from law and religion, has now expanded it beyond precedent. In some industrial societies social labelling has been medicalised to the point where all deviance has to have a medical label. The eclipse of the explicit moral component in medical diagnosis has thus invested Aesculapian authority with totalitarian power.

The divorce between medicine and morality has been defended on the ground that medical categories, unlike those of law and religion, rest on scientific foundations exempt from moral evaluation. Medical ethics have been secreted into a specialised department that brings theory into line with actual practice. The courts and the law, when they are not used to enforce the Aesculapian monopoly, are turned into doormen of the hospital who select from among the clients those who can meet the doctors' criteria. Hospitals turn into monuments of narcissistic scientism, concrete manifestations of those professional prejudices which were fashionable on the day their cornerstone was laid and which were often outdated when they came into use. The technical enterprise of the physician claims value-free power. It is obvious that in this kind of context it is easy to shun the issue of social iatrogenesis with which I am concerned. Politically mediated medical damage is thus seen as inherent in medicine's mandate, and its critics are viewed as sophists trying to justify lay intrusion into the medical bailiwick. Precisely for this reason, a lay review of social iatrogenesis is urgent. The assertion of value-free cure and care is obviously malignant nonsense.

Question
1. (a) *What is social iatrogenesis?* (4 marks)
    (b) *What are Illich's main criticisms of social iatrogenesis?*
    (11 marks)

86 David Tuckett: Doctors and Patients – Bargaining and Negotiation

Illich's writings underline the power and control of medical professionals (Reading 85). This reading begins with the theme of the power of doctors at an interactional rather than a structural level. It is interesting to see how, even at the micro level, class inequalities assert themselves.

The extract suggests that not all patients are passive in their relationship with doctors and that, to varying degrees, some may be able to counterbalance their power. Tuckett suggests that, in fact, a process of negotiation between doctor and patient often takes place before a particular form of treatment is arrived at. After some general reflections on the relative power of doctor and patient, Tuckett turns to a model of 'strategic interaction', first presented by the influential symbolic interactionist, Irving Goffman, to clarify his ideas. Goffman's model is based on an analogy by which consultation is compared to a game. The point of the model is, of course, to illuminate for doctors the intricacies of interaction during consultation, and to enable them to be more sensitive both to patients and themselves.

In looking for a reading to illustrate negotiation in a medical context, I had originally turned to Irving Goffman's *Asylums*. It was sobering to observe that although some patient-staff negotiation is described, most interaction involves patients either distancing themselves from, or succumbing to, the power of the establishment. In a total institution in which one party is virtually dependent on the other, little real negotiation seems to take place. In a 'normal' doctor-patient relationship there appears to be more room for manoeuvre.

Reading 86 From David Tuckett, 'Doctors and Patients' in David Tuckett *ed., An Introduction to Medical Sociology* (Tavistock Publications, 1976), pp. 202–10.

The doctor is in a complex and ambiguous situation. On the one hand since his role is to help the patient, it is his task to listen to what the patient has to say and to help the patient to communicate with him. On the other hand, since the patient's view of what he should present, how he should behave and how his problem should be treated may not always (indeed, not often) agree with the doctor's judgement, the doctor has to try and persuade the patient to change his view or his behaviour.

There are various ways in which doctors appear to try and control this dilemma and reduce conflict. One strategy is to restrict themselves to patients who are unlikely to differ in views, for example, those from a similar social and educational background who will share, to a large extent, their norms and values and may more readily agree with their recommendations. Many do seem to take this option. Tudor Hart, for example, has argued that practices with a more middle-class clientele are much more popular among doctors and get the best qualified new recruits (Tudor Hart, 1971: 406–7). But not all doctors could solve the problem this way. It is therefore interesting that Cartwright and O'Brien (1976: 89) after tape-recording consultations found that doctors spent longer talking with middle-class patients, taking up 6.2 minutes on average, compared to 4.7 minutes for working-class patients. Since working-class patients have more complaints this is an important difference. In fact, Cartwright and O'Brien (1976: 92) concluded a discussion of doctor-patient relationships by saying:

> Although the data suggest that doctors have a rather less sympathetic and understanding relationship with their working-class patients, and we would speculate that a middle-class patient is more likely to regard the doctor as a peer, to be more confident about his own opinions on the importance of his problems and so insist on their being discussed. This would suggest that working-class patients are likely to find it more difficult to raise additional problems at a consultation; and our observations that working-class patients discuss fewer problems, and are no more likely to talk about social problems although more of them regard these as appropriate issues to discuss with their doctor, support this.

Whether they are dealing with middle-class or working-class patients doctors seem to be most happy when they are in control of the situation. This is my interpretation of another finding by Cartwright, who also reports that doctors are more satisfied where consultations are kept short (1976: 92). A doctor has various ways in which he can control the relationship he has with patients and minimise the need to interact with them if he so desires. Doctors can and do 'educate' their patients to bring appropriate complaints to them in various ways. Seventy-six per cent of general practitioners in an earlier Cartwright study (1967: 31) agreed that a 'good general practitioner can train his patients not to make unnecessary or unreasonable demands on him'. One way doctors can control how often patients see them is by repeat prescriptions. If a patient is given a prescription which lasts for four weeks he may be discouraged from returning in two. The doctor can see the patient regularly but not too frequently. A repeat prescription for a medicine can ensure a regular dose of doctor. A patient may be more hesitant to return if not given a reason he can readily accept. As one doctor said about a patient in Cartwright's more recent study: 'It offers her a regular and legitimate occasion to come and see me – gives some structure to her life and she feels someone is bothering' (1974: 18).

Cartwright and O'Brien provide in a more recent paper further examples of the way doctors control their interaction with patients. Here are two tape-recorded consultations where the doctor cuts short the interaction:

Doctor: Apart from these palpitations you're really very healthy, aren't you?

Patient: Yes, yes. Well, I mean, I have varicose veins you know?

Doctor: Oh yes.

Patient: And I've got a small ulcer, but it's dry now.

Doctor: Mm.

Patient: On my right leg I have a small ulcer.

Doctor: Yes, that's very good.

Patient: But it's drying up gradually. One day I think it's gone completely but it hasn't. It comes back. But . . .

Doctor: Now here's the letter to see about your eyes.

Doctor: Righto, well that's it. Very good.

Patient: One or two other aches and pains but I suppose that's old age, I suppose? A bit of rheumatism in my shoulder.

Doctor: O.K.

Patient: As I say, the thing is that, well this here, though I've had these pains I've felt so good in myself, you know . . .

Doctor: That's right.

Patient: I've had – well . . .

    Doctor: That's right, if you develop further trouble, come back.
                    Otherwise you don't need to, just keep going.

These are negative examples but doctors can also encourage patients
to bring up additional problems or symptoms. Cartwright and
O'Brien quote an example from the beginning of a consultation:

    Doctor: You've been spitting blood?
    Patient: Yes.
    Doctor: It comes when you cough?
    Patient: Yes, but not always.
    Doctor: Any other trouble?
    Patient: Well, when I've taken that medicine I've been
                    prescribed that all comes up with it.
    Doctor: Have you noticed any other trouble at all?
    Patient: In what way?
    Doctor: Any other complaints?
    Patient: No.
    Doctor: Any pains anywhere?
    Patient: No.
    Doctor: Any trouble with your joints or your hands?
    Patient: Only my feet.

and another from the end of a consultation.

    Doctor: Now was there anything else that you might like to talk
                    about?
    Patient: No, I don't think so thank you.
    Doctor: Jolly good, fine. How's your wife by the way? Is she
                    alright?
    Patient: I think that the fact that I've not been well has done
                    her the world of good.
    Doctor: Oh good. Busy looking after you.

If a doctor is not confident that a patient will carry out the agreed
treatment he can attempt to extend the scope of his intervention in
a patient's life in order to exert direct control and thus ensure
recommendations are carried out. For example, patients can be
brought into the hospital as in-patients or the doctor and other
health workers can visit them in the home. A similar strategy would

involve enlisting the support of relatives or others in the treatment and 'control' process. A further alternative is to try and by-pass the patient to a large extent. The need to obtain reliable information from him, for example, can be circumvented by using tests and laboratory techniques that are largely independent of anything but his minimal co-operation. The need to involve the patient in treatment can be similarly reduced by using long-acting or slow-releasing drugs.

This examination of the ways doctors try to control the doctor-patient relationship should not hide the fact that patients are by no means passive. The point is made in Cartwright's 1974 paper where one doctor felt that patients often actively try to create their own diagnoses. Describing one consultation this doctor felt it was:

> a 'success' because the reason for the consultation was openly recognized as being for marital problems and depression. Two others he felt did not have this insight. One had been told he had asthma by the hospital – but the doctor did not think this was an appropriate diagnosis. In his view she had shortness of breath brought on by anxiety or hysteria. A third woman also suffered from depression and a dry mouth. She reckoned the dry mouth was caused by the drugs she was taking for depression. In the doctor's view the dry mouth preceded the treatment for depression and was 'a classical Jewish symptom of depression'. But he did not explain this to her as he felt it would be tantamount to calling her a liar. In the doctor's view these three consultations illustrated the way in which patients create their own diagnoses. They also show how doctor and patient may agree or disagree with an interpretation or collude. (Cartwright, 1974: 8).

A second patient, but from a different doctor, provides an example of the mutual negotiation that can go on.

> 'The doctor classified three of this patient's six prescriptions as "his" and three as "mine". "He's one of the few who has barbiturates. He says it's the only thing that gives him sound sleep. Ephedrine tablets are very important to him. I think they are useless. When he first came I wasn't going to give him barbiturates. I tried others which were useless – then Mogadon.

> Then I accepted barbiturates. It's an amicable arrangement" '
> (Cartwright, 1974: 17).

As I pointed out at the beginning of this chapter the basic consideration in situations of bargaining and negotiation is where the power
lies. This is a complex issue which has been much under-researched.

In one sense the patient is often in a weak power position. After
all, his illness may literally make him powerless. More frequently,
however, he has some latitude when deciding whether to visit the
doctor. But according to Parson's (1951) view of the sick-role, if
the patient does seek help he places himself in an inferior position
and accepts the doctor's superior wisdom. Like Szasz and Hollen-
der's analysis I think this view of Parson's accords more with what
the doctor hopes will happen (the rational model again) than with
the facts. We have already seen that patients have their own ideas
and this is confirmed by my own experience that patients often visit
a doctor without having finally made up their mind that they will
accept help. The doctor's right to determine what is wrong and
what to do about it, in short his right to carry out what he sees as
his task, is one issue that the patient will be out to negotiate in the
consultation. Correct, or not, this view is a possibility. In any case
what is certain is that if patients do not give up their right to
determine their future then the doctor, if he wishes to persuade a
patient, will need to establish he is in authority. Ritual activity in
the consulting room and the hospital helps the doctor to do this.
Through various devices, such as making patients wait, the white
coat, the filling in of forms, and other administrative procedures,
the patient and doctor are marked as of different status. Factors
such as social class and the doctor's high prestige in society will be
of help to a doctor wishing to establish his authority, although
conversely, they may hinder a relationship of mutual participation,
such as attempts at psychotherapy, with working-class patients.

There are a number of studies that analyse the negotiation and
bargaining that can occur between doctors and patients and the
strategies that each use to advance their points of view. Goffman's
(1968) participant observation study in a mental hospital and Roth's
(1963) participant observation (he developed tuberculosis whilst a
Ph.D student) in a tuberculosis sanitorium provide sensitive descriptions of the way patients and hospital staff manipulate one another.
The work of Davis (1963) on children with polio, Duff and Hollings-

head (1968) in an American teaching hospital, and Sudnow (1967) and Glaser and Strauss (1963) on dying are also especially interesting.

The relative power of doctor and patient, and hence the ability of each to get their way in the consultation, depends on a number of variables. In my view the most basic determinants are the relative needs of the actors involved. In the language of economics it depends on each actor's preference or utility function – on their wants in the interaction. If the patient does not particularly need the doctor's help, for example, if he is simply going to the doctor in order to placate a relative or friend, he will not be in a situation where he has much to win or lose. Conversely if his wants are great, if he has to get a sickness certificate or is in terrible pain, he needs the doctor's help very much and is thus dependent on him.

A doctor's utility function can be examined in the same way. He may need to succeed with some patients very badly. One need may be financial and, in their relationship with rich or powerful patients, doctors have often been in a difficult situation. If they insist on an unwelcome treatment the patients may leave. As Freidson (1970: 305–16) points out, the institutional arrangements through which doctors and patients meet will influence the doctor's power to carry out his wishes regardless of a patient's status. It is not surprising, therefore, that doctors in countries like the USA, where they are dependent for their income on the patient returning to them, have sought to limit the number of doctors and therefore improve their competitive position. A reduction of reliance on the patient is one of the gains that a doctor derives from the National Health Service, where he is paid in effect adequately regardless of the patient's views.

However, the rewards in a situation are not only financial. Doctors may wish to succeed for other reasons, for example, they may want to help patients in order to improve their own self-esteem or because they care for others. The point, for the purpose of this discussion, is that the doctor's power will be reduced the more his utility function depends on the patient, for example, a doctor who 'cares' not only that the patient does not come back but that he actually stays well and successfully carries out his various roles, will be much more dependent on his patients than one who does not. It is conceivable that a reward system for doctors could be designed (based on financial or other incentives) so that doctors gained from 'caring' in this way. Such a system would very much increase the power position of patients.

From the discussion so far it must be clear that patients often tend to be in a much weaker position than doctors. Their power is largely negative (they can refuse drugs or give up treatment or can simply sit it out in the doctor's surgery by bothering him until something happens) and depends very much on the doctor's utility function. Furthermore, patients are often likely to need the doctor's help badly. Also, for the patient, the patient role is more all-embracing (his 'illness' may affect all his other roles) whereas for the doctor his role is only one of several others he plays. Finally, whereas the patient is often dependent on one doctor, as in most systems there is a shortage of doctors or an agreement between doctors that shopping around is bad, the doctor has the opportunity of seeking rewards from other patients. For all these reasons the distribution of power in doctor-patient relationships, unless controlled by compensatory institutional arrangements, is potentially highly skewed.

Goffman (1969: 107–182) provided a model of social relationships which he termed strategic interaction and which may help us to think further about the relations that develop between doctors and patients. I shall briefly present it because I think it may help to provide a more useful way of looking at relationships than does the present alternative – the 'rational' or 'normatively biased' model. Relationships between doctors and patients, I suggest, are likely to be very frustrating for both parties if they assume the other is going to act in a 'sensible' manner.

Goffman's model is appropriate to a situation of 'mutual impingement', that is, where the actors involved have something to win or lose by interacting with one another (as we have seen this assumption may be unwarranted in the case of some doctors and some patients). Goffman conceives of a set of interactions (that is, consultations) *as* a game (he does not mean they *are* a game) in which individuals try to maximize rewards (he is therefore following the assumptions of exchange theorists who assess the costs and benefits to be derived from interaction). Individuals maximise rewards by making moves – that is acting in some purposive way. Before, and as they move, however, each player (an actor in the game) assesses the situation in various ways. The emphasis is on mutual assessment.

Each player attempts to assess the other player's *moves*, trying to find out what decisions he has taken and what plans he has for the game (why the patient has come, why the doctor does not get up when the patient enters the room, etc.). They each attempt to assess the *operational code* that the other is using, that is, the orientation towards the game that a player has and his preference pattern or utility function. This has been discussed earlier. What aims and goals does each player have and how does he order them in terms of possibilities? What is he willing to give up? What constraints are imposed on him by his values and norms (for example, religious or ideological or professional beliefs)? Another assessment can be made of each player's *style of play*; this is the particular way he presents himself in the situation. As I noted in an earlier chapter social class is likely to influence such styles of communication. Then there is the need to assess each other's *resolve* – how far is the individual willing to go in the game? What is he willing to put up with or lose? For how long will he persevere? Is he sincere?

Players will also wish to know each other's *information state* – what does each think the other knows about his own situation? Then there are the *resources* each has to help them play; records of past games (for example, patient records), techniques for discovery (for example, laboratory tests), and so on. And most important, in Goffman's view (1969: 121), there is the assessment of *gameworthiness* – the ability of an individual to assess all possible consequences of action and also his ability to act in the manner required by his judgement of the situation. Finally, there is the assessment of *integrity*, 'that is the strength of their propensity to remain loyal to [each other's] agreed interests once they have agreed to play . . . and not to instigate courses of action on behalf of [some other] interests, usually their own' (1969: 123).

These assessments are the elements of the situation that each player tries to '*dope-out*' in order to embark on courses of action. Actual moves will be made according to those assessments and according to the *position* in the game the players have arrived at (the history of the relationship). Moves and positions may be *viable* or *nonviable* depending on how far they sacrifice the game should they prove unsuccessful. At a certain point there is no turning back.

Goffman concentrates on the way in which assessments are made. Assessments are made by interpreting *expressions given off* by the other actor as well as by *communication transmitted*. In other words there are verbal and non-verbal elements of communication. Both may be intentional and a major concern of the actors involved will be to try and discriminate their *'correctness'*, whether or not they accord with the facts or are being created to make an impression. A great deal of the assessment that takes place will concern the *credibility* of information received. Is what the doctor says true? Is he really trying to help?

No study that I know has yet analysed doctor-patient relationships in terms of strategic interaction but I would regard it as a highly relevant perspective for doctors. What is the patient's *operational code?* Does the doctor understand the patient's *style of play?* How much *resolve* does a patient have? What *moves* has he made? What are his *resources* and his *information state?*

Certainly, whether or not doctors make these kinds of assessments, implicitly or explicitly, or find them useful, patients do. For example, in my own interviewing of psychiatric patients and in observation of general practice, I have been struck with the way patients are very sensitive to the *expressions given off* by doctors. Whether or not the phone rings in the consultation, the amount of time the doctor spends with a patient, the kinds of questions that are asked, all these are assessed by patients and not necessarily in the ways one might expect. Different patients, for example, interpreted long consultations as indicating they really were 'mad' whereas actually the psychiatrist was simply concerned to carry out a thorough interview. Other aspects of the consultation and of treatment, as well as the doctor's behaviour, were given all sorts of interpretation by patients (Tuckett, forthcoming). Given the fact that doctors and patients often come from very different backgrounds and often have opposing ideas about what consultations are about there can be many false assessments of operational codes, moves, resolve and the like. This often leads to frustration for doctors and patients. Thinking of what is happening in terms of strategic interaction, or some other similar model, may help to create a less frustrating situation.

The drug 'doctor'

The factors underlying the doctor-patient interaction have become all the more significant in recent years with the increased recognition that the actual relationship is itself a highly effective therapy. The importance of doctor-patient relationships is illustrated by a number of studies. For example, Egbert *et al's* (1964) study showing how pre-operative encouragement and instruction of patients can dramatically improve treatment efficacy has been quoted, so has Friedman *et al's* (1963) attempt to intervene to help the parents of dying children to cope with their loss. Other studies can be considered. Skipper and Leonard (1968) showed how a particular sort of social interaction with hospital personnel, providing information and emotional support, can reduce a mother's experience of stress and that this in turn will have profound indirect effects on the child's social, psychological, and even physiological responses to hospitalisation and recovery. Zola's (1963) suggestion, that failure to recognise the 'non-medical' element in help-seeking leads to drop out of treatment, may be put alongside Michael Balint's (1957) work arguing that harm is done to the patient through treating physical symptoms alone without recognising they are part of a wider presenting picture.

Furthermore, work with the placebo response underlines the significance of the doctor-patient interaction as a powerful therapeutic agent. Beecher (1955; 1961) in reviews of this literature suggests, for example, that up to one-third of the success of any drug or procedure may be attributable to placebo, that is to the patient's belief that something is being done for him.

Question

1. (a) Describe two ways in which doctors may seek to control the doctor-patient relationship.

(5 marks)

(b) Describe the main features of Goffman's model of 'strategic interaction'.

(10 marks)

(c) Why does the quality of the doctor-patient relationship matter?

(5 marks)

87 Edward Evans-Pritchard: Death and Illness as a Result of Witchcraft and Sorcery: A Primitive Paradigm of Health

The scientific, machine model or paradigm of health-illness described in the next reading will be regarded as familiar if not, indeed, as normal by most readers. Another paradigm of health is the holistic. In this case, the individual's health is regarded as the outcome of his/her relationship (active as well as passive) with the total environment – physical and mental. I have selected here an approach to death and illness which is as different as possible from the Western, scientific model.

Death and sickness are regarded by the Azande as the result of witchcraft and sorcery. Evans-Pritchard only deals with witchcraft in any detail here. Witchcraft, unlike sorcery, is regarded as an in-born ability to generate misfortune (including death and sickness) to others. Sorcery is an 'acquired skill'. Whereas disease is generally regarded as a materialistic phenomenon in the West, for the Azande it is produced psychically and spiritually.

Sheer curiosity compels the question 'is the Zande attitude to death-disease purely an illusion?' Dr Jonathan Miller in a television programme on the Azande virtually concluded that it is. But are there not illusionary elements in the scientific 'machine model' of medicine? Even dangerously illusionary elements? In fact, the question of medical effectiveness is not a sociological one. A sociologist or, in this case, an anthropologist is concerned first, to establish the framework of belief and explanation adopted by members of a given culture and, secondly, to explain it. One explanation of the Zande 'paradigm' of death-disease is, of course, their own. Evans-Pritchard almost seems to imply that he himself accepts it in the opening sentence of his account of the witchcraft he 'saw': 'I have only once seen witchcraft on its path . . .' This reminds us that in symbolic interactionist terms 'that which is defined as real becomes real in its consequences' (though cautiously one is inclined to qualify – at least, it becomes real to some extent and for those involved in the interaction).

Other explanations of the Zande paradigm are also possible besides the internal one. Evans-Pritchard himself provides the data for a materialistic explanation here although he does not develop it. It is notable that the beneficiaries of witchcraft are the wealthy and powerful. By successfully accusing witches they acquire forfeits. The system therefore works in accordance with their interests. From this point of view (broadly, neo-Marxist) witchcraft can be regarded as a major aspect of the dominant ideology and belief-system. André Singer and Brian V. Street have pursued such an explanation in *Zande Themes* (Basil

Blackwell, Oxford, 1972). As they imply, there is no need to suggest a conspiracy on the part of the more powerful Zande – both dominators and dominated may genuinely believe in the ideology of domination.

Reading 87 From Edward Evans-Pritchard, *Witchcraft, Oracles and Magic Among the Azande* (Oxford, Clarendon Press, 1937), pp. 21–2, 23–6, 32–4.

Azande believe that some people are witches and can injure them in virtue of an inherent quality. A witch performs no rite, utters no spell, and possesses no medicines. An act of witchcraft is a psychic act. They believe also that sorcerers may do them ill by performing magic rites with bad medicines. Azande distinguish clearly between witches and sorcerers. Against both they employ diviners, oracles, and medicines. The relations between these beliefs and rites are the subject of this book.

I describe witchcraft first because it is an indispensable background to the other beliefs. When Azande consult oracles they consult them mainly about witches. When they employ diviners it is for the same purpose. Their leechcraft and closed associations are directed against the same foe.

I had no difficulty in discovering what Azande think about witchcraft, nor in observing what they do to combat it. These ideas and actions are on the surface of their life and are accessible to any one who lives for a few weeks in their homesteads. Every Zande is an authority on witchcraft. There is no need to consult specialists. There is not even need to question Azande about it, for information flows freely from recurrent situations in their social life, and one has only to watch and listen. *Mangu*, witchcraft, was one of the first words I heard in Zandeland, and I heard it uttered day by day throughout the months.

Azande believe that witchcraft is a substance in the bodies of witches, a belief which is found among many people in Central and West Africa. Zandeland is the north-eastern limit of its distribution. It is difficult to say with what organ Azande associate witchcraft. I have never seen human witchcraft-substance, but it has been described to me as an oval blackish swelling or bag in which various small objects are sometimes found. When Azande describe its shape they often point to the elbow of their bent arm, and when they describe its location they point to just beneath the xiphoid cartilage which is said to 'cover witchcraft-substance' . . .

A witch shows no certain external symptoms of his condition though people say:

'One knows a witch by his red eyes. When one sees such a man one says he is a witch and this is true also of a woman with red eyes. But at present what happens is this: if they consult the poison oracle about a man and the oracle says that he is a witch the kinsmen of the sick man give him a fowl's wing that he may blow water on it. That man is a witch.'

It is also said that if maggots come out of the apertures of a dead man's body before burial it is a sign that he was a witch.

Witchcraft is not only a physical trait but is also inherited. It is transmitted by unilinear descent from parent to child. The sons of a male witch are all witches but his daughters are not, while the daughters of a female witch are all witches but her sons are not. Mgr. Lagae quotes a Zande text:

'If a man has witchcraft-substance in his belly and begets a male child, this child also has witchcraft-substance because his father was a witch. It is the same with women. If a woman has witchcraft-substance in her belly and gives birth to a female child, the child also has witchcraft-substance because her mother was a witch. Thus witchcraft does not trouble a person born free from it by entering into him.'

Biological transmission of witchcraft from one parent to all children of the same sex is complementary to Zande opinions about procreation and to their eschatological beliefs. Conception is thought to be due to a unison of psychical properties in man and woman. When the soul of the man is stronger a boy will be born; when the soul of the woman is stronger a girl will be born. Thus a child partakes of the psychical qualities of both parents, though a girl is thought to partake more of the soul of her mother and a boy of the soul of his father. Nevertheless in certain respects a child takes after one or other parent according to sex, namely, in the inheritance of sexual characters, of a body-soul, and of witchcraft-substance. There is a vague belief, hardly precise enough to be described as a doctrine, that man possesses two souls, a body-soul and a spirit-soul. At death the body-soul becomes a totem animal of the clan while its fellow soul becomes a ghost and leads a shadowy existence at the heads of streams. Many people say that the body-soul of a man becomes the totem animal of his father's clan while the body-soul of a woman becomes the totem animal of her mother's clan.

At first sight it seems strange to find a mode of matrilineal transmission in a society which is characterised by its strong patrilineal bias, but witchcraft like the body-soul is part of the body and might be expected to accompany inheritance of male or female characters from father or mother.

To our minds it appears evident that if a man is proven a witch the whole of his clan are *ipso facto* witches, since the Zande clan is a group of persons related biologically to one another through the male line. Azande see the sense of this argument but they do not accept its conclusions, and it would involve the whole notion of witchcraft in contradiction were they to do so. In practice they regard only close paternal kinsmen of a known witch as witches. It is only in theory that they extend the imputation to all a witch's clansmen. If in the eyes of the world payment for homicide by witchcraft stamps the kin of a guilty man as witches, a post-mortem in which no witchcraft-substance is discovered in a man clears his paternal kin of suspicion. Here again we might reason that if a man be found by post-mortem immune from witchcraft-substance all his clan must also be immune, but Azande do not act as though they were of this opinion.

Further elaborations of belief free Azande from having to admit what appear to us to be the logical consequences of beliefs in biological transmission of witchcraft. If a man is proven a witch beyond all doubt his kin, to establish their innocence, may use the very biological principles which would seem to involve them in disrepute. They admit that the man is a witch but deny that he is a member of their clan. They say he was a bastard, for among Azande a man is always of the clan of his *genitor* and not of his *pater*, and I was told that they may compel his mother if she is still alive to say who was her lover, beating her and asking her, 'What do you mean by going to the bush to get witchcraft in adultery?' More often they simply make the declaration that the witch must have been a bastard since they have no witchcraft in their bodies and that he could not therefore be one of their kinsmen, and they may support this contention by quoting cases where members of their kin have been shown by autopsy to have been free from witchcraft. It is unlikely that other people will accept this plea, but they are not asked either to accept it or reject it.

Also Zande doctrine includes the notion that even if a man is the son of a witch and has witchcraft-substance in his body he may not use it. It may remain inoperative, 'cool' as the Azande say, throughout his lifetime, and a man can hardly be classed as a witch if his witchcraft never functions. In point of fact, therefore, Azande generally regard witchcraft as an individual trait and it is treated as such in spite of its assocation with kinship. At the same time certain clans, especially the Abakunde and the Avundua clans, had a reputation for witchcraft in the reign of King Gbudwe. In Gangura's province this reputation clung to the Aböka and Abanzuma clans. No one thinks any worse of a man if he is a member of one of these clans.

Azande do not perceive the contradiction as we perceive it because they have no theoretical interest in the subject, and those situations in which they express their beliefs in witchcraft do not force the problem upon them. A man never asks the oracles, which alone are capable of disclosing the location of witchcraft-substance in the living, whether a certain man is a witch. He asks whether at the moment this man is bewitching him. One attempts to discover whether a man is bewitching some one in particular circumstances and not whether he is born a witch. If the oracles say that a certain man is injuring you at the moment you then know that he is a witch, whereas if they say that at the moment he is not injuring you you do not know whether he is a witch or not and have no interest to inquire into the matter. If he is a witch it is of no significance to you so long as you are not his victim. A Zande is interested in witchcraft only as an agent on definite occasions and in relation to his own interests, and not as a permanent condition of individuals. When he is sick he does not normally say: 'Now let us consider who are well-known witches of the neighbourhood and place their names before the poison oracle.' He does not consider the question in this light but asks himself who among his neighbours have grudges against him and then seeks to know from the poison oracle whether one of them is on this particular occasion bewitching him. Azande are interested solely in the dynamics of witchcraft in particular situations.

Lesser misfortunes are soon forgotten and those who caused them are looked upon by the sufferer and his kin as having bewitched some one on this occasion rather than as confirmed witches, for only persons who are constantly exposed by the oracles as responsible for sickness or loss are regarded as confirmed witches, and in the old days it was only when a witch had killed some one that he became a marked man in the community . . .

I have never known a case in which a man has been bewitched by a kinswoman or in which a woman has been bewitched by a kinsman. Moreover, I have heard of only one case in which a man was bewitched by a kinsman. A kinsman may do a man wrong in other ways but he would not bewitch him. It is evident that a sick man would not care to ask the oracles about his brothers and paternal cousins, because if the poison oracle declared them to have bewitched him, by the same declaration he would himself be a witch since witchcraft is inherited in the male line.

Members of the princely class, the Avongara, are not accused of witchcraft, for if a man were to say that the oracles had declared the son of a prince to have bewitched him, he would be asserting that the king and princes were also witches. However much a prince may detest members of his lineage he never allows them to be brought in disrepute by a commoner. Hence, although Azande will tell one privately that they believe some members of the noble class may be witches, they seldom consult the oracles about them, so that they are not accused of witchcraft. In the past they never consulted the oracles about them. There is an established fiction that Avongara are not witches, and it is maintained by the overwhelming power and prestige of the ruling princes.

Governors of provinces, deputies of districts, men of the court, leaders of military companies, and other commoners of position and wealth are not likely to be accused of witchcraft unless by a prince himself on account of his own hunting or on account of the death of some equally influential commoner. Generally lesser people do not dare to consult the oracles about influential persons because their lives would be a misery if they insulted the most important men in their neighbourhood. Therefore Bage, the chief's deputy in the settlement where I resided, could tell me that never in his life had he been accused of witchcraft and could challenge a crowd of listeners to instance a single occasion when this had happened to him. The rich and powerful are immune as a rule from accusations of witchcraft because no one consults the oracles to their names and therefore the oracles cannot give a verdict against them. It is only when the poison oracle has a name placed before it frequently that sooner or later it is sure to kill a fowl to the name. So we may say that the incidence of witchcraft in a Zande community falls equally upon both sexes in the commoner class while nobles are entirely, and powerful commoners largely, immune from accusations. All children are normally free from suspicion.

The relations of ruling princes to witchcraft are peculiar. Though immune from accusations they believe in witches as firmly as other people, and they constantly consult the poison oracle to find out who is bewitching them. They especially consult it about their wives. A prince's oracle is also the final authority which decides on all witchcraft cases involving homicide, and in the past it was also used to protect his subjects from witchcraft during warfare. When a lesser noble dies his death is attributed to a witch and is avenged in the same way as deaths of commoners, but the death of a king or ruling prince is not so avenged and is generally attributed to sorcery or cats.

While witchcraft itself is part of the human organism its action is psychic. What Azande call *mbisimo mangu*, the soul of witchcraft, is a concept that bridges over the distance between the person of the witch and the person of his victim. Some such explanation is necessary to account for the fact that a witch was in his hut at the time when he is supposed to have injured some one. The soul of witchcraft may leave its corporeal home at any time during the day or night, but Azande generally think of a witch sending his soul on errands by night when his victim is asleep. It sails through the air emitting a bright light. During the daytime this light can only be seen by witches, and by witchdoctors when they are primed with medicines, but any one may have the rare misfortune to observe it at night. Azande say that the light of witchcraft is like the gleam of fire-fly beetles, only it is ever so much larger and brighter than they. These beetles are in no way associated with witchcraft on account of their phosphorescence. Mgr. Lagae records a Zande text which runs:

'Those who see witchcraft on its way to injure some one at night say that when witchcraft moves along it shines just like flame. It shines a little and then goes out again.'

Azande say that a man may see witchcraft as it goes to rest on branches for 'Witchcraft is like fire, it lights a light'. If a man sees the light of witchcraft he picks up a piece of charcoal and throws it under his bed so that he may not suffer misfortune from the sight.

I have only once seen witchcraft on its path. I had been sitting late in my hut writing notes. About midnight, before retiring, I took a spear and went for my usual nocturnal stroll. I was walking in the garden at the back of my hut, amongst banana trees, when I noticed a bright light passing at the back of my servants' huts towards the homestead of a man called Tupoi. As this seemed worth investigation I followed its passage until a grass screen obscured the view. I ran quickly through my hut to the other side in order to see where the light was going to, but did not regain sight of it. I knew that only one man, a member of my household, had a lamp that might have given off so bright a light, but next morning he told me that he had neither been out late at night nor had he used his lamp. There did not lack ready informants to tell me that what I had seen was witchcraft. Shortly afterwards, on the same morning, an old relative of Tupoi and an inmate of his homestead died. This event fully explained the light I had seen. I never discovered its real origin, which was possibly a handful of grass lit by some one on his way to defecate, but the coincidence of the direction along which the light moved and the subsequent death accorded well with Zande ideas.

This light is not the witch in person stalking his prey but is an emanation from his body. On this point Zande opinion is quite decided. The witch is on his bed, but he has dispatched the soul of his witchcraft to remove the psychical part of his victim's organs, his *mbisimo pasio*, the soul of his flesh, which he and his fellow witches will devour. The whole act of vampirism is an incorporeal one: the soul of witchcraft removes the soul of the organ. I have not been able to obtain a precise explanation of what is meant by the soul of witchcraft and the soul of an organ. Azande know that people are killed in this way, but only a witch himself could give an exact account of what happens in the process. One man described an attack by witches as follows:

'Witches arise and beat their drum of witchcraft. The membrane of this drum is human skin. They stretch human skin across it so that they can sound their call on it to summon the members of their order. Their drum call is "human flesh, human flesh, human flesh".'

'They go to bewitch that man whose "condition" is bad.
That witch who hates him goes with a company of witches to
his dwelling-place. They dance around his hut. That witch who
hates him opens his door and in a witchcraft-struggle carries
him off his bed and throws him outside. All the witches collect
around him and worry him almost to death. When each witch
has seized part of his flesh they rise and return to their meeting-
place.

'They take a small witchcraft-pot and begin to cook the flesh
of this man in it. They place the lumps of flesh around the
edge of the pot. They tell one of their company to push his
lump so that it will fall into the pot. All of them act in this
manner, each pushing his portion so that it falls into the pot.
But that witch who was responsible for calling the assembly
cheats with his portion of flesh and hides it. The other witches
will die on account of the death of the man whose flesh they
have taken, for they all eat of his flesh. But that witch who was
responsible for calling the assembly cheats with his portion of
flesh. But that witch who summoned the assembly hides his
portion.

'The man falls sick and is sick nigh unto death and his
relatives consult the oracles about his welfare. The oracles
disclose to them the name of the man who called the assembly.
They consult the poison oracles and it kills a fowl to his name.
They take the wing of the fowl and give it to this witch and
say to him, "So-and-so, you are killing that man." He replies:
"Well, if it is I who am killing that man he will recover from
my witchcraft." He takes a draught of water and blows it out
and speaks thus: "I have blown water on the fowl's wing."

'When darkness falls he rises again as a witch and as a witch
(i.e. incorporeally) takes the flesh of this man and as a witch
returns it and places it on his body. He refrained from eating
human flesh in the company of witches and cheated the other
witches lest he should be slain in vengeance for the man's
death. He did this in order to take the flesh back again so that
when the man died and his relatives made magic the medicine
would come and merely look at him without striking him. It
would see that he had not eaten human flesh and would pass
him by to kill those other witches who ate the flesh of man.

'Therefore Azande speak thus about the matter: A man who

is a great witch is not likely to die on account of the deaths of men because he does not bewitch people to eat their flesh but bewitches a man to hide his flesh. It is for this reason that he continues to live because if he ate human flesh it would not be long before he died from magic of vengeance made on account of the deaths of men.'

Azande use the same word in describing the psychical parts of witchcraft-substance and other organs as they use for what we call the soul of a man. Anything the action of which is not subject to the sense may likewise be explained by the existence of a soul. Medicines act by means of their soul, an explanation which covers the void between a magical rite and the achievement of its purpose. The poison oracle also has a soul, which accounts for its power to see what a man cannot see.

The action of witchcraft is therefore not subject to the ordinary conditions which limit most objects of daily use, but its activity is thought to be limited to some extent by conditions of space. Witchcraft does not strike a man at a great distance, but only injures people in the vicinity. If a man leaves the district in which he is living when attacked by witchcraft it will not follow him far. Witchcraft needs, moreover, conscious direction. The witch cannot send out his witchcraft and leave it to find its victim for itself, but he must define its objective and determine its route. Hence a sick man can often elude its further ravages by withdrawing to the shelter of a grass hut in the bush unknown to all but his wife and children. The witch will dispatch his witchcraft after his victim and it will search his homestead in vain and return to its owner.

Likewise, a man will leave a homestead before dawn in order to escape witchcraft, because then witches are asleep and will not observe his departure. When they become aware that he has left he will already be out of range of their witchcraft. If, on the other hand, they see him starting they may bewitch him and some misfortune will befall him on his journey or after his return home. It is because witchcraft is believed to act only at a short range that if a wife falls sick on a visit to her parents' home they search for the responsible witch there and not at her husband's home, and if she dies in her parents' home her husband may hold them responsible because they have not protected her by consulting the oracles about her welfare.

The farther removed a man's homestead from his neighbours the safer he is from witchcraft. The wide extent of bush and cultivations that intervene between one Zande homestead and the next was remarked by the earliest travellers and has often puzzled visitors to Zanderland. When Azande of the Anglo-Egyptian Sudan were compelled to live in roadside settlements they did so with profound misgivings, and many fled to the Belgian Congo rather than face close contact with their neighbours. Azande say that their dislike of living in close proximity to others is partly due to a desire to place a stretch of country between their wives and possible lovers and partly to their belief that a witch can injure the more severely the nearer he is to his victim.

Question
1. (a) Describe the Azande 'paradigm' of misfortune (including ill-health).

(7 marks)

(b) Attempt to explain sociologically the Azande 'paradigm' of misfortune.

(8 marks)

88 Samuel Osherson and Lorna Amara Singham: The Influence of the Machine Metaphor in Contemporary Medicine as Exemplified by the Management of Death

The following is a brief extract from a contribution to Elliot Mishler, ed., *Social Contexts of Health, Illness and Patient Care*. In the first section of the book, Mishler himself describes the biomedical model of medicine predominant in Western society. He criticises health professionals for tending to regard this model as the only adequate representation of health and disease rather than as one of several models each of which, whatever its merits, reflects the culture which generated it. Essentially, the biomedical model reflects the dominance of the scientific paradigm (or 'way of looking at a problem') in Western culture. Positivistic science concentrates on cause and effect or, more broadly, the relationship between variables. In medicine this orientation takes the form of a concern with disease (effect) and its causes; for example, germs. The metaphor of the body as a machine fits in very well with the scientific way of approaching health-disease. When the body is seen as a system of inter-related parts, medicine can be conveniently reduced to a kind of machine-maintenance, and problems of the spirit and mind forgotten. Osherson and Amara Singham point out the conse-quences of this approach to the way death is dealt with in modern Western medical establishments. Death is explained and accepted as the breakdown of the 'body-machine' and human and spiritual issues – beyond the scope of professional medicine – tend to become marginalised. The authors usefully refer to other cultural approaches to death which reflect not only a different perspective on health-disease, but on the meaning of life.

Students might well be struck by the similarity of the machine model in medicine and the organic model used in functionalist sociology. Indeed, the machine model itself (though it is perhaps the crudest of all societal models) has sometimes been employed by sociologists. Such models further illustrate the dominance of the scientific paradigm within Western culture. Just as this model has been challenged in medicine, mechanistic models have been attacked within sociology from both phenom-enological and Marxist perspectives and, indeed, combinations of both.

Reading 88 From Samuel Osherson and Lorna Amara Singham, 'The Machine Metaphor in Medicine' in Elliot G. Mishler *ed.*, *Social Contexts of Health, Illness and Patient Care* (Cambridge University Press), 1981, 238–45.

In this section we shall discuss the management of death as an exemplar of the influence of the mechanical metaphor on contem-porary medical treatment. We need first to examine more closely the attributes of a machine organised into a model of the human body. For heuristic purposes we can conceive of three dimensions of a machine metaphor:

1. Machines are reducible to their component parts. They are capable of being understood entirely by analysis into their discrete subsystems or component parts. The whole is *not* more than the sum of its parts.
2. Machines are without emotion. As expressions of the interaction

of observable, objective physical forces, machines do not feel. Machines can be understood entirely from the outside, without reference to inner states (affect, mood, etc.).

3. Machines are instrumental (means, not ends in themselves) and non-purposive, and as such are not guided by considerations of value. A machine technology is one that emphasises efficiency and utility over (or in the absence of) purpose. Machines are neutral in relation to ends; machines 'do' and their value resides in the uses to which they are put by their operator.

How might this larger cultural model be expressed in medicine? When the body is being compared to a machine, do these three dimensions help us understand some of the attributes being applied to the body? Here is one possible description of a machine metaphor of the human body in terms of the three dimensions discussed:

1. *A mind-body split.* Because the body can be reduced to component parts, there is no more to the 'whole' and we can exclude considerations of 'spirit' and psyche. This is the central point of Descartes' distinction between the human body and mind: reason or thought was a separate faculty independent of the machinelike body. This position was reinforced by the decline of the 'vitalist' argument of the nineteenth century, in which little evidence was found to support the view of a 'life force' characterising the human organism. In modern times we see this tendency to exclude considerations of spirit from those of the body in the distinction between psychological and physical experience. The belief here would be that (psychosomatic medicine to the contrary) psyche and soma are easily separable, and that in dealing with the latter we need not deal with the former.

2. *An exclusion of emotion.* Machines, as merely the expression of the interaction of observable physical forces, do not feel. Similarly, the human body as 'a device for converting one form of energy into the one best suited to do the work at hand' or 'a physiochemical machine' can be seen as without affect. Emotion is not a part of mechanical systems composed of objectively observable, physical causes.

3. *Inattention to considerations of value.* Efficiency (what 'can' be done, how quickly, cleanly) is to be emphasised over consider-

ations of meaning and purpose (what 'should' be, which of several choices has salient meaning for the person).

To summarise, we can say that the dimensions of the metaphor of 'the body as machine' are the body as (1) spirit-free, (2) affect-free, and (3) value-free.

The question now becomes: How is this model of the body expressed in individual cases, on the level of specific doctors and patients? What is the impact of this model in treatment and practice? Because people cannot report directly their 'silent assumptions' derived from the machine metaphor, we are drawing on two experiences documented by a great deal of 'public', published material open to scrutiny. The management of death, the second of these, like childbirth, the first, offers a special advantage as a case example: Medical practices are in the process of evolution as our society attempts to redefine conceptions of both birth and death. In change, the underlying assumptions organising medical treatment and procedures are more apparent than they are in the static treatment of illnesses and application of procedures not so much open to recent questions. Note, too, that we have picked *extreme examples* from observational studies to illustrate our point.

Over the past five centuries there have been profound changes in Western attitudes towards death. Through the Middle Ages, death was seen as a nonmedical affair, with little attention paid to the body and far more to the individual experience of the dying person. Aires quotes *Don Quixote* to indicate the attentiveness of the doctor to 'the soul's health,' or what we might call psychological issues attendant to the end of life:

A physician was sent for, who, after feeling his pulse took a rather gloomy view of the case, and told him that he should provide for his soul's health, as that of his body was in a dangerous condition.

Aires also notes the intensely *personal* nature of death in earlier historical periods:

In the late Middle Ages . . . and the Renaissance, a man insisted upon participating in his own death because he saw in it an exceptional moment – a moment which gave his own individuality its definitive form . . .

681

After the Renaissance, however, the personal, individual experience of death gave way – as Illich shows – to a conception of death as a natural phenomenon, susceptible to the intervention and control that characterised humanity's evolving relation to the natural world. As the mechanistic world view of the West developed through the late Middle Ages and Renaissance, the machine metaphor allowed resolution of a problem in people's relation to death: How was one to understand and depersonalise the fact of death? In regard to the management of death, then, the machine metaphor of the body filled a vacuum in the post-Renaissance understanding of the world. The transformation of death from a psychological-religious event into a mechanical problem of bodily function allowed its depersonalisation and removed it from the arena of separate individual experience, blamable on personal failure or supernatural causation. As Illich comments, 'the new image of death helped to reduce the human body to an object.' In this postmedieval project of conquering death, medicine played a major role: Attention was directed to the body and – as with so many aspects of nature – it became a machine, susceptible to repair and intervention.

This shift in attention from the death of the person to the death of the body and the transformation of the human body into 'an object' has continued in modern medical approaches to the management of death. Before exploring the operation of a machine metaphor in this area, let us draw on a number of observational studies to describe traditional medical management of the dying.

Glaser and Strauss discuss 'closed awareness' situations in some hospitals where staff collude in hiding awareness of dying from the patient. The patient's mind – kept separate, then, from the event being experienced – is supposed to be directed to 'safe topics.' Glaser and Strauss quote the following conversation:

FIRST NURSE: A stern face, you don't have to communicate very much verbally, you put things short and formal . . . Yes, very much the nurse.

SECOND NURSE: Be tender but don't . . .

FIRST NURSE: Sort of distant, sort of sweet.

SECOND NURSE: Talk about everything but the condition of the patient.

FIRST NURSE: And if you do communicate with them, when you are not too much the nurse, you could

> talk about all kinds of other things; you
> know, carefully circling the question of
> death.

In addition to this deemphasis of the patient's awareness, we often find the attention of medical people to procedures and machinery in the management of death. There is as well the emphasis of mechanical functions in treatment of dying patients. Thus, during 'death watch,' Sudnow has noted that nurses' 'major items of interest became [the patient's] number of . . . heartbeats and the changing condition of his eyes.' Sudnow also describes the 'attention to parts' and the emphasis on 'getting practice' in the emergency ward. The former behaviour refers to the attention of specialists in specific anatomical areas to the posted lists of terminally ill patients, in the hope of obtaining such organs through donation after death. The concern with 'getting practice' refers to performing difficult treatments or mock surgical procedures on patients DOA (dead on arrival) so as to learn a technique better.

Finally, Glaser and Strauss describe what they found to be a consistent emphasis by hospital personnel on 'an acceptable style of dying.' This style emphasised control and avoided outbursts of emotion, despair, or noise. Composure, cheerfulness, and cooperation are the major components of the 'acceptable' style most emphasised. Other behaviour is seen as inappropriate:

> Miss Jones mentioned that Mr. James was giving a great deal of trouble today. They had been trying everything on him, and nothing worked. He was refusing all kinds of things, such as medication, pills, and food, and they were having trouble getting him to take his temperature. They had tried to be persuasive and now there was a nurse who was trying just the opposite. Miss Jones giggled and said it wasn't getting her anywhere either . . . To this the other nurse said, 'Tough customer, isn't he?' She looked stolid and said, 'He just wants to be ornery.' Then added, 'He's been ornery all day.'
>
> . . . Miss Smith came into the nursing station saying, 'I'm sick of insight.' According to her, this woman patient gets scared and there's nothing you can do, and then she gets more scared . . . At the staff meeting, Miss Smith said that this lady gags more and belches, and the nurse finally decided there was no physical reason for this. The nurse put on a big dramatic

act as she said this because she was in a big stew about it. She had spoken to the patient and told her it was just doing her harm and would hurt her more. Later I heard this lady belching pretty loudly, and the nurses just looked at each other.

To summarise, we can in general describe modern medical management of death in terms of the 'closed awareness' of the patient, an attention to mechanical functions on the part of the doctor, and an emphasis on an 'acceptable' way of dying. How do these dimensions of the medical management of death reflect a machine metaphor of the body? Let us consider each of our three dimensions of this metaphor, as discussed above: the body as spirit-free, value-free, and affect-free.

1 The mind-body split

The essence of a 'closed-awareness' situation in the management of death is that the patient's attention is directed away from what is happening to his or her body. The body is perceived in a machine metaphor as separate from psychological considerations ('spirit'), and thus death is approached as primarily a physical event, with specific attention to issues of bodily mechanism. Consideration of the person's attitude toward death or the problem of coming to terms with death are excluded. This can be seen in Glaser and Strauss' report on one doctor's manner of handling reports of carcinomas to his patients: The 'doctor walks into the patient's room, faces him, says "It's malignant," walks out.' In general we can ask whether instead of attention to 'the soul's health,' or providing care that allows for integration of the patient's experience, the emphasis today is on body mechanism and technological intervention in the process. And Cassell claims that in our society, 'death is a technical matter, a failure of technology in rescuing the body from a threat to its functioning and integrity.' A resulting problem is a *fragmentation of experience*, in which the individual's awareness is split off, and attention is directed away from what is happening to his or her body.

2 The body as value-free

We noted the emphasis on mechanical function and machinery in the management of death. We can see this as related to the emphasis on efficiency and utility in the machine metaphor of the body. Thus the ability exists – through a variety of mechanical and chemical interventions – to extend the functioning of the human body. But have considerations of what medicine can do in extending bodily functions obscured issues of individual choice, value, and meaning (what *is* as compared to what *should be* done)? Cassell has noted that exclusion of value considerations in the machine metaphor leads to technological, legal, and administrative solutions (when to 'pull the plug') to what are essentially questions of personal or social value and choice. This can be seen in the discomfort evinced when patients assert their individuality in the dying process or in their 'right to die.' A recent newspaper account reveals some of this sense of shock at a patient choosing *not* to further bodily function beyond what to him seems reasonable:

> The advent of improved kidney dialysis techniques for the treatment of acute renal failure has offered us probably the most clear-cut examples of patients themselves choosing to die. After noting that ' *only about three or four patients* of the 1400 that we have treated in this facility have withdrawn from therapy' one leading renal expert consented to tell the story of one such person. 'There was an elderly lawyer from in town who decided that coming here to be treated three times a week was arduous, who had difficulties with the treatments, such as vomiting, lack of sleep, and constant pain.' This man decided that it was not worth it at age 72 to extend his life. So he simply said, 'I will not have you touch me again.' It was his own decision, and his family agreed with it. *We made a very vigorous attempt to talk him out of it*, but he withdrew shortly thereafter. Within a week he was dead.
>
> 'Pain is not a predominant aspect of the life on dialysis,' he continued. 'The problems are emotional and social, and a commitment to be dependent on a machine' (italics added).

The emphasis on the 'commitment to be dependent on a machine' leads to a second aspect of the depersonalisation process: The attention to bodily mechanics easily results in an *abstraction of the individual* to a general category of mechanical function: 'heart failure,' 'stroke,' and so on. The attention of nurses to mechanical functions during 'death watch,' discussed earlier, is an example of such abstraction of the patient. The predominance of mechanical function in this approach to the human body can also be seen in the treatment of individuals in which such function is gone. Sudnow defines 'social death' as that period before biological death when hospital staff and others relate to the patient as if he or she were indeed dead. That the comatose individual, for example, is seen as 'almost dead' is not surprising. It is the content of the social behaviour toward the individual that is of note. Sudnow and Glaser and Strauss point to the *nonperson* status suddenly attached to the individual. The person loses his or her social prerogatives and is no longer attended to in the same manner by the physician – 'physicians lose their interest in the patient.' The 'sense of person' can easily fail when the mechanical function of the body breaks down. 'Nonperson status' reveals the problem of depersonalisation of the patient. So do the 'attention to parts' at social death and emphasis on 'getting practice' described by Sudnow.

Depersonalisation can also be seen in the *predominance of institutional values* in dying. As the salience of mechanical and chemical intervention increases, control of the process of dying passes, subtly, from the patient to the physician: because prolonging the mechanical operation of the body is the major consideration, the technical expertise of the doctor – seen especially in the specialised vocabulary of medicine – separates him or her from the patient and gives the doctor a special power. This subtle shift in agency characterises the whole process of dying. For example, the move from home to hospital as the context of dying means that the event is no longer a private, individual affair but rather a public, homogenised one, dominated, as Cassell points out, by 'symbols of interpersonal sameness.' Thus has Kastenbaum described the impact of institutional dynamics on the death of geriatric patients: '[They] often behave as though . . . attempting to make their demise as acceptable and unthreatening as possible [for the staff].' Glaser and Strauss offer many examples of the impact of these institutional values in teaching the patient 'how to die.'

3 The body as affect-free

Here the content of the 'acceptable style of dying' is of special interest. The emphasis is on unemotional, controlled, and standardised behaviour. We can see the impact of the 'affect-free' dimension of the metaphor in the *elimination of affectively rooted ritual* from the process. In part, this elimination dovetails with the depersonalisation of the patient in that personally meaningful opportunities for the experience of dying are not made available. Gorer years ago pointed to the absence of culturally sanctioned grief or mourning and the difficulty this absence presents to individuals in trying to cope with death, either their own or that of others.

Summary and conclusions

The primary message of this chapter is that to understand medicine truly we must look beyond it. Looking beyond it entails stating the ways in which medicine is responsive to, and productive of, forces in its larger sociocultural setting. We should note that in so doing we are engaging in a dialectic. Medicine not only responds to influences from the society in which it exists, but also generates changes within the society. We have tried to illustrate this mode of analysis by presenting the history of one image of the body: this mechanical image provides a focus for our examination of historical connections between the development of medicine and changes and strains in society itself.

Many discussions of the history of medicine center either on the history of ideas or on the history of people and events; they view medicine either as the evolution and advance of important concepts and theories or as the product of key discoveries by researchers. Both these approaches tend to stay *within* medicine: in them its development is isolated from significant social forces outside the profession. Their implication is that the way medicine developed is the only way in which it could have developed, and – 'should' replacing 'could' – that medicine has been a constant advance of 'better' theory and practice.

Our focus, in contrast, has been primarily on the social, political, and economical changes and strains that have shaped the medical profession. This focus is consistent with the perspective of such recent observers of medicine as Foucault and Illich, as well as other writers. The implication of this chapter is that the way in which medicine has developed is only one of many alternative ways in which it could have developed, and that medicine's growth reflects not the evolution of 'pure' concepts, ideas, and procedures, but rather the interplay of many different social forces and pressures.

Images of the body change over time. We have traced one

particular image, a model of the body as a machine. However, there are complementary and competing images. A 'war' metaphor can, for instance, be invoked when the body is 'fighting' an illness. Sontag has recently offered a rich description of the different kinds of metaphors applied to illness. It may be that the machine metaphor, which we have singled out, is appropriate for certain aspects of medicine (e.g., heart surgery, kidney dialysis, birth and death, where the body is producing or 'running down'), but less appropriate for others: the treatment of illnesses such as infections or cancer.

As we have seen in this chapter, medicine is constantly changing. The predominance of the machine metaphor has set up a counter-force within medicine. For example, in the domains of birth and death the machine model may be undergoing alteration – as evidenced by the increase in home births and living wills and hospices for the dying. Considerable work has been done recently on ethical issues in medicine, particularly in relation to the problems of the dying and patients' responsibility for decisions in the course of treatment. So, too, has there been an effort to integrate patients' feelings and concerns into medicine, as exemplified by the work of Kubler-Ross. Whether these innovations, designed to remove some of the mechanical, context-stripping features from a person's experience of childbirth and death, mean new ways of looking at the body, health, and illness is still unclear.

Question

1. (a) Describe the 'mechanical metaphor' of contemporary medicine.

(8 marks)

(b) Explain why the approach described by the 'mechanical metaphor' became widespread within medicine.

(8 marks)

(c) Critically review the approach to medicine described by the mechanical metaphor.

(9 marks)

SECTION 17

The Sociology of Knowledge, Ideology and Religion

Readings 89–92

Much sociology is, in a sense, the sociology of knowledge. This is because the sociology of knowledge is concerned with explaining how different groups and individuals perceive and understand the world in often radically different ways. Culture, ideology, education, religion and the media can all be viewed in the context of the sociology of knowledge because they are all concerned with how people come to 'know' society. An excellent illustration of how two different cultural groups can come to interpret apparently the same experience in totally dissimilar ways was given in the last section (Readings 87 and 88). In primitive Azande culture, illness is conceived of in terms of magic and sorcery, whereas in modern Western culture it is typically understood in terms of the malfunctioning of the biological 'machine'. Describing and explaining how and why these two forms of 'knowledge' are produced is an example of the sociology of knowledge. It is worth adding that both interpretations of illness are part of wider systems of knowledge by which members of the two cultures make sense of everyday life – the magical and scientific-rational modes of explanation.

The first reading in this section is an analysis of Karl Marx's contribution to the sociology of knowledge. Abercrombie discusses ideology (which he suggests Marx equates with 'knowledge') in terms of class interest and of the base-superstructure model. Abercrombie raises, in Marxist terms, a point fundamental to all sociology of knowledge – the relationship between social context and ideas. A particularly common theme is how subordinate groups acquire ideas contrary to their 'best interests'. Although no reading is given from Karl Mannheim, it is worth noting that he draws Marxism itself into a sociology of knowledge framework by analysing it within the social context of its origins. Following the Abercrombie reading, the rest of the section is largely devoted to analysing religion from the point of view of the sociology of knowledge. The brief extract from Karl Marx eloquently states this approach: that religion has helped delude working people into unprofitable conformity.

The next two readings in this section treat religion from a less theoretically taxing point of view. Both of them survey religion in the contemporary world. Bryan Wilson presents evidence for the secularisation thesis – that Britain has become a less religious society. Wayne Ellwood does not directly oppose this thesis but shows through a wide range of reference that religion is still alive and kicking.

Finally, it should be said that the sociology of religion is not concerned with the truth of religion but with its relationship to society.

89 Nicholas Abercrombie: Marx and the Sociology of Knowledge: Class Interest and Ideology, Base and Superstructure

Although the following extract from Nicholas Abercrombie is clear and full of insight, the subject matter precludes a simple presentation. A brief synopsis of the reading may help the student to follow it. Abercrombie first analyses ideology in terms of its relationship to social class. He then approaches the problem from the point of view of the relationship between the base and superstructure.

Abercrombie begins with Marx's dictum that social being 'determines' consciousness or, in other words, people's ideas and beliefs emerge out of and are formed by their social experience (some interpreters of Marx would put the relationship even more strongly than that). For Marx, the most important aspect of social being is class, so he appears to be saying that social class is the major, though not the only, *causal* factor in determining consciousness. Abercrombie asks how precisely class 'causes' consciousness. The 'causal mechanism', as Abercrombie calls it, is interest; specifically, class interest. Members of the same class have certain shared practical and material interests which collectively, if not always individually (subjectively), they attempt to justify. This justification is, in fact, what Marx means by class ideology. Thus, in a capitalist society, there are two major competing ideologies just as there are two major competing classes, the bourgeois and the proletarian. Bourgeois ideology justifies the interests of the bourgeoisie, and proletarian that of the proletariat. Abercrombie suggests that 'in Marxism, the sociology of knowledge is more or less equivalent to the sociology of ideology'. Part of the sociology of knowledge is, then, concerned with analysing class ideology and particularly the material interests that underlie it.

In approaching Marxist analysis of the sociology of knowledge from the point of view of the base and superstructure, Abercrombie maintains the link between the sociology of knowledge and ideology. Crudely, if the base is considered to cover class relations, the superstructure covers the rest of social activity including political, educational and religious institutions, as well as all systems of belief. The various sub-areas of the superstructure are 'shot through' with ideology. According to Marx, because 'the ideas of the ruling class are in every epoch the ruling ideas', their ideology tends to dominate and be transmitted through the superstructure at the expense of the subordinate class. The ideological as well as the material conflict tends, therefore, to be an unequal one. Abercrombie himself prefers the analysis of ideology based on class interest as it better recognises the development of distinctive belief systems between the classes than that premised on the base-superstructure model which stresses the dominance of ruling class ideology.

Reading 89 From Nicholas Abercrombie, *Class, Structure and Knowledge: Problems in the sociology of knowledge* (Basil Blackwell, 1980), pp. 12–26.

Class-interest and ideology

The orthodox starting place for a Marxist sociology of knowledge is the formula from the Preface to *A Contribution to the Critique of Political Economy:* 'It is not the consciousness of men that determines their being, but, on the contrary, their social being that determines their consciousness.' As I suggested at the beginning of this chapter, this kind of remark by Marx is intended polemically and requires some interpretation. At the least, Marx plainly means to say that consciousness is not some free-floating autonomous element but can be partially explained by reference to 'social being'.

But what is meant by 'social being'? Although in the Preface this phrase seems to refer to some rather unspecified category such as the 'social conditions of man's existence', what is in fact crucial to the determination of beliefs is an element of social being, namely 'the mode of production of material life'. So it is man's involvement in a particular mode of production of goods and services that determines his beliefs. However this formulation is still not adequate for we do not know what constitutes 'involvement'. Men are involved in a mode of production to the extent that the mode is embedded in a set of social relations – in the relations of production – and, in particular, in the system of social class relationships. A particular social class is involved in particular ways in a mode of production; social class determines consciousness. For any one individual it is his membership in a social class *as that class has a certain position in a mode of production that determines* his beliefs. As Marx puts it in *The Eighteenth Brumaire of Louis Bonaparte:*

> Upon the different forms of property, upon the social conditions of existence, rises an entire superstructure of distinct and peculiarly formed sentiments, illusions, modes of thought and views of life. The entire class creates and forms them out of its material foundations and out of the corresponding social relations. The single individual derives them through tradition and upbringing.

A reading of the original formula as 'social class, as it is involved in a mode of production, determines consciousness' requires further elucidation in that the meaning of both 'determines' and 'consciousness' is unclear. To say that A determines B is plainly to say that there is some kind of causal relationship between A and B. Commentators on Marx have assumed that the character of B is entirely and exclusively fixed by A, that given someone's class one can more or less read off their beliefs. One familiar way of understanding 'determine' is in terms of causal importance; to say that A determines B is to say that in the formation of B, A is causally important, more important than any other element, but not the only element contributing to B. In the formation of beliefs, classes are of crucial, but not final, causal importance. However not all kinds of belief are equally causally influenced by class. Marx occasionally speaks as though natural science and logic are categories of consciousness removed from determination by class or the mode of production.

Engels is even more specific in suggesting that those beliefs most involved in the productive process will be most influenced by class; aesthetic doctrines, for example, will be less shaped by class and more by other factors than will economic theories. So far I have read the basic formula of 'social being determines consciousness' as meaning 'social class, as it is involved in a mode of production, is of great causal importance in the formation of beliefs, more so for some kinds of belief than for others'. The other factors that may be involved in the formation of beliefs are not therefore necessarily reducible to class.

In one respect the analysis so far is rather artificial. In representing the theory as a causal theory, I have more or less suggested that what a conventional Marxist sociology of knowledge seeks to do is to describe the causal influences in the formation of any individual's belief-system and it seeks to locate the answer primarily in terms of social class *membership*. It can be argued, however, that such an approach is at altogether too superficial a level and that what is required is an analysis of the constitution of, and relations between, modes of production in a society, which will show how both social classes and systems of belief are effects of these relations . . .

To say that 'social class, as it is involved in a mode of production, is of great causal importance in the formation of beliefs' is still not theoretically adequate, for it does not tell us what causal mechanism is involved. What precisely is the link between membership in a social class and belief, or between a social class and the belief-system 'appropriate' to it? The answer lies in a particular use of the notion of *interest*, a notion crucial to conventional Marxist theories of belief, though unfortunately more often assumed than explicated.

Marx himself used interest in all sorts of different ways. He discussed the conflicts of interest between individuals and individuals, between individuals and the State, between individuals and the social classes of which they are members, between different elements within a social class, between different aspirations of a class, and between social class and social class. Despite this variety of use, however, in the *abstract* analysis of the sociology of knowledge it is the way that social classes conflict that is of importance: 'How is it that personal interests always develop, against the will of individuals, into class-interests, into common interests which acquire independent existence in relation to the individual persons, and in their independence assume the form of general interests?' However for the solution of a particular problem in a 'specific society at a specific time', Marx speaks of the interests of many different kinds of *groups*. In the *Eighteenth Brumaire*, for example, one of the most important features in the analysis is the way that different sections of the bourgeoisie, the landowners and the finance capitalists, have apparently quite different systems of belief, but, despite these differences, the basic difference underlying all the others, and the one which is ultimately the most important socially, is the conflict of interest and belief between the bourgeoisie, as a whole, and the proletariat.

Marx's discussion of interest implies a distinction between 'subjective interests', which are simply those wants, aspirations and preferences that people actually express, and 'real interests', which people may be said to have even if they are unaware of them and which they may actually deny. In opposition to the Marxist position, which takes real interests seriously, many political theorists believe that it is analytically absurd, and even morally disagreeable, to speak of real interests as something separate from expressed wants; it has the absurdity that is often felt in everyday life when someone says that he knows what is in someone else's 'best interests'. The traditional argument against real interests is that their ascription to any class or group is arbitrary; we have no reason for ascribing any one interest to a group rather than another; any such ascription merely depends on the personal preferences of the person making the ascription. The only way we have of deciding what a person's or group's interests are is to look at what they *say* their interests (or wants) are. Thus the only meaningful notion of interests is the subjective one.

It might be possible to construct a sociology of belief based on subjective interest as the causal mechanism but it would, I think, be rather uninteresting. It would, for example, make it difficult to say that beliefs were at variance with interests. However there are other serious difficulties in treating subjective interests as the only conception of interest. Firstly, it must be possible to be mistaken as to one's interest. Thus a man can have a want and favour a policy which he believes will satisfy the want, but be mistaken about the actual effectiveness of that policy. In this case, although he might declare that the policy is in his interests, in fact he is wrong. Secondly, it does seem possible, superficially at least, to have interests of which one is not aware. Thus some sense ought to attach to saying that it is not in a man's interests to drink six bottles of whisky a day (particularly if he does not know the effect). Typically, in everyday life, such arguments are used about children who do things 'not in their interests', the assumption being that they do not know what they are doing. Thirdly, an empirical difficulty is that it may actually be difficult for people to express their wants; they may simply be unable to articulate them . . .

Base and superstructure

In the previous section, I started from the conventional formula, 'It is not the consciousness of men that determines their being but, on the contrary, their social being that determines their consciousness.' It would have been equally conventional to have had another starting point, namely, 'base determines superstructure'. Although they may give rather different results, these two starting points are certainly not radically different, for they effectively deal with the problem at different levels. The first gives us a way of looking at the belief-systems of social classes, while the second supplies an account of those beliefs that dominate society.

We may start from Marx's Preface to *A Contribution to the Critique of Political Economy*:

> In the social production of their life, men enter into definite relations that are indispensable and independent of their will, relations of production which correspond to a definite stage of development of their material productive forces. The sum total of these relations of production constitutes the economic structure of society, the real foundation, on which rises a legal and political superstructure and to which correspond definite forms of social consciousness.

There is therefore an economic base and legal, political and ideational superstructure. The base is conventionally understood by commentators on Marx to comprise the forces plus the relations of production. For example, the former are said by Mills to comprise:

> (a) natural resources, such as land and minerals, so far as they are used as objects of labour; (b) physical equipment such as tools, machines, technology; (c) science and engineering, the skills of men who invent and improve this equipment; (d) those who do work with these skills and tools; (e) their division

of labour in so far as this social organisation increases their productivity.

The relations of production are often seen as something over and above the forces of production, which is misleading, since Marx clearly says that different elements within the forces of production were related to each other in different ways, and it was *these relations* that constituted the relations of production. In any event, conventional accounts tend to interpret the relations of production in a rather more straightforward way, simply as *class* relations. Thus, according to Cole:

> Marx held that these relations between men and men, involving the definition of rights of property and personal freedom and obligation, have in the past been embodied in successive class systems, so that each system has corresponded to a particular stage in the development of the social use of the powers of production, including both things and men.

The superstructure is then an avowedly residual category including political, educational and religious institutions, as well as all systems of belief.

So far I have left the exact relation between base and superstructure undefined. It is often suggested that Marx claimed that the base determines the character of the beliefs current in society. It is clear, however, that neither Marx nor Engels ever held such a doctrine. Firstly, they suggested that superstructural elements could be relatively antonomous of the base and have their own laws of development. Engels, for example, says that not all kinds of belief are equally determined by the base: 'The further the particular sphere we are investigating is removed from the economic sphere and approaches that of pure abstract ideology, the more shall we find it exhibiting accidents . . . in its development, the more will its course run in a zig-zag.' Thus the forms taken by art and literature may be much less closely related to the economic base than will political or economic theories. Secondly, and more radically, Marx and Engels argue that the superstructure will interact with, or influence, the base. In *Capital*, for example, Marx is at pains to show the independent importance of beliefs about the conditions of work. There is no reason inherent in the nature of capital why the working day should be limited: 'apart from extremely elastic bounds, the nature of the exchange of commodities itself imposes no limit to the working day, no limit to surplus-labour'. Nonetheless the length of the working day is regulated by the State, partially as the outcome of a struggle between competing classes and sets of beliefs. Again, as Engels points out:

> The economic situation is the basis, but the various elements of the superstructure – political forms of the class struggle and its results, to wit: constitutions established by the victorious class after a successful battle, etc, forms, and even the reflexes of all these actual struggles in the brains of the participants, political, juristic, philosophical theories, religious views . . . also exercise their influence upon the course of the historical struggles and in many cases preponderate in determining their *form*. There is an interaction of all these elements in which, amid all the endless hosts of accidents. . . . The economic movement finally asserts itself as necessary.

Engel's conclusion is thus that the economic is of final and decisive importance but the superstructure may still influence the economic. Such a formulation does not give any precise guide as to the *relative* importance of the base and superstructure.

From the point of view of the sociology of knowledge, Marx's distinction in the Preface between base and superstructure is interpreted generally as saying that the *dominant* ideas of an epoch or society reflect (in some way to be defined) the *dominant* form of economic organisation or more precisely, the dominant mode of production. For example, the various doctrines collectively referred to as individualism are often said to reflect the domination of the capitalist mode of production. Such doctrines emphasise the claims of the individual *vis-à-vis* some other entity such as the Church or the State and make him the final arbiter of his moral and political choices. Individualistic theories appeared in a number of different fields at different times. Thus religious individualism, effectively denying the importance of the Church as an intermediary between man and his God, appears significantly from about the fifteenth century onwards. The seventeenth and eighteenth centuries were the heyday of individualistic theories of political obligation, while individualism is a characteristic of the literature and economic theory of the eighteenth and early nineteenth centuries. It is suggested that individualism, as this very general *style* of thought, reflected capitalism in that that economic system has to treat people as autonomous units formally equal and separate as buyers and sellers in a market.

I suggested earlier that the relations of production are often interpreted simply as *class* relations. This has turned the notion that the dominant ideas of a society somehow reflect the dominant mode of production into the argument that the dominant ideas are the ideas of the dominant *class*. The inspiration for this position comes from *The German Ideology:*

> The ideas of the ruling class are in every epoch the ruling ideas: i.e. the class which is the ruling material force of society, is at the same time its ruling intellectual force. The class which has the means of material production at its disposal, has control at the same time over the means of mental production, so that thereby, generally speaking, the ideas of those who lack the means of mental production are subject to it. The ruling ideas are nothing more than the ideal expression of the dominant material relationships grasped as ideas . . . Insofar, therefore, as they (the individuals of the ruling class) rule as a class and determine the extent and compass of an epoch, it is self-evident that they do this in its whole range, hence among other things rule also as thinkers, as producers of ideas, and regulate the production and distribution of the ideas of their age. Thus their ideas are the ruling ideas of an epoch. For instance, in an age and in a country where royal power, aristocracy and bourgeoisie are contending for mastery, the doctrine of the separation of powers proves to be the dominant idea and is expressed in an eternal law . . .

(*Abercrombie then goes on to raise critical questions about the 'dominant ideology' perspective expressed in the above quote – editor.*)

It may well be that the dominant ideology functions chiefly towards the dominant class, perhaps in securing the measure of social coherence necessary for the preservation, transmission, and accumulation of private property so important in the feudal and early capitalist period. This would not, however, be to deny that the relative availability of dominant ideas might have the *secondary* effect of partially incorporating the subordinate classes. However, even with the last qualification, these arguments suggest that any simple conception of dominant ideas, as the ideas of a dominant class, being imposed on subordinate classes is not tenable. They also show the manner in which two doctrines which make up the conventional view of Marx's sociology of knowledge, relate to one another. The doctrine 'social being determines consciousness' tends to suggest that there are powerful reasons, chiefly class-interest, for supposing that each class will have its own distinctive system of belief. The 'base determines superstructure' doctrine, on the other hand, tends to argue that class-specific systems of belief become incorporated within a dominant ideology. The more that one stresses the significance of dominant ideas, the less easy is it to explain deviant, oppositional, or alternative beliefs. By showing the centrality of the concept of interest to conventional Marxist accounts and by suggesting that dominant ideas do not straightforwardly incorporate subordinate classes, I have been effectively arguing that conventional Marxist sociologies of knowledge stress the second doctrine to the neglect of the first.

Question
1. (a) *Briefly describe the relationship between*
     (i) *class interest and ideology*
     (ii) *the base and superstructure.*

(12 marks)

(b) *Why does Abercrombie suggest that the class interest model can be used to produce a less rigid view of 'dominant ideology' than the base-superstructure model often does?*

(13 marks)

90 Karl Marx: Religion as Ideology: 'The Opium of the People'

Marx is here claiming that 'the oppressed' seek in religion what they do not get in 'this world' – namely, some kind of fulfilment and content. Controversially (see below), Marx regards pursuit of fulfilment through religion as 'illusory' – a kind of spiritual opium.

Marx agrees that the majority are 'alienated' but urges a different solution. People must analyse ('unmask') the causes of their problems that relate to this world and act politically to change matters.

It is quite possible to accept Marx's argument that the

oppressed should tackle their oppression in this world without taking the view that religion is always 'illusory'. Some religious people do fully deal with the causes of oppression in 'the here and now'. others do not. Perhaps a fair revision of Marx would be that only for the latter group is religion 'illusory' in this given respect. In Reading 92 various groups are referred to whose members in part derive their commitment to social and political change from religion.

Despite the previous paragraph, this passage from Marx contains the essence of Marxist humanism – that social justice and, within realistic limits, the fulfilment of human potential should be sought in this world – that we should 'cull the living flower'.

Reading 90 From K. Marx and F. Engels, 'On Religion' reprinted in R. Bocock and K. Thompson *eds., Religion and Ideology* (Manchester University Press, 1985) pp. 11–12.

Religious distress is at the same time the *expression* of real distress and the *protest* against real distress. Religion is the sigh of the oppressed creature, the heart of a heartless world, just as it is the spirit of a spiritless situation. It is the *opium* of the people.

The abolition of religion as the *illusory* happiness of the people is required for their *real* happiness. The demand to give up the illusions about its condition is the *demand to give up a condition which needs illusions*. The criticism of religion is therefore *in embryo the criticism of the vale of woe*, the *halo* of which is religion.

Criticism has plucked the imaginary flowers from the chain not so that man will wear the chain without any fantasy or consolation but so that he will shake off the chain and cull the living flower. The criticism of religion disillusions man to make him think and act and shape his reality like a man who has been disillusioned and has come to reason, so that he will revolve round himself and therefore round his true sun. Religion is only the illusory sun which revolves round man as long as he does not revolve round himself.

The task of history, therefore, once the *world beyond the truth* has disappeared, is to establish the *truth of this world*. The immediate *task of philosophy*, which is at the service of history, once the *saintly form* of human self-alienation has been unmasked, is to unmask self-alienation in its *unholy forms*. Thus the criticism of heaven turns into the criticism of the earth, the *criticism of religion* into the *criticism of right* and the *criticism of theology* into the *criticism of politics*[. . .]

The philosophers have only *interpreted* the world, in various ways; the point, however, is to *change* it.

Question

1. *What does Marx mean when he writes 'Religion is the opium of the people'? Do you agree with him?*

(25 marks)

(You may find it helpful to refer to Readings 89, 92 and 98 before answering this question.)

91 Bryan Wilson: The Secularisation of Modern Life

The secularisation thesis contends that there has been a long-term decline of religion in Britain and, probably, most modern societies. Science and rationality have replaced religion as the dominant principle of explanation and social organisation. As Wilson puts it: 'To most people, society appears to be dependent not on divine providence, but rather on social planning.'

This point of view has its intellectual origins in the thought of Weber and Durkheim. Weber wrote of a process of 'disenchantment' by which predominantly irrational and emotional modes of thought were being replaced by rationality and calculation in the modern world. Durkheim saw the gradual advance of the 'profane' over the 'sacred', or, in Wilson's terms, the secular over the religious. In the following article, Wilson argues the secularisation thesis in several overlapping ways. He sees a steady erosion in the institutional power and influence of the church, a general decline in religious attitudes, and produces a battery of statistics to support his case.

It is essential for the student to be aware that the secularisation thesis is hotly debated: only lack of space has prevented the inclusion of an extract opposing the thesis. At least some of the major arguments against the thesis can be briefly mentioned. First is the point put forward by David Martin, Wilson's leading antagonist in the secularisation debate, that there is growing evidence of religious scepticism and laxity even in the Middle

Ages. The 'age of faith' may never have existed! Second is the argument that new, less institutionalised forms of religion have emerged to replace the old. To some extent, Wilson accepts this argument in his concluding paragraphs, but he still attempts to absorb it within the notion of 'the basic secularity of advanced industrial society'.

Reading 91 Bryan Wilson, 'How Religious Are We?' in *New Society*, 27 October 1977, pp. 176–8.

The writing on the church wall had already been there for some time in 1952: religion was declining in Britain. In that year, G. Stephens Spinks, editor of the intellectual religious periodical, the *Hibbert Journal*, wrote with two collaborators a book called *Religion in Britain since 1900*. The authors picked their way dolefully among the evidences of the steady decay of institutional religion in search of occasional signs of possible hope:

'In the years that followed the war, ministers of many denominations who had hoped for a "return to religion", experienced periods of great depression. Many a devoted parish priest . . . who had spent the greater part of his ministerial life in one area and who had been robbed by air-raids and evacuation both of church and congregation, found his life's work brought to a calamitous end. The "return to religion" did not come.'

Despite the horror of atomic war, people did not turn to God for reassurance. Only a small percentage of the nation joined in any form of regular public worship. People were even praying less, and when they prayed – so Mass Observation reported – they tended to use only the rote prayers learned in childhood. Religious attitudes to the dead were changing: war memorials had become virtually secular even after the first world war, and as Dr Spinks observed, after the second they were often not put up at all. Even the BBC, in 1947, had abandoned its earlier policy of not broadcasting opinions hostile to Christianity in favour of a liberal and high-minded pursuit of truth, which gave non-Christians the chance to state their case.

With apprehensive sidelong glances at the current progress of communism, Spinks and his associates no longer looked, in the words of the title of the Bishop of Rochester's report of seven years before, *Towards the Conversion of England*, but to the expansion of Christianity elsewhere:

'The fact that the leaven of English-speaking Christianity has been working in non-European minds with particular force during the last fifty years may be taken as an indication from the human end, that God, who does not leave Himself without witness, may, if the suicidal tendencies of the western world persist, found a new civilisation wherein the Christian praxis will continue, beyond our failure and infidelities, to redeem the world.'

Twenty-five years after Spinks wrote, even these tangential hopes seem quaintly antiquated. The churches have become even more completely separate compartments of the British social system; religious attitudes penetrate less and less effectively into social activities and individual lives; and the involvement of individuals in religious practice has become more emphatically a matter of private, individual choice.

Except under the ancient protocol of solemn processions, the church has now ceased to exercise even nominal presidency over our national life. A Prime Minister's correspondence 80 years ago dealt seriously with archepiscopal opinion; 40 years ago the bishops had a significant voice in the abdication crisis; today, we have even seen the occasion when the Prime Minister was 'too busy' to see the Archbishop of Canterbury. The mass media have virtually eclipsed the pulpit as a source of information and guidance. Armies of specialists now fulfil the educational, counselling, rehabilitative, and pastoral functions that were once the virtual monopoly of the clergy, or their religiously approved lay agents.

Religion itself is no longer news, except when a clergyman commits a moral misdemeanour, or when exorcism or the occult is involved. Convocations, assemblies, and synods are not now worth the cost of newsprint. Even a book like the recent *The Myth of God Incarnate* raises the temperature only in narrow church circles, and produces only a faint echo of the furore provoked in the early sixties by the Bishop of Woolwich's book, *Honest to God*. The type of material that shocked the press and stirred some of the public, when Margaret Knight broadcast on humanism in the early fifties, is now almost the staple fare of the early morning programme, *Thought for the Day* (itself the secularised successor to *Lift Up Your Hearts*).

The devaluation of religion is clear from the continuing decline in the relative rewards of the clergy. Even in the 1950s, the clergy shared something of the material and cultural standards and the social status of college teachers and professional classes. Today, the clergy are among our lowest paid occupations. Unskilled manual workers earn considerably more. Our society rewards technical expertise, but religion apparently requires no expertise; the clergy have no technical competences. They are merely amateur helpers, and British society rewards them as such.

The case of religious institutions is essentially similar. A poorer society built, repaired, elaborately decorated and serviced churches – even the basic fabric of which our affluent society cannot maintain. When churches qualify for special grants, it is their aesthetic merit not their religious service that renders them eligible. Our ancient shrines attract not pilgrims but tourists, and their keepers are not so much celebrants as custodians, paid as if they were janitors.

The content of the message that the churches seek to promote, and the attitudes and values that it tries to encourage, no longer inform much of our national life. The workplace is perhaps the environment most alien to religious values, and this has become more and more the case as work activities become increasingly more technological. Impersonal cost-efficiency, the operation of conveyor belts and electronic equipment, and the effort to make office administration as machine-like as possible, leave little place for either the substantive content of religious myth or the personal human values that it represents. To invoke God in political dispute would today be regarded as, at best, bad taste. The old correlations of religious affiliation and political preference appear of little consequence, except in Northern Ireland.

In schools, religious instruction has nowadays become often a travesty of the name: many teachers use the periods for current affairs, in which religion has little or no relevance. The growth of comprehensive education has led to schools so large that schools assemblies are impracticable, and the religious auspices under which such assemblies convened are no longer invoked.

Family practice in religious matters is harder to assess, but it is clear that in one respect parents no longer seek to provide religious instruction and a knowledge of worship for their children – they have allowed the Sunday school almost to die. In 1953, nearly 18 per cent of the children in England between the ages of three and fourteen were on the books of Church of England Sunday schools alone. If you add Nonconformist schools to these, certainly more than a third of children attended Sunday school. Today the proportion is probably less than 15 per cent. The effectiveness of Sunday school is disputable, but in the early fifties a much higher proportion of children were exposed to the rudiments of Christian ideas that are not so readily assimilated later on.

Quite apart from the penetration of religious ideas into the operation of other social institutions, lies the question of the extent to which individual consciousness is affected. Here, we have very little solid evidence. To most people, society appears to be dependent not on divine providence but rather on social planning. Men no longer appear to ask 'What is God's will?' so much as 'What shall I do to get on?' Modern man is, at least consciously, less concerned about death and the after-life than about happiness here and now. In particular, the permissive society that has evolved since the early 1950s has revealed the growing demand for spontaneity, immediacy, hedonism and the freedom to 'do our own thing', particularly among the young. These currents have affected religion itself, of course, as is evident in the expansion of the Charismatic Renewal movement. But it can be said that these trends represent a shift away from older ideas of man as God's creature, here to do his bidding, here to 'wait on God'.

Religious intimations about our personal dispositions are much less readily entertained, and are much less the subject even of clerical exhortation. One sees this in the shift of attitudes concerning sexual morality and birth control. Babies that were once the 'gift of God' are now in the vast majority of cases the result of deliberate personal decisions about family planning. The new techniques of birth control have opened the way to a much more rational exercise of personal choice, and slowly the churches have come increasingly to endorse this much more secular attitude to sex and even to marriage. The churches themselves demand less of us, religiously, than they used.

If organised religion influences the workings of society less than before, what about the individual's voluntary involvement in religious activities? The statistics are far from complete, but the story since 1952 is certainly one of general decline. In 1950, 67 per cent of the children born alive in England were baptised in the Church of England; in 1973, this was the case for only 47 per cent. In 1952, about 28 per cent of those aged 15 years in England were confirmed in the Anglican church: the proportion was below 20 per cent by the mid-70s. Some 6.5 per cent of the population took Easter communion in the Church of England in 1953 – but 20 years later, fewer than 4 per cent did so.

In the early 1950s, the Church of Scotland was still growing, according to its membership figures. By the mid-70s, however, decline had set in not only proportionately to population, but in absolute terms as well: the church had lost more than a fifth of its members in 20 years. The story of the Free Churches in England and Wales is one of even more rapid decline. The Methodists, who had three quarters of a million members in 1952, have fallen by nearly a third in 25 years. The Baptists, who numbered more than 300,000, have only 185,000. The Congregationalists and the Presbyterians once mustered well over 400,000. Today, as an amalgamated body (the United Reformed Church) they are even less numerous than the Baptists.

Even the Roman Catholics, who continued to grow both by virtue of immigration from Ireland and by differential fertility until the early 1960s, are today no longer the exception to the general rule of religious decline that they were in the early postwar years. It is not easy to arrive at an agreed number of Roman Catholics, but perhaps the best informed investigator, Dr Anthony Spencer, estimated in 1975 that although the Roman church might claim something like 15 per cent of the population of England and Wales, a leakage had begun in the 1960s that might amount to a quarter of a million a year.

It is not only that more and more people have ceased to support the institutional churches: we know from public opinion polls that a diminishing, though still sizeable, number now subscribe to the basic tenets of conventional Christian belief. In the early 1950s, no more than 10 per cent disavowed belief in God. By the mid-1970s, only 64 per cent affirmed that belief, and fewer than 40 per cent believed in life after death.

Despite all these evidences of decline, it would certainly be premature and perhaps quite mistaken, to conclude that religion was doomed to disappear altogether. Even though society becomes manifestly more secular, there is still a deeply committed minority of religious people, some of them in the traditional churches, and some of them among the sects. Periodically they can be mobilised in the cause of what has been called 'cultural defence', in support of traditions and cultural values – as, for instance, in the Festival of

Light. They may, in such cases, speak for a wider public which, since it is not religiously committed, cannot so easily be mobilised for moral causes.

While the majority of Christians and Jews have become steadily more secular during the last two and a half decades, some religious minorities have flourished. The growing influence of the evangelicals, well recognised in America, has yet to be documented in Britain. The Mormons have also won a significant constituency, with over 100,000 members; and Jehovah's Witnesses now claim more than 80,000 members in Great Britain. And there are the immigrants – Muslims, Sikhs, and Hindus – who together constitute the most exotic variant to the pattern of British religion in the last quarter of a century. We know neither the numbers in these faiths, nor the extent of their commitment. For some time, mosques and temples may serve as badges of ethnic and cultural identity as much as centres of religious dedication, in the same way that national churches functioned for immigrants to America early in this century. But assimilation, if it occurs, will demand compromise with religious principles for these groups, as they adjust to the basic secularity of advanced industrial society.

The pluralism of a multi-racial society relativises all religious beliefs. Christianity becomes just one tradition among others. The social order appears no longer to need religious legitimations, any more than individuals need religious justifications for their behaviour, and religion loses its best support when it ceases to be a higher expression of a particular culture. At the fringes, we shall continue to encounter the profoundly religious man, and he is more likely to be a sectarian than a churchman, since in society at large religion is becoming so much an 'optional extra'.

Question
1. *Is Britain now a 'secular' society?*

(25 marks)

(You may prefer to read Reading 92, including the introduction, before attempting this question.)

92 Wayne Ellwood: The Survival and Revival of Religion in the Contemporary World

This brief reading on contemporary religion needs some socio-logical 'beefing up' which I shall attempt to provide below. However, Ellwood covers a number of points with a journalist's incisiveness. First, he reviews the process of secularisation and the more recent return to religion in some quarters. Second, he illustrates the drive to social relevance strongly apparent in some of the new religious movements – of both the Right and Left. Third, he contrasts the 'new' religions with the traditional chur-ches which nevertheless have been stimulated to adopt more socially relevant perspectives by the former. Fourth, a constant theme of the article is that, for many, 'consumer culture' is not enough. Fifth, Ellwood makes the point that whether we accept or reject religion we should not 'lose our critical edge' – the hard issues of everyday life should not be fudged by sentimentalism, religious or otherwise.

A strength of Ellwood's approach is that he does not try to force a variety of facts and trends into a tight theoretical frame-work. There are, of course, many systematic sociological attempts to analyse religion. A theme touched on by Ellwood, more fully explored by others, is the distinction between church and sect. Ernst Troelsch sees the former as conservative and seeking to control and expand membership whereas the latter are more likely to reject 'the world' and turn inward to the sect for meaningful experience. It is the growth of sects and perhaps a general religious fundamentalism that has characterised the religious revival since the nineteen sixties. Sects are often formed as a split-off from established churches which are seen as having grown too accommodating to materialistic values and secular authority. In time, sects may acquire the characteristics of churches and produce breakaways. Though useful, these distinctions do not quite seem to explain the complexities of modern religion. For instance, a sharply critical statement of certain government attitudes and policies towards the inner cities, *Faith in the City* (1986), was published by a commission set up by the Archbishop of Canterbury who later in 1986 visited South Africa where he condemned apartheid. Here we have a key figure in an established church taking radical positions. It is not always predictable who will interpret Christian values radically or conservatively.

Similarly, the social and political orientations of modern sects defy simple explanation or prediction. However, Roy Wallis in *The Elementary Forms of the New Religious Life* (1984) provides a typology which makes broad sense of the complexity. He locates sects on a spectrum on the basis of their orientation to the material world:

World-affirming	World-accommodating	World-rejecting
e.g. Transcendental Meditation	e.g. Neo-Pentecostalism	e.g. Manson's Family

World-affirming movements tend to attract the comfortably off who seek a spiritual outlet (and perhaps moral justification). World-accommodating movements tend to attract the already religious who are seeking a more vital and active experience of religion. World-rejecting movements separate themselves from what they see as a corrupt world, often in anticipation of the second coming.

An important aspect of the relationship of religion to the material world is whether or not it tends to support social inequality. Bryan Turner's recent *Equality* (Tavistock, 1986) contains an interesting survey of the problem. Again, reality appears to be complex: sometimes religion sustains inequality and sometimes it undermines it. Examples of the former case are the Hindu and most other Asiatic religions and an example of the latter is Calvinism in the early modern period. As Turner observes, however, there were limits to Calvinists' support for a more open society of equal opportunity – it did not include slaves. Turner refers to Berger's typology of two 'theodicies' which tend to support inequality – one justifying the privilege of the rich, and the other making bearable the misery of the poor. However, I would add a third 'theodicy' which seeks to implement principles of human equality in the present world – such as the 'liberation theology' of certain Catholic priests in Latin America.

There is then no simple model to explain the social aspects

of religion. At root, perhaps, religion is an attempt to find meaning and fulfilment not as yet achieved in this world.

Reading 92 From Wayne Ellwood, 'Flame of Faith' in *New Internationalist*, No. 155, January 1986, pp. 8–9.

The 'Enlightenment' opened the first chink in the armour of organised religion. It began with thinkers like Copernicus, Galileo, Isaac Newton and Rene Descartes. Slowly but surely the twin gods of rational inquiry and scientific scepticism undermined supernatural explanations of the universe. Things magical or mysterious fell into place: the solar system, the working of the human body, the causes and cures for deadly diseases and eventually the secrets of life itself. The whole moral order of the Christian universe began to dissolve like a wet tissue before the onslaught of pragmatic science.

Instead of God sitting comfortably in the centre of the universe, people had to take responsibility for themselves. Life on earth was logically seen as the result of human action, not the result of some preordained plan made in Heaven. The omnipotent and omniscient force that had been the explanation and the reason for all of nature, history and human action, was forced to retreat to the sidelines. Christian theologians have been attempting to bring God back to centre field ever since.

New social order

This process of *secularisation* picked up steam with the great social dislocations of the Industrial Revolution in the early 1800s. The sacred was being slowly peeled away from the world of politics and economics. As the populations in the new industrial towns grew, the number of active churchgoers steadily declined. By 1851, only 42 per cent of the population of England and Wales attended church regularly. In the worst slum parishes the estimate was less than ten per cent.

The old authority of God and tradition no longer held sway in this new social order. It became clear to industrial workers that it was not God, but the factory managers and owners who were responsible for their lot.

Karl Marx and other social reformers spearheaded a growing opposition to organised religion. The church was criticised as a pie-in-the-sky diversion, promising comfort and contentment in the hereafter in exchange for social conformity and obedience to authority in the present.

Marx himself, in an infamous dictum, said that religion is 'the opium of the people'. But he put his finger on a more profound problem by adding: 'Religious distress is at the same time the *expression* of real distress and also the *protest* against real distress. Religion is the sigh of the oppressed creature, the heart of a heartless world, just as it is the spirit of *spiritless conditions.*'

It was precisely these 'spiritless conditions' that loomed larger as fantastic leaps in technology and industrial prowess ushered in the post-war age of consumerism. Philosophers like Friedrich Nietzsche had already announced the 'death of God' while 20th century Christian theologians were pushed into trying to define a new role for a modern God who had been supplanted by science. The buzz phrase was 'god-of-the-gaps' – a kind of spiritual mortar to plug the murky regions of doubt and dread that science and technology could not reach.

Denied its public role, hived off from the world of economics and industry, religion increasingly became a matter for private conscience and personal contemplation. God was not dead after all; he had merely retreated to the realm of the personal. Faith, for those who had it, was a source of spiritual strength and nourishment. It didn't matter that particle physics and genetics explained the physical workings of the world. Religion could not be pushed into a corner of the human psyche and forgotten like a bad dream. Faith, theologians like Marcel Eliade began to realise, 'is an element in the structure of consciousness, not a stage in the history of consciousness'.

By the early 1970s religion appeared to be making a comeback – in spite of hardening secular trends. Consumer culture offered the riches of the ages, but somehow it wasn't enough. According to American religion writer Harvey Cox, 'something had been lost; and what is lost seems to be religious: the sacred, the element of mystery in life, the transcendent, the spiritual dimension, a morality firmly grounded in revealed truth.'

The Nicaraguan priest and poet Ernesto Cardenal put this passion for the spiritual another way:

A New order. Or rather
a new heaven and a new earth.

New Jerusalem. Neither New York nor
Brasilia
A passion for change: the nostalgia
of that city. A beloved community
We are foreigners in Consumer City
The new man, and not the new
Oldsmobile.

At the very deepest levels our spiritual needs seem as great as ever. Believers want a full-blooded religion that packs an emotional punch. One that provides both meaning and values for us to live by and that offers us a purpose beyond the bottomless hollow of consumer culture.

In Western countries this search for a solid spiritual anchor has again put religion and the church at the very centre of an intense political debate. In countries like Canada, the US, Britain and Australia, fundamentalist Christianity has gained a new lease on life, pulling in adherents from mainstream churches and making loud noises about contentious social issues.

Fundamentalist preachers offer a clear prescription for both personal and social behaviour. They want not only to preserve the faith, to swing it back to its roots; they also want to inject an old-fashioned morality into our permissive secular era. Spokesmen like US preacher Jerry Falwell offer a smooth blend of personal salvation and down-home values.

'There is going to be an invasion of God on this planet, and changing of lives: real biblical evangelisation', Falwell says. And that means 'we must come back to the only principles that God can honour: the dignity of life, the traditional family, decency, morality'.

In practice, though, this fundamentalist morality is shot through with right-wing ideology. It poses a stark literalist vision of good and evil which neatly polarises the world into two warring camps. Mr Falwell and his supporters lay the blame for the world's ills on the twin demons of 'godless communism' and 'godless secularism'. The fundamentalist solution is to put women back in the kitchen, blacks in their place, gays in psychiatric hospitals and Marxists in church. It is a poisonous theology and a dangerous one. But it has to be taken seriously.

Speaking with authority

There is no question that fundamentalism scares the traditional churches – precisely because it works. Jerry Falwell and his Christian colleagues offer a theology that is simple, even crude. But it is also a faith which resonates with real life, which puts people at ease and which triggers the emotions as well as the intellect.

People have also turned to 'new' religions, from guru-based cults to scientology, in a frantic search for alternatives to the sterility of modern Christianity.

Partially in response to this and the overlap between fundamentalist theology and right-wing politics, mainstream Western churches have begun to come alive again. They now speak loudly about social justice and the need to build community. British churches have taken a strong lead in public education on Third World development; the US Catholic bishops have blasted the Reagan administration on its arms policy; the Canadian bishops have fired a stinging salvo at their government's orthodox economic policies. Established churches everywhere have taken clear positions on apartheid.

But other domestic concerns have also galvanised the major Western churches: unemployment, sexism, racism and the criminal justice system. The church is once again speaking with authority, conviction and confidence. And in the process it has vaulted back into the political limelight.

This religious revival has not been confined only to the West. In many ways it is a pale reflection of a fierce battle which is taking place in much of the Third World. There, the Western industrial model has stormed through in less than 40 years, upsetting patterns of community and worship which have been more or less stable for centuries. Fundamentalists of all stripes have leapt into this confused vortex.

The austere morality and severe vision of Iran's militant mullahs has won new converts to Islamic fundamentalism from Pakistan to Indonesia. And in black Africa and Latin America, fundamentalist Protestants continue to make inroads. According to the conservative US magazine, *Christianity Today*, there may be 100 million Protestants in Latin American by the year 2000 – most of them fundamentalists.

For Latin Americans concerned with social change, the impact of this conservative theology is a real threat. There is already clear evidence of Protestant groups in Central America being used to channel American funds to mercenaries attempting to overthrow Nicaragua's Sandinista government.

Another sort of 'people's' religion has also emerged in Latin America, a vibrant form of Christianity whose contagious energy has swept through the Roman Catholic Church from Korea and the Philippines to South Africa and Chile. Liberation theology came to life in the *favelas* of Brazil. But it has taken root wherever the poor have been brushed aside by modern development and the church hierarchy has catered to the rich and powerful.

Liberation theology puts God and the poor together at the centre of the world. Christ is seen as a liberator, the son of God who suffered and died for the rights of the poor – and for whom justice was an earthly as well as a heavenly concern. According to liberation theologians like Gustavo Gutierrez, poverty is not a fact of life but a result of sin by the powerful – and therefore a cause of God's wrath. Accepting poverty is akin to accepting sin. So being a Christian means not only changing your ideas, it also means changing your life. And that is why liberation theology is sending shock waves through the developing world. It challenges not only individuals but inept governments, corrupt bureaucrats, big landlords and greedy businessmen.

Critical edge

So where does all this leave us? In the end we still confront the same yawning void humankind has faced since the beginning. In the words of Cambridge theologian Don Cupitt, 'we are still prompted to religious dread and longing by the thought of our own death, our own littleness, and the precariousness of human values in the face of Nature's vast indifference'.

We all confront these profound questions in different ways. Some of us are actively religious, many of us are not. Yet we all need faith in something – beyond the soul-destroying consumer culture that threatens to enervate us completely. The main thing we must do is take each other's faith seriously, whether it's faith in a better world or faith in God. It's time we dropped our arrogance and snobbery and began to see we're all in the same predicament.

But one thing we can't do is lose our critical edge. That's because religion cuts both ways. While faith *can* offer us a pathway to understanding the human purpose, religion has also sparked the worst of human passions – hatred, bigotry, intolerance, pride and bloodshed. When that side of faith surfaces we must be on our guard against religion and be prepared to speak out forcefully against it.

In the meantime, if we cannot agree on our approach to God, let's at least agree on our approach to the enemy: the rootless nihilism of the modern age.

Questions

1. (a) *What evidence is there for a revival of religion since the late nineteen sixties?*

(10 marks)

(b) *How do you account for this revival?*

(15 marks)

2. (a) *Present and explain a case in which religion acts as a conservative force.*

(10 marks)

(b) *Present and explain a case in which religion acts as a force for change.*

(10 marks)

(c) *Do your examples suggest that religion frequently functions to legitimate the material interests of believers?*

(5 marks)

SECTION 18

Culture, Ideology and the Media

Readings 93–98

Culture and ideology are key sociological concepts which have recurred throughout this Reader. They are given 'top billing' in this section because the media, particularly the new technologically-based media, are the main means by which cultural and ideological 'messages' are conveyed. However, there is a range of useful readings on these concepts scattered throughout the book, some of which I shall indicate below.

Culture refers to a way of life, including elements of conflict with other ways of life (e.g. traditional working class culture was/is in conflict with aspects of 'bourgeois' culture). The concept of culture includes ideology. The latter term refers to the ideas by which people justify their actions, including, for instance, political and economic actions. People's ideas and emotions are formed by visual images as well as by words. We do not know the precise effects of the 'modern' media on the way people feel, think and behave. Neil Postman's bold if perhaps exaggerated attempt to chart the broad effects of the media on children is extracted in an earlier section (Reading 45). The reading which begins this section overviews the new technology of communications and discusses the issue of ownership. These matters are essential to understanding the power and effects of the media.

The second reading, from the Glasgow Media Group, deals directly with the issue of ideological bias and the media. The case study given here is the coverage of the Women's Peace Camp at Greenham Common. A sharply contrasting image of femininity to that of the Greenham Common women is presented by *Jackie*, the magazine for pre- and early teenage girls. Angela McRobbie describes the fit between the future roles of the girls and the ideology of femininity portrayed in the magazine.

Bhikhu Parekh's brief article, 'Prejudice and the Press', is one of the most political in this book – but perhaps racism is not an issue on which it is possible to be neutral. He argues angrily but factually that part of the British press is unscrupulously and dangerously racist.

The reading on the world's press agencies raises important issues of political and cultural influence but is included primarily to provide the necessary factual background without which discussion of these issues is meaningless.

Finally, the reading from Tony Bennett throws light on all that has gone before in this section. Through the work of Antonio Gramsci, particularly his concept of 'hegemony', Bennett raises the problem of power and culture. How precisely does hegemonic power operate and how culturally independent is it possible for subordinate groups to be?

For those interested in further exploring cultural analysis, see readings 41, 45, 47, 56, and 90.

93 Peter Golding and Graham Murdock: The New Communications: Scope, Control and Potential

It is necessary to describe recent rapid and far-reaching changes in communications before attempting to analyse their consequences. This extract describes basic developments in the technology of communications and in their ownership and control. In short, it is about who owns and controls what.

It is already well out of date to think of communications primarily as broadcasting and film, in addition to the longer established areas of the press and 'the arts'. The integration of computing and telecommunications technology has added an enormous new dimension to the transmission of information and image. Delivery, storage, processing and access to information is now of a quite different order of magnitude from even 20 years ago. The control of important means of communication offers great opportunity to make money and perhaps influence cultural consumption and ideas. Golding and Murdock stress the importance of the new systems of communication to big business and to the general economy. It is worth adding that the crucial role of communications in opening the city of London to international financial competition in 1986 sharply illustrates this point.

However, the specific focus of Golding and Murdock is on information and cultural provision. The new communications industries, like the older media, tend to be concentrated in the hands of a few corporations. Indeed, they seem to describe an emerging pattern of global concentration, particularly exemplified by Rupert Murdoch (though his communications 'empire' is still mainly based on the press). On the other hand, the balancing or 'countervailing' power of public intervention seems to be weakening. In Britain, this reflects the implementation of free-market principles by the Thatcher governments. The authors enumerate the ways in which they consider the application of Thatcherite free-market policies to communications has promoted corporate interests at the expense of the public interest.

Although I have omitted the policy section of the original article from which this extract is taken, the authors' socialist beliefs occasionally surface even in the more descriptive and analytical material given here. Their own views are more explicit in the final paragraph of the extract in which they write of the wider potential of the new communications.

Reading 93 Peter Golding and Graham Murdock, 'The New Communications Revolution' in James Curran *et al eds., Bending Reality: The State of the Media* (Pluto, 1986), pp. 175–83.

Developments in technology have combined with Thatcherite policies to create new centres of cultural power and alter established communication industries in important ways . . .

Although we concentrate here on their implications for information and cultural provision it is important to remember that communications technologies are also playing a major role in restructuring work and administration in pursuit of efficiency and profits. Current moves centre around improvements in computing and telecommunications technology and their convergence to form an integrated system which can transmit all kinds of information – speech, numerical data, written text, and visual images – over the same communications network. Applications include speeding the spread of automation in industry, rationalising clerical work, and replacing cash and cheque transactions with electronic funds transfers.

Most organisations buy the equipment and services they need

from companies specialising in advanced communications facilities, though leading firms, notably in the automobile industry, are beginning to move into these areas on their own account. In 1984 for example, the world's largest industrial company, General Motors, famous for its Chevrolet and Cadillac cars, took over the data processing company, Electronic Data systems. Its role is to integrate all of GM's computer and telecommunications systems into one worldwide paperless network linking everyone in the corporation, from executives and product designers to dealers running local car showrooms. Then in June 1985 GM branched out into the general communications marketplace by acquiring Hughes Aircraft, one of the world's leading space satellite companies. More recently, Daimler Benz, makers of the Mercedes, have bought a controlling interest in AEG whose interests span satellites, communications and micro-electronics. The new group is West Germany's biggest industrial corporation. Similar trends are also evident in Britain. BL's information systems division for example, is emerging as an important player in the market for electronic transfers of business data.

The centrality of the new communications industries to the economic structure of advanced capitalism means that communications policy can no longer concern itself solely with maximising the availability of cultural goods and services, promoting their diversity, and finding ways of making the cultural industries more accountable and responsive to consumer needs. These aims must remain at the core of any socialist cultural strategy, but in future they will need to be considered alongside economic goals in areas such as research and development and employment. Here we focus more narrowly on information and cultural provision, however, and in this area two sectors of the new communications industries are particularly relevant to policy: the electronic information industries and the new television industries.

The electronic information industries are based on the convergence of computing and telecommunications mentioned earlier and have two main sectors: videotex and interactive services. Videotex is the generic name for any system that allows electronic information to be transmitted for display on the screen of a domestic television set, computer monitor, or visual display unit (VDU). Teletext services use the spare capacity in the standard television signal for this, while viewdata systems use the telecommunications network.

At the moment, both basic teletext services (ITV's *Oracle* and the BBC's *Ceefax*) are free to anyone who has a set adapted for teletext reception, but they only operate one-way. Viewers cannot send messages back to the central information store or link up with each other. These interactive facilities are available on British Telecom's public viewdata system, *Prestel*, but access to them is much more expensive. As well as buying or renting the necessary equipment – and paying a quarterly subscription – users have to pay for the calls they make to the database, for the computer time they use and for the individual 'pages' of information they consult. Not surprisingly, *Prestel* is a luxury that most people cannot afford. At the end of 1984, there were only 21,801 viewdata terminals in private households, compared with 2.4 million teletext sets.

At the same time, *Prestel*'s interactive facilities have a number of positive features including messaging networks that allow personal computer owners to exchange information, and home shopping services which provide the electronic equivalent of a mail order catalogue. These could be particularly useful for groups like pensioners, the disabled and low income families. At the moment many members of these groups cannot take full advantage of the cheaper prices and greater range offered by city centre supermarkets or discount stores on the edge of towns, because they find travelling to them too difficult or expensive. However it is exactly the groups most in need who are least able to enter the new electronic marketplace. Half the senior citizens currently living alone on state pensions do not even have a telephone, let alone the other equipment they require. We need to come to grips with this situation by making telecommunications a central policy concern, and by devising practical proposals for increasing the diversity of information offered over public videotex systems and widening access to interactive facilities.

There is an equally pressing need to develop a comprehensive response to the rise of the new television industries. We already live in a television-centred culture. Virtually every household in the country has at least one television set and over a third (39 per cent) have two or more. In a normal week the average adult will watch around 31 hours of broadcasting as against seven hours spent reading the daily and Sunday papers. For most people, the screen will be their major source of information about events and issues outside their local area, and their main point of access to cultural and political life more generally. They will hardly ever go to the cinema or theatre but will watch a great many feature films and drama programmes. They will almost certainly never go to a political meeting or adult education class but may watch a considerable number of current affairs and feature programmes. Until recently, everything that appeared on the television screen was either pro-0duced or purchased by one of the main broadcasting organisations. This is no longer the case. Broadcast programmes still dominate people's viewing but they are now competing with the options offered by the new television industries of video, cable and, very soon, direct broadcasting by satellite (DBS). Like the electronic information industries, these developments present new problems as well as new opportunities for socialist policy. However, before we can devise a coherent response to either industry, we must look a little more closely at how they are organised.

Like the older media, the new communications industries tend to be highly concentrated, with a handful of firms dominating the key markets. Indeed they are quite often the same firms, as companies with significant stakes in established areas acquire interests in emerging sectors. One of the most spectacular examples is Reuters, which has long been among the top agencies supplying news stories to the world's press. Nowadays this business, though still lucrative, contributes less than ten per cent of the company's total profits. The rest comes from its electronic information services which supply business users with economic data and allow them to deal in currencies, bullion and bonds from their terminals. W. H. Smith provides another example of the growing links between the old and new media. As well as playing a key role in determining the general availability of books and magazines through its nation-wide chain of stores, it is now a major force in supplying programming for cable systems in Britain and Europe. It has a 35 per cent stake in the new Lifestyle channel, 19 per cent of Screen Sport, a substantial holding in the new Arts Channel and a significant interest in the rock video channel, Music Box, through its 30 per cent holding in Yorkshire Television, one of the three shareholders. However, the really significant players in the new communications system are the companies whose interests span the whole range of information and moving image industries, both old and new. Here again there are some very familiar names, including Robert Maxwell and Rupert Murdoch.

In addition to being the proprietor of the *Mirror, Sunday Mirror* and *Sunday People*, and owning publishing companies (such as Futura paperbacks) which account for 8 per cent of the British book market, Maxwell has extensive interests in electronic data services in the legal and scientific fields and significant stakes in the television industries. These include: a 13.8 per cent holding in the ITV company, Central Independent Television; 40 per cent of the independent production company, Antelope Productions; and sole ownership of the country's largest network of local cable systems. In August 1985 he extended his interests to Europe by buying a 20 per cent interest in the French broadcasting satellite TDF-1. This is due to be launched in mid-1986 with a signal capable of reaching 150 million people across the Continent through small dish receivers mounted on buildings. Rupert Murdoch is already well established in the satellite television market with his general entertainment service, Skychannel, which is piped into around 2 million households throughout Europe by local cable operators. He is now looking to expand his interests in this area through a partnership with the Belgian company, Group Bruxelles Lambert, one of the major shareholders in Radio Tele Luxembourg, another frontrunner for a channel on TDF-1. These ventures are part of Murdoch's ambitious plan to become a major force in the key markets for television-delivered entertainment. Other essential elements include: his purchase of the major Hollywood film and television studio 20th Century Fox (with its extensive back catalogue of productions); his acquisition of Metromedia, makers of the hit soap opera, *Dynasty;* his half share in one of the four major chains of American television stations; and his control of television stations in the two leading Australian markets, Sydney and Melbourne. This is in addition to owning one of the world's largest publishing empires which spans Australia and the USA as well as the *Sun, News of the World, Times* and *Sunday Times* in Britain.

Murdoch is one of the pioneers of a new style of megacorporation in the communications field, characterised by a wide spread of interests, integrated operations, and international reach. Their rise represents an unprecedented concentration of potential control over the production and flow of information and imagery. At the same time, the countervailing power of public intervention is being steadily weakened both institutionally, through the withdrawal of public ownership and subsidy, and philosophically, through the aggressive promotion of free market principles.

The most obvious British instance is the denationalisation programme. Since 1979 Conservative governments have privatised a number of public companies operating in key areas of the new communications industries. They include British Telecom, Cable and Wireless (the only company licensed to operate an alternative network to BT's until 1989), British Aerospace (the country's major satellite builder), Ferranti (the electronics company), ICL (Britain's only serious mainframe computer maker), Logica (one of the leading domestic companies in the computer software market), and INMOS (the microchip maker). Sales of shares in these companies represent a massive loss of public money at several levels.

First, there is the expense of arranging the sales themselves. It cost £323 million simply to dispose of 51.2 per cent of BT. Added to which, the shares were underpriced to attract small investors. As a result, eleven months after the sale they were worth a total of 3.4 billion pounds more than the asking price.

Secondly, there is the permanent loss of future revenues which could be used to subsidise access to telecommunications facilities and support initiatives in other areas of communications. In its first financial year as a private company for example, BT made £1.48 billion in pre-tax profits. . . This loss of direct control over a key part of the communications system makes developing an integrated public policy much more problematic.

This difficulty is aggravated by the current approach to regulating communications companies. Deregulation is not a particularly useful description of what is happening. The amount of regulation is less important than its direction. What we are seeing is a movement away from protection of the public interest and towards the promotion of corporate interests. Once again, telecommunications provides a good illustration. The main aim of current policies is to provide cheap and efficient services to business by allowing Cable and Wireless's Mercury network to compete on the best possible terms. To this end the new regulatory body, Oftel, has ruled that BT must connect Mercury's trunk network to its local and international networks and pay 50 per cent of the costs of providing any extra capacity required. The ensuing competition will undoubtedly keep costs down for business users but it will also mean higher line rentals and call charges for domestic customers, excluding even more low income

723

households from basic telecommunications facilities. This is entirely consistent with BT's steady retreat from the historic goal of making the telephone services geographically and financially accessible to everyone. Soon after the initial decision to license Mercury was announced, BT responded by cutting prices on the long distance and international routes most heavily used by business, increasing the price of domestic calls, and placing a question mark over the future of public call boxes in expensive-to-reach rural areas. Recent moves simply confirm the new wisdom that communication services are commodities not public utilities and that profitability takes precedence over accessibility.

This view also informs the developing cable television system. Because the present government defines cable very clearly as a commercial enterprise and not as a public service, most of the rules governing broadcasting are seen as irrelevant. Cable operators are basically in the business of selling additional entertainment channels showing sports, rock videos, feature films and mixed programming, plus additions such as arts, children's and lifestyle channels which can deliver audiences attractive to advertisers. They are not obliged to promote diversity if it does not correspond with market dynamics. There is no set limit on imported material and no positive requirement to provide reasonable access facilities or ensure that a wide range of views are presented. Cable operators may make concessions in these areas, to maintain good relations with the local community or earn 'brownie' points with the Cable Authority (who can cancel their franchise), but they are under no legal obligation to do so.

This attack on public service principles, coupled with cuts in public expenditure, is also having a powerful effect on the cultural and communications institutions that remain in the public sector. To survive in an increasingly harsh fiscal and political environment they are obliged to become more market oriented. The push to reintroduce museum charges and make users pay for library facilities is one aspect of this. The BBC's growing commercialism is another. This is particularly significant given the Corporation's centrality to the present cultural and communications system.

Faced with the growing gap between the licence fee revenue and the costs of maintaining its present range of programming, the BBC has adopted two main strategies: cutting costs by slimming down its operations, entering into more co-financing with outside investors; and raising extra revenues through the activities of its Enterprises division. These activities include: publishing the *Radio Times* (one of the country's top selling weekly magazines); producing books and records based on programmes; selling BBC productions in overseas markets; marketing an exclusive range of pre-recorded video cassettes through Marks and Spencer's stores; providing material for the *World Reporter*, the electronic information service; selling home computers in association with Acorn; and developing a range of educational materials on videodisc. Such commercial activities are expected to make around £100 million a year that can be ploughed back into original production and used to subsidise minority interest programmes. Although this could help to extend diversity, there is always the danger that the tail will end up wagging the dog and that projects will be selected for their attractiveness to outside investors, their spin-off possibilities, their suitability for video distribution, and their chances of selling in America and other major markets. This would mean more series and made-for-TV movies rather than single plays, more costume drama rather than contemporary fiction, more documentaries on wildlife and lifestyles rather than contemporary politics and contentious issues, and more attention to the Royal Family, the aristocracy, and the landmarks, celebrities and social types that make up the televisual tourism that is so saleable internationally.

In taking full advantage of the new communications marketplace the BBC risks reducing its ability to engage with the full range of contemporary British issues and experiences. The more successful it is commercially, the greater the risk.

Cost inflation and political pressures have also prompted the BBC to compromise its commitment to universal availability. Basic licence payers no longer have access to the full range of services. The Corporation broke with this fundamental tenet of public service when it agreed to provide programmes for the experimental commercial cable service in inner London, and to take a major role in the project to offer additional national channels by satellite available only on subscription. These schemes have been shelved, but both its major ventures into the business information market, *Datacast* and *World Reporter*, require additional payments. *Datacast* uses teletext technology to provide business users with a fast, confidential and nationally available service for transmitting business data. It is expected to earn the BBC at least £2 million a year by 1987. Once again, this money could provide a useful subsidy to general production, but it is also clear that as demand expands, capacity will have to be transferred from the public teletext service, reducing the range of information it carries.

Faced with contraction and commercialisation of publicly funded communications services and the rapid rise of the new megacorporations, it is easy to lapse into pessimism. However, this misses the opportunities in the developing situation. As Geoff Mulgan and Ken Worpole argue, building a socialist culture for the 1980s and beyond will entail using the full range of modern media and popular forms. Exploring the positive potential of new communications technologies is an essential part of this effort.

The possibility of using video as a cheap and flexible campaigning tool and means of expression is already widely accepted. Alternative computer applications are less well developed but potentially even more far-reaching. The scope for radical software is enormous. The possibilities of radical databases are even greater. Picture a continuously updated information store that contained and developed the kinds of materials that *Labour Research* now publishes monthly. Databases can also help to develop contact networks. In the USA for example, the National Women's Mailing List keeps a file with the names and interests of over 60,000 feminists who have agreed to be listed, making it very much easier for individuals and groups to contact people with similar interests or useful expertise. The word processing facilities of many micro computers can also be used to develop collective writing, since text can be added to, deleted or moved without having to retype. Computer networks can also be a valuable campaign tool. In the spring of 1985, for example, there were large demonstrations on campuses across America to urge university authorities to pull their investments out of companies operating in South Africa. Computer messaging was used extensively to exchange information and co-ordinate protests . . .

Question

1. (a) Summarise the information the extract gives on the ownership of the new communications.

(5 marks)

(b) Discuss the view that a free market in the new communications is not in the public interest.

(20 marks)

726

94 Glasgow Media Group: The Selective Coverage of the Women's Peace Camp at Greenham Common

The Glasgow Media Group has for long argued that the presentation of television news is not 'neutral' or 'objective'. In *Bad News* (1976), they write:

> Contrary to the claims, conventions, and culture of television journalism, the news is not a neutral product. For television news is a cultural artefact; it is a sequence of social manufactured messages, which carry many of the culturally dominant assumptions of our society. From the accents of the newscasters to the vocabulary of camera angles; from who gets on and what questions are asked, via selection of stories to presentation of bulletins, the news is a highly mediated product.

Television news, then, is not 'just the facts' but is the product of (i.e. 'mediated by') codes of selection and presentation. These 'codes' or hidden patterns of assumption tend to favour the establishment and status quo and to disfavour radicals and the forces of change. They argue that the priority broadcasters give to certain events (agenda setting) reflect their own class backgrounds and their attitudes to the political and social structure of the country. The fact that broadcasters usually believe in their own neutrality obscures their conservative, ideological role from themselves and their audience and thereby makes it more effective. The 'news' is easily perceived as the only or commonsense version of reality.

The strength of the Glasgow Media Group is that they provide detailed and substantial evidence to support their case. They consistently cite data to show that the news over-represents and favours 'official' versions of events and does the opposite with alternative or challenging versions. Their approach is well illustrated in the example given here – the news coverage of Greenham Common and the women's peace movement. What is most conspicuously absent from the news is an explanation of what political protest the camp was making as well as features considered central to the camp by its members. Another telling point is that the news very seldom conveyed the fact that opinion polls consistently showed more against than for the siting of

Cruise missiles at Greenham, i.e. more members of the public supported than opposed the cause of the Greenham women.

Reading 94 From The Glasgow Media Group, *War and Peace News* (Open University Press, 1985), pp. 196–204.

The women-only peace groups throughout the country, and particularly the women's peace camp at Greenham Common air force base, form a distinctive part of the British peace movement. We have taken them as a key example not because we believed they were particularly badly treated but because they provide the media as a whole with a reason to feature a series of stories. At the same time they are outside the main stream of sources for news journalism and do not 'fit' well into the routine way in which stories are assembled. In addition the women's movement has its own press which runs parallel to the rest of the media and offers its own account of events. There are also statements issued from other sources such as the police. As such it was important to lay out the range of perspectives which were available on the Greenham issue, to examine how each was treated in news accounts and to suggest why the coverage was as it was.

By the end of 1983 the women's peace movement had become highly visible in the media, the Greenham women in their woolly hats a familiar sight on our screens. BBC1's evening news on Christmas Eve 1983, for example, carried a film report about the women celebrating their third Christmas at the peace camp. We hear about donations arriving at the camp, about the women giving excess Christmas puddings to local children's homes, and a woman describing a campaign of attacks by local vigilantes: by now Greenham Common is well enough established to provide a seasonal news story without a mass demonstration or any arrests. The women even have the status of their own logo appearing behind the newscaster. Although the forms of protest varied, the television reporters seem to become quickly accustomed to them:

> Such scenes have become a familiar sight outside this particular court building.
>
> BBC1, 21.00, 15.2.83

> . . . members of the women's peace camp staging their now

familiar demonstration outside all seven of the entrances to the base.

> BBC1, 21.00, 31.3.83

Then they did what they often do: they sat down and started to sing.

> BBC1, 17.40, 8.7.83

Greenham Common was not always so well covered on the news. It came out of relative obscurity in December 1982, when 30,000 women were seen on television 'embracing the base': by then the camp had already been in existence for over sixteen months, virtually ignored by the media (although the fact that it attracted large numbers of women *before* it attracted much media coverage indicates that the camp and the national women's peace movement were already very active). In the earlier days, Greenham Common was not treated so seriously. In a brief report on BBC news of an incident not covered at all by ITN, it was dismissed as a 'so-called peace camp':

> Four women campaigning against nuclear weapons were arrested this afternoon after bailiffs arrived to demolish their *so-called peace camp* at Greenham Common near Newbury in Berkshire.
>
> BBC1, 21.30, 25.5.82

After the first sixteen months the Greenham Common camp did start to receive more coverage, but many events still were unreported. For example, on 25 June 1983, a large number of women arrived and put together a four-mile banner made up of embroidered sections from all over the world. Participants claimed that over 300 women entered the base but this was not covered on TV. Nor did the news report the regular break-ins, with small groups of women breaching security and entering the base, which continued on a daily or weekly basis throughout 1983. Another example of editorial selection was the treatment of International Women's Day for Disarmament on 24 May 1983. As the main BBC1 news reported:

> Thousands of women in Britain have been holding anti-nuclear demonstrations, they've been marking International Women's Day for Disarmament with protests in city centres and outside

> military bases . . . the organisers claiming that up to one
> million women had taken part nationwide.
>
> BBC1, 21.00, 24.5.83

Women were shown linking hands around the Ministry of Defence in London, protesting in a Kingston-upon-Thames supermarket, rallying in Glasgow, being dragged out of a military base in Devonport, and lying down in the main road in Bristol. The BBC report, lasting 1 minute 15 seconds, did not invite any of the women involved to explain their protest, and did not tell us about the full number of demonstrations across Britain (over 100) or about the simultaneous action in fourteen other countries; but it at least recognised that thousands of women participating in over 100 co-ordinated anti-nuclear and anti-military protests are making news.

By contrast, the Channel 4 and ITV news bulletins on the same night did not mention the women's actions at all. The absence of coverage of International Women's Day for Disarmament is even more striking since both ITN evening bulletins led with long items on defence and disarmament (discussing Labour's plans to scrap Polaris and the MX vote in Washington). Channel 4 news even appeared to run out of stories for its hour-long bulletin. Before the final item the newscaster is reduced to asking, 'Is there anything else out there?' The reply is a two-minute 'light' report on summer, beginning;

> It was just one of those great ideas that news editors sometimes
> pass on to reporters: has summer finally arrived? . . .

before the closing news summary, 'and that's Channel 4 news tonight, a day when the election campaign was dominated by defence' (Channel 4, 19.00, 24.5.83). ITN and Channel 4 chose to feature only debates within political parties or in the US Congress. So however 'familiar' Greenham Common's songs have become, the TV news can still leave out the women's peace movement.

We analysed the coverage of six women's peace demonstrations that appeared on the news between December 1982 and December 1983, in a total of thirty-eight bulletins; and compared it with other reports including some from the women who participated. We found that many features central to the camp were not covered in the news. First, why is the camp all-women? This is a fairly obvious question, asked by many visitors to the camp except apparently TV journalists; it does not seem to be prevalent in news reports and was not explained or raised in any of the coverage in our sample. How is the camp run? The women's peace movement has developed its own form of organising, based on collective decision-making and individual responsibility, run without leaders or any formal structure of bureaucracy. It's an exceptional method, quite distinct from the way CND, for example, or any political party works; but again the TV did not tell us about it. Instead, it gave the impression that the women's peace camp is run by the better-known disarmers of CND:

> At Greenham Common today women peace protesters have started a five-day attempted blockade. It's one of a number of events organised by CND to coincide with US 4th of July celebrations.
>
> BBC2, 19.35, 4.7.83

> Once again demonstrators from all over Britain converged on Greenham Common, and CND's hopes of a big turnout were fully realised.
>
> BBC1, 22.15, 11.12.83

The camp has always been independent from CND, and there are many differences between the two.

A further question is, what exactly is the political protest the camp is making? The broadcasters have grasped the fundamental idea that the camp is opposed to Cruise missiles – although even this is not always made clear. Coverage on the two ITV evening bulletins and BBC2's *Newsnight* of the opening of the five-day blockade at Greenham Common avoided giving any reason at all for the women's action. The full BBC2 report ran:

> Women peace compaigners have been trying without success to prevent workers entering or leaving Greenham Common air base. Police were there in strength and cleared a passage to allow workers in and out. There was one arrest. The protest began today on American Independence Day and is expected to continue until Friday.
>
> BBC2, 22.25, 4.7.83

On ITN the newscaster began: 'At Greenham Common police broke up an attempted blockade by women peace protesters' (ITN, 17.45, 4.7.83); and the correspondent concentrated on how the women were dragged away rather than why they were there. The BBC1 news did state that the protest was against Cruise. This is the full text of a BBC1 report.

> American Independence Day has been marked by more protests *against the siting of Cruise missiles* in Britain. The largest demonstration was at Greenham Common air base. Several dozen women tried to block coaches carrying base workers into the compound. There have been no reports of arrests.
> *Correspondent:* There are fewer protestors than previously at Greenham. Too few to succeed in their aim of blockading the base. A large force of police is apparently prepared if many more arrive as the five-day protest goes on. The main aim is publicity which helps explain the choice of today, American Independence Day.
>
> BBC1, 17.45, 4.7.83

Note the claim that 'the main aim is publicity'. The same point was made on International Women's Day for Disarmament: 'The women were more interested in putting across their anti-nuclear message than in inconveniencing the public'. (BBC1, 21.00, 24.5.83).

The news does not give any publicity to the women's *case*. Opposition to Cruise is mentioned, and some 'anti-nuclear message' is referred to, but the women have no chance to explain exactly *why* they oppose Cruise, *why* they are anti-nuclear. In particular, the broader anti-militarism of the women's peace movement, and the links they make between male supremacy, male violence, and nuclear weapons, are buried. Of course 'putting across their anti-nuclear message' is not the broadcasters' job; but they are falling down on the job of providing informative reporting if they cover the demonstrations without explaining (or allowing the demonstrators to explain) what they are trying to say.

Moreover the broadcasters *do* find space to give a full and proper explanation of the official pro-Cruise message. The BBC2 news story *Countdown to Cruise* on 9 November 1983 reports on:
1. (50 secs.) Mrs Thatcher's speech in Bonn urging the Soviet Union to accept the 'zero option'.
2. (18 secs.) The 24-hour peace camps set up at all the 102 US bases in Britain (though the newscaster adds that 'the government says they got their sums wrong and there are only 74').
3. (27 secs.) 'The effort of a group of Greenham women to take

their action to the other side of the Atlantic' with their court case against President Reagan for acting illegally in deploying Cruise.

4. (30 secs.) The visit of fourteen Labour MPs to the Greenham peace camp 'to show solidarity'.

5. (10 secs.) The government announcement that policing Greenham had cost £1.5 million over the past year.

6. (12 mins. 25 secs.) The correspondent's own story of how 'this morning I went down to Greenham to look as it were behind the wire'.

This is the background he gives to the decision to site Cruise in Europe:

These missiles, planned for Britain, Holland, Belgium, Germany and Italy, are intended to tell the Russians: Just in case you are tempted to try any attack, the West can now strike back from European soil, at selected military targets as far away as Kiev and Minsk, without having to risk certain annihilation by calling in America's intercontinental strategic system.

So the argument runs, these new Cruise missiles here at Greenham Common will actually make war *less* likely, by demonstrating to the Russians that if they attempted to lop off Western Europe from America, there would actually be a credible and still very demanding Western nuclear response.

Well, there's debate about the cogency of that nuclear strategy.

BBC2, 23.00, 9.11.83

At this point the reporter goes into the technical details of deployment: the training and organisation of missile crews, the composition of missile convoys, the construction of missiles, the timetable for deployment:

If all goes well, and all these tests are successfully passed, then the 501st will be awarded its Initial Operational Capability, its IOC. By the end of the year, Greenham will be a fully active nuclear weapons base.

BBC2, 23.00, 9.11.83

This is followed by the use of the silos, and the programme for convoy dispersal. Finally, he interviews a military specialist in a wood – 'an extremely good dispersal area' – about how the missiles would be fired. The official justification for Cruise – resting on the assumption of a Soviet threat ('to tell the Russians: "Just in case you're tempted to try any attack" '), and the deterrence arguments ('these new Cruise missiles here at Greenham will make war *less* likely') – presented in detail as 'news'.

This is scarcely in neutral terms, using such phrases as '*if all goes well* . . . Greenham will be a fully active nuclear weapons base'. Meanwhile, the case *against* Cruise is reduced to the single sentence: 'Well, there's debate about the cogency of that nuclear strategy' – even though the whole item is based on reports of active *opposition* to Cruise. In all, 1 minute and 15 seconds are devoted to the protest, and 12 minutes and 25 seconds to the 'technical background'. If it were not for the peace camp, the Greenham Common base would probably not be news at all, yet the political reasoning of the camp is virtually silenced.

The broadcasters sometimes argue that the business of TV news is to tell us about each day's events, and that 'background' issues and 'in-depth' explanations are properly left to current affairs programmes. However, it could be countered that the huge growth of a women-only movement, its unusual form of organisation, and the developing arguments against Cruise are all integral parts of the news about particular events, essential for allowing the viewers to come to an understanding of them. It is untrue to say that the news always confines itself to reporting merely 'what happened': it does attempt to explain the background to *some* issues. Consider, for instance, not only the 'in-depth' justification for Cruise missiles on BBC2 quoted above, but also the normal reporting of Westminster politics, with political correspondents offering their analysis of the arguments and the internal working of the parties. The problem is neither lack of space nor the news/current-affairs split – it is the journalists' assumption that Westminster politics are more important than the politics of grassroots opposition movements like the peace movement. (Which perhaps explains why BBC1 and BBC2's evening reports from Greenham Common on 9 November 1983 both carry an interview with a visiting, male MP, rather than with any of the peace women.) This may seem a 'natural' value judgement to the broadcasters, but it is a value judgement none the less.

Perhaps one of the reasons why the news captures so little of this innovative work is the women's refusal to tailor their activities to the needs of the media. A film about the camp records an incident of a TV journalist having difficulty coping with their obvious lack of respect for professional journalistic practices:

> *Journalist:* For God's sake, I'm doing a piece to camera to put your protest in a logical – in a way that people will understand – and make out that you're making some sense, and you go and clown around in the background and that doesn't do your case any good at all. . . . The bloody thing won't be used if you're doing cartwheels in the background because it will be distracting.
> *Peace camper:* But why should it be distracting? We're doing all kinds of things here.
> *Journalist:* I know you are, and when we film you doing them that's fine but when I'm doing a piece to camera . . . You were deliberately doing cartwheels in the background and you must know – all right I'm sorry I called you a tit.
> *Peace camper:* But there's a way of speaking to people . . .
> *Journalist:* I know there's a way of speaking to people – I've got a job to do and my job is completely messed up.

Public opinion and support

Another aspect of the Greenham Common peace camp not really dealt with in the news is the question of how much public support it has for its call that Cruise missiles should not be sited in Britain. There are hints given that, although the peace women themselves are sincere and confident, the television journalists from their position can see that they ought to pay more attention to 'criticism of their cause' and the fact that there is 'no hope':

> They left tonight having spent two days somewhat detached from dispute about and criticism of their cause, but full of confidence in it.
>
> BBC1, 21.00, 13.12.82

> [*Interview question*] Are you surprised by the level of support, given that there seems to be really no hope now of stopping the Cruise missiles?
>
> Channel 4, 19.00, 8.7.83

From this point of view, support would indeed be a surprise. On a

BBC World Service radio programme answering listeners' letters, we hear that:

> Our news editor's view is that it's obvious that the Greenham Common women are protesting against the views of the established majority. After all, if the Greenham Common women were supported by the majority, they'd have nothing to protest about, would they?
>
> BBC World Service, 25.11.83

In fact, though, as a range of public opinion polls over a period of time consistently show, more people are opposed to Cruise than in favour of it; and most polls show an absolute majority against Cruise. Here are the results:

Siting Cruise in Britain

	% against	% for	Don't know
April 1981 Marplan for *Guardian*	50	41	9
December 1982 Gallup for *Sanity*	58	31	11
January 1983 Marplan for *Guardian*	61	27	12
January 1983 MORI for *Sunday Times*	54	36	10
February 1983 Gallup for *Daily Telegraph*	54	36	10
May 1983 Marplan for *Guardian*	54	34	12
May 1983 Harris for *Observer*	55	32	13
October 1983 Marplan for *Guardian*	48	37	15
October 1983 MORI for *Sunday Times*	51	43	6
November 1983 NOP for *Daily Mail*	47	37	16
November 1983 Marplan for *Guardian* and *Panorama*	47	42	11
November 1983 Gallup for *Daily Telegraph*	48	41	11
December 1983 Marplan for *Weekend World**	66	28	6

*This poll question was about deployment rather than siting, as Cruise missiles had arrived by December 1983.

Note Some of the variations in results are attributable to variations in the sampling techniques and in the wording of poll questions, but the underlying trend is clear.

In other words, the repeated demonstrations at Greenham which the TV news (sometimes) covers are in some respects voicing majority opinion, and not the lost cause of a 'detached' few. The fact that the cause commands such widespread support could well be important in the viewers' perception of the Greenham demonstrations, but the TV news almost always fails to mention it.

Question
1. (a) *What evidence is given in the extract for selective bias in the news coverage of the women's peace movement at Greenham Common?*
(10 marks)
(b) *What explanations can you offer for the level of bias you established in question 1(a)?*

(15 marks)

95 Angela McRobbie: Teenage Girls, *Jackie*, and the Ideology of Adolescent 'Femininity'

Angela McRobbie uses the girls' 'teen' magazine, *Jackie*, to illustrate the socialisation of female adolescents into 'feminine' culture. Feminine culture ultimately reflects the sexual division of labour in capitalist society: the girls learn to be dependent on men, to service them in domestic labour, and thus to help maintain the capitalist system. According to Marxist feminists, the process of learning 'the female role' begins in babyhood within the family and is reinforced through the media and at school and work. McRobbie's contribution here is to show how, even within the apparently 'free' area of leisure and consumption – reading a 'teen' magazine – young females are caught within the framework of the dominant (capitalist) culture. Crudely, they pay to be brainwashed. This process continues as the girls grow older as they graduate through *19, Honey,* or *Over 21* to *Women's Own.*

'Femininity', as presented in *Jackie*, is based on an emphasis on the prime importance of the personal and of romance. Girls share these values but in order to 'catch' their man are forced to compete – a double-bind. Girls may appear to 'choose' their cultural and leisure activities but McRobbie suggests that this illusion of choice is perhaps the most effective way of ensuring their conformity.

Reading 95 From Angela McRobbie: *Teenage Girls,* Jackie *and the Ideology of Adolescent Femininity* in Bernard Waites *et al*, ' Popular Culture: Past and Present' (Croom Helm, 1983).

The world of *Jackie*

What then are the key features which characterise *Jackie?* First there is a 'lightness' of tone, a non-urgency, which holds true right through the magazine, particularly in the use of colour, graphics and advertisements. It asks to be read at a leisurely pace, indicating that its subject matter is not wholly serious, is certainly not 'news'. Since entertainment and leisure goods are designed to arouse feelings of pleasure as well as interest, the appearance of the magazine is inviting, its front cover shows a 'pretty' girl smiling happily. The dominance of the visual level, which is maintained throughout the magazine, reinforces this notion of leisure. It is to be glanced through, looked at and only finally read. Published at weekly intervals, the reader has time to peruse each item at her own speed. She also has time to pass it round her friends or swap it for another magazine.

Rigid adherence to a certain style of lay-out and patterning of features ensures a familiarity with its structure(s). The girl can rely on *Jackie* to *cheer her up, entertain her, or solve her problems each week*. The 'style' of the magazine, once established, facilitates and encourages partial and uneven reading, in much the same way as newspapers also do. The girl can quickly turn to the centre page for the pin-up, glance at the fashion page and leave the problems and picture stories which are the 'meat' of the magazine, till she has more time.

Articles and features are carefully arranged to avoid one 'heavy' feature following another. The black and white picture stories taking up between 2½ and 3 full pages are always broken up by a coloured advert, or beauty feature, and the magazine opens and closes by inviting the reader to participate directly through the letters or the problem pages.

This sense of solidness and resistance to change (*Jackie*'s style has not been substantially altered since it began publication) is reflected and paralleled in its thematic content. Each feature (as will be seen later) comprises workings and re-workings of a relatively small repertoire of specific themes or concerns which sum up the girls' world. These topics saturate the magazine. Entering the world of *Jackie* means suspending interest in the 'real' world of school, family or work, and participating in a sphere which is devoid of history and resistant to change.

Jackie deals primarily with the terrain of the personal and it makes a 'turning inwards' to the sphere of the 'soul', the 'heart', or less metaphorically, the emotions. On the one hand, of course, certain features do change – fashion is itself predicated upon change and upon being 'up to date'. But the degree of change even here is qualified – certain features remain the same, e.g. the models' 'looks', poses, the style of drawing and its positioning within the magazine and so on. All that does change is the length of the hem, shade of make-up, style of shoe, etc.

Above all, *Jackie*, like the girl she symbolises, is intended to be 'looked at'. This overriding concern with visuals affects every feature. But its visual appearance and style also reflect the spending power of its readers. There is little of the extravagant or exotic in *Jackie*. The paper on which it is printed is thin without being wafer-thin. The fashion and beauty pages show clothes priced within the girls' range and the adverts are similarly focused at a low budget market featuring, principally, personal toiletries, tampons, shampoos and lipsticks rather than larger consumer goods.[. . .]

The code of romance: the moment of bliss

> The hero of romance knows how to treat women. Flowers, little gifts, love letters, maybe poems to her eyes and hair, candlelit meals on moon-lit terraces and muted strings. Nothing hasty, physical. Some heavy breathing . . . Mystery, magic, champagne, ceremony . . . women never have enough of it. (Germaine Greer, *The Female Eunuch*.)

Jackie picture stories are similar *in form* to those comic strips, and tales of adventure, time travel, rivalry and intrigue which regularly fill the pages of children's weeklies. Yet there is something distinctive about these stories which indicates immediately their concern with romance. First the titles clearly announce a concern with 'you', 'me', 'love' and 'happiness'. Romantic connotations are conveyed through the relationship between titles and the names of 'pop' songs and ballads. (*Jackie* does not however use the older *Boyfriend* technique of using a well-known pop song and its singer to both inspire the story and give it moral weight!)

The title, then, anchors the story it introduces. In our sample these include:

'The Happiest Xmas Ever', 'Meet Me On The Corner', 'As Long As I've Got You', 'Come Fly With Me', and 'Where Have All The Flowers Gone?'

This concern with romance pervades every story and is built into them through the continued use of certain formal techniques and styles.

For a start, the way the characters look indicates clearly that this is serious, not 'kids' stuff'. They are all older and physically more mature than the intended reader. Each character conforms to a well-established and recognisable standard of beauty or handsomeness and they are all smart, fairly sophisticated young adults, rather than adolescents or 'teenagers'.

The most characteristic feature of 'romance' in *Jackie* is the concern with the narrow and restricted world of the emotions. No attempt is made to fill out social events or backgrounds. The picture story is the realm, *par excellence*, of the individual. Each story revolves round one figure and the tiny web of social relationships surrounding him or, usually, her. Rarely are there more than two or three characters in each plot and where they do exist it is merely as part of the background or scenery – in the cafe, at the disco or in the street.

Unlike comic strips, where the subject is fun, excitement or adventure, these stories purport to deal with the more serious side of life – hence the semi-naturalistic style of the drawings and the use of black and white. This, along with the boldness of the drawings, the starkness of stroke and angularity of the figures, conspires to create an impression of 'realism' and seriousness. The form of the stories alone tells us that romance is important, serious and relevant. Yet simultaneously in the content, we are told that it is fun; the essence and meaning of life; the key to happiness, etc. It is this blend which gives the *Jackie* romance its characteristic flavour. In general terms this is nothing new, these stories owe a great deal to popular cinema romances, and to novelettes. For a start the characters closely resemble the anonymous but distinctive type of the 'film star' – dewy-eyed women and granite-jawed heroes. Their poses are equally soaked in the language of film – the clinch, the rejected lover alone by herself as the sun sets – the moon comes up – to name but a few. But this cinematic resemblance is based on more than just *association*. The very form of the comic strip has close links with the film. Strung together, in a series of *clips*, set out across and down the page, the stories 'rise' to a climax and resolution, graphically illustrated in larger images erupting across the page.

From these clips we can see clearly that the emotional life is defined and lived in terms of *romance* which in turn is equated with *great moments* rather than long-term processes. Hence the centrality and visual impact of the clinch, the proposal, the wedding day. Together these *moments* constitute a kind of orchestration of *time;* through them the feminine career is constructed. The picture stories comprise a set of visual images composed and set within a series of frames laid out across the page to be 'read' like a text. But these frames communicate *visually*, resemble film-clips and tell the story by 'freezing' the action into sets of 'stills'. Unlike other comics (*Bunty* or *Judy*), *Jackie* stories do not conform to the convention of neatly mounted images set uniformly across the page. Instead a whole range of loose frames indicating different kinds of situations or emotions is used. This produces a greater continuity between 'form' and 'content', so that as the pace of the story accelerates, the visuals erupt *with* the breathless emotional feelings, spilling out over the page.

Each separate image which makes up the story is 'anchored' with sets of verbal messages illuminating the action and eliminating ambiguity. [. . .]Thus the moments of reading and looking are collapsed into one, and the reader is spared the boredom of having to read more lengthy descriptions; she merely 'takes it in' and hurries on to the next image. The techniques through which this relay operates are well known; – dialogue is indicated by the use of balloons issuing from the mouths of the speakers and filled with words; – and thoughts are conveyed through a series of small bubbles which drift upwards away from the character's mouth – thinking being associated with a 'higher' level of discourse, an 'intellectual' pursuit.

The central and most dramatic incident in each story is specified by the spilling out of one visual image over the page. This image sums up graphically the fraught nature of the moment; the moment when the timid shy heroine catches sight of her handsome boyfriend fascinated by her irresistible best friend at a party which she stupidly invited her to; or when the girl, let down by her boy, rushes out of the coffee bar across the street to be hit by a passing car . . . and so on.

Each frame represents a selection from the development of the plot, and is credited with an importance which those intervening moments are not. Thus the train, supermarket, and office have meaning, to the extent that they represent potential meeting-places where the girl *could well* bump into the prospective boyfriend, who lurks round every corner. It is this which determines their inclusion in the plot; the possibility that everyday life could be transformed into *social life*.

Within these frames themselves the way the figures look, act, and pose contributes also to the ideology of romance. For a start there is very little variation in types of physical appearance. This homogeneity hinges on a blend of modernity and conservatism which typifies the *Jackie* 'look'. The girls are 'mod' but neat and conventional, rarely are they 'way-out'. Boys may look acceptably scruffy and dishevelled by displaying a kind of managed untidiness . . .

Jackie asserts the absolute and natural separation of sex roles. Girls can take humiliation and be all the more attractive for it, as long as they are pretty and unassertive. Boys can *be* footballers, pop stars, even juvenile delinquents, but girls can only be feminine. The girl's life is defined through emotions – jealousy, possessiveness and devotion. Pervading the stories is an elemental fear, fear of losing your boy, or of never getting one. Romance as a code or a way of life, precipitates individual neurosis and prohibits collective action as a means of dealing with it.

By displacing all vestiges or traces of adolescent sexuality and replacing it with concepts of love, passion and eternity, romance gets trapped within its own contradictions, and hence we have the 'problem page'.

Once declared and reciprocated this love is meant to be lasting, and is based on fidelity and pre-marital monogamy. But the girl knows that where *she*, in most cases, will submit to these axioms, there is always the possibility that her boy's passion will, and can be, roused by almost any attractive girl at the bus-stop, outside the home, etc.

The way this paradox is handled is to introduce terms like resignation, despair, fatalism – it's 'all in the game'. Love has its losers, it must be admitted, but for the girl who has lost, there is always the chance that it will happen again, this time with a more reliable boy. Girls don't, then, fight back. Female 'flirts' always come to a 'bad end'; they are abandoned by their admirers who quickly turn their attention to the quiet, trusting best friend who had always been content to sit in the background.

Conclusion

What, then, are the central features of *Jackie* in so far as it presents its readers with an ideology of adolescent femininity? First it sets up, defines and focuses exclusively on 'the personal', locating it as the sphere of *prime* importance to the teenage girl. It presents this as a totality – and by implication all else is of secondary interest to the 'modern girl'. Romance problems, fashion, beauty and pop mark out the limits of the girl's concern – other possibilities are ignored or dismissed.

Second, *Jackie* presents 'romantic individualism' as the ethos, *par excellence*, for the teenage girl. The *Jackie* girl is alone in her quest for love; she refers back to her female peers for advice, comfort and reassurance *only* when she has problems in fulfilling this aim. Female solidarity, or more simply the idea of girls together – in *Jackie* terms – is an unambiguous sign of failure. To achieve self-respect, the girl has to escape the 'bitchy', 'catty' atmosphere of female company and find a boyfriend as fast as possible. But in doing this she has not only to be individualistic in outlook – she has to be prepared to fight ruthlessly – by plotting, intrigue and cunning, to 'trap her man'. Not surprisingly this independent-mindedness is short-lived. As soon as she finds a 'steady', she must renounce it altogether and capitulate to *his* demands, acknowledging his domination and resigning herself to her own subordination.

This whole ideological discourse, as it takes shape through the pages of *Jackie*, is immensely powerful. Judging by sales figures alone, *Jackie* is a force to be reckoned with by feminists. Of course this does not mean that its readers swallow its axioms unquestioningly. And indeed until we have a clearer idea of just how girls 'read' *Jackie* and encounter its ideological force, our analysis remains one-sided.

For feminists a related question must be how to go about countering *Jackie* and undermining its ideological power at the level of *cultural* intervention. One way of beginning this task would be for feminist teachers and youth leaders to involve girls in the task of 'deconstructing' this seemingly 'natural' ideology; and in breaking down the apparently timeless qualities of girls' and women's 'mags'.

Another more adventurous possibility would be the joint production of an alternative; a magazine where girls are depicted in situations other than the romantic, and where sexuality is discussed openly and frankly; not just contraception, masturbation and abortion, but the *social relations* of sexuality, especially the sexism of their male peers. Likewise girls would be encouraged to create their own music, learn instruments and listen to music without having to drool over idols. Their clothes would not simply reflect styles created by men to transform them into junior sex-objects, products of male imaginations and fantasies. But most of all, readers would be presented with an *active* image of female adolescence – one which pervades every page and is not just deceptively 'frozen' into a single 'energetic/glamorous' pose as in the fashion pages and Tampax adverts in *Jackie*.

Questions
1. *(a) How is 'romance' presented in* Jackie?

(10 marks)

(b) Explain how girls in Jackie *both support and compete with each other. What explanation does Angela McRobbie give for this behaviour?*

(15 marks)
2. *How does* Jackie *socialise girls for their likely future roles in the sexual division of labour?*

(15 marks)

Activity
Select a magazine that you read fairly regularly. Find examples of the presentation of gender roles (say, four or five). What messages do the presentations convey? Compare results.

96 Bhikhu Parekh: Racial Prejudice and the Press

Although written by a well-known academic, this is a personal rather than scholarly statement about racism. Parekh was clearly angered by the way certain sections of the press treated two racial issues occurring in late 1986. However, he does not allow his feelings to rule his pen and makes a factually based and tightly argued response.

He fully explains the background to the move by Brent Council to appoint teacher-advisers on racial matters. Towards the end of this section, he rightly points out that the tendency of much of the press to mix up the teacher-advisers issue with the controversy around the suspension of a headteacher could only lead to confusion. The second matter Parekh discusses is the imposition of visa requirements on visitors from five Commonwealth countries. The main reason given by government officials for this was the need to control the very large numbers of would-be visitors. In any case, the major issue of racism is the way in which some of the press described the Asian visitors. I myself will never forget the shock of the 'Liars' headline when it was drawn to my attention. My own view is that a 'free' press (though freedom is never absolute) is a condition of an 'open' society but the public need to be vigilant that the press itself does not abuse that freedom. Racism is such an abuse.

Reading 96 From Bhikhu Parekh, 'Personal View: Prejudice and the Press' in *New Society*, 7 November 1986, p. 28.

Our newspapers, including the best of them, have not shown much care and sensitivity in reporting racial matters. Two recent events have sharply brought this painful truth to the attention of even those otherwise inclined to doubt it.

Ever since the sixties it has been widely recognised that a local authority with a sizeable proportion of Commonwealth children should make requisite provisions to help them overcome the difficulties they are likely to face in their new environment. In order to help and encourage a local authority to do so, section 11 of the Local Government Act, 1966, entitles it to receive 75 per cent of the salary cost of the extra staff appointed by it. As is widely known, several local authorities have for years been improperly using the section 11 money to appoint general staff and allocating the money saved to other purposes. Despite years of complaints by the blacks, nothing was done.

During the last five years the Rampton, Swann and Egglestone reports have all highlighted the gross underachievement of ethnic minority children, and pointed to such factors as low teacher expectations, inadequate teacher attention and stimulus, lack of role models, poor regard for the children's culture and identity, and ethnocentric curriculum as among its major causes. Brent Council developed an interesting set of proposals to deal with the situation and applied for a staff of 177–103 to be placed in schools, 66 to be engaged in curriculum development projects and eight in the Directorate of Education. The proposals were prepared by its Conservative administration, had all-party support, were widely known, and had, after suitable revisions, been approved by the DES and the Home Office in April this year.

All of a sudden the storm broke loose last week. We were told the following by all the tabloid and some quality newspapers:

1. Brent was going to appoint 'race advisers.'
2. The 'race advisers' were really 'spies' reporting on their colleagues.
3. They were 'thought police' and 'commissars' who will tell our children what to think.
4. They represented a backdoor attempt to initiate a 'political revolution.'
5. Brent's ideas were all 'left-wing' and reflected the crazy educational philosophy of the 'loony left.'
6. Since Brent is Labour-controlled, its actions reflected Labour's policies and showed what it would do if it came to power.
7. The whole thing was 'suddenly' contrived and a 'shock' to the innocent British public.
8. Brent had violated section 11, for the latter was only meant to appoint English language teachers.

Now (1) was false as Brent was appointing teachers not race advisers. (2) was a distortion bordering on a lie for, although this may occur, it also may not, and this was not the intention. (3) was entirely untrue because periodically revising the curriculum is a part of a local authority's responsibility, was recommended by the three government reports mentioned earlier, and the new curriculum would be open to HMI's scrutiny. (4) was mischievous, as a mere 177 among several thousand staff can obviously do little, they were organisationally responsible to head teachers, and they had clearly allocated responsibilities. (5) was wrong because the ideas came from the three 'liberal' reports and were conceived by Brent's

Conservative administration. (6) was a mischievous and disgraceful way to malign a party and serve the interests of its opponents. (7) was totally false, for the Brent proposals had been known for nearly a year. (8) was a distortion, because section 11 covers a wide area. The Brent proposals do have obvious limitations and require critical examination. Misrepresenting and denouncing them, or mixing them up with a discussion of the case of Maureen McGoldrick (the headteacher suspended for alleged racism) was hardly the way to do so.

Thanks to these falsehoods and distortions, Brent might lose the posts. More importantly the black minorities feel deeply offended. When 'their' money was misused no one listened to their complaints. But now it was being put to what appeared to be good use, and their children seemed likely to progress, it looks like being taken away, and a demand made to abolish section 11 itself. They also feel that when their affairs are the subject of discussion, truth, sensitivity, objectivity and mutual respect apparently do not count.

The picture was little different when the visa requirement was imposed on visitors from five Commonwealth countries. The visa requirement was discriminatory; a case for it had not been made out; neither the governments concerned nor the Commission for Racial Equality had been consulted; and no provision had been made to send adequate and trained staff to the countries concerned. With a couple of exceptions, no newspaper took up these matters. When around 2,500 Asians arrived, the tabloid newspapers were awash with denigratory headlines. 'Asian flood swamps airport,' screamed the *Express*. '3,000 Asians flood Britain,' shouted the *Sun*. 'Migrants flood in,' echoed The *Mail*. *The Sun*, in a six-inch headline, called them 'liars.' Only the *Independent* and the *Guardian* agreed that the scenes at Heathrow were a 'disgrace' to Britain.

Once again, the newspaper reports contained falsehoods and distortions. The Asians were visitors not immigrants; a very large majority of them had a right to come; many came sooner than they had intended because of the uncertainty of the government policy; and the chaos was a result of inadequate planning. Tremendous inconvenience was caused to their sponsors travelling from long distances; and the whole Asian community was subjected to vicious moral mugging.

These are two of many disturbing instances. They show how much our sensibility has coarsened and the level of decency has declined in racial matters. The press is a paradoxical institution. A form of private property, it is also a public institution with considerable political power and responsibility. Its economic and political dimensions often pull in opposite directions. Its freedom is not and cannot be an absolute value. It is desirable because and insofar as it provides accurate information, uncovers and presents the truth (however inconvenient), analyses events from different points of view and helps its readers appreciate their complexity and formulate their own judgements.

When the press twists facts, tells lies, declares a cold war on a section of the community, uses editorials as party political broadcasts and subjects its readers to a daily breakfast of raw prejudices, it undermines the basic preconditions of democracy. It distorts public utterances and vitiates public debate, and the freedom of the *press* becomes an enemy of the freedom of *speech*.

One would have thought that the Press Council had a vital role to play here. As a council for and not merely of the press, it has a supreme responsibility to protect the integrity of public discourse, nurture a free flow of information and ideas, and preserve public confidence in the press. In racial matters its record so far has been rather patchy. Most of its adjudications relate to complaints about whether or not a newspaper was right to disclose a person's colour in criminal cases and riots. Sometimes it has dealt with offensive cartoons. And on rare occasions it has adjudicated on complaints about articles lacking 'balance, sensitivity and care.'

Surely all this is hardly enough. Complaints about the disclosure of a man's colour are rather trivial. Far more important issues relating to how we talk about each other and how much we respect truth and objectivity are at stake. The Press Council could periodically mount investigations of its own into the way certain types of event and groups of people are reported and commented upon. It could also issue guidelines, a kind of code of practice, in areas where it thinks the press has a tendency to slip up.

And it must really do something about the absurd situation when the force of its adjudication can be underminded by the newspaper concerned publishing and ridiculing it.

Activity
Divide the class into small groups of two or three. Each group carries out a content analysis of the racial coverage of a national newspaper for

a week. If possible, distinguish between news and comment. Compare results. (A similar exercise could be carried out on the local press.)

98 Tony Bennett *et al*: Culture, Structure and Gramsci's Concept of Hegemony

This section requires a more theoretical statement than has so far been offered. The student needs some overall conception of cultural analysis – even if only to reject it. The inclusion of this difficult reading is justified because it provides such a framework. So far, several readings in this section and the previous one have used the concept of ideology to analyse ideas and beliefs in relation to class or gender. Nicholas Abercrombie, for instance, examined class relations in terms of ideological domination and subordination. In this reading, Tony Bennett states his preference for Gramsci's term 'hegemony' to that of 'domination'. This concept is less rigid than that of domination and allows for some negotiation between bourgeois and working class culture within the overall influence of the former.

Bennett also attributes to Gramsci the important point that structure and culture are interdependent concepts and that cultural analysis recognises this. Many will say 'Amen' to that for it surely recognises the obvious. It is surely time that the polarised structuralist/culturalist debate was resolved in a way that appreciates the interplay of both processes. Perhaps Bennett's comments will be regarded as a fairly definitive statement that this is so.

The issues discussed by Bennett are present in a less explicit way in the work of Angela McRobbie (Reading 95). Like John Clarke (Reading 47), these two authors spent time at the Centre for Cultural Studies which has had great influence on cultural analysis in Britain.

Bennett nicely 'completes the circle' of the two sections on ideology. His presentation of the concept of hegemony provides a flexible framework for ideological analysis.

Reading 98 From Tony Bennett, Colin Mercer and Janet Woolacott, eds., *Popular Culture and Social Relations* (Open University Press 1986), pp. xiv-xvii.

For Gramsci too, of course, cultural and ideological practices are to be understood and assessed in terms of their functioning within the antagonistic relations between the bourgeoisie and the working class as the two fundamental classes of capitalist society. Indeed, Gramsci's insistence that these antagonistic class relations form the ultimately determining horizon within which cultural and ideological analysis must be located constitutes the outer limit to the programme of theoretical revision he inaugurated in relation to classical Marxist theories of ideology. Where Gramsci departed from the earlier Marxist tradition was in arguing that the cultural and ideological relations between ruling and subordinate classes in capitalist societies consist less in the *domination* of the latter by the former than in the struggle for *hegemony* – that is, for moral, cultural, intellectual and, thereby, political leadership over the whole of society – between the ruling class and, as the principal subordinate class, the working class.

This substitution of the concept of hegemony for that of domination is not, as some commentators have suggested, merely terminological; it brings in tow an entirely different conception of the means by which cultural and ideological struggles are conducted. Whereas, according to the dominant ideology thesis, bourgeois culture and ideology seek to take the place of working class culture and ideology and thus to become directly operative in framing working class experience, Gramsci argues that the bourgeoisie can become a hegemonic, leading class only to the degree that bourgeois ideology is able to accommodate, to find some space for, opposing class cultures and values. A bourgeois hegemony is secured not via the obliteration of working class culture, but via its *articulation to* bourgeois culture and ideology so that, in being associated with and expressed in the forms of the latter, its political affiliations are altered in the process.

As a consequence of its accommodating elements of opposing class cultures, 'bourgeois culture' ceases to be purely or entirely bourgeois. It becomes, instead, a mobile combination of cultural and ideological elements derived from different class locations which are, but only provisionally and for the duration of a specific historical conjuncture, affiliated to bourgeois values, interests and objectives. By the same token, of course, the members of subordinate classes never encounter or are oppressed by a dominant ideology in some pure or class essentialist form; bourgeois ideology is encountered only in the compromised forms it must take in order to provide some accommodation for opposing class values. As Robert Gray remarks, if the Gramscian concept of hegemony refers to the processes through which the ruling class seeks to negotiate opposing class cultures onto a cultural and ideological terrain which wins for it a position of leadership, it is also true that what is thereby consented to is a *negotiated version* of ruling class culture and ideology:

> Class hegemony is a dynamic and shifting relationship of social subordination, which operates in two directions. Certain aspects of the behaviour and consciousness of the subordinate classes may reproduce a version of the values of the ruling class. But in the process value systems are modified, through their necessary adaptation to diverse conditions of existence; the subordinate classes thus follow a 'negotiated version' of ruling-class values. On the other hand, structures of ideological hegemony transform and incorporate dissident values, so as effectively to prevent the working through of their full implications.

Although an over-rapid and somewhat abstract summary of a complex body of theory, the main point is, perhaps, clear enough: that the spheres of culture and ideology cannot be conceived as being divided into two hermetically separate and entirely opposing class cultures and ideologies. The effect of this is to disqualify the bipolar options of the structuralist and culturalist perspectives on popular culture, viewed as either the carrier of an undiluted bourgeois ideology or as the site of the people's authentic culture and potential self-awakening, as unmitigated villain or unsullied hero. To the contrary, to the degree that it is implicated in the struggle for hegemony – and, for Gramsci, the part played by the most taken-for-granted, sedimented cultural aspects of everyday life are crucially implicated in the processes whereby hegemony is fought for, won, lost, resisted – the field of popular culture is structured by the attempt of the ruling class to win hegemony and by the forms of opposition to this endeavour. As such, it consists not simply of an imposed mass culture that is coincident with dominant ideology, nor simply of spontaneously oppositional cultures, but is rather an area of negotiation between the two within which – in different particular types of popular culture – dominant, subordinate and oppositional cultural and ideological values and elements are 'mixed' in different permutations.

In sum, then, the 'turn to Gramsci' has been influential in both disputing the assumption that cultural forms can be assigned an essential class-belongingness and contesting a simply 'bourgeois versus working class' conception of the organisation of the cultural and ideological relationships. These reorientations have resulted in two decisive shifts of political emphasis within the study of popular culture. First, they have produced a perspective, within Marxism, from which it is possible to analyse popular culture without adopting a position that is either opposed to it or uncritically for it. The forms of political assessment of cultural practices which the theory of hegemony calls for are much more conjunctural and pliable than that. A cultural practice does not carry its politics with it, as if written upon its brow for ever and a day; rather, its political functioning depends on the network of social and ideological relations in which it is inscribed as a consequence of the ways in which, in a particular conjuncture, it is articulated to other practices. In brief, in suggesting that the political and ideological articulations of cultural practices are *movable* – that a practice which is articulated to bourgeois values today may be disconnected from those values and connected to socialist ones tomorrow – the theory of hegemony opens up the field of popular culture as one of enormous political possibilities. It is thus, for example, that in many recent debates, the call has been made that nationalism, and the forms in which it is constructed and celebrated, should be given a socialist articulation rather than be dismissed as essentially and irredeemably bourgeois.

Equally important, the Gramscian critique of class essentialist conceptions of culture and ideology and the associated principles of class reductionism enables due account to be taken of the relative separation of different regions of cultural struggle (class, race, gender) as well as of the complex and changing ways in which these may be overlapped on to one another in different historical circumstances. Apart from being an important advance on classical Marxism, this has also served as an important check on the Foucauldian tendency to view power and the struggle against it as equally diffuse and unrelated. Most important, though, it has offered a framework within which the relations between the cultural politics of socialist movements and those of, say, feminist or national liberation struggles can be productively debated without their respective specifications threatening either to engulf or be engulfed by the others.

This is not to suggest that Gramsci's writings contain the seeds of an answer to all problems in the field of popular culture analysis. There are specific and detailed technical and theoretical problems peculiar to television and film analysis, popular music, the study of lived cultures and the field of popular writings which no amount of general theorising might resolve. Likewise, questions concerning the relations between culture and class, culture and gender and culture and nation remained vexed and complex, requiring separate and detailed attention if progress is to be made. The value of the Gramscian theory of hegemony is that of providing an integrating framework within which both sets of issues might be addressed and worked through in relation to each other. By the same token, of course, it is liable to the criticism that it is too accommodating and expansive a framework, over-totalising in its analytical claims and ambit. The charge has certainly been made often enough, and it seems one likely to be pressed with increased vigour, particularly in the area of cultural studies.

Question

1. (a) For what reasons does Bennett prefer the term 'hegemony' to 'domination'?

(5 marks)

(b) How do the concepts of structure and culture complement each other? Give examples from areas such as gender, race and education.

(15 marks)

(If you wish to give a longer answer to part (a), material from Reading 89 could also be used.)

Sociological Theory and Method

Readings 99–101

This final section complements the opening section on theoretical perspectives and concepts. The major perspectives within sociology are again represented, this time at a slightly more demanding level. Ronald Fletcher's piece complements that of Durkheim in Section 1, Jack Douglas's that of Herbert Blumer; and Thomas Kuhn's extract on paradigms reminds us that science, as well as social science, must wrestle with the problem of the relationship between fact and theory, between the objective and the subjective.

I do not consider that the writings of the authors presented here or in the first section are essentially contradictory to one another, though in some respects they may be. Rather, I take C. Wright Mill's view that the perspectives or models developed by different sociologists or schools of sociologists all contribute, more or less, to our understanding of society. At the methodological level, it seems to me beyond question that the positivist-quantitative and the qualitative approaches are best suited to producing particular sorts of data, and that they can often be used in a complementary way to produce a more complete account of a given social process. In practice, they *are* often used together. It is artificial and, ultimately, illogical to exaggerate their different objectives to the point of making them appear mutually contradictory.

The major structuralist traditions of Functionalism and Marxism have more in common than many of their practitioners have been willing to admit. First, they *are* both structural. The individual is never conceived of in social isolation (as happens in the liberal tradition), but always within the social context. Most Functionalist and Marxist sociology is, in fact, concerned with describing and explaining the influence of social structures on individuals and groups, and vice versa. Second, both traditions are concerned to analyse the relationship between the various parts of society and of the parts to the whole: in that sense, both are functionalist sociologies. Marxism does this largely in terms of the relationship between the base and superstructure, and Functionalism does it by analysis of the interaction of the four sub-systems. Both models cover largely the same institutional and ideological areas, and frequently generate similar insights.

There are, of course, radical, and perhaps irreconcilable, differences between Functionalism and Marxism. Functionalism inadequately conceptualises social conflict and allows insufficient importance to class and class-related phenomena. By contrast, Marxism utilises a range of concepts which deal quite effectively with continuity and consensus within society, but it is arguable that Weber's concepts of status and party have an explanatory value in this context unappreciated by most Marxists. Certainly, Marxists have to address themselves to the persistent failure of 'the revolution' to occur where Marx expected it to, and in the socio-economic conditions that he anticipated.

The last point brings us to what is, perhaps, the crucial issue that any constructive critique of Functionalism and Marxism must face. It is arguable that the fundamental premises of the two traditions are at variance, and that this inevitably generates contradictory theoretical systems. Marxist analysis begins with relations to the means of production, and proceeds to explore the related social and economic contradictions of capitalism. Functionalism is a form of systems theory in which the relationship of the various sub-systems to one another and to the social system as a whole are assumed to tend towards integration and functionality, and analysed accordingly. To test the logical compatibility of those two approaches, and to achieve a theoretical synthesis more effective than either would be a mammoth undertaking which I do not propose to attempt here. For those who want to read an effort of this kind, Anthony Giddens has published a continuing, and now almost completed, series of books beginning with *New Rules of Sociological Method* in 1976. The series amounts to a total overview of sociological theory, including phenomenology and ethnomethodology.

It will not surprise the reader that, like Giddens, I also consider that both structuralism and phenomenology can live happily within sociology: neither has a rightful claim to dominate the discipline. Further, in combination with structural perspective, I also consider that positivist methodology is often highly suitable for establishing certain sorts of generalisations and correlations, particularly in respect of large social surveys with limited and clearly defined obejctives. Accordingly, I find Jack Douglas's critique of positivism, given below, a little too unsympathetic (though he himself by no means dismisses positivism out of hand). There are also specific areas of research to which phenomenology and qualitative methodology provide a much more appropriate analytical framework than structuralism/positivism. However, I can think of few, if any, areas of social life which cannot be illuminated by both approaches: in practice, much research does use both. Thus, the John Goldthorpe extract in Section 2 is a description of a piece of qualitative research in a predominantly quantitative survey. The works of Willmott and Young typically employ a whole battery of methods. Paul Willis's study *Learning to Labour* uses exclusively qualitative methodology, but is informed by a profound understanding of social structure mainly from the Marxist tradition. The same can be said of Ken Pryce's participant-observational study, *Endless Pressure*, except that he draws mainly from Weberian structural concepts.

Given the fact that many sociologists habitually use both structuralist and interpretist theory and method, perhaps what is needed is more work to link the two. Anthony Giddens has suggested that the concept of structuration effectively combines the notion that people are constrained by social structures which they also simultaneously maintain and change. Their action is informed by meaning and purpose, though particular outcomes are not always as intended. It may be that a whole range of such linking concepts would be useful. On the other hand, the relationship between the personal and social is so diverse and ubiquitous that it may be best left to specific description. It may not be possible to encapsulate it within a definitive theoretical framework.

My own theoretical interest and inclination is towards a more unified approach to sociological theory. However, I do not think that this should result in some homogenised theoretical compromise. Important theoretical issues cannot be glossed over, and I have not hesitated to 'take sides' on a number of key matters elsewhere (see *A New Introduction to Sociology*, Chapter 20).

My argument is as much for a more constructive attitude amongst sociologists as it is for a more constructive approach to theory. The perspectives approach to teaching sociology has polarised the discipline to an extreme degree – even granted that some of the differences presented are real enough. Very often, commitment to one or other perspective seems more a matter of ideology or personal inclination than a result of rigorous analysis and informed and tolerant debate. If internal communication within the discipline suffers a chronic breakdown, then so does the discipline. To outsiders, sociology has sometimes appeared to be in a state of breakdown, and sociologists themselves must bear much of the responsibility for this impression.

My own view is that any emerging unified sociological paradigm will combine structuralist and phenomenological theory. It will be necessary to include elements of consensus and conflict theory, although I believe there is little of worth within Functionalism that cannot be found elsewhere. I am too aware of the subtle and complex insight of Max Weber to call myself a Marxist. Nevertheless, it is primarily within the Marxist tradition that an adequate sense of structure can be found. However, there is no room for determinism within sociology, whether of a Marxist or any other kind.

99 Ronald Fletcher: The Comparative Method – 'The Only Alternative to Experiment'

The following extract is from the second of Fletcher's two-volume introduction to sociology: *Sociology: Its Nature, Scope and Elements* and *Sociology: The Study of Social Systems*. Fletcher's position in current sociology is a minority one but is interesting and significant. He regards the widespread tendency to conceive of the subject in terms of competing (and seemingly contradictory) perspectives as fundamentally wrong – and wrong is the term he uses. He argues that the founding fathers of sociology, including even Marx, were in fact in basic agreement about the fundamentals of the discipline. He considers that this general understanding and agreement lasted until about the Second World War when a number of misleading theoretical approaches, including Talcott Parsons' structural-functionalism, began to be developed. In Fletcher's view, fragmentation and faddism within sociology peaked when the 'perspectives approach' to teaching the subject became the norm in school sixth forms and further education as well as in higher education.

Like Comte and Durkheim, Fletcher regards sociology as a positive science which deals with a particular category of facts – social facts. I imagine he would find little to disagree with in Durkheim's account of social facts given in Section 1, page 25. In the first part of the reading, he describes the comparative method which he sees as the only alternative to experiment in providing an adequate means for analysing the relationship between social facts. The second part of Fletcher's piece examines the descriptive and explanatory methods of classifying social facts with particular reference to the classificatory typologies of Spencer, Durkheim and Hobhouse. Certainly, their typologies do provide a way of arranging and, to a certain extent, examining correlations between facts, but how far these correlations and the theories arising from them are wholly testable is, Fletcher notwithstanding, debatable. The term 'constant concomitance' refers to the repeated 'coming together' of given social facts which suggests a causal connection between them – e.g., a high suicide rate and low social integration. The same concomitances in different societies suggest the same causes at work.

The typologies presented here by Fletcher are extremely relevant to the community/society developmental theories described in Section 8 (see especially Readings 35 and 39).

See the end of this section for questions on method.

Reading 99 From Ronald Fletcher, *Sociology: The Study of Social Systems* (Batsford, 1981), pp. 76–83.

Why comparative studies?

In turning, now, to apply our general analysis of social systems to the study of actual societies, one basic question must be clearly asked and answered at the outset: 'What is the *point* of *comparing* societies?' To compare societies with each other does not, on the face of it, seem an especially profound or important thing to do.

Our earlier study of sociological theory showed, however, that there are crucial reasons for it.

Establishing systematic knowledge

In the first place, our objective is *not* simply to compare societies casually and arbitrarily, but to try to establish testable knowledge about all of them. This requires some systematic arrangement, some classification, so that we can – even if only provisionally – group societies into certain *types*. Then, with progressive detail and accuracy (and, no doubt, amendment as our studies proceed) we can compare and analyse the instances of each type: establishing an ever-increasing general knowledge about them, and becoming better able to move towards particular theories, definitive explanations, of whatever problematical aspects of them we may wish to investigate: of how it is, for example, that one type changes to give rise to another. It is important in establishing explanatory theories that we should be comparing *like* with *like*, not undertaking comparisons insufficiently formulated and therefore pointless.

Testing theories

This systematic arrangement of comparative knowledge could itself prove a ground for discerning regularities of connection within and between types of society, leading to the formulation of theories. This is not to claim that there is a *logic* of induction; only that detailed absorption in the systematic arrangement of the subject-matter is likely to throw up clues which can then be theoretically articulated and pursued further. But another point is more important. Whatever the *source* of theories (hypotheses), a systematic arrangement of knowledge of this kind is vitally important for *testing* them. The more systematic the body of descriptive and analytical knowledge we have, the more reliable will be our grounds for testing theories, and this is essential for scientific explanation.

The only alternative to experiment

This consideration leads to the most crucial point of all – which lies absolutely at the heart of sociological method. In sciences dealing with inanimate subject-matter, and with organic, physiological facts, some interconnections of which an explanation is sought can be *artificially isolated* from their normal contexts and examined in precisely measureable laboratory conditions. In sociology, except perhaps in the case of some small group interactions, this is completely impossible. We cannot put Great Britain, the Kwakiutl Indians, or the complex development of, say, Babylonian law, into laboratories. Furthermore, we know that any 'part' of a social system can only be understood in its essential interconnectedness with others. Even in comparative ethology, it has been seen that to *isolate* some components of 'animal psychology' in a laboratory is actually to *distort* them, and the new persuasion is that the behaviour and experience even of animals must essentially be seen in their 'social systems' in the wild before they can be correctly understood. Quite apart, then, from any *ethical* considerations (of which there are many) laboratory techniques are simply not appropriate to the nature and level of human associational facts.

We must, however, have some procedures for *testing* our theories, and the simple truth is that a careful formulation and use of *the comparative method* is sociology's *only alternative to experimentation.* (See *Nature, Scope and Elements*, p. 201, for the variations of the comparative method as an alternative to experiment: (i) systematic arrangement about a major hypothesis, (ii) the testing of constant concomitance, and (iii) testing the explanation of the particular case.) When we speak of comparative study then, we do not mean a loose or arbitrary comparison of specific instances but as rigorous a systematisation of knowledge as is possible to provide *crucial conditions of test* for any theories we propose. These can then be scrupulously checked by other investigators.

All this makes it clear that if comparative and historical studies are to be reliable, careful attention must be paid to the *principles of classification* employed . . .

The classification of types

As soon as we came to this question in our earlier discussion of the several theorists (see *Nature, Scope and Elements*, p. 200), it became clear that there was no such thing as *the* comparative method, and no such thing as *one* principle of classification, but *several:* depending on the kind of theory which was being formulated and tested. It is necessary, now, to say more about this. On the one hand, as indicated in our earlier outline, these different conceptions can themselves be quite clearly distinguished, and so much presuppose each other that, taken together, they can be seen to provide a firm comprehensive framework for the pursuit of knowledge. Here, we will simply elaborate our outline a little to show that this is so, filling in with some detail the diagram in which the conceptions of Spencer, Durkheim and Hobhouse were brought together, and which is reproduced here. Two other things, however, are important. First, we must consider a little further the extent and implications of this underlying agreement among the other sociological theorists of the time. And second – perhaps of more particular interest – we must note the firm continuity of this agreement in the comparative and historical sociology of *today:* in sociological studies in the Soviet Union, for example, and – strange juxtaposition! – in the sociological system of none other than the very controversial Talcott Parsons. To see the nature and extent of these agreements is of interest and importance in itself – demonstrating, yet again, the unitary nature of sociology which, in fact, underlies the supposed 'dissensus' of current controversies. It is much more important, however, in showing that there are certain *facts* about the types of society which can be distinguished in the complicated entirety of human history which are *true*, and which can therefore be used as firm, basic, commonly agreed elements in the task of achieving satisfactory principles of classification.

First, let us recall what we established earlier.

Methods of classification

It is of greater significance than is commonly appreciated, that each of the major classifications presented in sociology shared one or two major components – usually combining the two. On the one hand, social systems were thought to possess certain distinguishing *objective characteristics* according to which they could be arranged in a systematic order. On the other hand, it was also thought that this general, descriptive classification could be paralleled, substantiated, and illuminated by another which rested on some *central hypothesis*. In addition to offering a general objective and descriptive classification, each theorist proposed a particular interpretive or explanatory classification of his own. We noted Spencer, Durkheim and Hobhouse as having provided particularly clear examples of this.

Classification and comparison

Spencer		Durkheim		Hobhouse	
Descriptive (objective) criterion	'Explanatory' typology	Descriptive (objective) criterion	'Explanatory' typology	Descriptive (objective) criterion	'Explanatory' typology
Degree of composition	'Military Industrial'	Degree of aggregation	'Mechanical Organic'	Social bond	Levels of knowledge and mental development
(1) The simple society		(1) The horde		(1) Kinship	(1) Pre-literate societies Lower|hunters Higher|hunters Pastoral (1) / Agriculture (1) Pastoral (2) / Agriculture (2) Agriculture (3)
(2) The compound society (Clans, Tribes)	The military type	(2) The clan	Mechanical division of functions		
(3) Doubly compounded (city states, kingdoms)		(3) Simple polysegmental (tribe) (4) Polysegmental simply compounded (confederations of tribes)		(2) Despotism	Historical societies (2) Literacy and Proto-science (3) Stage of reflection in later East (spiritual regions) (4) Critical thought in Greece
(4) Trebly compounded (empires, modern nations and federations)	The industrial type	(5) Polysegmental doubly compounded (nations and federations)	Organic division of functions	(3) Citizenship	(5) Modern science
	The ethical type				

Herbert Spencer classified types of society from the simplest to the most complex according to their *degree of composition*. Societies had developed in history, he believed, in terms of growth, aggregation, specialisation and internal differentiation, and a more complex articulation of associations and institutions. *Simple societies* were those which formed 'simple working wholes unsubjected to any other, and of which the parts co-operated with or without a regulating centre for certain public ends' (e.g. Bush-men, Eskimos, Dyaks, Pueblo Indians). *Compound societies* were those 'in which the simple groups of which they are compounded had their own respective chiefs under a supreme chief' (e.g. Bedouins, some North American Indians, early Greek tribes). *Doubly compound societies* were 'those formed by the federation of these compound groups, giving rise to more settled forms of social organisation with more stable and more elaborate forms of government' (e.g. the Spartan and Athenian 'city states', Teutonic kingdoms from the sixth to the ninth centuries, the Ancient Egyptian Kingdom, and some federations of North American Indian tribes). *Trebly compound societies* were all the larger-scale empires and modern nations (e.g. the earlier empires of Mexico, Assyria, Egypt, Rome and modern Britain, France, Germany, Italy, Russia). These were all described and analysed in terms of *objective features* (whether they were nomadic, semi-settled, or settled, for example; whether they had no headship, occasional headship, or stable headship, etc.). An entire framework for arranging all the descriptive knowledge available about all societies (and which *could* be made available by further and more accurate studies) was provided. Henceforth, knowledge could be cumulative and increasingly exact.

Having established this classification resting on empirically observable characteristics of social organisation, Spencer then set up a theoretical *typology*, a construction of distinct *models*, which offered his own interpretation of how this actual development of societies had taken place. The first classification rested on *discernable objective* facts; the second postulated his *theory*.

His theoretical typology presented an extreme polarity between a militant and an industrial type of society. The first was one in which organisation for both offensive and defensive military action was predominant: with a centralised fusion of military, political and religious authority (total despotism) and a rigid hierarchy of ranks throughout society (even the 'religion' of society was one of militant command and allegiance), and in which social discipline was severe and characterised by *compulsory co-operation*. It was this type of social system which had first enlarged the range of human society, establishing a basis for subsequent development. Gradually, however, military activity increasingly took place on the extended frontiers of society, allowing a peaceful and settled development of civil activities over a larger protected area, and making possible a

763

focus of attention upon improved welfare. This gradually led to the development of the other type of society: the *industrial society*. Here, concentration was upon welfare. The social life of citizens was regulated on the basis of *voluntary co-operation*. Government (at all levels) was managed by elected committees and within a system of clarified rights and procedures whereby claims and counterclaims could be justly dealt with. Religion now allowed for individual discrimination in matters of faith, and it was in the interests of such societies to seek peace with others, not war.

Let us be completely clear about this. The second classification was not a *description* of what specific societies were actually like. It was a sharp polarity, a construction of extreme types, a deliberately exaggerated construction of two *models*, to provide a theoretical basis for interpreting, understanding, explaining the course of the change and development of societies from their earliest emergence to their present-day natures and conditions. A descriptive classification was accompanied by a theoretical analysis and interpretation.

Emile Durkheim followed the same procedure. First, he classified societies descriptively on exactly the same principle as Spencer: in terms of the nature and number of their component elements and their mode of combination. 'We know', he wrote, 'that societies are composed of various parts of combination; the constituent parts of every society are societies more simple than itself . . . to make our classification we have only to follow the way these simple societies form compounds and how these compound societies combine again to form more complex wholes'. But, like Spencer, he then offered a classification by *typology* embodying his own theory – which focused upon the kinds of social solidarity correlated with the changing collective conditions of the division of functions (division of labour) in society. His model of earlier, simpler societies sharply portrayed a condition of *mechanical solidarity*. A routine division of functions continued from generation to generation, requiring little responsible discrimination among individuals who were, in a simple way, bound together into a moral community by rigid rules of conduct, religious beliefs, and ritual practices. Thought, feeling belief, action, were intimately related with each other (in individual and society alike) in the entire mode of life. At the other extreme was the condition of *organic solidarity*. Here the division of functions was intricate and highly specialised. Objectively, individuals were inextricably caught up in this complex grasp of society's organisation, but there was a curious paradox. Subjectively, they did not feel themselves to be members of a community at all. On the contrary, the tasks they did had become so devoid of personal meaning that they had no sense of personal significance, no sense of personally belonging to society at all. They suffered a deep-rooted sense of normlessness, a malaise, a lack of personal direction. They lived in a vacuum devoid of social meaning. Durkheim's main concern was to analyse, diagnose, and remedy this situation.

L. T. Hobhouse offered the same kind of classification. To study societies systematically and objectively as wholes, he classified them first according to a clearly discernible characteristic – their *type of social bond*. One was the tie of kinship: the blood-tie. Another was the principle of 'despotism' (subdivided into personal despotism, the feudal type of monarchy, and despotism within international empires). A third was the principle of citizenship – 'incipient citizenship' (as in the Greek City States where the citizenship of the free citizens still rested upon a class in bondage) and 'full citizenship' (as in the modern nation state, where all men are citizens). In this classification, Hobhouse by no means thought that there had been some inevitable and continuous progress from one kind of social bond to another. The social bond was simply the clearly discernible criterion for classification. In all these *types* of total social system, he then undertook comparative studies to discover the kinds of correlation (inter-connection) which existed among all the elements of social structure within them.

Then, however, he also proposed a classification to explore his own theory (derived from Comte, Mill and others) that it was the *development of knowledge* which was the central feature underlying continuity and change in society: affecting all forms of associational activity because it brought new techniques and powers of control over natural resources and social organisation alike. The simpler societies, in the absence of written records, revealed their degrees of knowledge and control in their economic techniques. The early civilisations were distinguished by the emergence of 'Proto-Science' (pragmatic, rule-of-thumb science). Some later civilisations of the East were marked off by a refined development of the 'spiritual religions', themselves rooted in earlier traditional religions. The Greek city states were distinguished by the development of systematic and critical thought (which included the analysis of thought itself). Much of this was lost in the dark ages and in feudal society, but modern autonomous nation states – breaking away from Christendom and achieving independence – witnessed the full growth of science from the Renaissance onwards, and this period has seen the most extensive and rapid changes among societies in the whole of history – the very possession of this new range of knowledge and control having brought, simultaneously, enormous promise and enormous problems.

Spencer (in his *Principles of Sociology*) and Hobhouse (in *Social Development* and *Morals in Evolution*) then actually undertook a very detailed study of the interrelated institutions which characterised each type of society: showing how they were all correlated with each other, and correlated, too, with the central features emphasised in their theories. Hobhouse, for example, regarding *mind* itself as a correlating agency, traced the levels of development in mind (and its established knowledge) and then sought to show how the institutional complexes of each type of society were correlated with these. A very detailed and systematic body of knowledge was therefore achieved – all of which was (and is) amenable to *test*. In these respects, these two theorists were far more thorough-going in their studies than Durkheim. However, it is perfectly clear, that – in the case of all three – the *principles* of classification and comparison were the same.

100 Jack Douglas: Understanding Everyday Life (Phenomenology)

Parts of this extract from Jack Douglas's *Understanding Everyday Life* require close reading but the reward is a superb explanation of phenomenology. The passage begins familiarly enough with an exposure of the limitations of the positivistic tradition of sociology of which Durkheim is so celebrated a champion. Importantly, however, Douglas does not dismiss positivistic-structural perspective as useless but he does see it as 'less true' than phenomenological perspective. This greater truth lies in the fact that phenomenology starts with the expressed meanings, motives and actions of individuals whereas structural perspective is primarily concerned with establishing the external causes or, at least, influences on individuals and group behaviour. The orientation of structuralism, therefore, is at one remove from personal experience. Interestingly, Douglas claims that phenomenology offers a more appropriately scientific approach to understanding society (or 'everyday life') because it begins more closely than positivism to the subject of enquiry (the individual and inter-subjective interaction).

Douglas usefully distinguishes between three 'stances' towards everyday life. The first is the absolutist or objectivist adopted by positivists; the second is the natural stance assumed to be taken by all participants in the course of everyday life; the third is the theoretic stance of phenomenology which seeks to understand everyday life. He links the objectivistic and phenomenological stances with two contrasting methodological approaches. He suggests that a commitment to positivist methods creates the absolutist 'stance' (the tail wags the dog!) whereas those who adopt the theoretic stance of phenomenology find methods to suit their purpose of achieving human understanding. Douglas is right in implying that this enterprise involves scientific precision but essentially it is perhaps a humanistic undertaking.

Reading 100 From Jack D. Douglas, *The Understanding of Everyday Life: Towards the Reconstruction of Sociological Knowledge* (Routledge and Kegan Paul, 1974), pp. vii–x, 12–16.

We are all profoundly involved in everyday life and, because we human beings are necessarily social and thinking animals, we are all profoundly committed to understanding our everyday social lives. Our everyday, common-sense thinking includes an immense number of ideas about the human actors we encounter in our everyday lives. Our common-sense theories of motives, by which we try to explain and thereby anticipate and control what others will do, are an obvious example of how extensive and complex these theories are. There are literally hundreds, perhaps thousands, of possible 'motives', and each possible motive must be commonsensically analysed in the context of a number of basic motives and characteristics that are believed applicable to any motive – sincerity and insincerity, honesty and dishonesty, trustworthiness and untrustworthiness, and so on. In this sense, each man is necessarily his own sociologist; and *everyday sociology* is an extremely complex set of facts, ideas, theories, ideologies, and philosophies demanding expert knowledge of those who would practice it well.

It is an obvious question, then, whether there is any special purpose to be served by creating a *discipline* of sociological thought. Would not such a discipline be simply paralleling and competing with everyday sociologies? How would it differ, if at all, from literature or any of the many other forms of thought that are disciplined but firmly grounded in common-sense ideas about man and society? These are the kinds of questions that faced the social thinkers who created sociology as an independent discipline of social thought. The consideration of them in various forms took up a great deal of early 'sociological' thought in the nineteenth century. By the end of the nineteenth century those who called themselves sociologists had found the answer that satisfied them and that was to become the basic answer of all classical (or traditional) sociology. They had created sociology as a 'science of society', to be cast in the mold of classical natural sciences. It is this absolutist mold of classical science that was to remain dominant in sociology and the other social sciences long after it had been destroyed in the natural sciences by the revolutions wrought by relativity and quantum mechanics.

The 'obvious' answer to these traditional sociologists was that sociology must be created and developed in exactly the same way they believed the natural sciences were: sociology must be independent of and in opposition to common-sense ideas about man and society. The ideas of common sense were continually derided as imprecise, misleading, unsuited for scientific use, and so on. As is well known, this is the way Durkheim (1954) began *Suicide*, probably the most famous work of classical, positivistic sociology:

Since the word 'suicide' recurs constantly in the course of conversation, it might be thought that its sense is universally known and that the definition is superfluous. Actually, the words of everyday language, like the concepts they express, are always susceptible of more than one meaning, and the scholar employing them in their accepted use without further definition would risk serious misunderstanding. Not only is their meaning so indefinite as to vary, from case to case, with the needs of argument, but, as the classification from which they derive is not analytic, but merely translates the confused impressions of

768

the crowd, categories of very different sorts of fact are indistinctly combined under the same heading, or similar realities are differently named. So, if we follow common use, we risk distinguishing what should be combined, or combining what should be distinguished, thus mistaking the real affinities of things, and accordingly misapprehending their nature . . . But these natural affinities of entities cannot be made clear safely by such superficial examination as produces ordinary terminology; and so the scholar cannot take as the subject of his research roughly assembled groups of facts corresponding to words of common usage. He himself must establish the groups he wishes to study in order to give them the homogeneity and the specific meaning necessary for them to be susceptible of scientific treatment. Thus the botanist, speaking of flowers or fruit, the zoologist of fish or insects, employ these various terms in previously determined senses . . .

The essential thing is not to express with some precision what the average intelligence terms suicide, but to establish a category of objects permitting this classification, which are objectively established, that is, correspond to a definite aspect of things.

Sociology, then, was to be done outside of and in opposition to common sense and, thus, common-sense sociology. As Durkheim's statement suggests, if we follow 'common use' in studying social phenomena, we will surely wind up 'misapprehending their nature'. But there is a definite flaw in this conception of sociology as a natural science: as bodies, human beings may look like material stuff (in the same way rocks and planetary bodies do), but, as thinking bodies, humans are very unlike rocks and planetary bodies. The 'forces' that move human beings, *as* human beings rather than simply as physical bodies, are not gravitational forces or the forces of elementary particles. They are 'meaningful stuff'. They are internal ideas, feelings, motives. What Durkheim referred to as their nature is largely made of this meaningful stuff.

All human actions of any significance to sociology are meaningful actions. All significant orderings of human phenomena, which alone make any science of those phenomena possible, are the result of some kind of social meanings; and no significant scientific description, analysis, or explanation of those orderings is possible without some fundamental consideration of those social meanings. Although this may appear obvious, it took several centuries of misbegotten mechanistic social theories to convince those dedicated to the absolutist ideal of hard (natural) science (of treating man as an object) that what was commonsensically obvious was also true. By the time Durkheim and the many other founders of classical sociology began writing, the necessarily meaningful nature of all social phenomena was recognised, however vaguely and inconsistently. Geographic determinists, moon-phase theorists and even gene type theorists have all slowly disappeared from the ranks of social scientists.

But what was a *real* scientist to do with this quintessential form of 'subjective' stuff-meanings? It seemed obvious that a scientist would have to reject common-sense meanings, but what then? Durkheim and the other positivists found their solution in treating all social phenomena *as if* they were objects. That is, they looked for a way by which they could study and analyse social phenomena using the traditional methods of classical science (experimental controls, quantification, hypothesis testing, and so on). A way was found. They imposed their 'scientific' presuppositions upon the realm of social phenomena, but in doing so they distorted the fundamental nature of human existence – they boot-legged common-sense meanings into their object-like data and theories and created an *as if* science of man.

As I have shown elsewhere (Douglas, 1967), Durkheim was forced by his whole argument to inadvertently rely on the common-sense meanings of each of his fundamental variables (intention, suicide, education, and so on) for the relations he believed existed between those variables and for his explanations of those relations. The man who derided the common-sense meanings of suicide based his book on the subject and his whole argument for classical sociology on the 'official statistics' that have always been based on the common-sense meanings of suicide. The man who rejected intention as too subjective for any scientific consideration based his whole work on disembodied numbers (suicide rates) which may look object-like but are actually the outcome of necessarily commonsensical evaluations of the 'intentions' of individuals by unseen coroners, police, priests, medical examiners, and other officials. The man who so confidently and arrogantly derided common sense became the captive of common sense. This might be seen as simply another joke played on the hapless creature of reason by the absurdities of reality were it not for the fact that generations of functionalists, structuralists, experimentalists, and other absolutists in the social sciences have followed the same path in creating the *as if* social sciences and were it not for the fact that these 'experts' have increasingly used their scientific rhetoric to control our lives through their growing effect on government policies. There is no humor in the specter of technological tyranny.

Rather than imposing an *as if science* on our everyday lives, we must seek to understand everyday life. Rather than explicitly adopting the common-sense understandings of everyday life, or proposing to reject those understandings while covertly building our sociological understanding on them, we must begin all sociological understanding of human existence with an understanding of everyday life gained from a systematic and objective study of the common-sense meanings and actions of everyday life. We must always begin by studying these meaningful social phenomena on their own grounds, but, true to our goal of creating a science of man's existence, we must then seek an ever more general, transsituational (objective) understanding of everyday life. This is the fundamental program of all phenomenological and existential sociologies.

The accelerating progress in the realisation of this revolutionary program has begun to transform the sociological enterprise. This does not mean that we shall now sweep aside all other forms of sociology. All revolutions do produce rhetorical excess, but all revolutions also borrow far more from the ancient regimes than the revolutionaries care to admit. In sociology, as I have argued in Chapter 1, we shall long need certain forms of structural analyses of society that are not thoroughly based on more objective understandings of everyday life, for the simple reason that structural analyses are a practical necessity in a massive and complex society. Moreover, I believe that the calmer perspective of historical analysis will show that this intellectual revolution sought to replace absolutist perspectives on society that, although less true, were quite important in bringing us to this point of revolutionary change . . .

Everyday life as a phenomenon: the natural stance and the theoretical stance

We see, then, that we have no choice in our point of departure. We must agree that social phenomena must be studied in some way as (subjectively) meaningful phenomena and that our common goal as sociologists is to create a science of social actions. We then find that any scientific study of those phenomena necessarily begins with the systematic observation and analysis of everyday life, so this is where we necessarily begin. Finding the beginning, the fundamental questions to ask of nature, is always the most difficult thing for any science to accomplish. It has taken social scientists innumerable mis-steps, most of them inspired by simplistic analogies with the natural sciences, in the first century and half of their existence to find their proper beginning. Those of us who have recapitulated these mistakes in our own lives know the difficulties and the anguish of this search. And we know that we can never be certain that we have found a sure path to the knowledge we seek, but we feel that we have reached at least one clear and simple – fundamental – truth in all of our uncertainty. We have found our beginning in the analysis of everyday life. But where do we go from here? What is the best strategy for gaining an even better, a more scientific, understanding of everyday life?

The crucial questions we face in adopting a strategy for studying everyday life are what stance shall we adopt toward everyday life and what methods of analysis shall we use. The two questions are to some extent independent, but they also partially overlap because the stance or orientation we adopt toward everyday life from the beginning becomes an important determinant of our methods of analysis.

The first important point to note is that, instead of allowing our methods to determine our stance toward everyday life, we allow our stance to determine our methods. This is the opposite of the classical scientific approach to analysing man. The classical approach was to assume that there is only one general set of crieteria for scientific validity or truth and that it was embodied in the classical works of the natural sciences.

Thus the early social scientists adopted a conscious policy of studying man in the same way one would study any physical object. Having presupposed these methods, they adopted the stance most in accord with them. They adopted the absolutist perspective on man and society. That is, they viewed man as an object, causally determined (totally) by forces outside of his self. In accord with this perspective, they adopted an *absolutist (or objectivist) stance* toward everyday life. They assumed that the phenomena of everyday life could and should be studied only in terms of clear and distinct (scientific) formal categories defined by them in advance of their studies. They assumed that these categories should be both independent of and in opposition to the common-sense categories of men in everyday life. They assumed that all decisions about how one would decide that his results were true or false could and should be made in advance of studies of the everyday phenomena. And they assumed that the goal should be one of controlling the everyday phenomena in the way scientists seek to control the natural world. Sociologists will readily recognise the great similarity between these classical ideas and those stated so clearly in the 'methodological ideals' of many of today's statistics and methods textbooks (Blalock's widely used text is a good example). There is a direct historical lineage between the classical, 'scientistic' ideas, which go back to the seventeenth century, and the methods of present-day positivistic sociologists, though these present-day methodologists normally think of themselves as modern and 'working on the frontiers of sociological knowledge'. In general, the absolutist stance subsumed the everyday world under the methods of science and, in doing so, its users never realised that the everyday phenomena they observed were *scientified* phenomena. (The ultimate ideal, of course, has always been total experimental control. And, while only the academic psychologists have achieved this grand ideal with their carefully bred maze-rats and Skinner box pigeons, many sociologists, such as George Homans (1961), have extrapolated the beautifully simple theories derived from these mazes to all human action. If man cannot yet be put in the maze, at least we can assume that that is where he really belongs.)

The opposite extreme from the absolutist stance is the *natural stance*. The natural stance is that supposedly taken by men in everyday life, though whether or not they in fact take this stance is certainly an empirical question. It is the stance in which the everyday world is taken for granted as it is experienced in everyday life. It is that stance taken by the individual within the stream of everyday life. It is a stance that does not raise serious and persistent questions concerning the nature of the everyday experience as a fact. Husserl gave the idea its classical formulation:

> I find continually present and standing over against me the one spatio-temporal fact-world to which I myself belong, as do all other men found in it and related in the same way to it. This 'fact-world' as the word already tells us, I find *to be out there*, and also *take it just as it gives itself to me as something that exists out there*. All doubting and rejecting of the data of the natural world leaves standing the *general thesis of the natural stand-point*. 'The' world is as fact-world always there; at the most it is at odd points 'other' than I supposed, this or that under such names as 'illusion', 'hallucination', and the like, must be struck *out of it*, so to speak; but the 'it' remains ever, in the sense of the general thesis, a world that has its being out there.

The third general kind of stance toward the everyday world, as proposed by all phenomenologists since Husserl, is the *theoretic stance*. To take the theoretic stance toward the everyday world is to stand back from, to reflect upon, to re-view the experience taken for granted in the natural stance. To take the theoretic stance is to treat the everyday world as a phenomenon, as Zimmerman and Pollner have put it. At the most basic level, at its beginning, taking the theoretic stance involves what Husserl called the 'phenomenological suspension' (or *epoché*). Natanson (1962: pp. 12–13) has given what is probably the best general description of this phenomenological suspension:

> When I suspend or place in abeyance my common-sense belief in reality, I merely decide to make no use of the thesis which ordinarily guides our total cognitive and conative life; but this thesis is not to be understood as a proposition or a formulated article of faith. Rather, it is the unstated, utterly implicit theme of our common-sense relatedness to reality . . .
>
> Phenomenological suspension or, to use Husserl's term, *epoché*, consists in making explicit to consciousness the thesis which unconsciously underlies every individual judgement made within ordinary life about reality. Suspension means first of all coming into awareness of the very meaning of the natural attitude itself. Negatively put, suspension of the General Thesis of the natural standpoint most certainly does not include or

signify a denial of the reality of the external world or of the validity of our ordinary experience within it. Rather, as phenomenologist I place in phenomenological doubt (which is not psychological doubt) my traditional common-sense taking for granted of the very reality of the world within which things and events are noted and appraised. Suspension, then, involves a shift in modes of attention. The same reality I took for granted in typical fashion in naive attitude I now re-view in phenomenological attitude. The real world, everyday existence, etc., do not mysteriously vanish under *epoché:* they are merely seen in terms of a perspective hitherto unimagined and even unimaginable in common-sense terms . . . *Epoché* is the necessary condition to all other phenomenological procedures, for it guarantees the freedom of a starting point which refuses to remain within the metaphysical orientation of common-sense. And further, *epoché* is the clue to phenomenological method to the extent that it points to the kind of descriptive neutrality phenomenology encourages.

The commitment to the theoretic stance toward everyday experience is of crucial importance in determining the methods used to study everyday life and the further development of one's ideas about everyday life. The importance of the stance in these respects can be seen most clearly from an examination of the similarities and dissimilarities between sociology done from the theoretic standpoint and sociology done from the naturalistic standpoint.

The first fundamental methodological commitment of those phenomenological sociologists committed to taking the theoretic stance toward everyday life is to *study the phenomena of everyday life on their own terms, or to make use only of methods of observation and analysis that retain the integrity of the phenomena.* This means most simply that the phenomena to be studied must be the phenomena as experienced in everyday life, not phenomena created (or strained through) experimental situations. (The argument below that human actions are highly situational, and that human actors act in accord with their constructions of meanings for the concrete situations they face, will show further why experimentally induced acts cannot be taken as representative of everyday acts.) This is the basis of all phenomenological or existential methods.

101 Thomas S. Kuhn: Scientific Paradigms

Thomas Kuhn's famous essay, *The Structure of Scientific Revolutions*, is of interest to social scientists for two major reasons. First, he forces them to reconsider their assumptions about science itself – assumptions which they may carry over into social science. Second, Kuhn's notion of the paradigm described below has been very influential within social science.

Kuhn's comments on the nature of science and how scientific knowledge changes (by 'revolutions') has, perhaps, particular implications for positivists. The major meaning of paradigm (it has a second meaning with which we need not concern ourselves) is that 'it stands for the entire constellation of beliefs, values, techniques, and so on shared by members of a given community'. By 'community' Kuhn means the leading specialists in a given scientific area. His central point is that these beliefs and so on affect both the process of scientific inquiry and the way scientists 'see things' (an example is given below). This is a far cry from the positivist's confident claim that science is the objective pursuit of factually verifiable knowledge. Equally, the concept of paradigm challenges models of sociological theory-methods based on the view that sociology is exclusively concerned with establishing relationships between social facts.

The last point brings us to the second way in which Kuhn's concept of paradigm has been influential within sociology. He suggests that, at any given time, a particular scientific discipline tends to be dominated by a given paradigm. This is currently certainly not the case within sociology, and possibly never has been. Apart from the positivist-interpretist division, positivism itself is internally divided into Functionalism and various forms of conflict theory including Marxism (not all varieties of which are positivist, however). Likewise, interpretists are divided into symbolic interactionists and ethno-methodologists, although by no means all interpretists consider the two approaches to be logically exclusive. Arguably, then, sociology is characterised by several competing paradigms, and some consider that this detracts from its claims to be a science or, at least, a mature science. These are controversial observations and I discuss them further in my extended introduction to this section.

In what follows Kuhn's initial presentation of his theory of

paradigms is probably easier to understand than the examples
he concludes with. However, some examples must be included
as the theory stands or falls by them.

Reading 101 From Thomas S. Kuhn, *The Structure of Scientific Revolutions* (University of Chicago Press, 1970), pp. 10–11, 111, 114–7.

The route to normal science

In this essay, 'normal science' means research firmly based upon
one or more past scientific achievements, achievements that some
particular scientific community acknowledges for a time as
supplying the foundation for its further practice. Today such
achievements are recounted, though seldom in their original form,
by science textbooks, elementary and advanced. These textbooks
expound the body of accepted theory, illustrate many or all of its
successful applications, and compare these applications with exemplary observations and experiments. Before such books became
popular early in the nineteenth century (and until even more
recently in the newly matured sciences), many of the famous classics
of science fulfilled a similar function. Aristotle's *Physica*, Ptolemy's
Almagest, Newton's *Principia* and *Opticks*, Franklin's *Electricity*,
Lavoisier's *Chemistry*, and Lyell's *Geology* – these and many other
works served for a time implicitly to define the legitimate problems
and methods of a research field for succeeding generations of practitioners. They were able to do so because they shared two essential
characteristics. Their achievement was sufficiently unprecedented
to attract an enduring group of adherents away from competing
modes of scientific activity. Simultaneously, it was sufficiently open-
ended to leave all sorts of problems for the redefined group of
practitioners to resolve.

Achievements that share these two characteristics I shall henceforth refer to as 'paradigms', a term that relates closely to 'normal
science'. By choosing it, I mean to suggest that some accepted
examples of actual scientific practice – examples which include law,
theory, application, and instrumentation together – provide models
from which spring particular coherent traditions of scientific
research. These are the traditions which the historian describes
under such rubrics as 'Ptolemaic astronomy' (or 'Copernican'),
'Aristotelian dynamics' (or 'Newtonian'), 'corpuscular optics' (or
'wave optics'), and so on. The study of paradigms, including many

that are far more specialised than those named illustratively above, is what mainly prepares the student for membership in the particular scientific community with which he will later practice. Because he there joins men who learned the bases of their field from the same concrete models, his subsequent practice will seldom evoke overt disagreement over fundamentals. Men whose research is based on shared paradigms are committed to the same rules and standards for scientific practice. That commitment and the apparent consensus it produces are prerequisites for normal science, i.e., for the genesis and continuation of a particular research tradition . . .

Revolutions as changes of world view

Examining the record of past research from the vantage of contemporary historiography, the historian of science may be tempted to exclaim that when paradigms change, the world itself changes with them. Led by a new paradigm, scientists adopt new instruments and look in new places. Even more important, during revolutions scientists see new and different things when looking with familiar instruments in places they have looked before. It is rather as if the professional community had been suddenly transported to another planet where familiar objects are seen in a different light and are joined by unfamiliar ones as well. Of course, nothing of quite that sort does occur: there is no geographical transplantation; outside the laboratory everyday affairs usually continue as before. Nevertheless, paradigm changes do cause scientists to see the world of their research-engagement differently. In so far as their only recourse to that world is through what they see and do, we may want to say that after a revolution scientists are responding to a different world . . .

In the sciences, therefore, if perceptual switches accompany paradigm changes, we may not expect scientists to attest to these changes directly. Looking at the moon, the convert to Copernicanism does not say, 'I used to see a planet, but now I see a satellite'. That locution would imply a sense in which the Ptolemaic system had once been correct. Instead, a convert to the new astronomy says, 'I once took the moon to be (or saw the moon as) a planet, but I was mistaken'. That sort of statement does recur in the aftermath of scientific revolutions. If it ordinarily disguises a shift of scientific vision or some other mental transformation with the same effect, we may not expect direct testimony about that shift. Rather we must look for indirect and behavioral evidence that the scientist with a new paradigm sees differently from the way he had seen before.

Let us then return to the data and ask what sorts of transformations in the scientist's world the historian who believes in such changes can discover. Sir William Herschel's discovery of Uranus provides a first example and one that closely parallels the anomalous card experiment. On at least seventeen different occasions between 1690 and 1781, a number of astronomers, including several of Europe's most eminent observers, had seen a star in positions that we now suppose must have been occupied at the time by Uranus. One of the best observers in this group had actually seen the star on four successive nights in 1769 without noting the motion that could have suggested another identification. Herschel, when he first observed the same object twelve years later, did so with a much improved telescope of his own manufacture. As a result, he was able to notice an apparent disk-size that was at least unusual for stars. Something was awry, and he therefore postponed identification pending further scrutiny. The scrutiny disclosed Uranus' motion among the stars, and Herschel therefore announced that he had seen a new comet! Only several months later, after fruitless attempts to fit the observed motion to a cometary orbit, did Lexell suggest that the orbit was probably planetary. When that suggestion was accepted, there were several fewer stars and one more planet in the world of the professional astronomer. A celestial body that had been observed off and on for almost a century was seen differently after 1781 because, like an anomalous playing card, it could no longer be fitted to the perceptual categories (star or comet) provided by the paradigm that had previously prevailed.

The shift of vision that enabled astronomers to see Uranus, the planet, does not, however, seem to have affected only the perception of that previously observed object. Its consequences were more far-reaching. Probably, though the evidence is equivocal, the minor paradigm change forced by Herschel helped to prepare astronomers for the rapid discovery, after 1801, of the numerous minor planets or asteroids. Because of their small size, these did not display the anomalous magnification that had alerted Herschel. Nevertheless, astronomers prepared to find additional planets were able, with standard instruments, to identify twenty of them in the first fifty years of the nineteenth century. The history of astronomy provides many other examples of paradigm-induced changes in scientific perception, some of them even less equivocal. Can it conceivably be an accident, for example, that Western astronomers first saw change in the previously immutable heavens during the half-century after Copernicus' new paradigm was first proposed? The Chinese, whose cosmological beliefs did not preclude celestial change, had recorded the appearance of many new stars in the heavens at a much earlier date. Also, without even the aid of a telescope, the Chinese had systematically recorded the appearance of sunspots centuries before these were seen by Galileo and his contemporaries. Nor were sunspots and a new star the only examples of celestial change to emerge in the heavens of Western astronomy immediately after Copernicus. Using traditional instruments, some as simple as a piece of thread, late sixteenth-century astronomers repeatedly discovered that comets wandered at will through the space previously reserved for the immutable planets and stars. The very ease and rapidity with which astronomers saw new things when looking at old objects with old instruments may make us wish to say that, after Copernicus, astronomers lived in a different world. In any case, their research responded as though that were the case . . .

Questions on Theory (and Method)

1.   *'We must, however, have some procedures for* testing *our theories, and the simple truth is that a careful formulation and use of* the comparative method *is sociology's* only alternative to experimentation.'   (Ronald Fletcher)

   'We see, then, that we have no choice in our point of departure. We must agree that social phenomena must be studied in some way as (subjectively) meaningful phenomena and that our common goal as sociologists is to create a science of social actions.'
                                                                   (Jack Douglas)
   (a) Describe, with the help of examples, the comparative method.
                                                                   (6 marks)
   (b) Describe, with the help of examples, the main methods phenomenologists use to acquire data.
                                                                   (6 marks)
   (c) Do you consider 'knowledge' produced by the positivist and phenomenological approaches to research to be complementary or contradictory?   (13 marks)

2. (a) What role does the concept of 'means of production' play in Marx's theory of society?

(6 marks)

(b) Briefly explain Weber's use of the concepts of class, status and party.

(6 marks)

(c) Compare and contrast Marx and Weber's perspectives on the relationship between class and power.

(13 marks)

(Note: See Readings 2 and 3 and textbooks for relevant material.)

3. (a) Present and explain George Mead's concept of the 'self'.

(6 marks)

(b) Describe, with reference to one detailed example, what is meant by 'symbolic interaction'.

(6 marks)

(c) Do you consider that it is true that there is no room for the concept of the creative individual within sociological theory?

(13 marks)

4. (a) Explain, with illustrations, what is meant by a sociological 'perspective'.

(12 marks)

(b) To what extent do you consider Thomas Kuhn's paradigm theory to be applicable to sociology?

(13 marks)

5. Critically discuss the view that a single sociological paradigm is neither possible nor desirable.

(25 marks)

SOCIOLOGY

7

TITLES OF RELATED INTEREST FROM PINE FORGE PRESS

Sociology: Exploring the Architecture of Everyday Life, Sixth Edition, Readings by David M. Newman and Jodi O'Brien

The Globalization of Nothing by George Ritzer

The McDonaldization of Society, Revised New Century Edition by George Ritzer

McDonaldization: The Reader, Second Edition edited by George Ritzer

Second Thoughts: Seeing Conventional Wisdom Through the Sociological Eye, Third Edition by Janet M. Ruane and Karen A. Cerulo

Sociological Snapshots 4 by Jack Levin

Key Ideas in Sociology, Second Edition by Peter Kivisto

This Book Is Not Required, Third Edition by Inge Bell and Bernard McGrane

Women and Men at Work, Second Edition by Irene Padavic and Barbara Reskin

Race, Ethnicity, Gender, and Class: The Sociology of Group Conflict and Change, Fourth Edition by Joseph F. Healey

Diversity and Society: Race, Ethnicity, and Gender by Joseph F. Healey

Race, Ethnicity, and Gender: Selected Readings edited by Joseph F. Healey and Eileen O'Brien

Illuminating Social Life: Classical and Contemporary Theory, Third Edition by Peter Kivsito

The Production of Reality: Essays and Readings on Social Interaction, Fourth Edition, edited by Jodi O'Brien and Peter Kollock